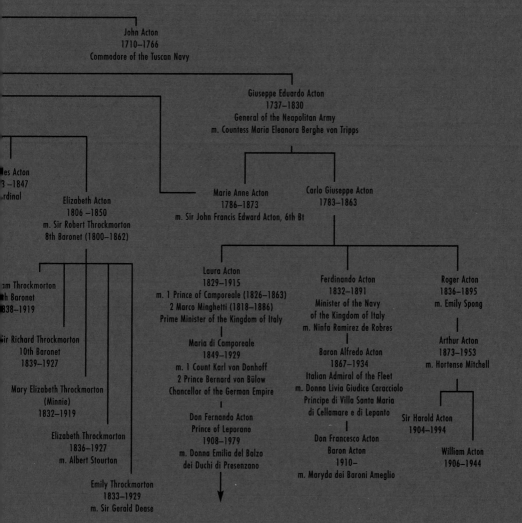

Richard Acton
d.1703
m. 1 Anna Llewellin
m. 2 Hester Gibbon
(mother of historian Edward Gibbon [1737–1794])

John Acton
1710–1766
Commodore of the Tuscan Navy

Giuseppe Eduardo Acton
1737–1830
General of the Neapolitan Army
m. Countess Maria Eleanora Berghe von Tripps

...es Acton
...3 –1847
...rdinal

Elizabeth Acton
1806 –1850
m. Sir Robert Throckmorton
8th Baronet (1800–1862)

Marie Anne Acton
1786–1873
m. Sir John Francis Edward Acton, 6th Bt

Carlo Giuseppe Acton
1783–1863

...am Throckmorton
...h Baronet
...838–1919

Laura Acton
1829–1915
m. 1 Prince of Camporeale (1826–1863)
2 Marco Minghetti (1818–1886)
Prime Minister of the Kingdom of Italy

Ferdinando Acton
1832–1891
Minister of the Navy
of the Kingdom of Italy
m. Ninfa Ramirez de Robres

Roger Acton
1836–1895
m. Emily Spong

...ir Richard Throckmorton
10th Baronet
1839–1927

Maria di Camporeale
1849–1929
m. 1 Count Karl von Donhoff
2 Prince Bernard von Bülow
Chancellor of the German Empire

Baron Alfredo Acton
1867–1934
Italian Admiral of the Fleet
m. Donna Livia Giudice Caracciolo
Principe di Villa Santa Maria
di Cellamare e di Lepanto

Arthur Acton
1873–1953
m. Hortense Mitchell

Mary Elizabeth Throckmorton
(Minnie)
1832–1919

Elizabeth Throckmorton
1836–1927
m. Albert Stourton

Don Fernando Acton
Prince of Leporano
1908–1979
m. Donna Emilia del Balzo
dei Duchi di Presenzano

Don Francesco Acton
Baron Acton
1910–
m. Maryda dei Baroni Ameglio

Sir Harold Acton
1904–1994

William Acton
1906–1944

Emily Throckmorton
1833–1929
m. Sir Gerald Dease

LORD ACTON

Lord Acton

ROLAND HILL

Foreword by Owen Chadwick

YALE UNIVERSITY PRESS

NEW HAVEN & LONDON

Published with assistance from the Mrs. L. D. Rope Third Charitable
Settlement.

Designed by Nancy Ovedovitz and set in Galos type by Tseng
Information Systems, Inc., Durham, North Carolina. Printed in
the United States of America by Vail-Ballou Press, Binghamton,
New York.

Library of Congress Cataloging-in-Publication Data
Hill, Roland, 1920–
Lord Acton / Roland Hill ; foreword by Owen Chadwick.
p.   cm.
Includes bibliographical references and index.
ISBN 0-300-07956-7 (alk. paper)
1. Acton, John Emerich Edward Dalberg Acton, Baron, 1834–1902.
2. Historians—Great Britain—Biography.   I. Title.
D15.A25 H487   2000
907'.202—dc21
[B]   99-053065

A catalogue record for this book is available from the British Library.

The paper in this book meets the guidelines for permanence and
durability of the Committee on Production Guidelines for Book
Longevity of the Council on Library Resources.

10   9   8   7   6   5   4   3   2   1

Title-page illustration: Lord Acton near the end of his life, 1899.
Reprinted by permission of the Syndics of Cambridge University
Library.

CONTENTS

A Word from Mia Woodruff, vii

Foreword by Owen Chadwick, ix

Acknowledgments, xiii

Introduction, xix

1   Birth in Naples, 1

2   A Cosmopolitan Background, 6

3   Onwards to Oscott, 16

4   Dr. Döllinger's Apprentice, 27

5   The Newfound Family, 40

6   The Squire, 51

7   Three Journeys, 63

8   Pleasing Lord Granville and Mama, 81

9   Editor in Chains, 108

10   Marie Consents, 157

11 Roman Courtesies, 173

12 The Unbidden Guest, 192

13 Papal Infallibility and Beyond, 212

14 A Misfortune for Religion, 226

15 Gladstone Fights Back, 252

16 Madonnas of the Future, Friendships of the Past, 273

17 "Power Tends to Corrupt . . . ," 296

18 Döllinger's Death, 308

19 Gladstone's Friend and the Queen's Lord, 333

20 Regius Professor, 365

21 Last Years, 392

Notes, 417

Select Bibliography, 503

Index, 525

Illustrations follow pp. 50, 272, and 364.

A WORD FROM MIA WOODRUFF

Author's note: The Hon. Marie Immaculée Antoinette (Mia) Woodruff was the eldest of seven daughters and two sons of the second Lord Acton. Although she never met her grandfather, the first Lord Acton, she was devoted to his memory and ideals and familiar with the painful struggle of his life. With her husband, Douglas Woodruff, who died in 1978, she temporarily had the care of the extensive family papers, which they made readily available to scholars once the family seat, Aldenham Hall, was sold. Ultimately the papers found a permanent home at the Cambridge University Library.

Like her husband, who for thirty-one years was the editor of the British Catholic weekly the *Tablet,* Mia Woodruff was a leading figure in the Catholic world of her generation. She was a veritable grande dame, a woman of great spirit, trenchant wit, and deep religious devotion who cared for others in numerous voluntary organizations, particularly for refugees of all races and creeds before, during, and after World War II. It was a fitting gesture, when she was buried next to her husband in the little Anglican churchyard of Lyford, Oxfordshire, that the tin hat she had worn as an air-raid warden in wartime London should have been placed in her grave. She died, aged eighty-nine, on 5 March 1994, not long after she prepared these words.

*   *   *

I never knew my grandfather. He died in 1902, and I was born in 1905. What I do know about him is what my Aunt Mamy told me. She was his favourite child, and he wrote the most wonderful letters to her as well as telling her many fine tales about himself. I think of him as a lonely young man spending much of his time at St. Martin's, the holiday home of the Arcos in Upper Austria, in the company of his future bride and his very beloved future mother-in-law, who was a great influence on his life. I imagine him at Aldenham in the vast library he built himself—which has since, alas, been demolished—surrounded by his thousands of books, now at the Cambridge University Library. I think of him at Tegernsee in Bavaria, where the Arcos had a lovely villa, and where we used to stay as young children, my brother and I. It was a most beautiful chalet with balconies all round, covered with verbena and wisteria, and the garden leading right down to the lakeside, where we used to fish. My grandfather spent the last days of his life there and is buried at Tegernsee. My grandmother and her two daughters remained there until the outbreak of the Great War in 1914 and then moved to Switzerland, where my aunts both died, Annie in 1917, Simmy in 1919. After that their mama came to live with us at Aldenham for the rest of her life, and there she died on 2 April 1923. There is a plaque in the church at Bridgnorth to the memory of my grandfather and various members of the Acton family. He was MP for Bridgnorth at one time, and he helped in the building of St. John's parish church.

I feel my grandfather lived by his conscience, which enabled him to fight his battle against Papal Infallibility in 1870 as well as practise a very simple private religion. I hope that from him I have inherited a great love for history and keen interest in the affairs of the Church. I hope that Roland Hill's sympathetic biography will interpret my grandfather's enigmatic personality for his readers and enhance his memory. He must have been a very fine man. May he rest in peace.

Marcham Priory, Oxon

Lord Acton, an eminent Victorian who was Gladstone's chief private adviser, made much difference to the development of historical studies in England, and one of his sayings has passed into common currency among English-speaking peoples. Most comparable eminences received biographies not long after their deaths, quite often in two volumes. Acton did not. The newspapers printed obituaries of varying quality, and his pupil Neville Figgis printed a short but valuable little life in the *Dictionary of National Biography*. Gladstone's daughter Mary, to whom Acton wrote brilliant letters, published his letters to her and drew the attention of everyone, not only to what an excellent letter writer he was but to aspects of his personality that were partly of stature and partly strange or at least complex. Herbert Paul, who edited these letters, produced another short life, which was useful. In more modern times others tried their hands at writing about Acton, and some of them illuminated various aspects or epochs of his life, but the only book that came anywhere near the target, if the goal was a proper biography, was that by the American historian Gertrude Himmelfarb, published in 1952.

Any plan for a life of Acton, however, encountered unusual difficulties. The first was that Acton was a compulsive taker of little notes, which he hoarded in the expectation that they would later be useful for historical research or writing. Therefore, after his death his chief relics were in a huge pile of paper, much of it in the form of a card index, and this pile included not only materials from past history but also writings about his contemporaries and his own experience. Because the pile was in the library of Cambridge University, it was accessible to any biographer, and every would-be biographer had to use it. Yet it was and is extraordinarily difficult to use with any confidence. It has never been easy to say what Acton meant in many of the notes: Was he was just copying someone else, or was an idea his own? Did he think this way all the time, or did a card represent only a passing judgement? Moreover, some of the cards are curious lists of historians all of whom held an idea—or something like the idea—that happened to interest his wide-ranging mind at a certain moment. Out of all this material researchers succeeded in obtaining information, which was useful. But from the material alone they could not get near the biography that was needed.

The second difficulty was that anyone who wanted to examine Acton's correspondence needed to range across the libraries of Western Europe. Acton, though an English squire, was only half English. In his near ancestry he had Italians and Germans. He was educated partly in France and partly in England and partly, with momentous consequences for his mind, in Germany. He had close friends in Paris and Bologna and Munich and Vienna as well as in London and Cambridge and Oxford. He used three languages in writing letters. And his German friends sometimes wrote with the old Gothic script, which in handwriting, as distinct from print, is still difficult to read for anyone but an old Gothic German. It might be said that anyone who wanted to write Acton's life needed to be almost as European as he.

The third difficulty was the worst. Acton was a Roman Catholic from birth, who for complex reasons became a profound critic of the Papacy at the time of the Italian Risorgimento, when the Papacy suffered and so called for extreme loyalty from the faithful. Acton's son and daughters, all good Roman Catholics, revered their father but did not share his views on the Papacy. This aspect of Acton had become prominent in various letters that had been published, and his children, who possessed a large collection of his private letters, did not wish it to become more prominent. No biographer could be successful, however, until these letters were made available.

The descendant of Acton who did most to help scholarship in this matter was his charming and scholarly granddaughter Mia Woodruff. As of the 1960s, interested scholars—Damian McElrath, James C. Holland, Josef L. Altholz, and Victor Conzemius—were allowed to publish some of the previously unpublished letters. Conzemius revolutionized Acton studies by printing the extensive correspondence between Acton and his teacher and father figure Ignaz von Döllinger of Munich, for in those letters Acton revealed far more of his mind and his inner personality than he had shown in the letters that were earlier published by Mary Gladstone or by his pupils Neville Figgis and Reginald Vere Laurence. Finally, in 1973 the entire body of the correspondence held by the family was passed to Cambridge University Library to join Acton's library and the earlier card index and other materials. For the first time, a comprehensive biography based on accessible materials was possible.

It was time for a reconsideration. Acton's reputation was at its height during the last years of his life, when Cambridge University Press believed, and rightly so, that it could sell a vast series of narrative histories of Europe with the magic of his name. The series—*Cambridge Modern History, Cambridge Medieval History, Cambridge Ancient History* (they travelled backwards in time, because Acton's primary concern was always the modern)—took long in publishing, more than thirty years, and each volume that appeared carried with it the name of Acton, who designed the plan and found the earliest contributors but died before the first of the volumes was published.

Then came the age of the dictators—Mussolini and then Hitler—and Acton achieved a different sort of fame. His historical instincts and his private moral convictions had made him hate despots. Mandell Creighton—who had edited the *English Historical Review,* which Acton helped to found—had written a history of the Papacy between the Great Schism and the Reformation, a subject that touched Acton's heart. Creighton's widow Louise had quickly published her husband's *Life and Letters* (1904), which included some of Acton's letters to Creighton; and in one of these he had written the sentence that became famous: "Power tends to corrupt; and absolute power corrupts absolutely."

Yet by 1960 Acton's reputation had faded. It was true that his Cambridge Histories were given a dusting and brought up to date with a new series of writers—sometimes valuably, though at other times the old seemed to be more use than the new. But a modern school judged historians by what they had published and not by the books that they owned or by the pile of facts that they were known to know. Acton had succeeded in publishing very little. Partly it was a matter of time—his career at first lay more in journalism and in politics than in professional history. But he did devote much time to history. He was always aware, however, of how much more there was still to know about anything that he studied. He was a perfectionist who refused to recognize that each historical book or tract or article must be an interim report on the evidence that is accessible at that moment. Also, he had so huge an appetite for knowledge of the past that he had to be always acquiring the new and resented the need to settle down to arrange what he had already amassed. Never neglected, for he was too famous for that, he has sometimes been regarded as a person who did not give the world what he ought to have achieved, and some have considered it a mistake to spend time in the study of a failure.

And yet, this character is one of the most fascinating and complex of all the Victorians. His biographer would need a sympathy for the historical process and Acton's particular work in it and for it; an understanding of Catholicism and especially of the sharp conflicts involving Catholicism during the nineteenth century—conflicts both with the world outside the Roman Catholic Church and within the Church; personal experience with Europe and cognizance of its history, with particular attention to South German and Austrian Catholicism and to the moderates among the people of the Italian Risorgimento; and a general knowledge of the upper class of Victorian intellectuals, whose excellent periodicals were able to provide the space for long articles that at times delved more profoundly into subjects than their smaller successors of the twentieth century have room to do.

Roland Hill meets all these criteria. He was a friend to Mia Woodruff and the family; he has historical training; he has reason and experience that enable him to penetrate the German and Italian backgrounds of Acton's life; and he is sympathetic to that liberal Catholicism towards which Acton, with whatever oddities or overstatements, pointed the way. The bulky materials that Acton left behind, now that they are at our disposal, do not negate his complexity, but they do enable us to understand him better. His political convictions, more even than any subtlety of his political expressions, still repay the attention of anyone who tries to examine that difficult theme, the nature of human freedom.

I greatly welcome Roland Hill's work and warmly commend it.

ACKNOWLEDGEMENTS

I owe my interest in Lord Acton's life and work to two men, Bishop (as he then was) David Mathew, author of two biographies of Acton, and Douglas Woodruff, editor for thirty-one years of the British Catholic weekly the *Tablet,* on the staff of which I began my journalistic career. Mathew was a longstanding friend whom I admired as an historian of English Catholicism and for his liberal views on Catholic matters. Woodruff's wife was the granddaughter of Lord Acton, and in the early 1950s I assisted her husband in the republication of some of Acton's early essays under the title *Essays on Church and State.* The decades immediately after World War II were the time of an Acton revival, especially in Britain and the United States, led by G. P. Gooch, who knew Acton at Cambridge, as well as Herbert Butterfield, Owen Chadwick, and Gertrude Himmelfarb. In Germany, Ulrich Noack published his Acton studies as early as 1935, 1936, and 1947. That generation of scholars still knew some of those who had known the great historian personally. Yet I was able to pursue my interest in Acton only after a lifetime spent as a staff correspondent of German and Austrian newspapers in London, when the Acton family, represented by the fourth Lord Acton and Douglas Woodruff's widow, the Hon. Mia Woodruff (who has since also died), supported the project. Her friendship and active interest were invaluable. Almost alone in her family she had preserved a special attachment to the grandfather she had never known and was particularly knowledgeable about his intricate family relationships. She had known Marie, Acton's wife; Mamy, his eldest daughter; and Mrs. Drew (Mary Gladstone). When Aldenham, the Actons' Shropshire seat, was sold, the Woodruffs kept the extensive collection of Acton's private papers in their home, Marcham Priory (near Abingdon), until they were permanently placed in the Cambridge University Library, which already housed Acton's vast personal library. Mia Woodruff's understanding of her grandfather's personality and life was a great help for me in the writing of his biography.

I am indebted, above all, to the selfless help and advice of Professor James C. Holland of Shepherd College, who is a leading Acton scholar. His great knowledge, rigorous historical discipline, and respect for the ideas of others are in the best Actonian tradition. He has given freely of his time and effort to knock my work into the shape it required (although I hasten to add that responsibility for the accuracy of the information in this book is mine alone). His belief in the book has meant much to me. I could not have had a better mentor, as Professor Holland (together with Josef L. Altholz and Damian McElrath) was part of the editorial team that republished the Acton-Simpson correspondence. Those important letters of Acton's early exuberant journalistic phase had to be rescued from the misguided partisan attempt at "rehabilitating" Acton's Catholic orthodoxy, undertaken by Abbot Gasquet in *Lord Acton and His Circle* (1906) after the unwise publication by Mary Gladstone of Acton's private letters to her seemed to cast doubt on his religious beliefs. As the publication of the bulk of Acton's correspondence has shown since, no such exoneration was in fact needed. To Dr. Mary Griset Holland—the other half of a partnership in learning—I owe much; her painstaking compression and revision of several chapters came at a critical moment. Professor and Mrs. Holland are currently preparing a scholarly edition of Acton's correspondence with Mr. Gladstone.

Basic for the understanding of Acton's life and thought is the admirable four-volume edition of the Acton-Döllinger-Blennerhassett correspondence by Dr. Victor Conzemius of Lucerne. This major work of scholarship has dispelled many ambiguities surrounding Acton's work. Moreover, Dr. Conzemius has, in numerous learned articles, illuminated many aspects of the life of the great Döllinger as well as his English pupil. I am grateful for his counsel, support, and hospitality. I owe much to the Reverend Professor Owen Chadwick, both for insights into Acton's personality and for his critical reading of my manuscript. I am honored to have his foreword included in this book. My former teacher and friend, Dr. Christopher Howard of the University of London, has contributed of his deep historical knowledge of the nineteenth century.

I acknowledge the Gracious Permission of Her Majesty the Queen to quote from Queen Victoria's journal, now in the Royal Archives, and also from letters from Lord Granville, W. E. Gladstone, and Lord Ponsonby relating to Lord Acton. I am obliged to Mr. Oliver Everett, the Librarian of Windsor Castle, and his courteous staff for frequent assistance. Invaluable was the support from Dr. A. E. B. Owen, formerly Keeper of Manuscripts in the Cambridge University Library (who was also instrumental in securing Lord Acton's private papers for the Library); from his successor, Dr. Patrick Zutshi; from Mr. Godfrey Waller, Superintendent of the CUL Manuscript Room; and from the ever-helpful members of the staff at that magnificent treasure house of learning. To Barendina Galloway, doctoral student in Trinity College, Cambridge, I am much indebted for detailed assistance with myriad references to archival and printed sources. I acknowledge gratefully the extensive professional assistance of Ann Hofstra Grogg, who copyedited the manuscript before it was submitted to the publisher. The skill and patience of Susan Burke, who typed the often-corrected drafts of the book, deserve particular recognition. Among my blessings has been a splendid manuscript editor from Yale University Press; I am most grateful to Jenya Weinreb for her astute eye for detail and her sense of connectedness in narrative. Special thanks to the Mrs. L. R. Rope Third Charitable Settlement for generous help and for the sympathetic understanding for Actonian thought shown by Mr. Crispin Rope. I received helpful information from the Biblioteca dell'Archiginnasio, Bologna, keepers of the Minghetti Papers. I thank the Provost and Scholars of King's College, Cambridge, for quotations from the Oscar Browning Papers, and the Master and Fellows of Pembroke College, Oxford, for quoted extracts from the papers of Sir Peter le Page Renouf. I am also grateful to Dr. Miroslav Kurelac, Director of the Historical Institute, Croatian Academy of Arts, Zagreb, which preserves letters from Acton to Bishop Josef Strossmayer; and to Mr. and Mrs. Roderick Swire, the present owners of Aldenham Park, Shropshire, who were kind enough to show me round the former Acton seat. Msgr. Charles Burns, of the Archivio Segreto Vaticano, kindly initiated me in the intricacies of that ancient library.

I have benefitted from conversation with Barone Francesco Leporanto di Acton, Naples, and with the late Sir Harold Acton, Florence. Valuable help was given by Countess Arco Valley, Schloss Adldorf, Bavaria; Baroness Ann Twickel, Coughton, Warwickshire; Professor Dr. Otto Bardong, M.E.P., Worms; Professor Adolf M. Birke, formerly Director of the German Historical Institute in London; Reverend Denis Cleary, Rosmini House, Durham; Countess Marion Dönhoff, Hamburg; Mrs. M. T. Halford, Shropshire County Council Record Office, Shrewsbury; Archbishop Bruno B. Heim, Olten, Switzerland; Baroness Heyl zu Herrnsheim, Worms; Msgr. Karel Kasteel, Rome; Professor Dr. Gottfried-Karl Kindermann, Munich; Canon Rudolf Laczka, Bridgnorth, Shropshire; Professor Dr. Maximilian Liebmann, Graz, Austria; Miss Nicolette Luthmer, Kurhessische Hausstiftung, Schloss Fasanerie, Fulda, Germany; Canon P. Marmion, Shrewsbury Diocesan Archives, Sale, Cheshire; Charles Edward Lord Mowbray, Segrave and Stourton, London; Canon J. S. Nurser, Cambridge, England; Dr. Maria Piacentini, Rome; Miss Elizabeth Poyser, former Archivist of the Westminster Diocesan Archives, and the present Archivist, Reverend Ian Dickie; Mr. and Mrs. Simon Reynolds, London; Prince Ludovic Rospigliosi, Rome; Dr. Robert Smart, Keeper of Manuscripts, University of St. Andrew's Library, Scotland; Mrs. Fabienne Smith, Edinburgh; Dr. Bernhard Stillfried, Vienna; Mr. Terence Weiler, London; Mr. John Wells, Cambridge, England; and the Very Reverend Gregory Winterton, of the Oratory, Birmingham, England.

To the Acton Institute of Grand Rapids, Michigan, I am greatly indebted. Its abiding interest and support has helped this work to come to print. It is my earnest hope that its fidelity to this effort will be rewarded by whatever are the merits of the book, and by advancing still Lord Acton's renown.

I am especially grateful to Dr. Martin Brett and Teresa Brett for their hospitality and kindness during my Cambridge research work. I owe much to Margit Crozier for years of loyal secretarial help. Last but not least, I pay tribute to my wife, Amelia, for her long sufferance and, particularly, for bringing her native Italian common sense and imagination to bear on the needful distinction between the true and the real meaning of words written in private letters in French and Italian a century and a half ago.

The Acton family tree, for which I am indebted to Leonardo Conte Visconti di Modrone, himself related to the Italian part of the Acton family, has naturally had to be compressed. A complete family tree, entitled *Genealogia degli Acton a cura di Fernando e Francesco Acton,* was privately published in Naples in 1969.

Regarding the spelling of names, consistency rather than certain correctness in every case had to be the aim, on account of the variety found even in British and Continental standard works on the peerage. In the case of Lord Acton's Italian maternal ancestors, the Genoese Brignole e Sale, the form Brignole-Sale (most common today) has been used throughout this book; similarly, the hyphen has been adopted in the case of Arco-Valley, the name of Acton's Munich relations. This usage would not have been allowed when Acton's uncle and future father-in-law, Maximilian Count Arco (1806–1875), having inherited a vast estate, received the additional title in 1827 from King Ludwig I of Bavaria in order to distinguish his branch from other Arcos.

INTRODUCTION

Lord Acton, the great scholar and historian, has long been considered an enigma, foxing his contemporaries as well as later scholars. His appearance was almost forbiddingly Victorian: he had a full black beard that turned grey in his last years, brilliant blue eyes, a fine resonant voice, and the beautiful manners of a patrician. He was at home equally in England, France, Germany, and Italy, and was fluent in French and German, less so in Italian. He possessed an extreme English reserve and routinely refused to explain himself. Yet, as his private letters show, he was able to open his heart to a few close friends and relatives: his "Professor," Ignaz von Döllinger; Countess Arco, his cousin and later his mother-in-law; Mary Drew, daughter of William Ewart Gladstone; the German-born writer Charlotte Blennerhassett; and his daughters.

His ideas on the nature and development of freedom are certainly relevant today; he indicated, for example, how important it is to protect freedom not only from its enemies but also, and even more so, from its well-meaning friends. He was devoted to the Catholic Church, whose communion, he said, was literally dearer to him than life. Yet Acton was not much preoccupied with "liberal Catholicism," although as a liberal and a Catholic, he naturally cared about liberty in and for the Church. Rather, his essential concern was with truth and how easily it could be manipulated by its apparent servants—in the name of religion or politics—so that the end would appear to have justified the means.

Sir John Acton was born in Naples on 10 January 1834 and died on 19 June 1902 at Tegernsee, Bavaria. These dates frame a cosmopolitan life favoured by outstanding intellectual gifts and promise as well as conservative family connections, altogether an unlikely background for a great liberal thinker. The Actons were Shropshire baronets—conservative, loyalist supporters of the monarchy and the Church of England. Occasionally they revived their family fortune by marrying rich heiresses. They had—as their kinsman, the historian Edward Gibbon, put it in his autobiography—"adequate connections . . . without being disgraced by the profession of trade" (pp. 272–73).

In the eighteenth century something of a jolt occurred in the Acton family. Three of its members, independently of each other, returned to the faith of their fathers. In 1762 Mass was said again at Aldenham, the family's seat in Shropshire. The head of the family, Sir Richard Acton, the fifth Baronet, had an attic converted into a chapel. Earlier, two of his cousins who belonged to a junior branch of the family had gone abroad, a not unusual move for adventurous young Englishmen without fortune or property. One of them, Dr. Edward Acton, went to Paris in 1732 to continue his medical studies. His elder brother joined the East India Company and, as Commodore John Acton, ended his career in command of the ships of Grand Duke Leopold of Tuscany. Dr. Edward Acton married a French woman in 1735 and settled at Besançon, and his change of religion was probably connected with his marriage. His seafaring brother, who remained a bachelor, thirty years later followed Edward's example, becoming a Catholic shortly before he died at Pisa.

In England at the time it was hardly possible for Catholics to rise professionally. So the surgeon's eldest son, John Francis Edward, was educated by the Jesuits at Besançon and went to join his uncle in Tuscany when he was fourteen, to be trained in the navy. After the Commodore's death, John Francis Edward took over his position. He was later sent to Naples to reorganize the navy of the Kingdom of the Two Sicilies, ruled by Grand Duke Leopold's sister, Queen Marie Caroline, and the Bourbon king, Ferdinand I. John Francis Edward Acton became their trusted prime minister and practically ruled the kingdom during the upheavals of the French Revolution and its Mediterranean repercussions under Napoleon and Nelson.

When the head of the Acton family in England, Sir Richard Acton, died without a male heir, title and property passed to John Francis Edward Acton, the English prime minister of Naples. He married late in life and had three children, the eldest of whom was Sir Ferdinand Richard Acton, the seventh Baronet, who continued in Bourbon service. His contribution to history was to marry the only child of the Duke of Dalberg and to die early, when their only son and heir, the subject of this biography, was just three years old. Sir Ferdinand Richard's young widow would marry again—into the top of the British Whig-Liberal establishment.

The boy, destined to follow his stepfather, Lord Granville, in a political career—though a far more limited one—went to an English boarding school. Young John Acton, whose mother was preoccupied with her second husband, was a lonely child. Rejected by Cambridge University because he was a Catholic, he was dispatched to Munich to study under the eminent Church historian Ignaz von Döllinger. There he discovered vast intellectual horizons and his vocation as a scholar and historian, but also a new home and real family life with his relatives, the Arcos. His cousin Anna, Countess Arco, loved him as a son; she was the first to understand his mind and heart. Resolved to consolidate this attachment, Acton eventually married her daughter Marie, his cousin. He returned to England with an idealist mission, to teach English Catholics what he had learned in Germany about the Church and history. As the editor of learned Catholic journals of liberal outlook, he was bound to be bitterly disappointed by the ghettolike mentality of English Catholics, who were just emerging from centuries of oppression.

Acton was twenty-three years old when he returned from Munich to England as a wealthy young man with a mission: to introduce to English Catholics some of the ideas and currents with which he had become familiar in Munich and which were behind the renewal of European Catholicism after the devastation wrought by the French Revolution and the Napoleonic Wars. At the same time, driven by his stepfather's pressure and influence, he also tried his hand at politics as a Liberal MP. But he had neither the political interest nor the ability to identify fully with the Westminster scene: it was too insular and shallow for him, although at least it led to his friendship with William Ewart Gladstone.

Acton clearly preferred being a writer and editor of learned reviews, on which at first he worked closely with John Henry Newman, whose ideas for raising the intellectual level of the Catholic laity Acton fully supported. And, more than the conservative Newman, Acton wanted the Catholic Church as far as possible to work with, not against, the forces of the century, modern science and scholarship, which were rapidly transforming European society and technology and leaving the Church behind like a bastion not even worth assailing anymore. In a telling image he compared the Church to a metal constantly exposed to the atmosphere, which every generation must cleanse anew from the accretions and the patina of time and place, which become mixed up with the essence of her faith.

Acton was particularly interested in the political education of Catholics. His writings reveal him as an English liberal to whom the anticlerical, nationalist, and State-centralized tendencies of European Continental liberalism were hateful. But his idea of reconciling the Catholic Church with the modern world came more than a century before its time. The numbers of educated and interested Catholic readers of his journals were minute—the circulation figures were never more than three thousand—and most were probably educated converts who had followed Newman into the Church. The Church authorities were hostile to the converts and disliked what they regarded as interference in theological issues, unheard of from a layman, however elevated. Besides, the influx of Irish and the growing number of poor Catholics needing work and schools in the age of industrialization concentrated the minds of English Catholic leaders on the more basic needs, those of the mind being considered a dispensable luxury. Moreover, the Pope, as head of the misgoverned Papal States, was under heavy attack from Italian liberals and nationalists and was threatened also by the big powers confronting each other in Italy. It was not the moment to question, as Acton and Döllinger dared to, whether the temporal power (by which was meant the Pope's exercise of political, secular sovereign power) was of the essence of the Papacy or was rather one of those accretions of the centuries, as the Catholic world has come to accept since.

This struggle came to a head in the Vatican Council of 1870 over the issue of the dogma of Papal Infallibility. Acton set out to support the minority, substantial though it was, of bishops who did not think that the proposed Infallibility of the Pope should be proclaimed as a dogma. In Rome that young Englishman, with style and moral fervour, proved an extraordinarily powerful force in rallying and influencing the various players on the stage, ecclesiastical and political. He acted as a kind of chief whip encouraging and warning his allies in multiple languages and inspiring them with confidence, a most unusual role for a thirty-six-year-old layman of his generation. His proven journalistic talent enabled him to discover what was going on behind the closed doors of the Vatican Council. He traced the political manoeuvres among the Papal majority to their sources, gathering information in high social circles into which he had easy access.

Acton sent daily reports to Döllinger in Munich, by diplomatic post or private messengers, to circumvent the Vatican secret police. Döllinger published these reports, edited by himself, in a Bavarian newspaper of liberal outlook. It gained some ten thousand new readers and was avidly read in the Vatican. These reports from the Council showed how well informed the anonymous writer was on the theological and political issues in and around the Council. They inspired greater confidence than the tendentious reports put out by each faction. Acton's and Döllinger's reports were not free from one-sidedness, tinged as they were by a veritable love-hate relationship with the cause they sought to serve. But they described that historical, political, and theological struggle in an exciting and understandable manner, and they are even readable and informative today, when the archives have surrendered most of the Vatican Council's secrets. Acton's role in Rome at that time has all the ingredients of a modern thriller, including its cloak-and-dagger dimension. It proved to a later generation, at least, that in the Church too, as in any government, exaggerated secrecy always brings about precisely what it wants to prevent. The proclamation of the dogma of Papal Infallibility by a majority of bishops stopped the advance of modern thinking within the Catholic Church for more than a century; the minority bishops were heavily routed. Acton's Professor was excommunicated by the Church, although Acton himself submitted outwardly to her decisions and escaped by a hair's-breadth being condemned as well. What saved him was probably his status as a leading English Catholic nobleman who had the British prime minister's ear and protection.

There was no enigma about Acton's religion. He had a simple and unostentatious faith. He was very serious about it, and was terrified that he might be excommunicated. His defeat in the great struggle over Papal Infallibility drove him near to despair. That fight, however, was not quite in vain. A century later, the Second Vatican Council redressed the imbalance of Infallibility by restoring the collegiate relationship of Pope and bishops. Newman, who had not thought the time was right for Papal Infallibility, was vindicated, and Acton along with him. Indeed, the Second Vatican Council also adopted Newman's ideas "on consulting the faithful in matters of doctrine." That was the prophetic title of his famous and controversial essay first published in Acton's journal the *Rambler* and denounced to Rome by an English Catholic Bishop.

Acton was to be vindicated in other ways, too. The century that followed

Victorian confidence and progress saw the full horrors of totalitarianism. In time there was good reason to recall what Acton had once written to the Anglican apologist of the Borgia popes, Bishop Mandell Creighton: "Power tends to corrupt, and absolute power corrupts absolutely." This lesson was aimed at Acton's liberal contemporaries, many of whom were inclined to make allowances for historical figures by citing their stage of historical development, but it had special relevance to the political developments of the twentieth century.

Acton's appointment, in 1895, to the Regius Chair of Modern History in Cambridge was the crowning moment of his life. In a famous Inaugural Lecture he warned his listeners "never to debase the moral currency." His emphasis on moral judgement in the writing of history has become distasteful to later historians, who seek to avoid the hypocrisy of the Victorians by doing without moral judgement altogether. But one may question whether Acton's concern with good and evil and conscience in history does not retain a validity beyond his age. His life seems to illustrate the importance of asking the right questions rather than finding the right answers, which in any case are likely to change in a changing world.

LORD ACTON

1

BIRTH IN NAPLES

At six in the evening on 10 January 1834, Marie Louisa, wife of Sir Ferdinand Richard Acton, gave birth to a son in their villa on the Riviera di Chiaja in Naples. The birth certificate, made out in Italian, described the father as Don Ferdinando Riccardo Acton, thirty-two years old, "Lord-in-Waiting to His Majesty Whom God preserve" and English Baronet. The mother was named as Baroness Donna Maria Luisa Pellina de Dalberg, twenty-one years old, domiciled with her husband in Naples at the Riviera di Chiaja.[1]

The baptism took place the next day. It is registered at St. Joseph's, the little parish church nearby on the Riviera. But it is more likely to have been held at the Villa Acton. The little chapel, situated in one of the porticoes through which carriages entered the Acton grounds, would not have held many guests. The child was christened John Emerich Edward Acton, the first two names after his paternal and maternal grandfathers, and Edward after a distinguished ancestor of the Aldenham Actons.

The Villa Acton was somewhat set back from the busy and fashionable sea promenade of the Bay of Naples. One entered upon an English landscaped garden with palm trees on the lawn, and beyond, just visible from the road, was the elegant and luxurious villa designed in the Neoclassical style, which Sir Richard Acton had had built for himself. He had been fastidious about the plans, employing a leading Naples architect, Pietro Valente, pupil of Antonio Niccolini, the designer of the Teatro San Carlo. However, a classical purist like Henry Edward Fox, later the fourth Lord Holland (1802–1859), felt that not much else in the Chiaja was "surpassed in hideousness by the vulgar, staring, ill-placed dwelling erected for Sir Ferdinand Acton."[2] And as we have Holland House to testify to his taste, his judgement is not to be disregarded lightly. There was some dispute in the Acton family over whether the palazzo should have been built at all. Richard's spirited younger sister, Elizabeth, implored him in her letters from England to put his money into the family seat at Aldenham, Shropshire, which had suffered from the owner's absence in Italy. Further to neglect it, she wrote, "would not only be wicked but mad. What would people say in seeing that beautiful property deserted, that old family mansion falling in ruins and to think that the money that ought to be spent on it is thrown away in foreign lands."[3] But Sir Richard Acton was not interested in his English inheritance; even so, his sister's nagging had at least some effect, as her mother wrote to her from Aldenham: "Richard is thinking so seriously of the Hall that he is going to name an architect to design a roof and skylight."[4]

Like their sister, Richard and his younger brother, Charles Acton, had been privately educated in England. In 1819 the two young men went to Magdalene College, Cambridge, but, as Catholics, were barred from taking their degrees. Having no stamina for studies, Richard left after barely a year to return to Naples and enter into the service of the Kingdom of the Two Sicilies, following in the footsteps of his father, who had been the prime minister. Richard first served briefly as a diplomat in St. Petersburg. But, restless, sickly, and spoiled as he was, he turned into a gambler and spendthrift. He preferred to travel and indulge his tastes as a cultured young gentleman of leisure and money.

Ferdinand II, the grandson of Ferdinand I and Queen Marie Caroline, inherited the throne in 1830, when he was just twenty and popular. Richard Acton was not as close to him as his father, General Sir John Francis Edward Acton, had been to the King's grandparents, but he was gratified to be made *gentilhomme de la chambre de Roi* (lord-in-waiting), as he wrote in a letter to his mother.[5]

Charles Acton had gone from Cambridge to the Roman Academia of young noblemen, where he studied for the priesthood and was grounded in papal diplomacy as Cardinal Luigi Lambruschini's secretary at the Paris nunciature;

then he returned to Rome to the Rota, the supreme ecclesiastical court. When Richard's son was baptized, he came to Naples. At that time he was already a monsignor and, being close to Gregory XVI, was soon to receive the Roman purple, at the age of thirty-nine. He died when he was only forty-four.[6]

The two brothers' own baptisms, in 1801 and 1803, had been conducted in splendour in the Royal Chapel. King Ferdinand I and Queen Caroline, whom their father had served as prime minister for nearly thirty years, were the godparents of Richard and Charles, respectively. The brothers were therefore given royal names and extravagant gifts. Sir Ferdinand Richard, however, dropped his "Ferdinand" and remained Richard, though not for any lack of political sympathy. The two Acton brothers were wholly on the side of legitimacy and restoration, and Charles, who had been held over the font by the turbulent Queen Caroline and whose second Christian name was Januarius (Gennaro),[7] represented the spirit of calm and pious conservatism in the Church in the age of Gregory XVI (1831–1846).

Sir Richard Acton's baby son was perhaps fortunate in being spared a similar royal and Bourbon baptism. For the future historian of liberty and friend of the British prime minister William Ewart Gladstone, the scourge of Neapolitan autocracy, that would have been even worse than being the descendant of the Bourbon King's most loyal English servant. It was left to another, later descendant of the Acton family, Sir Harold Acton, to vindicate the Bourbons of Naples from the calumnies to which Queen Caroline's prime minister was particularly prone, from his Italian and French revolutionary detractors.[8]

Baby John Emerich Edward was doted on by his parents, who called him their *petit chou* ("little cabbage," a common endearment for children). Writing to his mother in England, Sir Richard noted proudly that people said the baby looked more like him every day, "almost a Richard III," which was not perhaps as complimentary to the *petit chou* as it was meant to be. But soon after the birth, Sir Richard already felt the pull of the great world and the need to pursue his "projects," as he called them. He had been made a director of the newly funded Academy of Naples, a position that required him to travel abroad, and he wondered whether it would not be better for his mother to return to Naples to help look after Marie and the baby, rather than to take Marie and the baby abroad with him or leave them with his mother in England.[9]

In a letter to her mother-in-law, Marie praised her husband for his gentle ways with the baby. Marie's mother, the Duchess of Dalberg, was helping to look after him, but she tired easily. [10] The baby was putting on weight and seemed to be getting black hair, Marie noted in her next letter, and was taken out on the balcony for the first time on a springlike day at the end of January.[11] He was "magnificent," amazing visitors with his "embon point" (tummy) and strength and looking like a two-month-old baby rather than one of three weeks. Meanwhile, Richard, accompanied by Marie's aunt (Maria Brignole-Sale), was again claimed by the carnival season, "six balls a week." Their own house theatre was getting ready, and they were planning to put on *Le mariage de raison*.[12]

Three weeks after his birth, the baby was taken on his first outing, dressed in "a frock coat of white wool with blue piping and a small white hat." At the time, Richard was absorbed by preparations for a big ball with theatricals given by the Roman Academia. The King and Queen were expected, and Richard, who was going to open the ball by dancing with Queen Caroline, added a note to the letter hoping that it would be successful. Marie, for her part, was not sorry to see the dawn of Ash Wednesday, for "this year my carnival was my Lent," and she would go out again for the first time that Sunday.[13]

The ball was a success even though the King and Queen did not attend, although, as Richard and Marie later wrote to Nonna (as the infant's grandmother was called), the King showed Sir Richard much *bonté* (goodwill) and was to come to their next soirée. Among all the talk of preparations for this event, the doting references to *le petit,* increasingly left to the care of servants, took second place. Marie was preparing to play a small part in an Italian comedy they were rehearsing and was also taking part in *Le mariage de raison*. Weakened and thin after the difficult birth, she returned gradually to the social round.[14]

The Actons' big reception took place on 1 March 1834. The whole of the Riviera di Chiaja was illuminated by fires placed in iron baskets on poles, with cavalry assembled and two military bands playing, one in the Acton garden, the other in the entrance hall. It was St. David's Day (honoring the patron saint of Wales), and John Orlando Parry, the Victorian entertainer and a patriotic Welshman, recorded the occasion as "one of the grandest parties I ever was at. . . . Oh! what a magnificent house and what splendid style everything was in. The walls were covered with crimson and gold papers, every door was covered with gold leaf and the most splendid carving all embossed with gold! All the ottomans were white satin with gold embroidery! Looking glasses down to the magnificent carpets, chandeliers of the most exquisite forms and shapes, candlebras [*sic*] with wax lights in such profusion that it was as light as day!"[15]

At nine in the evening a flourish of trumpets and drums announced the arrival of the King and Queen and all the royal family. Parry's enthusiastic description continued: "They were recd by Sir [Richard] Acton at the street door and ushered into the splendid room." In the ballroom the other guests, Neapolitan nobility and English residents, were already assembled. The performance consisted of three pieces, all French vaudeville, "most excellently done indeed. The King amused many persons by his looking and touching the lamps in front of the stage to see how they were made. . . . What a splendid sight the ball-room presented—one sea of turbans, feathers, diamonds and jewels, etc." [16]

The host himself was less happy, particularly because of hordes of uninvited guests, of whom Parry may have been one. "It was far too crowded, five hundred people came . . . although we hoped there would be no more than three hundred. No one could move an inch. It was terribly hot and the strong wind prevented the opening of windows. Marie stayed with the royal family and I joined them in the interval." One might well wonder how the Villa Acton—today a much dilapidated site of concerts and exhibitions, known (after its later owners) as the Museo Pignatelli—could seat even three hundred guests in any comfort. "But . . . our guests stayed until two in the morning and enjoyed little hot pastries, cakes, ices, tea and hot soup. Naples had never seen a like concourse of carriages in the Chiaja." [17] No doubt, the baby in his nursery took little notice of the commotion.

2

A COSMOPOLITAN BACKGROUND

The early years of John Acton's childhood were dominated by women. His father was frequently away or, when he was home, did not want his pleasures interrupted. His mother was an overpowering influence, especially when it came to religion. Her firmly grounded Catholic piety was French rather than German in its loyalty to the Church of the Counter-Reformation. Born in Paris, she was brought up at Herrnsheim, the Dalbergs' Rhineland property, but the Dalbergs spent much of their lives at their Paris residence, 25 rue d'Anjou, in the Faubourg Saint-Honoré.

Another frequent presence in the young boy's life was his father's mother, who became known as Nonna Acton. She was only in her early forties and, with her warm Italian nature, remained attached to him, particularly later, when jealousies arose between the Dalbergs and the Actons over Marie's marriage settlement and Nonna felt bound to stick up for the orphaned boy. Then there were Johnny Acton's many cheerful Neapolitan cousins — Carlo Giuseppe Acton, his father's uncle and brother of Marie Caroline's prime minister, had no fewer than fourteen children with his German wife, Countess Berghe von Tripps. Acton's mother, brought up in the sophisticated Dalberg society in Paris, disliked the

Neapolitan provincial set, although she tried hard to adjust to her husband's environment.

Yet another early influence on John Acton was Pauline de la Ferronays, the eldest daughter of their Neapolitan neighbours. In later years he described her as "almost my earliest" friend and was sorry for being irritated by her somewhat gushing nature. "She was intimate with my mother before I was born. What does it matter that she also bores me a good deal by her restlessness, her curiosity and indiscretion, her want of serenity, etc.? I always liked her in spite of it, and she was always a great, but uncomfortable, admirer of Mr. Gladstone."[1] Acton was always somewhat vehement in his personal judgements. Pauline was twenty-six when he was born, and full of romantic neo-Gothic notions. She was married in the same year of his birth, in the Acton chapel, to Augustus Craven, son and heir of the immensely rich Keppel Craven and the Margravine of Ansbach, both staunch Protestants who disapproved of their son's Catholicism and friends. The most prominent characteristic of Pauline herself was her strong Catholic religious identity, acquired in her earliest years.

In Pauline Craven's edifying romance *Récit d'une sœur,* a schmaltzy saga of her own family and an international best seller of its day, the garden of the Acton villa was described as an enchanted paradise of childhood.[2] It is not without irony that the first seeds of the "ideal Catholicism," as the historian Lord Acton was later to describe the new and hopeful era of the Catholic Church in Europe, were planted, as it were, in his cradle by the intense and well-meaning Pauline Craven and at a time when he was not really conscious of her penetrating presence.

Given the small world of European aristocracy in the early nineteenth century, some surprise had been caused by the union between the only daughter of the Duke of Dalberg and the delicate Sir Richard Acton, her elder by twelve years. They had met about 1828 in Paris. Sir Richard's wooing of Marie was conducted with all the formalities, in the eighteenth-century manner of a careful business transaction. Rumours that he was sickly had reached her family, and the Duke wrote to him accordingly: "It would be hard for our daughter to become a nurse instead of a mother." Sir Richard persuaded a friend to dispel the Duke's concern on that score.[3] The negotiations dragged on through 1830. The Duchess seemed to be a major obstacle, pointing out that this suitor, aged thirty, was much older than her daughter, not yet eighteen. Marie herself was reluctant but ready to do her duty, which, for someone of her class, was the primary requirement.

Charles Greville, the cynical diarist, described Marie's parents: "The duc de Dalberg and his wife are a perpetual source of amusement to me, she with her devotion and believing everything, he with his *air moqueur* and believing nothing; she so merry, he so shrewd, and so they squabble about religion."[4] The embittered Henry Edward Fox, who had met the Dalbergs in Paris in 1821, found the Duke to be "a clever man, but a great projector . . . [who] spends his fortune in following up his theories and plans." Of the Duchess he wrote: "Mme Dalberg is not pretty, nor has she pleasing manners. She is pert and flippant; her teeth are fine, but she is *too* fair."[5] By contrast, Lady Harriet Granville, wife of the British ambassador in Paris, thought the Duchess "very agreeable and natural."[6]

Greville's dislike was no doubt strengthened by the Duchess's strong religious interests. She was keen on the Neapolitan miracle of the liquefaction of the blood of St. Gennaro (Januarius), which she extolled to Greville, the scoffer. He went with Sir Richard Acton to Naples cathedral to see the miracle and rather agreed with Sir Richard's assessment that nobody except the common people believed it, so the priests were obliged to go on pretending to perform a miracle in which it was known they did not believe themselves.[7]

As for Marie's father, Emmerich Josef Dalberg, like many Germans of his generation he was an admirer of Napoleon and entered his service after the peace of Schönbrunn, in 1809. In the following year Napoleon created him Duke and councillor of state and bestowed on him estates in Germany valued at some 7 million francs (£28 million). After Napoleon's fall in 1814, the Duke of Dalberg was a member of the French government of Louis XVIII and accompanied Charles Maurice de Talleyrand to the Congress of Vienna. In the eyes of German patriots fighting against Napoleon, the Duke was regarded as a traitor. (German historians think more kindly of him today.) The only way to save his estates on the left bank of the Rhine was then to become a French citizen. The family in any case was European, speaking French and Italian rather than German. Louis XVIII made the Duke a peer of France; he was French minister in Turin until he clashed over policy with the King and resigned. He lost a large part of his fortune in the crash of the Paris Bank and through the failure of a French coal mine in which he had invested much, so that he was compelled to sell his important collection of paintings. He also lost some of the Rhineland possessions because of dishonest stewards. Marie Louisa von Dalberg was not, therefore, quite as rich an heiress as was sometimes thought. According to the marriage contract, signed in Paris on 7 July 1832, she was given a dowry comprising household goods, linen, carriages, and other items, valued at 20,000 francs, and also the sum of 200,000 francs in gold, representing approximately £80,000 and £800,000, respectively, at today's valuation of the franc.

The wedding of the Duke's daughter and Sir Richard Acton took place in Paris in June 1832, even before the marriage contract was signed. It was a great social occasion, attended by some of Europe's oldest families. The bride's mother came from the ancient Genoan family Brignole-Sale; the Dalberg lineage was of even greater antiquity, and its family tree in the cathedral of Worms goes back to Abraham and to a Roman soldier who is supposed to have been a relative of Jesus Christ (some genealogical licence is not unusual in high circles). But more concretely they were descended from the twelfth-century chamberlain of the Bishop of Worms, whose office became hereditary. The *Kämmerer von Worms,* as they were called, came from the Middle Rhine region. The Prince Bishops of Worms held high office as electors, bishops, and canons in the Holy Roman Empire, their distinction being in the realm of intellect rather than military prowess. Their most famous ancestor was undoubtedly Carl Theodor (1744–1817), Archbishop Elector of Mainz and Worms, Prince Primate of the newly constituted Confederation of the Rhine. He played an important role in the late eighteenth-century nationalist stirrings in the German Catholic Church, the equivalent of the Gallican trend in France.

The Dalbergs were premier Dukes of the Holy Roman Empire, equivalent in rank to the Howards, the Dukes of Norfolk who held the rank of Earl Marshal, Hereditary Marshal, and Chief Butler of England. The special privilege of being the first in the imperial coronation to have their title confirmed by the new Emperor was granted to the Dalbergs in 1494 by Emperor Maximilian I at his coronation, and until the end of the Holy Roman Empire, in 1806, the herald's call "Ist kein Dalberg da?" (Is there no Dalberg present?) was customary at imperial coronations.

That the Neapolitan Actons and the Dalbergs came together at all was evidently part of that adventurous turn in the Acton family, when it suddenly developed a taste for foreign travel in the first half of the eighteenth century. In 1733 the young London doctor Edward Acton, who was studying surgery in Paris, travelled to Besançon in response to a call from a friend and kinsman who had fallen ill there. This was Edward Gibbon, father of the famous author of *The Decline and Fall of the Roman Empire,* who had gone to the Academie, an internationally known riding school attended by English gentlemen. While tending Gibbon for some months, Dr. Acton offered his skills also to the townspeople. One of these local patients was Anne Cathérine Loys, daughter of the president of the Besançon parliament. They fell in love, but the girl's mother at first displayed some resistance to the marriage, which was overcome when Dr. Acton converted to the Catholic faith. Dr. Acton became an honorary citizen of Besançon (though never a naturalized Frenchman) and attained fame as one of the first surgeons to introduce smallpox inoculation in France. In contrast to the reactionary views of his immediate descendants, Dr. Acton's liberal and reformist outlook corresponded to the French pre-revolutionary climate and was only to be taken up again a century later by his great-grandson, the subject of this book.

The origins of the Actons were Saxon, their earliest and pre-Conquest descendants being found in Worcestershire. The name is derived from the Saxon words *ac,* meaning "oak," and *tun,* meaning "sheltered habitation," which, by the early fourteenth century, was to be found at Aldenham (by the eldertree), a house situated on the winding road leading from Bridgnorth to Shrewsbury.

One Acton, Sir William, ventured as far as London. He became Sheriff of the City of London in 1625 and Lord Mayor of London in 1641, after he was made a Baronet by Charles I—only to be deposed when war broke out, on account of his attachment to the royal cause. His cousin's son, Sir Edward Acton, was even more loyal. He was granted a baronetcy for his services to the Stuarts, took part in the unsuccessful defence of Bridgnorth against its parliamentary besiegers, and sustained a leg wound at the Battle of Worcester in 1642, which was recorded exaggeratedly in the Acton coat of arms—a spurred leg encased in armour, still visible today in the Acton crest crowning the ornate arc of the Aldenham entrance gate. Sir Edward was succeeded as head of the family by Sir Walter, of whose seven stalwart sons Gibbon, the historian, wrote that they "all exceeded the ordinary proportion of the human stature. One of these, Francis . . . confessed or boasted that he was a pigmy [pygmy] of six feet two inches, the least of the seven," and he added that "such men had not been born since the Revolution." The young Gibbon, with a far less distinguished background, paid respectful tribute to the ancient and loyal family of Shropshire Baronets to whom he was related by "a triple-alliance": his grandmother was linked (in her first marriage) to one of Sir Walter Acton's sons; his father, Edward, married Anne Cathérine Loys; and Sir Whitmore Acton, who rebuilt Aldenham in the eighteenth-century taste, married the historian's aunt, Elizabeth Gibbon. All of this gave Gibbon "a deep and domestic interest" in the Acton family.[8]

A key figure in the broadening of the Acton horizons was Dr. Edward Acton's younger brother, Commodore John Acton, known as "the Commodore." He had joined the East India Company at the age of fourteen and at the age of twenty-five commanded his own ship, the *Lyell*. He then quit the company's service and made his way to Florence, where Grand Duke Leopold, the second son of Empress Maria Theresa of Austria, recognized his nautical skills. He was employed in the wars against the Barbary corsairs, the terrorists of their day, and was finally put in charge of the Tuscan navy. The doctor's eldest son, John Francis Edward Acton (1736–1811), after attending the Jesuit college at Besançon, joined his uncle at Leghorn in 1750, himself then only fourteen years of age.

John Francis Edward Acton had a remarkably adventurous career. He entered the Tuscan navy and underwent a short spell of naval training in England. It was on this occasion that he visited his kinsman and head of the family, the Sir Richard Acton of his day, who had recently lost his eldest son and probably hoped that his daughter would marry the young naval officer who would be next in line to inherit the title and property. But this marriage did not come about. The young woman married instead a Mr. Philip Langdale, and when she died without an heir, her part of the inheritance as well as Aldenham eventually fell to John Francis Acton, who had resumed his Tuscan career. Soon he commanded a frigate. It was because of him that his uncle, the Commodore, a lonely bachelor who had never learned to speak the language of the country in which he had settled, became a Catholic and consequently found himself shunned by English compatriots in Tuscany. When the Commodore died, in 1766, his nephew took over the command of the Tuscan navy. Grand Duke Leopold sent him to Naples to reform the navy of Ferdinand I, King of the Two Sicilies, and Queen Marie Caroline, the imposing sister of the Tuscan Grand Duke as well as of the unfortunate Queen Marie Antoinette.

John Francis Edward Acton rose to be general of the land and sea forces, controller of the ministries of war, finance, and foreign affairs, and prime minister of the Kingdom of the Two Sicilies, from 1780 virtually until 1804. He pursued a policy of relative independence, replacing the previous Spanish and French predominance with Austrian influence and the protection of the British navy, providing a relatively effective defence against Napoleon.[9] At the height of his career, aged sixty-four, he married his fourteen-year-old niece Marie Anne, daughter of his brother, General Giuseppe Eduardo Acton.

Sir John Francis Edward's unusual marriage needed a papal dispensation and was a sensation at the time, devised, it appears chiefly, by Queen Caroline and the girl's German mother, Countess Berghe von Tripps, to keep outsiders from gaining political influence over the affairs of the kingdom and the fortune and property that the prime minister had amassed in Naples and Palermo. The marriage was solemnized in a Catholic ceremony in the presence of the King and Queen of the Two Sicilies at Palermo, where the royal family, accompanied by Acton and their ministers, had fled under Admiral Horatio Nelson's protection when Naples was temporarily occupied by French revolutionary forces. To comply with English law, an Anglican marriage service was held on 2 February 1800 aboard HMS *Foudroyant,* lying in Palermo harbour. Having sustained much damage while serving as Nelson's flagship during the blockade of Malta, she was sent back to Sicily for a refit while the admiral remained at sea. But Emma Hamilton, by then accepted as the English colony's leading lady and a trusted friend of Queen Caroline's, was present with her husband, Sir William Hamilton, the British envoy to the court of Naples. They both signed the marriage register with five other witnesses. When Nelson returned to Palermo in April 1800, he gave a ball on board the *Foudroyant* in the newlyweds' honour and to mark his own capture of the French flagship, the *Guillaume Tell,* off Malta, as well as the final departure of the Hamiltons for England. (Sir William Hamilton's retirement had been curtly accepted by King George III, and he was being replaced by Sir Arthur Paget.) Nelson had informed his superiors at the admiralty of the excitement, almost scandal, caused by the Acton marriage in Palermo. "Acton is married to his niece, not fourteen years of age; so you hear it is never too late to do well. He is only sixty-seven."[10] Nelson had earlier conveyed to their lordships what he thought of his fellow countryman Sir John Francis Acton, the prime minister of the Two Sicilies: "I need not say more than he has the wisest and most honest head in this Kingdom."[11]

Family legends conflict as to the reactions of the child bride, who eventually became known as "Nonna" Acton. One story has it that when her uncle, resplendent in court uniform and cocked hat, came to ask for his niece's hand, the girl was so frightened that she hid under a sofa, whence she could only be coaxed forth with a box of chocolates. That night, it is said, she tried to escape but, wearing her maid's cloak, was challenged by a sentry and brought back.[12] Another version was given, more than a century later, by a descendant, Emily Dease, who wrote to her niece, Annie Acton: "I think Nonna was even more terrified of her German mother than of her husband. She told me once she wanted to dress in boys' clothes as a sailor, to run away from her. My impression is that she was completely under her mother's rule for many years after she married."[13]

The marriage turned out much better than anyone expected, however. Sir John was a devoted husband, full of solicitude for his young wife. She, for her part, appears to have taken in stride her sudden rise to importance. A plucky girl of great character, she was small in stature with long brown hair and large, striking brown eyes, and was liked and admired by all because of her lively nature. She was destined to outlive her husband by many years: Sir John Francis Edward Acton, the prime minister, died in Palermo in 1811 at the age of seventy-five, loaded with honours and riches, although, like Nelson, he had neglected to take up the Neapolitan dukedom conferred on him. Mourned particularly by Queen Caroline, whom he had served for thirty-six years, he was given a state funeral and buried in the Church of the Cruciferi in Palermo.

Soon afterwards, Nonna Acton departed for England, accompanied by her younger brother, to take up residence in London at 44 Montagu Square, later at 71 Pall Mall and also at Aldenham, and devote herself to the education of her three children.[14] The youngest, Elizabeth, was to marry, in 1829, Sir Robert Throckmorton, the eighth Baronet of that old English Catholic family, and her home became the splendid country seat of Coughton Court (near Alcester, Warwickshire), which dates from the fifteenth century, and the Georgian Buckland House near Faringdon, Berkshire. The many letters that Elizabeth's mother wrote to her children from there showed that she, too, made her home there in between travels to Aldenham, London, Paris, and Naples. Coughton Court—a long Tudor house with a square tower, priest-hiding holes, and Throckmorton family pictures—became a particular favourite for Elizabeth's brother Charles, the Cardinal, and also for his young nephew, in whose upbringing he had taken a close interest before his early death in 1847.

Attempts to send Elizabeth's two brothers to Westminster School failed because of the school's insistence on their learning the Anglican catechism and because "Lady Acton's scruples are probably invincible."[15] So, beginning in 1813, Charles Acton went instead to a Catholic establishment, the Academy of the Abbé Quequet in Parsons Green, and both boys—after their application to St. John's, Cambridge, was objected to by the college's "spiritual guides"— ultimately went to Magdalene College, Cambridge.[16]

The picture that emerges from Sir Richard Acton's letters to his mother, written in French in his plodding, regular hand, is that of a vain man, living for the moment, although the attachment to his family showed his good side. He had plenty of opportunity to indulge in gambling in Naples and on his frequent visits to Paris, where he often went on his own, much to his young wife's displeasure. But he was devoted to his little Johnny, writing, when the child was one year old: "This is the birthday of my little angel and son whom I love with all my heart. He is altogether delightful." [17]

An imposing life-size portrait of Sir Richard used to hang on the grand staircase at Aldenham. Painted in Naples about 1835, it shows him in characteristic pose of the late Romantic age, on a rearing thoroughbred, self-assured if not entirely relaxed. He is dressed in black with his coat billowing behind him, his top hat in his right hand as in greeting; he has a thin face with fair hair and long side-whiskers, and he wears a white choker. Behind him an attendant is struggling up a craggy ravine, and beneath his horse's hoofs can be glimpsed the Bay of Naples, with smoke from Vesuvius rising up in the background. His wife encouraged him to assume this gentlemanly pose, which fate was to allow him little time to enjoy.

Sir Richard's sudden death in Paris, on 31 January 1837, cut deep into the lives of his wife and three-year-old son. The cause was pneumonia, caught, according to the family's own account, when he returned late one night from the gambling table. By order of his wife the door had been locked against him. Drunk and red-faced, he stood knocking at the door in the bitter cold and caught the chill that carried him off. Some six hundred people attended the funeral at the Church of St. Thomas Aquinas, among them the ambassadors of Russia, Prussia, and Austria; the King of France also sent a representative. The French paper *Le moniteur universel* described Sir Richard Acton as "a gentleman from England, citizen of Naples, Conservative at home, and Liberal in his adopted country. This was because his reason told him that the institutions of the one, being good and tested by time, must be preserved, while those of the other country, being defective and incomplete, must be reformed gradually without doubt, but with no hesitation." [18]

Sir Richard's remains were taken to England and buried in the chapel at Aldenham, where his widow had a monument made in his memory "in testimony of affection and regret." The sculpture, made in the Romantic manner, shows a weeping woman sitting in front of a closed door with a small boy by her side whose hand rests lovingly on her lowered head. "Thy will be done" and "I.H.S." are written over it. The motif of the shut door might well have been chosen by the contrite Marie to commemorate the Paris portal outside of which the wretched husband knocked in vain. The fine monument, unfortunately consigned to the vault below when the chapel was demolished, was the work of Richard Westmacott, son of Sir Richard Westmacott, the pupil of Antonio Canova and one of the foremost sculptors of his day. Westmacott the Younger was a school friend of John Henry Newman's and designed a somewhat similar memorial to Newman's mother Jemima for the church at Littlemore.[19]

The English estate of Sir Richard Acton was heavily mortgaged for the then-large sum of £49,213 12s. 6d. In Naples he left 89,000 ducats (worth about £30,000–40,000 at that time). The young John Acton inherited his father's title as the eighth Baronet, with his mother acting as guardian until his twenty-first birthday, when he would take over Aldenham and, after her death, also the Dalberg property. For the time being mother and son remained in Paris with the Duchess of Dalberg, who by then was also a widow. Marie was not sorry to cut her ties with Naples. Aldenham was to be their future home, and her brother-in-law, Charles, just appointed Auditor of the Roman Rota, came to London after his brother's death to help with legal matters, among these the naturalization of his sister-in-law and his nephew.

Though born abroad like his father and grandfather, Sir Richard Acton had been a British subject, domiciled in England with residence on his estates in Shropshire, where he was a magistrate and deputy lieutenant. According to the British Nationality Act of 1772, however, the third generation born abroad was excluded from British nationality, and so the "Act for Naturalising Dame Marie L.P. de Dalberg and Sir John E. E. Dalberg Acton, Bart." was issued by Parliament. Restrictions that would have barred the son and heir from becoming a member of either House of Parliament, or from holding any public office, were afterwards repealed. By the private Act of 1859 and the Acton Nationality Act of 1911 these rights of British citizenship were also ensured for later generations.[20]

Although in later life John Acton liked to describe himself jocularly as "a Neapolitan," it was the Naples conquered by Giuseppe Garibaldi, rather than the Kingdom of the Two Sicilies of his father and grandfather, that left its mark on him. Acton made a point of not wanting to benefit from the riches amassed by his grandfather.

3

ONWARDS TO OSCOTT

It was probably in Paris at one of her mother's receptions that the widowed Lady Dalberg-Acton met George Leveson-Gower, the eldest son and heir of the first Earl Granville, British minister in Paris for seventeen years. Lord Leveson was twenty-three and had also been briefly attaché in Paris at his father's legation; he was about to advance quickly to the top of the Whig-Liberal establishment. When Marie and her son, evidently about again after the bereavement, came to see the Granvilles at their country house at Longchamps in June 1838, Leveson's mother described them as "Lady Acton and her beautiful boy, like Lawrence's picture of young Lambton and the infant John in some 'Holy Family.'"[1] Leveson and Marie fell deeply in love. The fact that she was five years older than he mattered to her rather more than it did to him. The major obstacle to the marriage was their religious differences. Neither the Duchess of Dalberg nor her daughter was prepared to give way regarding the Catholic upbringing of any children. Monsignor Acton, in Rome, was also worried about Marie's wanting to marry the Anglican Granville's son. Earl Granville was equally adamant that his grandchildren should remain in the Established Church. But Lady Acton refused to give in on the religious issue.

The engagement was actually broken off, to everyone's regret, until Lady Georgiana Fullerton, Leveson's sister, enlisted the aid of Abbé Félix Dupanloup (1802–1878). The Abbé was a great showman and charmer, an elegant priest with politically liberal views, and was later to play an important role with Acton at the Vatican Council. He was a friend to Charles Forbes-René de Montalembert, popular among the wealthy Catholics of the Faubourg Saint-Germain as a preacher and confessor. He had also been present at Sir Richard Acton's death and consoled his widow in her grief. The wily Dupanloup saved the Acton-Leveson marriage with a compromise: any sons were to be brought up as Anglicans, any daughters as Catholics. They need not have worried, for the future Lady Leveson was to have no more children.

The marriage of George Leveson-Gower and Marie Dalberg-Acton took place on 25 July 1840 in a double London ceremony, at Devonshire House (the bridegroom was a nephew of the Duke of Devonshire) and in the Spanish Chapel. Leveson was, that same year, appointed undersecretary of state for foreign affairs. He succeeded to his father's title as the second Earl Granville in 1846. Marie soon enchanted and won over her new husband's family, and indeed the entire English establishment, including the young Queen Victoria. On the first Earl's death, they settled in the Granville house in Bruton Street and were seen to be blissfully happy. Leveson's sister wrote about her new sister-in-law:

> My mother is enchanted with Lady Acton and my father also, though he would rather Leveson had married an English girl. . . . Small eyes, but of a pretty blue, a pink and white complexion, a quantity of light hair, beautiful arms, a pretty white neck. . . . She speaks English well, though with an accent, but a pleasant one. She is much loved by every one that knows her well. I think she has a quick temper, but never disagreeable, and her gaity is pleasant to see. My mother writes from Chiswick, "Here come Leveson and Lady Acton in a little carriage as happy as two children, he teaching her to drive. They go boating every day and she is learning to row. She tries to please all the family. . . ." What pleases me in my future sister-in-law, is her perfect frankness, extreme honesty, and her deep religious feelings, though these are not quite according to my ideas.[2]

Nonetheless, Lady Georgiana Fullerton was later to share these ideas by following her husband into the Roman Catholic Church.

Lady Georgiana's mother, Lady Granville, was also pleased with her new daughter-in-law: "I never saw a couple so well suited to each other. She is charming, good, gay, pretty and as a wife the happiest mixture of spirit and sub-mission." Referring to their disagreement on religion, she noted that Marie's mother, the Duchess of Dalberg, "has been all satisfaction and gracious kind-ness, which she must have great credit for, as there was strong feeling excited and only laid [to rest] by amiable ones."[3]

Meanwhile, Johnny lived mainly at Aldenham, but from time to time he was whisked off to share his stepfather's grand life in the capital. His Italian grandmother, Nonna Acton, felt pity for him. From Aldenham she wrote to her granddaughter Minnie: "*Le petit* left this morning at eight, sorry to go, and myself very sad. This departure seems to me something so unnatural—from what he says it seems that they will go to Chiswick tomorrow, then settle them-selves in Grosvenor Square where she has taken a house. . . . Here people appear disturbed and they know nothing. Her maid came with *le petit* to take all her summer frocks, work and other things. Yesterday we dined with *le petit* and had a very happy day." Nonna disapproved of the boy's being dragged around in London society, as "he felt lost in it."[4]

When, after her eldest son's death, it emerged that her daughter-in-law would have £1,600 a year for herself and the boy £500, to be augmented when he grew older, Nonna Acton vented her irritation: "This ought to show the Dalbergs how wrong they had been in the disagreeable things they used to say about the Actons."[5] There was a gulf opening between the Actons and the young Lady Leveson, and in the year in which the second Earl inherited his father's title, Nonna Acton, in a letter to her daughter, Elizabeth, again expressed pent-up feelings. That the memory of her eldest son was fading for others but not for her, was made the more painful by Marie's determination to cut what emotional ties still linked her with her past and to make her new marriage work: "If I were with you I would not dare speak of it—I would not have the strength and it would hurt you—the same with Charles—we understand each other without words. The more the years pass, the more we feel the cruel void."[6]

In the family's consultations over young Johnny's education, three ecclesi-astic personages made their influence felt. Two of them met at Aldenham in October 1840: Mgr. Charles Acton, the boy's uncle, and Nicholas Wiseman, who, after twelve years as Rector of the English College in Rome, had just re-turned to England to take up his new duties as Coadjutor for the Midlands District. The occasion was the blessing by Bishop Wiseman of the new chapel that Lady Dalberg-Acton had completed after her husband's death. She and Nonna Acton decided that the boy, when he was eight, should go to St. Mary's

College, Oscott, where Wiseman was president. At first a private tutor for him was found, mainly to perfect his English, because he had been used to speaking French and German at home. This was Charles Anselm Spink (1816–1885), who had been educated at Oscott and had given up the idea of becoming a priest. He seems to have been a good influence and was much liked, and his popularity in the Acton household was later extended to the German cousins, the sons and daughters of Count Arco in Munich, whom he taught English.

The third ecclesiastic to be consulted about young Acton's education was Dupanloup. He had recently been put in charge of the seminary and boys' school St. Nicholas du Chardonnet at Gentilly, on the outskirts of Paris, where he was applying his educational theories, which were critical of Jean-Jacques Rousseau and espoused the gentler spirit of François de Fénelon: they involved work, strong discipline, avoidance of dissipation, encouragement of the competitive spirit, much reward, and little punishment. Religion, in Dupanloup's view, was inseparable from good breeding and that modicum of common sense that is derived from a classical education. In the late summer of 1842, the eight-year-old Johnny Acton, accompanied by Mr. Spink, entered Gentilly. Dupanloup wrote to his mother about her *cher enfant:* "I like him very much. He is frank, open, resolute, firm. His German is natural, he is getting into his stride in history, geography, Latin."[7] Dupanloup cared little for theology or the natural sciences. His popularity with his penitents or pupils—he even earned the praises of his former seminarian Ernest Renan, later the great apostate of the century—was based on his positive and encouraging attitude, although his sincerity was sometimes in doubt. He was the favourite religious instructor of ladies of rank and taught the catechism to Talleyrand's niece. That is how one day in the spring of 1838 Talleyrand had invited him to dine, wanting to consult him on various forms of his submission to the Church. And his success in reclaiming the soul of the old sinner became one of Dupanloup's greatest coups.[8]

The boy's letters home were a mixture of adult language and a small child's mind and heart:

Dear Mama, I am afraid you will find very bad news in this letter. I was fourth; I am afraid I am now no better and yesterday I was nearly being worse, today however has proved favourable to me, and next Friday I hope to be first! However, I will not trouble you about these affairs—let us return to our former practice and here is a riddle: "I am long I am short, I am pretty I am ugly I belong to a beggar and to a king, I belong to a theif [*sic*] and belong to a saint. — A name." I have made this riddle myself. I must now finish the letter. Love to all, ever yours J. E. D. A.[9]

Dear Mama, I am very happy here and hope you are also happy too. . . . I know several boys here. Tell Lord Leveson that I have written this letter without my master having read it, pray write to me as soon as is possible, and write your letters very plainly, for if I could not read them it would be a bore. Good-bye dear Mama. I send my love to you and to all. I remain your affectionate son J. E. D. A.[10]

And there is a very short letter, dated 8 December 1842, without any further explanation: "Dear Mama, . . . I am very, very, very unhappy here and I beg you to come and fetch me as soon as possible."[11]

After not even nine months at Gentilly, John Acton was dispatched to St. Mary's, Oscott, where first impressions seemed better: "I must quickly tell you that I am very happy here, though I should still be happier with you, for as you know I cannot be happy anywhere without you and Lord Leveson. I find the boys much nicer here than they were at Gentilly, though the first night I was here, I was very unhappy."[12] John Acton was putting on the brave face expected of young Englishmen. His letters to his mother are reminiscent of those that the young Winston Churchill sent from Harrow (although Lady Leveson could not have competed with Churchill's frivolous American mother, with her beauty, energy, and sense of adventure). With both boys in a comparable parental setting, and with both having acute sensibility and needing more than anything to be loved, the English boarding school system was probably the worst form of education that their parents had the means to afford.

In a pathetic letter John Acton told his mother that the masters and boys had sung the praises of Stonyhurst, the Jesuit college, then the leading English Catholic public school:

I do not feel at all happy here and I therefore beg in the most earnest terms, that you will send me to Stonehurst [*sic*]. I do not wish to encroach upon your kindness, but still, I cannot stop here. My health is rather on the decline on account of not being with you, of the bad weather at Oscott and from the ill-treatment of the boys here, and even some of the masters are grown unkind to me. If, as I hope, you will comply with what I ask you in this letter. . . . I believe and trust you will save me from what I consider almost as bad as death. I hope you will not forget either to take away or else soon come to see J. E. Dalberg Acton.[13]

Acton was probably right about Stonyhurst's being the better school, but Oscott was the school frequented by the Midlands Catholic gentry. Bishop Wiseman had been rector in 1840–1841, and Acton's mother was unlikely to upset her relationship with him. Anyway, the boy regained some happiness when his skills made him shine. He bragged just after his tenth birthday: "I am a perfect linguist, knowing, perfectly, that is so as to be able to speak it, English, French, German and can almost speak Latin. I can speak a few words of Chinese, Greek, Italian, Spanish and Irish. I also know Chemistry, Astronomy, Mechanics and many other sciences, but do not know Botany. I am very happy here and perfectly reconciled to the thoughts of stopping here seven more years. I am in a hurry, therefore goodbye, Caesar Agamemnon John Dalberg Acton."[14] Agamemnon—a valiant fighter, proud and passionate, but vacillating in purpose and easily discouraged—was an appropriate hero for young Johnny. The boy, too, was subject to changing moods of doom and exultation. "I am very much liked by the boys, and excel in two principal things: I am the best chess-player of all the boys except four, and am the best pick-pocket (of pocket-handkerchiefs) ever known. I hope you will soon be here. . . . I went to Communion the Sunday after the anniversary of Papa's death."[15]

It was remarkable that John Acton's first two famous headmasters were also to play an important role in his later life, both ultimately as opponents. Wiseman, intellectually Dupanloup's superior, was an erudite man of great emotional power and vision. He stood on the sidelines of the Oxford Movement, an attempt, originating in England's oldest university, to make members of the Church of England recognize its primitive and Catholic principles that were being attacked by liberal theologies of the day. The movement was started by Edward Pusey in 1833 through one of his "Tracts of the Times," and its members therefore became known as Tractarians. It reached its peak in 1843, when John Henry Newman, one of its leaders, resigned the living of St. Mary's in Oxford. Two years later Newman was received into the Catholic Church, a step that rocked the Church of England to its foundations. Wiseman, soon to be Cardinal and lead the restored hierarchy of England and Wales, welcomed the stream of Anglican converts. Newman came to Oscott to be confirmed in October 1845, and Wiseman offered the Oxford converts the use of the old college building, later renamed Maryvale by Newman, as a place of refuge and study.

The Oscott boys were proud of their president. "He was approachable and gracious, and no great friend of discipline," Acton later recalled. The boys used to see him with the great Catholic benefactor Lord Shrewsbury; with Daniel O'Connell; with Father Theobald Mathew, the Irish temperance apostle; with a Mesopotamian patriarch; with Newman and A. W. Pugin—"and we had a feeling that Oscott, next to Pekin[g], was a centre of the world."[16]

Oscott's new buildings, full of pinnacles, had been put up by Pugin. Gothic narrowness was the architectural fashion, and Acton told an anecdote from Buckland, the Throckmorton seat, where someone had said: "What a narrow door!" and was answered: "Oh, of course, to keep the Cardinal out."[17] Wiseman was a big man physically, but the story illustrated the clash between the old English Catholic families, relaxed in their country houses and their outlook, and the "foreign ways" that Wiseman, with the more Ultramontanist spirit and his own Spanish-Irish background, brought with him from Rome.

The college served mainly as a seminary, but the school attracted the sons of the Midlands gentry, including one of the wealthy Jerninghams and John O'Reilly, who was to become Acton's closest friend at Oscott and later also to study at Dr. Ignaz von Döllinger's in Munich. Closer to the boys than Wiseman was Dr. George Errington, who arrived at Oscott about the same time as Acton did, to act as Wiseman's confidant and *locum tenens,* allowing him to attend to other things. Errington also attended classes as a student himself.

"There have just been examinations in history," John Acton wrote home, "for which, if you get fifty points, you have half a play day; if sixty-six, a whole one. I had only a half. Those who got the whole went with Dr. George Errington to Manchester, and we who had half, had a little feast in the evening."[18] Acton found Errington "a hard-headed, grim, rather vigorous man with little general cultivation or humility. But I used to be in disgrace and only recall his avenging countenance as it was presented to me. In later years we were on more pleasant terms together, but I rarely got hold of the inner man. He gave boys religious instructions and often preached. But there was no apparent spirituality. His religion seemed to be made of leather, and I think we profited more from the alternating discourses of Father Spencer."[19] This was the Hon. George Spencer, the youngest son of Earl Spencer, an ardent and ascetic priest better known as Father Ignatius, a member of the Passionist Order, who supported Wiseman's ideas for the conversion of England and whose cause as a saint of the Catholic Church is in preparation.

But John Acton had other things on his mind. One of these was to win over his stepfather, who had usurped his mother's love and who must have seemed something of a threatening presence, looming in distant London or closer, when he came to Aldenham on holidays. Leveson was a worldly man, relaxed about everything in life, whereas his precocious stepson had an anxious as well as a serious religious disposition. What may have attracted Marie to the future second Earl Granville was some foreign, mild, and gentle quality about him, unusual in an Englishman of his class, which earned him the nickname Pussy. Leveson was talented, knew about foreign countries, and spoke fluent French; he was observant and undemonstrative and liked good living. Johnny Acton must have felt that he was faced with a formidable enemy at his mother's side.

"Dear Lord Leveson," he wrote after his tenth birthday:

> I am very sorry I have not written for such a long time, but I could not get leave to a room and therefore could not write well. I am rather at a loss for not knowing your direction properly; however, I shall direct it as well as I can, to Woburn. I hope you and Mama are quite well. Will you soon come to see me? Mr. Nichols thinks that my pecuniary arrangements are going on very well. I should very much like to have coffee instead of milk for breakfast and tea, so if you would please write to Mr. Nichols about it, I should be able to have it. I cannot write any more as it is study time now. Good bye, ever yours, John Acton.[20]

Four days later Acton wrote to his mother: "I suppose you were at the opening of Parliament. How is Lord Granville's foot? Please to tell him that I am studying Herodotus and Cicero's oration *Pro Plaucio* (which is dreadfully hard). Good bye, dear Mama, John Emerich Dalberg Acton."[21] The next month he wrote, "Dear Mama, I renew my demands for a letter and should be thankful for a little money, as a pound of mine has been taken away, by somebody."[22]

There were outings from Oscott. Once his mother invited him and a party of friends to come to Aldenham for the day. They went by train to Birmingham and Wolverhampton, then by open carriage to Bridgnorth and Aldenham, where John Acton showed the boys round. They looked at King Charles's coat and sat down to a large meal prepared for them by the housekeeper (his mother was not there). They also visited Wenlock Abbey and arrived back at Oscott early the next morning.[23] Because his parents were often away from Aldenham, young Johnny enjoyed spending his holidays at Buckland with his Throckmorton relations. Nonna Acton complained occasionally to her daughter that Acton's mother and stepfather seemed to keep the boy away from the Throckmortons by insisting that he join them in their London life: "It is rendering him a bad service for his future happiness to keep him a stranger from the only true relations he has in England; he would amuse himself so much with his cousins."[24] Young Johnny came to be particularly fond of Minnie, four years older than he was, whom he used to describe as "my favourite cousin."

A desperate and revealing letter came from Oscott when John Acton was fourteen: "It is really impossible for me in this college, in whatever class I am and especially in my own class, to carry out my duties towards God, towards you and towards myself. This may be a very good place for some, but it does not suit me." He went on to say that he would prefer to study in Aldenham with someone to oversee his work. "My strongest passion is the desire to re-nown which, I know very well, can only be acquired by study, jointly with the gifts I have received. This will serve at keeping me at my studies in a way that is no longer possible here. Believe me, my dear Mama, that I tell you the truth. Apart from all this I am quite happy here and my friendship with the young Irishman John O'Reilly is increasing every day. It is extraordinary that after five years he is the only one with whom I am totally in accord."[25]

Lord Granville, with his own recollections of Eton, later bluntly told his stepson that he believed him to have been idle at Oscott, to have quarrelled with his masters, and to have failed to avail himself of the advantage of study to be found there. Lord Granville may have been right, but the two had different sensitivities, and for whatever reason, Acton found the Oscott atmosphere stifling. There was, however, a grand finale to those years when, aged fourteen, Acton accompanied Bishop Wiseman to the solemn opening of Pugin's St. George's Cathedral, Southwark, on 4 July 1848. Preceded by torchbearers, acting as incense bearer, and swinging the thurifer, John Acton walked by the side of the architect, who had the face of a Romantic poet. They led a long procession of bishops and priests. The event was one of the highlights of the English Catholic "Second Spring." Bishop Wiseman preached the sermon. The slim Gothic spire that Pugin had designed for the cathedral was, however, never built. The cathedral itself was rebuilt after being wrecked in an air raid in World War II.

After the Oscott years, there followed a "polar exile" in the form of two years of private tuition in Edinburgh, which Lord Granville found to be necessary to improve the boy's Latin, Greek, English, mathematics, and history. John Acton stayed with a former vice-president from Oscott, Dr. Henry John Charles Logan, a Scot, at Belleville, Blackheath Place, Newington, outside Edinburgh, in a small house that Dr. Logan had rented. It was "comfortable, with magnificent furniture," the boy noted, "like the villas near Frankfurt."[26] The plan was to prepare Acton for entry to one of the Cambridge colleges, in order to follow in his father's and uncle's footsteps. He described his day: "Mass at seven-thirty and afterwards Greek preparation. Breakfast at nine and I leave at once to go to Mr. Veitch [his math teacher] at ten. I stay with him till midday and then, after a little walk, return for lunch at one o'clock. After that I study Latin, Greek and history for three-and-a-half hours. We dine at five o'clock and from six to eight-thirty I read history or write an essay for Dr. Logan. After that I read Burke or Macaulay for half an hour before going to sleep after ten o'clock. Twice a week I do mathematics with Dr. Logan. I am thus reading or studying for sometimes nine-and-a-half hours except Saturday." [27]

Edmund Burke and Thomas Babington Macaulay were early influences. The first two volumes of Macaulay's five-volume *History of England* had just been published and were much discussed. Dr. Logan was critical of Macaulay "for sacrificing everything to his brilliant style." [28] Edinburgh had recently rejected Macaulay as its Liberal MP, and controversy still raged about that. Yet Acton was captivated by Macaulay's *History;* he read it four times. Later, under German influence, he came to be extremely critical of Macaulay as a prejudiced and insular historian, ignorant of religion and philosophy, overtaken by Leopold von Ranke. Acton described his younger self as "a raw English schoolboy, primed to the brim with Whig politics," and recalled that it was "not Whiggism only, but Macaulay in particular that I was so full of." [29] Despite his growing reservations regarding Macaulay's historical technique, Acton's regard for Macaulay remained high as "very nearly the greatest of English writers." [30]

Whether young Johnny profited much from the crash course with the Scottish tutor, famous for his knowledge of Greek, may be doubted. "He told me," recorded Sir Mountstuart E. Grant Duff, "that at sixteen he did not think he knew more than five hundred words of that language." [31] But things were soon to change. While Acton was in Edinburgh, his applications to three Cambridge colleges were turned down because he was a Catholic. The idea of his going to Germany was then discussed between his mother and Anna, Countess Arco, her Munich cousin. At first they thought of his living with a young Catholic Englishman, Richard Raby, son of a Leicester cloth manufacturer, who lived in Munich as a writer and tutor and took in young Englishmen on cultural tours. Acton was horrified by the idea; he did not care for Raby, and, what was worse, two of his fellow students at Dr. Logan's whom he disliked would also be there. The alternative was the old friend of the Arcos', Dr. Ignaz von Döllinger. Döllinger was well known, also in England, as the most celebrated German Catholic scholar since the deaths of Johann Adam Möhler and Johann

Joseph von Görres. Wiseman had visited him in Munich and asked him for his support for raising the intellectual level of English Catholics. He was in touch with Newman and other converts, and among Anglicans with Edward Pusey, John Sherren Brewer, and also with Gladstone. Acton pleaded with Lord Granville to send him to Döllinger and not to Raby, "at most a moderately good master in the classics, and a person in whose hands I would not willingly place the direction of my reading. . . . I believe you will not think it unnatural that I should be anxious to attend a person of great acquirements and enlarged views; and as I have read no philosophy, I could hardly begin with a better master than a German such as Professor Döllinger." Acton went on to flatter his stepfather in having been right in sending him to Edinburgh, and himself wrong in having opposed it, because it had induced him "to think long and deeply on important points, and to make several resolutions for the regulation of my conduct. . . . Accordingly I have resolved to spend my time in hard study, and am diligently preparing for it."[32]

As usual in Acton's letters to his stepfather, there was an element of special pleading. Lord Granville wanted the boy, in due course, to go into politics. Acton's refusal was part of the tug-of-war that was going on, underneath the surface, between him and his stepfather. The transient and worldly pleasures that Lord Granville valued and his stepson, on that account, despised, turned the prospect of staying with Dr. Döllinger into a kind of ideal escape. Acton was delighted to hear, as he wrote to his mother, that the Professor was agreeable to his coming. From all that he had heard, Dr. Döllinger would give him more freedom and fulfilment than he had been used to in his education so far.[33] In June 1850, at the age of sixteen, Acton arrived in Munich, at Frühlingsstrasse 11, eager to put his expectation to the test.

4
___

DR. DÖLLINGER'S APPRENTICE

John Acton's initiation into his new German surroundings was agreeably gradual—in the holiday month of August. There was a relaxing first week spent in
the Bavarian mountains at Tegernsee, some fifty kilometres from Munich, at
the lakeside chalet that was the summer residence of his relations, the Arcos.
It was the first of many visits to that romantic landscape, with its monastery
dating from 719, and with here and there an onion-domed little church and
gaily painted wooden and stone chalets dotted about amidst the wooded lakeside; the whole scenery gradually and softly merged with that of the neighbouring Austrian territory. Johnny Acton could not imagine on that first visit how
much that beautiful Tegernsee setting and its people would come to mean to
him soon, indeed for his whole future life. After Johnny had returned to Munich, Dr. Döllinger reported to Lady Granville his first impression, "which, I
am happy to say, is in every respect a favourable one," he wrote in his careful
English. "Finding him endowed with more than ordinary natural abilities I see
also, that these abilities hitherto have been carefully cultivated; for his years he
is a good proficient in classical studies, and, which is more, his remarks upon
persons and books he has become acquainted with, often exhibit strong traits

of good sound judgement and reflective power, although of course the time of our being together is too short, and the communication on his side not yet sufficiently divested of a certain shyness, for enabling me to pretend that he had already revealed to me fully the measure of his mind."[1]

The boy had no reservations. After his Tegernsee visit he wrote to his mother (as usual in French):

> It is impossible to be more amiable than my aunt and the Count. All the children are very cheerful and have pleased me very much. . . . Tegernsee is delightful. We have made several excursions into the mountains nearby. The Professor speaks English well and talks to me never in another language. . . . I like him immensely. His knowledge of the history and literature of all countries and all times is just extensive. I am not sure that he knows much about physical science. He is very simple and speaks to me very openly and kindly. He has lent me a lot of books and allowed me to look through his great library. When he has time he even takes me for walks into the English Garden. Otherwise I don't see him until dinner. He has given me a German-teacher, a Swiss, whom he praised. He has arranged my day so that I have five hours for the classics and German. The rest of the day is my own for history and literature. I don't know about his political opinions, but he detests Lord Palmerston.[2]

To his stepfather Acton described the Professor as follows: Dr. Döllinger's "personal appearance is certainly not prepossessing. His forehead is not particularly large, and a somewhat malevolent grin seems constantly to reside about his wide, low mouth."[3] But the Professor's harsh appearance was mitigated by his inward spiritual beauty. His stony expression often concealed the twinkle in his eye when he was listening or making an observation. There was a child-like quality about him; he could never believe evil of anyone without proof. Gladstone noted a resemblance to Newman. On Döllinger's deathbed someone remarked about his facial resemblance to Dante. He had a touching way with children; when he walked in the Englische Garten they often came up to him to shake hands. To Anna Gramich, one of his young intellectual women friends, he admitted that he had often wished to have children around him "for a change, for relaxation. But they must not take up too much of my time—perhaps at midday or of an evening, for half an hour, but that is too much to ask."[4]

Dr. Döllinger was a priest-scholar who made no show of his learning and intellectual superiority. "I am inclined to think that he owes more to his character and industry than to his innate genius," his pupil wrote, impressed by Döl-linger's cool-headed and original judgement. "He prefers Byron, and probably Dryden and Moore, to Milton, and thinks Wellington the greatest of modern generals. He is minutely conversant with English literature—and indeed is like a book of reference upon every question I have had occasion to propose—yet he gives no more than the requisite answer."[5]

Like other German professors, Döllinger took in students to supplement an initially meagre income. His boarders were mainly sons of the English Catho-lic gentry, a veritable "English colony" that, on the death of his mother, had moved with him to the larger apartment of Frühlingsstrasse (today called Von-der-Tann-Strasse), closer to the new university buildings near the Englische Garten. At one time or another Dr. Döllinger had staying with him various Joneses, members of the Herbert family, one of the sons of Lord Clifford of Chudleigh, and members from other well-known Catholic families: Wyse, Vavasour, Hencage, Bunbury, Jerningham, and O'Reilly. Döllinger's apartment consisted of as many as twelve rooms with high ceilings. Acton described his room as conveniently furnished. He was even given a fine bookcase with a glass front.

Acton noted that Dr. Döllinger's library was "as dusty and as valuable as the most fastidious taste could desire. I have free access to it—and he can procure me any books from the great library which is close by."[6] It was said that Dr. Döl-linger's apartment was inhabited by books rather than by himself. They were his "better half," piled on the floor in hundreds, on the shelves in thousands, al-together some thirty thousand. As *Oberbibliothekar* (chief librarian), since 1838, of the University of Munich Library, with its two hundred thousand books, manuscripts, and archives—then one of the finest in Europe—he was able to borrow books freely and take them home, indeed, keep them for months and years. When he died, no fewer than two thousand books in his possession were found to belong to the university library. "He knew every book in the library that he cared for," Acton noted after Döllinger's death, "made great catalogues for his own use, and easily caused whatever he wished to be purchased. . . . He made his own large collection out of the duplicates."[7] Döllinger's avidity for books stimulated Acton in his own efforts to establish at Aldenham one of the largest private libraries in Britain. Lord Granville agreed to raise the boy's allowance so that he would have an extra £120 per year to spend on books, and Döllinger advised him to buy cheaply.

"I like Munich exceedingly," Acton wrote home. "Fortunately I am not skilful enough to be displeased with what is incorrect in architecture, and the general effect is certainly very fine."[8] That comment was meant for the farrago of palaces, theatres, churches, and public buildings on which the autocratic Ludwig I had spent millions to remodel Baroque Munich according to his pompous pro-Hellenic taste. The ordinary Munich citizens, or Münchener, whose tenement houses were not included in the royal, marble-smooth, classical facelift did not care much for the modernization process, even though it turned Munich into a modern capital city. The Münchener tended to dislike all pomposity, conceit, and Romanticism, which did not agree with their down-to-earth roughness. They took to their hearts the Baroque Catholicism with its angels and saints writhing in pain or joy on the altars, a reminder of the time when Munich was a Jesuit stronghold.

Some Catholic nucleus remained. As far as Protestant Europe was concerned, Munich had become the first Catholic centre in Germany, "a headquarters of Catholic conservatism," as Acton described it later,[9] but, like most of the Continental princely capitals, it was not a particularly religious place. There was not much crime, nor much education. There were few devout Catholics among the upper classes, but many among the ordinary people. Bavarian Catholicism had not been remarkable either in enlightenment or fervour. Superstition was rampant, but the many intellectual and sectarian currents such as the Freemasons and Rosicrucians made little impact on the ordinary citizens.

The seventeenth century, with the Thirty Years' War and its horrors, was, in Acton's day, still closer to the popular imagination than the recent French Revolution. Thanks to the Bavarian princes and the Catholic faithful, the Reformation did not cross the Danube. The average Bavarian continued to be surprised that Protestants, too, believed in Christ. The fact that Martin Luther, pursued by horsemen on his flight from Augsburg, had made off without paying for his fried sausage at the inn was remembered and seemed to tell more about him than any of his teaching. The countryside remained fervently, superstitiously, Catholic.

Munich was unique in Europe, in the first half of the nineteenth century, in its intellectual openness. It was because of Napoleon that in 1806, after the Holy Roman Empire's demise, a new kingdom, Bavaria, under the ruling house of Wittelsbach, had been created out of the old principalities with added Austrian territories. It was twice the size of the present Bavaria, one of the largest Länder (states) in today's united Germany. Munich's university was backed by the resources of the state, a situation that Döllinger disliked. In a city of ninety thousand inhabitants the presence of three thousand students was noticeable, not least by their facial "ornaments" due to duelling, the favourite sport in the student societies. "Sometimes the hair has been shorn off their head, . . . sometimes a bit off their nose," Acton described his surroundings to his cousin, Minnie Throckmorton. "For they always stop fighting at the first wound. I may expect to come back to England with one eye singularly sharp-sighted from the extermination of the other, with my nose chopped off, or with one of my ears in my pocket." [10] And he drew some appropriately frightening illustrations.

In an account of the daily routine that Döllinger had devised for him, Acton wrote: "I breakfast at eight, then two hours of Plutarch and an hour of Tacitus. We dine a little before two—I see the Professor then for the first time in the day. At three my German master comes, from four to seven I am out—I read modern history for an hour—having had an hour's ancient history just before dinner. I have some tea at eight and study English literature and composition till ten—when the curtain falls." [11] Döllinger intended Acton to go on with the study of Greek and Latin classics till he was equal to Oxford and Cambridge standards; he was to study the constitutions and government of the principal nations, the growth and decline of ancient and modern empires, and the causes of both. "These are the pursuits, which will, I hope impart method and discipline to his mind and occupations, and prevent him from getting into a habit, which has been the bane of many a gifted youth, the habit, I mean, of idly turning over a chance variety of books forgotten as soon as read." [12]

Acton's foremost task was to perfect his knowledge of German so as to be able to attend lectures at the university. Döllinger also introduced him to the works of François de Fénelon and to those of Jacques Bénigne Bossuet, Louis Bourdaloue, and Jean-Baptiste Massillon, the famous preachers at the courts of Louis XIV and XV. Döllinger thought highly of the writers of the French classical tradition and regarded them as invaluable for imparting the truths of religion in an elegant fashion instead of the drab style customary in Germany. A confessor was found for Acton: Mgr. Friedrich Windischmann, a Sanskrit scholar and expert in Eastern religions, who was a close friend of Döllinger's. When Acton's mother asked Döllinger about her son's spiritual state, Döllinger replied that Acton was punctual in the fulfilment of his religious duties. When Döllinger had once reminded Acton of going to confession, the tutor was pleased to find that his pupil had just been. "I feel a certain repugnance to speak to him much about religion, but I gladly seize every opportunity he gives me of rectifying his ideas and strengthening his principles." [13] Döllinger disliked talking about personal religion, which, to him, was more a matter of reason, of what one ought to do rather than what one had feelings about. It was a very different atmosphere from Oscott. Dr. Döllinger seemed the living contradiction of the theory that Catholic priests, because they are used to the confessional, tended to be particularly suspicious of evil and ready to see sin everywhere. Döllinger, by contrast, dwelt much more "on folly and ignorance" as man's chief defects, on time and place, on influences of education, and on nationality and authority—on everything that "can excuse error and diminish responsibility."[14] Here was the seed of differences that were to develop, decades later, between the student and his teacher on the matter of moral judgement in history.

Dr. Döllinger's household reflected the atmosphere of its celibate master, as a friend, Louise von Kobell, noted.[15] His cook, his housekeeper, and his manservant had been with him as long as anyone could remember. His study, according to Kobell, was comfortable. Döllinger sat in a high chair with arm support at his writing desk, which was a kind of home-made contraption, with drawers and extensions added on all sides as it was found too short to support the books and manuscripts he needed. A cardboard box with two divisions contained some thirty penholders, penknives, india rubbers, and pencils. A large black inkstand, a sandbox, and a penwiper were in daily use. A few birthday presents in the shape of paperweights formed the only ornaments. On the walls were engravings of great churchmen: Julius II, the enemy of the Borgias and architect of the modern Papacy; Leo X, the Medici Pope, powerless to stop the rise of Luther; the seventeenth-century Jesuit general Thyrsus Gonzales, who was sharply opposed to the doctrine of Probabilism, widely regarded as Jesuit moral theology; and the famous French Gallican theologian Jean de Launoy, who rejected Papal Infallibility, the Immaculate Conception, and the bodily Assumption of the Virgin Mary. There were also views of Paris, London, and Oxford, which Döllinger had visited (he was especially fond of Paris). The furnishing was modest: an old-fashioned sofa where he sat next to a visitor, and an embroidered prie-dieu and a flower basket, presents from pious lady friends.

Döllinger rose early, about four in the morning, so that he had already some hours' work behind him when the rest of the household got up. He went to bed at half past nine in the evening, but with rare visitors like Gladstone, whom he admired as a politician with whom he could discuss theology, he sat up late in eager conversation. For breakfast he had only a glass of water; he ate a copious lunch, then a glass of milk or lemon juice before he went to bed. He drank no beer, and wine only diluted with water, and he ascribed his health to hard work, cold baths, and daily walks. He was severe on the self-indulgence of others who smoked or who, before midday, indulged in beer or tea, then a German luxury. Once he congratulated Acton on coming back to his "good German bed." The pupil observed: "Of all the congratulations this is the last to quiet the traveller in Germany, and D[öllinger] himself admitted, in later years, that there were better beds than he himself had been used to."[16]

The teacher-student relationship—Döllinger was Acton's senior by thirty-five years—was soon to develop into a genuine friendship, centred on their travels together during vacations. The four years that Acton spent in Munich, and frequent additional visits, were an important phase in both their lives that outlasted all later crises and even estrangement. It was significant that Döllinger gave the beautiful portrait of the mature Acton, painted by Franz von Lenbach, the place of honour in his study over his desk at the time when Acton was becoming increasingly critical of him. Lenbach had given the portrait to Döllinger as a present in 1883, and Döllinger was delighted with it.[17]

Döllinger and his pupil travelled together in the north of Italy, in Austria, in Switzerland, and also in England. They visited friends, worked in archives, did some sightseeing. Often they stayed at the Dalberg *Schloss,* Herrnsheim, near Worms. Acton returned to England frequently. In March 1853 he went on his own to Paris, spending three days there, "some of the happiest days of my life," although there was an outbreak of typhoid fever and his mother was anxious for him.[18] Acton was made much of by his relations, among them the Marquis, Antonio Brignole-Sale, whose salon was a centre of the Catholic nobility. He went about the bookshops and, introduced by Döllinger, was received by Montalembert "like an old friend." Acton also made a "pilgrimage" to Saint-Germain-des-Prés to pay his respects to the memory of Clement XI (1700–1721), the Pope who had condemned both Jansenists and Jesuits, and to the tombs of the great Benedictine scholars of St. Maur, Jean Mabillon (1623–1707) and Bernard de Montfauçon (1655–1741), the founder of paleography.

At the Brignoles', Acton was introduced to the famous Madame Swetchine (1782–1857), who, born into the Russian high nobility, was forced into a marriage when she was barely seventeen. Through her friendship with French émigrés, among them Joseph de Maistre (1757–1821), she converted to Catholicism in 1815 and with her husband, who had remained Russian Orthodox, went to live in Paris, where her salon attracted many writers and artists. Her biography was written by Alfred de Falloux, the Catholic minister of education of 1848, who, along with Louis Veuillot and *L'univers,* which Veuillot edited and turned into the organ of international Ultramontanism, was much admired among the *bons Catholiques*—Acton's relatives—and much preferred to the liberal Montalembert.

In the summer of 1854, Acton and Döllinger went on a long trip to Switzerland and Italy, starting from Herrnsheim and stopping at Freiburg, where they were hospitably entertained by Döllinger's publishers, the brothers Karl Raffael and Benjamin Herder. Acton and Döllinger crossed to Switzerland by *Lohnkutsche* (a kind of coach taxi), took a steamer from Basle to Interlaken, visited Gruyère—famous for its cheese—then Lausanne and Geneva. They met Gaspard Mermillod, later Bishop of Fribourg-Lausanne-Geneva and Cardinal, and one of the leading infallibilists at the Vatican Council.

When they reached Venice, Acton renewed his acquaintance with the English historian Rawdon Lubbock Brown, who had lived there for twenty years. Brown was the first to recognize the value of the reports from London of the Venetian ambassadors in the sixteenth century. He introduced Acton and Döllinger to the Marciano, which was still in the ducal palace (but has since moved to the monastery adjacent to the Franciscan church, the Frari). It was to become Acton's favourite among the Italian archives.

Acton loved Venice because he had seen it first with his newfound family, the Arcos, and also because it was there that he was initiated into working in archives, learning "history for myself apart from historians—more even than in Rome."[19] Brown also introduced the young man to Madame Foscarina Rosa Mocenigo, who remembered having let her palazzo to Lord Byron and having danced with the last doge—her illustrious family having supplied its share of doges in earlier centuries. Unfortunately, Brown's favour and friendship ceased soon afterwards. Acton had discovered a howler in one of the calendars Brown published and pointed it out in a review, only to discover that Brown could not take criticism. So, on a later visit to Venice, Acton sent up his card by basket to his window, with Dante's words addressed to Vergil (*Inferno* 1.83–84): "Vagliami 'l lungo studio e 'l grande amore che m'ha fatto cercar lo tuo volume" (Make allowances for the sake of learning and great love which has made me search in your book). No response descended, however, and Acton was unforgiven when Brown died.[20]

On Acton's frequent visits to Paris, he always called on his friend Ferdinand Eckstein, known as Baron D'Eckstein (1790–1861). Eckstein had the greatest influence on the young Acton, impressing him more than the brilliant Montalembert or the celebrated Jean-Baptiste-Henri Lacordaire, and strengthening the young man's dream of a reconciliation between Catholicism and liberalism. Eckstein was born in Copenhagen, the son of a German Jew of middle-class origins. From Denmark his family returned to Hamburg-Altona, but mystery surrounds his early history and his ennoblement—in fact, his title was probably self-bestowed. Acton and Döllinger were captivated by Eckstein's intellectual gifts and independent mind. The elderly man, still an elegant figure in silk brocade dressing gown and blond wig, lived in poverty and alone. He did not care that the world thought of him as an intriguer and a sham. He was, as it happened, a man of deep religious faith, whom his turbulent life had left with a passion for truth and liberty. He had studied, at Heidelberg, ancient religions and Oriental languages and was a friend of the founder of the early Romantic movement, Friedrich von Schlegel, whom he followed into the Catholic Church.

After the Napoleonic upheavals, Eckstein turned up in France, where he worked for the Foreign Ministry and wrote for the royalist press. As a friend of Montalembert's he came to support the cause of civil and religious liberty of *Le correspondent* and, from 1826 to 1829, was editor of *Le catholique,* the sixteen volumes of which contain his major writings. Later he contributed articles to the *Rambler,* which Acton translated, having to iron out any "Ecksteinese" (Eckstein's awkward style). The Baron would have little influence on Acton by his middle age.[21] He would later write to Döllinger of a self-confessed delayed maturity, evidenced through "banal enthusiasm" for the work of freshly encountered thinkers, including Baron Eckstein.[22] In hindsight, he would view Eckstein and many others with increasing severity. Still, he stayed in touch with the Baron until the latter's death in 1862 and always remained faithful to his advice not to become involved in controversies, which were a special mark of Catholic political partisanship, and instead "to fight for wholeness."[23]

The main influence was and remained Ignaz von Döllinger. He was not one of the great original thinkers of the nineteenth century, which his life almost spans. For Acton he proved to be not a good teacher of historical method. But he was one of the great formative minds of the Catholic Church in Germany and in Europe. When Acton came to him Döllinger was, at fifty-one, in the middle of his career, Professor in the Theological Faculty of the University of Munich, a member of the Bavarian Academy of Sciences, and the university's representative in the Bavarian *Landtag* (Diet). He was *Stiftsprobst* of St. Cajetan, the congregation of canons regular, called Theatines. He was thus the equivalent of a provost or dean of the Royal Chapter, which entitled him to wear a mitre ceremonially and entailed his attendance at ecclesiastical functions, such as walking in the Corpus Christi procession, a popular event in Munich which he disliked because it kept him away from his books for hours.

Together with the converted Jacobin, Johann Joseph von Görres, Döllinger led the Catholic or Ultramontane Party—calling for control of Church affairs by Church officials—as an elected deputy to the Frankfurt Assembly in 1848. He made a great plea for toleration and basic rights for Catholics, Jews, and Poles, and he defended religious liberty against state absolutism. At Frankfurt, in the revolutionary beginnings of German parliamentary democracy, Döllinger, according to Acton, "got as near to being as liberal as he ever did—a potential liberal."[24] In 1848 Döllinger also acted as adviser to the first German Catholic Bishops' Conference at Würzburg, and in 1850 to the Bavarian Bishops' Conference at Freising, and there were rumours that the vacant Archbishopric of Salzburg was to be offered to him. As it would have meant giving up his academic work, he refused.

By profession and disposition Dr. Döllinger was a theologian, not an historian. He was born on 28 February 1799 at Bamberg, where both his father and grandfather had been eminent physicians. His father, Ignaz Christoph Döllinger, had philosophical interests, too, and was a friend to Friedrich Wilhelm von Schelling (1775–1854), the leading thinker of the German Romantic and Idealist School. The father looked on religion as largely superseded by the natural sciences. Young Döllinger was more attached to his mother, a devout woman, who made him read to her from books of devotion, which he did grudgingly; he would rather have devoted himself to his collection of butterflies. Entomology and nature studies remained a lifelong hobby.

When studying for the priesthood, Döllinger fell in love with a young girl who wanted to marry him. But her parents had someone in mind with better prospects, and, rather than upset her family, he resigned himself to giving her up. She married the other man. But he kept a bundle of her letters with a miniature, showing a pretty face surrounded by long curls, in a shoulder-free lilac dress in the fashion of the early *Biedermeier* period. Döllinger accepted the celibacy of priesthood without question. But in his friendship and correspondence with women of intellectual interests he was able to break out of his usual reserve—his dry, seemingly cold manner.

His correspondence with these women, especially with Countess Leyden (edited by Dr. Victor Conzemius), showed Döllinger from his most attractive and human side. Whatever erotic element there may have been in these friendships, it was sublimated by Döllinger's tact and sensitivity. He was a conscientious director of souls and a teacher ready to share his great store of knowledge with anyone in whom he sensed the thirst for truth.

An impression of Döllinger's alleged intellectual arrogance persisted, nevertheless, beyond his death. This false view goes back to ill-disposed friends like Josef Edmund Jörg (1819–1901), his former student and early assistant, who gave Acton German lessons. The maligned image of a haughty intellectual also seemed to fit his reputation as an apostate, which after his excommunication in 1871 became widespread in the Catholic world. Döllinger certainly lacked the gift of suffering fools gladly, leaving, for example, an English visitor sitting in his drawing room while he went back to his study because he felt that the man had merely come to chat and waste his time.

After his ordination in 1822, Döllinger had a short and happy spell as a young curate in a Bavarian village. But soon he was called to teach at the *Lyceum* at Aschaffenburg and, in 1826, to become Professor at the University of Munich. Readily he gave up this professorship of ecclesiastical history to enable his friend, the famous Johann Adam Möhler, author of *Symbolik,* to come to Munich in 1832. When Möhler died six years later, Döllinger returned to his subject and also lectured on canon law, church history, ecclesiastical literature, symbolism, and the philosophy of religion. Generations of bishops and priests passed through his lecture rooms in nearly half a century.

When Acton came to him in 1850, Dr. Döllinger had ended his political activity as the university's representative in the Bavarian diet. It was also the end of the short-lived German liberal experiment. Döllinger had resumed the professorship that he, along with other colleagues, had lost over the affair of the royal mistress, Lola Montez, which had forced the autocratic Ludwig I to abdicate in 1848. Henceforth Döllinger concentrated on teaching and writing. The year 1850 was therefore a watershed both for him and for his English pupil. Döllinger was about to reject much of the German Idealism and Catholic Romanticism of his own past and retrace his learning processes. He had become known as the author of a primer on Church history (1840) and adopted the remark of a contemporary scholar who, after having written a similar work, had said that it was now time to begin to learn it. Döllinger had also become famous, especially among Protestants, for his three-volume work on the Reformation (1846–1848), at a time when German historical and religious scholarship was still deeply divided by denominational disputes. A Catholic scholar who was prepared to admit a share of the Church's responsibility for the Reformation was still a rarity. While remaining critical of Martin Luther's articles of faith, Döllinger always had a high regard for the German reformer's person and actions as one of Germany's national heroes. Increasingly Dr. Döllinger disliked all "systems," as his pupil discovered—Thomism, Augustinianism, and the Calvinists as much as the Jesuits or Jansenists. Döllinger dreaded flights of imagination, combinations, fancies, divination. Where certainty ended, he liked to stop.

Born a Franconian, as were Johann Wolfgang von Goethe and Albrecht Dürer, Döllinger shared with them the cultural characteristics of the people from the Middle Rhine and Main region: an open mind, a quick brain, a religious spirit, and a capacity for the enjoyment of life. Döllinger combined the German characteristics of intense patriotism and understanding of other cultures, a combination that had not, as yet, been channelled into militant and overbearing nationalism. His father had taught him French and learned Greek himself in order to teach it to his son. A monk of the *Schottenkloster* (the name given to Benedictine monasteries in Germany and Austria, founded by Irish-Scottish monks arriving from "Scotia") was his English master. His uncle, a Cistercian monk, taught him Latin. He was at home in the literature of Europe and, in short, was a European German.

The dearth of Catholic ideas in early nineteenth-century Germany made Döllinger seek inspiration in the new and flourishing post-revolutionary Catholicism of France. Félicité Robert de Lamennais, Charles de Montalembert, Bishop Félix Dupanloup of Orléans, Cardinal Guillaume-René Meignan of Bourges, and the theologians Alphonse Gratry and Henri Louis Charles Maret were among his earliest friends. But he became gradually disillusioned by them. Döllinger seemed to have more in common with the great Archbishop of Cambrai, François de Salignac de la Mothe Fénelon (1651–1715). Like Fénelon at the court of Louis XIV, Döllinger was a royal tutor. Fénelon's mysticism, his distinction and nobleness, and his outspoken opposition to absolute monarchy attracted the young German scholar,[25] and Fénelon's friendship and correspondence with Madame Jeanne Bouviér de La Motte Guyon is reminiscent of Döllinger's with Charlotte von Leyden, later Lady Blennerhassett.

Döllinger gained a reputation, abroad rather than in Germany, of a leading "Catholic liberal," which he seemed to enjoy and never contradicted. Young Acton, however, soon found that Döllinger's so-called liberalism had no justification in fact. In the great conflict between Catholic liberalism and Ultramontanism, which dominated both their lives, Döllinger's role was that of an enlightened Catholic conservative, a defender of political liberty against state oppression. In Germany, which had strong conservative and weak liberal-revolutionary traditions, this position did not make one a liberal. Acton saw Döllinger as belonging to the Ultramontane Catholicism of the German South, indeed as a man whose singular contribution was to make Munich the Ultramontane ("beyond the Alps") capital of the Catholic world. He was really not Ultramontane (in the modern sense of favouring papal absolutions) or Gallican or liberal, and he seemed to have been caught totally unawares by the final clash over Papal Infallibility.

Döllinger's knowledge of modern European languages was widely acclaimed, and he had a considerable ability, based on his reading, to express himself well in writing. It prompted English Catholic friends to invite him to teach in England; in 1839 there was mention of a chair at the recently founded Durham University, and John Henry Newman wanted him for his Dublin University project in 1854. Döllinger's spoken English, however, suffered, according to Acton, from "a defective ear."[26] And Döllinger probably had not been used to paying as much attention to English pronunciation as to grammar. It is arguable whether Döllinger's links with France went deeper than those with England. He was a francophile as well as an anglophile; he knew English literature and history well and was particularly conversant with the seventeenth-century Anglican spiritual writers. He took the closest interest in the Tractarian movement and other tendencies within the Church of England and was well known in British Anglican and Roman Catholic circles. He was a bit of a snob in English matters, as his pupil observed in a masterly study of the Professor written forty years later: "Early acquaintance with Sir Edward Vavasour and Lord Clifford had planted a lasting prejudice in favour of the English Catholic families, which sometimes tinged his judgments."[27] And when Acton returned to England and was faced with the controversies of the English Catholic body, he once vented his impatience with Döllinger, who, as always, thought only the best of the English: "You are far from having taken the measure of the Anglo-Catholic limitations."[28]

Döllinger's name was known in England. His books were translated and widely read. Wiseman, Newman, and E. B. Pusey visited him. Gladstone came in September 1845, one month before "that earthquake"—Newman's reception into the Catholic Church—and found him "a remarkable and very pleasing man." As he wrote to his wife, "I have lost my heart to him."[29]

5

THE NEWFOUND FAMILY

What Acton owed to Dr. Döllinger in terms of intellectual development, he owed to his Munich relations, the Arcos, as far as his heart was concerned. On Sundays he escaped from the austere Döllinger household to Theatinerstrasse 7, the palatial home of his cousins Count Maximilian von Arco-Valley and his beautiful Italian wife, Anna, born Countess Marescalchi, and their children.[1] It was a house full of life and laughter. It also had an English touch—an English coachman and an English tutor, Mr. Spink from Oscott, were among the household's numerous retinue. Acton and the Countess went riding together and on carriage drives. He spent holidays at the Arcos' summer-house at Tegernsee or at their castle near Ried in Upper Austria, ten miles from the Bavarian frontier, within easy reach of Austria's mountain scenery, including Gmunden, Bad Ischl, Hallstatt, and Bad Aussee. It was, for Acton, like a dream come true. He had hardly known his father. His mother always cared for him, wrote to him regularly, and found the best teachers for him to form his religious outlook, but she had other priorities and was not able to give him what he wanted more than anything—to be loved and understood by her. Yet in the Arcos he had suddenly acquired what he had never had before: a family and a real home.

"La bella contessa"—a temperamental Italian, intelligent and religious, educated at the Rue de Varennes Convent in Paris, and devoted to her Acton-Dalberg relations—accepted Acton as though he were the ninth of her children. The Arco-Valleys were old and close friends of Dr. Döllinger; he had advised them on the education of their children. Yet his advice was not always taken. Döllinger, for instance, evinced an irrational dislike of Jesuit education, but the Arcos supported the movement for the Jesuits' return to Bavaria (they had been banished in the eighteenth century) to open a boarding school. The Arcos represented the elite of the Munich milieu, being royalist, rich, and Catholic. The Count was something of a libertine who caused his wife much anguish with his many amours, but he was a great philanthropist and patron of many Catholic charities. During the outbreaks of cholera, then frequent in Munich, he turned parts of the Palais Arco into a hospital.

Of Acton's cousins, originally ten, two had died quite young, and their portraits—which, in the manner of the age, depicted them as angels—hung in the Arco drawing room. All six Arco boys became cavalry colonels and Knights of the Royal Bavarian Order of St. George, and they all fought in the Franco-Prussian War of 1870–71. With their many affairs, unfortunate marriages, duels fought, or other scrapes they got themselves into, they were a constant source of anxiety to their mother. Cousin Acton took a close interest in their lives and advised on their education, and one of them wrote to him: "Having your support was worth much when I realized how little I was fitted for the realities of the world."[2] He might have been speaking for all of them. Of the two daughters, Leopoldine, known jocularly as Tini because she was so large, lost all her original charm; she became a disgruntled old maid and Dame of the Royal Order of St. Teresa.

In Munich, John Acton was roped into the new Society of St. Vincent de Paul, which the Count supported. Its purpose was to encourage well-to-do Catholic laymen to take a regular interest in a particular poor family and provide them with help beyond whatever public assistance they received. The Count, born in 1806, with King Maximilian I as godfather, had literally overnight come into the inheritance of a distant cousin, Count Tattenbach, who, preferring him to his own nephew, had left to Count Arco castles, vast estates, and art treasures.

It was in connection with this inheritance that King Ludwig I bestowed on the Count the right to be styled Arco auf Valley, to distinguish himself from other Arco branches (the county of Valley belonged at one time to the counts of Scheyern-Wittelsbach, who came to constitute the Bavarian royal line). Maximilian Arco was a hereditary member of the Reichsrat (in the Upper House or First Chamber, as it was called) and leader of the Catholic opposition. Unlike Dr. Döllinger, who was a member of the Lower House, or Second Chamber, Arco had little talent as a parliamentarian or party leader.

Count Arco had wanted, originally, to marry the only daughter of the Duke of Dalberg—Acton's mother. But she was already promised to Sir Richard Acton. Seeing how disappointed he was, her mother, the Duchess of Dalberg, advised him to go to Bologna, where her sister's daughter, Anna Marescalchi, was still unmarried. He took her advice and returned from Bologna engaged to Anna. Their marriage took place in Bologna on 6 June 1832, five days after the Acton-Dalberg wedding, and the fates of the Actons and Arcos were to be still more closely entwined.

The Brignole-Sales, grandparents of Anna, Countesss Arco, and Marie, Lady Granville, were members of an ancient Genoese family famous for their beautiful women, some of whom were painted by Sir Anthony van Dyck. One of these, Angela, married a Bolognese commoner, Buoncompagni, and was the mother of Pope Gregory XIII (1572–1585), who was responsible for the Gregorian calendar reform. Later, one of three Brignole-Sale sisters—Caterina, a clever woman—married Count Carlo Alfonso Marescalchi, a charming grand-seigneur from that well-known Bolognese family, and their daughter was Acton's cousin Anna. Thus Acton's Italian relations, taking into account both his father's and his mother's sides, extended to such Italian aristocrats as the Littas, Viscontis, Lavaggis, and Brusqui-Fulgaris, and, through his aunt's brother, Ferdinando, who lived in Paris and was married to Matilda de Pange, also into the French nobility.

In the summer holidays after his first arrival in Munich, Acton and Döllinger went via Innsbruck and Milan to Venice, and back through Trieste and Austria. They called on monasteries on the way and visited such friends as, in Milan, the historian and literary critic Cesare Cantù (1804–1895), one of the Italian patriots who combined loyalty to the Pope, longing for national unity, and hatred of Austrian domination. In Venice they met up with the Arcos. Anna Arco clearly turned Acton's head, as she had turned those of many other admirers. That encounter and its beautiful setting consolidated the romantic attachment, if such it was, between Acton, not yet seventeen, and his cousin, then just thirty-seven. She was a cultivated and well-read woman. In Munich she had a regular salon where, on the first Tuesday of the month, Döllinger, the Catholic physician Johann Nepomuk von Ringseis, and poets and artists came to her "at home." She was also a sparkling hostess, and the balls at Palais Arco often lasted until four in the morning. Once Anna Arco caused a sensation at a fancy dress ball at the court in Munich by appearing with all the diamonds of the three Arco branches (Valley, Zinneberg, Stoppberg) sewn to her black velvet bodice. Acton at once came under the spell of this affectionate, dramatic Italian beauty.

Acton spent his first Christmas at Munich with the Arcos. There were a lot of presents; the Countess gave him a golden pin for his cravat and the Count gave him an illustrated edition of the *Nibelungenlied,* and they all went to midnight Mass, celebrated by Döllinger, at the Royal Chapel. A lighthearted account of a later Christmas, 1852, appears in a letter to Minnie Throckmorton:

> At the Arco's, where I have 8 cousins, and where I reckon as the 9th we had 9 little trees, each on its own table-benches, a great pine in the middle of the room, all groaning with the exertion of carrying innumerable sweetmeats, which wailing and exertion are presently shared by certain little boys who sacrifice their stomachs out of a charitable desire of alleviating the overbur-dened trees. On each table, which bares [*sic*] the name of its owner, was a quantity of presents, for it is usual to be sparing in presents on odd occasions in order to give an indigestion of them now. On this occasion the indiges-tion was not without cause or consolation, for among the presents were two ponies and a billiard table.[3]

On 6 January 1857, Epiphany, when Catholic Munich celebrated the Feast of the Adoration of the Magi, there were to be theatricals performed by the Arco children Toni and Marie, but they had scarlet fever, so the event was cancelled. To console Acton, the Countess visited him, bringing chocolates, a prayer-book in German, and, from the Count, Friedrich von Schiller's poems.

Anna Arco often talked with John Acton about his interests. From her he learned to overcome his shyness with women, and she was the first of those very few women who knew him intimately. In the countless letters they ex-changed—in English or French—he poured out his heart to her as to no one else, and she supplied him with a mother's love. Apparently disguising his love for her, he decided pointedly to address her as "my own dear Mama" long be-fore his own mother had died and before Anna became his mother-in-law. The emotional tone of Acton's many letters might suggest an affair between them. Anna's eldest daughter, Marie, who eventually became Acton's wife, was nine years old when he came to Munich in 1850, and still a child when he left with the understanding that they would ultimately marry. During his Munich years

Marie tended to tease the earnest cousin, while he became devoted to her in a protective, brotherly fashion. Some years later he wrote to her mother from Aldenham: "I lack the happiness to have a brother like Toni and a sister like Marie."[4]

Were his hopes of marrying Marie influenced by his feelings for her mother? The determination with which he pursued Marie suggests an element of wishful thinking, for he must have been aware that the love he thought he had for her was not returned. After years of to-ing and fro-ing the girl gave in, beaten by both her family's pressure and her own uncertainty. The age in which they lived, if nothing else, made the older woman and her young charge keep to the formality of their relationship.

Countess Arco was fond of Acton's mother and, indeed, sometimes rebuked him for his apparent coolness to Lady Granville. Once he replied:

> I should like you not to be anxious about my relationship with my mother. . . . It is impossible for me to show affection which would be easily suspected and which she would certainly reject. Every difference between myself and Lord Granville will make her doubt my friendship and respect for him, the more so since he still has enough influence to destroy my credit with her. I should like you to understand truly this complicated state of affairs which has made me so unhappy and has always deprived me of the feelings of "home." This has played and does play such a great and painful role in my life that you ought to appreciate it and stop reproaching me about it. It is you who have given me all the consolation and compensation that I have had.[5]

Back in England, and writing to Countess Arco on a lonely New Year's Eve from Aldenham, Acton reminded her that his uncle Charles, who, as Papal Legate in Bologna, had known her family, had once expressed the wish that his father might have married her rather than her cousin: "What a pity for me at least that it was never realised. What would Aldenham be now! See how selfish I am to wish to deprive you of so much of your children instead of giving you one more. . . . My own dear Mama, you alone have been the source by your kindness and affection of all my happiness and of all my sorrow for your absence."[6]

But in the happiness of the Munich days, Acton's letters to his stepfather and mother reflect only his anxiety not to have his stay limited, as Lord Granville would have liked: "I am still of the opinion that it would be an advantage to you to finish your studies in England, if a method likely to be agreeable as well as profitable to you, could be agreed," he wrote. And he went on to suggest that in thinking that Munich was absolutely the only place in the world that could afford him the benefits of pursuing the course of studies he had begun, "It appears to me that you prove a little too much."[7] Persuaded by the progress he was making and by Dr. Döllinger's glowing reports, Lord and Lady Granville finally agreed to having him stay on.

Acton's knowledge of German was soon proficient enough for him to go to university lectures. He attended two of Döllinger's courses—one on the history of the Church until the French Revolution, the other on the general history of the Church. He described the Professor's lecturing as "quiet, restrained, with a voice which could only be heard over the vast assembly by absolute quiet. [He dealt with much that was] obvious, necessary, unavoidable. Then when there were points to be explained, a difficulty got over, a view taken, there was an impressive jerk of the whole body."[8] Another of Döllinger's students, Dr. Hyazinth Holland, a friend of the Arcos', recorded: "He used to carry a large leather folder containing what he required in the way of quotations, written down on bits of paper. The rest he delivered freely. He was excellent in describing historical figures, allowing them to come alive in their historical settings. . . . Döllinger kept the utmost cool, also in Parliament, the more excited his listeners became. When he spoke in the Bavarian Chamber as rapporteur on the emancipation of Jews, he spoke for two hours without losing his voice. He spoke frankly, with deliberate bluntness, but with such accomplished elegance that no one was offended."[9]

Next door to Döllinger lectured Ernst von Lasaulx, professor of philology, Greek literature, and philosophy. Acton was enthusiastic about him, and Lasaulx took a liking to the young man and became a trusted friend. When Lasaulx died in 1861, Acton acquired his library. Lasaulx, also son-in-law of the philosopher Franz von Baader, was a key figure of the Munich Romantics; Döllinger was part of that circle but about to distance himself from it.

Acton just missed a man who had a major influence on Döllinger. This was Johann Joseph von Görres, champion of the Rhenish Republic and the famous editor of Germany's first political newspaper, *Rheinischer Merkur,* in which he had preached resistance to Napoleon. His opinions had led to his being exiled to Strasbourg, where he discovered the ideas of the Catholic revival in France, in particular those of Louis-Gabriel-Ambroise, Vicomte de Bonald, and Joseph de Maistre. In 1827 Görres was invited by King Ludwig I to the University of

Munich, where, as a Catholic convert and moderate conservative, he acquired a large following. Together with Döllinger, he wrote for the *Historisch-politische Blätter*. He died in 1848.

Just as Döllinger cut himself loose from Görres's influence, Acton became, in later life, highly critical of Lasaulx's "indistinct mixture of dates and authorities, and the spell which his unchastened idealism cast over students"—among them Acton himself, who at that time was far from casting off the spell.[10] It was said of Lasaulx, who was basically a man of creative imagination, that he put many Christian elements into ancient myths and then delightedly welcomed what he found there. The Christian elements did not prevent some of his writings from being put on the Index of forbidden books because of their Christian Platonist and pantheist tendencies. But he accepted the condemnation and died reconciled with the Catholic Church.[11]

Lasaulx was among the participants in the Munich Romantics' "Sunday Suppers," held at Dr. Döllinger's because most of the members lived in his neighbourhood. A glimpse of the suppers was given by Gladstone in 1845, in a letter to his wife: "I never saw men who spoke together in a way to make one another inaudible as they did, always excepting Dr. Döllinger . . . [who] is a much more refined man. But of the others I assure you always two, sometimes three, and once all four, were speaking at once, very loud, each not trying to force the attention of the others, but to be following the current of his own thoughts. One of them was Dr. Görres. . . . Unfortunately he spoke more thickly than any of them."[12] Görres once accused Döllinger: "I always see analogies and you always see differences."[13] That opposition characterized the distinction between the Romantic School and the Critical School that followed it.

Acton later defined the Romantic School disapprovingly as a "preference for obscurity and divination; the use of imagination and dislike of criticism; the preference for literature over law, and poetry over prose; the sympathy with irrational thinking, thinking by myths and symbols; the inclination to early times, and contempt for modern [times]; . . . [preference for the] instinct of masses, the forces of nature against reflection."[14] Döllinger, as Acton noted, outgrew most of the characteristics of the *Romantik*, but what he retained opened up the gulf between him and Acton concerning the question of historical judgement. *Romantik* was another name for the permissive society of the early nineteenth century in the often-misquoted sense of Madame de Staël's "To understand all is to forgive all."[15] The mature Acton recorded in 1892: "The Romantic School was feeble as to morals. Schlegel ran away with another man's wife, and wrote a voluptious [*sic*] novel, to which Schleiermacher supplied a commentary. Later on, he [Schlegel] became noted for his good appetite— and Metternich, who took him to Rome, reports that he was enchanted by the Pope's own cook. They tended to debase the currency, to bend the standard of morality. They established the theory that every age must be understood and judged on its own terms."[16]

Acton's boxes of notes, kept at the Cambridge University Library, contain a mass of material on Döllinger as historian, collected after the Professor's death for the biography that the pupil would have been uniquely qualified to write but never wrote. These notes contain many brilliant flashes of insight into the Professor's entire outlook. It was from the history of the Church that Döllinger sought to know its mind, Acton noted. Döllinger's own mind was formed by the works of the ecclesiastical historians who preceded him.[17] He thought that the historical method of approaching truth was the method of the Church, and the speculative method the method of the schools. His idea of deriving truth from history was Hegelian, although he had disliked G. W. F. Hegel at first. Independent of Hegel, Döllinger came to the theory of development that became as important to his thinking as it was to Newman's: "The methods of Church (ecclesiastical) history led away from the methods of eccl[esiastical] authority. Authority restricted the range of study, promoted approved authors, by long acceptance, discouraged the study, acknowledgment, recognition, of hostile writers, heretics, unbelievers, sceptics. . . . The scholar, in history, learned to make his sheaves where he could, was uneasy in his position until he had exhausted the objectives of opponents, the difficulties which they suggested indirectly." Acton went on in this recorded note to emphasize that Döllinger "carried this far. He was always for gleaning away from the main path—for the byways—for exploring the unexpected."[18] His leading idea was that there was more religion in history than in theology, and that the annals of mankind make man feel the presence of Christ and his action on the soul, on society, on history.[19] Döllinger thought that history reconciled those whom theology divided.[20] He disliked comparisons and analogy and excluded all personal elements.[21] Döllinger's interest in history was always linked to particular events or needs of his time, influenced by practical experiences of having lived in many European cities and been a member of three parliaments; he had been consulted in the formation of ministries, had advised the policy of statesmen, and had seen how history is made.[22]

Döllinger's pupil, soon to come of age and take over the running of his estate at Aldenham, was to follow up the Professor's teaching in England. The Munich years—though by no means the links forged there—were at an end. For John Acton the parting from the Arcos was tearful. But first, in August 1854, he and Countess Arco as well as Marie, nearly fourteen years old, had some pleasant days together at Wildbad, the spa in the Black Forest, and at Herrnsheim, the Dalberg Schloss. It was, as usual, full of varied, interesting guests, this time Lord Shaftesbury, the social reformer and prominent Whig; a Polish poet; and a Catholic priest from London, a friend of Acton's mother's.

For Acton, this summer was "part of the sweetest memories" he would take back with him to England. He wrote to his "aunt" soon after from Freiburg, where he had travelled with Döllinger:

> You have made me so happy in these short moments together, that I am now quite sad on this first evening without you. I went to bed yesterday reproaching myself, because there were so many things I still wanted to tell you. This morning I stood beneath your window which you had opened, hoping for a glance of you and to say adieu again but you didn't even show the tip of your nose, and your discretion deprived me of a real solace. Do you think sometime of the good moments we have passed together at the end? Shall I in your eyes always remain that strong John Emerich who, as you sometimes believe, gives you a lot of worries without loving you at all? When I think of my incomparable luck in being with you, I can't bear the idea that you might want to diminish this closeness by doubts. I would love to write to you always during my travels until that certain day when we shall see each other again. But you have other worries into which I do not want to interfere. I hope that we shall be such close and good friends as we were in our parting after this happiest span of my life in Munich.[23]

Countess Arco responded no less fervently, full of affection for her young cousin. Whether there was more to the emotions shown by both parties in this and their later voluminous correspondence remains unclear. Anna was a temperamental Italian, suffering in private over a wayward husband and unruly sons. John Acton, deeply attached in his mind and heart to the Munich world, was unsure over his personal future in England, his inheritance, himself. "I always feel the same sorrow on saying goodbye to you," she once wrote,

> and it is with joy that I look forward to your return, my dear Johnny. . . . I get upset at the nice things of life to which one abandons oneself, but I feel at the same time that my friendship for you will survive anything in this world

and I always want your greatest happiness. . . . Tomorrow we will go to Bonn and I will trace our steps from the time we were there together five years ago. Then later we shall meet again at Tegernsee, the place of your first arrival. I don't think it will be too late to send this letter to Annecy.[24] Pray for me. . . . Tell me about everything you hold dear and that worries you, my dear John Emerich. I want to convince you that you will always have a real friend in your affectionate aunt A. Marescalchi.[25]

Acton had met up with the Professor at Herrnsheim. At their first stop, Freiburg, they were guests of Döllinger's publisher Benjamin Herder (1818–1888) and met some prominent Herder authors: Johann Baptist von Hirscher (1788–1865), the moral theologian and writer of popular Catholic books; and Franz Joseph von Buss (1803–1878), the canon lawyer who had been close to Döllinger as a member of the 1848 Frankfurt Assembly and president of the German *Katholikentag*. Buss was an advocate of a "South German" solution involving a federal Germany under the Austrian emperor. Accompanying them all on walks into the fine scenery of Freiburg's surroundings was Alban Stolz (1808–1883), a best-selling Catholic writer and professor of pastoral theology and education at Freiburg University, whose striking appearance seemed to Acton to resemble that of the devil.[26]

Acton and Döllinger then spent some days in Geneva, where they visited their friends the Menthons and the Abbé Mermillod. Gaspard Mermillod (1824–1892) was a strong advocate of Papal Infallibility, an issue over which he was later to clash with Döllinger. As the first "apostolic vicar" of Geneva, he met with much hostility in staunchly anti-Catholic Switzerland. His interests in Catholic social thinking on an international basis played an important part in preparations for the publication of the first encyclical on social questions, *Rerum Novarum,* of Leo XIII (1891).

After crossing over the Simplon Pass into Italy and visiting Milan, Döllinger and Acton went to see the Certosa and on to Bologna to indulge in what was to become their favourite vacation activity—enjoying the manuscript treasures made accessible only recently in the Continental archives. Bologna, with its Marescalchi palazzo on top of a hill, the residence of Acton's energetic great-aunt (Countess Arco's mother), was conveniently situated for the two travellers, enabling them to visit archives in the region, including those in Venice.

Acton returned on his own to Munich and, in September, eventually via Paris to England. The Professor spent the rest of his vacation in Salzburg with his old friend from the 1848 Frankfurt Assembly, George Phillips (1804–1874), the historian and canon lawyer of English extraction, pupil of the famous Friedrich Karl von Savigny, the founder of the School of Historical Jurisprudence in Berlin. Phillips, who was a contemporary of Görres in Munich, a member of the Romantic School, and a Catholic convert, played a prominent role as a leading conservative in the early nineteenth-century German Catholic renewal.

Acton's summer trip with the Professor was a memorable and fitting conclusion to Acton's Munich years of study, though by no means to his links of mind and heart with the Bavarian world. The England of his ancestors beckoned him with uncertainties and hopes.

Il merci, et je me suis échappé pour aller passer ces derniers jours de Carême en repos à Edgbaston. Je tâcherai d'être à temps pour dîner avec vous le jour de Pâques.

L'abbé Domenech a écrit un fort bon livre qui a été beaucoup approuvé par la presse en Angleterre, avec plus d'intérêt personnel que les voyages de [...]. J'aurais aimé faire sa connaissance.

J'espère que Mr. Leveson fait des progrès avec son couvent à Bodmin. Bowyer est sûr de Dundalk, car il est aidé à la fois par l'influence du Cardinal et par celle de Lord Roden.

Croyez ma chère Maman
Votre affué fils
J Acton

Ce mardi

Ma chère Maman,
Je retrouve Aldenham par ce plus beau soleil, charmant, et c'est avec peine que je m'en vais demain. Tout est en ordre, excepté Mr. Morris qui a mal à l'oeil. La vieille Mrs. Taylor et old Day sont morts depuis mon départ.

J'ai vu cette fois une partie de l'intérieur de l'Irlande, ce qui m'a fort intéressé, et beaucoup plu. En comparant ce que je voyais avec mon guide, de 1854, je suis étonné de l'immense progrès que ce pays a fait, et continue à faire. On ne trouve presque plus de mendiants, et plus assez

A specimen of Acton's even handwriting, which scarcely changed throughout his life. Family letters were often written in French, the lingua franca of the European elite of his day. This letter, written by Sir John Acton when he was twenty-four, was, significantly, meant not for his own "Maman" but for Anna, Countess Arco, his maternal "aunt" (actually his cousin), who with her large Munich family took the place of his own remarried mother and gave him the first taste of a loving home he had known. Courtesy of Cambridge University Library.

A sketch (ca. 1879) for the oil painting of Acton by Franz von Lenbach. In 1882 the Munich painter presented the finished picture to his friend Ignaz von Döllinger, who gave it pride of place in his study over his writing desk, where it remained even after the estrangement between the "Professor" and his English pupil. Courtesy of the National Portrait Gallery, London.

The Regius Professor of Modern History at the University of Cambridge, ca. 1896.
Photo by Elliott and Fry, London.

The family of Sir John Francis Edward Acton, the prime minister of Queen Marie Caroline of the Two Sicilies: (left) Sir Ferdinand Richard Acton (1801–1837), the father of the historian; (right) Charles (1803–1847), the future Cardinal Acton; and Elizabeth (1806–1850), the future Lady Throckmorton, in the arms of her mother, who became known as Nonna ("Granny") Acton. Courtesy of Mrs. Theodore Donahane, Palm Beach, Fla.

Marriage certificate of Acton's grandfather, Sir John Francis Edward Acton, and Lady Marie Anne Acton, dated Palermo 22 February 1800. Among the witnesses' signatures are the names of Sir William Hamilton, the British ambassador, and Lady Emma Hamilton.

Emma
1791

A drawing entitled "Emma," made by Thomas Lawrence in 1791, after the adventuress had married the British ambassador at Naples, Sir William Hamilton, having lived with him for five years and fascinated the great world of which Naples was then a centre; seven years later she became the mistress of Nelson. © The British Museum, London.

King Ferdinand I of the Two
Sicilies with Queen Marie
Caroline and their seven chil-
dren. Painting by Angelica
Kauffmann (1741–1806).
Reprinted by permission
of Museo di Capodimonte,
Naples.

Sir John Francis Edward
Acton, sixth Baronet (1736–
1811), Acton's grandfather,
who as prime minister of the
Kingdom of the Two Sicilies
steered the Bourbon King-
dom from its Spanish ties into
the Austro-British alliance
against Napoleon. Private
owner.

Cardinal Charles Acton (1803–1847), uncle of the historian, interpreting between Pope Gregory XVI and Tsar Nicholas I during the tsar's visit to Rome, an occasion used for a diplomatic protest against the tsarist oppression of Polish Catholics. Private owner.

Villa Acton on the Riviera di Chiaja, Bay of Naples, in the year of Acton's birth (1834). Private owner.

Lady Acton, née Marie Louisa Pelline von Dalberg (1812–1860), daughter of the Duc de
Dalberg. *After the early death of Sir Richard Acton, the young widow married Earl
Granville. This painting by Ary Scheffer (1795–1858), a Dutch-French artist popular in the
Paris Salon, shows the historian's mother as an elegant embodiment of the post-Napoleonic
Biedermeier fashion in the age of Restoration. Private owner.*

Sir Ferdinand Richard Acton (1801–1837), father of the historian. This portrait, made in the Romantic manner of the 1820s, was intended to reflect his grand status in Neapolitan society: behind the horseman a servant is seen struggling up the ravine; just visible between the horse's legs is the smoking top of Mount Vesuvius. Private owner.

A cartoon showing King Ferdinand II of the Two Sicilies (1810–1859) at the lavish party given on 1 March 1834 by Acton's parents two months after the birth of their only son. The Bourbon King's reign opened in 1830 with promises of constitutional reforms, but his bombardment of the chief Sicilian cities in 1849 caused European liberals to dub him "King Bomba."

Tombstone of Sir Ferdinand Richard Acton. The historian's father died in Paris in 1837, having caught a chill after one of his late nights of gambling. The monument, now lost in the vaults of the former Aldenham chapel, depicts the sorrowing widow and son, aged three, at the door of death. The sculpture is by Richard West-macott the Younger, a school friend of Cardinal Newman's. Private owner.

George Leveson-Gower (1815–1891) married Acton's widowed mother in 1840 and rose to high offices in Liberal Governments as the second Earl Granville. Photo by W. and D. Dawney from the Royal Archives, Windsor Castle, reprinted by permission of Her Majesty Queen Elizabeth II, © The Royal Archives.

The Dalberg tomb in Worms Cathedral, Germany. Acton's maternal ancestors, an ancient family of dukes of the Holy Roman Empire, even claimed descent from one Gaius Marcellus, an officer in the Roman army and a supposed relative of Jesus Christ. Photo Stadtarchiv, Worms, Germany.

Schloss Herrnsheim, the residence of Acton's Dalberg ancestors. The round tower at the right contained one of the many libraries that Acton accumulated wherever he lived. Herrnsheim was the scene of memorable meetings prior to the First Vatican Council between Acton, Döllinger, Bishops Dupanloup and Ketteler, and others opposed to the dogma of Papal Infallibility. Photo courtesy of James C. Holland.

Tomb of Carl Theodor von Dalberg, last of the Electors of Mainz (1744–1817). During the Napoleonic wars, this most famous of Acton's maternal ancestors endeavoured, as Primate of the Catholic Church in Germany, to secure its greater national independence from Rome. Photo Stadtarchiv, Worms, Germany.

6

THE SQUIRE

Early in December 1854, Acton was back at Aldenham, where only part of the house was habitable because of restoration work at the front. His mother was having the eighteenth-century windows replaced (an innovation much disapproved of today because it destroyed the original façade). She had also had many improvements carried out in the park and gardens. Three rooms were prepared for his use, and everything was done to make him feel at home and—he suspected when writing to the Professor—"to counter the attraction of Germany and they overlook that it will equally draw me away from London where people most wish to see me."[1] Acton felt his first solitary days in the big house to be a foretaste of the life he would lead. His mother and Lord Granville had been running the estate, which covered more than six thousand acres, during his minority, and between his arrival and the date of his twenty-first birthday, on 10 January 1855, he was called upon to make a major decision. Should he sell Aldenham to Lord Granville or keep it for himself and for whatever family he would have in the future?

Acton's stepfather had grown fond of the place that, apart from his London house, had become his permanent residence. He loved country life. Aldenham was ideal for partridge shoots: "Lowe, the fat keeper, gave me a day's shooting on his own preserve," Lord Granville wrote to his old Eton chum Lord Canning, son of the famous statesman, then governor of India. "I know of no one more agreeable. I asked him whether Acton did not manage to kill the deer. 'Well, my Lord, I don't think he ever takes aim,' adding with much feeling, 'I am sorry to say.'"[2] For some time Lord Granville had wanted to acquire Aldenham. Now Acton had to make up his mind, and, in view of the hidden tension among the three of them, he had to tread carefully. His mother, who had certain rights in the matter, left the decision to him.

"At first I was in doubt whether I should take these rights from her," Acton wrote to Döllinger. If he were to cede Aldenham to his mother he would never become independent. Lord Granville "promised to leave my rooms free for me, but as long as my mother lived he would remain master at Aldenham (over the house, not the estate)."[3] He consulted his grandmother, who advised—indeed, implored—him not to give up Aldenham to his mother, but to preserve it for the family. To Countess Arco, his only other confidant, he wrote that he "had not realized before this conversation how much love and confidence she [Nonna] had for me."[4] Sir Robert Throckmorton was also consulted and agreed with Nonna's view.

Late at night, on 7 January 1855, Acton wrote to his stepfather telling him that he wanted to remain "master of Aldenham" and that the decision was made regrettably in direct contradiction to the advice of J. W. Freshfield, Acton's lawyer and trustee of the estate.[5] Acton told Granville as diplomatically as he could to stay at Aldenham "until my marriage or entrance into public life. . . . It will always be open to you, and if you find it convenient to stay here any longer time, it will, of course, be most pleasant for me." If Granville resolved on taking another country house, he should not hasten his departure from Aldenham. "The subsidy which my mother proposed to fix for part of the household expenses I accept with the greatest thankfulness."[6]

In spite of the gracious way Acton's decision was wrapped up, it came as a surprise and disappointment to Lord Granville. He evidently did not think much of Acton's ability to maintain Aldenham. Acton's mother, by contrast, was pleased with the fondness he had shown for his heritage. "Johnny is a charming host," Granville noted a year later. "It is rather a curious feeling coming as a guest to one who has always been one to me, and to a place where for years I was master, and where many little objects of interest have ceased. . . . It is a pleasure to see Lady Granville's happiness here; I think her zest about it is

not in the least diminished by her having to give it up. Johnny is very affectionate to her, and nice to me."[7] There was little love lost between Acton and his
stepfather; however, they learned to rationalize their close relationship, which
was soon extended also to the common bond of Liberal politics.

The twenty-first birthday celebrations of the new squire were to be conducted fittingly. The house filled with family and guests. Acton consulted Newman regarding the line he, as a Catholic should take when he had to propose
the loyal toast. Answer came:

> My first impression is, that it would be best to avoid the subject of religion
> altogether—or at least to speak of it as little as possible—and in the most
> general terms. . . .
>   As to the Queen, everyone must respect her private conduct. There is but
> one opinion as to the excellent way in which she brings up her family—and
> she is the keystone of the social fabric—so that all our political happiness is
> bound up in her welfare. Moreover, as being a lady it is right to have certain
> chivalrous feelings about her. Yet I doubt whether I could be enthusiastic in
> her favor, knowing how opposed she is to the Catholic religion.[8]

On the great day, at ten in the morning, a procession came up the Aldenham
avenue, led by the rich farmers on horseback, with two oxen on a cart, followed
by a large crowd and packs of foxhounds of the neighbourhood. They were met
by Acton and family in front of the house. The Anglican parson gave an address.
The huntsmen who accompanied the hounds were entertained to breakfast. A
toast was drunk to the health of Sir John Acton with beer labelled with the date
of his twenty-first birthday. That evening there was dancing, eating, and drinking that lasted till half past two in the morning, when Acton chased the last
revellers from his house. Altogether 250 bottles of wine were consumed.

That night, before he went to bed, Acton's mother came to his room with
her present, a mantel clock, and the promise of a writing table for his study. She
showed him much affection, he told Countess Arco; his speech had evidently
pleased her. To his beloved cousin he wrote that her letter and Marie's had been
delivered the moment the procession arrived in Aldenham. When he read them
later, they had given him the greatest joy of the day. He was clearly beginning
to think of the Countess and Marie Arco as sharing the future life at Aldenham.

But after the heady delights came the time to return to work. The Aldenham estate required the new master's attention, and then there were his books
and writing plans. Acton also talked to his lawyers about his financial posi-

tion, which, as he learned, required him to be economical. He reckoned that he would have less than £1,000 a year, one-tenth of his revenue, to spend. The property was run down and heavily in debt. Acton hoped that the land he owned at Bridgnorth, whose value would increase with the coming of the railway, could be sold to pay off the debts. But the value of agricultural land in general was diminishing. When the Aldenham estate, with some fifty tenants and tithes from twenty cottages, came to be valued again, in 1883, it had decreased from £10,000 to £7,500 per annum for 6,231 acres. The estimated yearly rental amounted to £4,521, but even six months into the new year only £3,366 of the previous year's rent had been received.

Acton's mother had founded a little elementary school in the neighbouring village of Morville, where the Aldenham chaplain was expected to give religious instruction to a few of the Catholic children. Acton decided that because most of the children belonged to the Established Church, it would not be just to appoint a Catholic as schoolmaster. So he addressed himself to the task of finding someone who would not promote anti-Catholic bias against the Catholic landlord.[9]

It was also difficult to find a suitable chaplain. The growth of an industrial urban population in the nineteenth century was changing the demographics of the Roman Catholic Church. In the eighteenth century the organization of the Church had often centred round the chaplains of a few big country houses. The Aldenham chaplain was expected to hold services on Sundays at Bridgnorth, which, at four miles each ride, made his life arduous. Acton gave a piece of land for a school-chapel to be built at Bridgnorth. This gift involved him in contacts with the Bishop of Shrewsbury, James Brown, who, while acknowledging Acton's contribution, pointed out that it was little more than sufficient for the building. The problem would be how to maintain it. The relationship with Bishop Brown was friendly at first. He came to stay at Aldenham for a few days in July 1856, when they agreed that in future Acton's chaplain would not have to serve Bridgnorth as well. The Bridgnorth school-chapel was officially opened in October 1856.

The growth of the English Catholic body due to the influx from Ireland was clearly illustrated at Bridgnorth. In 1851, the Bridgnorth congregation (including the Aldenham area) numbered 110, with sixty Easter communions, three baptisms, and one marriage. It was a minute part of the new diocese of Shrewsbury, which also covered parts of Wales and was then estimated to comprise

10,284 Mass-attending Catholics. By 1870 the numbers in that area had increased fourfold, to 41,000, with 16,099 Easter communions and 2,371 baptisms.[10]

With the greater needs of the urban Catholics, it was not easy to find a suitable man for the more restricted activity of a squire's chaplain. As a young bachelor, Acton was looking for a mature and scholarly priest who would share his life and also take an interest in his growing library. He negotiated at length to get John Brande Morris (1812–1880), a forty-two-year-old convert since 1846 who had recently been made a canon of Plymouth. Morris, a former Balliol man, was a classical scholar and Orientalist, Petrean Fellow of Exeter College, university lecturer in Syrian, and Pusey's assistant in Hebrew. He seemed ideal, and Acton imagined them both sitting in front of the log fire in the long winter evenings, engaged in deep discussion. Unfortunately, Canon Morris was also quarrelsome and decidedly odd, and his delicate health and restless character prevented him from staying anywhere for long. He had briefly joined the Newman converts at Maryvale and had taught at Oscott, where he was popular with the boys, Acton included. He had a weakness for the gentry. That made him move from one country house to another—not a good omen.

His last position, as Morris wrote to Acton in one of his long-winded letters spiced with Greek quotations, was with Edward Rodney Pollexfen Bastard, Esq., of Kiltey and Ashburton Court in Devon, a wealthy young landowner who had recently become a Catholic and taken a wife. Unfortunately, his choice fell not on the one his chaplain had favoured, but on her sister, whom the Canon thought "unlikely to breed." So, not unexpectedly, Morris was turned out by the new Mrs. Bastard. At Aldenham, Morris was supposed to live in the roomy priest's house, which Lady Granville had built in the garden behind the new chapel. But Morris made difficulties: "I am weakly. I need . . . the comforts I could get in the house," he wrote. Acton gave in. So "Jack" Morris, as he came to be known, describing himself as "Aristotelian virtue personified," arrived and was put in the Yellow Room at Aldenham.[11]

Morris was clearly a nut case; even his intimate friend F. W. Faber recalled: "You had always some little screw loose at Oxford."[12] He had acquired, on account of his extravagant sermons, the nickname Simon Stylites, after the Syrian monk who spent years of his life on a pillar. He also delighted in a style of gentlemanly bawdiness that, like his "sunshiny old Phiz" and "eternal laugh," as Faber called it, were better suited to eighteenth-century Oxford common rooms than to sober Aldenham.[13] Acton soon found Morris fatally ignorant of history and lacking in historical sense, serving indeed the purpose, as he wrote to Döllinger, "of convincing me more and more of the great asset of historical studies."[14]

Acton was horrified by Morris's strange views, which included considering the seventeenth-century Spanish Jesuit, Juan de Lugo, as the greatest of all theologians, and admiring Faber as Newman's equal. Morris also was soon bored with life at Aldenham but would not decide either to leave or to stay. Finally Acton felt impelled to write to Bishop Brown to say that Mr. Morris had apparently "misinformed" his Lordship on various matters. Probably incited by the heresy-hunting paranoiac Faber, Morris had gone around accusing Acton of supporting a "Protestant" school at Morville and refusing to support a Catholic school at Bridgnorth. The truth was that, long before the idea of the Catholic school at Bridgnorth was discussed, the Morville school had been founded by Acton's mother, so that the Catholic children of the place should have a school to go to at all.

Now Acton felt compelled to tell the Bishop that "the openness and coarseness with which things, hardly ever alluded to among Christians, were constantly discussed in the canon's sermons, and in catechising children were really alarming and a continual source of apprehension and distress to me."[15] After one of these sermons Acton reported: "Jack Morris has just preached about Our Lady—that we ought to pray for a fervid desire of leaning on those beautiful breasts."[16]

A successor was found in the person of Thomas Louis Green (1799–1883), called "Old Green" or "Verdant Green," with the stipend raised from £100 to £105 a year (plus winter fuel and garden produce). Green came from an old Catholic family, had been prefect at Oscott and afterwards parish priest. Before he came he was warned—so he told Acton later—by the Vicar General of the diocese to be on his guard, because Acton was said to have found terrible weapons in the German infidel literature and to want to undermine the Catholic faith, which he had lost himself. Green admitted that he had always believed all that until he had got to know Acton better. He left Aldenham, to Acton's great regret, after twenty-three years because of increasing deafness.

Apart from the question of the chaplain, the building also needed attention. What alterations the nineteenth century made to Aldenham has not enhanced the Actons' reputation as had the work and taste of their eighteenth-century ancestors.[17] The imposing entrance of Aldenham Hall—a large gate screen set between grey stone pillars through which the house, at the far end of a long avenue of lime trees, can just be seen—is a reminder of that more elegant age. One comes across the fine gate quite suddenly on the meandering road from Bridgnorth to Shrewsbury, after passing the village of Morville. The gate's pillars bear carved military trophies; the two flanking the central gate are capped by jovial lions holding their escutcheons. The ornate arch of the gate is crowned by the Acton crest.

In the late seventeenth and early eighteenth centuries, Sir Edward Acton's marriage to a rich heiress enabled him to rebuild much, as an inscription on the northwest wall of the house records: "Sir Edward Acton, Barronett, built this house in ye Yeare of Our Lord 1691." As in many old English country houses, however, this date is not to be taken too literally. Parts of the sprawling house are from the sixteenth and seventeenth centuries; others the eighteenth century added and rebuilt. Sir Edward's son, Sir Whitmore Acton, continued these extensive renovations. The initials "WWA and E" can be found on the lead rainwater heads on the front of the house. (The "E" stands for Elizabeth Gibbon, part of the "triple alliance" that linked the historian of *Decline and Fall* with the "worthy" Actons.)

After much pestering from his sister, Elizabeth Throckmorton, around 1826 Acton's father had finally decided to do something about basic renovation at Aldenham. Elizabeth had written: "Mama has made the most beautiful plan, the entrance to be behind the present hall and drawing room. As you will be obliged to repair it, for it is in a sad state and some of the rooms upstairs begin to sink, it will be much better to alter it at once, which will cost you little more trouble and money."[18]

When Sir John Acton's mother was left Aldenham, in 1837, she completed the renovations initiated by her husband. She was responsible for reglazing the windows, thereby introducing plate glass. And if the seventh Baronet, Sir Richard, loved the ostentations of the Neapolitan and French Empires, the eighth Baronet, by the time he came of age, was accustomed to the Romantic pomposity of Ludwig's Bavarian castles and palaces. John Acton's aesthetic taste was not on a par with his other gifts. He wanted "a library for 30,000 books, that is to be also a pretty drawing room," which he put up in Aldenham in 1863.[19] A building as far as he was concerned had to be "commodious"; books, too, served a functional purpose.

The chapel that Acton's mother completed is today a sorry sight. It became a kind of bathing pavilion and storage place for the swimming pool that replaced the garden southeast of the house, which had an elaborate flower parterre laid out by Acton's mother with her monogram "MA" and the Dalberg coat of arms. On ascending the worn chapel stairs, the inscription over the door can just be made out: "A.M.D.G. In Hon. Beatae Mariae Dei Mater in Coelo Assumpta." Acton's mother had a particular devotion to the Virgin Mary. She also furnished the chapel, which had originally been a kind of Neoclassical temple with an Ionic façade. On entering it, one came into a "gallery" where the members of the family and guests sat. A few steps led down to the altar, the front of which was covered with an embroidery of the Last Supper. Behind the altar were some panels of carved oak. There was an east window of stained glass depicting Christ with the dove descending.

When the chaplain was about to begin Mass, he rang a little bell on the chapel roof, on Sundays at eleven in the morning, on weekdays at nine, or earlier in summer. On Sunday afternoons there was Benediction at half past three, depending on a sufficient number of singers from the neighbourhood being available. In the chapel vault several generations of Actons were laid to rest.

Acton's mother had brought with her to England something of the Zeitgeist of Continental Catholicism, and this shaped liturgical and devotional practices at Aldenham. The late Romantics were not ashamed of intense religious feelings; they liked their religion to be more personal and mystical, less purely theatrical and aesthetic than that of the Baroque era, although they continued to cherish its art in the absence of anything better of their own. "Latin" hearts never took to the rediscovery of the sombre Middle Ages and the Neo-Gothic spirit.

The spirit of nineteenth-century Marian devotions at La Salette and Lourdes came to dominate the popular Catholicism, and its statuary was also found in the Acton chapels at Herrnsheim, Naples, and Aldenham. In December 1854, when Acton was back at Aldenham, Pius IX proclaimed the dogma of the Immaculate Conception. It did not disturb the young Acton, still in his apostolic zeal. Döllinger's misgivings about the dogma were expressed in the negative opinion that the Munich theological faculty had voiced, but which the Munich nuncio had somehow "failed" to forward to Rome.[20] In Döllinger's article on Duns Scotus, written in 1851 for the *Kirchenlexikon,* he noted that Scotus, the Church's great *Doctor subtilis et marianus* (teacher of wit and Marian devotion) had expressed only with great hesitancy his theological opinion that the Mother of God was herself conceived without the stain of Original Sin.

If one compares Aldenham with Acton's maternal Schloss, Herrnsheim, which was also rebuilt in the early nineteenth century (Herrnsheim serves the city of Worms today as a stately home for municipal receptions), it seems that the Aldenham alterations resembled, perhaps deliberately, the Dalberg ancestral home. But two centuries of wars, industrialization, and acid rain have scarred the Rhineland more deeply. Shropshire, or Salop, is still part of the "heart of England," the "heart of oaks," a land of rich undulating pasture, arable land, and woodlands. Aldenham still shelters under the Clee Hills. Nearby is Much Wenlock, where the Actons, though not Sir John, frequently attended the horse races. This region, like the Rhineland, is rich in history and bloody wars, strewn with the ruins of abbeys and religious houses sacked by Henry VIII and Thomas Cromwell. At Aldenham Hall one is shown the heavy buff jerkin that King Charles, who according to Acton family tradition stayed there one night, had left behind, having exchanged it for the owner's garments. After the Royalists' defeat at Bridgnorth the Actons had to pay heavily for the upkeep of Cromwell's Roundheads. Aldenham, at least, was spared the past two centuries of foreign invasion and the multiple military occupations that Herrnsheim suffered after the Napoleonic Wars and again in 1918 and 1945.

It was to the task of building up his library that the young Baronet devoted himself initially. "I have ordered book shelves for four thousand books so that I no longer need restrict myself," he wrote to the Professor.[21] And a little later Lord Granville was reporting to Canning on the matter: Johnny Acton's "library is becoming immense. He has remodelled the old library. He has entirely filled the hall; he has furnished his own room with books, and he has bagged a bedroom for the same purpose. I can hardly open a book without finding notes or marks of his."[22] Acton had learned from Döllinger to read with pen and pencil, to note down every striking passage, mark the page with small pieces of newspaper cut in oblong shape as a signal, and make a reference in his notebook. His books were becoming his best friends, and he devoted much time and money to them, perhaps along the lines of the adage that "a man puts the best of himself into his books and the worst into his life." The original library in the south corner of the house was probably designed by Acton's father. It was the nucleus of the "Aldenham Library," which Acton later added on the chapel side to the northeast corner of the house. (Where it stood is today a yawning space, and its disappearance has not been regretted by architectural aesthetes.)

Acton's books eventually found a new and permanent home in Cambridge, and after they had gone the large space served as a ballroom. The historian's granddaughter, Mia Woodruff, remembered dances held there when she was in her teens. The enormous cruciform structure, intended to be "a nice drawing room," had an iron gallery all round—the gilding and moulded ironwork remind one of Sir Anthony Panizzi's Reading Room at the British Museum and of the London Library in St. James's Square. "My only positive dogma is that books should not be against a wall," Acton told Gladstone many years later, "but in double rows, with nothing between, and the backs looking both ways." Gladstone was thinking about how to arrange his own library, his cherished project, at St. Deiniol's in Hawarden village, and wondered about imitating the ideas of their mutual friend Panizzi. Acton replied that his own library experience was "rich in lessons of what to avoid. . . . Panizzi was an immense spender of money." Acton also expressed doubts about slate shelves, which were popular then, because of the rising prices at Bangor.[23] The Aldenham Library was lighted from the top, from a large bay window and by lantern lights. From two corners of the room narrow staircases led to the gallery, and iron passages connected on two levels with the house. From floor to ceiling the walls were fitted with bookcases. A large canvas with the Dalberg family tree and numerous coats of arms used to hang in the room.

The books eventually numbered about seventy thousand. The bookseller John H. Bohn, whom Acton employed as one of his first librarians, confessed himself "fairly beaten" by the quantity: "I find the space allotted to England not quite sufficient. Germany will require nearly as much more as it now occupies. Universal History, I think, would completely fill No. 1–9 in the Gallery, if you have no objection to its removal. No. 10–17 are filled with Belgium and Holland."[24]

Acton spent a fortune on these books, purchased particularly on his travels in France, Germany, and Italy, with the majority in the languages of those countries. Book parcels constantly arrived from everywhere. Dr. Döllinger never saw the completed library, but he watched its growth with amused envy, and quoted Friedrich von Schiller:

> Du wühlest, reicher Mann, in deinen Manuskripten
> Du lebst in Canaan, wir aber in Ägypten.

> [You, rich man, are wallowing in your manuscripts,
> You live in the Promised Land, we only in Egypt.][25]

Dr. Döllinger's frugal habits had enabled him "on an income of a couple of hundreds to form a library of 30,000 volumes," Acton noted.[26] For him as for Acton, these books were his pride. Acton's books had a strictly functional purpose: to help his search for truth. His library was divided into three parts:

(1) ecclesiastical history and subjects directly connected with it; (2) political history arranged according to countries; (3) other subjects such as biography, theology, philosophy, ethics, letter writers, belles lettres and fine art, and the outstanding collection of the leading academies and periodicals of the era. The object of the classification was to concentrate on the main purpose, namely, tracing the struggle in the Church between authority and freedom, between the papal policy and centralization and the advocates of local autonomy and liberty, the conflict of the papacy with particular national churches or states. And there was another consideration: "Browsing among its shelves, the reader cannot help feeling that nothing is petty, nothing mean-minded, nothing blink-ered, in the man who garnered and studied and organised these books. It all issued from a purity in the quest for truth."[27]

Aldenham and its library became something of an intellectual centre. It served as the editorial offices of the Catholic journals edited by Acton from 1858 onwards. There were constant visitors. Acton's old friend Montalembert spent the summer there in 1855. Dr. Döllinger came in the autumn in 1858, on his third and last trip to England.

An interesting account of Aldenham and its library in its heyday, when Acton was long married, was given by the German historian Reinhold Pauli (1825–1888), who, with his colleague Georg Waitz (1813–1886), a pupil of Leopold von Ranke, stayed there for a few days in 1877. "At Bridgnorth," Pauli recorded, an elegant phaeton two-seater,

> drawn by two black horses, was waiting for us in which we soon reached Aldenham. . . . Dinner was not before 9:00, and until midnight we had the most lively conversation in German. Life there is the height of luxury. A grand avenue leads to the chateaulike building, to one side a terrace and flower garden in the style of Versailles, also with a small chapel, while to the other side the park extends far over undulating land, fields, and lakes, pleasant for long walks with ever new views over the infinitely variable hilly landscape with the Welsh mountains as background. It is difficult to find one's way in the rambling but comfortable house. The rooms, often with wooden panel-ling, are furnished stylishly and with the greatest comfort. I have a large room with a delightful view of the park, a servant at my disposal.[28]

The visitors were overwhelmed by the great library. Its owner, Pauli went on,

> could be envied by many a German university. To this collection a separate annexe is devoted, reached easily by iron galleries, and the whole centre hall

and other living and bedrooms are filled with books. We have hardly any comparable royal or state library. . . . Acton really knows his way about his books and is the most gracious of hosts. He is quite like a German scholar, so that one is completely among one's own kind.

His lady speaks German, French, and English equally well like her husband, is blond, delicate, still exhausted from her care over their sick children. . . . The dinner consists of few but excellent courses, and as main wine ice-cooled champagne, and we also had milkpunch. A fine flower arrangement set in a low china receptacle, like a pond; the main decoration was at the centre of the dining table with seats for four. We are served by a butler in black and by a liveried servant. Nothing is pretentious, everything even unostentatious, but, of course, evening dress and white tie are worn.[29]

A year after this visit, in 1878, the Acton grandeur that was Aldenham came to a premature end. The maintenance of two seigniorial establishments, Herrnsheim and Aldenham, with many servants and decreasing returns from their farms, was no longer possible, and the Acton family decided to move to the Riviera, where not only was the climate better but also, at that time, life was cheaper and the English way of keeping up appearances less costly.

$$7$$

THREE JOURNEYS

Lord Granville's endeavours to persuade his stepson of the attractions of a public career led to some important trips. The first, in the spring of 1853 and while Acton was still in Munich, was for Acton to accompany the English delegation to the New York industrial exhibition. "He wants me to meet the great personages of the country," Acton explained to Countess Arco.[1] Leading the delegation was Lord Granville's cousin, the first Earl of Ellesmere (Francis Leveson-Gower Egerton, 1800–1857), who had inherited the wealth of the Egertons, Dukes of Bridgewater. Acton liked him. The knowledgeable Ellesmere had been a follower of George Canning, a free trader before Sir Robert Peel, chief secretary to the Lord Lieutenant in Ireland, and minister of war. He was also an art collector and had published some poor translations of Friedrich von Schiller and Johann Wolfgang von Goethe. Lady Ellesmere, a sister of Charles Greville, the diarist (who lodged with the Granvilles in Bruton Street), was both literary and religious, the author of such Protestant tracts as *Questions on the Epistles* and *Believers' Guide to Holy Communion*. Acton thought she feared that he might try to convert her daughters—two pleasant girls aged twenty-two and twenty-three—whom he had recently met at a ball given by his mother in London.

The delegation embarked, on 10 May 1853, from Plymouth on the *Leander,* a new frigate of five hundred men and fifty guns. Others in their group were the famous geologist Sir Charles Lyell and a young German naval lieutenant, Prince Victor of Hohenlohe-Schillingfürst, whose two younger brothers, friends of Dr. Döllinger, were to attain eminence—Chlodwig as chancellor of Germany and Gustav Adolf as a Cardinal. Acton's diary of this American trip is interesting on account of some apt as well as many trite observations (he was, after all, only nineteen years old).[2] The passengers passed the time by playing games: one person had to discover an historical figure or event that another had thought of. Acton could not resist playing on Lady Ellesmere's anti-Catholic prejudices by choosing such personages as St. Dominic, St. Dunstan, St. Ignatius of Loyola, and St. Thomas Aquinas. He wrote to Döllinger that the temptation "of destroying some of what Görres called the stuffed elephants of Semiramis" was too strong.[3]

The *Leander* pursued a leisurely course, stopping in the Azores and taking a month to cross the Atlantic. On 11 June, in great summer heat, the *Leander* anchored off Staten Island, and the delegation remained in New York for five days, using the ship as their headquarters. Lady Ellesmere was put off that they were not received with greater honours, and the exhibition itself, its opening postponed, turned out to be something of a flop. This mattered little to Acton. With some of the ship's officers he went on a four-day trip to see Niagara Falls, which he enjoyed; it included, he recorded, a late, drunken night.[4]

Neither New York nor its wealth-dominated society met with Acton's approval. Dinners were cheap at one dollar, though the wines were dear, and he delighted in American ice cream. "There is much less talk and liveliness than I have seen at a German table d'hôte. I was not at first struck with the voraciousness with which they dispatched their dinner, but I have since observed that many people eat very quick. . . . [The] Yankee type of countenance . . . is not a very intelligent face, and a selfish face. They are generally thin, and their hair turns white early, perhaps partly by the quantity of drink and profuse perspiration. They are seldom fine men, but tall. They are fond of wearing hair all around their chins, or else a goat's beard." He noted great uniformity in dress, straw hats or white hats worn in the hot season. "Smoking is very much practised. I was not so much struck, perhaps from accident, with the custom of chewing and spitting at N.Y. as I have since been, elsewhere."[5]

The company of the Ellesmeres seems to have brought out Acton's aggressive Catholicism. He "thirsted after a Catholic prelate," he wrote to Döllinger. As the nephew of a Roman Cardinal and the stepson of an English Liberal politician, and equipped with introductory letters, Acton found doors open to him. In New York he called on Archbishop John Joseph Hughes and elsewhere on various other bishops, but most of them were away. The most interesting part of the diary is his account, written very much from a superior Munich perspective, of Boston and Harvard, "the only university in the States," he reported to Döllinger, "very incomplete. History is ignored there, the classics little studied. They have no editions of their own. There seems to be no call for accurate learning here. *Multa non multum.* Many things are wanted to be known. Mathematics and the natural sciences are most studied." Acton met the poet Henry Wadsworth Longfellow (1807–1882), who was a professor of modern languages, and attended an examination in German: "All pronounced German execrably, but translated well enough. I have read some of Longfellow's poems here and some are beautiful. He might rank with Tennyson. . . . There is nothing of great genius about him, but he is a fine man."[6]

Acton also met the scholar-statesman Edward Everett (1794–1865), then secretary of state, a former ambassador in London and former president of Harvard, who had been the first American to receive a doctoral degree at Göttingen; the natural scientist Jean Louis Agassiz (1807–1873); and the historian Jared Sparks (1789–1866). Acton summed up: "I have seen enough of America to see that there are much greater lessons to be learned here than I imagined and much more than I can as yet take advantage of. My ideas will be set in order by this journey, and I shall have gained a great interest in the country; but the full profit of examining the country I shall be able to derive only from a second visit."[7] That visit never took place, but in later life Acton deepened his interest in American history, especially the Civil War and the concept of democracy, through his studies for his history of liberty. Acton came to believe that political freedom originated among the Quakers in the forests of Pennsylvania, not in the forests of Germany, as his generation tended to think. In the very last lecture he was to deliver nearly half a century later as Regius Professor at Cambridge, Acton expressed his admiration for American federalism, which "has produced a community more powerful, more prosperous, more intelligent, and more free than any other which the world has seen."[8]

Acton's keen Catholicism accounts for the deep impression that the American writer and convert Orestes Brownson made upon him. Armed with an introduction from Bishop Dupanloup, Acton spent three days at Mount St. Mary's College in Emmitsburg, Maryland, the largest Catholic college in the United States, where he stayed with Brownson. Acton reported to Döllinger:

> He really is a wonderful person. Intellectually no American I have met comes near him. He has no real historical knowledge and avoids historical issues in the Review [that he edits]. He is a large man, an ugly Cardinal Wiseman, without manners, rough, uncouth, much given to grimacing when talking, is obstinate, he judges usually very severely, has much respect for you but for few others. Thomas [Aquinas] and Augustine he knows well and takes his theology from them. . . . He puts Burke and de Maistre above all other political writers, but has a high regard for Donoso Cortes. . . . Brownson, as you know, is no Democrat. . . . He has such a very lively mind, that he has thought about everything and formed theories without really having studied the matter.[9]

Acton saw American democracy in action at a Massachusetts State Constitutional Convention that happened to meet for the first time since 1820, and he did not like what he saw. "Not a single speech deserved to be called good. . . . One half-madman made a loud speech for equality of all things. . . . Mr. [George Washington] Greene, a doctrinaire, a horrid-looking fellow . . . advocates women voting and such like. . . . The standard of politics is much lower than in England, or anywhere, almost, in Europe; for in no European assembly would such democratical views pass without censure. It reminded me most of the Swiss assembly, but the speeches are not so good nor so violent. There is plenty of decorum, no solemnity. Few look like gentlemen."[10]

Acton had seen a great deal on his trip, although he failed in his ambition to visit the Deep South and witness slavery. He had been scheduled to visit a South Carolina plantation but did not go owing to reports of malaria. Eventually the party embarked on the *Leander* bound for Plymouth (England) and home. Lord Ellesmere was to be a house guest at Aldenham. At the time, the royal yacht was lying at anchor at Holyhead. Lord Granville was in attendance, accompanying Queen Victoria on a visit to Dublin. On the Queen's return journey Acton's mother was invited to dine on board, and Acton came, too, "telling the Queen and Prince Albert much about America," as he wrote to the Professor.[11] Acton must have also mentioned his library plans, for there are occasional references that Prince Albert, via Lord Granville, recommended German books to him, for example, the recent work of the well-known German historian and philosopher Kuno Fischer (1824–1907) on Francis Bacon. When, some years later, Acton's essay "Human Sacrifice" appeared as part of a debate on the subject, the Prince Consort congratulated Lord Granville on his stepson's achievement.[12]

Three years later, in the summer of 1856, Lord Granville took his stepson to Russia. Granville, then Lord President of the Council, represented the Queen at the coronation of Tsar Alexander II. Acton went along with the English delegation as an attaché, a position that entitled him to wear the handsome, gold-braided uniform of a diplomat. The Crimean War was barely over, and the coronation was to further the improvement of relations between the Tsar and the Court of St. James's. "My travel companions . . . are likely to look upon the Russian character from the heights of their Liberal wisdom—the delegation consists of young Whig lords and heirs," Acton wrote to Dr. Döllinger.[13] Two weeks later he observed, "I wish I had more joy and keenness for the Russian trip."[14] The delegation went from Stettin, Germany, by steamboat to Swinemünde, then by warship to Kronstadt and on to St. Petersburg with countless other official visitors.

Lord Granville asked Acton to find suitable accommodations for the English delegation for about a week's stay at St. Petersburg. According to Granville's instructions, in Moscow Acton was to look for a furnished Palais suitable for "giving dinners of 70, balls and parties—a Palais near the Kremlin would be the best . . . although Economy is a great object, a fine apartment is absolutely necessary. . . . My expenditure in Russia must be limited to £10,000."[15]

Apart from the British embassy staff in Russia, the special mission comprised some twenty members and their servants. There were Lord and Lady Granville; his brother Freddy; Lady Margaret Leveson-Gower; the Robert Peels; the George Byngs; Lords Lichfield, Villiers, Lister, Burghersh, Seymour, Cavendish, Lincoln, and Dalkeith; Gerald Ponsonby; and Sandwith, the doctor. The sixth Duke of Devonshire, who had been on a similar special mission for the coronation of Nicholas I, in 1825, lent the Chatsworth plate. Lady Granville had her diamonds reset; she and Lord Granville prepared themselves for the festivities by taking the waters at Carlsbad. Lady Granville was to be in charge of bringing over, by sea, a dozen English horses with coachmen, grooms, five carriages, and some harness; from his stable Lord Granville kept for his own use the horses Woronzonow and Marlborough. "My carriages are magnificent," he wrote enthusiastically to Acton, "liveries and harness to match. Would it be of use to you to send you cloth & lace for the Coachmens Clothes . . . ? The livery hats are plain black with a black cockade . . . short red feathers on the inside of the back, the same of white feathers on the inside of the flap—do you understand, like a uniform hat?" [16] Vases were brought out from Minton. Missing was a portrait of Queen Victoria, and one was hastily painted by one of the attachés.

Acton threw himself into organizing things. He went to see Count Borch, a Pole who, as master of ceremonies, was responsible for the direction of the coronation. The order of the ceremonies was not yet completed, but it was clear that things had changed since the last coronation, so that the recollections of the Duke of Devonshire could not be relied on. For example, the coronation was to be a purely religious ceremony. All the events were to take place inside the Kremlin, where space was limited. Lord Granville therefore had to do without the extravagant equipages and display on which he had set his heart. Acton had some difficulty in finding out even whether the Russian court approved of grand receptions at the ambassadorial residences at all. Alexander II was apparently less in favour of them than his predecessor. Given the tacit rivalry of so many embassies, one had to tread carefully. The festivities were to last three weeks. There were to be several great occasions at Court, a masked ball, balls given by various officials and grandees, a popular fête, and a troop review of the guards and troops from the Austrian frontier, some 150,000 men. "I may find a house with very fine furniture," Acton reported to Granville, "but it is imperatively necessary that the house and table linen, china, and every better sort of glass should come from England." Any amount of handsome glass could afterwards be sold in Russia. At St. Petersburg, Acton rented the first floor of the Hotel Demouth. "You will find the beds at the Hotel Demouth a bit hard, but that is a security against bugs which otherwise have to be chased with Persian powder." The atmosphere was friendly, he reported after sounding out French and Austrian colleagues. The foreign guests were certain of a good reception. "I have seen many officers who were extremely cordial and spoke with the greatest freedom of the [Crimean] War. The ladies are somewhat more martial and patriotic." [17]

Acton telegraphed the result of his enquiries about horses to London: because nobody was to have six horses at Moscow and the distances were enormous, it was necessary to have the means of driving tolerably fast. The state carriage must have four English horses. Russian horses could not possibly be driven in English harness. To his mother he wrote how helpful Prince Esterhazy of the Austrian special mission had been. Austria and England agreed to combine matters of protocol in Moscow as far as that was possible. It was rumoured, reported Acton, that the great Russian ladies turned their noses up at the company of the Duke of Morny, the French special envoy. But this remark appears to have been an exaggeration; the French were more than able competitors and spent an enormous amount of money on their embassy. Acton also wrote that he had very little time for sight-seeing, yet he was impressed by the churches. He continued:

> People chant beautifully, the congregation is very fervent, incessantly crossing themselves. They make the sign of the cross the wrong way round as we would when calling the devil, throw themselves on the ground with head bowed at every moment during Mass. The priests are very good-looking and venerable, with long hair and long silk robes. The dress of the lower people is strange, very different from anything we have ever seen. The outside of the churches is very imposing, the dome, the roof, all covered with gold. It makes a great and imposing effect, but they are all ruined by the rejection of anything that, in other countries, would be considered artistic. The centre of town is all government offices—they alone cover the space of a big city. Altogether Petersburg is bigger than Paris with half the inhabitants. There are no pretty shops, because the cold inhibits big windows, and the majority of the big stores are on the first floor. Fears of Russian cold seem to be exaggerated, the summer is likely to be very hot.[18]

Acton performed all the tasks expected of a twenty-two-year-old attaché. Once he was given a message for the Duchess of Sutherland. He knocked at her door; she called "Come in," thinking it was her maid, and he found her without any clothes on and withdrew in confusion. That aside, he had to see to it that the members of the English mission appeared at the various events on time and in the right attire. The entries in the Moscow Functions Book, which is preserved among the Actonia at Cambridge, are in part in his hand, and he allowed himself some ironic license: "It is particularly requested that the members of the Embassy will for some days at least be punctual at breakfast. . . . 17 August: Balls at the French embassy and at Prince Galitzine (white trousers); Tickets for opera, ballet and French play (108, 48 and 54 rubles), best private boxes taken—apply to John Dalberg Acton; The Nuncio's Reception (blue trousers); 19 September: The Popular Feast takes place at Petinowski. Carriages at 11.45 (uniform, not necessarily diplomatic); 21 September: Whole embassy is invited to ball and supper at Kremlin at 9 o'clock (no trousers)."[19] The young man's little joke meant that uniforms were to be worn.

French was the lingua franca of the event.[20] The diplomatic result of the mission was negligible. However, two thousand decorations besides medals were distributed, and Lord Granville, with an eye for human vanity, noted that "everybody is said to be dissatisfied." At the coronation, the corps diplomatique missed the sight of the Emperor coming out of church. "Our compensation was seeing Mr. Murphy, the Irish correspondent of the *Daily News,* emerging from behind the altar with the priests. He has been secreted there by them for a consideration."[21]

"Lady G[ranville]," her husband noted with pride, "is a host in herself. She is in great health and spirits, keeps English and foreign in good order. She holds her own with all, and chaffs and orders about the Russian grandees as if they were so many young admirers. She is with all this very civil, and her popularity great."[22] Accustomed, like the grand seigneur he was, to dividing the world largely into bores and nonentities, Lord Granville thought that the only really pleasant member of the imperial family was the Grand Duchess Marie Nicolaievna, the Tsar's sister, widow of Maximilian de Beauharnais, with whom he had danced; he found her "so easy, so *grande dame,* so clever, so insolent, so civil."[23] John Acton, moving at ease in a world he pretended to disdain, made many friends and acquaintances whom he would meet again in the small international world of Europe's aristocratic society. The Russian trip, while remaining an extravagant interlude, had proved his ability to feel at home in different social environments. Could this ability be combined, he wondered, with scholarly, political, Catholic pursuits? Back in England and stopping in London on his return, he saw Cardinal Wiseman, who, without Acton's having broached the subject, said to him that he might have a good chance to be elected if he stood as a candidate for an Irish constituency. Lord Granville was to pull some strings for him in this direction in the following year.

Acton went to the British Museum, as he told Döllinger, where the magnificent, domed Reading Room was nearly completed and where he found the historical manuscripts section in "very good order." He looked at a newly bound quarto volume collection of "Papal Registers Relating to England, Scotland and Ireland" from 1216, including many documents of the fourteenth century and the seventeenth-century period of James I and Charles I, which interested him and Döllinger. In London Acton also got to know Henry William Wilberforce (1807–1873), with whom he had been in correspondence for some time. Wilberforce, the youngest son of the Emancipator of the Slaves, was Newman's pupil at Oriel, and Newman's novel *Callista* was dedicated to him. Wilberforce had followed Newman into the Catholic Church, then turned to journalism and became proprietor and editor of the *Weekly Register,* which, with a circulation of only 1,800 copies, had a difficult stand against the rival Catholic weekly, *The Tablet,* edited by another convert, the barrister Frederick Lucas. Wilberforce asked Acton to contribute, and Acton's first journalistic products appeared in the "Weakly Register," as he, not thinking very highly of Wilberforce's ability, maliciously called it. Acton's first article was "The Influence of the Reformation on Morality," with quotations from the German reformers. A further article, "The Political Working of the Austrian Concordat," showed Acton's pro-Austrian sympathies by extolling the Concordat and criticising its prejudiced reception among Catholics everywhere.[24] Neither of these early articles was particularly noteworthy. Both articles were apparently much corrected by Wilberforce, whose interference with his contributors' work caused Acton constant irritation.

"I request your criticism," Acton asked the Professor, whose response is lost. "I would be glad to have suggestions for further pieces. I like to do it for exercise, partly because I still find writing a great struggle and jeopardizing my other work too much. However, I do not want to neglect form altogether like some Germans, as it is handled with great splendour by those of other convictions." The English chauvinist and anti-Catholic historian James Anthony Froude (1814–1894) was a case in point. Froude's *History of England from the Fall of Wolsey to the Defeat of the Spanish Armada,* brilliantly written but given to the personality cult of English national heroes like Henry VIII, had just been published.

As for his other activities, "I was in Birmingham to see the cattle-show, in my capacity as farmer," Acton reported.[25] But other interests obtruded. Lord Granville had asked his stepson to suggest a Catholic, but a nonconvert, for the government post of school inspector. Acton mentioned the request to the Bishop of Birmingham, William Bernard Ullathorne (1806–1889), whom he met at the cattle show, and one may imagine them walking past the prize bulls and discussing Catholic affairs. Bishop Ullathorne declined to propose a candidate because the Catholic bishops had not been consulted as a body about the appointment, but, being an "old" Catholic himself, expressed his pleasure that no convert was to be appointed.[26]

Points of scholarship, books, and Catholic affairs are discussed in the stream of letters to Munich. Acton was as yet unsure of the world in which he wanted to shine. In the English Catholics he noted an increase of "that corrupt tendency, prevalent in France, a necessary consequence perhaps, of limited knowledge."[27] This comment referred to a controversy between Cardinal Wiseman and the *Rambler,* a periodical that Acton, in the same letter, called the "sole protagonist of the more intelligent views," a year before his own association with that publication began.[28] But before the controversy had been settled, Acton set out on another mind-broadening journey, in the spring of 1857, this time with Dr. Döllinger to Rome. They were away for more than six weeks. The weather was atrocious, with both the Splügen Pass and St. Bernard blocked by snowstorms. Eventually they reached Milan by post-coach. They stayed briefly with Acton's grandmother at Bologna and reached Rome by the end of April, Acton staying at the Hotel d'Angleterre, Döllinger at the Jesuits. There was a welcome reunion with the Arcos, who were spending Easter in Rome.

This visit was the first time since his childhood that Acton had been back in Rome, and the only time Dr. Döllinger ever went there. It was to have significance for both of them in their attitude to Pope Pius IX, to Roman ecclesiastical authority, and to the temporal power in its last desperate decade. They were, on the whole, received well. In his Rome journal, Acton quotes the Professor as saying that "he would have come to Rome long ago if he had foreseen that he would be received with so much kindness and liberality."[29] But that impression did not prevail. In retrospect Acton seems to have seen 1857 as much more of a watershed than it was, as some of his undated Cambridge notes suggest and in view of his later clash with Roman authority: "1857 destroyed the halo—abolished confidence, admiration, respect. But did not produce any strong sense of condemnation." But he also noted that Döllinger's "journey to Rome had not exposed to him the weakness of the church," and again: "Change in Rome—not perceived in 1857."[30] The Professor was happy with his quest for manuscripts, and it was in his own field of studies rather than what he sensed in the Roman intellectual atmosphere that the visit was seen by him, Acton noted, as "an epoch of emancipation."[31]

Döllinger seemed not to have "the remotest presentiment," he wrote later, of the things that were to happen within the next twelve or thirteen years in Italy—politically, in the Papal States, and in the Papacy itself: "When I was in Rome in 1857, I gave myself to historical pursuits and artistic enjoyment with an untroubled mind," he recalled in 1870.[32] Acton was more conscious—whether in 1857 or in retrospect—of Döllinger's transition. What is clear is that Döllinger was profoundly disillusioned with the quality of Roman scholarship.[33] And in his Rome journal Acton noted the growing impact of Ultramontanism in the Roman teaching in theology and history: "St. Peter's leaves one cold—

can pray better in Gothic churches. Gallicanism is dead and buried. What is so called now was never known as such formerly. The matter of the breviary for instance. In Germany several dioceses, as Cologne and Munster, have breviaries differing from the Roman, and have never been complained of as Germanicans. The Roman breviary ought to be improved first of all."[34]

In the atmosphere of Rome one was conscious of heresies. And the Ultramontanist school emphasized the danger. For nearly forty years the teaching of dogmatics at the Collegio Romano, the Roman seminary, had been in the hands of Giovanni Perrone (1794–1876), a leader of the Neo-Scholastics. The study of dogma had moved to the dialectical approach, which was safer than the study of original sources. Perrone roused Acton's ire by his assertion, contrary to the historical evidence, that in Rome the Inquisition executed few or no heretics. His way of dealing with the reformers was to emphasize Martin Luther's and John Calvin's moral defects rather than to try to rebut their ideas. At the Gregoriana, the Jesuit university, theology was taught by its German prefect of studies, Josef Kleutgen (1811–1878), who was a leading Neo-Scholastic and had written ten volumes to vindicate Catholic truth as derived from the Fathers of the Church and the medieval authors. He was to play a leading part in preparing the dogma of Papal Infallibility.

An example of what happened when someone deviated from the Roman line is provided by Carlo Passaglia (1812–1887), an eminent theologian of patristic orientation. He played a leading role in the preparation of the dogma of the Immaculate Conception in 1854, but left the Jesuits and became a secular priest and professor of moral philosophy at the University of Turin, then the capital of united Italy. He was an Italian patriot, became a collaborator of Camillo Cavour, and, in 1861, published anonymously a pamphlet in Florence in which he criticized the temporal power. This pamphlet was put on the Index, and Passaglia was suspended from his priestly functions. His books and papers were confiscated by the Inquisition, but he escaped arrest by fleeing to Florence.

When Acton visited Passaglia in Turin in 1865, he found him a broken man in despair about the state of religion in Italy. All kinds of pressures were put on him to make him recant. In Rome, Acton was told by Cardinal Karl August von Reisach that Passaglia had "gone astray" with his attacks on Scholasticism and the elevated status accorded to St. Thomas Aquinas. The Pope, when told of Passaglia's pamphlet and flight, exclaimed that he deserved three years in prison. Nevertheless, Passaglia (who before his death reconciled himself with the Church) would say no more about his persecutors, the Jesuits, than "Mi rincresce che questi buoni padri siano caduti cosi basso" (I am sorry that these good Fathers have fallen so low).[35]

The militant spirit of Ultramontanism—and indeed the trend towards centralized institutions in which the Catholic Church of the nineteenth century was following in the footsteps of the State—was not likely to lessen authoritarianism. In the past, controversy and argument had taken place at the level of theological seminaries and universities and only ultimately involved ecclesiastical authority. But now that authority came to be involved at once in beleaguered situations in which the Church saw herself as a bastion holding out against enemies all round. It was not the time to make allowances for the liberal spirit and the objective search for truth: "He who is not with me is against me, and he who does not gather with me scatters" (Matt. 12:30). Christ's admonition became the watchword of Ultramontanists for establishing uniformity of thought and rigorous punishment for intellectual deviation.

In Rome, Döllinger spent every day in the archives of the Dominicans, in the Piazza della Minerva, working on manuscripts relating to the medieval heresies, and also at the Secret Vatican Archives, where the Oratorian Father, Augustin Theiner, was in charge as prefect. As far as sight-seeing was concerned, Döllinger's interest in Renaissance and Baroque Rome was limited. He was, as Acton observed, "not a good traveller. Too thoughtful to be observant."[36] Döllinger's scholarly interests dominated all others. Acton wanted to know about recent Roman history, particularly the effects of the Revolution of 1848, the papal struggle over Italy, and above all what sort of man Pius IX was. French troops were still in occupation in Rome, the Austrians in Lombardy, soon also in Veneto, and the Italian nationalists were disillusioned with Pius IX for abandoning, with the help of French bayonets, the cause of Italian independence that he had so enthusiastically espoused.

Acton's liberalism was then of the English Burkean constitutional sort, very different from the Continental kind, which supported State intervention in education and trade. There was a natural Erastian element in his attitude towards the State Church of members of his class, not infrequently also members of his religion. Vienna's absolutist Imperial Chancellor, Prince Metternich, whose government system was the chief target of the European revolutions of 1848, when he himself was driven into exile in England, accurately foresaw the contradictions that would involve Pope Pius IX in his early championship of Italian national and liberal causes. "Each day the Pope shows himself more lacking in any practical sense," Metternich wrote in October 1847 to the Austrian Ambassador Count Rudolf Apponyi at Paris. "Born and brought up in a *liberal* family, he has been formed in a bad school; a good priest, he has never turned his mind towards matters of government. Warm of heart and weak of intellect, he has allowed himself to be taken and ensnared, since assuming the tiara, in a net from which he no longer knows how to disentangle himself, and if matters follow their natural course, he will be driven out of Rome." And in a letter in December to his agent Count Karl Ludwig von Ficquelmont at Milan, he emphasized the point: "A *liberal* Pope is not a possibility. A Gregory VII could become the master of the world, a Pius IX cannot become that. He can destroy, but he cannot build. What the Pope has already destroyed by his liberalism is his own temporal power; what he is unable to destroy is his spiritual power; it is that power which will cancel the harm done by his worthless counsellors. But to what dangerous conflicts have not these men exposed the man and the cause they wanted to serve!"[37]

Acton's impression of the Papal States was that they "can never be well governed according to modern ideas because it [*sic*] has not gone through that which has influenced other states. Many things are not done by the government because it has not acquired the power of doing it. . . . Men can only do one thing well—not both spiritual and temporal power. . . . One or the other must suffer."[38]

Acton's opinion of the Pope who proved to be the great challenge to many of his ideas in religion and history remained remarkably objective and dispassionate. Writing to Döllinger after the death of Pius IX, Acton concluded that the Pope's life produced no sort of unity if one looked for a theological purpose as its leitmotiv. His early years in office seemed to Acton to provide the key.[39] Giovanni Maria Mastai, who came from the provincial nobility in the Marches, the impoverished and backward part of the Papal States, was born in 1792 and educated by the Piarist Fathers. He was handicapped by epilepsy and chose the priesthood when an officer's career proved impossible. Ordained in 1819, he was raised to the Archbishopric of Spoleto in 1832 but later transferred to Imola as mere Bishop, in punishment, so it was said, for having helped Prince Louis Napoleon, afterwards Napoleon III, to escape from the Papal States, where he had fought against the Pope's troops.

After the repressive administration of Gregory XVI, the new Pope seemed to encourage Roman hopes for change. He allowed greater access to his audiences and released thousands of political prisoners against the advice of his cardinals. What he intended as a humane gesture increased the impression that he was an

Italian patriot, eager to lead Italy to independence. Pius IX seemed not to realize the political effects of his actions; he wanted reforms, but he did not want to upset anything, least of all to curtail the temporal power.

The Pope's actions played into the hands of both the "populists" and the conservatives, who wanted to use the Church for the restoration of the ancien régime. He was attacked from all sides and was implored at least to do something to free Italy from foreign rule. After much hesitation he wrote to the Austrian Emperor, Franz Josef, asking him voluntarily to give up Lombardy and the Veneto. Predictably, he was told that the Austrian rights rested on the same Treaty of Vienna as the Pope's to his own territories. Pius then sought the support of French arms. On 16 September 1848, Pius IX had appointed Pellegrino Rossi as prime minister so that he would restore papal rule in the States of the Church. Rossi was a former French ambassador who had stayed on in Rome as a naturalized citizen. Confusion in Rome grew, owing to the revolutionary mob increasingly under the influence of Mazzini, who had returned from his Swiss exile to Florence and was eventually elected triumvir of the Roman Republic.

This was the moment that Antonio Rosmini-Serbati made the historic intervention that could have changed the fate of Italy. Born at Rovereto in the Alto Adige, he was an Austrian citizen, Count of the Holy Roman Empire, and also an Italian patriot. He was a friend to Alessandro Manzoni, an eminent but controversial philosopher and political thinker, opposed to the conservative forces in the Church. Rosmini was also the founder, in 1828, of the Institute of Charity, a missionary congregation inspired by the Jesuit rule, which proved successful at a time when the Jesuits themselves were only slowly emerging from their eighteenth-century suspension and which, not unnaturally, elicited their envy and resentment through Rosmini's criticism of their moral teachings.

Acton was greatly interested in Rosmini, as the many references in the Cambridge manuscripts show. He noted the "remarkable moment" when "the two greatest Liberals in the clergy were one [Vincenzo Gioberti], minister at Turin, the other [Antonio Rosmini], his ambassador in Rome."[40] The ambassador's mission was to offer the Pope the idea of an Italian federation, to be presided over by him, in which the integrity of the papal territory would be guaranteed. But the Austrians were already incensed with Rosmini over his book *Delle cinque piaghe della Santa Chiesa* (On the five wounds of the Holy Church), published in 1848, which they took as a veiled criticism of their ("Josephinist") system of State control of the Church. When Rosmini's position in Rome was weakened because of the removal of Vincenzo Gioberti, the Pope, much impressed by him, proposed even to make him a Cardinal.

But it did not come to that. Prime Minister Rossi was murdered in Rome on 15 November 1848. Turmoil and anarchy ensued. The Pope escaped to Gaeta and went over to the conservative opposition, the majority of the cardinals and the Jesuits, who had warned him all along against dangerous political experiments.

Courageously, Rosmini went to Gaeta in June 1849 to remonstrate with the Pope and save the temporal power. But Pius IX, now in Cardinal Giacomo Antonelli's hands, told him: "Caro Abbate, non siamo piu costituzionali" (Dear Father, we are no longer constitutionalists) and informed him that two of his books were being examined for heresy; however (in a manner typical of Rome), the Pope kept from him that the books had already been condemned.[41] The ruling Roman junta had meanwhile dissolved the governmental Chamber. On 9 February 1849 a Roman Republic and the end of the temporal power were proclaimed.

Acton's analysis of Rosmini's failure and personal tragedy is revealing because of his own clashes with the Church. Rosmini belonged to the "ideal Catholicism" of which Acton was becoming increasingly critical: "Rosmini had no great diplomatic skill or popular appeal. He was in a false position, for a man of delicate conscience and scrupulous honour, accustomed to the discipline of a religious order, unused to the glare of publicity."[42] But even a much stronger man could hardly have withstood that hostile phalanx of absolutists and conservatives in the Church or in the Austrian government. The skilful Antonelli, "anxious not to offend the Austrians, dropped the man who, technically an Austrian citizen, enticed the Pope to make war on his own country" and emerged from these events as "the most intelligent Roman statesman since [Ercole] Consalvi—and yet the most inefficient and sterile."[43] In the last resort "Rosmini was not made for the victories of this world."[44]

Pius IX had returned to Rome a changed man. "It seems to me," Acton later wrote to Döllinger, "that when he [Pius IX] lost his crown on the field of liberty, he became easily convinced that it was to be regained only in the opposite way, and so he went over to the Jesuits who were able to exploit his changed circumstances the more easily for their purposes, as the fulfilment of their teaching aims also involved an increase of papal power."[45] The Pope was personally responsible for the launching, in April 1850, of the Jesuit bimonthly *Civiltà Cattolica* as the organ of the new Ultramontane spirit. It became the authoritative journal of the Holy See but in its early decades contributed to the ideological conflicts in the Church, particularly regarding the extent of Papal Infallibility, by unhappy formulations of articles purporting to be inspired by the Pope.

Acton's Rome journal records a conversation with Marchese Carlo Bevilaqua, a supporter of Cavour and a friend of Acton's Brignole-Sale relations, who regarded the situation in the Papal States as "hopeless" and change as impossible.[46] The Pope allowed Antonelli and the papal delegates outside Rome to govern as they saw fit, and the general trend was to oppose change. Worst was the administration of justice, corruption, bankruptcy, nepotism, the conditions in the prisons housing nearly ten thousand political prisoners. It was thus, gradually and necessarily in opposition to the Pope, that Piedmont became the embodiment of all Italian liberal and reformist aspirations. Acton and Döllinger's dilemma was that, though loyal Catholics, they could support neither the papal nor the anticlerical Italian liberal government.

The Rome of 1857 seemed to remind Döllinger of the Reformation. There is the surprising note (as usual, undated) in Acton's hand when enumerating the development of Döllinger: "Experience of Rome. Luther not wrong after all." And walking with Döllinger from the Capitol to the Colosseum, Acton asked him: "How long will all this last?" The Professor replied: "As long as it is felt to be beneficial to religion, and no longer."[47] In this reaction to the Roman atmosphere Döllinger's raw nerve as German scholar had been touched. "We have been here three weeks, and today the Professor said he had not been asked a single sensible question about Germany since he came."[48]

Still, Angelo Vincenzo Modena, the secretary of the Inquisition, came to consult Döllinger in the affair of the Munich philosopher Jakob Frohschammer (1821–1893), who upheld the independence of speculation and had refused to submit to a censure from Rome. Döllinger advised that they should let the matter rest, as the Bavarian king would certainly protect him.[49] But the advice was not taken.

Acton and Döllinger had an audience with the Pope, possibly on 25 April. Theiner was present. They spoke French. The Pope, Acton noted, did not speak it well. He "spoke of the importance of unity in the Church, for strength, and the Professor told him that no clergy was more thoroughly devoted to the Holy See than the German — which pleased him. T[heiner] said [Johann Adam] M[öhler] and [Döllinger] had done most for ecclesiastical literature in Germany, and the Pope said that there were many new French books on eccles[iastical] history etc., in which the good was apparent, but not comparable to the

Germans. . . . The P[ope] gave the impression of great kindness and suavity, well acquainted with religious questions, but not with the state of other countries."[50]

There was a further—family—audience, which took place in one of Raphael's *Stanze,* attended by Nonna, Acton's grandmother, and her daughter and son-in-law, Lady Elizabeth and Sir Robert Throckmorton, as well as Acton. "Nonna introduced us as we knelt down successively. . . . He leaned forward and gave us his hand rather to shake than merely to kiss, very gracefully and raised us by it—without allowing us to kiss his red-shoed foot. He made us all sit down. I stood. Nonna alone spoke, until she turned to appeal to me." Seeing Acton's diplomat's uniform, hat, sword, and gloves, the Pope asked what it was. Nonna Acton explained that he had been to Russia—with the embassy—and that his mother, whom the Pope seemed to think Nonna's daughter, was ambassadress. This he remembered, but asked the ambassador's name. The Pope said that he had heard so much "of our brilliancy, and of my mother's religiousness from [Flavio Prince] Chigi. . . . [He] gave us his blessing, and his hand again, calling each up successively, with a wave of the hand, and stood by the side of the table till we were all out of the room." Afterwards everyone remarked on the Pope's obesity, almost torpidity, and found him old and weak. "He took a deal of snuff, and spoke very quietly, distinctly and slowly, with no affectation whatever of impressiveness. My impression is not of any ability and he seems less banally good-natured, than his smiling pictures represent him to be." Nonna was pained that he never mentioned her son, Acton's uncle, the Cardinal.[51]

In a third audience, on 12 June 1857, Acton, introduced by the two papal chamberlains, George Talbot and Bartolomeo Pacca, was received alone. The Pope asked what the English Catholics expected from the new Parliament. "I said we had very little—*da sperare,* he interrupted. I said yes, but little also to fear. He said oh yes, Palmerston had made himself quite necessary in the present crisis, and appeared useful. I said he was less dangerous at home than abroad. Yes, he said, because he is quite an infidel, and cares not about Catholics, but seems restless to disturb Catholic countries abroad. I observed that he disliked Catholics too, and that was part of his reasons for interference, especially in the [papal] states." Acton mentioned that the husband of his mother was a minister. "Oh yes, you are the son of Lady Gr[anville], but Gladstone I believe was better, and as a Puseyite near Cath[olicism]." Acton replied: "Ambition made him useless, as it was a very bad thing."—"Oh," he said, "*secondo me ei passioni inubbriacono gli uomini come il vino* [I am of the opinion that passion can make men drunk like wine], and when it masters them makes them incapable of good. Then I said G[ladstone] was also unsafe in foreign affairs, and he said, yes, he had been carried away and deceived in Nap[les]."[52] This comment referred to Gladstone's criticism of prison conditions in Naples. As yet there was no hint of the Acton-Gladstone friendship—that was still in the future.

It seems that only after their departure was it noted in Rome that Döllinger had been allowed to leave without the usual award. So, on his return to Munich, he was notified that he had been made *cameriere segreto sopranumerario,* which entitled him to the title of Monsignor; it was not the usual rank of "domestic prelate" but a slightly lower one. This rank was thought by some to be an intended slight, as it was simultaneously bestowed on a Bavarian priest of no scholarly distinction. Dr. Döllinger never remarked on this matter. Back in Munich he duly notified the Archbishop's office and the royal chamberlain of the foreign honour he had received and was told by the palace that he was allowed to wear prelate's dress, but not at Church functions, when he would have to wear the vestments of *Stiftsprobst* (provost) of his Munich abbey. In fact, Döllinger never made use of the Roman title.

PLEASING LORD GRANVILLE

AND MAMA

Acton's entry into politics—a hesitant entry, it must be said—was largely the work of his stepfather. "I am trying to get Johnny Acton in for some place in Ireland," wrote Lord Granville in 1857. "I am glad to find that, although he is only a moderate Whig, he is also a very moderate Catholic."[1] There seemed to be some wishful thinking on Lord Granville's part, believing as he did: "He has, I am glad to say, a yearning for public life."[2] This perception contradicted what Acton had told his stepfather earlier: "I am conscious of no political ambition, and I have an aversion and an incapacity for official life." In this letter Acton, with the thought of possibly representing the Irish seat of Clare, expressed gratitude for Lord Granville's support of his "entering the noblest assembly in the world." But he added haughtily: "I am bound to tell you at once that you would be rendering an uncertain service to your party by supporting my election with Government influence. I put this in the most uncompromising way, because I know your great kindness for me, and your desire of helping me to distinction, and I should feel disgraced if you could ever say that I had taken advantage of your kindness to deceive and disappoint you." Acton's conviction was based on his antipathy for Lord Palmerston's rejection of reform in the Lord John Russell government: "There is a sort of fastidiousness produced by long study which public life possibly tends to dissipate, but although the profession of anything like independence of party appears ridiculous, I am of the opinion that, to a Catholic, a certain sort of independence is indispensable. Reasons of religion must separate me occasionally from the Whigs, and political convictions from the Irish party."[3]

In those days a seat in Ireland could be relatively easily obtained, and without great expense. Some effort was required, however, even by Lord Granville's stepson, and Acton tried his luck at several places—Dungarvon, Clare, Cashel, Waterford City, Dublin. "I have not the slightest regret that my projects to be elected had no success," he told Countess Arco after a week in Dublin, his first visit there.[4]

Nevertheless, Acton dutifully sought out the Archbishop of Dublin, Paul Cullen, who, as a former rector of the Irish College in Rome, knew his uncle, Cardinal Acton, and the family. Like most of the Irish Catholics in the nineteenth century, Cullen was strongly opposed to the radical and violent elements in Irish nationalism. He wanted to obtain concessions from the British government for Catholic education in Ireland. "I would be happy to see you Member of Parliament for Dungarvon or any other place in Ireland," he answered Acton, "for I am persuaded that your knowledge of ecclesiastical matters as well as your zeal for religion would render your presence of great advantage to us in the House."[5]

On Cullen's suggestion, Acton wrote to Cardinal Wiseman, who replied in similar terms: "It would give me the greatest pleasure to see you in Parliament. I am sure you would discharge your duties there with independence, and in a thorough Catholic spirit. If this expression of my high opinion of you can be of any service to you in your efforts to attain an honourable position, which I think you well deserve, you are at liberty to make use of what I write with any of our Bishops and Clergy."[6] It was a recommendation that the Cardinal was to regret ever having made when he encountered young Acton's views on Church and State in print.

Two years passed in tentative explorations. "I fear I shall be obliged to try [my chance in Ireland]," wrote the reluctant Acton from Munich in 1859, "*pour acquit de conscience,* and because an election is cheaper than being sheriff, but I do not feel *sanguine*."[7] Lord Granville wrote to his stepson: "If you will stand £700 to be spent legitimately and not on bribery, you may be certainly returned for Carlow."[8] Carlow Borough, some fifty miles south-southwest of Dublin, "had an unenviable reputation for bribery."[9] The seat was held by a Tory, John

Alexander, who was an Anglican and a local landlord and who hardly ever appeared at Westminster. Of the population of nine thousand, 85 percent were
Roman Catholics, but only 236 had the eight-pound household franchise that,
after 1850, qualified for a vote in Ireland.

Acton did not return his expenses, but in a note of Lord Granville the sum
of five hundred pounds is mentioned, to be paid to the agent approved of by
Father James Maher, parish priest of the neighbouring township of Graigue,
a powerful local influence (and also the uncle of Archbishop Cullen), who,
though not himself an elector, canvassed in the Liberal interest for Acton.[10]
The election was spirited even by Irish standards. On nomination night, 3 May
1859, the Dragoons from the nearby barracks had to charge the drunken mob,
although no one was hurt. Acton was not present to witness the event. He had
a throat infection from which he suffered frequently.[11] "Farewell, I depart in
peace tonight," he wrote to his friend Richard Simpson. "I am advised that I
had better not appear there just at first—the importunity of the constituents
being probably in proportion to the popularity of the new member. So I will
let both subside a little, and meantime make the most of my throat. In fact I
cannot open my mouth properly yet."[12]

In a letter to Father Maher from London, dated 8 May, Acton explained that
the old political divisions no longer catered for all shades of opinion; he therefore could not attach himself to any existing party but felt it his duty to expose
the one in power, Lord Derby's administration. Acton stood for a Reform Bill
and improvements in tenant rights. Having no confidence in the foreign policy
of either party, he was in favour of non-intervention in Continental politics.
He emphasized his Catholicism. As an English Catholic he paid tribute to the
Irish for owing to them "not only our political emancipation but the revival
of religion among us. The Irish in our towns have been the occasion of great
efforts that have been made to provide for spiritual wants. . . . It is for the English Catholics to assume the office of mediators between those who are their
brethren in religion and those who are their brethren in blood. It is for them
to provide reasons for conciliation, to soften down the aspects of national and
religious differences and remove national prejudice."[13]

The *Times,* having, unusually, published Acton's address in the form of his
letter to Father Maher on 17 May, supported Acton the next day in a leading
article. Commenting on the general result of the election—in which, for the first
time since Catholic Emancipation, the Liberals were in a minority in Ireland as
a whole, with forty-eight against fifty-seven Conservative seats (Carlow being

one of the three constituencies that were Liberal gains) — the paper noted: "Sir John Acton speaks the language of the old English Roman Catholic. We know by personal acquaintance with the various parties in this island what are their feelings towards his communion. Neither High Church nor Low Church nor any Protestant churches do really and honestly love the Church of Rome." And the paper went on to declare: "Whatever the Liberals may do for the Roman Catholic Church or the dissenter, they do from a principle which will stand the test of varying circumstances. Whatever the Tories do can only be from sheer necessity. . . . The Irish Roman Catholics, it appears, have thought the latter their best friends in the present instance. They will find out their mistake before long, and then, of course, we shall hear the Tories as well abused as most of Ireland's friends have been abused in their time. In this case, however, the abuse will be better deserved than it usually has been."[14]

Amidst great Liberal rejoicing and Conservative complaints of "much priestly influence, intimidation, mob violence and, it is feared, wholesale bribery," Acton had unexpectedly won his seat with 117 against 103 votes.[15] The ten Roman Catholics who had voted for Alexander, the Protestant candidate, were made to feel the fury of the non-voting mob; three had their houses and shops badly damaged and had to be awarded compensation by the court. As for allegations of intimidation or bribery, Father Maher was able to assure the new MP that there were not the slightest grounds for them. "All the Tories voted on one side (not one for you). All the Liberals, with few exceptions, on the other. . . . I believe there was not a shilling spent on either side in bribery. On the eve of the election, a number of the voters remained together, in the reading rooms, with a view to keep each other out of the way of temptation. They have had some punch to drink, but who supplied it, or paid for it, I have not heard; but of this I am certain that not one penny of your money has been used for such purpose."[16]

Alexander, who had ritually challenged the result on both these counts, withdrew his petition. The victor arrived in Carlow only a month after his election, to be the guest at a great banquet at Cullen's hotel. The *Carlow Post* of 4 June 1859 wrote that Acton was drawn from the station to his hotel by a crowd of three or four thousand who cheered him or shouted "Soupers" (a name given to those who went over to Protestantism for food at the time of the Irish famine). "I am received with enthusiasm by the people and great cordiality by all the educated Catholics," the new MP wrote to Countess Arco. "The priests of the seminary have been very kind and hospitable. They gave me a champagne breakfast yesterday. . . . The professor of theology has become my intimate friend and spent all his evening yesterday drinking punch with me, and discussing questions of theology! . . . My popularity is as great as possible." Acton's letter to Father Maher had made him, as he put it, *une puissance* (a force) in Ireland, and every Catholic newspaper drew attention to it. People say, he wrote, that he was the first Englishman who had done justice to Ireland. "I have the good fortune to find that precisely my ideas are shared by all the leading Catholics here. They say it seems as if I had studied Carlow politics all my life, as I hit the right tone so well." [17]

At the celebration dinner Acton said that he was merely reaping the fruits of Father Maher's labours. The priest sitting beside Acton expressed confidence in him, going on to say that "the road from Carlow to the House of Commons can be travelled by anyone who is a friend of the people." [18] There were ten toasts and as many speeches. It was a very Irish occasion, and Acton not the first Englishman to be captivated by it. The young MP was recommended to take a local bride. The *Carlow Post* made no bones about how things had been actually conducted, and in a fine piece of blarney concluded: "Whenever Father Maher found an elector hesitating to do his duty to his country, he was anxious to have a chat with his mistress. . . . One said that if her sick husband did not do his duty in the election, she would never show her face in Carlow—that she would go to America." Not surprisingly, of all the votes promised only one "failed in delivery." [19]

On Friday, 10 June, Acton was back in London to take the obnoxious oath still imposed on Roman Catholic officeholders under the Emancipation Act of 1829:

> I do further declare that it is not an article of my faith, and that I do renounce, reject and abjure the opinion, that princes excommunicated or deprived by the Pope . . . may be deposed or murdered by their subjects or by any person whatsoever; and I do declare that I do not believe that the Pope of Rome . . . hath or ought to have any temporal or civil jurisdiction, power, superiority or pre-eminence, directly or indirectly, within this realm. I do swear that I will defend to the utmost of my power the settlement of property within this realm . . . and I do so solemnly swear that I will never exercise any privilege to which I am or may become entitled, to disturb or weaken the Protestant religion or Protestant government in the United Kingdom. [20]

Acton took his seat on the opposition bench, among the radicals.

When Acton arrived at Westminster, Queen Victoria had reigned for more than twenty years and the monarchy was, in constitutional theory, still an independent source of initiative and leadership. Parliamentarians enjoyed enormous prestige, although the business transacted was small compared with today's huge legislative load. But it was an essentially insular assembly. Acton was ill at ease in it. With his slightly sallow complexion, Continental manners, fastidious tastes, and scholarly interests, he was the proverbial square peg in a round hole. Lord Granville nevertheless was convinced that Acton was enjoying himself. He believed that his stepson's new position "has taken away from him the suspicion that people undervalued him, and he appears to appreciate some of the fine ladies being coquettish with him."[21] Almost immediately Acton was called upon to cast his first vote, helping thereby, early in March 1859, to defeat Lord Derby's Conservative government on a vote of no confidence by thirteen votes (323 against 310). There was a certain amount of to-and-froing over who should form the new government. The Queen first sent for Lord Granville, but, in June, Lord Palmerston replaced the Conservative government.

Even before the new Liberal MP had stood for election, he had taken the opportunity of calling on W. E. Gladstone, who was to be the new chancellor of the exchequer, at Carlton House Terrace. Accepting office in Lord Palmerston's government marked for Gladstone the final step of his passage from the Conservative Party. Switching parties was then not as unusual for party leaders and followers as it has become under today's more rigid party structures, and Sir Robert Peel, W. E. Gladstone, and Joseph Chamberlain were the most eminent of those who, in Acton's time, "crossed the floor of the House." Gladstone recorded Acton's visit in a letter to his wife: "Of all the birds in the air, Sir John Acton called on me this morning (before going to Ireland to stand) to ask a lot of questions about politics. This, I concluded, was a fishing visit prompted by senior persons."[22] No doubt Acton's stepfather, subsequently Lord President of the Council in the Palmerston government, was one of these "senior persons," one of the powerful old Whigs compared with a "Peelite" like Gladstone. They were something of a worry to Gladstone, the newcomer, although he was to reshape British Liberal politics in his image.

Gladstone had come back to England from his special mission as high commissioner in the Ionian Islands, to which he had been appointed by the Derby government. He was then fifty, an MP since 1832; Acton was half his age. They had first met in the early 1850s; their common bond was Dr. Döllinger, whom Gladstone had visited in Munich in 1845. Professor Döllinger admired the English politician and devout Anglican with whom he could talk late into the night about the Eucharist and Church affairs. That—and Ireland—was also what interested Acton in Gladstone. But the young Baronet was not alone in having to overcome considerable prejudices. Their friendship, probably the only lasting benefit that Acton derived from his years in Westminster, was slow in ripening.

As Acton had told Pope Pius IX in 1857, he found Gladstone "ambitious" and "unsafe" in foreign affairs.[23] Gladstone's intemperate outbursts in the Commons against the Pope as a tyrant caused Acton's special "wrathfulness" and also criticism in the *Rambler,* as they had "neither the merit of sincerity nor the excuse of blindness."[24] However, he had, as he put it, "not lost all hope in Gladstone, but all faith and most of my charity."[25]

To the young Baronet, Gladstone with his Low Church image and wealthy Liverpool origins lacked "the instincts of a gentleman" and did "nothing handsome or chivalrous."[26] But in July 1860 came the first invitation to breakfast, Gladstone's favourite discussion time, at Carlton House Terrace, and many were to follow.[27] At the end of July, Acton reported to Döllinger: "I have seen much of Gladstone. He has played rough with the ministry [by earlier voting with Benjamin Disraeli and the Derby government] . . . but it seems that he nevertheless remains in it. He is very much on edge and has become rather unpopular. I have at his request written a paper for him on what German books there are on Hellenic mythology since he plans to develop his ideas about the excellence of Homeric thought in the autumn. What I told him about Lasaulx's ideas greatly interested him in the man and, aided by him, he will exceed even Lasaulx in his fancies."[28]

Gladstone had recently published the results of his Homeric researches in which he showed his indebtedness to German scholars like Döllinger, C. W. F. Nägelsbach, and Johann Friedrich.[29] Acton did not think much of this particular hobby of Gladstone and characterized his views as "highly uncritical and antiquated."[30] Gladstone "treats me with the greatest kindness, and three days ago we had a long discussion about Homer. I learned that he had never read Plato and urgently recommended him to read *The Laws.*"[31] An article by Acton titled "Political Causes of the American Revolution" increased Gladstone's admiration for him: "I have read your valuable and remarkable paper. Its principles of politics I embrace: its research and wealth of knowledge I admire: and its whole atmosphere, if I may so speak, is that which I desire to breathe. It is a truly English paper."[32] It was the first of many studies of federal government that were to preoccupy Acton for more than four decades, and this one showed him siding openly with the South in the American Civil War.

What appealed to Gladstone in Acton's *Rambler* article was his constitutionalism, the rejection of the infallibility both of the people and of the State. "For it is a most striking thing," Acton wrote, "that the views of pure democracy, which we are accustomed to associate with American politics, were almost entirely unrepresented in the convention [the Constitutional Convention in Philadelphia, in 1787]. Far from being the product of a democratic revolution, and of an opposition to English institutions, the constitution of the United States was the result of a powerful reaction against democracy, and in favour of the traditions of the mother country. On this point nearly all the leading statesmen were agreed."[33] To find the reason for the dissolution of the Union, Acton argued, one had to determine how far the rights of the states were merged in the federal power and how far they retained their independence. By abuse of federal authority, South and North had each alternately attempted policies of economic victimization against the other. The Northern manufacturers, unable to compete with European manufacturers (unlike their English counterparts), wanted protection of the home market; the agricultural producers in the South wanted free trade, moderate taxes, cuts in government spending. Slavery became the lever by which the abolitionists attacked the constitutional rights of the South, and that attack led to its secession.

The Church's system of Christian liberty "is essentially incompatible with slavery and the power of masters over their slaves was one of the bulwarks of corruption and vice which most seriously impeded her progress. Yet the Apostles never condemned slavery even within the Christian fold. The sort of civil liberty which came with Christianity into the world, and was one of her postulates, did not require the abolition of slavery. . . . St. Paul prescribed to the Christian slave to remain content with his condition [1 Cor. 7:21]." Acton noted at the bottom of the page, "The opposite interpretation, common among Protestant commentators, is inconsistent with verses 20 and 24, and with the traditions of the Greek Fathers."[34]

Acton was to return to the subject of the American Civil War in a lecture he delivered a few years later at the Literary and Scientific Institution at Bridgnorth.[35] He did not change his view that slavery has been "a mighty instrument not for evil only, but for good in the providential order of the world," by awakening the spirit of sacrifice and charity. But Negro slavery, as it existed in America, he was now convinced, was essentially immoral. Emancipation in the United States "has been an act of war, not of statesmanship, or humanity. They have treated the slave-owner as an enemy, and have used the slave as an instrument for his destruction. They have not protected the white man from the vengeance of barbarians, nor the black from the pitiless cruelty of a selfish civilisation."[36]

In all this Gladstone could agree with Acton, but there were the dark spots in Gladstone's private life that troubled the early relationship between the two. "I understand that he is being spied upon. He could be ruined," Acton wrote to Döllinger.[37] Acton was referring to Gladstone's evangelical "rescue work" among London's prostitutes and the dangers that it represented for his reputation. The matter was much rumoured about. Gladstone, the chancellor of the exchequer and later prime minister, used to set out from his home at Carlton House Terrace on nightly errands to the nearby Haymarket, which was then the West End's foremost parade ground for prostitutes. Gladstone genuinely believed that he was playing an active part in an important Christian city apostolate, though looked at in a modern, post-Freudian, and non-Christian age, his motivation would seem suspect. Gladstone was a man of strong sexuality. He was also much interested in pornography, and his and Acton's common friend Monckton Milnes had a well-known and remarkable pornographic library.

Gladstone's wife, Catherine, was nine times pregnant and frequently recovering from childbirth and miscarriages in the first fourteen years after their marriage in 1839. "There is no indication," as the editor of *The Gladstone Diaries* and Gladstone's biographer, H. C. G. Matthew, has noted, "of any sexual incompatibility between the two, but it is clear that there were considerable periods of enforced sexual abstinence, caused by the Victorian middle-class convention of abstaining from sexual relations during most of pregnancy, nursing and menstruation."[38] Moreover, as a devout Anglican, Gladstone probably took literally the Prayer Book's injunction that marriage was "first . . . for the procreation of children." There were also frequent periods of separation between Gladstone, in London, and his wife, at Hawarden Castle, and as his diaries show, during those periods his rate of rescue work increased. The Greek letters eta and upsilon and a character resembling a pair of crossed whips, all of which appear frequently in *The Gladstone Diaries,* were used to indicate that Gladstone scourged himself after returning home from these encounters or because of sinful thoughts after his conversations with particular prostitutes. The women are named by initials or full names. Gladstone helped them with gifts of money, trying to induce them to change their way of life.

Gladstone's activity was known at the time to a small circle of London society and naturally caused considerable gossip and anxiety among the Liberal leadership and friends like Acton over his apparent imperviousness to criticism regarding the political dangers involved. Catherine Gladstone must have known about her husband's activities because the prostitutes were frequently invited to the Gladstone house. Gladstone was well aware of the moral dangers of an activity that had become "a craving," and as he admitted to himself in his diaries, he deliberately "courted evil" or "trod the path of danger," especially because his rescue work met with little success. "A nasty story against Lord Palmerston is making the rounds," Acton wrote to Munich, "but serves only to add to his popularity. That sort of thing would mean ruin for Gladstone."[39] To the young idealist MP there seemed, as yet, little to choose between Lord Palmerston, the aged womanizer, and Gladstone.

From the back benches, Acton concerned himself with religious education in the Irish schools and consulted with others about how to take account of the wishes of the Irish episcopate. "I was urgently asked to come to this consultation [meeting]," he wrote to Döllinger, "but I am glad that I didn't have to go. My opinion is that the religious character which is necessary in the teaching of elementary schools and in universities cannot be derived from the same principle." In the case of the younger children, Acton believed, religion and teaching could very well be separated according to time and place. In higher studies they must be united.[40]

Meanwhile Acton was drawing closer to three other Irish MPs: Richard More O'Farrell (1797–1880), MP for Kildare; Thomas (later Lord) O'Hagan of Tullalogue (1812–1885), who became the widely respected first Catholic Lord Chancellor of Ireland in 1881; and William Monsell (1812–1894), later Lord Emly, a convert and close friend of Newman's. Monsell's refusal to swear the oath imposed on Roman Catholics when he was nominated as privy councillor caused no little embarrassment to Lord Granville. On Catholic issues the Catholic MPs tended to act independently of party affiliation. And in August 1860, during a debate on the Roman Question, they protested against the ministry's policy by rising as one body and leaving the chamber. "Johnny Acton has thrown us over," the irritated stepfather noted.[41]

In more than six years at Westminster, Acton asked only three questions, one of them in the form of a short speech. When his fellow MP, Sir Mountstuart Grant Duff, tackled him about his lack of participation, "he replied that he agreed with nobody, and nobody agreed with him."[42] Acton's reluctance to speak on the various issues, particularly on the Roman Question, was due to his fear of doing more harm than good. As for the temporal power—one of the great questions of the day, as much in politics and in religion, and particularly crucial for a Catholic MP—his fear of having to speak in Parliament on the issue was caused by the fact that he could not express his true mind. The papal government was in serious danger, and the great majority of Catholics throughout the world were anxious over the fate of the Pope. The future Cardinal Manning held support of the temporal power to be a matter of faith, "an ordinance of God," rather than a question of political expediency.[43] The generation preceding Acton's had seen the Pope being driven into exile, as he was again in 1848, and Catholics in all countries were called upon to rally round him. The fall of most of the papal territories to France and Austria forced the issue, in 1860. Acton in this regard was conscious of being "antiquatedly conservative," almost "Burkean," and confessed to Simpson that he was "a partisan of sinking ships, and I know none more ostensibly sinking just now than St. Peter's."[44] Acton was groping for some sort of international solution, guaranteed by the Catholic powers. His real thoughts on the subject did not emerge in Parliament but, gradually and at length, surfaced in articles in the *Rambler* (see Chapter 9).

Not wanting to attack the government merely because he disagreed with it on its Italian policy, which supported the country's unification, Acton addressed a parliamentary question to the foreign secretary, Lord John Russell, asking him to publish the dispatches, relating to the condition and administration of the Roman states, of Richard (later Lord) Lyons, the English representative at Florence from 1855 who for two years (1856–58) was under orders to reside at Rome. These dispatches would enable the House to form a reliable opinion on the situation. The Catholic MPs wanted to make public information showing the papal government in a favourable light and thought that one of Lyons's dispatches would support their case. Acton was firmly convinced that it would not and, by asking that all of Lyons's dispatches be made public, turned the tables on those of his co-religionists in the House who, in their uncritical support of the temporal power, merely wanted to embarrass the government. "I am speaking in the interests of all Catholics," he said. "We do not wish that it should be believed that the Catholics of this country . . . are indifferent to the political welfare of their fellow Catholics abroad, or that we are blinded by attachment to our religion to facts by which, if they are true, that religion is injured and disgraced."[45]

That speech made some impression in the House. Lord Granville, who had listened from the gallery, sent a copy of Acton's speech to Countess Arco with the note: "Spoken in the House of Commons by Johnny, looking pale, but was perfectly self-collected; both admirable voice and manner. His future success in the House is certain."[46] It was not the customary maiden speech that the young MP had envisioned, on a subject like Irish education or national defence, but never delivered. His brief intervention nevertheless brought him congratulations all round. He was quite at ease standing up in the crowded chamber for the first time, he wrote to Countess Arco, and was glad not to have let down his stepfather. What he really felt, he told Richard Simpson: "If I could only get turned out of Parliament in an honest way, and settle down among my books."[47]

When the Lyons dispatches were made public, Acton found that they confirmed his assessment of the papal government and also of the reform policy of the Italian liberals. Summarizing Lord Lyons's view, Acton noted:

> [He] recognizes the good will of the Roman government to make reforms and also the determination of the people—of the discontented part of it—not to accept them.
>
> The opposition is not to definite grievances, but to the government altogether—not because it is bad, but because it is clerical, and therefore not suited to the spirit of the time.
>
> Therefore the disaffection in the papal states is like that in Tuscany against the Grand duke, not like the Sicilian movement, a protest against real, distinct wrongs. The Grand duke [is] attacked because he was an Austrian—the pope because he is a priest. The readiness to concede very much on one side, the resolution to be satisfied with nothing on the other—is the most striking result of these papers.

Secularization would satisfy nobody, yet it was Lyons's great remedy. But the Italian liberals were no less hostile to the Catholic system than to English ideas of liberty. Moderates and conservatives among the Italian liberals, like Lyons's Bologna friend Marchese Carlo Bevilaqua, felt "baffled by their unscrupulous allies who strive to make things worse under the present system in order that they may become better only by the supremacy of their own system—Revolution is the great enemy of reform—it makes a wise and just reform impossible."[48]

The ability of Lord Palmerston's government to survive seemed uncertain and to depend, as Acton wrote to Döllinger, on Gladstone's budget as well as on the Conservatives' finding a sufficiently broad basis for attack in order to win Catholic support. If the Liberal government fell owing to an alliance of Tories and Catholics on the Roman Question, the Liberals would hold the Catholics responsible, Acton believed, and would revive the "no popery" cry.[49]

The Liberal decline was due not only to the Conservatives but to what Acton called "the disorganisation of positive Whiggism. It had fallen into mere abstract Liberalism. Whiggism is a doctrine, but Liberalism is merely negative and has no particular end, or boundary. So it merges in radicalism and democracy and revolution. . . . It is only a vessel, but has no cargo, and only a temporary organisation. Now the philosophic radicals *have* a theory and doctrine and so they carry the undogmatic Liberals with them. Remedy: Redogmatize Whiggism."[50] This was what Acton set out to do in regard to Gladstone.

With the premature death, in 1861, of the Prince Consort, a new phase of the Victorian age was beginning. "It is a great misfortune for Queen and country," Acton wrote. "He was awfully Gothaic, and not very Christian, but he guided the Queen loyally and skilfully in the negotiations with the leaders of both parties. *Il nous manque quand nous en avons besoin* [We miss him when we have need of him]. For Lord Granville probably a real loss."[51] The "heroic age" of the Industrial Revolution was passing. Now the effects of the "dark satanic mills" and of the transformation of England's green and pleasant land were being felt: poverty, social deprivation, drunkenness, crime.

Prime Minister Lord Palmerston, who had dominated the world scene for decades as foreign secretary, the embodiment of the Pax Britannica, was not really interested in home affairs or social reforms. And in foreign affairs, too, the old master was losing his grip. New players were about to dominate world politics—Camillo Cavour, Napoleon III, Otto von Bismarck. Acton's attitude towards Palmerston was influenced by the prime minister's anti-Catholicism, which coloured Great Britain's policy towards the Pope and Italian nationalism. There was also the Turnbull affair. The prime minister gave his approval to what appears to have been the dismissal, because of alleged dishonesty, of William Turnbull (1811–1863) from the Historical Commission. Turnbull was a respected editor of English historical documents and a Catholic convert. But the allegations were made by Protestant members of the board and were later proved to be groundless. When Acton took the case up with Palmerston, he incurred a rebuke from his stepfather in his governmental capacity as Lord President of the Council. Lord Granville evidently found it difficult, as shown by a much-corrected draft of his short letter:

In your place I should not have felt myself justified in communicating to Mr. Turnbull the content of the letters from the prime minister without that permission from him which you thought it necessary to give him as to your letter, but of which he did not avail himself. They were marked private on the outside, they were written in unreserved, non-official style and no action was taken upon them by either you or Lord Palmerston. You hold a different opinion as to the character of these letters and you acted accordingly. No one who has the pleasure of being personally acquainted with you or who knows the . . . estimation of your high character can suspect you of intentionally committing a breach of confidence.[52]

In temperament and ideas the young Liberal MP was worlds apart from Lord Palmerston. Acton did not disguise his wish to leave Parliament. Lord Granville warned, "It would be a sort of moral cowardice to run away."[53]

The confidence that Gladstone showed Acton led to a discussion of Gladstone's political aims when both were spending a weekend at Cliveden, Buckinghamshire, as the guests of the Duke of Sutherland. This exchange was very important for him, as Acton wrote to Munich. Gladstone "explained with rare trust his whole policy—with all personal judgements, intentions, hopes. I can say that I can approve of everything in his home policy—especially because of Ireland and the Catholics. . . . My hopes for his future ministry are much increased. I discovered an energy of the will, a resolve and an indignation . . . that were salutary and that foreshadow consequences for world history. His trust in Cavour's love of liberty, however, I was able, with some effort, to undermine."[54] Acton marked this discussion, as Herbert Butterfield records, as a red-letter day, and more than twenty years later he still looked back to "the date of getting the future policy of Liberalism quite clear before me."[55]

Gladstone had told Acton about his planned great domestic measures, among them the Disestablishment of the Church of Ireland, which became law in 1871. Acton shared with Gladstone the conviction that, in regard to Ireland, Great Britain must seek an opportunity of righting past wrongs. In April 1864 Gladstone noted in his diary a conversation with Acton, "whom the more I see, the more I like. *Si sic omnes*" (If only everyone were like that).[56] By the time of the general election of 1865, however, the electors of Carlow made the decision for their reluctant MP by unseating him and finding someone who would better nurture the constituency and also prove more amenable to their wishes. A story had also circulated that Acton had a bloodhound with a passion for biting Irishmen, which, true or not, indirectly reflected British attitudes towards the people of the neighbouring island.[57] But Acton's happiness at having escaped was of short duration. The Liberals of Bridgnorth begged him to stand for the 1865 July election, as their Conservative MP had lost popularity by opposing the railway link that the town, Acton's tenants, and Acton himself had warmly supported. Reluctantly, Acton consented. Among other reasons, a refusal would have appeared as though, as a Roman Catholic, he felt incapacitated to stand as a candidate for an English constituency and was not anxious to break through the ghetto seclusion of English Catholics.

Acton wrote to Marie:

> We went in with four horses and took our places on a great balcony erected for the purpose; and my opponents spoke first, very respectfully of me, and not very wisely, against my principles, as an adversary of their religion. I answered them with great generosity, and, I think, with perfect success. So that I have had a splendid ovation, and have gained immense popularity in the town . . . today I am quite victorious. Tomorrow, in the urns, I shall be defeated, but fairly, and my defeat will only be obtained by buying the votes of the poor people. Not one unfriendly word has been spoken and though I spoke long of religious matters, there never was the least outcry, interruption or disapproval. The great point is gained: a Catholic has been well received by the electors of a Protestant town, has been the popular candidate and has had the first victory. Such a thing has never happened in England since the restoration of the hierarchy in 1850.[58]

And in another letter: "I hear the people are strongly with me. Some are afraid of my Ultramontanist views. . . . I am to speak in the High Street this evening. If they don't interrupt me and I don't lose the thread, I shall have important things to say."[59]

A handwritten poetic "Appeal to the Working Electors of Bridgnorth" seems to have been circulated, the eighth verse of which read:

> Then do your duty, working men, be early at the poll,
> Be zealous for your country's cause, and vote with heart and soul
> Strike terror in the Tory breast, its owner crush and bruise,
> And honour bring to Gladstone's name, and Acton proudly choose.
> Vote for Acton, the true friend of Progress![60]

When the result of the Bridgnorth election was finally declared, Acton was elected by a majority of one vote, but the result was overturned by a scrutiny early in the following year.

Prematurely, the *Times* welcomed Acton's election as the first Roman Catholic to win a seat in Great Britain: "It is satisfactory to find that religious zeal does not in all cases urge the British elector to vote against a papist. The Bridgnorth people in returning Sir John Acton have not only shown themselves superior to the prejudice that has hitherto prevailed, but they have placed in the House an accomplished man and one of the most thoughtful and judicious among the members of his Church."[61] Newman also congratulated Acton on being the first to break through the impediments raised against Catholics since the restoration of the hierarchy, in 1850.[62] Fine words barely concealed the fiasco of having the election overturned. But Acton himself wrote later to Marie, by then his wife: "I can say with perfect truth that I have never regretted my defeat for one moment since this time last week. The joy of being with you and the children, and among my books, doing something for Catholic studies is beyond all other joys."[63]

Nevertheless, Acton had to stand once more as a candidate for Bridgnorth. The general election of November 1868 was the first test of the newly enfranchised electorate of the 1867 Reform Act, and the local Liberals thought that only Acton would be able to beat the sitting Tory MP. So he took up his cross once more for the sake of the party. Because one of the chief planks of the Liberal programme was the Disestablishment of the Church of Ireland, Acton had to deal with the full fury of the "no popery" cry. He was accused by opponents of using the Irish issue to establish papal absolutism in England. The *Spectator* came to his rescue. Calling Acton "the most Liberal and able of the English Catholics," the *Spectator* hoped that he might be "a member of the House which will have the duty of disestablishing the Irish Church. No Roman Catholic member will command the weight on such a subject which he can command, for he will combine with sincere Catholicism a width of intellect, a depth of learning, a sobriety of judgment, and a hearty dread of Papal despotism, such as will secure for him the deep respect of the Protestants as well as the sympathy of the Catholic part of the House."[64]

But in Shropshire a less elevated tone prevailed. It made no difference outside the Liberal election meetings that Acton said he was just as keen to defend the Irish people's right to be governed in the way that suited them best as to defend the Romans' right in the matter of the temporal power. Acton had at least the satisfaction of being supported by an Anglican clergyman, his friend Horatio James Ward, a master at the grammar school. The support caused a local stir.

There was a landslide Liberal victory. The new voters showed no thanks to Disraeli for extending the franchise, but instead elected Gladstone's party with a surprising majority of 112 seats. "It is shown generally that the real working class is more receptive to ideas and principles than the egoistic middle class, or rather, shopkeeping class," wrote Acton to Döllinger.[65] But the Liberal Party no less than the Conservatives had yet to learn the lessons of that development. For instance, in Lancashire where the Protestant "orange" won over the "green" Irish vote, even Gladstone lost his seat, although he got himself elected at Greenwich. One of the Liberal casualties, however, was Sir John Acton at Bridgnorth. Lord Granville wrote to him: "I cannot tell you how sorry I am (possibly more than you are). I cannot, however, regret the opportunity you have had of making the speeches which have done you so much credit."[66] "Alas, alas," wrote Simpson, "but you will have more time for the Quarterly."[67] The reference was to the *North British Review,* which was to conclude Acton's decade of intense journalism. He had conducted his editorial activities simultaneously with his parliamentary career, and they were one of the main causes of his decidedly muted impact as an MP.

What Acton felt, he had revealed earlier in an undated letter to Marie Arco, at the time of his engagement. The letter was written from 32 St. James's Place, where Acton lodged before his wedding in 1865, and shows his earnest and priggish side:

> I will try to explain to you why I do not wish to be in Parliament during the early years of our married life. You know that the one supreme object of all my thoughts is the good of the Church; and I wish to arrange all things so that this may be accomplished as well as my means allow. The greatest good that I can do is by means of literature, for there I have resources greater than any other person, and I have collected materials of immense extent. The time has come when I ought to make something of these collections, and it is impossible while I am in Parliament. The good that I can do in the House of Commons is not greater than that which is in the power of several other Catholic members. I should therefore be sacrificing one sort of activity in which I have advantages such as no other person enjoys, for another in which I should not do anything which is beyond the reach of others. Political influence, and that of a very valuable kind, I shall always continue to possess while my friendship with Gladstone lasts, and while he is a leading statesman—for in Catholic matters he trusts me more than anybody. . . . For the next few years at least I am sure that I am better out of Parliament. . . . Let me enjoy a period of quiet and comparative obscurity in private life, with my home made happy by my wife, and my time still devoted to the good cause.[68]

This was, in many ways, a sad period in Acton's life. His mother died, after a grave illness, in March 1860. In addition to this loss, his hopes of marrying Marie Arco suffered ups and downs. There had been a mutual attachment between his mother and Marie, as there was between himself and Marie's mother during his Munich days. These ties were further complicated by his Hamletlike feelings about his mother, whom he loved but who, he also felt, had neglected him in her anxiety to please Lord Granville.

At Carlsbad, in October 1859, Lady Granville suffered a stroke and was brought by a doctor, her husband, and her son to Herrnsheim, where she recovered slightly but felt that her end was near. She asked her son to note down various last wishes, bequests to servants, what should be done about her jewellery, and similar matters. Acton recorded the following:

> I am to give her best and tenderest love to Anna [Arco]. Then she said, "*Et la petite* Marie — partly as a question. I made them leave me alone with her, and asked *Si j'avais l'espoir d'épouser Marie, est-ce-que vous l'aimeriez?* [If there was a chance of my marrying Marie, would that please you?] These words seemed to give my poor mother more pleasure than anything which happened during her illness. She said the thought made her so very happy, and she prayed that [Marie] might make me happy. She told me to give her her love, and to tell her this. This was when she asked most eagerly: *Est-ce-[que] vraisemblable?* [Is it really likely?] and I answered: "*Je l'ai désiré beaucoup depuis des anneés.* [I have wanted it for years.] She was extremely agitated with the pleasure this gave her, and seemed to have waited for it long.
>
> Then I opened the door, and she asked leave to tell Lord Granville, and told him with great eagerness that I had hopes of marrying Marie. Then she called for her jewel box and said she wanted to give Marie her rings and a brooch. I said: *Seulement un petit souvenir* [only a little keepsake], but she insisted. She took out and gave Lord Granville what belonged to him, pulled a ring off her finger and put it on mine, and began giving away her presents. . . . She cut off a long lock of her hair for Lord Granville. . . . She put on earrings her father gave her, in which she wished to be buried. . . . Then she gave me for Marie a beautiful brooch, a smaller one for Anna. She gave me a bracelet of her mother's hair, lockets with my father's and my own, all her rings, a cross which had been blessed by the pope. . . .
>
> Towards five in the evening she laid her head smiling on my shoulder and asked me to repeat the words which had conveyed the news which gave her so much pleasure in the morning. Then she repeated them with delight to Lord Granville. They were: *Si j'épousais Marie, l'aimeriez vous?* [If I married Marie, would you like that?] When I repeated them she said: *Oui! Oui! de tout mon coeur!* [Yes, yes, with all my heart.] [69]

Marie Arco, then eighteen, visited Lady Granville at Herrnsheim, and in November Acton took his sick mother back to England. They stopped in Paris, and he wrote to Marie: "You entered into our family like a ray of light, like an angel whose apparition alone is enough to change suffering into joy. The good that your sight has done makes her feel better."[70] In her joy Lady Granville talked to everybody as though there were already an engagement, and, considering her heart condition, no one wanted to disillusion her.

In fact there had been a tacit understanding since Acton had left Munich, subject to Marie's final consent, that they would marry one day. She had formally allowed him to "entertain hope." Her parents were for the marriage, but she was unsure. She was fond of her cousin and admired his gifts, but she had none of his intellectual interests. She was a typical comtesse of Munich's cosmopolitan society set: she loved gaiety and was fond of dancing. She played the piano tolerably, often accompanied her mother, who had a fine voice, and liked to sing Italian, French, and German songs. But Marie's character and mind needed shaping. Acton set to work, trying—unsuccessfully—to persuade her to write to him in English, which she never learned to speak as well as French. He suggested books for her to read, introducing her to a current best seller, Charles Reade's *Love Me Little, Love Me Long*. The novel dealt with the doubts and uncertainties of a young woman with several admirers and with how she finally made her choice. Acton warned Marie against identifying with characters from the novel: "Modern novels describe contemporary society so realistically that one is more easily deceived than by those of Scott and Manzoni which you have read hitherto."[71]

Marie Arco found it difficult to imagine having to live with Johnny Acton in remote Shropshire, giving up her life and her friends in Munich. Not only was he seven years older than she, but he was also so serious and forbiddingly clever. He was entering Parliament and moving among people with whom she had little in common. Nevertheless, in November 1859 there was a form of engagement, but it seems to have been more of a charade enacted to please Acton's mother, who was not expected to live long. "She was so happy about it that for the first time in her life she embraced me," Acton wrote to Marie. But he emphasized: "Don't forget when reading my letters that your liberty and independence are sacred to me. I shall never ask of you anything that, for my part, I would not be ready to give. You will pain me more by saying yes without loving me than by refusing me definitely. While I would suffer in the one case as in the other, you would risk being unhappy as well, and your happiness is no less precious to me than my own."[72]

Nevertheless, engagement presents arrived at the Granvilles' house in Bruton Street. Lord Granville's mother sent a sum of money with which a toilet case for travelling was bought. Although Marie had not fully consented, it was difficult to keep news of the engagement secret. Acton's mother told her friends. Lord Granville wrote to the Queen,

> begging to state what he believed will give Your Majesty and His Royal Highness pleasure, that Lady Granville arrived safely in London late last night. The journey which was a trying one on account of two days of snow and cold on the French Lines had done her positive good. When Lady Granville was at the [hospital] ward, she told Lord Granville that she should die with pleasure, if she could be sure that her son would be well married. She has now reason to believe that he will marry his second cousin, Marie d'Arco Valley. Nothing is settled and therefore nothing can be said or announced about it, but it has made her a very happy mother.[73]

The Queen congratulated Lord Granville and passed on the news to the Prussian Crown Princess (the future Queen Augusta), who, as Acton said, told everybody.

At the end of January 1860, Acton wrote to Marie that his mother's thoughts were entirely devoted to her. She was making all sorts of plans for her future daughter-in-law to come to England; a personal maid was to be sent to Munich and later accompany her back to England. Acton commissioned a design of her future coat of arms. Lady Granville was enchanted with a little locket with Marie's hair, which Marie had sent to her. But between February and March, as Lady Granville's condition deteriorated, Marie wrote to Acton that she did not want to commit herself finally before having seen him again. He was unable to go to Munich there and then because of his mother's condition, and there was also uncertainty about the validity of his election as an MP. So he implored Marie's mother not to tell anyone about the cause of the delay and to impose an absolute silence on all the family.[74]

At the end of February, Lady Granville was taken to Brighton; it was hoped that the sea air would do her good. Her mother, the Duchess of Dalberg, came over from Germany; Lord Granville's mother, brother, and sisters came to visit. Lord Granville wanted to resign from the Foreign Office to be with her, but Lord Palmerston, compassionately, assured him that this was not necessary.

Acton was with her most of the time. A Jesuit priest gave her the Sacrament for the Dying and sat at her bedside, reading to her from books of devotion.

Lady Granville's lingering agony ended at midnight on 14 March 1860. "They have laid my mother out, and I went up to see her," Acton wrote to Countess Arco. "I placed upon her heart the crucifix you gave me. It is three o'clock; I have induced Lord Granville to go to bed. . . . I never felt how much I love you more than now, and I have never had such need of you. Remember of my mother her childhood, her long expiation and her love for your daughter."[75] The funeral took place at Aldenham. Late at night, accompanied by torch-bearers, the hearse with the coffin arrived at the chapel, a sad sight for the son watching from the house alone. But the greatest pain for him at his mother's death was the absence of his "aunt" and Marie, who had refused to face his mother with a lie. Countess Arco instead sent a consoling telegram on the day of the funeral: "Close to you with all my soul and with all that is dear to you on earth."[76]

Acton carried out "my poor mother's last wishes": rewarding the servants at Herrnsheim and founding a perpetual Mass stipend. She also stipulated that the pearl necklace that his father had given her in 1834, when he was born, was to be given to his wife "by degrees as fast as her children are born."[77]

"I doubt whether a purer, brighter, truer creature ever left this world," Granville wrote to Lord Canning.[78] In Paris, Jean Lemoine paid tribute to Lady Granville in the *Journal des débats:* "One who was much admired in foreign as in English society, a lady still young who, in addition to all the gifts of providence, combined the treasure of the most amiable and most solid virtues. Lady Granville is dead after a long malady in England, surrounded by her family. Theirs doubtless is the principal loss, but they do not stand alone. On the Continent Lady Granville leaves a numerous domestic circle of which she was the soul and centre. In France, where she was born, there are many friends who comprehend our feelings, who share our regrets, and of whose grief we are satisfied in being the interpreters."[79]

Granville disconsolately went abroad, to Paris and Munich, to see some of his wife's relations. Because Marie's betrothal to Johnny had given so much happiness to his wife's last days, he tried to mediate between his stepson and Marie. If, Granville suggested, Acton could not give her up, he should try to offer her his friendship and tenderness in the hope that it would gain for her later what she clearly did not feel now.[80] This, in a way, was what eventually happened. Granville warned Marie "not to keep Johnny dangling. He is capable of very strong decisions, and there are women here, married and unmarried, who would like to win him over from you."[81] One who had caught Acton's eye was the beautiful Miss Ellis, the youngest of the three daughters of Lt. Col. Augustus Frederic Ellis. Of her Acton wrote that he "almost regret[ted]" he had not succeeded better.[82] On Acton's part, however, these women friends seemed to be part of an elaborate scheme designed to keep Marie interested in him.

Acton's resolve to marry Countess Arco's daughter became something of an idée fixe and certainly caused Acton to ignore the love and devotion his cousin Emily Throckmorton had for him. She had a great interest in his ideas, too, and in later years told Acton's daughter, Mamy, that never a day passed without her praying for him. Knowing of her great passion, her elder sister, Minnie Throckmorton, was even said to have written to him asking whether Emily had any chance of becoming his wife. He replied in an affectionate manner, saying that they were first cousins and that he had always thought of his Throckmorton cousins as taking the place of the brothers and sisters he never had. However, for his marriage to Marie Arco, a second cousin, a papal dispensation had to be obtained, and presumably it would have been granted for an Acton-Throckmorton marriage, too. But that was not to be. Emily later married Sir Gerald Dease, chamberlain to the Lord Lieutenant at Dublin Castle. Acton attended the wedding and offered to let them spend their honeymoon at Aldenham while he himself went to London for a few days. It must have been a strange honeymoon for Emily, tinged by her secret love for John Acton. As for his feelings, Acton wrote to Döllinger: "My dear cousin . . . has found an excellent husband and will be the best possible wife for him; but I lose the most intimate friend who was more than a sister to me."[83]

Acton's duties at Westminster had involved his move from his stepfather's house in Bruton Street, with its lively comings and goings, to a dismal rented apartment at 37 Half Moon Street and the life of a lonely clubman. For all that, his name, according to an authority on Acton's parliamentary career, appears in only twenty-seven out of forty-eight lists on important divisions.[84] He seems to have been particularly remiss regarding his own Irish constituency, failing to vote on various occasions of importance to Irish interests (although other Irish MPs also missed these votes). Acton's poor parliamentary performance was mainly due to his other absorbing activity—his work for the Catholic reviews he edited during these years as an MP. He wrote no fewer than six hundred closely printed pages of learned articles and commentaries on current affairs. As a champion of freedom of intellectual enquiry, he fought battles with the

Church authorities. All this activity earned him reproaches of neglecting his duties. "You must take an early opportunity of visiting your constituents," his own Bishop wrote to him. "I heard on Thursday from a former candidate that your absence, justifiable as it was, had not been welcome to them, and might be resented at the next Election."[85]

And there were other obligations or diversions that, willy-nilly, Acton had to assume during these years. In October 1861, Acton accompanied his stepfather, then Lord President of the Council, as the British government's representative to Berlin, to attend the coronation of the King of Prussia, William I. They were housed in an apartment next to the Berlin residence of the British ambassador, where the foreign secretary, Lord Clarendon, who represented the Queen, also stayed. There was a week of festivities with international attendance following upon the coronation in Königsberg. The British suite was in some prominence because the Prussian Crown Prince had been married in 1858 to Queen Victoria's eldest daughter, *die Engländerin*. "The queen [of Prussia (Augusta)] has distinguished me by more than once talking to me long and in a very friendly fashion," Acton wrote to Dr. Döllinger.[86] Acton's success with Queen Augusta may have had something to do with her liberal sympathies. The daughter of the Grand Duke Karl August of Saxe-Weimar and the Grand Duchess Maria Pavlova of Russia favoured constitutional and liberal reforms and Prussia's connection with Britain rather than Russia.

Whenever he could, Acton escaped from the royal events to visit German scholars. He had already met Ranke at his earlier Berlin visit, in 1855, and had attended one of his lectures. Acton had written to Dr. Döllinger at the time: "It is not worthwhile, listening to him. He is very small and ugly, very lively, speaks so quickly that I can hardly understand him, and there is no seriousness or dignity in his nature."[87] Ranke had invited Acton to spend one evening with him. They had met again in London in 1857, at an "historians' dinner" that Lord and Lady Granville had given in Ranke's honour and at which Charles Babington Macaulay and George Grote had also been present. "There is a somewhat greater mellowness and religious air about him," Acton wrote to Döllinger in 1861. Ranke now told him that he had been reading Richard Baxter, the English seventeenth-century nonconformist theologian whose efforts for Christian reunion had influenced the German Pietists. That, Ranke said, was the true and real Protestantism.[88]

Acton's relationship with Ranke, the recognized leader of the Continental school of historians, was changing with his own development as an historian.

Döllinger and other Catholic writers of the German South found Ranke, a native of Thuringian Saxony and a Protestant, uncongenial and narrow, preferring even the Protestant Heinrich Leo. "Slack and trivial" was Döllinger's pronouncement on Ranke's five-volume *Deutsche Geschichte im Zeitalter der Reformation* (1839–47),[89] while Ranke was offended by what he thought of as Döllinger's having slighted his history of the Popes in the sixteenth and seventeenth centuries, which he regarded as his preserve. But in 1865, when Ranke visited England, Acton reported that Ranke had spoken of the deep impression Döllinger had made on him. They had had their disagreements on the German Historical Commission, he said, but discussed these without rancour. Döllinger's view of the Church seemed to him the right one: "After all," he said, "we are not attacking the positive sides of Catholicism, but its aberrations," which Döllinger also recognized. "That was the road to reconciliation."[90]

Probably still under Döllinger's influence, Acton wrote in the early 1860s of Ranke's history of England:

> His history is all plums and no suet. It is all garnish, but no beef. He is a great historical decorator, and avoids whatever is dull or unpleasant, whatever cannot be told in a lively way, or cannot help to his end. He is an epicure and likes only titbits. He is the staff officer who leaves all the rough work to the regimental officers. He appears always in pumps and kid gloves. This is his great art, the art of selection and of proportion and perspective. . . . His art becomes artifice, and his ingenuity treachery. No historian has told fewer untruths, few have committed so few mistakes. None is a more unsafe guide. All that he says is often true, yet the whole is untrue, but the element of untruth is most difficult to detect.[91]

When, in 1864, Acton reviewed the fourth volume of Ranke's *English History,* which extends from the death of Cromwell to the year 1674, based on Ranke's research in Paris, Oxford, the British Museum, and the Public Record Office, he acknowledged that Ranke was "free from conventional influences, and presents many new points of view." And yet Ranke's

> strength does not lie in the history of free communities. He is the historian of courts and statesmen, incomparable at unravelling the web of an intrigue, and divining the hidden, changing schemes of the most expert politician; and he understands the force of convictions, the influence of literature, and the progress of theories. . . . His miniature-painting preserves with a fidelity amounting to genius the features of royal and illustrious persons; but he has not the breadth of touch requisite to do justice to great popular and national

movements, and to dramas in which the actors are whole classes and provinces of men.[92]

This was the time when Döllinger and Acton together discovered the value of the Continental archives hitherto sealed to them, which they came to regard as the essential tools of the serious historians. The discovery was to change Acton's attitude towards Ranke, too. When he saw the German historian again years later, in 1877, Ranke reminded him of their meeting in London in March 1857, together with Macaulay, and of how Macaulay had resented that he, Ranke, was following his tracks in English history. "He says," Acton wrote to Marie, "it was Macaulay's narrow Whiggism that induced him to undertake the task for a more universal point of view, and I refrained from saying that I hoped I was a good Whig, and yet had a universal view." That Berlin visit in 1877 finally confirmed what Ranke meant for Acton—less, of course, than Döllinger, but, Acton wrote earlier in his letter to Marie, Ranke had been his

> guide to all the original sources of modern history. . . . It is by his means that I became *mündig* [of age] in historical study, so that my debt has been very great. He is above eighty-two, blind in one eye, and feeble; yet as lively and quick as possible; more gentle and genial than ever in his opinions, gracious and generous and joyous, and showing me a degree of friendship and affection that I never dreamed of. . . . His powers of work for a little, funny, redfaced old man are quite extraordinary. The doctor was announced. Ranke literally clung to me with both hands, and with tears in his eyes, entreating me to stay, and tell him many things. But I knew it was time to take my leave; and we shall meet no more in this world.

Although they did not meet again, the following year the feeble Ranke, at eighty-three, surprised Acton and the world by beginning his monumental *Universal History,* which, according to Acton, "is not without traces of weakness" but which, in seventeen volumes, reached far into the Middle Ages and brought "to a close the most astonishing career in literature."[93]

In April 1864 Giuseppe Garibaldi came to London, ostensibly to thank the English for their assistance to the Italian national cause. His twelve-day visit produced a tremendous stir that was welcome to Lord Palmerston's Liberal government, not least because it distracted attention from the diplomatic and political difficulties Great Britain was facing over the Schleswig question and intervention in Poland (the Danes had invaded Schleswig only to be expelled from the province by cooperating Prussian and Austrian forces). The Italian hero was received with enormous enthusiasm by the London crowds; one hundred thousand people turned up to greet him on his arrival at Nine Elms station, Vauxhall. He was met by the Duchess of Sutherland and led in triumphal carriage procession to Stafford House (today Lancaster House), where he was staying as the Duke's guest.[94] So dense were the crowds on the three-mile route from the station that it took more than five hours to reach Stafford House. People were delirious with excitement, all wanting to shake the hero's hand, touch his clothes. "Women, more or less in full dress, flew upon him," reported *The Scotsman,* "touched his beard, his poncho, his trousers, any part of him that they could reach. . . . Would any class of people in any other country under the sun—always, of course, excepting America—conduct themselves in such an indecent manner?"[95]

Garibaldi's red shirts and blouses became fashionable, and biscuits, sweets, streets, and pubs were named after him. Queen Victoria did not approve of the adulation because of its effect abroad, especially on other European courts, and was furious that the Prince of Wales called on Garibaldi. Lord Palmerston gave the Italian hero a private dinner and also attended the banquet to which the Duke of Sutherland had invited everybody in London society. Lord Granville, leader of the House of Lords, cleverly explained to Queen Victoria that Garibaldi has

> all the qualifications for becoming a popular idol in this country. He is of low extraction, he is physically and morally brave, he is a good guerilla soldier, he has achieved great things by "dash," he has a simple manner with a sort of nautical dignity, and a pleasing smile. He has no religion, but he hates the Pope. He is a goose, but that is considered to be an absence of diplomatic guile. His mountebank dress, which betrays a desire for effect, has a certain dramatic effect. . . . His political principles, which are nearly as dangerous to the progress and maintenance of real liberty as the most despotic systems, are thought admirably applicable to foreign countries.[96]

Garibaldi dined with Palmerston and with Gladstone, then chancellor of the exchequer; he lunched with the foreign secretary, Lord Russell; met the leading members of the opposition, Lord Derby and Lord Malmesbury; visited Alfred Tennyson and Florence Nightingale; and had his portrait painted by G. F. Watts. The Marquess of Bath, the Tory chief whip in the House of Lords, was the only politician who resigned over the visit. Acton, too, had himself invited to the great Sutherland reception. "As a native Neapolitan I do not despise the destroyer of Bourbon rule as much as some," he wrote to Döllinger. "My purpose thus was curiosity, and I avoided being introduced to him."[97] But that did not save him from various rebukes, for example from his old friend Pauline Craven, who, though also a liberal Catholic, firmly drew the line when it came to fêting the advocates of the Red Revolution, such as Giuseppe Garibaldi and Giuseppe Mazzini, and told Acton so.[98]

The worst offenders in that hero cult were the great Whig ladies like the Duchess of Sutherland, who gave Garibaldi lunch at Chiswick House, receiving him royally in all her diamond splendour. The old warrior allowed himself to be entertained without being impressed. He appeared in gilded staterooms in his red flannel shirt, wearing his black hat with a red feather, and did not disguise how thoroughly bored he was by all the feasting, and especially by elderly women, whether they were duchesses or not. After the Stafford House banquet he said that he was not used to dining so late and asked for his pipe. The dowager Duchess, Acton's friend from the St. Petersburg mission (the Duke and Lord Granville were cousins), overcame her loathing for tobacco smoke and took him to that most sacred of places, her boudoir, where she lighted his pipe and heroically conversed with him until he had finished smoking.

With the general election to be due in 1865, Acton was relieved that his time at the House of Commons was coming to an end. Having tried to be both a Member of Parliament and an editor, he would now be able to shift the main thrust of his energies to Catholic journalism and to the even more congenial ground that he hoped his marriage would be.

EDITOR IN CHAINS

While struggling with the pressure to continue in politics, Acton was also looking for an opening in Catholic journalism that would enable him to combine the two ideals he had brought with him from Munich: the service of his Church and the quest for historical truth. He was well positioned. Through his maternal family links he had an easy entrée to the aristocratic elite in Italy, France, and Germany. Through his father's family he was part of the English old landed gentry that had returned to their ancestors' Catholicism. And Lord Granville, his stepfather, opened to him the inner circles of the Whig establishment, still a potent force in English public life and society. Yet Acton and Granville, never easy with one another on a personal level, saw the world of ambition and possibility in vastly different terms. An urbane man, Granville was at home in the arena of power and practicality, while Acton was drawn to the world of ideas and ideals. Moreover, Acton's Munich education colored his comprehension of English ways and means so familiar to his stepfather.

Acton's Munich was a centre of high Catholic culture where intellectuals and public leaders intermingled. In England, conditions were far more complex, especially for a Catholic. Clearly, intellectual life was relatively open in

England, but it was more fragmented in outlook; on the one hand, it was narrower—as, for instance, in the study of history—but, on the other, it spanned a broader universe. The new learning in historical studies was centered in German schools, not at Cambridge or Oxford. Still, in England at midcentury, intellectual life was becoming more secular, scientific, and egalitarian in tone, producing a kaleidoscope of voices seemingly lacking a unified theme. This was a time of quite unprecedented material and technological change. It was the age of reform bills, of the repeal of the corn laws and subsequent free trade, of unique educational university reforms. In one sense it was a bleak age, in that suddenly the effects of the Industrial Revolution were felt in the destruction of the English countryside and the towns, producing human misery and social ills but also social improvement in the form of human control over the material environment. It was the age of George Stephenson's railway, Marc Isambard Brunel's engineering advance, Joseph Lister's surgery, Humphry Davy's inventiveness, Rowland Hill's introduction of the penny postage, Florence Nightingale's hospital reforms, to say nothing of the impact made by the more familiar figures, the political leaders, great writers, artists, scholars. Seldom have so many intellectual giants appeared together: Tennyson, Darwin, Mill, Macaulay, Carlyle, Newman, Gladstone, Disraeli, Arnold, Dickens.

The principal vehicle of expression for this Victorian diversity was the journal, dominated not, as is the case today, by the academic communities, but rather by a broad spectrum of leadership in the life of the mind. W. F. Poole put it well in 1882: "The best writers and great statesmen of the world, where they formerly wrote a book or pamphlet, now contribute an article to a leading review or magazine, and it is read before the month is ended in every country in Europe. . . . Every question in literature, religion, politics, social science, political economy . . . finds its latest and freshest interpretation in the current periodicals."[1]

Acton's entry into journalism occurred at a moment of supreme sensitivity in the English Catholic community, itself in a state of unrest and transformation. The Oxford Movement added to the rich divisiveness of Old Catholics and converts, while the massive influx of Irish occasioned by the famine brought unprecedented challenges. The restoration of the English Catholic hierarchy in 1850, which occasioned an intense "no popery" reaction, was an important milestone in the Romanization of English Catholicism that characterized this period. English Catholicism had enjoyed a tradition of lay—aristocratic—supremacy in the centuries following the English Reformation. The Old Catholic landed families had provided refuge and protection for clergy and worship during the most turbulent years of the Reformation and continued to exert their influence over Catholic life well into the nineteenth century. For all those years the liturgy had remained decidedly Anglo-Saxon in expression and taste. No longer. A triumphant Rome now set about bringing the faithful within the clerical discipline and pietistic practices of the Latin aesthetic, an agenda that was reflected in the broad variety of Catholic periodical publications of the time. Moreover, those journals, which were woefully inferior in quality to the best that Victorian talent was then offering, championed the renewed authority of the Papacy and its Vatican Curia. It was precisely to remedy that situation— to elevate the intellectual tone of his co-religionists by bringing to bear the fruit of his Continental education—that Acton decided to become a journalist. Time would prove that in his youthful optimism Acton underestimated the enormity of the challenge.

Victorian earnestness and a widespread thirst for knowledge inspired the new periodical literature. "The writer had a moral duty to meet the intellectual needs of his time," commented John Morley's *Fortnightly*.[2] Gerturde Himmelfarb, surveying this particular Victorian literary achievement, emphasized its "peculiar amalgam of philosophy, history, politics and sociology that was the distinct quality of the English essay in the age of the great Reviews. They are the product of a lively, cultivated, interested and engaged mind, in which all the resources of thought are brought to bear upon any subject, and in which any subject may be made to bear the burden of truth."[3]

According to Matthew Arnold, the arbiter of Victorian criticism, "it is by communicating fresh knowledge and letting his own judgment pass along with it—but insensibly, and in the second place, not the first, as a sort of companion and clue, not as an abstract lawgiver,—that the critic will generally do much good to his readers."[4] Having considered the leading French *Revue des deux mondes,* Arnold noted with fine irony that

> our organs of criticism are organs of men and parties having practical ends to serve, and with them those practical ends are the first thing and the play of mind the second; . . . But we have the *Edinburgh Review,* existing as an organ of the old Whigs, and for as much play of the mind as may suit its being that; and we have the *Quarterly Review,* existing as an organ of the Tories, and for as much play of mind as may suit its being that; we have the *British Quarterly Review,* existing as an organ of the political Dissenters, and for as much play of mind as may suit its being that; we have *The Times,* existing as an organ of

the common, satisfied, well-to-do Englishman, and for as much play of mind as may suit its being that.[5]

These reviews governed intelligent conversation. They addressed themselves to an educated public limited in numbers, in the London clubs, in the higher civil service, in the country houses and rectories, in the universities, in Bench and Bar, among the leaders of industry, the chiefs of political parties, the members of Parliament. In the London clubs one copy of a periodical had countless readers; the readership thus tended considerably to exceed circulation figures: *Edinburgh Review,* 7,000; *Quarterly Review,* 8,000; *Westminster,* 4,000; *North British,* 2,000; *National Review,* 1,000.

The golden age of the monthlies and quarterlies extended to the weekly reviews like the *Spectator* (not that of Sir Richard Steele and Joseph Addison but a new one under the old name), the *Athenaeum,* the *Examiner,* and Walter Bagehot's *Economist.* There were also *Punch, Illustrated London News, Chambers Journal,* and as of 1855 the newly established and vigorous *Saturday Review.* The mid-Victorian press and periodicals were a factor of great social and political significance.

For a century and a half the ruling class's fear of what might happen if newspaper reading were allowed to become general had led to the imposition of a stamp tax of 1d. a sheet in 1712, which had progressively increased to 4d. a copy by 1815, and the tax was not finally abolished until 1855. There were also taxes on advertisements that remained in force until 1853 and paper duties that lasted until 1861. Besides, newspaper reading, apart from its unaffordability for the majority, was literally a dirty business owing to the blackening effect of handling these printed products.

The political purpose of the taxes was to tame the press if it could no longer be suppressed, and if all else failed, circulation should at least be confined to the "responsible" middle and upper classes where the periodicals could perhaps do no great harm. "Newspapers," said Alexis de Tocqueville, "become more necessary in proportion as men become more equal."[6] Thus five London morning papers (*Times, Morning Advertiser, Morning Chronicle, Morning Post, Morning Herald*) and four evening papers (*Sun, Globe, Express, Standard*) held the virtual monopoly at a cost of 5d. a copy. Outside London, until 1853, there was no single successful newspaper; no city except Manchester and Liverpool had even a biweekly. The rest of the country depended on small weeklies largely filled with items cut from the London dailies.

Richard Cobden, John Bright, and the working-class radicals were foremost in the long campaign for the abolition of these taxes. This campaign, according to Francis Williams, "served a great principle, the final removal of the hated taxes on knowledge, and it hit *The Times*," disliked for long holding the monopoly of the governing classes when it was a bad newspaper and, even more so, when, under great editors like Thomas Barnes (1817) and John Thaddeus Delane (1841), it became one of the most influential newspapers in the world, able to make or break political leaders and governments.[7] When, on 2 July 1855, the *Times* came out, for the first time, priced 4d. owing to the abolished penny tax, the stage was set generally for the modern popular and independent press, very much as, a century later, the computer revolution paved the way for cheaper newspapers by enabling the British press to break out of Fleet Street and the stranglehold of the printing unions.

Acton's chosen field of Catholic journalism was small. Significant as the Catholic advance was by virtue of Catholic Emancipation and the Oxford Movement, its effect on the country as a whole remained relatively insignificant. As the historian Elie Halévy observed, "The Catholics by nature or choice were something of an interior emigration, and the history of their advance cannot be considered as forming an integral part of English history."[8] Catholicism was far from penetrating the social consciousness or affecting the national way of life until the legal and social equality of Catholics was fully achieved in the second half of the twentieth century. There were actually only five Catholic journals at the time, none of which reached beyond a Catholic readership.[9]

First in seniority was the quarterly *Dublin Review,* founded in 1836 by Nicholas Wiseman, later the first Cardinal-Archbishop of Westminster, while he was still Rector of the English College at Rome, with support from Daniel O'Connell, the Irish "Liberator" and politician. But the active "makers" were Michael J. Quin, a journalist from Tipperary, and Dr. Charles Russell of Maynooth. O'Connell, Quin, and Russell were wholly Irish, Wiseman only partly Irish, but the *Dublin,* first produced in Dublin, later in London, was intended to be a rival to the formidable Whig *Edinburgh Review* and the Tory *Quarterly Review.* Wiseman's aim was to arouse the torpid English Catholic body, "old" Catholics and "new" converts, and put English Catholicism "on the map," with support from Continental Catholics whom he knew like Montalembert, Lamennais, Görres, Döllinger, Gioberti, and Rosmini, but he was unable to devote much time to what he continued to regard as his pet project. In 1863, with the review still under Wiseman's overall direction, William George Ward (1812–1882), a lay professor of theology and Oxford convert, but poles apart from Newman, took over as editor. His friend, the gentle Lord Tennyson, described him kindly as "the most generous of Ultramontanes," but that was the understatement of the age.[10] Ward was the most extreme and vituperative of Ultramontanists, the English parallel to Louis Veuillot. Edward Manning, who was to succeed Wiseman not only at Westminster but also in charge of the *Dublin,* was amply justified in his choice of Ward. He proved to be a strong editor, proud of his views opposed to all forms of liberalism, especially the liberalizing of Catholicism. Acton, the Munich school, Montalembert, and Lacordaire were his chief targets for attack. He was in favour of the *Syllabus* of 1864 (the papal condemnation of the errors of the age), a promoter of Papal Infallibility with an insatiable appetite for doctrinal definitions, famous for daily desiring an infallible Papal pronouncement on his breakfast table. He made the *Dublin* into a combative platform of narrow orthodoxy, denouncing Catholics who didn't agree with him as disloyal and heretical. There was no doubt that Newman meant Ward in his famous denunciation of "tyrannous ipsedixits" and the "aggressive and insolent faction."[11] Ward, friend to the scientist Thomas Henry Huxley and other prominent contemporaries, mellowed in later years, when he was one of the honorary secretaries of the Synthetic Society, which imitated and vied with the distinguished Metaphysical Society.

Next among Catholic weeklies came the *Tablet,* founded by Frederic Lucas in 1840 and edited by him until his untimely death in 1855. Lucas was a barrister, a cousin of John Bright, one of the leading Victorian nonconformist politicians; Lucas was also a convert from the Quakers, not, however, equipped with their pacific qualities. After a period in Dublin under Daniel O'Connell's influence, the *Tablet* returned to London, selling at 6d., an expensive purchase for its readers.[12] Loyalty to the Crown, adherence to the government of the day (Melbourne), and support for Ireland were Lucas's political principles. In regard to Ireland, where he was deeply affected by the consequences of the famine, he experienced another conversion, this time political, which won him the support of O'Connell and five hundred new subscribers. Unfortunately, Lucas was a robust polemicist, which got him into trouble with Catholic aristocrats like the wealthy Lord Shrewsbury, Bishop Wiseman, and the Irish bishops; complaints came even from the papal court concerning lack of respect towards the Holy See. Lucas's flamboyant character, style, and sense of humour were reflected in the quaint appearance of the paper, with its tiny print and the general appearance of a newspaper and, in its first year, its catering for popular interests with stories of murders and accounts of the trial of Louis Napoleon. Under its second editor, John Edward Wallis (1856–1859), the *Tablet* established a link with Conservative ideas, following Benjamin Disraeli's early dictum, modified later, that Catholics and Tories were natural allies. The *Tablet,* according to Michael Walsh, was addressed to an educated and wealthy Catholic public whose natural political stance was Tory.[13] It was acquired in 1868 by Herbert Vaughan (later Bishop of Salford and, later still, the Cardinal-Archbishop of Westminster) and became the organ of Infallibilism and strict Ultramontanism; in the late 1930s it returned to private ownership and lay editors as an internationally recognized organ of intelligent Catholic opinion.

Wallis, who had some money, improved the look of the paper and was able to pay its contributors better. His aim was to knock out the rival *Weekly Register,* edited by Henry William Wilberforce, who remained devoted to Newman. Wilberforce, the convert son of William Wilberforce, the Emancipator of the Slaves, had acquired the *Catholic Standard* in 1849, when Lucas transferred the *Tablet* to Dublin. Wilberforce then reissued it in amalgamated form as the *Weekly Register and Catholic Standard,* running it until 1863. It was later acquired by Cardinal Manning, who gave it to his admirer and follower Wilfrid Meynell to edit and operate as a rival to the *Tablet*. Wilberforce had published Acton's first articles. But although the *Weekly Register* was useful to Acton in providing an outlet for his views as an MP, he was not happy with Wilberforce, who seemed to interfere too much with his contributors' copy and to have the convert's exaggerated subservience to cardinal and clergy. Wilberforce was especially reluctant to publish original (that is, Actonian) views that might not agree with the ghetto mentality that remained after the Catholics' only recent emergence from centuries of oppression.

In 1860, belatedly taking account of the abolition of the penny tax, the *Universe* entered the popular Catholic market as a penny paper. It was backed by Cardinals Wiseman and Manning. Inspired by Louis Veuillot's *L'univers,* the *Universe* became a cheerleader for the papal cause, courting the popular audience by banning, for example, "intellectual" book reviews.

This left, as far as Acton was concerned, the *Rambler* as "sole mouthpiece of the more sensible views."[14] The *Rambler* was founded in 1848 by John Moore Capes, a Balliol convert, as an organ for the lay converts.[15] Its motto *In necessariis unitas, in dubiis libertas, in omnibus caritas* (In important matters unity, in doubtful matters liberty, in everything charity), originally coined by the seventeenth-century German Lutheran theologian Peter Meiderlin, conveyed the right kind of topical emphasis. The paper was started as a weekly, became a monthly, and then, in 1858, when Acton joined it as co-editor, a bimonthly. It ended its sixteen-year existence as a quarterly under the title *Home and Foreign Review*.

Under Acton's editorship, the *Rambler* became one of the outstanding periodicals of the nineteenth century—independent, critical, and of high intellectual calibre. Richard Simpson, a rebellious convert then in his forties, played a large part in its development. Simpson was an admirer of John Henry Newman and John Keble from Oriel College, Oxford. When, in 1846, he and his wife became Catholics, he had to resign the valuable living as Vicar of Mitcham. Simpson had contributed spirited articles to the *Rambler* from 1850, became assistant editor in 1854, and took on an increasing share of the editorial work in 1856 when Capes, who was having qualms about his conversion, gradually withdrew. That year a series of articles by Simpson on Original Sin caused offence, and a committee of theologians was appointed to look into them. It was to prove a recurrent problem. The brilliant Simpson could not help being provocative: he had an impish spirit and was the born enfant terrible, particularly where, as in theological matters, it was least wanted.

Acton's friendship with Simpson sprang from an intellectual and political affinity. They respected each other's talents. Simpson admired Acton's learning and integrity, and Acton could not have done without Simpson's support and application. Simpson shouldered many of the day-to-day editorial burdens. He "is brilliant and has much energy," wrote Acton, "but little general knowledge. He has always studied only to write particular articles, but lacks prudence and a general view of world affairs. But he is very much our main man." [16] With Simpson, Acton was able to relax, and that was more than he could do with the many he came to describe as his friends. After one of his frequent trips to Aldenham, Simpson wrote to his wife: "Acton and I spent yesterday afternoon, first in fishing, then in mud-larking, like babes in a brook—damming up first one stream, and opening another, he working with a rotten stick, and I with a stop horn I picked up on the park. I think my visit will do me good." [17] Their innocent pastime seemed symbolic of the opening and damming up that they would later undertake in the realm of Catholic journals.

When Acton embarked on his editorship, Newman was just emerging from the defeat that his Irish Catholic University scheme had suffered from the ecclesiastical authorities. Newman was sympathetic to Acton, but more prudent and less confrontational. No doubt the clergy-layman differences loomed large in all of this, as they also played a part in the rift that later opened up between Döllinger and his pupil.

Acton agreed with Newman's conviction, basic to his Dublin University discourses, of the wholeness of intellectual knowledge and truth. Religion and knowledge were not opposed to each other, contrary to the prevailing view of their age, which held that one or the other was likely to be either disproved or at least proved irrelevant. Newman and Acton felt that those who, like Catholics, had an absolute faith in revelation need not be nervous or frightened at every new scientific discovery.[18] The Church "fears no knowledge," Newman wrote, "for all branches of knowledge are connected together because the subject-matter of knowledge is intimately united in itself, as being the acts and work of the Creator."[19] That was Newman's message and challenge to all those "of little faith," be they in secular or religious folds.

The *Rambler* wanted to raise the intellectual level of English Catholics by introducing the methods and thought patterns of the new German historical scholarship. But the English Catholic bishops, largely products of a sheltered seminary education, did not believe in a reconciliation with the increasingly godless tenets of the modern world. Their one concern was to protect priests and laity from its dangers, real or suspected, and because elementary schooling was of major importance in the growing Catholic body, Newman's ideas for Catholic higher education, no less than Döllinger's, were regarded as a dispensable luxury at a time of more basic educational needs.

Acton saw the role of the *Rambler* and the *Home and Foreign Review* as somewhat parallel to Newman's efforts to bring Catholics to Oxford, thirty years before they were allowed by their bishops to go there. Like Döllinger, Acton shared Newman's vision of an educated laity, devoted to intellectual free enquiry. Acton was also aware of the pressure exercised by fellow Oratorians like John Dalgairns and Frederick William Faber, who were opposed to seeing the new German theological influence spread in England via Acton. "Of course there is war to the knife between the Bromptoratory and all theology pursued by the German method, independently of conclusions," Acton wrote to Simpson. "Dalgairns said that all Germans struck him as having something wrong about them. So I told him in my answer that 'I hoped his bad opinion would not prevent him from studying them, which would probably diminish the severity of his judgment, and would materially add to its weight.'"[20] That was not likely to appease.

Surveying the English scene, Acton found it depressingly characterized by the hatred and endless controversies of Gallicans and Jansenists and felt no reason to be sanguine about finding support and respect for his ideas among the English Catholics.[21] Even the new and educated Anglican converts generated opposition, as Acton found to his surprise. The issue in question was a public school for boys that, under Newman's aegis and with the convert and Oratorian priest Nicholas Darnell as first headmaster, was opened at the Birmingham Oratory in May 1859. The idea for its foundation actually came from the *Rambler*, which had criticized the existing Catholic school system as inadequate and demanded a school modeled after the English public school. If the new school turned out to be successful, it might eventually become separated from the seminary education of Oratorians and necessitate the building up of an English Catholic University for the laity.

Acton was involved with Serjeant Edward Bellasis, the convert and close supporter of Newman's, in the negotiation of this scheme.[22] Acton hoped that the project might, in some way, be connected with the great library he was accumulating at Aldenham. He had offered Newman a piece of land for buildings at Bridgnorth and a house at Morville, part of the Aldenham property, where he wanted to make fifteen rooms available as a centre for studies comparable to Dr. Döllinger's in Munich. Acton had ideas for a Catholic University in England to be linked with Newman's Edgbaston school and, as it would be near Oxford, to profit from Oxford's increasing liberality towards Catholicism. He tried to enlist Peter le Page Renouf, the Egyptologist, who had joined Newman's University scheme in Dublin and had to find a new opening when it came to an end, continuing as a contributor to Newman's *Atlantis* and to Acton's *Rambler*, whose editorial board he joined shortly before it ceased publication.[23]

Regarding the wisdom or even the possibility of an English Catholic University, Renouf expressed his doubts. It was more desirable, he considered, for the old universities to allow Catholic halls or colleges to exist on equal terms with Anglican. Acton, however, with his German experience and unfamiliar with the tutorial system at Oxford and Cambridge, had a "pleasing dream," as he called it, "which I shall not willingly give up, for I have always trusted to the professorial system to make Catholic students some day superior to Oxford and Cambridge men—at which, of course, all my Oxford friends laugh."[24]

While this exchange of views about a Catholic college continued, the Catholic bishops meeting at Oscott spoke much of the plan for Catholic colleges at Oxford, condemned it as a surrender of the principle of denominational education, then consulted Rome, with the result that the bishops' view prevailed.

On educational matters, moreover, Acton and Newman were confronted also by "Bromptoratory" opposition, motivated by fears that the Edgbaston Catholic school run by converts would have inadequate discipline. Even Newman's bishop, William Bernard Ullathorne, initially in favour of the project, was influenced by Wiseman and Faber and by dark hints about "goings on in Dublin," as though a university and a boys' school were comparable to each other as far as discipline was concerned.[25] After the trouble caused him by the University scheme, the Oratory school, and another abortive project, the translation of the Bible in cooperation with Archbishop Francis Patrick Kenrick of Baltimore, Newman entered a phase of depression and despondency in regard to his new co-religionists. To his private spiritual journal, he confided these bitter thoughts:

> Jany 8. 1860
>   . . . I am nobody. I have no friend at Rome. I have laboured in England, to be misrepresented, backbitten, and scorned. I have laboured in Ireland, with a door ever shut in my face. I seem to have had many failures, and what I did well was not understood. I do not think I am saying this in any bitterness.
>   "Not understood"—this is the point. . . .
>   . . . O my God, I seem to have wasted these years that I have been a Catholic. What I wrote as a Protestant had far greater power, force, meaning, success, than my Catholic works—& this troubles me a great deal—though it is a fresh subject, on which I cannot enter now.

> Jany 21. 1863
>   . . . O how forlorn & dreary has been my course since I have been a Catholic! here has been the contrast—as a Protestant, I felt my religion dreary, but not my life—but as a Catholic, my life dreary, not my religion. . . .
>   . . . Persons who would naturally look towards me, converts who would naturally come to me, inquirers who would naturally consult me, are stopped by some light or unkind word said against me. I am passé, in decay, I am untrustworthy; I am strange, odd; I have my own ways & cannot get on with others; something or other is said in disparagement. . . . I shrink from a society which is so unjust towards me. I must say, that the converts have behaved to *me* much worse than old Catholics, when they might have had a little gratitude, to say the least.[26]

Similarly discouraged, Acton wrote to Döllinger, "I am here so alone in my ideas and convictions that I want to test them sometimes against your judgement. Here I have no one with whom I can communicate or who could put me right."[27] But encouraged by his rapport with Simpson, Acton threw himself into *Rambler* work. From July 1858 the *Rambler* made a new start. Despite his trouble with Cardinal Wiseman, Simpson was to remain responsible for the actual editorial running, with history as his special field, a responsibility that would allow him to continue his work on English Reformation martyrs like Edmund Campion. Acton took over politics. That would give him practice in writing and becoming familiar with political questions that, as he told Döllinger, would be useful for him. "It will give me a position and an influence among Catholics which I hope to use well, and which must be of great advantage to me." He would also use his knowledge of persons abroad to improve the *Rambler*'s foreign affairs compared to other journals. "Above all I embraced this chance of obtaining for your ideas and judgments an organ in England, and I trusted that you would allow me constantly to appeal to you for direction and advice."[28]

The *Rambler*'s philosophy section was to be looked after by Charles Meynell (1828–1882), Acton's fellow-pupil at Oscott who, after being ordained, was appointed professor of philosophy there. "He has written some good essays on philosophy and has more talent and energy than actual knowledge," wrote Acton to Döllinger.[29] The Irish priest and writer Dr. Charles William Russell (1812–1880), with whom Acton was friendly, was also to be made use of. Russell, who taught Church history at Maynooth College, the Irish seminary, was liked at Oxford, where he exerted some influence on the Tractarian Anglicans. He temporarily edited, with Cardinal Wiseman, the *Dublin Review,* and that association, Acton hoped, would diminish antagonism from that quarter.

Then there was the theology section. Oddly, Simpson wanted control to be given to William George Ward, who was to become one of Acton's chief opponents. Fortunately Ward declined, saying he wanted to concentrate on the preparation of his lectures as professor of dogmatics at St. Edmund's College, to which position Cardinal Wiseman had appointed him. In Ward's place, Simpson wanted the Catholic theologian Dr. William Gowan Todd (1827–1877), who, to Acton, seemed "a very unlikely person to infuse into English theology the new blood that it requires," and he cited Todd's "dictum" that Ward was, next to Carlo Passaglia, "the most learned divine in Europe." Acton managed to talk Simpson out of his idea to have a theologian at all. Thus Acton could have "things much more my own way."[30]

Ward had peculiar ideas about the "unspirituality" of the English Roman

Catholic priesthood: "If we are to remain the godless body which we are, I hope we may also remain the ignorant, uncivilised, disunited, intellectually contemptible body that we are," he wrote.[31] As far as Acton was concerned, they were well rid of that "dangerous firebrand": "Our clergy have other deficiencies besides a want of spirituality, and not less needing correction."[32] He could do without Ward's paradox about the necessity of ignorance.

Ward's refusal actually stemmed from the anxiety that both he and Cardinal Wiseman felt about "ecclesiastical liberalism," which they saw spreading among English Catholics, from Montalembert and Lacordaire in France, and from Döllinger in Germany. "Great is the evil," Ward wrote, if the Church possess "no children who can defend her cause with fully adequate intellectual power. But then there is another evil possible and greater still, namely, that her nominal children may assail her cause with fully adequate intellectual power."[33] And Simpson and Acton were suspected to be such assailants. At Cardinal Wiseman's request, Ward contributed articles to the *Dublin Review,* and, as editor from 1863, Ward wanted to rescue that moribund journal that Wiseman had founded in 1836 as the herald of the English Catholic "Second Spring." Its new task was to combat the *Rambler*'s liberalism, and it became the organ of extreme Ultramontane Catholicism.

Cardinal Wiseman expressed—outwardly—satisfaction with the new *Rambler* plans and told Acton that he hoped there would be less trouble now that Acton had joined the journal.[34] Acton was actually negotiating with Wiseman, in the summer of 1858, to associate the *Dublin Review* and the *Rambler* under one publisher, Burns, but under separate control—one to continue as a quarterly, edited by Acton, the other as a monthly, run by Simpson. But this scheme came to nothing because the Cardinal, as Acton suspected, really wanted to separate him from the *Rambler* in order to crush it more easily, while the bishops wanted "tacit" censorship. "I want neither," he wrote to Döllinger, "and expect a hard struggle. Only literary excellence and good taste in contributions can serve us. . . . All I need is support. Simpson will be co-editor. . . . Unfortunately he has a bad reputation as a mad fellow. It is my task to keep him quiet."[35]

Early in September 1858 Dr. Döllinger came to Aldenham—it was his third visit to England—and took part in an editorial conference of *Rambler* associates: John Acton, Richard Simpson, Richard Macmullen, John Moore Capes, and T. W. Allies. Newman was unable to come, although Acton urged him twice.[36] It had become known that Capes was undergoing a crisis of conscience about his conversion; indeed, he returned to the Church of England and later published a book titled *To Rome and Back* (1873), but he died reconciled with the Catholic Church.

The Capes affair was the cause of some wild rumours probably started by Acton's chaplain, Jack Morris. Morris had told his friend Faber about "goings-on" at Aldenham and, on Faber's advice, pointedly told everyone that he had never been consulted by the *Rambler* people. It was said that a number of converts were plotting at Aldenham, half of them determined to apostatize, the others to remain in the Church and, as Catholics in appearance only, to damage it further through the pages of the *Rambler*. Cardinal Wiseman himself made various enquiries as to who had taken part in the Aldenham meeting, particularly whether Newman had been there.[37] Wiseman had been told by the indefatigable Mgr. Talbot in Rome that the purpose of the meeting was to attack the hierarchy. Certain people, Newman wrote, were "looking at everything I do in the way of theology," so that he was in constant danger of being "whispered about at Rome," where he knew he had no friends (apart from the Pope).[38] "Summa," as Acton reported. "Faber, now wholly against Newman, has won over the cardinal, the weak duke of Norfolk, bishop Errington. Also against Newman in the issue of school and Catholic University are many old Catholics and most of the Irish bishops, especially [Cardinal Paul] Cullen. Loyal friends are almost only his Oratorians and not even all the English ones, professors in Dublin, Manning, Hope and Badeley. [Henry] Wilberforce resides too much in the shadow of the London [Faber] Oratory, Hope believes in the possibility of a reconciliation which I consider quite impossible."[39]

In the situation thus outlined Acton hoped that the *Rambler* "could do good, particularly in leading people back from such personal dissensions to important questions. Our public we shall first have to create: I fear hostility from outside less than inner disunity."[40] Even that assessment proved wildly optimistic. Acton suggested to Simpson that he, Acton, should be paid for his contributions on the understanding that he would use this money for extending the foreign coverage of the *Rambler*. Acton wanted, above all, to recruit distinguished political writers. The weakness of British journals, he felt, was their limited knowledge of the outside world. There was a noticeable lack of a true Catholic view of public affairs and a true constitutional doctrine, he wrote to Simpson. What he meant by that was Edmund Burke's "Catholic view of political principles and of history."[41]

The circulation of the *Rambler* was always small, about 750, certainly not more than 1,000.[42] It cost three shillings, and contributors received payments of two guineas per thousand words. The general tone of the review was heavy. Victorian readers were used to that. But the English Catholic climate was not conducive to the exchange of free ideas regardless of where they might lead, which was Acton's Germanic message. After three centuries of persecution and victimization by lies and calumnies, Catholics found it difficult to become disinterested and coolly objective defenders of their faith. The very motto of Acton's *Rambler* was seen as provocative: *Seu vetus est verum diligo, sive novum* (I value truth whether it is old or new).

As Simpson was inclined to be overawed by fellow converts like Ward and Faber as "formed theologians," as he called them, and they in their turn looked down on the "bumptious" *Rambler* editors, Acton felt compelled to explain his purpose more clearly to his friend. After his own three-year Munich course of theology—which Döllinger had made a part of his studies—Acton admitted he had not exhausted any subject, nor was he an authority on any question. "Yet I know very well the method on which it is necessary to proceed, and can at once detect a writer who even with immense readings of theologians, is but a dilettante in theology." The "Bromptorians"—Faber, Morris, Ward, Dalgairns—belonged, he said, in that latter category. "They have all got a *regia via* which leads them astray, and for scientific purposes all their labour is wasted. It is this absence of scientific method, and of original learning in nearly all our best writers, that makes it impossible for me to be really interested in their writings." He was prepared to exempt Newman from dilettantism on account of an essay on St. Cyril, "which on a minute point was original and progressive, was a bit of *theology*" and accorded with his own norms learned in Munich and described by the Germans as "quellenmässig [*ex ipsissimus fontibus*—according to the best sources or authorities] and . . . Wissenschaftlichkeit [scientific or scholarly method]." And he concluded with what he described as "my profession of faith": "You want things to be brought to bear, to have an effect. I think our studies ought to be all but purposeless. They want to be pursued with chastity, like mathematics. . . . And it is on this ground that I shall say when we are condemned Eppur si muove ['But it does move'], for we shall be condemned on what the same Germans would call a subordinate standpoint."[43]

Acton felt he was waging a double contest both "with those who are of little faith and with those who have none at all—with those who for the sake of religion fear science, and with the followers of science who despise religion." Fighting on both fronts weakened and was the cause of much "scandal and vexation in the Church. The devil must be equally gratified with the zeal of either party; for they equally serve his purpose, by confirming the fatal notion of the incompatibility of faith and reason." He wrote this in his article "The Catholic Press," an example of the young editor in his idealist phase, with a gift for writing purple passages. "The common reluctance on the part of Catholics to consent to the results of science indicates as much a defect of faith as of knowledge," he maintained. Writing in the midst of the age that had begun to reverse the former biased accounts of the Reformation, he claimed that "all the lies of the Protestants of the sixteenth century are being rapidly refuted by their descendants of the nineteenth. . . . A really scientifically learned work, written without any religious interest, helps the truth in spite of its author; whilst a superficial apology will do little or no good, and probably some harm, in spite of the zeal and good intention with which it is written." Acton ended pointedly with the story Cardinal Robert Bellarmine told in his autobiography—how Pope Sixtus V, after applauding his learning, had put Bellarmine's work on the Index. "The edition of the Vulgate that Sixtus V had prepared, was found after his death to be so full of faults that some were for prohibiting it altogether. But, in order to save his memory from the indignity, Bellarmine undertook to correct it himself; showing how little he was moved by the intemperate attack of which he had been the object."[44]

But among the English Catholics there was little inclination for intellectual generosity. In the June 1858 *Rambler,* J. M. Capes had expressed the notion that Jansenism was "Augustinian."[45] That equation would cause little upset to twentieth-century Roman Catholics, used to the novels of Graham Greene and the repressive effects of the Augustinian-Jansenist attitudes towards marriage and sex. But when Acton, in a book review arguing for openness in Catholic historical study, reemphasized the point in passing, there was a wild outcry. All he had said was: "Nor because St. Augustine was the greatest doctor of the West, need we conceal the fact that he was also the father of Jansenism."[46] Cardinal Wiseman placed the passage before an investigating committee of ten theologians.

Charles Meynell, the philosophy editor, wrote to Acton: "You startled us by saying St. Augustine was the Father of Jansenism—you put your hand into the lion's mouth—Why didn't you put the glove on? You did not put the glove on Sir, but you thrust your fist straight down the throat of the infuriated monster—your naked fist—without glove!" But putting gloves on was not Acton's way, nor could Simpson be induced, as Meynell put it in the same letter, graciously to "triumph and not crow."[47] Dr. Döllinger added to the uproar with an unsigned letter (translated by Acton) on the paternity of Jansenism. St. Augustine could not be accused of fathering Jansenism, he wrote, in the sense that Martin Luther fathered Lutheranism, but there was no doubt that he had exceeded the teaching of the Church in a sense in which it was later taken up by Jansenism. The appellation "Augustine—Father of Jansenism" was therefore justified.[48] This letter caused a stir, and Acton kept the pot on the boil by sending the letter to all the Catholic bishops, colleges, and priests he knew to be interested.[49]

In their correspondence Acton and Simpson discussed a prefatory note recommending Döllinger's letter to *Rambler* readers, describing it as "some consolation for those who have at heart the reputation of English theology to know that not a single divine whose opinion deserved attention mistook or disliked the passage" (in the end, the controversial passage was omitted). "Newman thoroughly approved of it, and was the only person in England who did. Faber was very wrathful, and [J. B.] Morris [Acton's chaplain] is miserable about it. I feel almost certain that not a convert will be made by Döllinger's admirable paper."[50]

The *Weekly Register* for 12 December published two letters against the *Rambler* and Döllinger's letter, which was delated by Faber to Cardinal Wiseman, who denounced it to the Index in Rome, where, however, no further action was taken. This was the background of the significant three-hour meeting Acton had with Newman, "the venerable Noggs," as he called him.[51] Newman

came out at last with his real sentiments to an extent which startled me, with respect both to things and persons, as HE [His Eminence], Ward, Dalgairns etc. etc., natural inclination of men in power to tyrannize, ignorance and presumption of our would-be theologians, in short what you and I would comfortably say over a glass of whiskey. I did not think he could ever cast aside his diplomacy and buttonment so entirely, and was quite surprised at the intense interest he betrayed in the Rambler. He was quite miserable when I told him the news, and moaned for a long time rocking himself backwards and forwards over the fire, like an old woman with a toothache.[52]

Nevertheless Newman advised that the *Rambler* should keep away from theology. He wrote to Acton that it should aim at escaping the displeasure of ecclesiastical superiors without prejudicing the promotion or the good ends of the journal: "Let it be instructive, clever, and amusing. Let it cultivate a general temper of good humour and courtesy. Let it praise as many persons as it can, and gain friends in neutral quarters. . . . Then it will be able to plant a good blow at a fitting time with great effect."[53] But Acton was against the idea of the *Rambler*'s complete secularization, its confinement to historical and political articles, because that would destroy it as an organ of Catholic thought. He wanted to enlarge rather than restrict the range of the review.

In fact, Newman, too, found it difficult to practise what he preached. In April 1859, he took over the editing of two issues of the *Rambler* in order to soothe the Catholic authorities incensed by Simpson and Acton. "He is in great spirits at having the Rambler, although he bitterly complains of his old age, and of the time he is going to devote to it. But he throws himself into it vigorously, and has large plans."[54] However, when Newman's famous article "On Consulting the Faithful in Matters of Doctrine" was published in the July issue, this caused worse offence in theological terms than anything that had gone before.[55]

Newman, anticipating criticism, had defended his use of the word *consulting*. In ordinary English, Newman wrote, the word "includes the idea of inquiring into a matter of *fact,* as well as asking a judgment. A physician consults the pulse of his patient; but not in the same sense in which his patient consults *him*."[56] It is in the first sense that the Church "consults," "regards," the faith of the laity before defining a doctrine "because the body of the faithful is one of the witnesses of the fact of the tradition of revealed doctrine, and because their *consensus* through Christendom is the voice of the Infallible Church." While the hierarchy has sole responsibility for "discerning, discriminating, defining, promulgating, and enforcing any portion of that tradition" that the Apostles committed to the Church, it "manifests itself variously at various times."[57]

Newman then cites the celebrated historical example from the Early Church during the Arian heresy of the fourth century. "In that time of immense confusion the divine dogma of our Lord's divinity was proclaimed, enforced, maintained and (humanly speaking) preserved, far more by the 'Ecclesia docta' than the 'Ecclesia docens.' . . . The body of the episcopate was unfaithful to its commission, while the body of the laity was faithful to its baptism." And Newman concluded boldly: "I think certainly that the *Ecclesia docens* is more happy when she has such enthusiastic partisans about her . . . than when she cuts off the faithful from the study of her divine doctrines and the sympathy of her divine contemplations, and requires from them a *fides implicita* in her word, which in the educated classes will terminate in indifference, and in the poorer in superstition."[58]

This very passage formed the basis of the delation to Rome of Newman's article as "totally subversive of the essential authority of the Church in matters of faith" by Bishop Thomas Joseph Brown of Menevia.[59] He had consulted Cardinal Wiseman; Newman's bishop, Ullathorne; and Manning. Bishop Ullathorne, too, objected to Newman's English and interpreted the faith of the laity as a "reflection" of the teaching of the Church, which drew from Newman the ironical comment: "Reflection; that is, the people are a mirror, in which the Bishops see themselves. Well, I suppose a person may *consult* his glass, and in that may know things about himself which he can learn in no other way."[60] The fact that Newman retracted the word *consult* and, indeed, withdrew the offending essay from the edition of his works published in his lifetime, made no difference to his reputation in Rome.[61] The essay was "the chief cause of our Bishop's dissatisfaction with me,"[62] but this was increased by what he wrote in the July *Rambler* in "The Mission of the Isles of the North." The *Tablet* took him to task for criticizing the current Catholic biographies of saints. "I take but a secondary interest in books which chop up a saint into chapters of faith, hope, charity and the cardinal virtues. . . . They do not manifest a saint, they mince him into spiritual lessons."[63]

Newman's trials at the hands of the English bishops and the Roman authorities caused the following outburst to his friend and penitent Emily Bowles: "This country is under Propaganda, and Propaganda is too shallow to have the wish to use such as me. . . . If I know myself, no one can have been more loyal to the Holy See than I am. I love the Pope personally into the bargain. But Propaganda is a quasi-military power, extraordinary, for missionary countries, rough and ready. It does not understand an intellectual movement. It likes quick results—scalps from beaten foes by the hundred." And referring to his offending *Rambler* article, he went on:

> What did Propaganda know of the niceties of the English language? Yet a message came (not a formal one) asking explanations, and on the other hand, dangling before my eyes the vision of a Bishoprick, if I explained well. It seems they fancied that I was soured because a Bishoprick was to be given me in 1854 (six years before) and Dr. Cullen had stopped it. How little they knew of me! but I suppose they have to deal with low minded men. As what was said to me was very indirect and required no answer, I kept silence and the whole matter was hushed up. I suppose so—for I have heard no more of it—but I suppose it might (*pel bisogno*) be revived at any time. Don't you see that this, if nothing else, puts a great obex to my writing? This age of the

Church is peculiar—in former times, primitive and medieval, there was not the extreme centralisation which now is in use. If a private theologian said any thing free, another answered him. If the controversy grew, then it went to a Bishop, a theological faculty, or to some foreign University. The Holy See was not but the court of last appeal. *Now,* if I, as a private priest, put any thing into print, *Propaganda* answers me at once. How can I fight with such a chain on my arm? It is like the Persians driven on to fight *under the lash*.[64]

A hundred years later, the teaching of Newman's article "On Consulting the Faithful in Matters of Doctrine" was solemnly expounded in the decrees of the Second Vatican Council.

It was, however, the Italian events concerning the temporal power of the Papacy that ultimately sealed the fate of the *Rambler*. By 1860 Pius IX had lost all his dominions except the patrimony of St. Peter. Catholics everywhere were rallying to the Pope's support, many speaking as though the temporal power were of the essence of the Papacy. This was not Acton's view, nor Newman's. But the first publicly to speak out was Döllinger. In April 1861 he delivered a series of lectures at the Odeon Hall in Munich that made a sensational impact. The temporal power, he said, was not essential to the Church but an historical accident. It had begun late in the history of the Church and was then something quite different from what it afterwards became. If the temporal power was destroyed at the present time, it should be restored. But Catholics need not despair over its disappearance, nor should Protestants rejoice. The Church would continue without it. Indeed, it had become an oppressive burden. But when Döllinger referred to the Italian situation and the abuses in the Papal States, the audience grew restless and the papal nuncio, Prince Flavio Chigi, rose and left in protest.

Döllinger was hailed all over the world by liberal and anti-Catholic elements, and equally vehemently attacked by Ultramontane Catholics for stabbing the Pope in the back and sowing dissension in the Church. In fact, Döllinger defended Pius IX against the charges that the abuses in the Papal States were due to him, saying that he personally had done his best to achieve reform, but his effort went unheeded in the general clamour. Reading these lectures today, one can hardly understand the furore they caused. What Döllinger said is today accepted by the whole Catholic world. His facts—how the temporal power and the Pope's power to depose kings and princes had grown in history—were incontrovertible. But he could not have chosen a worse moment to express them.[65]

This was also the turning point in Acton's attitude towards Newman. Common interest and work for the *Rambler* had increased the spell Newman cast on him. At night in Aldenham he read Newman's sermons to his friends. After a visit to Birmingham to see "my dear friend Newman," he movingly described a service of the Stations of the Cross that Newman conducted: "The dark church was full; many protestants were there, but not a sound was to be heard but the beautiful voice of the great preacher, praying in the midst and in the name of the people. Nothing could exceed the touching simplicity of his discourse."[66]

Newman, however, soon joined the many former idols of the young Acton who, having been "found out," were totally rejected. The numerous entries in Acton's index cards (now at Cambridge) concerned with Newman, illustrate this process of disillusionment, although, unfortunately, the lack of dates makes it difficult to establish a time sequence. "Newman came over for the sake of the Pope. That was his purpose and reward."[67] This was one of the later entries, when their divergences came to a head over Infallibility. Newman was clearly in favour of Infallibility, yet thought the dogma inopportune. Acton was suspicious of Newman's strong feelings for authority: because he regarded history as insufficient, authority was needed. "Without a supreme authority, sceptics win," was Acton's interpretation of Newman's position. "The Church most given to authority is the true Church."[68]

Acton quoted from Newman's *Apologia:* "There are but two alternatives—the way to Rome and the way to atheism: Anglicanism is the halfway house on the one side, and liberalism is the halfway house on the other."[69] And he noted that, while Newman's opposition to liberalism was the key to almost all his life, he objected to political even more than to religious liberalism. Catholic emancipation had been achieved, in 1829, by political liberalism and was therefore disliked by Newman, as he came to object to Home Rule for Ireland because of its Liberal and Gladstonian connotation.[70] With glee Acton published an article by his friend Baron Ferdinand d'Eckstein, critical of Napoleon III whom Newman favoured, although the latter might have retorted that the young pro-Austrian Acton had his Tory leanings, too, in foreign affairs despite his Whig-gism in home politics: "Austria is the only continental state with which I have any sympathy," he told Simpson.[71]

Acton was also becoming aware of the temperamental and philosophical incompatibility between Newman and Döllinger despite their outward signs of friendship. In Acton's words, Newman "sometimes agreed with Doellinger in the letter but not in the spirit, and distrusted him as a man in whom the priest lived at the mercy of the scholar," and further, that "the burden of unnecessary learning weighed on the point and the play of his mind."[72] No date is attached to this observation, but it links with the remark Newman made after Döllinger, accompanied by Acton, then seventeen years old, had visited him at Birmingham in 1851: "It was like a dog and a fish trying to make friends."[73] Presumably Newman cast himself in the role of the fish and Döllinger in that of the tail-wagging dog. Döllinger held Newman in highest regard among all his English contemporaries, above all "because of Newman's constant opposition to liberalism and his constant respect for authority."[74]

The gulf between Döllinger and Newman was probably due mainly to Newman's English insularity and instinctive rejection of what, not least under the pressure of his fellow converts and Oratorians like Faber, was "the enemy" —that is, German (religious) liberalism, by which, in fact, Döllinger was untainted. However, Döllinger liked, especially in his earlier life, to be regarded as "liberal" when he was close to French Catholic liberals like Montalembert, and he also assumed a temporary liberal political aura in the heady days of the Frankfurt Parliament of 1848 and the young German democratic movement. But Newman's Toryism basically appealed to Döllinger. What he could not understand—in spite of his anglophile outlook and profound understanding of the English character and of British history, literature, and especially its religious history—was the complicated mixture of puritan, Evangelical, and Catholic elements, the strange disposition for the Italianate moral theology and casuistry of St. Alphonsus, which constituted Newman's religiosity. And Döllinger was quite unable to come to grips with Newman's fresh and revolutionary mind, which made him a poet and mystic rather than a reasoning philosopher or trained theologian.

"Ignorance of later history, as you always say [after that of the Early Church up to the Arian controversy] explains much of Newman," Acton wrote to Döllinger. "At heart he is against Rome, but is unable to clarify the evidence for himself."[75] Newman lacked Döllinger's intellectual curiosity and passion for knowledge, the urgent sense of letting the chips fall where they may. He knew little of European philosophy, hardly any Plato, and little more of Aristotle than what the Oxford of his time studied—for instance, the *Metaphysics*. Newman's very Englishness—he was basically a man of sentiment, not, as was Döllinger, a man of science, used always to verifying his knowledge—foxed the German, as it was later to turn Acton, too, against Newman. Sir Rowland Blennerhassett reported to Acton Newman's way of coming to terms with the dogma of Papal

Infallibility, which he had previously opposed. Only someone like Döllinger, who always believed the best in people, could assume that Newman sincerely believed what he said.[76] And Döllinger "understood prejudice, but not precaution. He had no idea of hedging."[77] Newman's precaution, indeed his silence, enabled him to complete his perilous voyage in the barque of St. Peter and emerge ultimately so triumphant, while Döllinger was to be shipwrecked in it.

In the end, after Newman's death, there was Acton's famous observation made in a letter to Gladstone: "You know that in this instance I am forced to use the ambiguous word *great* as I should in speaking of Napoleon or Bismarck, Hegel or Renan. But I should quarrel with every friend I have, in almost every camp or group, if I said all I know, or half of what I think, of that splendid Sophist."[78] And six years later to the same: "Some day I shall say to a pupil: . . . Read Newman; he is by far the best writer the Church of Rome has had in England since the Reformation. And the pupil will come back and say: But do you think his arguments sound, or his religion Catholic? And I shall have to say: No; if you work it out, it is a school of Infidelity."[79] This opinion did not, however, prevent Acton from giving his daughter Annie the complete edition of Newman's works as a Christmas present in 1895.[80]

That Acton admired Newman as one of the greatest minds of his age gave his criticism its special, almost obsessive note. And one looks for hidden meaning in one of Acton's cards: "D never felt that he lived in a very grotesque company of professing Xians!"[81] He registered that Newman had passed on to him, with seeming approval, the remark of a Dominican who, after reading one of Simpson's articles, said that "he would like to have the burning of the Author."[82] Whether or not this was meant light-heartedly, for Acton it was not a joking matter.

When, years later, in his dispute with Döllinger, Acton tried to account for his intellectual development as relying on great minds rather than on his own research, he singled out Joseph de Maistre and Newman as two of the most brilliant outward defenders of religion who came to appear to him as "advocates of deceit and murder." And he emphasized that they were to be placed far above the common herd, that they were not "incapable men, victims of a bad training, or a narrow sphere, or a backward age. I am thinking of men with whom I should not venture for an instant to compare myself, in knowledge, or talent, or yet greater gifts of God." While common writers could deceive nobody, the clever writer deceives without a downright lie, and he "seems to me much the worse of the two. De Maistre says, no priest ever sent a heretic to death. Newman says, no heretic was ever put to death in Rome, excepting one mentioned in the life of St. Philip [Neri], an exception that proves the rule. Here is the brutal liar, and the artful deceiver, who seems so scrupulous, and certainly does his work, the devil's work, best."[83]

In 1861 Acton wrote in the *Rambler* of the realization among Italian priests that the temporal power was in fact harming the Church. And he went on, in his veiled manner, to suggest: "England is no exception to the rule, that where the greatest sanctity and the greatest wisdom are united, there is a belief that the revolution which has overthrown the temporal power has been directly a blessing to the Church."[84] The reference was to Newman, who had voiced these sentiments privately. In a letter to Acton he had remarked that people wished him to speak out on the other side and to maintain the temporal power. "Accordingly I think I fulfil my duty in keeping silence. . . . The very fact that I do not repudiate the sentiment ascribed to me there [in the *Rambler*], is in some measure avowing that sentiment myself."[85]

The response only confirmed Acton's view of Newman as a trimmer, as having the obedience rather than the courage of a saint. Privately or in his letters Newman spoke out on matters concerning the *Rambler* about which Acton knew he felt deeply, but in public he kept silence. When Döllinger's lectures on the temporal power appeared in book form and Acton reviewed them, he criticized the silence of the minority who agreed with Döllinger but refrained from saying so, through either prudence or fear.[86]

In a Whitsun sermon, Faber warned of "dangers from within" and clearly alluded to Acton and the *Rambler* when he said:

> We must be upon our guard even against Catholic books, periodicals, journals, pamphlets, however specious they may be. Our Blessed Redeemer said of the false prophets that they should deceive, if possible, even the elect. . . . There is something very horrible in a Catholic disloyalty to the Church, but there is surely a peculiar horror about it in a misbelieving land. Unfortunate and singularly graceless as it is when it comes from the imperfect Catholicism or reluctant submission of a convert, it is worse when it comes from the ungenerous timidity of intellectual pride of one who has had the inestimable happiness of being born in the bosom of the Church.[87]

Faber had struck the popular Catholic note. Simpson was itching to respond to the attack that had found a wide and favourable echo. Acton tried hard to restrain him, to keep controversy impersonal.

In June 1861, Manning, then Provost of Westminster and speaking for Cardinal Wiseman, who was gravely ill in Rome, called on Acton. He was carrying out an instruction of the secretary of state, Cardinal Giacomo Antonelli. The upshot of the long interview, which Acton described in letters to Newman and Döllinger, was that it was thought that the *Rambler* was becoming less Catholic in spirit and tendency, and it was highly desirable to put an end to it altogether. If Acton did not do that, he should at least disengage himself from it so as not to suffer later from the effects of an ecclesiastical censure that was impending from Rome. He was to promise that whatever the wishes of the Holy Father might be, he would make them his own.[88]

Acton was resolved to say nothing in reply, as he felt that the Church authority had no jurisdiction over the *Rambler* and its criticism of the temporal power. Both he and Newman regarded the unwarranted interference of Antonelli as preposterous, particularly the insinuation that when the Catholic MPs failed to support the temporal power, they were following the editorial policy of the *Rambler* rather than the British Liberal government's support for Italian nationalism. But Acton realized that the Italian involvement could only damage the *Rambler*. He limited himself to historical observations in the *Rambler* and criticized merely the evident shortcomings of the papal government, until Döllinger spoke out in his Odeon Lectures. But the *Rambler,* he felt, should carry on.[89]

Newman did not agree. "If they do not allow the *Rambler* to speak against the temporal power, they seem to me tyrannical—but they have the right to disallow it—and a Magazine, with a censure upon it from authority, continues at an enormous disadvantage."[90] So, in order to keep Newman in good humour and ensure his support in case the censure came, the July 1861 issue was kept deliberately innocuous. In his article on Camillo Cavour, Acton even refrained from drawing the obvious conclusion about the coming end of the temporal power.

Nevertheless, the publisher, Burns, under pressure from Manning, refused to bring out another issue if Dr. Newman's name as editor was connected with it; a new publisher had to be found. That was Williams and Norgate, London and Edinburgh, a Protestant firm, and the *Rambler,* now a bimonthly, was advertised as remaining "under the exclusive direction of Sir John Acton, Bart., MP" and as continuing "to advocate the same principles as heretofore, namely, harmony of implicit faith with free enquiry of religion, with the just claim of special progress, and of political right and freedom."[91]

The withdrawal of Burns, who later published the *Dublin Review,* acquired by Manning, opened Acton's eyes to "Manning's Mephistophelian treachery and craft."[92] Manning had initially overwhelmed the young Baronet with flattery, extolling his influence and generally softening him up, as was his way also with Newman. When Acton returned to England from Munich in 1854, there was talk of Manning's coming to stay at Aldenham to recover from an illness, even to accompany Acton on a visit to Munich in August 1855, although nothing came of that. Manning's involvement in a council of four, also including Acton, to control the *Rambler* had been under discussion before Acton and Simpson acquired the journal. All seemed fine. Manning "was very affectionate, and pressed me to go to lunch and have a talk with him," Simpson wrote to Acton, and to Döllinger Acton wrote that he had the friendliest contacts with the excellent Manning.[93]

Because of Cardinal Wiseman's illness, his plan to establish in England a branch of the Roman Academia as an intellectual centre for the Catholic laity was actually carried out by Manning. Manning, however, had in mind a centre not for free discussions on literary and scientific questions of the day but for drumming up support for the temporal power and spreading the "Roman" or Ultramontane spirit among the laity. He invited Acton to join as one of the censors and even proposed Simpson and Macmullen of the *Rambler* staff as members. Manning wanted Acton's name as one of the old Catholics to add attraction to the enterprise. His tactics were by now obvious. Simpson told Acton that he, Simpson, was going to play "the Devil's advocate in a place where otherwise pious interests only would be represented."[94]

Describing his own very different ideas of the role of the Academia, Acton wrote: "The great error of the day . . . is that Catholics, men of science, and politicians are inclined to recognise only one authority. In the domain of learning, as well as in civil society, there is an authority distinct from that of the Church, and not derived from it, and we are bound in each sphere to render to Caesar the things that are Caesar's. There can be no conflict of duties or of allegiance between them, except inasmuch as one of them abandons its true purpose, the realization of right in the civil order, and the discovery of truth in the intellectual."[95]

A general condemnation of the *Rambler* by the English hierarchy was initiated with the Cardinal's pastoral letter, read from the pulpit by the Vicar General on 17 December 1861, in which Wiseman wrote: "Laymen seem to have assumed a mission to instruct the clergy on the difficulties of the faith as revealed by God and taught in His Church. . . . The Church seems to be habitually put on her defence by her own children, and, forgive me the use of such a word, wrangles almost are raised amongst us on matters of ecclesiastical, even theological magnitude. We have permitted men to speak flippantly and irreverently about sacred things instead of reproving them with dignity and even with virtuous indignation."[96]

Acton did not reply to that generalized attack, but it was to be intensified in the following year, prepared by various complaints sent to Propaganda by English bishops. The most detailed dossier came from the Bishop of Birmingham, William Ullathorne, who wrote to Cardinal Alessandro Barnabò: "The *Rambler* demands the greatest and most prompt attention. For there is a general tendency in that publication—professing to be the organ of Catholic sentiments—to exalt the rights of the laity, to discuss and propound doctrine, to lower the intellectual competency of the clergy, to raise obtuse questions and discuss them by the light of reason, even when they are intimately linked with the truths of Revelation, and one or two of the writers seem to delight in enunciating daring propositions such as startle and scandalise the faithful." Ullathorne enclosed extracts from contributions by Acton and Simpson. "If these writers are not themselves sceptical, and I believe they are not, but only delight in being bold, daring and provoking, from pride of intellect, yet the result may ultimately be to awaken scepticism in minds that are ill-instructed, weak and pretentious."[97]

Quoting extensively from the May and July 1861 issues of the *Rambler,* Ullathorne, in his submission to Rome, took particular exception to the sentiments enunciated against the Pope's temporal power. "Where the writer [Acton] takes the view that, though the invasion of the Pope's states and the criminal acts of the adversaries cannot be approved, they are yet providential, and that after they are terminated we may exclaim *felix culpa*."[98] Equally pernicious was held to be the view expressed in Simpson's articles on Edmund Campion, which suggested that the Reformation Popes, Paul III and Pius V,

> sacrificed the church of this country to their desire of maintaining all the temporal prerogatives exercised or claimed by their predecessors. . . . They rendered simply impossible the coexistence of the government of Henry VIII and Elizabeth with the obedience of their subjects to the supreme authority of the pope. . . . Those popes lost England to the faith, and were so far from securing the prerogative for which they were contending, that in the contro-

versy with France in the next century it was resigned, not without debate, but without any great struggle. If Henry VIII and Elizabeth had been treated with the same delicacy and circumspection that Louis XIV experienced, the end might have been very different from what it was; and if Louis XIV had been treated like Henry VIII, the most Christian king would probably have proved as bad a churchman as the Defender of the Faith.[99]

To counteract the hierarchy's criticism it was necessary to drop the name *Rambler,* present a more peaceable and conciliatory face, and publish quarterly. The name chosen, *Home and Foreign Review,* was originally intended as a subtitle denoting the strength of the review in home and foreign affairs. The motto *Seu vetus est verum diligo, sive novum* was to demonstrate continuity with the *Rambler.* Acton kept the editorial chair, guaranteeing, as it were, the magazine's journalistic freedom, scholarship, and independence. In fact, he alone was able to maintain the foreign connections, win Protestant support, and make the sacrifices needed in money, time, effort, and, indeed, reputation. For the July 1862 issue, the first number of the *Home and Foreign Review,* Acton contributed two major articles, "Nationality" and "The Secret History of Charles II."[100] He also wrote the foreign political chronicle and the literary notices, altogether about one hundred densely printed pages.

Acton was full of enthusiasm and ideas, finding liberal-minded correspondents from Belgium, Spain, and Poland and mobilizing an array of writing talent and intellect unique among British periodicals. He secured the collaboration of historians like Charles Henry Pearson, who was to write about the dissolution of the monasteries; Joseph Stevenson, on the Elizabethan State Papers; John Sherren Brewer, on Cardinal Thomas Wolsey; and Dean Church. He planned a series of articles on the leaders of Catholic parties—Joseph de Maistre, Gioacchino Ventura di Raulica, Vincenzo Gioberti, Jaime Balmès, Louis Veuillot, Pierre-Paul Royer Collard, Wilhelm Roscher, Georg Anton von Stahl—and also on new historical research. The German philosopher and historian Constantin Frantz, a prominent opponent of Bismarck, also promised to write.

Informing Renouf of the changeover and asking him for further contributions, Acton explained that he wanted the new quarterly "to embrace subjects of a more serious and permanent interest, and to receive articles, if they can be obtained, of enduring scientific value." Contributed articles would be signed so that the authors need not be committed to the views of the editor. There would be a political summary, which no other quarterly had, and as full a survey of the literature of the previous months abroad as could be obtained. For this section as well as for the weightier articles Acton asked for Renouf's support, and, as Renouf was still in Dublin, Acton also asked him to get contributions from Irish scholars so that, without trespassing on Newman's *Atlantis* and apart from some strictly scientific subjects, the Irish University should regard the *Home and Foreign Review* as its organ. He would pay contributors five pounds a sheet, and for literary notices a proportionate fee. And so that Renouf might set minds at rest in Dublin, Acton told him that the change of the *Rambler* was to be seen as "a natural development" and not as an attack on the *Dublin Review*. This journal had started as Cardinal Wiseman's organ and, as the leading Catholic periodical in Britain, was "now in so deplorable a state that I am only attempting to redeem the literary honour of the Catholic body by enlarging the Rambler."[101]

"If all goes well," Acton wrote to Döllinger, "this Catholic Review will turn out to be the best of all English Reviews—provided, of course, that the Catholics themselves do not prevent it."[102] He had sent the first number to Gladstone with the gloomy note: "I should beg leave not only to present, but to dedicate it to you if there was any present prospect of the objects for which it was founded being fulfilled in the reality. One of the foremost of these objects is by instructing English readers generally concerning Catholic ideas."[103] The editorial team consisted of Acton, Simpson (his most intimate literary ally, but now acting in a non-official capacity), Thomas Frederick Wetherell, and Daniel Connor Lathbury. In the autumn of 1863 Renouf, whose expertise included theology, Egyptology, and foreign languages, also joined. Acton offered him a regular payment of a hundred pounds a year plus remuneration for contributions.[104]

The quarterly's reception was impressive. The *Irish Universal News*, one of the three London Catholic papers, described the *Home and Foreign Review* as the best of the English reviews, even better than the *Edinburgh*; the *Daily News*, the Liberal organ, was full of admiration. "We have nothing to say of the *H&F Review* that is not to its praise," wrote the *National Review*, a monthly, representing an enlightened Protestant point of view and departing from its practice of not noticing rivals in the periodicals field, even though its idea of Ultramontanism was rather superficial. "It is evidently conducted and written with singular ability. . . . The great merit of the *Home and Foreign Quarterly* [*sic*] is that, being a Catholic organ, even Ultramontane in principle, it represents a living idea, which, if the prelates of its own church do not suppress it, after the fashion of superiors, may go as far to make Catholicism tenable by thinking men in the nineteenth century as the conditions of the case allow." [105]

Simpson's open character helped to ease the painful transition from the *Rambler* to the *Home and Foreign Review*. He withdrew from editorial responsibility and gave up his share in the ownership, but he continued to work behind the scenes. He also wrote an answer to Bishop Ullathorne's open letters against the *Rambler* in which he revealed himself to have been the author of the incriminating passages, thus publicly and clearly distancing himself from the *Rambler* and drawing the enemy's fire upon himself.[106] Acton now shared most of the editorial work with Wetherell, whose judgement and intelligence he valued. Wetherell was more exact and critical than Simpson in assessing manuscripts that poured in for publication. Wetherell's greater circumspection was one of the reasons why he never got on with Simpson. But Acton was now aware that the attacks on himself and on Simpson disguised reasons for the bishops' more fundamental rejection of the *Rambler*'s principle "that the defence of the Church should only be conducted with moral weapons." [107]

What angered his enemies appeared to be that Acton remained calm under attack, or reacted coolly and impersonally, which, wrote Acton to Döllinger, "irritates feminine, proud natures of ignorant people and the whole lot of so-called *bien pensants*." But attempting to unite orthodoxy and scientific truth had always met with calumnies. Acton wanted to teach something that was entirely new among English Catholics, not, as was customary, to deceive opponents but to argue with, and instruct, them. The authorities, however, found the *Rambler* insolent and accused it of claiming to know everything better. Robert Cornthwaite, the Bishop of Beverley, said that he had not come across a more dangerous heretic than Acton since Pelagius. "I live surrounded by this atmosphere of lies," wrote Acton. "But I can honestly say that I have never printed or spoken an angry word against it and refuse to fight back even with legitimate weapons. Please do not think that I am arrogant." [108]

But Cardinal Wiseman's anger broke out again over a reference in the first *Home and Foreign Review* to a report in the French newspaper *La patrie* about the bishops' meeting in Rome. The most violent attack on all the fundamental principles of modern society, so *La patrie* reported, had been made in the address to the Pope for which Cardinal Wiseman carried the responsibility, and he had advocated the excommunication of leading opponents of the temporal power. Addressing the Westminster clergy, the Cardinal interpreted this reference as a deliberate personal attack and denounced the *Home and Foreign Review* for spreading a false report. This kind of report was not, he said, surprising in view of the past history of that journal "under another name, the absence for years of all reserve or reverence in its treatment of persons or of things deemed sacred." In warning against such dangerous leadership, the Cardinal was "only obeying a higher direction than my own impulses, and acting under much more solemn sanctions."[109]

Acton did not, at first, want to answer the charges, vague as they were, but in the meantime the "more solemn sanctions" alluded to by the Cardinal had been activated. The Cardinal's public attack on the *Home and Foreign Review* was answered in moderate tone in an article written by Simpson and Wetherell, with material provided by Acton, reaffirming the *Review*'s loyalty to the Church and then driving home the main point of the dispute: "A false religion fears the progress of all truth; a true religion seeks and recognises truth wherever it can be found, and claims the power of regulating and controlling, not the progress, but the dispensation of knowledge." Intellectually, the Church had reacted to the development of society of the past hundred years, at first, when absolutism and infidelity were in the ascendant in the eighteenth century, by an attitude of timidity and concession, then, in the great Catholic revival of the early nineteenth century, by the opposite—an attitude of confidence, triumph, defiance. A third attitude, with which the *Home and Foreign Review* identified itself, was influencing contemporary science and the progress of learning. It required an apparent sacrifice, a risk. It would seem to the men of the Church to introduce "nothing but new and unwelcome difficulties—trial and distraction to themselves, temptation and danger to their flocks." But in time they would learn that there is a higher course for Catholics than one "which begins in fear and does not lead to security. . . . They will remember that, while the office of ecclesiastical authority is to tolerate, to warn, and to guide, that of religious intelligence and zeal is not to leave the great work of intellectual and social civilisation to be the monopoly and privilege of others, but to save it from debasement by giving to it for leaders the children, not the enemies of the Church."[110] That was no more likely to appease the opposition than what Acton had earlier written about the Catholic press.

"You see," Acton wrote to Döllinger, "one is not your pupil with impunity."[111] The fame Acton had achieved by having produced two distinguished English Catholic journals drew opposition from powerful quarters. Manning was mobilizing a "big counterblast" with the newly arisen *Dublin Review* and the support of W. G. Ward, F. W. Faber, David Lewis, T. W. Allies, and J. Spencer Northcote—the "obscurantists," as some of the Ultramontanists were called. According to Acton, Newman had declared himself "for the first time openly to be on my side, writing most encouragingly, saying that his school, the future University, progress and science—all that was bound up with our cause." But he had restrained himself so as not also to suffer the Cardinal's blow. "So," Acton wrote in his letter to Döllinger, "I am taking upon myself the whole weight of public denunciation, the cardinal's, Propaganda's, the English episcopate's, the entire Catholic press, for I alone answer for these ideas, and my hand is recognisable throughout the article." Henceforth, he added, he had only his own real friends to rely on, among them three bishops—William J. H. Clifford, William Hogarth, Richard Roskell—more liberal in this regard at least than the others, as well as a few Irish bishops and Newman, William Waterworth (a Jesuit theologian) and other Jesuits, and some Benedictines.[112]

Acton felt all this as a bitter trial:

> You cannot imagine how angry those churchmen in authority, how much calumny this matter is causing. It will cost thousands if it goes on like this. My own career in public life has become quite impossible, and you know that in this issue I had to sacrifice things much dearer to me. However, really great work can be accomplished, to which I gladly devote myself. The Review's point of view can do much among Protestants. There are signs enough that people of greater insight understand that in Catholicism not all is so perverse or limited as they thought. Upon Gladstone, after all, the effect is profound and visible.[113]

Money worries also increased; Catholics stopped their subscriptions. Nevertheless, Acton concentrated on producing an outstanding quarterly that would be talked about. Simpson felt the attacks more directly. His Bishop, Thomas Grant of Southwark, urged him to stop writing on subjects affecting the Church and the Holy See. Even the Redemptorist priest to whom he went regularly to confession refused him absolution, and when he asked what he should do, the answer was: Write no more in the *Home and Foreign Review*.[114]

The July 1863 issue of the *Home and Foreign Review* contained an important contribution by Acton, in which Simpson had had a hand, on Ultramontanism.[115] It was an attempt to vindicate the concept for the aims of the *Review* by differentiating between the right and wrong sorts of Ultramontanism: Acton's kind and that of his opponents, that is, those who advocated the rights and prin-

ciples of the Catholic Church in party terms. Just as Gallicanism was the instrument by which absolute monarchs extended their power over the Church, so
Ultramontanism introduced the same principle of absolutism into the Church
herself. Both were expedients by which ecclesiastical liberty was curtailed: this
was Acton's point.

Acton showed how the Catholic Church had survived the general prostration
of religion in the eighteenth century. A more hopeful era dawned for her liberty
and restoration with the advent of the Romantic age, the defeat of Napoleon
in 1815, and the new anti-revolutionary Europe emerging from the Congress
of Vienna. The temporal power—that is, the States of the Church ruled by the
Pope in Italy—was almost completely restored. Absolutism in both Church and
State marked the European historical picture of the eighteenth century. Catholic and Protestant sovereigns closely controlled religion in their dominions and
decided how far the voice of the Holy See should be heard.

The assumption of Gallicanism was that not Rome or the Curia but the
French King, particularly when he was a devout believer like Louis XVI, was the
proper source of the freedom and independence of the Church. The Gallican system was strengthened in the eighteenth century against abuses of the
Papal or episcopal prerogatives; it extended to the influence that Catholic rulers
wielded in papal elections. As chief opponents to this trend, the Society of Jesus
was suppressed in 1773, with Catholic monarchs pressing for the expulsion of
the Jesuits.

Jansenism and Febronianism were particular sprouts of Gallicanism.[116] In the
Habsburg Empire and among the Bavarian Wittelsbach a similar system reigned
beyond the French Revolution, far into the nineteenth century. This system was
named Josephinism (Josephism) after the Emperor Joseph II (Maria Theresa's
son), who established it, with the bishops functioning as higher-grade civil servants and the clergy as lower-grade ones. In Protestant countries like Prussia
the dependence of the Church on the State was greater still.

Acton's own celebrated maternal ancestor Carl Theodor von Dalberg, Arch-
bishop-Elect of Mainz and the last Arch-Chancellor of the Holy Roman Empire, and his Vicar-General, Heinrich Ignaz von Wessenberg (1774–1860), were
renowned for their efforts towards the creation of a quasi-national Church,
a German equivalent of Gallicanism. They recognized the need for spiritual,
moral, and educational reform at a low point of the papal power; they supported episcopal rights against the increasing power of the Roman Curia and
wanted to protect the Pope in his political weakness. As German territorial

magnates, they were, in fact, as much opposed to a national Church as to a global Church. For them the problems of Church renewal were paramount. The whole temper of the modern age was against Catholicism. In France and in the Latin countries there were anticlerical, even atheist stirrings. The Church seemed insolubly allied to the old reactionary order, and there grew up a corresponding aversion, particularly among the middle classes, to any sort of clerical or "monkish" attitudes.[117] Voltaire's "Ecraser l'infâme" (Crush the Beast), by which he meant to oppose not religion as such but the superstitions tolerated by the Church, became the slogan of the century.

The Gallican equivalent in Great Britain was Erastianism, deriving from Thomas Erastus (1524–1583), the German-Swiss theologian of the reformed (Zwinglian) Zurich school, whose ideas subordinating ecclesiastical to secular power influenced Anglican development. As far as English Catholics were concerned, on their road from suppression and recusancy to nineteenth-century toleration, Emancipation (marked by the Catholic Relief Bill of 1829), and the restoration of the hierarchy in 1850, they were in a different category. In the British Isles the Catholic Church was neither established nor persecuted but free to develop, once it had attained legal emancipation. The Irish Catholics, under their liberator Daniel O'Connell (1775–1847), impressed someone like Montalembert because their Catholic life and culture flourished despite persecution and yet it owed nothing to the State and was all the more robust on that account. In England, the home of free discussion, the same was about to happen through the movement of conversions, thus setting a remarkable example to Continental Catholics, who were used to the progress of the Church only as an agency of the State.

In the fifty years leading up to Catholic Emancipation in 1829, the English Roman Catholics produced their own equivalent of the Gallicans, that is, the Cisalpines, represented chiefly by the wealthier element of the land-owning old Catholic families, who had borne the brunt of past persecution and oppression. After the English Reformation, Catholics were imprisoned or executed for practising their religion. In the relatively more tolerant eighteenth century, fines were imposed for those holding Roman Catholic services on their estates and for those attending them. The rich were naturally able to pay these fines more easily than the poor. Moreover, Catholics continued to be deprived of official positions and possibilities for professional advancement. However, toleration was in the air. The old Catholics were anxious to prove themselves acceptable members of their society, not to show up as religiously or otherwise "different," and to assure their Protestant fellow-citizens of their peaceful and patriotic intentions and the groundlessness of the fear of "papists" and "papal aggression." The real core of the deeply ingrained objection to Catholicism in the English character and its basic sense of liberty, as Newman recognized, was not so much the Papacy as the Church and the idea that Christ should have set up a visible society or rather kingdom on earth for the propagation and maintenance of his religion on earth.[118]

The English Cisalpines, according to David Mathew, thus put the interests of the State before that of the Church organization; they were against the Italianate, neo-Gothic fashion of the times, a club of like-minded Englishmen, loyal to the Pope but not abjectly so, "anticlerical," "exclusive," "non-intellectualist," "querulous."[119] Sir Robert Throckmorton, who had married Acton's aunt Elizabeth, was one of these Cisalpine leaders. The Cisalpines were understandably critical of the new school of brashly triumphant Ultramontanists (and vice-versa) who after 1850 replaced them in the English Catholic leadership. But the old families had kept the faith alive during the centuries of persecution. Suddenly they found themselves ignored at Rome in favour of the "prodigal sons" like the Italian-trained Nicholas Wiseman, the future first Archbishop of Westminster, and his successor, Henry Edward Manning, the convert from the Established Church. They were altogether more self-confident and aggressive than their Cisalpine predecessors had ever dared to be. They expected the conversion of England to be close, either through the disintegration of the Anglican Church from internal dissension or from mass desertion of converts. Moreover, their desire was to discard the old minority stance, reminiscent of the ghetto spirit, of not being too conspicuous. A new spirit of Catholic assertiveness ruled.

First used only in the geographical sense of the term, Ultramontanism thus developed between the Reformation and the French Revolution into a party term aiming at the liberty of the Church, the converse of Gallicanism. Gallicans accused their opponents of looking *ultra montes,* across the mountains, to take their cue from Rome. As a product of an absolutist age, Ultramontanism introduced absolutism into the Church herself by attempting to revive the medieval ideas of Gregory VII and Innocent III, but this occurred at a time when the Papacy had actually reached its lowest point in modern history. Ecclesiastical liberty everywhere was curtailed. "In one sense the designation [of Ultramontane] was just; in another it was a strange inversion of the meaning which had hitherto attached to the word," Acton wrote.[120]

In this context it is worth noting the symbolic Ultramontanist significance that the Concordat of 1801 had for the coming century.[121] Under the impact of the French occupation, the Pope and his secretary of state, Ercole Consalvi, were forced to make important concessions, but they also secured decisive advantages for the Church. These involved nothing less than the resignation of all French bishops, indeed the deposition even of those legitimately appointed, and the creation of a totally new diocesan structure. It was a unique and striking show of papal power over the whole Church, such as had never happened before. The enormous precedent soon sparked a similar reform of Church structure in Germany. But again this occurred at a time of the Papacy's extreme political weakness. Pius VII, too, was soon (in 1806) to become Napoleon's prisoner, as Pius VI had been.

The theological implications of this Ultramontanist advance found expression in further "stages" of the papal absolutism. There was, first of all, the strengthening, in the 1830s, of a Roman school of theology, Traditionalism, which was Jesuit-led, neoscholastic, and ahistorical. Next came the dogmatizing of the Immaculate Conception in 1854, followed by the publication in 1864 of the encyclical *Quanta Cura* with the *Syllabus Errorum,* in which Pius IX condemned eighty political and philosophical "Errors of the Age." When Acton and Döllinger were in Rome in 1857, the government of Pius IX was about to enter the last desperate decade of the temporal power. The ambitions of the House of Savoy were advancing alongside its claim to Rome as the predestined capital of united Italy. The French troops stationed outside Rome were the Pope's only protection. When they eventually left, on the outbreak of the Franco-Prussian War, the day after the Vatican Council of 1870 had ended, Rome was occupied by the forces of united Italy within a few weeks.

But in Papal Rome no alternative to the temporal power could be envisaged. Pius IX was mesmerized by the Jacobin menace. The Italian nationalists and liberals, for their part, did not mince their anticlericalism inherited from the French Revolution. Cavour might talk reasonably, supported by the England of Russell and Palmerston, but what security had the Pope that Cavour might not be swept away like those Roman revolutionaries who, in 1849, had frightened Pius IX out of his own tentative nationalism and liberalism into his Gaeta exile? There was talk that he might again have to flee Rome and seek shelter in another country willing to accept and protect him. Eventually, he reconciled himself to his fate as a self-styled "Prisoner of the Vatican" until he and the times were readier to accept the idea, first voiced by Dr. Döllinger, that the Pope might possibly be able to exercise his spiritual function much better, unencumbered by secular rule, in an international agreed enclave of the modern State as was only to come about in Mussolini's Italy in 1929.

But neo-Ultramontanism also was a means and political weapon, by which the temporal power and the aspirations for Papal Infallibility became confused. The principal inspiration for the mid-nineteenth-century neo-Ultramontanism was the ideas of the French publicist and philosopher Joseph Marie Comte de Maistre (1754–1821). In the steep decline of Catholic theological education during and immediately after the French Revolution, with the educated clergy on the Continent everywhere marked by rationalism, laymen like de Maistre came to fill the vacancy. They were often recent converts, seldom trained scholars, but all under the impact of recent history, the Revolution and the Revolutionary Wars, and the powerful Romantic current. Thinking Catholics, after 1814, thus dreamed of a Holy Alliance, a league between Church and State, in which men of goodwill would support the revival of religion. It was hoped that the Church in her new freedom would enable the State to protect society against a recurrence of the recent revolutionary and anti-religious catastrophe.

De Maistre, at first, had upheld a love of freedom coupled with admiration for England's resistance to Napoleon and against the violence of the French Revolution. But his dread of revolutionary despotism had then given way to a horror of constitutionalism. Catholicism, he maintained, inculcates the absolute authority of the sovereign and forbids resistance even to the greatest wrong. The unity and absolutism of authority spring from the very nature of religion and are not only necessary for the State but essential to the Church. Just as civil society cannot subsist without the maxim that the King can do no wrong, the Church requires the same privilege for the Pope. Absolute Infallibility in the one is a corollary of despotism in the other. Denying to the people any part in the vindication of right, de Maistre transferred to the Pope alone the whole duty of moderating Kings. To want to limit the Holy See in Church or State was tantamount to attacking religion and to open the door to Jansenism, Protestantism, and infidelity.

The philosophy developed by Hugo Félicité Robert de Lamennais (1782–1854) seemed at first to support de Maistre's Ultramontanism and right-wing argument for the papal authority, although it ended in decided contradiction of it. According to Lamennais's philosophy, no evidence amounts to certain demonstration unless confirmed by the universal consent of the general reason, and the organ of this general reason is the Holy See. He thus rejected the theory of the absolute authority of the civil power that de Maistre had used to such effect. But if the Infallibility of universal opinion is the origin of certainty, it is the source of authority; and the Holy See is therefore exalted over princes as much as over philosophers and thinkers. When, therefore, the restored Bourbon monarchy became despotic, Lamennais, the enthusiastic royalist turned liberal, appealed against it to the people as the source of power, and to the Pope as their organ. That was the spirit of the *Avenir,* the first Catholic daily of the modern era, which found enthusiastic support all over Europe.

Gregory XVI, however, rejected the democratic and liberal ideas of Lamennais in the encyclical *Mirari Vos* (1832). Lamennais, not being specifically named in it, made his submission in Rome. With his internationally popular book *Paroles d'un croyant* (1834), he soon earned condemnation as a socialist revolutionary, this time by name, in the encyclical *Singulari Nos.* He himself died in obscurity, with friends having tried vainly to reconcile him with the Church, but his social Catholic ideas continued to influence a wide range of Ultramontanist Catholic thinkers such as, in France, Jean-Baptiste-Henri Lacordaire, Prosper Guéranger, Charles de Montalembert, Louis-Eugène-Marie Bautain, and Augustin Bonetty; in Spain, Jaime-Luciano Balmez and J. Donoso Cortes; in Italy, Vincenzo Gioberti and Antonio Rosmini; in Great Britain, Nicholas Wiseman and John Henry Newman; and in Germany, Johann Joseph Ignaz von Döllinger and Joseph von Gorrës. Ultramontanism became a popular movement in the Church, serving the interests of the Papacy in its widest sense.

This was precisely Acton's objection to this particular expression of Ultramontanism. He saw it as a form of Catholic escapism into the teaching of the Church as the sole foundation and test of all certain knowledge. Behind that he saw the small-minded Catholic distrust and fear that the modern scientific method could not be reconciled to truth. Catholics everywhere were particularly suspicious of historical study, because, as the study of facts, it was less amenable to authority and less controllable by interest than philosophical speculation. Partly because of the denial of historical certainty and partly because of the fear of it, the historical study of dogma in its original sources was abandoned, and the dialectical systematic treatment preferred.

Acton's experiences in Germany had shown him, in particular, that whereas Protestants had shared the eighteenth-century decline of religion in equal measure, they were also the first to recover from it. They, rather than Catholics, dominated the German literary revival culminating in the work of Goethe. To Acton this movement, though it had no specific religious impulse, seemed comparable to the revival of the Medicean age. It spread to the German universities, producing a renascence of medieval historical studies borne by the new scientific approach. The lesson he drew from this was as follows:

> A school of historians arose who made it their business to write of the Middle Ages as they wrote on the Persian War; who spoke of the Church as they spoke of the Areopagus, and applied to the most obscure moments of her history those tests of credibility and authenticity which had been lavished on Herodotus and Livy. They had nothing of the spirit of panegyrists or accusers; but with all their learning, acuteness, and equity, most of these men were destitute of that faculty or experience which would have enabled them to understand the significance of religion. They understood, better than any Catholic writers before them, the outward action of the ecclesiastical organism, the moral, intellectual, and social influence of the Church; but they knew nothing of her religious character. They betrayed the same incapacity in the study of paganism; and their interpretation of the Hellenic theology was often as superficial as their explanation of Catholic doctrine. . . .
>
> Catholics were astonished to find that men who wrote with fairness, and often with admiration, of the Church, who made themselves the champions of her maligned or forgotten heroes . . . cared nothing for the doctrines of the institution they labouriously defended, and repudiated with indignation the proposal to submit to its authority. . . . But the method they pursued in the investigation of truth prevailed against all hostile inclination; and the scientific spirit which arose out of the decomposition of Protestantism became in the hands of Catholics the safeguard of religious truth, and the most efficient weapon of controversy.[122]

This was the form of Ultramontanism that Acton advocated, aiming at the freedom of the Church against the civil power, but "not specifically for the interests of religion, but on behalf of a general principle which, while it asserted freedom for the Church, extended it likewise to other communities and institutions." And his test of true Ultramontanism was: "The Catholic is subject to the correction of the Church when he is in contradiction with her truth, not when he stands in the way of her interests." And in a fine passage he illustrated his faith in Catholicism and the modern spirit of scientific enquiry:

> But there is an outward shell of variable opinions constantly forming round this inward core of irreversible dogma, by its contact with human science or philosophy, as a coating of oxide forms round the mass of metal where it comes in contact with the shifting atmosphere. The Church must always put

herself in harmony with existing ideas, and speak to each age and nation in its own language. A kind of amalgam between the eternal faith and temporal opinion is thus in constant process of generation, and by it Christians explain to themselves the bearings of their religion, so far as their knowledge allows.

The real Ultramontane is thus a Catholic in the highest sense of Catholicism,

> who makes no parade of his religion; who meets his adversaries on ground which they understand and acknowledge; who appeals to no extrinsic con-sideration—benevolence, or force, or interest, or artifice—in order to estab-lish his point. . . . He finds that there is a system of metaphysics, and ethics, singularly agreeable to Catholicism but entirely independent of it. . . . It is a process never to be terminated, till God has finished the work of educating the human race to know Him and to love Him. . . .
>
> Authority may put itself in opposition to its own code; but the code is vin-dicated by the defeat of authority. Thus it was in politics during the drama of the Sicilian Vespers, and in physical science during the opposition to Galileo. Those experiments have taught authority its own bounds, and subjects the limits of obedience; and they have destroyed the last conceivable obstacle to the freedom with which a Catholic can move in the sphere of inductive truth.[123]

This article was a last clarion call. It had a wide response, provoking anger, as expected, on the part of opponents but no serious objections. It made a strong impression on Protestants, Acton wrote to Döllinger. One journal had observed that if the Church followed that line, Englishmen would have to re-vise their attitude towards Roman Catholics. Newman was in favour. Bishop Thomas Brown of Newport told a Jesuit that that number of the *Home and Foreign Review* was the best that English Catholics had produced since the Ref-ormation.[124] Acton was gratified by Döllinger's compliments and replied that it was strange that the distinction he drew in principle between the two types of Catholics had not been made so clearly before. In Germany, for instance, Görres had failed to see that point and had thus been unable to make his influ-ence felt in an enlightened way. In Dublin, Cardinal Cullen's paper commented favourably and, as Acton learned, preferred the *Home and Foreign Review* to Manning's new *Dublin Review,* now the weapon of the opposition. Gladstone told Acton's friend Anthony Panizzi of the British Museum: "If only all Catho-lics were like him." [125] Acton felt that sooner or later he would be the victim of Roman censorship, and on an issue in which he could not give in, for simply to ignore Roman authority could only cause a scandal.[126]

Acton was in Munich in September 1863, for the congress of Catholic scholars that Dr. Döllinger had organized and over which he presided. Nearly a hundred professors, authors, and theologians assembled at St. Bonifaz monastery, for the four-day conference, some deputed by their bishops. Only about a dozen laymen were present, among them the Munich physician Johann Nepomuk von Ringseis; the historian Johann Nepomuk Sepp, disciple of Görres, working on a reply to David Friedrich Strauss's *Das Leben Jesu* (1835–36); and Josef Edmund Jörg, Döllinger's former student, editor of the *Historisch-politische Blätter*. Acton wrote about the congress, showing his familiarity with the intellectual currents of German Catholics, which are well described in his article.[127]

The real key to the proceedings, as Acton realized, was the antagonism between the overwhelming personal authority that Dr. Döllinger exercised and the partly tacit reaction against it, the reasons for which Döllinger seemed unable to fathom at all. He wanted to persuade the bishops to support a proposed modus vivendi between claims of ecclesiastical authority and the spirit of free enquiry, to reconcile the theological camps as though there were not the deepest ideological divisions between the advocates of "scholastic theology" and Italian, French, and German theology: "A real dogmatic error against the clear and universal teaching of the Church must be pointed out and retracted, but a purely theological error must be assailed only with the resources of scientific discussion." Yet it was only two years since the storm had broken over Döllinger's lectures on the temporal power. To pass over this as though nothing had happened was, according to Acton, to cast a shadow of unreality over these deliberations.[128]

Reality dawned on 21 December 1863, when the Pope addressed a brief to the Archbishop of Munich, which was published only later, on 5 March 1864. The document explained that the Holy Father had originally been led to suspect the recent congress of Munich of a tendency similar to that of Dr. Jakob Frohschammer, suspended from his priesthood (and banned from the congress) for propounding the view that philosophy should be "emancipated" from the conflict of religion and revelation and that the Pope had consequently viewed it with great distrust. These feelings had been removed by the filial address adopted by the congress and by the Archbishop's report. Yet, there followed several propositions that, Acton believed, had an important bearing on his review.

The gist of these propositions was that in the present condition of society the supreme authority in the Church was more than ever necessary and must not surrender in the smallest degree the exclusive direction of ecclesiastical knowledge. Entire obedience to the decrees of the Holy See and the Roman Congregations (which included the Index) was not inconsistent with the freedom and progress of science. The disposition to criticize scholastic theology and dispute the conclusions and methods of its teachers threatened the authority of the Church. Catholic writers were not only bound by those decisions of the infallible Church in regard to articles of faith; they also had to submit to the theological decisions of the Roman Congregations and to the opinions that are commonly received in the schools. And it was wrong, though not heretical, to reject those decisions or opinions.[129]

Döllinger sent a copy of the letter to Aldenham. Acton replied at once: "You see exactly how you are feared, and how far they dare go against you. It is like an accumulation of malicious views of many years so perfidiously to mix up Frohschammer's teaching with yours and to give the passage concerning error this kind of meaning. It is the effect of a revenge long cherished, the existence of which you must have been aware of." Moreover, several passages of the papal letter referred to ideas Acton had also publicly maintained and defended. Submission was not possible, he wrote, nor was the thought of going against the letter. "Silently to ignore it would sooner or later lead to severe reprimand. . . . The scandal caused [in Britain] by a rebellion against Rome and in view of the lack of an educated Catholic opinion would be so enormous that I dare not provoke it, not to mention the glee among Protestants, which would wipe out all the good our theories have done." Renouf, Simpson, and he would henceforth have more time to write books. For the permanence of a review leads, Acton reasoned, to a constant state of hostilities with Rome, which does not exist in the case of individual books. He would therefore suppress the *Review* after the April issue.[130]

Acton similarly informed Newman, who replied that he was grieved at the news.

The Review seemed to me improving, number after number, both in religious character and in literary excellence. It had gained a high place among the periodicals of the day, and that in a singularly short time. Protestants prophesied of it, that it was too able to be allowed to last. I wished it to take its place, not only with the Protestant public, but in the confidence of our bishops. There seemed no extravagance in this wish; no inconsistency between my submitting to my own bishop's judgment, when the Review began, and hoping for a reversal of that judgment, as it proceeded.

On the "Munich Brief," Newman wrote that he had no difficulties in "acquiescing" in its main points.

> But I dread their application. I suppose they mean much more than they say. And thus there are serious grounds for apprehension, lest there may be some ultimate intention of proceeding against you, and that the more easily, because we in England are under the military regime of Propaganda.
>
> But good may come out of this disappointment. There is life, and increasing life in the English Catholic body; and, if there is life, there must be reaction. It seems impossible that active and sensible men can remain still under the dull tyranny of Manning and Ward.[131]

Newman's hopeful note was to be justified at least in one respect. He was working on his reply to the pamphlets of Charles Kingsley and Frederick Meyrick on the Catholic notion of truthfulness and his own understanding of it, the great controversy that caused his *Apologia* to be written.[132]

Acton realized that Kingsley and Meyrick, like contemporary England, were basically less adverse to Newman's idea of truthfulness than to the confusion that existed because of the alleged Catholic practice of proscribing truth and positively encouraging falsehood in the interest of the Church. Acton therefore reminded Newman that to meet Kingsley and Meyrick head on as well as to fulfil the expectations of those who were eagerly awaiting his *Apologia*, he must deal with the question of truthfulness not only *pro domo* but *pro ecclesia*.[133]

Newman was grateful for the reminder. "I am writing from morning till night, and against time, which is not pleasant," he replied. "As to the points you mention, you may be sure I shall go as far as ever I can."[134] Thus Acton indirectly had a hand in the last chapter of the *Apologia*, completed on 26 May 1864, in which Newman is "brought to the direct question of truth, and of the truthfulness of Catholic priests generally in their dealings with the world, as bearing on their general question of their honesty, and of their internal belief in their religious professions."[135]

This issue involved the moral theology of Alfonso Maria di Liguori (1696–1787), founder of the Redemptorist order, who was canonized in 1839. As an opponent of the dominant rationalism of the eighteenth century, he developed a pastoral approach or system of casuistry that, on disputed questions of conscience, was more compassionate and relied more on divine grace than did harsh and pessimistic judgements. The system was intended to counter the Jansenists, Liguori's particular opponents, who admitted only a model of perfection. On these disputed questions Liguori's "probabilism" allowed a more liberal course to be followed, if that is "equally or near-equally probable." Newman's view of equivocation, which Liguori permitted under certain circumstances, was: "Much as I admire the high points of the Italian character, I like the English rule of conduct better" and "follow other guidance in preference to his." And rejecting the charge that he allows the maxim of doing good that evil may come, Newman went on to say: "There is a way of winning men from greater sins by winking for the time at the less, or at mere improprieties or faults; and this is the key to the difficulty which Catholic books of moral theology so often cause to the Protestant. They are intended for the Confessor, and Protestants view them as intended for the Preacher."[136] That was as far as Newman would go.

Acton told Simpson that if the *Home and Foreign Review* accepted the Munich Brief it would "lose its identity, and the very breath of its nostrils. If it is rejected, and the proclamation of the Holy See defied, the *Review* cannot long escape condemnation, and cannot any longer efficiently profess to represent the true, authoritative Catholic opinion."[137] Simpson consented to and approved of Acton's decision to suspend publication. So did others, "but all believe it to be a great misfortune for religion. They think it will make an equally bad impression on gleeful Protestants, obscurantist Catholics and those for whom the existence of the Review was a reason for remaining in the Church."[138]

Dr. Döllinger did not agree with Acton's reasons at first. His letter in which he advised him not to submit to a mere threat is lost, but in replying to it Acton begged him to consider all the points he was unable to state officially in the *Review*. And he listed these points: eleven of thirteen bishops had condemned the *Review;* only two were on his side (Bishop William Clifford of Clifton and Bishop Richard Roskell of Nottingham). Even more zealous than the bishops were Manning and Ward, all of them besieging Rome for a censure, which, now that the general threat was issued, could be expected at any time. As for the English Protestant perspective, the collision would have appeared even stronger if Acton had waited for the censure, for no Protestant would have accepted the message of the *Review* as pure Catholic teaching. They would have agreed with Manning rather than him. Moreover, he would not be justified in involving his friends who were not as independent as he was in such a struggle. Very few English Catholics would have clearly understood the ideas at stake.[139]

In the final issue of the *Home and Foreign Review* Acton published his explanation under the heading "Conflicts with Rome," and he signed the article with his full name to show that the responsibility was to be his rather than the *Re-*

view's.[140] He gave an outline of the Catholic Church's condemnation of Hugo Félicité Robert de Lamennais and Jakob Frohschammer (1821–1895) as two men who despaired of the reconciliation between science and religion, Lamennais by subordinating one to the other, Frohschammer by positing their complete separation and estrangement. Lamennais had so exaggerated the Infallibility of the Pope as the oracle of eternal truth that he confounded the human element with the divine, which finally proved fatal to his faith.

The case of Dr. Frohschammer was different. He was not highly rated as a theologian, according to Acton, and when he found himself censured by the Holy See, unjustly, as he thought, instead of believing in his own conscience that he was in agreement with the true faith of the Church, he allowed himself to be driven into heresy. He came to consider the whole Church as infected with the liability to err. Far from aiding the cause of freedom, his errors provoked a reaction against it, which must be regarded with deep anxiety. The first symptom of this reaction was the Pope's letter to the Archbishop of Munich, and that affected the position of the *Home and Foreign Review*. It was faced with the summons to submit.

Acton concluded that the *Review* would have to cease: "It would be wrong to abandon principles which have been well considered and are sincerely held, and it would also be wrong to assail the authority which contradicts them. The principles have not ceased to be true, nor the authority to be legitimate because the two are in contradiction." He would not challenge a conflict that could only deceive the world into a belief that religion cannot be harmonized with all that is right and true in the progress of the present age. "But I will sacrifice the existence of the *Review* to the defence of its principles, in order that I may combine the obedience which is due to legitimate ecclesiastical authority with an equally conscientious maintenance of the rightful and necessary liberty of thought."[141]

And Acton took leave of his readers with the humble thought "that the principles it has upheld will not die with it, but will find their destined advocates, and triumph in their appointed time. From the beginning of the Church it has been a law of her nature, that the truths which eventually proved themselves the legitimate products of her doctrine, have had to make their slow way upwards through a phalanx of hostile habits and tradition, and to be rescued, not only from open enemies, but also from friendly hands that were not worthy to defend them." The extinction of the *Review* could not shake the principles, the hopes, the confidence of its supporters: "It was but a partial and temporary embodiment of an imperishable idea—the faint reflection of a light which still lives and burns in the hearts of the silent thinkers of the Church."[142]

Acton emerged from his six years of Catholic journalism exhausted, but with his spirit unbroken. The English Catholics had had no time for that young layman with pretensions to teach them to think and act for themselves, not on matters of faith, but on those disputed questions in the middle ground which the English laity of that time were also used to leave to bishops and priests to settle for them. They had rejected the message not by argument, but by the tried old method of getting rid of the messenger. They could see themselves only as minorities have traditionally seen themselves, rightly or wrongly: Catholics were used to responding to partisan attacks in a partisan way, by adopting the esprit de corps of a fighting community and rallying round their ecclesiastical leaders.

As a group they were bound to agree with Wiseman's words, warning them

> of one of the great dangers of our time, the influx into ecclesiastical and spiritual affairs of principles belonging to temporal and social interest. For the sake of peace, of charity, and good understanding let us keep a well-drawn boundary line between our respective spheres of action. . . . The Church of God does indeed often want your zealous co-operation, your social influence, your learned or ready pen, your skilful pencil, your brilliant talents, your weighty name, your abundant means. But the direction, the rule, belongs to us. . . . Think not that these will prosper while insubordinate to those whom God has placed to direct them. We will always gladly see you working with us, but we cannot permit you to lead where religious interests are concerned.[143]

Fortunately for the Church of later generations, Acton took no notice of these words. He had produced only eight issues of the *Home and Foreign Review*, but part of his reward was a glowing tribute from Matthew Arnold (whose convert brother was a contributor) regretting the extinction of the *Review*:

> Perhaps in no organ of criticism in this country was there so much knowledge, so much play of mind; but these could not save it. The *Dublin Review* subordinates play of mind to the practical business of English and Irish Catholicism, and lives. It must needs be that men should act in sects and parties, that each of these sects and parties should have its organ, and should make its organ subserve the interests of its action; but it would be well, too, that there should be a criticism, not the minister of these interests, not their

enemy, but absolutely and entirely independent of them. No other criticism will ever attain any real authority or make any real way towards its end,—the creating a current of true and fresh ideas.[144]

It was not, however, quite the end of Acton's journalism. In May 1864, he and Irish fellow MPs Thomas O'Hagan and William Monsell were discussing the idea of a new Catholic paper, "but without the risky principles of the *H & F Review,* more like the French *Correspondant.*" As Acton told Döllinger, he favoured something along the lines of *Blackwood's Magazine,* with stories and as little to remind people of the *Home and Foreign Review* as possible. But he was keeping in the background, feeling that his name could only do damage.[145] A committee was formed to collect funds and eventually to act as trustees. The editor was to be Wetherell. Involved were Newman, James Hope-Scott, the Catholic peers Lord Dunraven and Lord Petre, Thomas O'Hagan, and Bishop David Moriarty of Kerry, who was friendly with Newman and had been a supporter of the *Home and Foreign Review*.

Nothing came from these plans, but eventually the *Chronicle* was launched, attached to the Gladstone cause, in March 1867, with Wetherell in sole control.[146] "I am sorry to say that he was originally a Tory, and made conservative speeches at the Union," Acton ironically informed Gladstone, who had come a similar way.[147] George Lathbury left the *Daily News* to take on the post of assistant editor. The paper was financed by Sir Rowland Blennerhassett, the young Liberal MP, Acton's and Newman's friend. It was not to be a Catholic journal, not out to propagate Catholicism, although Wetherell held that its religion would be Catholic. He was content to tread softly, without flourish, without a programme. Acton congratulated Wetherell on the literary part of the first issue, but was otherwise critical: "Current events ought to embrace more countries. . . . A certain number of idle readers are caught by neat titles or articles. You are excessively sincere and matter of fact. There is some want of fun in the articles themselves, but that is what everybody has a better right to complain of than I have."[148]

The moment chosen for the publication of the *Chronicle* was unfortunate. The British public was preoccupied with a new Reform Bill and with the rights of householders, and less than ever with foreign affairs, Ireland, and the disestablishment of the Church of Ireland, or with the learned books to which the *Chronicle* devoted much space. Inadequate finances, the paper's espousal of a purely Gladstonian brand of liberalism—with its support for social reform in England and religious, political, and social reform in Ireland—and a liberal point of view on religious topics such as the coming Vatican Council, probably alienated the small circle of enlightened Catholics and Protestants likely to be its readers. Sir Rowland Blennerhassett's promised support was not forthcoming, and when the hoped-for rescue by Gladstone or the Liberal Party failed to materialize, Wetherell had no alternative but to stop publication after not even a full year, in February 1868. Acton, who was paying Wetherell's salary, was not prepared to finance the paper as well.

Acton had proposed to Gladstone to rescue the *Chronicle* as a link between the Liberal Party and Catholics and to take a financial interest in it, provided that a number of others would do the same.[149] But Gladstone, still lamenting the *Home and Foreign Review,* preferred a different idea. This was to revive the *North British Review,* once the organ of the Free Kirk Party and a serious rival of the *Edinburgh* and *Quarterly Review* but now fallen into decline. This time, the Liberal Party bore the major part of the costs.[150] Acton contributed £250 per year out of his own pocket, plus the proceeds from all his articles and reviews. Simpson contributed £50, also waiving his fees; Wetherell contributed his editor's salary of £500 as his share, and there were three amounts of £50 each from Liberal friends George Glyn, Mountstuart E. Grant Duff, and Thomas O'Hagan as well as, again, an unknown sum from Blennerhassett. Acton's contributions amounted to four major articles on his religious preoccupations of the moment.[151] It was Wetherell's failing health rather than financial worries that put an end to the quarterly in January 1871, after six issues.

The *North British Review,* like its weekly predecessor the *Chronicle,* attained a remarkable breadth of intellectual vision encompassing the literary, the religious, and the political, comparable to the best in Victorian periodical journalism. Its unique contribution, showing Acton's influence, was its treatment of foreign affairs—Catholic, non-nationalistic, and prophetically critical of the growing military predominance of Prussianized Germany in Europe. These were the views expressed by the principal correspondent, the widely travelled and cosmopolitan Saxon, Aurelio Buddeus (1817–1880), editor of a journal for lawyers in Frankfurt, and by Constantin Frantz (1817–1891), whom Acton had already won to write for the *Home and Foreign Review.* Frantz was a highly interesting political philosopher, a pupil of Friedrich Wilhelm von Schelling and a political outsider in the sense that, as a devout Protestant Christian and a German federalist and sworn enemy of Otto von Bismarck, he stood against the dominant nationalist-imperialist current of German history. With the disappearance, after World War II, of Bismarck's legacy, the centralized German national state, and its replacement by the Federal Republic of Germany, the far-sightedness of Frantz's understanding of German and European history is again finding deserved recognition.[152]

It was the events of 1869 and 1870, as Josef Altholz contended, that persuaded Acton and his friends and sympathizers that no useful purpose could any longer be accomplished through Catholic journalism in the monolithic, centralized, and triumphalist Ultramontanist system of the Church. Their efforts could not, they realized, gain them any significant support.[153] In their day, Catholicism and Catholic liberalism could not be reconciled. Nevertheless, Acton switched his own journalistic activities to Rome and to a great final effect at the Vatican Council.

MARIE CONSENTS

The seven years of Acton's experience at Westminster and as a Catholic editor had a good ending after all, in that they brought him private happiness. Towards the end of 1864 Marie Arco finally accepted his proposal of marriage. This happy conclusion came after a long struggle, because several years earlier she had fallen in love with someone else: the young Count Ludwig Heinrich von Lerchenfeld. For Marie, an added element of romantic attraction in her affair with the Count was its apparent hopelessness, for he was afflicted with epilepsy. His fits were rare, but they could happen at inconvenient moments, such as the occasion when he fell at the feet of Marie's father while asking for her hand. Acton knew of his rival. He had met him and told Marie that, for the sake of his love for her, he was even prepared to withdraw from the field if she really wanted to marry the other man. Lerchenfeld eventually married the Bavarian Countess Klara von Bray-Steinburg, in 1867.

Döllinger followed his pupil's problems with warm sympathy but was careful not to intervene. "It is a delicate matter between us, for it is the only one where I have not consulted him and where he knows that all his counsels would be of no avail," Acton wrote to Marie in 1860.[1] In June 1863, Dr. Döllinger told

Acton that the Arcos were still looking to him as their son-in-law: there had been some who had asked for her hand, but they were not acceptable.[2] Acton held out for another year. At the beginning of 1864, soon after his thirtieth birthday, he wrote to the Professor: "You will surely agree with me that I must no longer think of a girl who persists so stubbornly in other ideas. If my heart was momentarily too strong or too weak for my reason, that is past now. . . . From this London season onwards I shall consider myself no longer wholly *hors de jeu*."[3]

Yet Acton continued to write to Marie. Their engagement was not "off." Even Pope Pius IX congratulated Count Arco. This was a formal courtesy towards the head of one of the leading Catholic families of Bavaria (the Arcos were friendly with the Munich nuncio, Prince Flavio Chigi, who would have procured such a letter in Rome). Acton himself was in the midst of his struggles with the English bishops over the *Rambler* and relished the irony of it. "My felicitations on the Holy Father's letter," he wrote to Marie. "For my part, I am ever expecting his attention in the form of an Index decree that some devout souls are trying to procure for me, notwithstanding my having no other aim in my intellectual and public life than the good of the Church and the progress of religion."[4]

One of these "devout souls" was the oily Monsignor Francesco Nardi (1808–1877), an old friend of the Arcos, a Roman prelate, auditor of the Rota, and a member of the Congregation of the Index. He was a keen advocate of the temporal power and had written various pamphlets about it. He knew and disapproved of the Arcos' friendship with Döllinger and his pupil at the time when Döllinger's views on the Papal States had aroused world opinion. The "treacherous Nardi" tried his best to block the marriage by sending to Munich any derogatory information he could obtain on Acton (Acton surmised that it was supplied by Manning).[5]

Count Arco was not the sort of man to take notice of such a defamation, however, and Marie herself cared less for the temporal power than for the Munich ball season. Acton continued to write tender letters and clung to her desperately. After the Christmas Eve Midnight Mass in the Aldenham chapel, "where the tombs of my parents are," and his return to his lonely house, he wrote to her: "The affection I have for you grows all the time and despite all doubts. The more I need you, the stronger it becomes. . . . Everybody here is incensed about me, and in his Christmas Pastoral Letter the Cardinal has denounced me, and all the other dignitaries having done it before him. All that does not disturb my sleep, but it gives me an importance which I do not seek."[6] But Marie wanted to be courted differently and with more ostentation. His devotion seemed to her one-sided. "You never ask about my feelings," she wrote. She felt that Acton took her too much for granted, that he gave her presents as though thereby wanting to establish his claim on her. Besides, he was full of strange ideas—ideas very different, at least, from those she was used to. Evidently, she wrote to him, he cared for her only because of her mother, for whom he showed more affection than for her.[7]

Acton kept on patiently urging Marie, hoping and waiting: "I always fear you are keeping something from me. But my life is only with you—in my country I am like an exile. Believe me, it is only your letters which do me good. My request is always: No favours please, but trust. Remember my friendship for all of you."[8] And in another letter: "I have nothing in the world than the future you will make for me."[9] In the summer of 1863, the papal dispensation for their marriage, needed because of their near relationship (they were second-degree cousins), arrived.[10]

Relieved of his work as an editor after the demise of the *Home and Foreign Review*, Acton took advantage of the long parliamentary vacations of the summer of 1864 for an extensive working holiday with Dr. Döllinger, spent in various archives in Austria and Italy. When Döllinger had to return to Munich in the autumn, Acton stayed on, working at San Marco's in Venice and also in Mantua and Verona. In October he went to see his Marescalchi relations in Bologna. Everyone was there, including Marie: Nonna Acton, Countess Arco with Marie's sister Leopoldine, and also Lord Granville. It was a kind of family reunion. "I was very well received despite the pope's view of me," Acton wrote to Döllinger.[11] To have anything to do with that young Englishman whose clashes with the Church were widely publicized required some independence of status and means, which Acton's aristocratic relations, though loyally Catholic, possessed.

The occasion served for an unexpected reconciliation between Acton and Marie and their re-engagement under general acclaim. His persistence had finally borne fruit. He had lost in his fight as a Catholic journalist, and he was about to lose his seat in the House of Commons. But with Marie's hand he had at least gained the happiest prize. And she may have seen his persistence as a token of a good marriage. "It will have dawned on her that finding a husband like Acton is one of the rarest fortunes," Döllinger commented.[12] But the Professor was prejudiced in favour of his pupil and was also used to considering personal relations as coolly and rationally as an historical problem. That was not Marie's way.

Among those present in Bologna was another happy couple, Marco Minghetti, the prime minister of Piedmont, just married to Acton's cousin Laura, the widowed Princess Camporeale. Acton was fond of the beautiful, flirtatious Laura but did not approve of her frivolous ways. She was clever and ambitious, always surrounded by numerous famous admirers. She had set her eyes on the widowed Lord Granville, who said, however, that he loved her in every capacity except that of wife, and, to Acton's relief, nothing came of the matter.[13] Minghetti was picked by Laura out of her circle of devotees. He was born of a middle-class family in Bologna, then part of the Papal States, and had entered the papal government as a young official belonging to the camp of the liberal regent, Charles Albert of Sardinia.

After Cavour's death, in 1861, Minghetti became Italy's leading statesman, apart from the three national heroes: King Victor Emmanuel, Giuseppe Garibaldi, and Giuseppe Mazzini. Minghetti was a good-looking man, tall, like many North Italians, with fair hair and rosy cheeks, a man of letters with the manners of a man of the world, and a great orator. Acton liked him because he was a moderate liberal and a free trader and had a good understanding of Gladstone—"the only man who has any appreciation of Mr. Gladstone's policy"— and approved of him because he was as opposed to the anticlericalism and collectivism of the Italian liberals as to the extreme papalism of some Italian Catholics.[14]

Minghetti was Italian prime minister from 1863 to 1864 and again from 1873 to 1876. The Piedmontese deposed him when he transferred the capital from Turin to Florence as a result of the September Convention with Napoleon III. Later the Florentines also overturned Minghetti when they fell into debt because of their enhanced status as a capital. Minghetti was a scholarly man, and Donna Laura came to describe her marriage to him as *un giorno di scirocco* (a sirocco day), by which she meant it was as humid, enervating, and dulling as the warm, dust-laden wind sweeping Italy from the Sahara. He was clearly not up to her expectations of an exciting husband.

Acton kept his distance from the enticing Laura, but he put a word in for her teenage son from her first marriage, Prince Paul Beccadelli di Bologna (Camporeale), so that he was accepted into Newman's school, run by Father Nicholas Darnell. Expressing his cousin's gratitude for the arrangement, Acton introduced Laura's new husband to Newman in a somewhat apologetic fashion as "a man who observes outwardly at least the duties of religion, and is politically a most decided supporter of religious liberty. Within the last year or two he has advanced a good deal in this direction, and he is particularly unpopular just now, as a friend of the clerical party. I don't think he has an[y] unbelieving theories, and he is not a scoffer, but his education must have been neglected as far as religion is concerned."[15]

The spoilt young prince's stay at Birmingham was a disaster. He was expelled under dramatic circumstances for using bad language but seems to have improved in a less strict atmosphere at another school at Oxford. Laura's daughter Maria also had a stormy life. She married Count Karl von Dönhoff. Only after that marriage was annulled by the Church—a condition on which her stepfather, Minghetti, strictly insisted—was she allowed to marry Prince Bernhard von Bülow, who was to become chancellor of the German Reich. Donna Laura, surviving Minghetti by nearly thirty years, extended her fame as a great society hostess to Berlin and died at the advanced age of eighty-six at the Villa Mezzaratta near Bologna.

With general relief over the reconciliation with Marie at Bologna, Acton accompanied the Arcos to Venice, where he remained until the end of October 1864. He spent his time working in the Marciana, the famous library then housed in the Ducal Palace, where he discovered and copied the private notes of Paolo Sarpi (1552–1623). The Servite monk and Venetian historian hostile to Rome was the author of a history of the Council of Trent that aroused the interest of those concerned over the plans of Pope Pius IX for another Church Council.

Acton spent that November and December with the Arcos in Geneva and then continued on his own to Turin, still the capital of Piedmontese Italy but soon to be supplanted in this capacity by Florence. In his eight-day stay Acton heard from Minghetti, as he told Döllinger, how displeased the Piedmontese were about the Convention just concluded between them and their ally, Napoleon III. Their finances were in a bad state: they were obliged to pay some of the debts of the papal government and yet had to respect the status quo of what remained of the Papal States. In return for the payments, France had offered to withdraw her troops from Rome within two years.[16]

Acton went on to Milan and Florence, but his mind was not on sixteenth-century manuscript studies or contemporary Italian politics. "I could not bear the separation from my happiness and shall soon be reunited with my Marie in Rome," he wrote to Döllinger.[17] Unexpectedly, Acton met up with the Arcos again at Livorno, and together they travelled in a ramshackle steamship to Civitavecchia. He spent Christmas in Rome with the Arcos and early in February 1865 went with them to Naples, on one of his rare return journeys to the place of his birth. The past months of his travels through northern Italy and the Italian South were bound up with his newfound happiness and concluded his "seven years of scarcity," with little joy or fulfilment either in his parliamentary or in his journalistic life. Because of Marie's final surrender to the persistent cousin, "There now opens up for me the only chance of a truly happy and quiet life for me," he wrote to Döllinger in his new gladness. "Not only my hopes are fulfilled, but my ideals have been exceeded. My expectations were not as elevated as what I have now found. It will be no disadvantage for my future work in the service of the Church, to share with her the joys of life, also the inevitable sorrows, and sad experiences, and to have a nearer, surer consolation than the undetermined and even uncertain outlook for a better future. Through this influence which she has already won, and through the continuous reminder of the ordinary duties of a devout and Christian life, this union has been for me an extraordinary grace." [18]

The couple agreed, for a variety of reasons, among them the uncertainty of his final parliamentary phase, to hold off their wedding until the summer of 1865. Their mutual love of Italy was a bond meanwhile. "There is scarcely a part of Italy," Acton wrote to Marie about this time, "that has not been enchanted by the history of our love, and this charm will remain upon the country as long as I live." [19] There is a series of letters to Marie (who was staying on in Rome with her mother), undated but datable by their joyous mood, written from various places on his journey back to England. "It seems strange indeed when I think of last October, before Bologna, and the very different expectations I then had of spending the winter." [20]

From Munich, Acton wrote exuberantly: "To me, the revelation of happiness which I have derived from the time we spent together is something so great and new that it fills my thoughts and throws a brightness over the time to come which nothing can darken, so long as I am sure of you. Everything is transformed by it. What is wrong seems more hateful and remote than ever, and all that is pious and good seems to me secured, sweetened and made easy. Spiritually as well as domestically you have inspired me with a wonderful confidence and repose." [21] In his old rooms at Professor Döllinger's he now felt himself to be crossing another divide in his life, "from the old existence into a new one which you will wholly fill. . . . Do not let me forget, in the midst of my new happiness, all that I owe to the time I have spent in these rooms, and to the incomparable friendship of my great master. His reign is over. But if you are happy in your life with me remember always that it is due in great part to the habits of thoughtfulness, the patience, the clearness and the confidence which I have learnt from him."[22]

Back in London Acton told Marie of a dinner given by his friend Lord Houghton (Richard Monckton Milnes) at which he met Thomas Carlyle, "who is one of the most original and celebrated English writers, and who first introduced into England those German studies to which I am so much devoted. He was clever, but grotesque, and often absurd. He has just written a long life of Frederic the Great, about whom his judgment is very different from mine."[23] And then he returned to Aldenham, "to my last lonely bachelor days and solitary dinners" and walks over the fields with the chaplain, Dr. Thomas Green. Aldenham was, as he told Marie, "the scene of my best thoughts and of my most frequent and silent meditations on my absent love," and he ended with his constant and wishful plea: "It is delightful to hear you say that you really care for me—all the future of my life depends on that."[24] Richard Simpson congratulated Acton on his re-engagement and added: "I don't think any body observed the way in which you bore your long troubles with more respect & sympathy than I did."[25]

Sometimes in their early happiness Acton wrote to Marie of the things that interested him. The news of President Abraham Lincoln's assassination on 14 April 1865, for example, came as a deep shock to Acton, who was a fervent supporter of the American South. He expatiated on complicated matters like the Italian political parties, which actually were of little interest to Marie. "There is nothing more delightful to me than to explain my whole life to you, its motives, causes, intentions and prospects; and you may suppose how glad I am to find that you care for these interests, and are ready to be quite in harmony with me."[26] He discussed religious problems with Marie, who had attended the Holy Week ceremonies in Rome but disliked the pomp of the liturgy at St. Peter's. She wished for something less noisy and ostentatious, she wrote to him. He agreed with her: "But the Church is so formed by our Lord that real edification and piety are as great in the poorest and . . . humblest congregations. . . . Perhaps you will be more deeply struck by the simple zeal of the poor Catholics in this Protestant country than by the splendours of St. Peter."[27]

The wedding had to be postponed yet again, until the end of July 1865, because of Acton's sudden candidature at Bridgnorth in the general election. They decided that Marie was to be known as Lady Dalberg Acton. As he had not inherited the Dalbergs' French title, there was to be no "de." The bridegroom made the arrangements for the presents for the bridesmaids: a locket of rock crystal surrounded by pearls set in a turquoise enamel border with Marie's initials on the front. Familiar as he was with English etiquette, he explained to Marie the finer points of social usages, for example that she must not write to "The Right Honourable Earl of Granville" but to "The Earl Granville, KG." Acton addressed her as "my sweet child." He told her how Aldenham was preparing for the new mistress. The little room next to the oak room was to be her boudoir, "although so very small. I like to think that nobody is supposed to be admitted there, except myself, and the sacredness which has hitherto belonged to my study will be transferred to that new room."[28] Shortly before the wedding he wrote to Dr. Döllinger, who was to marry them: "Everything is uniting to make this summer the most peaceful and happiest time of my life."[29]

But neither Acton nor Marie could have had any illusions about the nature of the bond that they were entering. She was finally being "sensible" in the way girls of her kind were told to be when faced with the prospect of marrying a man they did not dislike but did not love. For his part, he had talked and thought himself into this love for her on the model of what he had felt for her mother. He hoped that it would kindle the flame in her heart. "God bless you, my own sweet child! Pray for your old husband, and trust his tender love."[30] That was how he ended one of his last letters to her from 32 St. James's Place before their marriage—an affectionate if unpromising beginning.

Acton and Marie were married by Dr. Döllinger on 1 August 1865 at St. Martin's, the Arco castle in Upper Austria. The bridegroom's cousin, Sir William Throckmorton, was best man. The purpose of this peculiarly English function, Acton explained to Marie, was to keep up the bridegroom's courage and prevent him from running away![31] Lord Granville and English, Italian, and German members of both families were among the many guests. A *Heiratsschiessen,* a wedding target shoot, in which the guests could show their skills, was organized by the bridegroom according to Austrian country custom. Then the couple went to Aldenham and later, on their honeymoon, again to Italy. A reminder of this trip, kept among the personal papers at Cambridge, is the passport issued by John Earl Russell, Viscount Amberley, etc. etc., Her Majesty's Secretary of State for Foreign Affairs, etc. etc., dated 24 July 1865, requesting "all those whom it may concern to allow Sir John Acton, baronet and member of Parliament, accompanied by his wife—travelling on the continent with a maid servant—to pass freely without let or hindrance, and to afford him assistance and protection of which he may stand in need."[32]

There is a fine charcoal drawing of Marie, the young Contessa Arco, made before her wedding by Franz von Lenbach, which depicts her with a fringe, her hair pulled back, showing her open oval face, big eyes, and hint of a smile. She is wearing a flowing robe and is shown leaning forward over the back of a chair, delicate hands stretched out in front of her. She was pretty rather than strikingly beautiful, as her mother had been at her age. Marie had bright blue eyes, a good complexion, and a lovely figure. Everything about her seems attractive. It is worth recalling that Lenbach was said to catch the real character only of sitters with whom he had a real rapport. Döllinger, Acton, and the Arcos were evidently among those.

Marie turned into the most dutiful and devoted of wives. "Will you send me one of your socks for a pattern for the woollen ones that I am to get for you?" she urged.[33] Their first daughter was born in London, at 15a Hill Street, on Assumption Day (15 August) 1866, the name day of Marie's mother, who was present at the birth, and also the name day of Acton's mother. "Everything went so well, Marie is so well and happy, she was excellently cared for by doctor and nurse, and the little girl is so healthy that we feel we have received a special grace. She was baptized Marie Elisabeth Anna."[34]

"I forgot to ask you whether you wish me to be churched here or at Aldenham, RSVP," Marie wrote to Acton at Aldenham.[35] It was the new Archbishop of Westminster, Henry Manning, who arranged for this to be done at the Jesuit Church, Farm Street, London. "It is not considered a parochial rite," Manning wrote to Acton, and he added: "You will be doing great good if you utilise your abilities and your time in the manner I suggested."[36] Manning was referring to the edited publication of papers from the Vatican Archives relating to English Catholic seventeenth-century history at the time of James II, which he evidently believed that Acton in his Aldenham Library could more safely be entrusted with than anything more journalistic and concerned with the present. Marie's churching, one may assume, was regarded by Acton and his wife as a pious custom in the Roman ritual's traditional sense. It had, at that time, popularly attached to it the Old Testament notion of cleansing from bodily impurities after birth, which Catholics today no longer hold. Acton was not otherwise given to puritan or Jansenist interpretations of his faith, but his devotional life was, considering the high level of his intellectual understanding of his religion, both very simple and time bound.

The early years of their marriage were spent at Aldenham and on visits to Munich and Italy. Marie played the role expected of her, consorting with their Shropshire neighbours. She used to run a stall at the church's Easter bazaar, and Acton's friend Sir Rowland Blennerhassett, a frequent visitor, was always asked to bring from London a supply of picture cards of famous contemporaries for her to sell. In special demand were two contemporary foreign heroes: the unfortunate Austrian Archduke Maximilian (1832–1867), known for his liberal and enlightened views, who, in 1864, allowed himself, with French support, to be proclaimed Emperor of Mexico; and Benito Pablo Juárez (1806–1872), the Mexican liberal revolutionist who probably ordered the Emperor to be shot at Querétaro, when he was captured and imprisoned after the French troops had withdrawn. Popular British cards were those of Benjamin Disraeli, Henry Morton Stanley, Lord Derby, W. E. Gladstone, John Bright, Lord Palmerston, Richard Cobden, John Stuart Mill, Charles Dickens, Anthony Trollope, Benjamin Jowett, John Henry Newman, Arthur Stanley, and Alfred Tennyson. Acton's letters to Marie now began "Dear wife," "Dearest wife," "My dear wife"; she usually wrote to him as "Mon cher Johnny." Her early letters, most written in French, are tender, full of affection, gossipy. The wise old Professor wrote to Anna Gramich, herself only recently married: "Until now nothing has disturbed the happiness of their marriage, but you will know from your experience about the trouble likely to come out of the blue."[37]

Their first child, Marie Elisabeth Anne, came to be known as Mamy. She was always very close to her father. "Our Mamy is the sun of our life," Acton wrote to Döllinger when she was nearly six:

We have rather neglected to get her to study, but she learns with great facility. Her memory and observation are excellent, quite out of the ordinary, and the clarity and sharpness of her thinking is almost disquieting. No sophism passes muster with her. There are no inconsistencies in her well-ordered little mind. She knows well how to distinguish between legend and history and always prefers the latter. And for her it is all natural, not affected, also her devoutness. Her evening prayer is something Raphael has never painted. She is stronger than she was, but still a delicate child. The English winter is still a danger for her.[38]

She was somewhat naughty. "I am so glad you whipped Mamy, and successfully. I am sure it will do her good," Acton wrote to Marie when Mamy was seven.[39] And on another occasion: "I am so very much pleased at the idea of your putting Mamy *en pénitence*. A very little severity will go a long way at her time of life, when all impressions are so vivid and immediate. It shows how much courage you have."[40] It appears that this Victorian method paid off in Mamy's case. Her attachment to her father (more than to her mother) did not prevent her from developing in relative independence from what must have been his overpowering influence. Mamy's bronchitis persuaded the family, from 1878 onwards, to spend the winter months in the south of France, where it was cured. When in May of that year, Mamy, aged twelve, made her First Communion, he wrote to Döllinger about "the inexpressible joy" that her spiritual state gave him after his own religious conviction had suffered a severe shock at the Vatican Council. "I have . . . seen that she was not disturbed by the wrong-headedness of priests—I chose the oldest I could find—in her calm and unaffected faith."[41]

The Actons' second child, Anne Mary Catherine Georgiana, also born in London, on 26 September 1868, was serious and pensive, a great reader, and closer to Acton intellectually than all his other children. Their relationship caused her, when grown up, to research the material for a life of her great-grandfather, the much-maligned prime minister of Naples, which was, however, not published. She never married, kept house for the family, and died, aged thirty-nine, at Thun, Switzerland (Thun is near Berne, where Acton's son served at the British embassy during and after World War I). Acton's happiness as a young father was immense despite his preoccupations with the Vatican Council and its effects. "My own love," reads an undated note from him, "I have just been upstairs to wish you good bye, and found you sleeping so soundly, I was afraid to wake you. God bless you! I am quite out of spirits at going away, and will manage not to stay long. Kiss our darlings for their old papa."[42]

The third child was the long-expected son and heir, Richard Maximilian, born at Tegernsee on 7 August 1870, just after the turmoil of the Vatican Council. When the boy was twelve, Dr. Döllinger expressed the wish that he might become for his father what Barclay junior had been for Barclay senior: "You know they are my special favourites in history."[43] The reference was to the Scottish Catholic jurist William Barclay (1543–1608), professor of law at the universities of Pont-à-Mousson and Angers, and his son, John Barclay (1582–1681), both famous for their disputes with the Jesuits over the temporal power of the Pope. Richard, called Dick, did not, however, emulate that model. Still, his father delighted in being able to guide his intellectual development. But he failed to complete his studies at Magdalen College, Oxford, and although he entered the diplomatic service and Acton was proud of his advancement, they were not very close.

Dick probably felt overpowered by his father's intellect. After Acton's death, Andrew Carnegie left the Aldenham Library, which he had purchased and thus saved from dispersal, to John Morley. Describing what happened then, Acton's daughter Mamy wrote that Carnegie had first asked Morley if he thought Dick might like to keep some of the volumes. John Morley replied, according to Mamy, that "he never opens a book." Richard Acton heard of this unkind re-mark, and when he was asked if he would care to have any of his father's books, he asked for "Punch from the commencement." "But knowing John Morley as I did," Mamy went on, "the subtle sarcasm must have been lost on him. John Morley left most of the library to Cambridge as a memorial to my father."[44]

Jeanne, known as Simmy, the third daughter, born in London on 17 March 1876, was a backward child and had to have a nurse to attend her. She often had screaming fits. It was because of her that, in later years, her mother never went out, devoting her entire life to her care. Simmy was very musical and fell in love with a music teacher but had to break off the relationship because of their social differences; she suffered badly from the episode emotionally. The family recalled that she played Chopin with tears streaming down her cheeks. She be-came obese from unhappiness and died, aged forty-three, at Thun, Switzerland.

Marie bore her share of the physical and psychological burdens that child-birth imposed on Victorian wives regardless of social status. Her children were frequently ill. They had scarlet fever, pneumonia, and tonsillitis, and sickness made for rows between the anxious parents. The father took a rational view: "My principle. . . is always to obey the Doctor's orders, if it is a good doctor, and if the facts are plainly before him. . . . Doctors are often wrong, but more often more right than eager parents." When Simmy was very small, she once had a high fever. Acton became very anxious and, meeting the famous Sir William Jenner in the street, brought him back to the house at Princes Gate. The great physician showed himself alarmed and advised that Lady Acton should not feed the baby but have a wet nurse. Marie, feeling that she was suspected of infect-ing her own child, was most upset and made Acton understand that she would never get over it. He felt that he had to insist on her accepting the doctor's ad-vice. After all, Jenner was an expert. He had discovered the distinction between typhus and typhoid, though his autocratic manner was notorious. Acton went to look for a wet nurse, but fortunately, because of a change in the child's con-dition, she was not brought into the house. Marie never forgave Acton for his apparent readiness in sacrificing her tenderest feelings for her child to the word of a doctor whom she had never seen before. "Our life has been less happy since that day," Acton said to his son.[45]

Sorrow came with the death of their baby boy, John, born in London in 1872, who lived only just over twelve months. A yet greater blow was the tragic death from scarlet fever of their fourth daughter, Elisabeth, aged seven. The surviving children were Acton's consolation. All of them adored him because, when he was at home, he looked after them even more than their mother did. It was he who took them to the doctor or to the dentist or even to the chiropodist and who instilled the love of history in them by telling them stories "with always an attractive touch of the romantic," as Mamy recalled.[46] Her earliest memory of her father was of being pushed in her pram in the Aldenham flower garden while he was eagerly discussing some problem with his friend Thomas Wetherell. If she could not go to sleep at night, he would leave his guests and come up to the nursery and sing her to sleep. He had a fine voice and had sung in the chapel choir at Oscott. He read to the children when they were ill, from Charles Dickens, George Eliot, William Makepeace Thackeray, and Sir Walter Scott.

In a letter on Mamy's fourteenth birthday, Acton reminded her of three obligations for her future life: the love of prayer, charity towards others, and self-denial. "Remember that Our Lord came down and died not for mankind in general, but for you in particular. He had each of us in his thoughts and saw the little nursery at Tegernsee and gave his life for each of its inmates." She must strengthen her habits of economy, self-control, and sacrifice, he went on, "doing without things we wish for, even if it is a very little thing. To deny oneself something is always useful and makes one strong and happy and master one's actions and feelings. Another source of happiness is the habit of thinking charitably and kindly of people, not only wishing them well, but making out the best case for them we can."[47]

Thinking over her childhood, Mamy came perhaps nearest to an understanding of her father's character when she said of him that he was "a man starved of either the love or the understanding his rich nature required."[48] She is also reported to have told a member of the family—one would like to know by whom she was told this Victorian bedroom secret, could it have been by her mother?—that after her father made love to her mother he used to get out of bed to kneel down and pray that a child had been conceived.[49] That would have been in keeping with the widespread Victorian religious conviction that the primary purpose of marriage was procreative, that the child and the child alone must be the object of love-making between husband and wife.

John Acton's marriage was evidently flawed, and not least by himself. The fact that, at first and for some years, Marie did not want to marry him and finally came round to it only under family pressure and for what was considered to be, at that time, a *mariage du convenance,* probably hurt his pride and left its mark on him. If she did not love him, however, she cared for him, looked after the children devotedly in their sickness, and stood loyally by him during the trials in the wake of the Vatican Council. Even though they did not get on well in later years, she was with him throughout his last illness at Tegernsee and shielded his reputation from malicious attacks after his death.

Acton, for his part, always imagined that he loved Marie, but he evidently transferred to Marie the love he had felt for her mother, Countess Arco. His relationship with the temperamental Countess was at times stormy. In his letters to her he constantly pleaded with her, no matter how badly she treated him, and he put up with much unreasonableness on her part. Their love, whether maternal on her part and filial on his, or mixed up with other emotions, was strong enough to weather any such setbacks. His love for Marie was different. He seems not to have afforded her the same patience and regard. He became unbending in his attitude to others as well, especially after the shattering impact of the Vatican Council, which was the great divide in his life. The stubbornness of his character was demonstrated as much in his political views as in his later moral judgements. In his intellectual estrangement from Dr. Döllinger one of his famous sayings was "Politics come nearer religion with me, a party is more like a Church, error more like heresy, prejudice more like sin."[50]

In their later years, John Acton and Marie were used to living much apart—he travelling frequently to London and elsewhere, she house-bound in the South of France, at Tegernsee, and at Munich, looking after their handicapped daughter, Simmy. Their letters, full of each other's activities, and especially his letters to his children, show no trace of discord. But their correspondence also includes a strange batch of letters, torn up, but with the pieces retained in an envelope and thereby adding to the mystery, as the curious reader can reassemble them like a jigsaw puzzle.

These letters are undated, but postmarks and internal evidence show them to have been written in the early 1890s. As usual, Marie wrote in French. They are emotional, pathetic cries for help in an evident crisis of their marriage, full of apologies—but for what? One may think, given the difference in their ages and interests, that Marie, middle-aged but still attractive, living alone with her children, may have had an affair of which the husband had got to know. He was away on prolonged visits to England, attending the House of Lords, busy behind the scenes in Gladstone's final administration and as Lord-in-Waiting to Queen Victoria. We know nothing beyond what the letters reveal, a lonely woman near despair and the apparent stony silence of the remote and unforgiving husband. There is no hard evidence that she had had an affair. The impression given is rather as though something had happened that reinforced her previous misjudgement of her husband's character and gifts. She was frightened of his growing coolness towards her. Whatever the cause, it seems to have been a turning point in their marriage.

In a letter dated 3 May, possibly 1893 or 1894, she wrote:

> I will tell you imperfectly what I wanted to express more clearly: that the causes which you, outraged, thought due to prejudice on the family's part, were actually your religious beliefs which astonished me and which I disliked. They caused a lack of confidence between us, and my misjudgement of you. . . . If he has these odd and newfangled ideas in religion, people used to say, can we be sure that his moral and social ideas are any better and needing respect? . . . Since it proved impossible what I had always dreamed of, spending some years with you here [at Tegernsee], I did the best I could for myself to discover your real self. My trouble was that I lack serious reflection, always stop short at things of lesser importance which matter, but not all that much. I was always afraid of losing myself in the depths. Your present work is something that interests me much and that I find inspiring. It makes me feel how much is in you and how much I have missed while you knew me and I was fighting my own life's battles. There remains the hope of showing you my deep regret, and finding a better life with you until our girls are married. And there is also the hope of accompanying you on your visits to Cambridge.[51]

A fortnight later, she wrote to him: "It is eight days that I am waiting for you to forgive me, a word of pity even if you do not want to believe me. In the meantime I feel my sadness and solitude having been thus abandoned by you, though my resolve is firm that you ought to show me the means of reconciling myself with God despite my having been untrue to my promises [the French text has "*mon infidelité a mes promesses,*" which could also refer to marital vows] and I have believed that you could save something for the love of our children, rather than be so mercilessly cruel."[52] A week later she wrote again: "I swear to you that I have never felt the pain so much as when your unspoken reproaches go to my heart and I must accept them as being deserved. If only you could give me a little of your confidence once more, I swear to you that I should not abuse it ever again. I want you to guide me in everything. I have made my peace with God in telling him that I have wronged you in refusing you the relationship which you asked of me. Let me, towards the end of our lives, make reparation and, on your side, have a little pity for your Marie."[53]

And a month later, on 24 June, she pleaded:

> Will you never write to me again and give me a sign of forgiveness and kindness on your part? Put me on the way of recovering them. The sadness in which your silence and indifference leave me for weeks has been a real penance. I long for a letter from you. . . . Be good and sweet and forgiving and you shall not regret it. . . . Last winter I often thought of talking to you, but it was always with fear and in the knowledge that I have not the gift of expressing myself as you have. Soon after our marriage I knew that your ideas of affection and confidence were far above my comprehension. When I saw later that there was nothing left of attachment and affection, I resolved to win you back. The idea of your leaving me seemed always the worst of disasters that could befall me. Forgive me for what I have done and allow me to win you over once more for the time left to us.[54]

With Marie living in Munich and Tegernsee, her place in London society was often taken by her daughters Mamy and Annie. "One has heard of a gentleman as *le mari et sa femme* [husband and wife], but I find that I am widely known as *le père et ses filles* [father and his daughters]," Acton wrote to Mamy.[55] On their visits to England, the girls accompanied him on weekend invitations to the great Whig houses, the Bedfords at Woburn Abbey, the Devonshires at Chatsworth, the Roseberys and Rothschilds. Acton was proud to show them off to the smart set, which bored Marie, and to introduce his son, Richard, to his political and academic friends. "Taking you out has made me lose all my shyness," he told Mamy. But the children remembered the time when they were all in awe of their father. "He could be very strict and used to beat us if we told an untruth, but for nothing else," Mamy recalled.[56]

Whether or not there was a formal reconciliation between Acton and Marie after their difficulties—their letters preclude a judgement either way—life went on, and they came to terms with it. A few years later she wrote to him: "I wanted to tell you how much I reproached myself having made life hard and difficult in the old days. I am now convinced that I was not educated at all, insufficiently formed to be your wife, too obstinate to accept you. After many years I see now the beauty of your qualities and mind. I had just no idea of a sure and quiet affection."[57]

11

ROMAN COURTESIES

In November 1864, before his marriage, Acton accompanied the Arcos to Venice and thence to Geneva and later journeyed with them to Rome to spend Christmas there. In Geneva, Gaspard Mermillod, who had recently been consecrated Titular Bishop of Hebron, told him in confidence which way the wind was blowing in Rome: a great universal Council was to be summoned, with the main purpose of clarifying the Church's authority in matters of faith and knowledge. The object of the Council seemed to be to condemn the errors of the age and confirm the temporal power. Infallibility was not mentioned, but apart from that the prediction turned out to be accurate. Mermillod recommended that when Acton got to Rome he should "cultivate" Cardinal Giacomo Antonelli, who was involved in the preparations, in order to mediate between Döllinger and the Curia. Acton described Mermillod as very skilful in the best Roman tradition (rare in a Frenchman) of conveying his intended message only vaguely, but with many words. On this occasion the message was evidently meant for Döllinger: that Pius IX continued to hold him in high regard as a Church historian although, according to the Pope—and Acton passed this on with particular relish—he was "deficient in the good traditions of the Italian schools of theology." [1] Both he and Döllinger were becoming adept at decoding such Roman compliments, which seldom meant what they said.

When Acton and the Arcos, travelling by steamship from Livorno to Civitavecchia, arrived at Rome on 21 December 1864, a sensation awaited them. Pius IX had just published his encyclical *Quanta Cura,* in which he condemned rationalism, Gallicanism, liberalism, communism, capitalism, and the modern State-Church separation. The encyclical was sent out to all bishops together with a letter from Cardinal Antonelli and accompanied by the notorious *Syllabus Errorum,* the list of eighty "errors of the age." These propositions were not classified theologically, and although it is generally accepted today that they were not infallible pronouncements, this was by no means the understanding at the time. In Italy the encyclical was talked about everywhere, but the storm broke because of protests from abroad.

The French government forbade the bishops to publish the encyclical (although this order was hardly observed) because it was thought to contravene principles of the French imperial constitution.[2] Montalembert's acceptance of the encyclical, "with secret indignation," earned him Acton's contemptuous comment: "That foolish man!" The official Roman explanation given to anxious diplomats was that only theories, not constitutions, were condemned. Cardinal Antonelli, as Acton observed in a letter to Döllinger, was forced into issuing various excuses, such as that the condemnations had been requested by the bishops to enable them to deal with local opponents, or that he had had no part in it, or had seen the necessity of the matter.[3]

Acton kept quiet about his own opinion. He was anxious only to get on with collecting material for his planned history of the Roman Index (one of his many projects that was never completed), the mere mention of which would have closed his Rome sources at once. So he emphasized his more innocuous aim of collecting material on English Catholic history relating to Cardinal Reginald Pole, St. Charles Borromeo, and Pope Benedict XIV. He also wanted to ease things with the Arcos, his future in-laws, and took care not to go around Rome proclaiming himself a victim of the *Syllabus.*

Such restraint paid off. Acton worked quietly at the Angelica, which, apart from the Vatican Library, was the oldest library in Rome. Ferdinand Gregorovius, the German historian of medieval Rome, introduced him there. Four times a week Acton went to the Corsiniana, which was part of the Academia dei Lincei, where he consulted various eighteenth-century manuscripts. He was less cordially received at the Vallicelliana, the library of the Oratorian Fathers, which had the papers of Caesar Baronius and of St. Philip Neri. Acton had worked there before, in 1857, but this time he was put off by the librarian. When he went to the Jesuits, he was informed that their papers had been removed to a safe place, which was kept secret. The archivist, Father Giuseppe Boero, received Acton rather coldly at the outer door. He was not allowed in. Afterwards he wondered whether this rebuff had had something to do with his review of an essay by Boero about King Charles II, which may have lacked sufficient respect.

At a dinner party, however, Acton was introduced to Cardinal Antonelli, who, bearing out what Mermillod had told Acton in Geneva, showed himself unexpectedly friendly. He knew all about Acton's family and what he was doing in Rome. "Our library has great treasures," he said. Acton replied that he had not been to the Vatican Library because he did not know whether he might request that privilege. "Why not?" said the Cardinal. "You shall have everything. What is the purpose of your search?" Acton replied, "The sixteenth and seventeenth century, Your Eminence, for the history of the Church. I know that much of it is reserved and I dare not apply." The response: "For you nothing is reserved. You shall have it all."[4] Antonelli gave the necessary instructions to Mgr. Carlo de San Marzano to issue the permit and wished Acton well for his "noble studies."[5] Rome seemed to have adopted a new policy towards him. Perhaps it was considered useful to remain on good terms with a man of his social position and influence. Yet the Protestant Kurd von Schlözer, the historian and counsellor of the Prussian legation in Rome, heard that Sir John Acton, "a leading English Catholic MP, was considered a heretic in the Vatican because of his opposition to Ultramontanism."[6]

Acton had various encounters with Antonelli and recorded his impression in a letter to Döllinger: "He treats me with the greatest courtesy, but tells lies to such an extent that what he says can be regarded as interesting merely for psychological reasons. . . . He chats a good deal, wants to know nothing, has no originality, no depth, no knowledge, but great dexterity in small things." As Acton went into Antonelli's office, Simplicio Pappalettere, the Abbot of Monte Cassino, who had fallen into disgrace because of his efforts to reconcile the Church and the Italian states, came out and whispered meaningfully to Acton: "É il tipo della furberia romana" (He is the typically crafty Roman). Giacomo Antonelli (1806–1876) was made a Cardinal-Deacon, the lower order of the cardinalate, in 1847. He was thus obliged to celibacy but appears not to have abided by the vow of chastity, as the Roman rumours about his numerous illegitimate children testified. As secretary of state for twenty-six years after 1850, he became the prototype of conservatism on the Roman Question. "He seems to me to have absolutely no moral sense," Acton wrote. "He said to me literally: *'C'est un bonheur pour nous que les Piemontais persécutent la Réligion. Sans cela nos affaires seraient allées mal'* [It is fortunate for us that the Piedmontese persecute the Church, otherwise things would have gone badly for us]. He regards retaining a few provinces more important than saving souls. . . . In important questions he has a great influence over the Pope insofar as such a volatile and yet weak creature can be dominated by one person."[7]

"But Pius IX," Acton went on in his long letter to Döllinger,

whose health is much better than was thought, has mentally become almost childish, occupying himself only with the silliest of pastimes and simple-minded, meaningless gossip, in which people like [Mgr. George] Talbot and [Mgr. Bartolomeo] Pacca readily encourage him. Last year he instructed that Lord Palmerston be thanked for allowing Cardinal Wiseman to give a public lecture in some hall or other. [Odo] Russell told him that it was really nothing to do with the government, nor would it have been able to stop him, which he could not understand at all. Finally he replied: "I have always said that there are two kinds of people, the English who can do things for themselves, and the others who cannot." He thus remains ignorant in most things—incapable of making up his mind and holding on to an opinion, to the despair of his ministers. Dupanloup said during his last visit: *"Le Pape est bien malheureux et mal entouré. Il ne dit la même chose deux fois de suite"* [The Pope is unfortunate and badly advised in the people with whom he surrounds himself. He never says the same thing twice in a row].

But at the same time he pursues his aim of calmly extending his power to an unlimited extent, in which he is especially encouraged by the Jesuits. I am assured that both Antonelli and [François Xavier de] Mérode despise him from the bottom of their hearts. . . . It is said that he is not all that popular, but whenever I saw him driving through the streets he was greeted with respect.[8]

Acton's peace was disturbed when, in January 1865, English Catholics in Rome were encouraged to sign an address to the Pope by foreigners thanking him for his encyclical and *Syllabus*. Count Arco was among those who would have preferred a general, unpolitical address of support, but that had been changed. Acton found the address unacceptable for various reasons, which he was then asked to specify to Lord Stafford, the president of the committee preparing the address. When he proposed a text of his own without political content as requested, objections to that were raised by someone close to Louis Veuillot, the leading French Catholic conservative journalist, who said that Cardinal Antonelli had indicated that the Pope would prefer to have no address rather than one that was silent on the encyclical and *Syllabus*. For a moment Acton feared that he might have to state his views on the encyclical openly, an act that would damage both his access to the archives and his standing with the Arcos.

Count Arco, however, had promised German Catholic friends that he would sign no commitments on Italian politics. Lord Vaux of Hawarden was another English Catholic who declined to sign, thus some confusion was caused in the Ultramontane ranks that, Acton feared, would be detrimental to him. Wanting to make it clear that he himself had no hostility towards the Holy Father, Count Arco showed the text of Acton's nonpolitical address, which both of them had been willing to sign, to his friend Cardinal Karl August von Reisach. The Cardinal, formerly Archbishop of Munich and known to be hostile to Döllinger, nevertheless decided to show Acton's text to the Pope to prove that Arco and Acton were loyal. At the same time the Pope was told about the forthcoming marriage of Arco's daughter to Acton, with a request for the papal blessing for Marie, which was duly given.

Manning, who was in Rome early in February, had been recalled by telegram because Wiseman was dying. Manning was not generally seen as the obvious candidate to succeed Wiseman as Archbishop of Westminster. Acton, surprisingly, remained one of the few defenders of Manning's appointment when it was made. Was he a victim of Manning's flattery, or had he merely recognized Manning's obvious talent? "I think the Pope chose the better man," he wrote of his future and most bitter opponent. "He makes himself as amiable as possible and his reception of me as friendly as that which I met with at the Vatican. I have no doubt his policy will be as conciliatory as he can make it at first, for nearly everybody is displeased at his election."[9] And to Marie he wrote: "We hear that Manning will be Archbishop. He is the ablest of all the candidates, and will do in some respects very well; but I fear not so well in others."[10]

In his long letter to Döllinger already quoted, Acton reported extensively about conditions in the Eternal City. Among the Roman nobility, the Princes Doria and Massimo represented the Italian outlook but had no political or intellectual weight. The Duke of Sermoneta, head of the Caetani, is "the only man of stature among the aristocracy, with an extraordinary clear judgment. His conversation is extremely funny, sometimes even grotesque; his knowledge of the Court is immense, also his repugnance. He considers they lacked the ordinary pagan virtues and did not even think of the spiritual ones. . . . He is an expert on Dante and a good classicist. But as a liberal he dare not attend the Florentine celebrations [of Dante's six hundredth birthday] because he believes he would not be allowed to return [to Rome]."[11]

As for the Pope, Pius IX depended in spiritual matters on Cardinal Prospero Caterini (1795–1881), Cardinal Karl August von Reisach (1800–1869), and Bishop Antonio Cagiano de Azevedo (1797–1867). The Pope's closer entourage was badly split; they were fighting each other. Mérode was the only talent among them, Mgr. George Talbot quite senile.[12] The most intelligent observer of Roman conditions, Acton went on, was the Austrian minister in Rome, Alexander von Bach, who is told "everything, and very exactly" by Antonelli. Odo Russell, the English agent, had told Acton that he had compared notes with Bach, and their accounts of Antonelli's conversations tallied completely. Acton also met the Prussian minister, Harry von Arnim-Suckow, a Protestant, who had a high regard for Döllinger and "was interested in Catholic affairs." Acton was to have close contacts with Arnim during the Vatican Council. Arnim's deputy was the historian Kurd von Schlözer, "who, however, has forgotten all about his studies in the whirl of society." Acton summed up his impressions of this Roman visit as follows: "Some exhibit Italian patriotism, others complain about the sufferings of religion and would like to give way for the sake of peace. Many are in opposition from purely personal motives. People with strong convictions, however, ready to sacrifice their existence to it, and who understand the true evils of the age, do not exist."[13]

Together with his future father-in-law, Count Arco, and one of the Arco cousins, Acton visited his native Naples in February, for the first time since the Garibaldi landings in 1860 and since Naples was made part of the kingdom of the newly crowned King of Italy, Victor Emmanuel. "Your father amuses himself," Acton wrote to Marie, "by throwing money into the sea, from the Villa Reale, and two men instantly stripped and went in after it, to the horror of several ladies and, believe me, to mine."[14] He described Naples as "quite calm, doing well business-wise, the churches well attended." The lazzaroni, the traditional beggars of Naples, were not to be seen. But the Italian government insulted the feelings of the people by destroying the religious symbols in the streets and public places. He was also told by Augusto Vera, the Italian Hegelian philosopher, an opponent of the Italian Idealist School of Vincenzo Gioberti and Antonio Rosmini-Serbati, that Vera's position in the University of Naples was becoming difficult. Three former priests had been given posts, one of them teaching Church history.[15]

"The charm of Naples is nothing to me when I think of our sweet moments together," Acton wrote to Marie, who had stayed in Rome, "and you must not think I want to amuse myself away from you." The purpose of his visit was to see some old relatives while his grandmother, Nonna Acton, was there. There was also an idea of bringing the remains of his uncle, Cardinal Acton, to England. He had died in Naples and was interred in the vaults of the cathedral. "It would be an act of respect which I owe his memory," he told Marie, if his remains "could be brought to England, to be buried under the Chapel at Aldenham where my father and mother lie buried."[16] But nothing came of that.

Acton also looked in briefly at the archives, which he found in magnificent order and very rich in material: Naples holds the archives of the Dukes of Farnese, the literature concerning the Spanish occupation of Sicily. At the Brancacciana, Naples's first public library, founded by Cardinal Francesco Maria Brancaccia in 1647, there were, Acton wrote to Döllinger, many manuscripts, for example by Girolamo Seripando (1492/3–1563), the eminent Italian theologian.[17] An Augustinian anchorite since 1507, Archbishop of Salerno in 1554, and Cardinal Legate of the Council of Trent, at which he chaired the debates on dogma, Seripando was accused of being too conciliatory in his theological discussion with Protestantism.

In Naples, Acton's meeting with Cardinal Girolamo Marchese d'Andrea was of particular interest in that it reflected how moderate Catholic elements, and also liberal Catholics, were feeling about the intransigence shown by Rome towards the Italian Liberal government. The Cardinal was an old friend of Nonna Acton and the family.[18] To Döllinger, Acton described him as a

very reasonable and thinking man, with a generous outlook and nothing petty in his nature. He may lack worldly wisdom, depth of learning, knowledge of people and sureness of judgement. But his goals, his bent are like ours. He let me talk at length, and was delighted with my views as though he heard them for the first time. He represents the reaction of a straight character and healthy intellect against all the bad tendencies here. . . . He disapproves of the Encyclical [*Quanta Cura*], as a severe aberration, wants to save the Papal States by a prudent peace with Italy and big internal reforms. He describes the Roman policy as wicked, doing bad things for the sake of good. Nothing could be expected of this Pope. He has no initiative, no more ideas, is driven here and there by his bad entourage.[19]

The Church must accept all established governments, Acton wrote to Marie. The Pope had the best intentions, but he was pushed around by the Jesuits. When Acton said that Veuillot predominated at Rome and that his party encouraged the Holy See in these steps, Cardinal d'Andrea quoted a French bishop, who said of Louis Veuillot: "Il est fou par foi" (His faith has made him mad). And when Acton replied how distressed he was to find that, at Rome, they were actually glad of the religious persecutions under the secular, liberal Italian government, the Cardinal replied with emotion: "Yes, it is quite true. They rejoice at the harm done to religion, because they think it will serve their own purposes. It is a most wicked and scandalous thing. It was quite right to defend the temporal power of the Pope, like the crown of any other prince. But it is not a dogma, and yet they try to make people believe it is one."[20]

Acton also met a sympathetic group of Neapolitan priests and laymen, among them the Oratorian Alfonso Capecelatro, who had been to see him in England in 1863.[21] Summing up his impressions, Acton told Döllinger that these high-minded priests and laymen in Naples were "respected at Rome, for they have an important influence and submit to the decisions; yet their general bent is feared. They are so careful that none has visited Cardinal d'Andrea. . . . I spoke out against their anxious attitude and said harsh things; but these men do not want to cause offence in matters of discipline, and the ablest among them believe that the Pope in such decisions is infallible. No argument is of use, only history can help. Here you can grasp tangibly the evil that is caused to religion due to clinging to temporal power."[22]

In view of the task Acton had set himself—making the archives accessible for unfettered research—nothing was more important than to cultivate his links with Augustin Theiner, prefect, since 1855, of the Vatican Archives. They had first met, in 1857, with Döllinger. Theiner's views seemed sympathetic outwardly, but Acton came to describe him later as that "gross prevaricator."[23] A friendship between the cosmopolitan aristocrat and the Oratorian priest, a Silesian cobbler's son with a rough and unsubtle mind, was difficult. They had little in common except their passion for the sources of history, for which Theiner literally had the key, being in charge of some eight thousand volumes of secret documents, chiefly from the nuncios' reports in the sixteenth and seventeenth centuries, when Rome was the centre of world politics and diplomacy. They had hardly been penetrated by scholars.

Theiner showed a reformist bent in his legal studies by writing a book on celibacy, which necessitated the continuance of his studies elsewhere. He went to work on medieval documents in England, France, and Rome. Acton, with his fondness for the backstairs of history, delighted in telling—in his celebrated Eranus Society lecture at Cambridge—how Theiner was originally sent to Rome by Louis Adolphe Thiers, the historian, then French minister of the interior, as his Vatican spy. He went to Cardinal Thomas Bernetti, secretary of state, fell on his knees, and confessed the purpose of his mission. The Cardinal told him to continue his reports but to show them to him before sending them off, and "so Theiner was installed as a man who served two masters and betrayed each impartially to the other."[24]

Theiner's vindication (1853) of Pope Clement XIV, the Pope who suppressed the Jesuits in the eighteenth century, added to Acton's sympathy for him, because he was on account of that correspondingly disliked by the Jesuits when these were back in favour with Pius IX. Theiner's influence in Rome widened when he reported on German books for the Pope, for example, positively, on Döllinger's book based on his Munich lectures on the temporal power, in 1861. Acton frequently visited Theiner in his apartment, on the top of a winding staircase, the *Himmelsleiter* (Jacob's ladder), as Acton called it, perhaps thinking of the archives as "heavenly revelation" and feasting with him "on the spoils of Eternal Rome."[25] It was a compensation for the prefect, badly paid as he was, to be able to reside high up in a papal grace-and-favour apartment, one of the most beautiful abodes in Rome, in the tower in which Galileo was imprisoned, overlooking the Vatican gardens and the city. Theiner had his own little private door and key leading directly to the archives.

Theiner had just published a volume of documents on medieval Scottish and Irish history. Acton, as Theiner knew, shared his interests in Reformation and Counter-Reformation history. But the Jesuits were suspected by Theiner of having delayed the printing of the minutes of the Council of Trent, which Theiner had been given the Pope's permission to publish. The German and Austrian bishops donated money for the edition. The project was, however, opposed by Father Tommaso della Tosa, a Dominican member of the papal commission who had originally supported Theiner, on the grounds that publication might provide ammunition for Protestant attacks on the Catholic Church and the Council of Trent.[26]

As a result of Acton's closer contacts with Theiner, the prefect made him an intriguing offer: under Theiner's overall authorship Acton was to edit and write the historical introduction to a collection of some hundred documents on the Spanish-English marriage negotiations between the future Charles I and the Infanta Maria of Spain, which included far-reaching concessions regarding greater religious freedom for English Roman Catholics. These negotiations came to nothing when Charles instead married the French Princess Henrietta Maria, in 1625. In addition to Acton's misgivings about Theiner's scholarship, which he once had expressed when reviewing "Father Theiner's Publications,"[27] he wondered about the motive for this flattering offer for which Theiner claimed to have been given permission. Was it part of the conciliatory ways Acton was encountering during his visit to Rome? But there might also have been the consideration that these papers were mainly of English interest and that it was useful for Theiner to have a competent English assistant.

In the talk on the opening of the European archives that Acton, when Regius Professor at Cambridge, gave to the Eranus Society, he mentioned that he still had the draft of a preface Theiner had actually proposed to him, in which he was to extol Theiner's virtues: how truthful, religious, and generous to students Theiner was! And he concluded: "That any man should spend years in acquiring many thousands of documents, for nobody's use but his own, and with no better purpose than to form a defined and certain judgment on the problems of controverted history that bear on the living world, was a form of mental infirmity not dreamed of in his pedestrian philosophy."[28]

Acton decided to accept Theiner's offer at face value, because he needed his help even more in regard to material on the history of the Index and the Vatican papers on James II.[29] He paid Theiner generously for the papers on the Spanish marriage negotiations that he took home with him;[30] the James II transcripts were to follow. But before they were sent, Theiner showed the papers to Manning to determine whether they might possibly cause a scandal, because they contained material detrimental to Sir Edward Petre (1631–1699), who entered the Society of Jesus, succeeded to the baronetcy in 1679, and was privy councillor to James II (1687–88). Manning had no objections to publication,[31] but it occurred to others in Rome, as Acton put it, that he "was not of all people the one chosen to possess the secret revelations of the Vatican."[32] It was then that the old misgivings about Theiner were revived in Rome. It was rumoured that he had sold Acton not only copies but originals and that they were conspiring to damage the Jesuits. Theiner was alarmed and wrote to Acton, who, feeling himself suspected, was also getting nervous.

Before leaving Rome in March 1865, Acton had an audience with the Pope. His own account is missing, but Döllinger, writing to a friend, referred to it, remarking on the "strange way" the Pope seemed to express himself on the controversial encyclical *Quanta Cura,* to which the *Syllabus Errorum* had been attached. The Pope talked about it, Acton reported, like a genial old man: such were his views that he had gradually formed and "noted" and wanted to express once and for all. He just could not help it if Döllinger or some other persons—this was literally what he said to Acton—were of a different opinion. Actually, the Pope could have had no notion of Döllinger's attitude towards the encyclical unless the nuncio had reported his views from hearsay. The Professor was impressed, however, by the courtesy shown to Acton in Rome and by his unexpected access to the archives, from the results of which Döllinger, too, hoped to profit.[33]

Meanwhile, Acton was back in England for the fiasco, as far as he was concerned, of the July 1865 general election. Then, at last, his wedding took place in August and was followed by further travels. The young couple happened to be in Paris when their uncle, Count Ferdinando Marescalchi, died there. They visited Aldenham with Marie's mother, and all of them attended the wedding in September of Lord Granville, who married Castalia Rosalind, the daughter of Frederic Campbell of the Isle of Islay in the Inner Hebrides, Scotland. Then they went back to Bologna, where the Duchess of Dalberg, Acton's grandmother, also died that year. The death of Lord Palmerston, in October, had the effect of increasing Gladstone's importance in the government. "The first weeks of my honeymoon were occupied with the idea," Acton wrote to the Professor, "of so comparing paganism and Christianity, as to be able to discover how much man knew by his own natural ability and what could not be anticipated. I want to talk about this subject in our Academy when I have better mastered the rich material. . . . For the benefit of my studies I shall probably not remain in parliament. Otherwise, and not only otherwise, my life is only too full of happiness."[34]

The Italian archives proved, when the material was reviewed, to be literally an *embarras de richesses.* There was no coping with them. In Venice on his honeymoon trip, Acton discovered the private notebooks of Fra Paolo Sarpi (1552–1623), the Venetian Servite monk and Procurator General of his order, who represented the Venetian interest in Rome in opposition to Pope Paul V. Sarpi was a virulent enemy of the Jesuits and also of the Roman Curia, which was believed to have organized an attempt on his life. He was influenced by Gallican and Reformation ideas and was excommunicated in 1607. He was certainly one of the most brilliant opponents of the post-Tridentine Papacy, and he came into renewed importance as the Vatican Council approached. Acton's point in writing on Sarpi had been to counter the current Roman attempt of concealing the wickedness of the Inquisition (Pedro de Arbues, a leading figure of the Spanish Inquisition, was beatified in 1867) by showing that saints and popes, too, had blessed acts of murder, for instance of Protestants, carried out in the name of religion.

In his essay on Paolo Sarpi, published in 1867, Acton made a gratuitous attack on two saints, Pope Pius V and the then Archbishop of Milan, Charles Borromeo, for supporting a decree that promised pardon for the murder of heretics.[35] The attack had nothing to do with Sarpi. A storm of protest arose in Catholic circles. Newman took umbrage at the passage in question and, while admitting that canonization should not provide exemption from criticism, implied that Acton was indulging in sensationalism by criticizing the moral standards of two great saints.[36] Marie Acton—having read the article, which her husband had left her to mail—expressed her misgivings about the passage.[37] Later it turned out that Acton had confused St. Pius V with his predecessor, Pius IV, and that the decree he quoted made no provision for the lawful murder of heretics. Acton had relied for his facts on the Italian historian Cesare Cantù and had not checked them himself.

It was only two months later that Acton realized what he had done and wrote to Wetherell, the editor of the *Chronicle,* in which his article had appeared: "There is no excuse for my blunder about Pius IV. The fact is I had not seen the book for a year, and ought not to have written a historical article away from Aldenham. Pius IV and St. Charles amount to the same thing. Pius IV has not otherwise shown bloodthirsty fanaticism; Pius V has. I suppose that is how, in the dark recesses of my memory, one name supplanted the other. This is said only to explain the thing to yourself—not in mitigation."[38]

Worse for his reputation as an historian was the famous article on the Massacre of St. Bartholomew, although it was one of the most learned and heavily researched pieces he ever produced. Its purpose was to attack the prevailing view that the massacre of the Huguenots was the result of a sudden and unpremeditated decision. Acton admitted that there was no conclusive evidence but marshalled an impressive array of facts arguing that the evidence for premeditation was even stronger. According to Herbert Butterfield's detailed study, however, Acton made various mistakes in interpretation and was guilty of what, among professional historians, is regarded as the worst of sins: manipulating the evidence and, contrary to his own ruling principle, omitting what was unfavourable to his own case. Acton, in fact, while suspecting the Roman motives, pointed out that no evidence had ever been produced to confirm the belief, common at the time, that the massacre had been promoted or sanctioned by the court of Rome or the Catholic party; he perhaps understated the case for the responsibility of the French government.[39]

Acton made much use of the papal nuncio, Anton Maria Salviati, to prove premeditation, but failed to mention Salviati's own stated belief that the murders could have happened only in sudden reaction to the attempt to assassinate Gaspard de Coligny. Butterfield referred to Ranke's investigation of the same subject fifteen years before Acton and concluded, damningly for Acton: "Not being deflected by any strong feeling into imagining that even bad men will be pointlessly bad, Ranke had penetrated the subtleties of a situation in which the apparent evidence for premeditation required to be handled with great care." According to Butterfield, Acton was guilty of behaving like a journalist.[40] But in fairness it should be remembered that the academic seeker after truth, too, is not always free from the sin of special pleading.

Acton employed copyists all over the Continent. They and his constant new acquisitions for the Aldenham Library consumed his fortune: copies of some five hundred of Cardinal Reginald Pole's letters came from the Parma archives; the James II material from Theiner, 620 pages, was to be supplemented from the Paris archives, hopefully also from the correspondence of Cardinal César d'Estrées (1628–1714) in the Vatican Secret Archives, and from the countless letters of Queen Christina of Sweden, and so on. "It is getting difficult to master the material which my own library offers on James I," Acton wrote to Döllinger.[41] By the 1890s these private purchases amounted to some hundreds of volumes. "My extracts and transcripts," Acton explained, "have been made in above forty collections and are the product of many labourious years." This is how his conviction grew that "by going on from book to manuscript and from library to archive, we exchange doubt for certainty, and become our own masters. We explore a new heaven and a new earth, and at each step forward, the world moves with us."[42]

Acton's optimism about reaching certainty by consulting the archives changed, however, in later life. Finally he thought that the ultimate disclosures were not to be found in the formal documents but in the private letters and revelations of public figures. But such totally unguarded private revelations, too, were not free from wilful or involuntary deception. Acton remained "the old-fashioned historian, collecting sources in every field, and assembling materials for many historical topics at once."[43]

In November 1866 the young couple returned to Rome, and Acton continued his intricate dealings with Theiner. On the way to Rome from Munich he had calculated, in a letter to the Master of the Rolls, Lord Romilly, the costs of the Vatican material, including transcribing and collating, to be between £1,200 and £1,500. This sum could be distributed over three or four years and be still made profitable for Theiner. The British government should negotiate with Cardinal Antonelli and the Curia on these terms: "It will be a matter of some delicacy, because Theiner would be giving up materials which might have served to enhance his literary fame, and because it will be necessary to establish some control and revision over copies made by his own secretaries. Also he would easily be frightened if jealousy were awakened and an outcry raised in Rome. But a discreet pension coming to him with an offer of £400 for the James II papers, with a prospect of twice as much for copies of the other English historical papers in his charge, would obtain all that is worth having."[44]

Acton knew of the uncertainties of human affairs in Rome: the Pope or Cardinal Antonelli might change his mind; Theiner, growing old and ill, could disappear, and no one better to deal with was likely to succeed him. His "charming Stevenson plot," as Simpson called it, namely, to secure government funds for the copying of the English historical documents in the Vatican Archives and to avoid the Roman opposition to Acton himself, involved Joseph Stevenson (1806–1895).[45] He was a former Presbyterian minister, then Vicar of Leighton Buzzard for thirteen years, and had resigned, in 1862, to become a Roman Catholic. He worked in the Public Record Office and poorly edited many volumes of the Church Historians of England series. It was not until six years after his conversion, however, that Stevenson was sent to Rome. The result of his work, which lasted only six months, was meagre. But by then, April 1870, Theiner had been dropped in disgrace. He was barred from the treasure, the lock of his private door to the archives having been changed overnight. Among other malpractices he was accused of having given or sold the secrets of the archives, such as the Council of Trent minutes, to opponents of Papal Infallibility at the Vatican Council, including Cardinal Gustav Adolf Hohenlohe and Acton. And by then, in Rome, any link with Acton would have been the kiss of death. "If all his confidants had been as discreet as I was, he might have lived to his death in the lustre of office; and he did not stipulate for discretion."[46]

Another of Acton's Rome visits, in October 1866, coincided with one by Gladstone, his wife, and two elder daughters, Anna and Mary. Gladstone looked forward to a respite from Westminster politics, and the family settled in an apartment at the Piazza di Spagna. They had a private audience with the Pope, met Cardinal Antonelli, and wandered around the city. Mary Gladstone, very English and Anglican, found the audience with Pope Pius IX "excessively ludicrous." Like others of her generation she preferred ancient Rome to Baroque and Catholic Rome. With due disapproval she noted Monsignor Francesco Nardi's behaviour. He was taking the English ladies round, even though "Monsignores are not allowed to drive with females in Rome. And he said some odd things."[47]

"Nothing can be more unlikely," Gladstone wrote to Acton when announcing his Rome visit, "than that I should meddle with the prisons, or anything else of the kind. The case of Rome in 1866 is very different from that of Naples in 1850 when the whole Royal Government was nothing but one gross and flagrant illegality."[48] This was a reference to his denunciation of Neapolitan prison conditions during the 1850 visit. But this time it was Acton who stirred up a similar hornet's nest with a visit to the Ergastolo, the penitentiary for recalcitrant priests at Corneto, near Civitavecchia. This was the only institution of its kind in the Papal States, and the evil conditions he saw there caused Acton to send a long report to Cardinal Antonelli, who, as the Pope's secretary of state, was the responsible minister. There were sixteen prisoners when Acton was shown round. He noted that priests who had been sent there were regarded as so totally lost that Italian bishops thought twice about sending anyone there. So the inmates were mainly from Rome.[49]

One of the convicts, a Piedmontese who had written books, was found guilty as a schismatic, and because it was feared that he would go mad, the Pope had him sent to the Ergastolo without any formal condemnation. Another had persuaded a child to steal some money from his father; another had attempted to poison a papal pallbearer so that one of his relations should be able to take on the position. There were sexual offenders, and some cases of heresy. The prisoners were able to communicate easily with each other in gangways and even in their cells. One had escaped by making a rope from sheets he had forced others to give him; four or five others had also recently escaped. The convicts were not recognizable as priests; they were in rags and dirty, and seemed to have lost all dignity and shame.

Madness was often mentioned as an explanation for the priests' crimes. Or they said that imprisonment had made them go mad. The cells measured about twelve square feet and had high ceilings; the gangways were dirty. There were three warders, uncouth men who were paid only six scudi per month, and they had got rid of a fourth warder so they could share out his pay. As punishment for misbehavior, prisoners were deprived of their daily exercise in the garden, or put on dry-bread ration, or forced to sleep in a worse cell than their own, on the floor and without a mattress. They would not say Mass but read the breviary together. Three or four of them had formed a group with a former Jesuit for voluntary exercises, penitence, and meditation. They were paid nine *baioceni* a day, which they could freely spend.[50] Twice a year they were given clothes, and they had a barber. The best-behaved inmate was made sacristan. He and others were at their prayers when Acton's party visited the chapel during recreation; a third was binding books. Acton was impressed by how well they copied manuscripts and music, but they had no books to read or study. The warders were complaining that the prisoners were treated better financially than they themselves were, but no trace of that was seen. Acton requested permission to send a chest of books. His letter to Antonelli concluded with the assurance that he had not mentioned what he had seen at Corneto to anyone except the Cardinal.[51] When no answer came for three weeks, Acton no longer felt obliged to remain silent. At a dinner party given by Odo Russell he described his visit to Gladstone, who was predictably incensed.

The following day Acton had occasion to meet Antonelli and brought the matter up again. The Cardinal promised that the prisoners should have books and seemed to be grateful for Acton's intervention. What actually went on behind the scenes is shown by an angry note marked "most secret," which Antonelli appended to Acton's letter, in which the Bishop of Civitavecchia, responsible for the Corneto prison, was taken to task for allowing foreigners like Lord Acton, however distinguished, not only to visit the prison but to penetrate its most private places.[52]

It was shortly afterwards that Döllinger wrote to Acton about rumours he had heard regarding a Council to proclaim Papal Infallibility. Could Acton find out more about it in Rome? Why had the bishops from all the world again been called to Rome? The occasion was the canonization of Pedro de Arbues. "And what a canonization!" Döllinger exclaimed. "A Spanish Inquisitor struck dead by the people who were driven to despair at the height of the persecution (about 1485). And he is now to be canonized as a martyr of the Inquisition. One can only wonder at such deliberate provocation of public opinion."[53]

Acton was unable to find out anything more definite than rumours. Soon, however, the news broke. In the June issue of *Civiltà Cattolica,* a Council was powerfully advocated. On 26 June 1867 the Pope told the bishops assembled at Rome of his intention, and on 29 June 1868 the Bull of Invitation, *Aeterni Patris,* went out to all the bishops and others entitled to assemble in the Vatican Basilica on 8 December 1869. Infallibility was not mentioned.

But then an ominous article appeared in *Civiltà Cattolica,* on 6 February 1869.[54] It played a major part on the eve of the Vatican Council in producing two bitterly opposed camps. In the form of a report from a Paris correspondent, the article claimed that *true* Catholics (that is, the great majority of the faithful as opposed to the liberal minority) wanted the Council to give affirmative expression and dogmatic form to the propositions of the *Syllabus Errorum.* They were also said to want the dogmatic Infallibility of the Pope to be confirmed by acclamation of the Council Fathers. They also wanted, it was said, the proclamation of the dogma of the Assumption into heaven of the Blessed Virgin. The material of this article was originally part of two memoranda that the Paris nuncio, Chigi, had sent to Cardinal Antonelli. They described the expectations of extreme Ultramontane elements as though they represented the majority opinion of French Catholics. Recognizing their propaganda value for the Vatican Council, Antonelli passed the memoranda to the Jesuit review, which published them as coming from a French correspondent. An ugly mood was being created in all parts of the Catholic world.

Acton spent the summer of 1869 at his Rhineland home, Herrnsheim, where an important pre-Council meeting was to take place, in October 1869, with Döllinger and Bishop Dupanloup, in order to discuss what they could do to activate the forces opposed to Infallibility. "The front seems to be hardening," Döllinger wrote from Munich, having heard from Louis Arco, a diplomat at the Bavarian legation in Rome: "*Consilium sine spiritu consilii*" (A Council without the spirit of counsel).[55] Acton's wife and the children were at Tegernsee. "It is lonely here without you and I cannot accustom myself to it. Whenever I go to the library, it is a shock to remember that I need not walk on [the tips of] my toes," wrote the young father (the library occupied the magnificent round tower at the east end of the Schloss, near the nursery). "I am busy from morning to night and tired with writing," Acton recounted.[56] He supplied Wetherell with material for the first issue of the *North British Review,* the former nonconformist journal, a quarterly, that was to take the place of the *Chronicle,* which had had to close down in February 1868 after a brilliant but short-lived existence. Acton's contributions comprised two substantial articles as well as sixteen reviews of historical books. Among them was one on Acton's Council of Trent "hero," Fra Paolo Sarpi, by Arabella G. Campbell, which Acton reviewed negatively.[57] The two major articles were, in fact, also book reviews; the topical one was "The Pope and the Council"; "The Massacre of St. Bartholomew" could claim topicality because of the number of books published at that time on the same subject, particularly by Catholic apologists.[58]

In the article on the Council, Acton reviewed Döllinger's *Der Papst und das Konzil,* which had been published earlier, in October 1869, under the pseudonym Janus. Acton's review of the book, in which Döllinger had the assistance of his pupil and later biographer, Johann Friedrich, and Johannes Nepomuk Huber, appeared under the heading "Communicated" so as not necessarily to implicate the new journal in its viewpoint, with the reviewer even mentioning Döllinger's name as though he was unaware of who Janus really was. Acton entered the fray without equivocation: "The attempt to establish the infallibility of the Pope by decree of a General Council is a phase of controversy which the internal disputes of the Church of Rome have made almost inevitable. The Catholic opposition in its several forms, national in Italy, scientific in Germany, liberal in France, has uniformly been directed against one or other of the Papal claims."[59]

The episcopate had allowed the Pope to proclaim a new dogma (1854), pronounced almost unanimously in favour of the temporal power (1862), accepted the *Syllabus* (1864), and "assured the Pope that they were ready to believe whatever he should teach" (1867). "The most sanguine opponent can hardly expect, if the Council meets, that the dogma will not be proposed, or that it will be rejected in principle, or on any higher ground than that of present expediency."[60]

Even before Bishop Dupanloup arrived at Herrnsheim, Acton had his doubts about the man who had been his mother's friend and his own first headmaster. Would the bishop who was to lead the minority opposition to Infallibility really refuse to give in *jusqu'à la mort*? Alphonse Gratry, the French philosopher and opponent of Infallibility with whom Acton had discussed the question in Paris on his way to Herrnsheim, would not swear to it.[61] And when Marie had been about to meet Dupanloup in Paris, shortly before their marriage, Acton wrote to her in one of his fine characterizations: "You will find Dupanloup very brilliant, though less so than Montalembert, very adroit, but less than Mermillod, and not as deep as Gratry."[62] But the gloomy prospect of what was to come made no difference to Acton's girding himself for the battle and writing to Peter le Page Renouf almost gaily: "I am on my way, an unbidden guest, to the Council. I am afraid that before we meet again we shall be heretics."[63]

The German bishops seemed more unanimous than the French in their opposition to the proposed dogma. Their Fulda pastoral letter of 6 September 1869 was clear in that respect, Acton noted, "but they may have been prompted to act under pressure from [Karl Josef von] Hefele, the bishop of Rotten-burg. However, not one of them would not be ready, in case of need, to go against his conviction; at any rate, it is difficult for the laity to speak out after the bishops. Reisach knows perfectly the mood in Germany."[64] Hefele, too, had visited Herrnsheim briefly that September, and so had Bishop Wilhelm Ketteler, the old friend of the Dalbergs. Ketteler's opposition to Infallibility was "on grounds of expediency, not, like Hefele, of Doctrine. Dupanloup looks forward to the question of opportunity as his vantage ground. They expect to get off on a quibble like a condemned criminal."[65] And a week later he wrote: "You may bind these men with links of iron and they will elude you."[66] This was his view of the reliability of the German bishops' stance. They had written privately, but collectively, to the Pope to entreat him not to bring Infallibility forward at the Council. This letter was drawn up jointly with Cardinal Prince Schwarzenberg of Prague, who was the highest-ranking leader of the minority at the Council and thus had more than German backing.[67]

THE UNBIDDEN GUEST

One of the direct consequences of Acton's failure to get elected MP for Bridg-north was Gladstone's offer of a peerage, in November 1869. His character "is of the first order," the prime minister told Queen Victoria, "and he is one of the most learned and accomplished, though one of the most modest and unassum-ing, men of the day."[1] Justifying the choice of two Catholic peers (the other was Acton's fellow MP Edward Fitzalan-Howard, second son of the thirteenth Duke of Norfolk), Lord Granville countered the objection that the Queen said might be raised: "The policy of Your Majesty's government is to treat Roman Catholics for the future with equality in proportion to their numbers," and, evi-dently defending his stepson's suitability, he pointed out that most of the other Catholic peers "cannot think for themselves and are under the direction of their bishops, and Sir John Acton would be excluded if Dr. Manning had power to do so."[2] That would have weighed with the Queen.

Gladstone wrote to Acton, who was already on his way to the Vatican Coun-cil, of the pleasure it gave him to offer the peerage. "Suffice it to say I think you will confer honour by your acceptance, no less than you will receive it," he wrote.[3] Acton, in his letter of thanks, replied from Rome: "I wish there were public services in the past to justify my acceptance of a peerage; but I cannot decline an honour, however undeserved, which is proposed by you."[4]

There was some discussion of his title. The Acton baronetcy was "of Aldenham Hall." The College of Arms objected to "Dalberg Acton" because the Dukedom of Dalberg was a foreign title, possibly extinct since the death of his mother, and there was no precedent for granting such a title. Acton cabled from Rome that he wished "to be gazetted Lord Acton without changing my name."[5] So Lord Acton of Aldenham it was from 11 December 1869, a day after the first working session of the Vatican Council. It was clearly Gladstone's intention to strengthen Acton's hand. "I habitually attach very great weight to information received from you. . . . as much as I should like to have you here, I am glad you are there." And addressing his friend by his new title, he added that it was not meant "as a mere decoration, which you could want less than any other man, but because I trust it opens to you a sphere of influence and action."[6]

Being an English peer helped in Rome with the European bishops, because many of them came from noble families. Italians remembered that Acton was the nephew of a Cardinal; Germans and Austrians remembered that his mother was the last of the Dalbergs and that his wife was an Arco. That he was Döllinger's pupil was, according to one's point of view, either a recommendation or a hindrance. Döllinger was especially delighted to hear about the honour, and Acton wrote to him that the reactions of the English Liberal press "make me blush. Even the Tory *Times* was more favourable to me than to the other peers."[7]

Earlier, on his way to Rome, Acton had stopped in Florence to see Marco Minghetti, his cousin Laura's husband, then demoted from prime minister of the Kingdom of Italy to minister for trade and industry. Acton wanted to find out what preparations the Italians were making for the Vatican Council and "to exert the legitimate influences of a great Catholic nation inseparably linked with the future of the papacy."[8] After the encounter, however, he wrote to Marie: "People here do not seem very curious about the Council, which shows how thoroughly indifferent they have become to the things of the Church. . . . Fetched my own letters at the post. I came home to read them with some proscuitto, salami and parmesan."[9] At least he had not lost his taste for Italian specialities.

Acton arrived in Rome on 10 November 1869 and immediately threw himself into a whirl of activity to which his journal bears witness.[10] Owing to increased pressure of work he was, however, soon unable to continue his daily entries. "Please keep my letters; have not been able to keep up the Journal for more than eighteen days," he wrote in a postscript to Döllinger.[11] Similarly, he wanted Marie to keep the letters in which he wrote of memorable events.

The opposition bishops were divided. There was distrust between the French-speaking and the German-speaking bishops. The Bavarian Cardinal Gustav Albert Hohenlohe and Cardinal Friedrich Schwarzenberg were estranged. Among the Americans, Acton developed close links with Archbishop Francis Patrick Kenrick of St. Louis. He came to know Father Isaac Hecker, who attended the Council as theologian to Archbishop Martin John Spalding of Baltimore and was also procurator for the absent Bishop Sylvester Roscreans of Columbus.[12] Döllinger, whom Hecker had visited in Munich, was impressed by him and wrote to Acton in Rome that, according to Hecker, the American bishops were opposed to the doctrine of Infallibility but also very loyal to the Pope personally and that "a triumphalist Ultramontanism if victorious would be particularly damaging to the Church in the United States."[13] Acton was glad to find a sympathizer in Father Hecker but soon discovered that, in his enthusiasm, Hecker had greatly overestimated the number of liberal-minded American bishops like Kenrick of St. Louis, believing, for example, that not five of the forty-five American bishops would sign the address to the Pope demanding the proclamation of Infallibility (in fact, ten of them signed).[14]

Considering the lack of political *nous* in many of the bishops of the minority, compared with the more single-minded Roman advocates of Infallibility, Acton realized the importance of not only mobilizing the minority bishops into some sort of viable force but also stirring up the governments. They, however, were reluctant to become involved. A lead was to be expected, above all, from France, which had the military hold over the Roman Question and was also divided because of internal opposition to Infallibility. Yet no special envoy to the Council, as was customarily sent by Catholic countries, was appointed by France, and therefore Austria would not nominate one either, nor Prussia, which, within little more than a year, would hold sway over the whole of Germany. The liberal government of Bavaria at least, as Acton had been told in secrecy, was going to replace its clerical-minded and incompetent minister in Rome with one of its ablest diplomats.[15]

His widespread diplomatic contacts in Rome would be useful, too, Acton felt. But to rouse the government at home from calculated apathy was beyond his capacity. A letter to his stepfather, Lord Granville, contained a shrewd assessment of the situation of the minority bishops: "They do not form a compact group. Some are acting on this side because they think the definition [of Infalli-bility] dangerous; some, because they think it difficult, and some because they think it utterly inadmissible." Acton estimated the majority-minority propor-tion to be "something like four to one. . . . Therefore the greatest force that can be brought to bear upon the Council is the certain and distinct manifestation of European opinion in favour of the minority. It may not, indeed person-ally I hope it will not, check the Court of Rome. But it will add strength and numbers to the opposition, by assuring them that, if at the last moment they are compelled to protest, and to appeal to the nations, the governments, and the educated laity, will stand by them. That will secure the weak and doubting men."[16]

The invaluable Louis Arco had found a flat for Acton and Marie, their two little girls and the nanny, and temporarily also for Acton's grandmother, Nonna Acton, who, however, was becoming very frail and turning out to be some-thing of a burden to Marie, who was expecting her third child. The spacious and sunny apartment was on the second (top) floor of a house in Via della Croce, a little side alley off the busy Corso Umberto, close to the centre of Rome, the Via Condotti and Piazza di Spagna. There were three well-furnished living rooms (one of which served as a spare bedroom), two bedrooms, and two rooms for servants. The flat cost seven thousand lire for seven months, with service and laundry included—only £350 at the current exchange rate.[17] This was the Actons' home from the end of November 1869, for what was perhaps the most intense period of their lives, and also a kind of headquarters of the anti-infallibilists, where friends and like-minded bishops came to dine and talk.

Among the bishops assembled in Rome, leaders emerged: from the infalli-bilists, Henry Edward Manning and Gaspard Mermillod, "in a certain rivalry" with each other; the opposition was less organized because their leaders—Félix Dupanloup, Friedrich Schwarzenberg, and Georges Darboy, the Archbishop of Paris—arrived late. "Many, very many are wavering and are likely to be bagged by clever leaders."[18] There was the Croatian Josef Strossmayer, "the bravest of the bishops," who was to be one of Acton's closest allies.[19] "It is impossible to describe the diversity and briskness of what goes on," Acton wrote to Countess Arco, "and for anyone who knows the majority of the players and the inside of their interests, the fascination is such that one is tempted at times to forget the deadly gravity of the crisis."[20]

Gloomily but clearly Acton perceived the trend. "No bishop has hitherto declared publicly that he rejects the doctrine [of Infallibility] as erroneous," he wrote to Gladstone, "and the opposition intends to take its stand on the ground of expediency. At present, a majority of French, German, and Austrian bishops mean to take that line. Some, no doubt, will give way under the influences of Rome; and the rest will find their position very difficult to defend. It will be very easy to drive a wedge between those who deny the expediency of the decree and those who deny the truth of the doctrine."[21] The "inopportunists" existed only to be beaten. Who would risk a schism in a mere question of inopportunism?

In his Council journal, Acton recalled his and Döllinger's visit to Mermillod in Geneva, in November 1864, and noted how accurate Mermillod's information about the forthcoming Council had proved to be. Now he invited Mermillod to dinner. The Bishop wanted to meet Marie and hear her play the piano and sing. That dinner party impressed itself on Acton's mind because of Mermillod's shallowness. "Mermillod dined here and is still talking," he noted, having left his guests. "I have come to write down what he said. He talked the whole evening, very readily, fluently, and cleverly, but he gave us all the impression of being a charlatan. It is a serious reflection that the fortunes of the Church should be in the hands of seven hundred such men. For he is decidedly superior to the average of the bishops. . . . People seem to be aware how thin his mind is. He is however a most successful bishop and told us of his achievements at Geneva."[22]

A very different personality, and much admired by Acton, was the Archbishop of Paris and confessor of Emperor Napoleon III, Georges Darboy, whom, together with Strossmayer, Kenrick, and Karl Josef von Hefele, he came to regard as "the best men" among the bishops of the minority.[23] This opinion seemed to be confirmed by "the coldness and suspicion" he sensed between Darboy and Dupanloup.[24] Darboy "shows a certain reserve like someone carrying great responsibility and swallowing a threatening *quos ego*.[25] Nobody speaks more skilfully, beautifully and brilliantly than he does. . . . He has, as he told me at once, the Northern calm, and disdains violent ardour or extremes. His attitude is gentle, almost humble. But he thinks already, quite deliberately, of the *ultima ratio,* of protest and departure. The hope is, with the threat of such a step, to prevent the acclamation acceptance"[26] — acceptance of Papal Infallibility not by a vote but merely by acclamation, as rumours were predicting.

Acton recorded that Manning, on his way to the Vatican Council, visited Darboy in Paris and said to him: "Why don't you write a few lines to the Pope? You would get the red hat at once, and it would be nice if the two largest towns in Europe had cardinals as archbishops." What Manning meant was that he himself would also get the hat if he brought about Darboy's submission.[27] But when, on 19 January, Darboy, in an outspoken attack on procedure, asserted that, regarding Canon Law, they were discussing trivialities rather than what needed reform, and regarding the schema of the bishops, that it was concerned with the duties rather than the status, power, jurisdiction, and rights of bishops, Acton commented prophetically: "Today Darboy has gambled away his cardinal's hat."[28]

With his own Roman experiences and his recent editorial conflicts in mind, Acton saw the Vatican Council as a culmination of the struggle between authority and liberty in the Church. In the nineteenth century, the Church had imitated in her institutions the centralizing and increasingly authoritarian trend of the modern national state. The Pope's own history reflected that process, the changeover from his idealist, liberal pre-1848 phase to his clash with revolutionary forces, and the extreme conservative reaction. Pius IX found the spearheads of his aims in the Jesuits, a defence of the spiritual and temporal claims against the onslaughts of the time. To declare the Infallibility of the Pope an article of the Catholic faith was in a sense a logical development, though not the Council's declared original intention.

The doctrine that the Pope was infallible whenever he pronounced in his official character—*ex cathedra,* as it was to be formulated—on questions of faith and morals, had been held by such sixteenth-century proponents as Caesar Baronius and Robert Bellarmine. Since then, the conflict between papalists and conciliar theories had often engaged great theologians on both sides and, indeed, stimulated theological controversy. Acton's opposition to the Infallibility of the Pope was mainly historical and moral rather than grounded in dogma, as was Dr. Döllinger's. From the historian's point of view, Papal Infallibility would operate retrospectively and would include the authority of General Councils in the Church, thus enhancing papal responsibility for the discredited "acts of the buried and repented past." Acton listed what seemed likely to get him to get retrospective papal blessings: "The Bulls which imposed a belief in the deposing power, the Bulls which prescribed the tortures and kindled the flames of the Inquisition, the Bulls which erected witchcraft into a system and made the extermination of witches a frightful reality, would become as venerable as the decrees of Nicaea, as incontrovertible as the writing of S. Luke. . . . And the sentences of every Protestant judge (by the Bull *Cum ex Apostolatus Officio*) would be invalid."[29]

To Gladstone, Acton outlined the gloomy prospects; according to the regulations of the Council, the Pope alone could propose decrees and refuse his sanction to any act of the Council: "I am bound to say that I do not believe that the means of preventing the worse excess exist within the Council. In the case of almost every bishop it would be possible to point out the way in which his position may be forced or turned. The only invincible opponent is the man who is prepared, in extremity, to defy excommunication, that is, who is as sure of the fallibility of the Pope as of revealed truth. Excepting Strossmayer and perhaps Hefele, I don't know of such a man among the bishops."[30]

When the Vatican Council began, Acton requested Gladstone's authorization to make clear the British government's fears regarding possible secular consequences of Papal Infallibility, if adopted in the sense then widely expected, namely, that the Pope's authority might override the authority of governments regarding the social and political obligations of their citizens. This was an obvious concern in non-Catholic countries such as Britain, which remembered the excommunication and deposition of Queen Elizabeth I by Pope Pius V, by which English Catholics had been formally absolved of their civic obedience and loyalty. The papal bulls had unleashed and legally justified the bloody persecution of English Roman Catholics for the crime of high treason in the sense in which, ever since, it has successfully been applied by totalitarian governments against those they consider "enemies of the state." Under the harsh English penal laws that were applied to the small remnant surviving the destruction of the Catholic Church in England, a different attitude thus naturally developed: the Cisalpine, in sympathy with the national government rather than with Rome, and comparable to the Gallican trend in France.

One of Acton's maternal ancestors, the powerful Primate and Prince Elector Carl Theodor von Dalberg, had supported a controversial plan of a German national church, advocated by his own Vicar General, Ignaz von Wessenberg (1774–1860). On the side of Acton's English ancestors, Sir John Throckmorton (1753–1819), of that old Catholic family, played a leading role in the Catholic Committee of the 1790s when, under the French revolutionary storm blowing across the English Channel, the campaign for Catholic Emancipation became an irresistible political force under the leadership of Daniel O'Connell. Opposed to the Irish Catholic democracy, Throckmorton published three tracts in 1790 arguing for a lay voice in the appointments of English bishops. It was vicious slander to suggest that the idea of Papal Infallibility could be considered a dogma of the Church. English Catholics wanted to show that national loyalty and civic conduct were not at the Pope's disposal and control, and they so declared. This was a widely held English view, expressed in official catechisms and manuals of theology right into the 1860s. The fears of "papal aggression" that the new Cardinal Archbishop Wiseman's triumphant return from Rome evoked in Protestant England contributed in their turn to a new aggressive Ultramontane element in Rome.[31]

From Rome, Acton wrote to Gladstone that Dupanloup wanted to make use of the English arguments regarding the dogma's effect on the Catholic subjects of the Queen in any Council measure that was expected to weaken their defenders and strengthen their enemies. "In all this he will be contradicted by Manning, who will make the most of his acquaintance with you, and will give all manner of assurances that the Irish and English Catholics have much to gain and nothing to lose by the establishment of his favourite doctrines."[32] Gladstone gave the desired authorization by cable via the unaccredited British agent at Rome, Odo Russell: "Please tell Lord Acton he may use the strongest language he thinks fit respecting my opinion on the subject about which he desires it should be known."[33]

Acton's closeness to Gladstone infuriated Manning, who described it as "poisoning [Gladstone's] mind" against Papal Infallibility and the Pope's friends and supporters.[34] With his semi-official status as the British prime minister's confidant and his contacts with diplomats and leading prelates, Acton knew that he was under constant surveillance. Odo Russell reported to Lord Clarendon, the foreign secretary, that Acton was regarded in the Vatican as "un diable dans un bénitier" (a devil in a holy-water stoop).[35] For his correspondence with Gladstone he was able to use the English diplomatic courier. Letters to Döllinger usually went by Bavarian diplomatic bag, or the address of the Prussian representative in Florence was used to forward them. Then there were occasional travellers like the famous Abbé Franz von Liszt, who acted as mail carrier. In Rome, Liszt, who had received lower orders, was pursued by Princess Caroline von Sayn-Wittgenstein, a sister-in-law of Cardinal Hohenlohe. Liszt and the Princess were friends of Döllinger and the Arcos and in sympathy with the liberal Catholic cause.[36]

The Papal States were full of political spies. There were some mysterious incidents. The fearless Josef Strossmayer just escaped being poisoned by his Bosnian cook, although Acton was inclined to blame the man's cooking. Dr. Johann Friedrich, Döllinger's friend and Council theologian to Cardinal Hohenlohe, was stabbed on the train to Rome. A cloak-and-dagger atmosphere seemed to surround the Council. Those supporting the minority felt threatened and watched.

Acton devised a secret code for his letters to Döllinger when they were posted in the normal way. Dupanloup became "Padre Giovanni"; the talkative Roman archaeologist Giovanni de Rossi became "Madame Auguste"; Manning was "Miranda," from the Catholic convert in Robert Browning's poem who wanted to serve two masters—ease and religion; Cardinal Antonelli was "Melander"; and for himself Acton chose "Monsignor."[37]

In his notes on the Council, Acton recorded, "Nobody molested on account of hostile opinions. Letters carefully examined, and much espionage. But no serious hindrance put in the way of distributing documents, pamphlets, etc. Newspapers frequently stopped; but distributed to the bishops, so that their effect on the course of events was not prevented."[38] There were all kinds of minor pressures, however, such as attempts at character assassination against the leaders of the opposition. The good-looking Bishop Strossmayer, for example, was accused of affairs with female admirers.[39]

Making use of Acton's reports—and those of others—Döllinger published highly descriptive accounts of the Council in the Augsburg *Allgemeine Zeitung,* a newspaper of liberal tendency, under the title "Roman Letters from the Council."[40] He used the pseudonym Quirinus, recalling a third-century Roman martyr whose relics were actually taken to Tegernsee in Bavaria and were especially venerated in the Benedictine monastery, founded beside various Quirinus shrines on its shore, near the Acton-Arco house. These letters were the sensation of their day, an extraordinary journalistic feat that added some ten thousand subscribers internationally to that provincial newspaper's circulation. It was then, however, a respected, indeed the most important, newspaper in German. Translations of the reports into French and Italian appeared in newspapers at the time, and they were published in book form shortly after the Council. There was also an English translation by Henry Nutcombe Oxenham, a former Anglican parson and convert, and Döllinger's friend.

The letters were remarkable because they were evidently written by someone with firsthand and astonishingly accurate information of the Council proceedings, and this at a time when there were no press offices or official documents made available to the press. Indeed, anyone obtaining such a document was liable to the most severe penalties of the Church. The 750 Church Fathers were sworn to secrecy. Thus no official denials could be issued by the Vatican regarding distorted accounts of any kind. With some hundreds of journalists and diplomats eager to know what went on in the daily sessions at St. Peter, Quirinus illustrated the ease with which secrecy rules can be broken by an outsider with sufficient know-how and the right contacts.

The *Allgemeine Zeitung* was eagerly read in Rome. Even for the participants of the Council, Quirinus provided an all-round assessment by someone deeply versed in Church history and theology, even though the writer's sense of irony was bound to annoy the Ultramontane party among the bishops. Quirinus was evidently a passionate partisan of the anti-infallibilist and "inopportunist" camp. Acton reported to Döllinger that in Rome everybody was saying that the *Allgemeine Zeitung* had the best reports on the Council:[41] "For the *A[llgemeine] Z[eitung]* is a power in Rome, greater than many bishops, and much feared— greater even than many states."[42] Quirinus was superior to the ordinary reporters of the Catholic press, also to much that was published in the secular press, because of his familiarity with both Church affairs and international politics. Only a few like Veuillot, favoured by the Vatican with inside information, managed to sound equally authoritative.

The sarcastic tone of some of the letters, however, employed by Döllinger in the classical tradition of polemical literature, diminished their impact and confirmed the instinctive distrust widely felt even towards serious journalistic products of this kind. Odo Russell, for example, did not exempt the *Allgemeine Zeitung* reports from his condemnation. He warned his father-in-law, Lord Clarendon, in a private letter as early as December, not to have any confidence even in the reports of renowned newspapers: "The press is misleading the public in a manner which can only be explained and excused by the overwhelming amount of false reports in Rome in which 'Our Correspondents' believe and propagate *faute de mieux*."[43] There was great puzzlement as to who Quirinus was. The regular Rome correspondent of the *Allgemeine Zeitung*, an elderly, half-blind German scholar who had lived in Rome for decades, was suspected and almost expelled by the papal police. The minister of the Bavarian legation at Rome, Karl Tauffkirchen-Guttenburg, intervened and saved him and the equally suspected Dr. Friedrich, Cardinal Hohenlohe's Council theologian. The Augsburger *Allgemeine Zeitung* eventually told its readers, with evident *Schadenfreude* (malicious delight), that "the source from which we obtain our information on the Council has not been muddied by this grave incident. We shall carry on publishing the 'Rome Letters' to the end, and, God willing, to a victorious end."[44]

Altogether sixty-nine letters were published. Clearly, several informants were responsible; no single person could have written them all. Who they were, and their role in the operation, has been admirably researched by Victor Conzemius, the editor of the Acton-Döllinger correspondence.[45] According to his list, Döllinger was the author of fifteen letters and compiled thirty-eight others for which Acton was the main source of information. Döllinger's role was evidently paramount, and he put his own stamp on the letters. Acton wrote only fifteen, but these were the most important ones, and he provided information for most of the others. The other contributors were Louis Arco, an ideal decoy, as no one suspected the suave Bavarian diplomat of theological spying, and Dr. Friedrich, who was a trained theologian but lacked Acton's sense of history and political know-how.

Friedrich was *peritus* (expert) to the liberal Bavarian Cardinal Hohenlohe, whose brother was prime minister of Bavaria from 1866 to 1870, which explains how some of the Bavarian dispatches from Rome were made available to Döllinger. This connection became embarrassing for the Bavarian minister in Rome, Count Tauffkirchen, and for the Roman and Council personalities, when their confidential conversations, reported to Munich, appeared in the Quirinus letters. The Austrian ambassador, Count Ferdinand Trautmannsdorff, not knowing of Acton's role, noticed a definite decline in the quality of the letters in June 1870, before the Council was terminated, when Acton had already left Rome.[46]

The letters of Quirinus remain a major source for the history of the First Vatican Council and are of growing importance to historians. One puzzle remains, however. When Döllinger published the letters in book form, he lifted the secret surrounding Quirinus insofar as he mentioned in his preface that the correspondents were three friends from three nations. Only two nations, however, are known to be represented: Acton was an Englishman, and Friedrich and Arco were both Bavarians. According to Conzemius, there were no other contributors to these letters. Dupanloup and Strossmayer, two intellectual leaders of the minority, were also—falsely—regarded as possible sources. Perhaps Döllinger made a mistake in the heat of the great battle in which he was involved.

Acton's own activities during the seven months of his Roman stay were astonishing. He met bishops and diplomats daily. Leading members of the minority dined frequently at his apartment in the Via della Croce. He attended receptions where he might find out what was going on, afterwards noting down carefully what he had heard. He was always on the go, encouraging and organizing the opposition bishops, bridging national and language barriers among Germans, French, Austrians, Italians, English, Americans. He truly merited the title of "Chief Whip" for the minority.[47] Late at night Acton came home, sitting up till four or five in the morning to write his long letters to Döllinger or Gladstone, to catch the courier in time. As Acton explained the task confronting him: "We are dealing with people who, at best, will do what is needed but no more. They have not their books, their notes, not their friends with whom they would discuss these matters at home." All superfluous things have to be avoided. "It is true that the real opponents of Infallibility are incorrigible, but the fickle crowd, even the Dupanloups and their followers, can be easily deterred. Our party, that is to say, consists of tender, resistant material. One has to work at it every day, mould it, support the good, warn against all ruses, guide the weak, frighten the bad."[48]

Acton's contacts in Rome were mainly with the group of minority bishops. He knew many well among the Curia cardinals, such as Antonino de Luca, Girolamo d'Andrea, and Camillo Di Pietro, and bishops of the majority like Manning and Mermillod, but managing the minority left him no time for anything else. The Roman social round alone was taxing. On Friday evenings, Augustus and Pauline Craven, the friends of Acton's parents, were "at home" in their apartment in the Via dei Maroniti. Among those who might be there were Bishops Mermillod and François Alexandre Roullet de la Bouillerie of the infallibilists, or, among the opposition, Archbishop Kenrick of St. Louis, Archbishop Ludwig Haynald of Kalosca, the leader of the Hungarians, and Bishop Strossmayer. On Sunday evenings, Bishop Dupanloup was "at home" at the Villa Grazioli, where he stayed with one of the richest Roman families.

Acton recalled a memorable scene on Sunday, 13 March 1870, when the news of the death of Montalembert, Dupanloup's old friend, arrived and the family wanted the many guests to leave as quickly as possible. The Pope then stopped the Requiem Mass, which Archbishop François Xavier Mérode, Montalembert's brother-in-law, was organizing at the Church of Santa Maria in Aracoeli, in case it turned into a liberal demonstration. For his defence of the rights of the Holy See in the Revolution of 1849, Montalembert had been made a Patricius Romanus and was thus entitled to a public funeral service at the Aracoeli Church near the Capitol. The service took place all the same, but quietly, in the presence of some hundred people. Dupanloup and Acton and other well-known figures of the opposition thought it wiser not to provoke matters by their attendance.

The Pope's ban was much resented in Rome, especially among the French bishops. "Il parait qu'il n'est plus permis de prier pour les morts ici" (It seems that one isn't allowed to pray for the dead here any longer), the old Duke Scipione Salviati exclaimed at a Borghese reception.[49] The Pope's first public reaction to the death of the great French Catholic was uncharitable enough: "A man had just died who at one time had great merit, but had forgotten all about that and, worst of all, had become a liberal Catholic."[50] The Pope's anger was due to the famous letter written shortly before Montalembert died.[51] In this letter, addressed to his friend Paule de Lallemand, the jurist, Montalembert welcomed the opposition that Dupanloup and Alphonse Gratry were organizing in Rome to the new servile spirit in the Catholic Church. In particular, he attacked the theological theoreticians of absolutism, meaning Veuillot and his circle, "who have made a bonfire of all our liberties in praise of Napoleon III, in order then to sacrifice justice and truth, reason and history, in a holocaust to the idol they created in the Vatican." Acton, who had become estranged from Montalembert because of the latter's defence of the temporal power, paid tribute to him for his courage: "It is part of the fulfilment of his life that after his death he should have done so great a service to the good cause of the Church."[52]

But the Pope, perhaps advised by Veuillot, who had attended the Aracoeli service, bethought himself and ordered a Memorial Mass to be said for Montalembert on 18 March, which he attended at Santa Maria Traspontina, the Vatican's parish church. The Pope was driven there on his own in his phaeton. The bishops on their way to the Council passed the church draped in black, but no one knew for whom the Mass was intended, as it was announced only *per un nominato Carlo* (for someone named Charles). The secret, however, leaked out when two French priests saw the Pope enter the church. Pius IX was capable of the fiercest of outbursts of temper, but he was not vindictive by nature. And this fact may also discredit the story that, on an outing in the Pincio Gardens and seeing Acton's two little girls with their nanny, the Pope, on being told who they were, denied them his blessing.[53] According to the story, Acton was so deeply upset that he fled to Russell's Palazzo Chigi to spend a sleepless night there. But the astute Odo Russell, always eager to record any significant Roman scandal, made no mention of it anywhere, nor does Acton in his extensive Roman correspondence with Döllinger or any of his close friends.

Albert du Boys, the French diplomat and writer who was staying with Dupanloup, recorded that Acton called there frequently to find out what was going on and that he also met him at other Roman salons.[54] There was the palazzo of Prince Rospigliosi, whose wife, Françoise de Nompère de Champagny, from the house of the Dukes of Cadore, was a renowned Roman hostess; there were "at homes" at the palazzo of the Marquise de Spinola, at Princess Borghese's, at the Duchess Salviati's. Acton noted in his journal that at Duke Salviati's, George Rose, an English convert and writer, once said that Dupanloup remarkably resembled Borghese, and there came a dead silence. It was afterwards explained to him that Dupanloup was Borghese's half-brother, a son of Camillo Borghese (1775–1832). Dupanloup's mother, Anne Dechosal, was a servant attached to several rich families in the Haute Savoie, where Borghese was in exile from Rome. Félix-Antoine was born there, on 3 January 1802. A local labourer by name of Dupanloup acknowledged the boy as his own but disowned paternity ten years later with a notation on the baptismal register.[55]

A well-known liberal rendezvous was the Caetanis, where the old and blind Duke, head of the family, recounted how he had smuggled copies of Döllinger's polemical book *Pope and Council,* published under the pseudonym Janus, into the College of Cardinals.[56] "The Bodenhams have a reception for bishops every Wednesday evening," wrote Bishop Francis Kerrill Amherst of Northampton to his sister, "and have fitted up an oriental divan for the Easterns, where they sit cross-legged and smoke and drink coffee. The hour for the reception is 8.30; but the Orientals seem to like it so much that, yesterday, they arrived at six, before their hosts had dined!"[57] There were "at homes" at the Actons' and at English residents' like John, third Marquess of Bute, who provided the basis for Disraeli's *Lothair* (1870), and Rudolph, eighth Earl of Denbigh, both recent converts; and among old Catholics at the John Dormers', at the John Arthur Farrells', the Joseph Monteiths', Albert J. Stourton's, George Lake-Fox's, and at Mgr. Edmund Stonor's. Stonor, the third son of the third Lord Camoys and a chamberlain to Pius IX, sympathized with Acton's views.

The Bavarian Countess Charlotte von Leyden, Döllinger's ardent disciple and friend, who was in Rome early on during the Vatican Council, had an eye for the hilarious side of the Roman social scene. "In every salon there are people of the most different opinions, who all sit in different corners like conspirators, telling each other the latest gossip. No one trusts anyone else and with the exception of our friends no one says what he really thinks."[58] She was chaperoned by her friends, the Menthons. They were trying to find a husband for the twenty-seven-year-old Bavarian, who was something of a blue-stocking with great intellectual depth. She had heard about Döllinger's great pupil but not met Acton before. Now she saw him almost every day and formed a friendship with him and his wife. The Professor was their common bond, and Döllinger wrote to her that it had always been his most ardent wish that "the two dearest people I have on earth should meet and become friends."[59]

Countess Leyden was impressed by Acton and by his passionate engagement in the Council. She was probably also a little in love with him. "I see him frequently," she wrote to Döllinger, "but there is something funny between us. Now and then he thaws, tells me everything he knows and likes talking to me. Some hours later he is shut away in his shell like an oyster and becomes a stranger, so that I am quite intimidated and do not like to ask any more questions."[60] She suspected that she bored him, but it made no difference to her feelings and admiration for him. The Menthons' efforts on behalf of Charlotte proved successful. Through the Actons she met Sir Rowland Blennerhassett, Liberal MP for Galway. He came from an old Catholic family in County Kerry, read law at Christ Church, Oxford, and then studied political sciences at Louvain. Acton had introduced him to the Arcos and to Dr. Döllinger. Blennerhassett was also close to Newman. As an owner of land in Ireland, he became increasingly critical, however, of Acton's and Gladstone's ideas for Home Rule and also of Charles Stewart Parnell's National Land League, which aimed at securing the ownership of land in Ireland for the occupiers.

Countess Leyden fell for the good-looking Irishman as second best and, to Döllinger, confessed herself being "in complete theological harmony" with him.[61] It was her way of indicating an attachment in which closeness to Döllinger and Acton played a part. She told Lady Acton of her attraction to Blennerhassett, and Acton was deputed to find out about his "intentions." It was done in Victorian intellectual style — Acton writing a note (Blennerhassett was staying with him in Rome) and asking him, if he was agreeable, just to leave his card and write on it "Barkis is willing," which he did.[62] Charlotte von Leyden expressed her happiness about "entering the family," meaning the three people — Döllinger, Blennerhassett, and Acton — who were closest to her. And she was grateful to Acton for his mediation "carried out with as much discretion as friendship," as she put it.[63] Döllinger married the couple in June 1870 in Munich.

The leaders of the opposition bishops — Darboy, Schwarzenberg, Heinrich Förster, Haynald, and Strossmayer — met regularly at the villa of Count Arnim, the Prussian minister, Acton's friend. Odo Russell, newly married to Lady Emily Villiers, the daughter of his chief, the British foreign secretary, Lord Clarendon, was installed at the Palazzo Chigi. Russell loved Rome and after ten years of Italian residence spoke Italian well though with a strong English accent. He was an amiable character, always wearing large-size suits, in the summer a tall white top hat on his enormous head. With his jovial temperament, distinctive beard, and gold-rimmed spectacles, he was a striking figure.[64]

If Russell got on well with Acton, however, he also made it his diplomatic business during the Vatican Council to be on equally good terms with Manning. He was aware of, and reported to the British government on, Acton's influence on the minority bishops. But Russell was not a religious man; he saw the world, and indeed the Catholic Church, in pragmatic terms, as a political and international power. He observed the diplomat's rule that it was dangerous either to fight or to be too friendly with the Pope, according to the old French saying: *Qui mange du Pape en meurt* (He who eats of the Pope dies). During the Council, Russell never wavered in his belief that Pius would triumph with Infallibility. International intervention would therefore be a mistake and would, besides, increase the British government's difficulties with its Roman Catholic subjects in Ireland. Russell advised the government, and Lord Clarendon, in this sense.

These diverging concerns were behind the letters that Odo Russell sent to the foreign secretary and the prime minister. Lord Clarendon, an English Protestant, had no interest in saving Catholicism from itself. This would have been a wish closer to Gladstone's High Anglicanism and thoughts of Christian reunion. Gladstone, more than Acton, feared for Christianity as a result of an extremist form of Papal Infallibility. He was "immensely excited about the Council," Acton noted in his journal, "more than about events in England." Gladstone "wished the views of the English government to be communicated officially to the Court of Rome. Clarendon objected, and got Odo Russell to draw up a statement of the reasons against such a step. Gladstone reluctantly gave way, but asked Russell to say what G[ladstone]'s private opinion is. This he has done, to Cardinal Antonelli."[65] But when, in January 1870, Acton wanted to involve Gladstone and "the counsel of England" officially to effect the necessary change of policy in France—to have the government oppose Papal Infallibility—Gladstone backed away.[66] "Acton must know how difficult it is for England to take any ostensible initiative," Gladstone told Clarendon.[67]

Russell's regard for what Acton did in Rome was undoubtedly genuine. "The party he has so powerfully helped to create is filled with respect and admiration for him. On the other hand, the Infallibilists think him the Devil! I admire his creation, I bow before his genius, and I wish the Opposition all the success they have so earnestly at heart, but I adhere to my conviction that humanity will gain more in the end by the dogmatic definition of Papal Infallibility than by the contrary."[68]

A few weeks later Russell was writing to Lord Clarendon, supporting Acton's letter to Gladstone on the urgent necessity of assisting the opposition bishops, "because I cannot say more or write better on this subject than he has done. The only difference between us is that I do not believe the governments of Europe can be persuaded to interfere in unison at Rome. Single and separate interference would be worse than useless."[69] Lord Clarendon could only conclude, four months before the dogma was proclaimed, that "everything tends to prove that the Pope is infallible and Odo the only true prophet."[70]

Acton wrote to Gladstone as well as to his stepfather, Lord Granville, about his fears that, worse than being regarded as the evil one, he might be in some personal danger. Lord Clarendon asked Russell if he would "with special instructions throw your aegis over him."[71] Cardinal Antonelli should be given to understand how much more the papal Court would lose than gain by the banishment of an English peer and a devoted Catholic because he differed with a Council at which the freest expression of opinion was promised. Odo Russell replied, on 9 March 1870, that he had taken steps to protect Lord Acton, but he did not apprehend that he would be molested. Acton was, of course, watched by spies but was unlikely to be physically threatened or harassed, and he ended with characteristic irony: "If later he resists the infallibility dogma, he will naturally be excommunicated, but nothing worse."[72]

Among the German "inopportunists," Bishop Wilhelm Emmanuel, Freiherr von Ketteler of Mainz, played a significant role that also illustrates the defects of Acton's own opposition to Papal Infallibility. Ketteler had acquired the reputation of a waverer because of his changes, during the Vatican Council, from an infallibilist to an inopportunist anti-infallibilist, and again to an infallibilist. His vacillation was the principal reason for Acton's distrust of him even though he was also Döllinger's student. Döllinger and Ketteler had been united by a common idealism at the Frankfurt Assembly of 1848. Acton's grandmother, the Duchess of Dalberg, knew Ketteler well when he became Bishop of Mainz, and he was her frequent guest at Schloss Herrnsheim. Döllinger's teaching on the Mass, he told her, had left an indelible impression of true religious devotion on him.[73] Yet pupil and teacher had become estranged by the time of the Vatican Council. What later divided them was Döllinger's emphasis on the importance of history in theology, which, in Ketteler's view, had "something of the inevitability of the laws of natural science."[74]

Acton's attitude towards Infallibility, as he explained later, in 1872, was that the infallibilists of the "pre-July Church" were worse than those of the "post-July Church," that is, after the dogma was proclaimed.[75] Acton's objections to Infallibility had no direct connection with theology but rather with morality and politics, and in particular with the development of the Ultramontane theories identifying the temporal power, historically spurious and hopelessly out of date, with the spiritual prerogatives of the Pope. Acton noted how Ketteler had been shaken by the Pope, who repeatedly put Christ's question to Peter to him—"*Amas me?*" (Do you love me?)—and had wavered.[76] That is why Acton thought that the so-called inopportunists were really more dangerous than the supporters of Infallibility. They were liable, at any moment, to desert to the majority camp, many of whose ideas they shared. Bishop Dupanloup was the perfect embodiment of this group. He supported the *Syllabus Errorum,* the Roman opposition to the leading ideas of the century, but rejected Infallibility yet, proving Acton's point, went on to accept it in the end.

Ketteler replied to an attack on him that appeared in one of the Quirinus letters for which Acton was responsible. He was, however, not aware that Acton was the author. In a short polemical pamphlet, which he published against the letters of Quirinus, he suggested that the Roman correspondent must be a German professor, for no one else could be so full of himself. Ketteler believed that the Infallibility dogma was not opportune for pastoral and theological reasons. He wanted to avoid the separation of the Roman primacy from the episcopate and to preserve the collegiate character of the Church's supreme exercise of her teaching and her authority.[77] Victor Conzemius has drawn attention to the fact that Bishop Ketteler's understanding of Papal Infallibility and primacy has become the widely accepted theological interpretation of this doctrine in Roman Catholic thinking after Vatican II.[78]

In regard to Ketteler, Acton may have been particularly sensitive, suspecting him perhaps of wanting to revive the old, elevated German concept of the episcopal office, an equivalent of the Gallican tradition. This concept was ripe among Acton's own episcopal ancestors, the Rhineland prince bishops of the House of Dalberg.

And then, sometime in June 1870, the storm broke over the head of the unfortunate Theiner, Acton's friend and ally in the Vatican Archives. Theiner had gone to Naples for a rest after Easter, but was told to return to Rome at once and was immediately sent to Pius IX. The Pope, trembling with rage on seeing him, asked Theiner to hand over the keys to the archives to Archbishop Giuseppe Cardoni. The Pope's behaviour so upset Theiner that he began to cry like a child. After he regained his composure and the Pope, too, calmed down, Theiner asked for the reason for his dismissal. The Pope replied that Theiner had supplied those ignorants—Pius IX used the Italian word *somari* (donkeys)— with secret books and documents in order to combat "my dogma." Moreover, he had given advice and information to Cardinal Joseph Othmar Ritter von Rauscher and Schwarzenberg, the two leaders of the German-speaking minority, to Gregorius Yussef, the Melchite Patriarch of Antioch (Yussef had spoken up in the Council for preserving the old *consuetudines* of the Eastern Church and was then forced by the Pope to resign) and also "to that *caposetta Croatino* [Croatian ringleader], Strossmayer." And to crown it all, he had given documents and access to the archives to that *briccone* [rascal] Acton, "who licks my feet and at the same time works with the opposition." In reply, Theiner admitted that as prefect of the Vatican Archives he was in correspondence with the more learned German, French, Slav, and American bishops, but he denied— by giving his word of honour as a priest—that he had ever communicated any secret documents to them. As far as Lord Acton was concerned, he declared that he had never confided any documents to Acton except for those the Pope had ordered him to give. Cardinal Antonelli, Theiner said, had been intermediary in this matter. He reminded the pontiff that at that time he did not know Acton, nor did he ever allow him to pass the threshold of the archives. The Pope, after having listened to him calmly, said: "You are not one of us, and you cannot be in charge of the archives."[79]

That was the end of Theiner, the "reward," as Ferdinand Gregorovius put it, "for all the volumes that he has compiled in the archives on the rights to the dominium of S. Peter." The German historian, who had lived in Rome for nearly twenty years, felt "disgusted" about so much fanaticism in the Vatican, "at the sight of this idolatry, of these old and new idols and this perpetual condition of falsehood, hypocrisy and the crassest superstition. Could almost despair of mankind, not alone on account of the priests, who are obliged to continue their handiwork, but on account of their vassals."[80]

The Pope's charge that Acton had been sold the Vatican's secrets by Theiner was apparently a piece of gossip. Count Johann Konrad Preysing (1843–1903), a young Bavarian politician related to the Arcos, had spoken insultingly about

Janus (Döllinger). Acton had answered him that the views of Janus would not seem exaggerated compared to the material that he, Acton, had obtained from the Vatican. Preysing mentioned this reply to Ketteler, who told the Jesuits, and they passed it on to the Pope.[81] Before the Actons left Rome, Ketteler visited them to say farewell. One may wonder whether he would have done so if he had indeed denounced Acton to the Jesuits. Actually, Acton was on weak ground in his complaint, having himself just fired off another of his Quirinus missiles in which he praised Ketteler ironically for "coming along nicely," that is, on the road to Infallibility, but blaming him for his inconsistencies.[82]

13

PAPAL INFALLIBILITY

AND BEYOND

By the middle of February 1870, the inopportunists were beginning to disintegrate and the unqualified anti-infallibilists almost alone were left. International action therefore became paramount, and Acton urged it explicitly at the request, made via Dupanloup, of the French minority bishops who were also asking their own government for support. But not for the first or the last time, the European governments found it difficult to act in unison. The major obstacle in this case was the disagreement between France and Italy on the Roman Question.

Acton wrote to Gladstone that England should press the powers, France first of all, to send a joint note on what, in his view, directly touched Church-State relations. This was the draft *Schema de Ecclesia,* published early in 1869, which, on the model of the *Syllabus Errorum* of 1864, condemned most of what modern liberal governments stood for: the separation of Church and State, freedom of worship, civil marriages, non-religious education.[1] The intended measures would mean, Acton warned Gladstone in a later letter, that Catholics should be "bound not only by the will of future Popes, but by that of former Popes, so far as it has been solemnly declared. They will not be at liberty to reject the deposing power, or the system of the Inquisition, or any other criminal practice or idea which has been established under penalty of excommunication. They at once become irreconcilable enemies of civil and religious liberty. They will have to profess a false system of morality, and to repudiate literary and scientific sincerity. They will be as dangerous to civilized society in the school as in the state."[2]

Acton sent this more urgent appeal after it was made public, on 6 March, that Infallibility would be put on the Council agenda and the proposed formula was distributed among the bishops. The Pope had now joined the extremist party, Acton wrote to Döllinger; the Papacy would never recover from this move. It was now a question of "either the Pope prevails to the detriment of the Church, or the Church prevails at the expense of the Pope."[3]

Döllinger followed Acton's appeal to Gladstone with a similar request that the British prime minister issue a public warning that perseverance in the dogmas would lead to hostile legislation in Britain against Roman Catholics. But this was prevented by the foreign secretary, the Earl of Clarendon. Gladstone's failure to do something on the international level prompted Odo Russell's telegram to Lord Clarendon: "Lord Acton is anxious the French government should know that further loss of time will be fatal to the bishops of the opposition."[4] But the foreign secretary cabled back saying that, monstrous as the Pope's assault on the reason of mankind might be, "the British dwarf could be of little aid to the French giant who was responsible for there being any Council at all, and who ought to bestir himself in preventing its evil effects."[5]

Three weeks later, Lord Clarendon put his case ironically and bluntly to Gladstone:

> Döllinger and Acton, like good Catholics as they are, feel distressed at the dangers which beset their Church from the Pope's audacious assault on human reason and they catch at every straw to save it. Far be it from me to consider you a straw or to underrate the power of your words, but I am sure that if the angel Gabriel trumpet-tongued were to rise from the treasury bench and hold the language recommended by Döllinger, it would have no more effect in arresting the car of Juggernaut at Rome than it would have in changing the East wind. . . .
>
> Whether the Pope is infallible or not, he would infallibly reply to your threats by deed, and we should soon find Cullen and Co., who are now rather favourably disposed, the bitter enemies of every measure proposed by the Protestant first minister of England who did not understand the true interest of the Catholic Church and should do no good at Rome and much harm at home.[6]

In the end, Clarendon's line, which could be described as unfriendly neutrality, prevailed. British public opinion, with its firm anti-Catholic bias, was not especially exercised over Infallibility any more than over all other Catholic dogmas. The English bishops were divided. On Manning's side was only one bishop, Robert Cornthwaite, but all the Irish bishops, Acton believed, calculated that Infallibility would strengthen their influence, a consideration that played no part in Britain. In Rome some of the English Catholic bishops, among them William Clifford and George Errington, supported by the sole Irish inopportunist Bishop David Moriarty of Kerry, presented, in March and on Acton's initiative, a declaration to the Council in which they recalled that Catholic Emancipation had been obtained by the English bishops' denying the teaching that was now proposed as a dogma and that they could not, in honour, now go back on their solemnly given word.[7]

Acton also asked Odo Russell to inform Gladstone about this presentation. His request was a ruse to get round the fact that the bishops' statement, as a Council document, could not be published outside the Council. If the matter came up in Parliament, Gladstone could refer to Acton's letter to him. But this issue naturally had little weight with the large majority of the Catholic countries. The French foreign minister, Napoleon Daru, a practising Catholic, was eventually prevailed upon to send a special envoy, the Marquis Gaston-Robert Morin Banneville, to the Council and to mention—if not to threaten—the withdrawal of French troops from Rome if the Council adopted social and educational policies likely to encroach upon the realms of government. But this strategy proved ineffective. Cardinal Antonelli and the Pope responded by stalling, making declarations of gratitude for French financial support and protection, and trusting, rightly, that the anticipated majority for Infallibility would quell any opposition in the French bishops' ranks.

When the Bavarian Hohenlohe government was driven out of office by the Ultramontanes in Munich, in February 1870, Acton lost an important ally in his international endeavours. Not much was to be expected from the reactionary Austrian foreign minister, Count Ferdinand von Beust. He forewarned Rome, on 10 February, that Austria would ban the publication of any Council decrees regarded as hostile to its state laws and prosecute those who obeyed them. Austria's curious indifference was perhaps due to the fact that the country had greater worries than the Council, namely, worries over rivalry with France in Italy, and over its enemy, Piedmont, Prussia's ally. It was said that the ambassador in Rome (Count Ferdinand Trautmannsdorff), a Catholic conservative, did not read the Council decrees, and Count Beust did not read his dispatches.[8]

As for Prussia, Otto von Bismarck played a cool "wait and see" card at first, unlike Count Harry von Arnim-Sucknow, his minister in Rome, Acton's friend, who was personally, and as a Protestant Christian, interested in international action. Bismarck's instructions to Arnim were "to encourage and morally support the German bishops and any bishops sympathising with them" and, if the worst came to the worst, to safeguard the bishops' rights in their own lands.[9] Some 13 million people were at that time subjects of the North German Federation. Sometime in March, however, Bismarck's reluctance to intervene changed suddenly. An explanation for this change of policy has been suggested by the Austrian historian Erika Weinzierl-Fischer, and related to the report of the ambassador of the North German Federation in London, Count Albrecht von Bernstorff, of his conversation with Lord Clarendon on 9 March.[10]

The British government evidently had made another of its attempts to persuade Prussia to give up its reserved attitude. Bismarck would also have known of the discontent in the ranks of the bishops of the minority, some of whom (Darboy, Dupanloup, and some Austrians) had contacted Arnim, knowing that he was keen on international action. Odo Russell, in a private letter to Lord Clarendon, referred to the "war measures," in fact recommended by these bishops, "as the best means of fighting the Pope,—which shows how hopeless they must feel.—You will probably hear of this from Berlin, for the German and Austrian Bishops seem to expect a great deal from Count Bismarck."[11]

The Austro-Hungarian bishops were almost united in opposition to Infallibility, as were the Germans. The Munich nuncio, Mgr. Pier Francesco Meglia, had reported before the Council opened that Catholics loyal to the Holy See were not in favour of the dogma.[12] The educated laity in Germany, Austria, Hungary, and Ireland could generally be said to be on the liberal side of opposition to Infallibility. Of the lesser Catholic powers, almost unrepresented in Rome, Spain (under a liberal and anticlerical government) and Portugal supported French expressions of concern in oral communications to Cardinal Antonelli; Belgium, governed by an anti-Catholic prime minister, played no significant part. Russia was the only power showing open hostility, forbidding its Catholic bishops to attend the Council and hoping that their absence would strengthen the schism.

Italy, whose King Victor Emmanuel II had been excommunicated in 1861, was of course deeply affected by the events at the Council. Rome counted on more than a hundred votes of Italian bishops, but in November 1869 the anticlerical trend of the government in Florence was strengthened, and Rome then had to fear more from what the government would do by way of administrative measures than on the international stage. On 20 March, however, Acton had to record "the complete fiasco" of the French policy in regard to the Council. Cardinal Antonelli had countered French diplomacy by accepting the protection of French troops and France's financial support, but he made it clear that he could not allow the French special envoy, Marquis de Banneville, to exact any influence over the Council.[13]

Meanwhile, the minority bishops had fared little better in the Council. Quite apart from the issues of the Council, the debates themselves were a major problem. The appalling acoustics in the echoing spaces of St. Peter's made it difficult to understand the seven hundred bishops, speaking Latin with different intonations and accents. The Pope, moreover, used every public and private occasion to express his impatience with the Council's slow progress. The extremists among the Ultramontanists wanted to get on with Infallibility. They felt that it was a matter of acclaiming a belief already widely held in the Church and opposed merely by a small minority of misguided, obstinate, or heretical theologians, like Karl Josef von Hefele of Rottenburg, Henri Louis Charles Maret of the Sorbonne, Döllinger of Munich, or that gadfly layman and English peer, Acton. The minority bishops, for their part, felt constantly under pressure, with the result that their reactions were equally one-sided and highly charged.

When Odo Russell, in a conversation with Antonelli, mentioned the new Council procedure to improve acoustics, a system about which the minority complained because it curtailed their freedom of speech, the Cardinal replied with a smile that "minorities always thought majorities in the wrong and wished to set them aside or ignore their existence, but that the Oecumenical Council would never end if the majority were deprived by the minority of the power to express and assert their opinions."[14]

Clearly there was a dilemma, the age-old one concerning the exercise of majority powers. But the First Vatican Council was not the occasion to absorb what lessons the British and American political experience had taught, as Acton himself was later to express in the observation: "The test of liberty is the position and security of minorities," and he was thinking especially of unpopular minorities.[15] Not to protect these, but to speed up the debate, was the intention of the amended *regolamento* (regulation), which stipulated that henceforth a simple majority would suffice for the acceptance of all decisions introducing dogmatic questions. On the Council sessions the presidents were empowered to close debates if so requested by at least ten of the Council Fathers, to cut speeches short, and to silence any speakers who were talking off the point. The presidents (chosen from the Ultramontane majority) held decisive power in the sessions.

This old method of managing unruly assemblies with a semblance of democracy always assured that the ruling party would hold the advantage. The first to feel the new rule was the Hungarian inopportunist Archbishop Ludwig Haynald of Kalocsa, who, during the catechism debate, attacked the autocratic Roman system. He was stopped by Annibale Capalti's ringing his bell and telling him to stop and get down from the *ambo* (rostrum).[16]

Acton spent much time persuading Dupanloup, Darboy, Strossmayer, and Haynald to make their intended protest vigorous enough through the International Committee that they had formed. "The matter is of immeasurable importance," he wrote to Munich, for if the minority accepted the new procedure lying down, he felt, they would surrender the very principle of the Church— ecumenicity.[17] The majority were resolved to press on, as Manning indicated on one of his "Sabattinos," as he called his customary Saturday walks and exchange of views with Odo Russell. When Russell asked him whether he saw any way of preventing Infallibility from getting through, he replied, Yes—by cutting our throats. Russell passed the remark on to Acton, who reported it to Döllinger. It thus crept into one of the Quirinus reports in the Augsburg *Allgemeine Zeitung* and incidentally enabled Manning to identify Döllinger's man in Rome when Russell assured him he had told the story to no one but Acton.

Yet the minority bishops were not willing to fight with equal weaponry what many of them regarded as more attempts of frightening them into submission. Only Darboy talked of open defiance. "Si nous partons," he told Acton, "environ 80, nous emporterons le Concile dans la semelle de nos souliers" (If we leave, some 80 of us, we shall carry the Council away with us on the soles of our shoes).[18] Eventually thirty-four French bishops signed a protest drawn up by Dupanloup. It was a milder version of what Acton, with the support of Strossmayer, had suggested. But Dupanloup objected by saying that the time was not yet ripe. Acton had wanted them to say that the minority would not take part in any further Council sessions unless the ambiguities in the amended rules were removed, nor should there be any simple majority decision in dogmatic questions. A group of forty bishops, mainly Germans, Ketteler among them, also signed a mild protest comparable to the letter of the French bishops. The episode showed that Acton's influence extended even to Council documents.

Early in March, the issue of Infallibility came before the Council. Acton felt compelled to note that the Curia could draw no other conclusion from the timidity shown by Dupanloup, or from waverers like Ketteler, than that these minority bishops would ultimately accept the doctrine, or that they believed it would be proclaimed and merely wanted to safeguard their own options.[19] The one bishop who impressed Acton among all others by his courage was the Croat, Josef Strossmayer. "If you had created a bishop and instructed and prepared [him] for the Council," Acton wrote to Döllinger, "the result would have been Strossmayer. He is Janus personified. . . . What I believe in my deepest heart about the Church and the world, he put into words of burning zeal. . . . I discovered no weak point in him. On the Church, the papacy, the cardinals, the rights of bishops, the rights of the laity, on the Curia, on mendaciousness, forgeries, the lack of priestly concern, the love of souls, the union with Gr[eeks] and Prot[estants], . . . he thinks exactly as I do. . . . If the whole Council were against him and for inf[allibility], Strossmayer will remain firm."[20]

But that expectation was not to be fulfilled. Strossmayer had all the Slavonic passion and panache, deep conviction, and gift of the Latin style, but he tended to be too rash and, Acton thought, lacked deeper scholarship.[21] Not surprisingly, it was Strossmayer who caused the one real "scene," on 22 March, when speaking in the debate on the dogmatic constitution of Catholic faith. He repudiated majority voting in matters of faith and was shouted down by some four hundred furious bishops. He had provoked this audience by asserting that the Schema had assigned responsibility for the unbelief of modern society to Protestantism. Against that, he referred to the Catholic show of religious indifference before the Reformation and to the atrocities of the French Revolution as having caused unbelief among Catholics, not Protestants. Then he went on to say that all Christians ought to be grateful to men like Gottfried Wilhelm von Leibniz and François Guizot for the refutation of errors. Loud groans greeted those names.

The president of the Council, Filippo de Angelis, rang his bell, shouting, "Hicce non est locus laudandi Protestantes" (This is not the place to praise Protestants). Some bishops even threatened the speaker with raised fists. Greatly excited, Strossmayer repeated that no article of faith must be imposed on the faithful unless the bishops were unanimous. When the Bishop of Marseilles, Charles Philippe Place, one of Dupanloup's supporters, called out in defence of Strossmayer, "Ego illum non damno" (I do not condemn him), the answer was shouted from all sides, "Omnes, omnes illum damnamus!" (All, all of us condemn him). Capalti called Strossmayer to order, and, protesting, Strossmayer came down while some were shouting, "These people don't want the infallibility of the Pope; this man regards himself as infallible!" and others: "He is Lucifer, anathema, anathema!" or "He is another Luther, let him be cast out!"[22] Afterwards Cardinal Friedrich Schwarzenberg went to see Strossmayer to tell him off; he was talking too much, compromising the others of the opposition. Strossmayer left in tears. It was Acton who calmed things down, and serenity returned.[23]

Was Acton too gullible in his estimate of Strossmayer, as he had been in his original opinion of Manning? Strossmayer's charm and warm-hearted, open nature seemed irresistible. Already in his earlier speech, on 24 January, he had made a passionate plea for the universalization of the Church. The Papacy had merely become an Italian institution, he said, and therefore the Pope's moral influence had been infinitely reduced in the world. In the early days of the Council, that statement had made a great impact. Only Manning remained deaf to it: "At the end we asked ourselves, 'What did he say?' Nothing, only he said it in excellent Latin and as a born orator."[24]

The English Archbishop certainly lacked any understanding for the sort of Church reforms that Strossmayer, like Acton, advocated a hundred years in advance of Vatican II. Strossmayer's ideas on the Church were influenced by his pan-Slav political ideas. Like the Hungarian, Transylvanian, and other bishops of the far-flung Austrian Empire—indeed, of the Catholic Eastern churches— he opposed Infallibility largely through fear that it would endanger the reunion of the Eastern Orthodox churches with the Catholic Church of the West, just as a similar fear existed in the Western countries for the chances of Catholic-Protestant reunion.[25]

By the "universalization" of the Catholic Church that Strossmayer advocated, he meant more, however, than strengthening the pan-Slav cultural current against the dominant German influence. In a letter to Gladstone, written at the beginning of the subsequent pontificate, Strossmayer observed that the Italians had certainly a natural talent for running "the Roman prelature" competently enough. But their competence fell far short of what, in his view, was required. He envisaged the Catholic Church evidently as a kind of spiritual United Nations, long before its time, and not just as an international bureaucracy but as "capable of entering into the most delicate matters touching upon the universal conscience of mankind and leading them to a happy solution corresponding to the real needs of society."[26] Despite his pessimism concerning the Church of his day, Strossmayer was a great dreamer of dreams.

Acton's own thoughts about his Church were expressed in an important letter to Döllinger, in which he voiced strong criticism of the liberal Catholics with whom he was so easily but falsely identified.[27] He accepted the label, Acton wrote, inasmuch as it applied to those who wanted liberty not only for, but in, the Church, and wanted arbitrary rule in State and religion to be subject to law and tradition. But important though this perspective was for the religious struggles of his age, "it is an aspiration, a means, a hope, not a principle or method." The problem was not so much how to relate to authority or liberty but to truth. The Church as the redemptive institution, the dispenser of grace, was primarily concerned with millions of ordinary people. For their protection the Church had developed a popular type of Catholicism in which everything shone in an ideal light and everything that was difficult and offensive to pious ears was avoided or dissembled.

This "sham Catholicism" related to Infallibility inasmuch as the glorification of the Papacy was needed so as not to clash with its evident lack of Infallibility in past centuries. Acton recalled the observation, ascribed to Manning, that the dogma has prevailed over history. "In fact, it was not a battle of dogmas at all, but of theological views on history through which truth, error, good and evil, in short, conscience, became the victims." He went on to link the old maxim "The end justifies the means" with Infallibility. What used to be wrong and sinful was suddenly considered good if it served the Church or the good of souls. He recalled his essay on the Massacre of St. Bartholomew, in which he stated: "Pius V demanded the death sentence for imprisoned Huguenots—he is a Pope and saint and has thus done right. Charles Borromeo approved of the murder of Protestants by private individuals. He has been canonised. . . . This mentality is the worst defect of Catholicism today."[28] In his letter Acton went on to blame the liberal Catholics for sharing this attitude: "Falloux,[29] writing in praise of Pius V, Montalembert fighting under the banner of religion and liberty against absolutism in France and for exonerating the double absolutism in Rome, Dupanloup in defending the *Syllabus,* all showing that sinister influence." But the true Catholic who also wants to be a good Christian cannot thus divorce love for his Church from love of goodness and truth.

Quite apart from whether Acton's judgement on Pius V and Charles Borromeo would or would not be regarded as tenable by modern historians, one can see, with Victor Conzemius,[30] in this letter a first sign of that element that later obtruded in regard to moral judgement in history and was in the early 1880s to estrange Acton even from the revered Döllinger. The letter also shows the effects of the unbearable strain of the past five months. The relentless pace of activity was beginning to take its toll on Acton, both physically and mentally.

Towards the end of April, Acton had a breakdown from sheer nervous exhaustion, constant excitement, and lack of sleep; he developed a high fever and was ordered to rest for two weeks. Earlier the Actons' Irish maid had suddenly died from an infection that the Roman climate and the unclean water had made it only too easy for her to catch. Then their two little girls caught the measles, and finally Marie, too, fell ill under all the strain, with an attack of pneumonia. Fortunately her mother, Countess Arco, was there to help look after all the patients. Döllinger, dependent on Acton's dispatches, had to make do for his Quirinus letters with bits of information that Acton had previously supplied and with the compilation of a critical survey of various pamphlets on Infallibility written by bishops of the minority. By May, Acton was out and about again, in time for the general debate on Infallibility on the basis of amended theological texts. They had been issued to all the bishops in two folios of 104 and 242 pages.[31]

The debate began on 14 May, a very hot day, foreshadowing the tremendous heat of that Roman summer, which proved a serious health risk for many of the elderly bishops. "The fight is on," Acton wrote. "The heat is a disadvantage for the opposition. [Cardinal Camillo] Di Pietro says that the Pope is facing the possibility of letting the Council sit through the hot months, [in order] to come to a conclusion with the Italians and in the absence of the Northerners," who cannot stand this heat.[32] That his sense of sardonic humour was restored is shown in his account of the pious and meaningless speech of the Archbishop of Messina, Luigi Natoli, who, as Acton put it, produced "quite a new argument for the Sicilians' belief in infallibility. When St. Peter preached in Sicily where there were already some Christians and told them that he was infallible, they were astonished at his claim and decided to investigate the matter. They sent a deputation to Our Lady. Had she heard of it? Yes, she replied, and remembered to have been present when Christ entrusted Peter with this special prerogative. Content with that testimony the Sicilians had since preserved belief in papal infallibility in their hearts!"[33]

Towards the end of May, Acton felt that he could do no more in Rome. His wife, expecting their third child, and the two little girls went back to Tegernsee. He stayed on for another ten days, not to await the outcome but to see what the opposition would want to do next. He reported only briefly, as though there were no point to it any more, the excellent speech of his friend and ally Bishop William Clifford, which clearly showed Acton's influence. He had argued against Manning's formulation of Papal Infallibility as separate from that of the Church. Clifford caused disapproving murmurs when he said, "It must first be shown to the satisfaction of countless Anglicans that the Roman Church was not a despotic institution."[34]

There was a farewell dinner given by Countess Arco for Strossmayer, the favourite bishop of everyone in the Acton household. On Acton's last day in Rome, Arnim, Strossmayer, Hefele, and Förster (Prince Archbishop of Breslau) came to say farewell. Acton himself went to call on Darboy, Clifford, Gregor von Scherr (Archbishop of Munich), and some others who were not at home. The Archbishop of Munich was under some pressure from the Pope because of the liberal theologians in the Bavarian capital. He urged Acton to stop publishing articles signed with his name. The Bavarian minister in Rome, Tauffkirchen, reported to the King on the Archbishop's audience with Pius IX. Scherr warned the Pope of dangers in Germany if the Council passed the extremists' resolution on Infallibility. The Pope seemed to react almost lightheartedly, saying, "I know those Germans; they know everything better, everyone there wants to be Pope." The Archbishop retorted excitedly that it was a serious matter concerning souls. Tauffkirchen wrote in his report: "This seemed to make some impression on His Holiness." The diplomat, however, used the word *seemed* deliberately, because the Pope, that same evening, received some hundred French priests whom Louis Veuillot had sent to assure him of their faith in his Infallibility, and he used the occasion to make some very critical remarks about people of the opposite view.[35] Scherr's attitude must be seen in the light of his later volte-face, of which Döllinger became the chief victim.

Sitting up late the night before he left Rome, Acton summed up these farewells. He had put the abstract-seeming question to some of these friends: What was a man to do who had seen and learned much during the Council? Understanding what he meant in view of the secrecy of the Council, Archbishop Francis Patrick Kenrick of St. Louis replied that he must now tell everything and publish. The Pope had no right to impose silence on the bishops—only the Council could have done that, but had not done so. And Darboy answered his question: "Il faut agir pour l'Eglise par la verité et la loyauté" (We must act for the Church through truth and loyalty). Kenrick and Darboy "clearly want me to say openly what I have learned and observed. I stick to my original view: Strossmayer, Kenrick, Darboy, Hefele are the best men."[36]

Commenting on Acton's departure, Odo Russell wrote: "As he has been the soul of the opposition, we all expect the body to collapse the moment he goes."[37] It was a permissible exaggeration. But Lord Clarendon could not suppress his admiration for Pius IX: "How right Odo has been throughout in declaring that the Pope would end by having his own way in all things. He has stood alone against all the representation of the Catholic powers and all the opposition bishops plus Acton, who is worth them all put together."[38] In a final tribute to Acton "on record in the annals of Your Lordship's office," Russell summed up Acton's achievements: "Without his personal intervention the bishops of the opposition could scarcely have known each other. Without his knowledge of language and of theology, the theologians of the various nations represented in the Council could not have understood each other, without his talents as a leader they could not have remained united amongst each other, and without his high virtues they could not have accepted and followed the lead of a layman so much younger than any of the Fathers of the Council."[39]

Archbishop Manning's thoughts on Acton were expressed in a letter to Gladstone: "The shadow of Lord Acton between you and the Catholics of Great Britain would do what I could never undo." To which Gladstone replied: "I regard his character and admire his abilities and attainments, but I have never supposed him to be a man representative of the general body of English Roman Catholics. You will not be surprised at my adding that I wish he were such. For though I have noticed a great circumspection in his gifts, I have never seen anything that bore the slightest resemblance to a fraudulent reserve. Meanwhile you need not assure me as to your motives, as one-twentieth of the time I have known you would have sufficed to show how absolutely incapable you were of any spiteful act."[40] Three days later Manning wrote again: "I will say no more of Lord Acton whose career has been a disappointment to his truest friends, not Catholics only. He might have done much both in public life, and among us. Of the former you can judge; of the latter—I am sorry to say—he has lost all hold on England and abroad except upon individuals."[41]

Gladstone showed the letter to Lord Granville, who sent it back commenting: "I presume there is no Protestant, or atheist, whom he dislikes more than Acton. I am, however, afraid, he may be right about the latter's success in public life. If anything will spur him into action, it will be the knowledge of Manning triumphing in his not having done so."[42] To his stepson he wrote: "Manning had had great hopes of your distinguishing yourself in political life, and of your being in service to Catholicism. In both things you have failed completely. Put that into your pipe and smoke it."[43]

When the final vote was taken in the Council, on 13 July, on the whole constitution *Pastor Aeternus* concerning Infallibility, there were, of the 601 bishops who voted, 451 *placet* (accepted), 88 *non placet* (rejected), 62 *placet iuxta modum* (in favour of modification of the definition). As for the rest of the bishops, 76 absented themselves and gave no vote; others had returned home on account of illness or other reasons.[44] And when finally, on 18 July, the constitution was voted on again—this time in public session and to the accompaniment of a violent storm, with each of the Council Fathers shouting his *placet,* followed as in response by a terrible clap of thunder and renewed lightning—the result was 535 *placet,* 2 *non placet.* The two nay votes were given by Edward Fitzgerald of Little Rock, Arkansas, and Luigi Riccio Cajazzo of the Kingdom of Naples; both, however, signified their acceptance afterwards. Most of the eighty-eight bishops of the opposition had either left Rome by then or stayed away from St. Peter's because they wanted to avoid the scandal of a negative demonstration.

Naturally, much was made of the drama of St. Peter's, underlined by the elements: the Pope reading out the votes with the aid of a taper, and the lightning bursting out again as though the heavens were—so the opponents said—displeased at the actions of Man. "They forgot Sinai and the Ten Commandments," was Manning's riposte. As far as he was concerned "the Day was won and the Truth was safe as it was after the Council of Nicea."[45]

When the final voting figures were analysed and the uncertain element in the middle camp of both sides was discarded, the base camps appeared to number 470 for, 130 against, or the rock-bottom figure of 430 to 88 (Acton's January estimate of 137 looked surprisingly accurate when deaths and departures are included). Writing after the most explicit and telling first ballot, on 13 July, Acton estimated the opposition to have included thirty-six German, Austrian, and Hungarian bishops, twenty-five Anglo-American bishops, and twenty-five French bishops. Among the opposition were three cardinals (Rauscher of Vienna, Schwarzenberg of Prague, and Césaire Mathieu of Besançon), the archbishops of the metropolitan sees of Paris, Lyons, Milan, Cologne, Munich, Halifax, and St. Louis, and two Patriarchs. Acton was able to conclude that at least "after all that has been said and has happened, the Pope cannot regard . . . [this] as a moral victory that will secure the future of his cause."[46] He saw in the events of those July days "a terrible grandeur."[47]

Döllinger, completing his last Quirinus letter, number 69, on 19 July, anticipated "the second phase of the Roman conquest" to begin with the subjection of the individual bishops of the minority. A *transfugae,* a wholesale desertion, was likely.[48] He expressed his anxiety over the fate of Herrnsheim, then threatened by French troops crossing the Rhine in the Franco-Prussian War and occupying Worms nearby. But Herrnsheim was protected by the neutral Union Jack flying from its round tower. It was used as an army hospital but saved from the destruction it had suffered in the Napoleonic Wars.

Acton's plan to see Darboy at Easter 1871 came to nothing because of the tragic events in Paris. The Archbishop was arrested by the Communards on 4 April and held as a hostage, and on 24 May 1871 he was shot, blessing his executioners. Earlier, when the German siege of Paris had begun, on 2 March, Darboy had written to the Pope to declare his acceptance, "purely and simply," of the decrees of 18 July 1870. When the Pope heard of the death of the most determined opponent of the definition, he exclaimed: "He has washed away his defects in his own blood, and put on the martyr's robe."[49] Acton wrote to his wife: "I had so much to say to him—for I loved him and I knew that he loved me—and now that he is dead I feel that I am so much nearer to him than when he was in prison, and that he knows the thoughts I have. Teach Mamy to say a prayer daily for the good archbishop who loved Papa. They showed me the account in *The Times* yesterday, but I could not read it because I knew I should cry."[50]

One of the immediate effects of the Vatican Council in the newly founded German Empire was the *Kulturkampf* (struggle of cultures). Otto von Bismarck, who had refused to join any international action in connection with the Vatican Council on the ground that entire freedom in Church matters was granted in Prussia, now proceeded to attack "Rome-ruled" Catholic institutions as encroaching on the rights of the State. Roman Catholics were made to feel that Rome was in conflict with their patriotism and with the militant nationalism of the new German Reich. The German bishops, who before the Vatican Council had issued a pastoral letter expressing their misgivings, met again at Fulda and declared their humble and unconditional acceptance of its conclusions.[51]

Among the bishops who stayed away from Fulda was Hefele of Rottenburg. Having publicly declared, in November 1870, that he would not proclaim the new decrees in his own diocese, he nevertheless did publish them in April 1871, justifying his change of mind five months later by saying that it had restored his "peace of mind." Acton characterized the submissions of the most active and most learned of the German members of the minority bishops as pathetic. As by that time Strossmayer, too, as the last of the Austrian bishops, had given in, Döllinger concluded: "Thus not a single bishop is left who has not bowed before Baal. That has never happened before in the Church. Judgment will not fail to come."[52]

14

A MISFORTUNE FOR RELIGION

The Archbishop of Munich, Gregor von Scherr, who had voted *non placet* on 13 July 1870 and signed the opposition's protest on 17 July, changed his mind by the time he returned to Munich on 19 July. "*Roma locuta est*. Gentlemen, you know what that involves. We can do nothing but submit," he told the members of the theological faculty whom he had called to his palace on 21 July and who appeared in a group led by Döllinger. A few days later he went to work on Döllinger separately. In that meeting, which lasted an hour and a half and which cost Döllinger, as he told Louise von Kobell, the first sleepless night in all his life, the Archbishop asked him to declare publicly that it was just and right to accept the fait accompli and recognize the Council and the dogma. Döllinger replied that such a declaration would mean revoking what he had held from even before the Council and would give the impression that he was bowing to fear. He wanted to study the Church's teaching again and would retract his views publicly if he was shown to have been wrong. The meeting ended with an ominous exchange. Archbishop: "Let us now begin to work again for our Holy Church." Döllinger (his voice on edge, as always happened when he was greatly moved): "Indeed, for the Church of old." Archbishop: "There is only one Church that is neither new nor old." Döllinger: "They have made a new Church."[1] Describing for Acton's benefit the memorable encounter, Döllinger said, "Now begins the second part of the Roman Conquest campaign." He summed up: "I need not tell you what my reaction was."[2]

But Döllinger was uncertain what he should do next. To say what he thought would bring immediate excommunication, and he did not want to let down his followers, theologians and clergy, all over Germany. But he took part in the Nuremberg meeting of German professors of theology, on 26 August, which was arranged by Josef Hubert Reinkens of Breslau, already suspended as professor of Church history, and Franz Heinrich Reusch of Bonn, who were to become the first Old Catholic Bishop and his Vicar General, respectively. A protest declaration was issued. Acton had been invited to the meeting but declined to attend.

While the lay professors of Munich University signed a protest against the Council and the dogma, Archbishop Scherr sent a written request to the theological faculty in October, asking for their submission to the dogma. On 29 November, the faculty complied by recognizing the ecumenical character of the Vatican Council. Döllinger and Johann Friedrich distanced themselves from their colleagues. Early in January 1871, the Archbishop formally urged Döllinger to accept the decrees, warning him not to provoke the Archbishop's powers. This step was followed, on 5 January, by a pastoral letter in which the Archbishop used the traditional arguments for the justification of Papal Infallibility. Döllinger responded in an article published in a supplement of the Augsburg *Allgemeine Zeitung,* and in a letter to the Archbishop, of 29 January, he asked for time for a renewed and full study "of the great question."[3]

In the middle of February, the Archbishop urged Döllinger again to declare himself but granted him, on 14 March, at his request, a final fortnight's grace. On 20 March, Döllinger requested a free exchange of views with a recognized theologian to take place before the Cathedral Chapter or the German Bishops Conference. He undertook publicly to withdraw everything he had written on the matter and to give the lie to his own words, if he could be shown to have been wrong in his evidence and facts. At the same time he gave the reasons for his refusal to recognize the dogma and had this letter also published in the *Allgemeine Zeitung* of 31 March.[4]

The Archbishop replied at once in a pastoral letter, read out in all the churches on Palm Sunday (2 April), rejecting Döllinger's request to have the matter discussed before theologians or bishops. The issue had already been decided by the

Council, he said. It was not, as Döllinger stated, a purely historical question; he was subordinating Church and Catholic truth to historical research. The Archbishop rejected as untrue Döllinger's argument that the decrees of 18 July 1870 were irreconcilable with the constitutions of European states such as Bavaria. Döllinger, "this man so far highly placed in Church and State and until now of greatest merit," had, by his public statement, come out in open rebellion against the Catholic Church. Indicating further "necessary measures," the Archbishop asked for prayers "for the gravely endangered spiritual welfare of the author of these statements inimical to the Church."[5]

Somewhat late in the day Archbishop Scherr seemed to have realized the irrevocable course of events on which he had embarked, and the full implications of Döllinger's case. He consulted Rome about what he should do. But Cardinal Antonelli coolly left the decision to him, writing to the nuncio in Munich, Archbishop Pier Francesco Meglia, that the Archbishop had all the authority and powers he needed.[6] Scherr then decided to go ahead. The Munich Cathedral Chapter voted for excommunication, with three votes opposing the majority. As a final measure, seminary students attending lectures by Döllinger and Friedrich were threatened with severe Church penalties. Finally, on 17 April 1871, Ignaz von Döllinger was excommunicated; his pupil, Friedrich, was excommunicated on the following day.

The solemn decree of public excommunication was read out from the pulpit of the Royal Chapel, St. Cajetan's Church, where Döllinger was provost, and in other Munich churches. This kind of public punishment was usually reserved for priests guilty of the grossest immorality, and only rarely inflicted even upon them. On purely technical grounds the sentence was not justifiable, for the First Vatican Council was never formally dissolved but postponed *sine die* because of the outbreak of the Franco-Prussian War, and therefore its decrees were not yet absolute. Döllinger was condemned because he continued to reject what he believed to be false and what the man who pronounced the sentence had himself rejected only shortly before. Contrary to the Canon Law provisions, Döllinger was not given the right to defend himself or even to be heard and explain his conduct, but simply had to submit.

Even this disgraceful treatment did not drive Döllinger into rebellion. He abided by the penalties imposed on him and remained a Catholic priest in his heart and outlook, if not in his acts. He clearly sympathized with the Old Catholic movement, which looked upon him as its intellectual leader, but he never wanted a schismatic church separated from the Roman Catholic Church. When, in September 1871, the first Conference of Old Catholics protesting against the new dogma was held in Munich's Crystal Palace, Dr. Döllinger warned against "setting altar against altar, forming independent congregations."[7] His firm rejection of a separate German national church is well documented, but his repeated warnings to his Old Catholic allies were inconvenient to them, even suppressed; they were intent on going ahead.

To his English friend and translator Henry Nutcombe Oxenham, Döllinger wrote: "Our position in the Church is quite plain. We abide by the old teaching, reject the innovation, discard the unfree Vatican Council, but make no separation and will not permit our right and property to be infringed just as did the countless opponents of the Bull *Unigenitus*. We continue to receive the sacraments from the servants of the church regardless of whether they are infallibilists or not. If a priest or bishop should require us to subscribe to the new dogma, we refuse."[8] But this was not what the leadership wanted.

Döllinger clung to the hope of an ultimate correction of the dogma. While considering his excommunication invalid, he nevertheless accepted it in obedience. In a vivid phrase noted by Lady Blennerhassett (née Leyden), he compared himself to "the fascine that is thrown into the ditch so that others may be able to cross it." The reference was to the traditional practice, used by army engineers in times of war, of throwing bundles of long faggots into trenches and ditches that they wanted to cross. Conscious of the traditional use of faggots for a funeral pyre, Döllinger evidently saw himself as being made an example of. Lady Blennerhassett, writing after Döllinger's death, added that she had never been able to forget the phrase and the sadness in Döllinger's voice when he used it. And she heard him use it more than once.[9] It seemed to her—and she was perhaps as close to Döllinger as Acton was—to express all that the excommunication of 17 April 1871 meant to him. And yet it also contained an element of hope that his sacrifice might not be altogether in vain.

The Old Catholic movement contained from the beginning the seeds of its more extremist and de-Romanizing elements that were to reject also the Catholic dogmas of the Immaculate Conception and Transubstantiation, and the Church's rule of celibacy. Acton recognized these elements from the start and therefore assumed an attitude of circumspection towards it, fearing a schism and having experienced, during the Vatican Council, the truth of the old dictum: "God defend me from my friends, from my enemies I can defend myself." Döllinger understood that the Old Catholics were clinging to his inspiration and name. He wanted them to make an effective protest, but no more. When, without their explicit agreement, Acton's and Blennerhassett's names were used to lend international support to the Munich Declaration of Whitsuntide, in May 1871, they were greatly annoyed. But only Sir Rowland Blennerhassett wrote to the *Times* to say that neither his nor Acton's signature had been authorized.[10] Lady Blennerhassett explained the reason for her husband's immediate protest: "I believe his excommunication would [otherwise] have been inevitable."[11]

The wordy Munich Declaration of Whitsuntide professed adherence to the old Catholic faith while rejecting the Vatican decrees that were described as a serious danger for state and society.[12] The German Bishops Conference at Fulda had tried to explain away and minimize these decrees and threatened to impose the punishment of heresy by force, and for the first time in eighteen hundred years not on those who advocated a new doctrine but on those who remained loyal to the old faith. A genuine reform of the abuses in the Church could serve the supreme aim of Christian development: the union with the now-separated Christian brethren. First among the thirty signatures of mainly laymen was Döllinger's, followed by those of the Bavarian attorney general and the King's chamberlain, Count Karl Ernst Moy de Sons, and the director of the Royal Theatre, Baron Karl von Perfall. Among the clergy already excommunicated were the canon lawyer Professor Johann Friedrich von Schulte of Prague; Josef Hubert Reinkens, as yet only suspended as professor of Church history at Breslau; and Dr. Johann Friedrich, Döllinger's student and biographer.

The apparent inclusion of two non-German signatories of the Old Catholics' unilateral declaration of independence—the odd spellings of Acton's and Blennerhassett's names would have been noticed at once in England—misled one of Acton's biographers to say that for him the episode constituted "only a tactical retreat."[13] Gertrude Himmelfarb would rather accept the version of the affair put out by the secretary of the Munich Conference, Professor Josef Berchtold, according to which the publication of Acton's name had been vouched for by Döllinger, because Acton (unlike Blennerhassett) had not been present at the final session of the Congress at which the declaration was drafted.[14]

It is, however, clear from the Acton-Döllinger correspondence that Berchtold was wrong in his assumption. Neither Acton nor Döllinger was present at the drafting session. Acton was not shown the text beforehand, although he had asked to see it. His sympathies for the Munich protest against the Vatican decrees did not extend to unconditional support for the Munich movement. Indeed, Berchtold's letter seemed to justify the charges of dishonesty that the German Ultramontanes were levelling against the Old Catholic leader, and Acton, writing to Döllinger, felt that there was not much to choose between the lies of either party. But to protest publicly would have created "the impression that I wanted to dissociate myself or, even in the naked formulation chosen by Blennerhassett, wanted to blame those gentlemen."[15]

Döllinger, too, felt bad about the "disagreeable signature affair." Not having been present at the drafting session of the declaration, he afterwards appeared before the Munich Committee, putting in Acton's request for a correction and for admission that a mistake had been made by the secretary. But he met with "obstinate resistance." "They said that we would be giving an all too convenient excuse to the Ultramontane press to denigrate and suspect the Committee and its cause. They also said that if I insisted, it could be done, but the Committee would then resign. I am at a loss what to do." And in a later letter he admitted that the matter had caused him even more annoyance and hurt than the lack of consideration shown to Acton. Berchtold was not the only one to blame. "But I keep silence for the sake of the cause."[16]

The refusal of the Committee to admit the mistake angered Acton so much that he wanted to have nothing more to do with these men and tried also to distance Döllinger from them. "I must confess that the moral disgust which separates me from the infallibilists also cuts me off from some of those near you. That is why I shall in future keep my distance from them, and why I wish above all to have you here with us. Come, if possibly you can." And again writing from Schloss Herrnsheim about the Munich Committee: "These are men who do not deserve one's trust; and these are men whom you are not in a position either to guide or dominate and for whose actions you must not be held responsible."[17] Lady Blennerhassett, who was staying with the Actons, confirmed in her diary that Acton had told her that he had declared war on the *Museumsmänner,* as he called them, after the conference room in the Munich Museum in which they had met.[18]

But Döllinger was not willing to be put off his Old Catholic allies by Acton:

You are right to warn me and point to the mantraps along those difficult paths which I really walk against my will. . . . But looking back I cannot detect the moment or occasion when I should have acted essentially differently from the way I have acted. . . . In order not to allow the false teaching to become dominant in the Church or for it to be expelled again one day, there must be a number of men who deny and reject it [the teaching] loudly, openly, again and again, while not separating themselves from the Church.

That is what we have in mind—that requires a certain modus vivendi and it is now the task to find that. It pains me that you deny us your advice and co-operation, and that you deliberately keep your distance. I myself have no other choice. I must do what I can not to allow the movement to degenerate. I will not, must not let down the men at Bonn, Breslau, etc. who loyally were on my side from the beginning.[19]

It was a turning point in their relations.

There was the usual coming and going among the Herrnsheim house guests that autumn: Rose Blennerhassett, Sir Rowland's sister; Thomas Frederick Wetherell; Dean Arthur Penrhyn Stanley, the Anglican theologian of the Broad Church wing, and his wife; Eugene Michaud, the French Old Catholic theologian; and later Döllinger. Archbishop Ludwig Haynald of Kalocsa, Hungary, came briefly to tell Acton that he was about to send off his letter of submission. Thus all the Hungarian bishops had accepted, Acton noted ironically. "He even says he believes firmly in the doctrine [of infallibility] and is cross with those such as Kenrick and Hefele who had accepted it without actually believing it. But in reality he does not believe in it either."[20]

Lady Blennerhassett, recording a conversation with Acton that took place in the castle's round tower library, noted Acton's deep regret at Döllinger's involvement with the Old Catholics. One ought to remain in the Church, he had told her, as long as one was not forced to declare whether or not one accepted Infallibility, as Döllinger had been. "The Church after all is the God-given instrument of salvation and each person has ever to be ready to die, and thus to do what is necessary at a particular moment."[21]

Gradually their differences in regard to Infallibility were becoming more evident. Döllinger appealed to the tradition of the Church, to the truth of history; Acton feared that Infallibility would destroy liberty and legitimize the countless acts and crimes committed by the fallible men of the Church throughout her history. He was obsessed by the moral argument. Neither of them appeared to have any clear theological concept of Infallibility. They, no less than their opponents, the advocates of Infallibility, were victims of traditional concepts of the divine right applied to the temporal order. Döllinger remained close to the Old Catholics but never became one himself, although the fierce and one-sided post-Council antagonism towards any Catholic not fully loyal to the Vatican decrees naturally tended to identify both Acton and him with heresy and the enemies of the Church. Döllinger continued his work as Church historian. He became more interested in the reunion of the churches and the reformation of moral ideas, and in these aims he found much support and sympathy outside Germany, especially in Great Britain.

Dr. Döllinger never accepted the rebel image imposed on him. The Archbishop's sentence was said to be due to his "deliberate, persistent and public denial of clear and certain dogmatic decrees of the Church."[22] When this statement was read out in Döllinger's own church during the Sunday Mass, a woman rose and walked out in protest. This was the German-born Lady Renouf, of the well-known Brentano family, wife of the Egyptologist, Acton's and Döllinger's friend. She later started various initiatives to bring about a reconciliation between Döllinger and the Holy See under Pius IX's successor, Pope Leo XIII, whose brother, Cardinal Vincenzo Giocchino Pecci, also appeared ready to respond to a move from Döllinger. But Döllinger retained his original belief that nothing short of his "absolute recantation" would be acceptable. In November 1889 Lady Renouf, who did not think that Rome could be expected to make the first move, as Döllinger wished, asked her old friend point-blank for his word that he really did want reconciliation, and Döllinger gave her his hand upon it. She then wrote to her husband in England, who, for various reasons, delayed calling in this matter upon Cardinal Mariano Rampolla del Tindaro, the Vatican secretary of state, until January 1890, when Döllinger was already dead. The Renoufs were later urged to make public these attempts at reconciliation while Pope Leo XIII and his brother were still alive. Renouf hesitated, as he was unsure whether they would wish their unconventional approach to Döllinger via various ecclesiastics to be known. Acton viewed the Renouf demarches on Döllinger's behalf sceptically, as is apparent from a brief commentary in 1878.[23]

Not the least obstacle to a reconciliation between Döllinger and the Church was the temper of the times—the authoritarian manner in which opinion in the Church was made to tow the official, Ultramontane line—which affected especially the way official historians dealt with the Vatican Council and the opposition until the mid-twentieth century, when E. C. Butler's *The Vatican Council*, Roger Aubert's *Vatican I*, and, even later, Klaus Schatz's *Vaticanum I, 1869–1870* paved the way for different interpretations.[24]

In Germany, the fall of Döllinger, the most illustrious German Catholic scholar, evoked sorrow as well as rejoicing. His claim in one of his letters to the Archbishop of Munich that "thousands among the clergy, hundreds of thousands in the laity think as I do" was put to the test when signatures of loyalty to the Archbishop, linked with a protest against Döllinger's claim, were collected.[25] In Munich, and in spite of various pressures applied, it was said that all the clergy had voted unanimously. The reality belied these claims: only 6,401 signatures were collected from seventeen German dioceses with a total of 12,625 secular priests, but not even a thousand of the laity voted their support for the Archbishop.[26] Döllinger's expectation had proved accurate enough.

John Henry Newman, while making no public comment on Döllinger's excommunication, wrote to him: "You are continually in my thoughts and in my prayer. I am sure you must have hearts feeling and praying for you, and that so true a servant and son of the Catholic Church should be so tried."[27] It was just a year before, on 19 March 1870, that Döllinger had appealed to Newman to break his silence on the Vatican Council, quoting the Spanish proverb "Quien no parece, perece" (He who hesitates is lost): "Your silence becomes a snare for thousands."[28] And in his reply Newman wrote: "Can any thing I should say move a single Bishop? and if not, what is the good of writing? . . . I suppose in all Councils there has been intrigue, violence, management, because the truth is held in earthen vessels. But God overrules. I do not see that the Vatican Council or the Council of Florence, is worse than the Second General Council in this respect, or than the Third. And the Fathers of the Fourth may be said to have turned around at the word of a Pope."[29]

Blennerhassett, who visited Newman in Birmingham in early April, found him, as he told Acton, "in an extremely odd state of mind." Newman "expressed himself strongly against the Archbishop of Munich for having asked Döllinger for a declaration on the subject of infallibility, and at the same time professed his own belief in the new dogma although unable to reconcile it with well-ascertained historical facts." Newman rejected Döllinger's views on the truth of the doctrine of Infallibility and on the validity of the definition.[30] When, some time later, Newman visited the Blennerhassetts in London, he expressed his sorrow about the German developments and wanted to know whether Döllinger had taken part in the election of Josef Reinkens, and also whether he approved of it. Newman said that he had found more evidence for Papal Infallibility in the early centuries of the Church than Dr. Döllinger would give him credit for. Lady Blennerhassett gave her own largely negative impressions of Newman's visit in a letter to Döllinger.[31]

Replying to this letter, Döllinger wrote that Newman had by now, and not without great energy of will and mind, worked himself into accepting the new dogma, and into thinking that he believed. "How one does that, how the mind can force itself to find firm supports and certain proofs where the unsophisticated person is incapable of discovering not even the very semblance of evidence—that I know only too well; often enough I have noted it in myself and others. Of one thing I am certain: if the Vatican decrees had been proclaimed before Newman's conversion, he would never have gone over and would still be a member of the Anglican Church."[32]

Having said his last Mass on the Sunday before his excommunication, Döllinger abstained from all further priestly functions, even from saying Mass privately, for instance in the Arco castle chapel. What that must have cost him after being a priest for nearly fifty years! There was a temporary rupture in the close Arco-Döllinger links, but about two years later the Arco family felt that they had to apologize to their old friend. Marie, Acton's wife, and her brother Toni were instrumental in bringing about the reconciliation.[33]

Acton was in Bavaria when the Franco-Prussian War broke out, on 19 July 1870. It made the world temporarily forget the Vatican Council and its impact. Bavaria joined the war on Prussia's side. Two Arco sons were officers in the German army and one in the Austro-Hungarian army, and when Max and Toni fell into the hands of French guerilla fighters, the family was deeply worried about their fate because of the atrocities committed in that war on both sides. They returned home eventually, however, broken in health, as did the Arco nephew, Antonio Marescalchi, who as Marshal Patrice Maurice de MacMahon's aide-de-camp had been taken prisoner of war by the Germans. In London, Lord Granville, the foreign secretary, was able to intervene through diplomatic channels for their release.

Acton, who had joined Marie and the girls at Tegernsee in June, went on a brief trip to England, where, on 28 June, he took his seat in the House of Lords, his sponsors being Lord Granville and his old Irish friend and former fellow MP Thomas O'Hagan, also raised to the peerage as the first Catholic Lord Chancellor of Ireland since the reign of James II. The dressing-up part in the scarlet velvet robe and ermine, and the actual ceremony, were quickly got over with, as Acton wrote to his family. After the oath, he took his seat at the lower end of the barons' bench. "There is a splendid library in the H[ouse] of Lords, which I propose to enjoy greatly."[34]

Early in August Acton was back again at Tegernsee, and on Sunday, 7 August, his son was born, the third child, after Mamy and Annie. The father movingly recorded the event: "Our son was born this morning at twenty minutes to five. The doctor cried out *'Ein Sohn. Ich gratuliere!'* as I went into the room. My mother-in-law was sitting in a corner, and met me at the door. Thank God, all is well. Mamy is delighted with her little brother, and expects to be allowed to nurse him in a fortnight. She wishes to carry a light at the christening tomorrow, and is afraid of burning her fingers. I asked Annie what she had got upstairs, and she said at first: chocolatty—but then corrected herself and said: tiny brother. He will be named after his two grandfathers, Richard Maximilian. God grant that he may grow up to make good his father's faults!"[35] Döllinger, despite his other preoccupations, fully shared the Actons' joy over the birth of "the son whom God has given you. May his blessing protect the precious child! I feel as though this son was born to me."[36] It was an interlude of happiness in that fateful year for all the Acton circle.

Acton was in Vienna in October 1870, irresistibly drawn, it seemed, to what was happening in the Eternal City. The withdrawal on 4 August of French troops needed to fight in the Franco-Prussian War had been followed, on 22 September, by the occupation of Rome by Italian troops after only brief resistance by the papal army under General Raffaele Cadorna. On 2 October a plebiscite confirming Rome as the new capital of the Italian Kingdom sealed the fall of the temporal power. From Vienna, Acton wrote home: "I got Granville's dispatch as I came here. What I wrote to him from Munich may have suggested to him that it would be well to do something at Rome."[37] What that "something" was has become something of a mystery.

Acton's stepfather had inherited the seals of the Foreign Office after the death of the Earl of Clarendon in July, but with the British government's concerns over the Franco-Prussian War and a cabinet divided and wavering over whether British neutrality should favour Paris or Berlin, Lord Granville's priority was clearly not the Roman Question in its changed form.[38]

Having arrived in Vienna earlier than expected, Acton went first to see his friend Alfred von Arneth, keeper of the Austrian State Archives, where he saw Ranke and Don Pascual de Gayangos y Arcre (the Spanish scholar and Orientalist) at work but did not disturb them. Next he called on his cousin by marriage, Marco Minghetti, the Italian ambassador, whom he found "favourable to France, but he says that Thiers had failed most completely everywhere." Louis Adolphe Thiers, then republican in sentiment, was on a diplomatic mission to the capitals, trying to reconcile the interests of defeated France and the other powers. Minghetti had "some strange views about Rome and promises to give me papers." Then his cousin Laura took him to Nonna Acton, who happened to be in Vienna accompanied by her granddaughter Minnie (Throckmorton), Acton's devoted cousin. Minnie "jumped into my arms," Acton reported to Marie, "and kissed me aloud. Nonna (in her eighties) is looking well though as *distraite* as possible. I swallowed some breakfast and drove off with Minnie to Schönbrunn where I spent an hour or two with her. She is quite cheerful and content but not attached."[39] Minnie Throckmorton had found a position as a lady-in-waiting to Empress Elisabeth (Sissy), but when it was discovered that her riding ability was limited, she became instead an English tutor and governess to the Archduchess Valerie, the youngest daughter of the Empress.

The details of this Vienna visit are of some importance because of the story subsequently spread by the Austrian historian Theodor von Sickel.[40] He said that he met Acton on 16 or 17 September to take him to a dinner with Ranke. Coming down the hotel stairs he met the Italian ambassador, and Acton then told him in great confidence that he had just heard from Minghetti that Italian troops would occupy Rome within a few days and take possession in the name of King Victor Emmanuel. Accordingly, Acton excused himself from their dinner. He wanted to take the night express train to Rome to be there with the troops in time to carry off the Vatican Archives and secure important manuscripts such as the *Liber Diurnus* for international scholarship so that they might not be spirited away by some other interested party. "Anyone who knew the rash and resolute Acton will understand that for such a prize he would be ready for any adventure," wrote Sickel, and Herbert Butterfield agreed with that observation.[41]

But Sickel's story, written down twenty years later, sounds unlikely. His memory may have misled him, especially about the dates. He was also an interested party in that, like Acton, he had searched for the *Liber Diurnus* because he was interested in it as an historian, and indeed would later, having discovered it by chance in the Vatican Secret Archives, produce his own edited version (1889). At the time he told the Roman archaeologist Giovanni de Rossi, a notorious gossip, about Acton's intended "raid." Sickel had reasons for keeping in well with the Vatican authorities. Minghetti, knowing that it was impossible to stop Acton (so Sickel wrote), had wired a warning to Rome, and when Acton arrived (before 20 September) he was detained temporarily by the Italians until order was restored in Rome.

One might imagine Acton capable of such a mad plan, if he thought that some Ultramontanist would suppress an important historical document. He had a great belief in historical truth gradually emerging from the European archives that had been opened only in his own lifetime, and he also knew to what lengths those holding power in Church or State would go to make vital documentary evidence disappear in order to establish a particular version of events.

But he was certainly averse to using evil means for a morally good end.[42] According to Sickel, Acton told him on a later visit to Vienna that his mission in Rome had failed. When Sickel visited Acton again at Merano shortly before his death, however, Acton's memory was blurred. But it seems unlikely that Minghetti, close as he was to Acton through family bonds and in his liberal politics, would go behind his back to frustrate his plans. When Sickel later mentioned his story to Laura Minghetti, praising her husband for forestalling Acton, she retorted angrily: "Non Monsieur, mon mari n'a jamais été méchant" (No, Sir, my husband was never malicious).[43]

The Sickel version of events is disproved by a series of letters in the Italian State Papers, which contradict Acton's alleged dash to Rome and arrest, "honourable" or not, on 20 September, and his intention of raiding the Archivio Segreto.[44] In the first letter, dated "Vienna, 23 September 1870," Marco Minghetti wrote to Acton, who was then evidently still at Tegernsee, about the latest Roman developments. He reminded him of their last meeting in Rome on 1 January of that year. "You were then convinced that the Pope's temporal power was near its end: more quickly than seemed possible to me at that time, but events have proved you right and we are now in the capital."

Minghetti went on to tell Acton about the proposals that the Italian government, through its emissary Count Ponza di San Matino, had put to the Pope, to the effect that for surrendering the temporal power, the Pope's legal and spiritual sovereignty over the Leonine City (the parts around St. Peter's as fortified by Leo IV [847–55]) would be fully recognized nationally and internationally. This was in fact the policy of Camillo Cavour (who had died in 1862), which the Italian government was determined to carry out against the opposition of the Roman Republicans. According to Minghetti, "Cardinal Antonelli, the Pope's Secretary of State, expressed no basic objections, was even conciliatory while objecting to the use of force. It was the Pope himself who refused all dealings on the alleged grounds of his ties with his predecessors and successors. . . . [Now] the Pope's presence in Rome gives hope for a deal." The Italian troops would not occupy the Leonine City. As for the Papal States, there would probably be a referendum, as there had been elsewhere in the occupied territories, with the recalled Parliament in Florence voting on the capital's move to Rome and granting the necessary funds. There would be great "material and moral" difficulties, but one could not act otherwise in view of public opinion. Cavour's programme had been accepted by the country, and it had to be realized to its full extent. Minghetti added that the French Republic's influence in Italy was insignificant and that the fears of a revolution in Italy, expressed in the German newspapers, were "totally mistaken": "The whole country was quiet; Mazzini imprisoned for the past two months, and Garibaldi going on about being hindered from leaving Caprera, which however nobody minded."

At the time Minghetti was evidently over-optimistic about a settlement with the Pope, perhaps because of the smooth Antonelli's diplomatic assurances. Between the rigid opinions of the two extremist parties—the Pope as head of the priestly obscurantist, notoriously mismanaged, cosmopolitan States of the Church, and Garibaldi, the champion of Italian national liberation—there could be no compromise. Nearly a century had to elapse before the various parts of Italy fully accepted unification and the Pope renounced his status, allegedly as "prisoner of the Vatican."

Another dispatch was sent by Minghetti, dated "Vienna, 11. Ottobre 1870, ore 19.45," to Emilio Visconti-Venosta (1829–1914), five times the Italian foreign minister, upon Thiers's departure from the Austrian capital to Florence, saying that a letter was on the way by courier that the minister should read before seeing the French emissary. "Lord Acton is here on his way to Rome. He will see you on Saturday. I recommend showing him the project concerning guaranteeing the Pope's spiritual power and consult Acton about it. He represents all that is most intelligent and most liberal among Catholics." On the following day Minghetti sent a further communication to the foreign minister regarding the "guarantees for the Pope," writing that Acton shared his (Minghetti's) opinion that matters should be speeded up, that the Italian proposals should be put confidentially to the powers in order to secure their support, and that they should be voted on as soon as possible in the Italian Parliament. That would improve the government's standing, even if the Pope were to think of leaving Rome. "Our enemies are out to embarrass us, we must do what we can to render our position as correct as possible before the conclusion of peace and the reestablishment of diplomatic relations among all the Powers. Lord Acton recognizes that the Leonine City project is no longer viable. He has seen Count Bray [the Bavarian minister in Vienna] here, who told him that unless having previously agreed with Prussia and Austria, Bavaria would do nothing for the Pope."

These letters show Acton's continued diplomatic influence on post-Vatican Council Rome and also dispel the myth spread by Sickel. Acton's arrival in Rome could not have taken place before "Sunday," which would have been 17 October 1870, that is, after the relatively peaceful Italian occupation of Rome had been concluded and confirmed by a huge majority of the referendum and order had been restored in Rome, thus making unnecessary Acton's alleged "arrest."

Acton left Florence, where he had spent a tiring day, on "Saturday," and this is confirmed also by a letter to Marie.[45] In Florence there was "first the learned part of my business": meeting one of the copyists he employed in the State Archives, then their keeper Cesare Guasti, followed by a call on the National Library of Florence to meet its learned head, Giuseppe Canestrini, after which he lunched with Giuseppe Massari (1821–1884), who was the *Rambler*'s Italian correspondent. In the afternoon Acton called on Isaac Artom (1829–1900), formerly Cavour's private secretary, now "the chief man under the Foreign office," who spoke to him "about the Roman Question with great wisdom." There followed an hour with Visconti-Venosta, "who explained all his policy about Rome and was not surprised when I showed him that it could not succeed." Thence to the British minister to Victor Emmanuel, Sir Augustus Paget, "whom I had already met at Visconti's door, and who is rather a Tory. I made acquaintance with his handsome wife, née Hohenthal, rather uninteresting."[46] Acton concluded that day: "Came home tired to write to my dearest wife and pack up." He dined with Artom and Massari at Doney's, and "met Thiers in the street. He has failed here as everywhere. . . . You cannot think how well all my friends, literary and political, have received me. I have got to understand what they are about, and have given, I think, very good advice which was well received. They cannot settle the Roman Question, but they can put it in a position which will be secure for the future, both for the Church and the State. There is a chance of such blessings as will almost make up for the Council."

What Acton was about at Rome is explained in a long letter that, like many of his letters, was evidently meant as much as for his own later records as for the recipient.[47] The letter does not refer to the saving of the *Liber Diurnus* or the Vatican Archives, which anyhow were closed. Their future was part of the general negotiations between the Papacy and the Italian government. No doubt, Acton would have preferred it if the Pope's library were "nationalized" and open to any scholar, but for the time being it became an "unapproachable sanctuary," and to keep it more firmly locked than ever was part of the exercise of papal sovereignty. Surprisingly, the deposed prefect of the Secret Archives, Acton's friend Theiner, had been allowed to stay on in his apartment in Galileo's "Tower of the Winds"; he even continued to receive his meagre stipend of thirty scudi a month. But his private door to the Archives was bricked up to prevent him from having perhaps another key made, and he was not allowed access except under the stringent conditions of other scholars, "conditions which pride forbade him to accept."[48]

Theiner had not got over the terrible scene of his dismissal by the Pope in June. He was ill and put Acton's visit off to another day; all energy seemed to have been drained out of him, but he was working on his *Acta Genuina Concilii Tridentini,* three volumes of which were to be published with financial help from Bishop Strossmayer (without the express permission of the Pope) at Zagreb, but shortly before this occurred Theiner died in isolation at Civitavecchia, on 10 August 1874. He left his correspondence and other written material to Canon Nikolaus Vorzak, Strossmayer's aide at the Council. Under pressure from the Curia, Vorzak surrendered all these papers to the Holy See, in 1878. It was suggested by a fellow Croat that the surprisingly kind treatment Theiner, the alleged enemy of Pope Pius IX, received might have been caused by fear that he was in possession of personal letters of the Pope's that would discredit him and that Theiner's dismissal was because of pressure by the Jesuits and revenge for his anti-Jesuit writings rather than because he had given secret documents to the opposition during the Council.[49]

In Rome, Acton renewed his contacts with Arnim, the Prussian minister; Trautmannsdorff, the Austrian ambassador; Harry Jervoise, who had taken Odo Russell's place; his friends among the old Roman families like Michelangelo Caetani; and representatives of the Italian government. On the basis of these talks he concluded that no accord between the Pope and Italy was likely in the foreseeable future. The European governments were forced into nonintervention either because, like France and Germany, they did not want to drive the Italians into joining the war on one side or the other, or because of divided opinion among their own Catholic population, or because of strong republican trends in the Latin Catholic countries, France, Italy, and Spain. The lesser evil for most governments was to accept as fait accompli the inevitable fall of the temporal power and to work towards some alleviation of the spiritual and political dependence of the Pope as "prisoner of the Vatican." "Antonelli has triumphed," wrote Acton in his long letter to Marie. "His [the Pope's] power has grown through the fall of his system. . . . Antonelli has told the Pope that the Italians want him to leave. That has encouraged him to stay. And staying, he is becoming an embarrassment for them, prevents them from taking radical measures, contains them and makes it a bitter war . . . and adds to the world's impression that the Italians are his gaolers and that he is not really free."

Acton developed what he had seen and heard in Rome in a notable address he gave a few months later at Kidderminster, a market town in the Midland county of Worcestershire.[50] The purpose of that unusual, non-partisan, indeed ecumenical meeting was to appeal on behalf of the Pope. Acton, receiving "immense applause" and frequently interrupted by "loud cheers," proposed a resolution "that it is the true policy of free states to protect the liberty of the Holy See, irrespective of treaty obligations, and to secure its independence of national and political influence." It was carried unanimously by acclamation.

There was a clash, Acton said, between Catholics associated with authority and other Catholics associated with liberty. "We were accused of inconsistency and insincerity. People said that we were weak, and denied it when we were strong . . . and that we were liberal from interest, but illiberal and intolerant in principle." Even the most bitter enemies of Pius IX were conscious, however, that this "Pope, in his eightieth year, at the close of the longest and most unfortunate pontificate on record, going forth once more to eat the bread of exile and to die in a strange land, would afford a spectacle that would rouse the feeling of many millions of men." But instead of fleeing "when he lost the corruptible crown of earthly monarchy," the Pope stayed on "in the midst of the people he had ceased to govern," his position still threatened now in his spiritual liberty.

The Pope's position was of concern not only to Catholics but to the whole civilized world. For it was necessary that the Pope should exercise his spiritual functions without impediments or without the suspicion of undue foreign and political influence. And as he could not guarantee his own independence, it must be done by the powers and with international securities. "No difference in religion can justify blindness to what is right and wrong in policy. The independence of the Holy See was neither a dynastic matter nor one of political expediency. Religious liberty is one of the chief objects for which civil society exists, because liberty is the medium of religious truth." That was a remarkable plea for the Pope's liberty from the man who had not long ago opposed him more than other "enemies."

Did the Vatican City State, established by the Lateran Treaty of 1929, fifty-nine years after the fall of the Pope's temporal power, answer to Acton's demand for the political and spiritual independence of the Papacy? It certainly paved the way, another fifty years on, for the Church's headquarters to become more international and even for a non-Italian to become Pope. But that was not what, above all, mattered to Acton. This speech, given after all by one of the bitterest opponents of the temporal power, was actually understood by some of his allies at the Vatican Council as deserting their cause. Had he not condemned the temporal power as an "immoral regime" and seemed now to continue it "by other means"? This was the accusation made by Charles Loyson,[51] although he later accepted Acton's explanation, but he did make a point with which Acton agreed: "Far from restraining the spiritual power of the Holy Father, Italy on the contrary has added to his spiritual power, and, as has been well said, if the Council made the Pope infallible, the [Italian] parliament has made him all powerful."[52]

The main reason why Acton was so opposed to the unilateral Italian solution of the Roman Question—without international guarantees—was that it left the European powers open to pressure from the Pope towards a solution more favourable to his interests. The outcome, he feared, would be the increased centralization of the Church's government by strengthening the power of the Pope and the Roman Curia at the expense of the Italian lower clergy and laity. Marco Minghetti, who also anticipated this outcome, wrote that the government expected no reconciliation to be possible under Pius IX, but that perhaps a future pontiff would be more amenable to a settlement.[53]

In September 1870 Acton's pamphlet *Sendschreiben* (Circular Letter) was published in Germany.[54] It was written in German in the form of a letter to an anonymous bishop of the minority of Council Fathers. Acton's contribution covers about half the text; the remainder is taken up by verbatim Latin quotations that some of the minority bishops had made during the Council. (These quotations were taken from the printed *Synopsis observationum,* a secret document drawn up for the Council Fathers, in which were collected various criticisms of the first draft of chapter 4 of the constitution on the Pope.) The attitude of the minority bishops had found the trust of many throughout the Catholic world, Acton wrote. But when the hour of decision struck, suddenly they were silent. There was a "disturbing" contrast between their former language and the present silence. Just when individual Catholics were most troubled in their conscience, these bishops were failing them by neither explaining their own conduct nor providing the necessary leadership. Acton referred to these bishops as having been opposed to the new decrees "in principle" (p. 3), thus implying that they were all outright opponents of Infallibility, which, as far as the inopportunists were concerned, was of course not the case.

One of these bishops had said that he would rather die than accept the decrees (*Synopsis observationum,* no. 86, p. 3); another had spoken of the "suicide of the Church" (*Synopsis observationum,* no. 134, p. 4). Cardinal Schwarzenberg in his *Desideria* had warned that the bases of the faith in the hearts of the most devout Catholics would be shaken and the opponents strengthened in their attacks. Archbishop Kenrick of St. Louis said that the new Catholicism could be defended only by laughable subterfuges against the unshakable witness of history, for the lives and teachings of popes were only evidence that they were incapable instruments of Infallibility (*Synopsis observationum,* no. 37, p. 4). An Irish Bishop had declared that the new teaching would be rejected by many and regarded as an unheard-of innovation; the authority not only of the Pope but also of General Councils would founder and a terrible unbelief would follow (*Synopsis observationum,* no. 83, p. 5).

Countries with different denominations (Germany, England, America) had said that the definition would impede, indeed prevent, the return of Protestants to the Catholic Church (*Synopsis observationum,* no. 4, p. 5). Archbishop Sheridan Purcell of Cincinnati said that in their dispute with Protestants, Catholics would now be told that the new teaching had been previously described as a free opinion in the Church which they could hold or reject: "Now you have turned it into a dogma; either you have lied before or the teaching of the Church has changed" (*Synopsis observationum,* no. 100, p. 6). Bishop Wilhelm Emmanuel Ketteler of Mainz, in a treatise distributed in Rome, had said that Infallibility would cause a schism in the Church and irreconcilable hatred of non-Catholics (*Synopsis observationum,* no. 65, p. 6). The Irish-born Archbishop Kenrick said that Papal Infallibility was not taught in any book of religious instruction in the English-speaking world (Kenrick, *Concio habenda,* p. 7).

English and Irish bishops had solemnly denied holding the belief in Papal Infallibility before Catholic Emancipation and in order to counter anti-Catholic prejudice (*Synopsis observationum,* no. 97, p. 8). That the Pope's powers over secular rulers, his power to depose kings and discipline heretics, were implied in Papal Infallibility was recognized by Bishop Dupanloup of Orléans, who also described the new dogma as "absurd and unheard-of" (*Synopsis observationum,* no. 22, p. 8). Archbishop Kenrick denied that the Church could declare as an article of faith what she had failed to teach for eighteen hundred years (*Synopsis observationum,* no. 1, p. 10).

Some of the ablest men of the Vatican Council—Schwarzenberg, Rauscher, Dupanloup, Haynald, Ketteler, Clifford, Purcell, Thomas Connolly, Darboy, Hefele, Strossmayer, and Kenrick—had declared the new Council to be a conspiracy against truth and right. The new dogmas were said to have been neither taught by the apostles nor believed by the Fathers; they were soul-destroying errors, contrary to the genuine teaching of the Church, based on deception, a shame for Catholics (*Synopsis observationum,* p. 16).

The puzzle was that these minority bishops, even in their farewell message to the Pope, had reiterated their opposition and said that, departing early and before the proclamation, they did not want to detract from their loyalty to him. And it was generally believed that they would continue their opposition at home. But as one of the signatories of the document (Archbishop Paul Melchers of Cologne) had said: "Before the proclamation [of the dogma] we are bishops obliged to vote according to our conscience and conviction. After the papal proclamation we are merely Christians and owe the world the example of humble submission to the judgment of the Church" (*Synopsis observationum,* p. 18). It appeared that there was a distinction between the teaching of the Church and that of Scripture and tradition, and that a teaching could be imposed, the truth of which, according to the Catholic method of dogmatic verification, was not either proved or provable.

"If you and others have really gone over to this view, you would have to make up for a deplorable number of mistakes and slanders," wrote Acton. "Highly placed men in the Roman Curia used to say that the opposition misused their liberty to spread heresies. If the bishops themselves have now adopted this position, accepting the opposite of what they stood for as the teaching and law of the Church, they will inevitably feel the impulse to atone for the scandal they have caused." And Acton ended his *Sendschreiben:* "I believe that you will not forget your words and you will not disown your work; for I place my trust in those bishops—there were Germans among them—who, in the last hour of the Council, admonished their colleagues, saying that 'one must persevere to the end and give the world an example of courage and constancy of which it stands so much in need'" (pp. 18–19). And he concluded, "I remain, my most reverend Bishop, with sincere respect, yours most truly, Acton," with the dateline Tegernsee, 30 August 1870.

It is not clear what Acton's pamphlet was meant to achieve. Undoubtedly he hoped, through the pressure of public opinion, to hold the bishops to their clearly stated words and to inspire them to act as true "witnesses of the faith" as they had defended it at the Vatican Council; to stop their moral defection; and to show the worried faithful a way out of their spiritual dilemma—but which way? The schismatic way? There was just a hint of that in the *Sendschreiben.* Acton made himself clear in a letter to Döllinger when the *Sendschreiben* was already out and he was trying to keep Döllinger away from these men "or you will have the responsibility and no control. You cannot know what individuals will say or whether the direction of Schulte, or the opposite, which is mine too, will eventually prevail."[55]

Acton was resolved to stay in the Church almost at any price, as was Döllinger, who as a priest had no choice in the matter. There are certainly no grounds to confirm the speculation that Acton aimed at a national Church independent of Rome.[56] The *Sendschreiben* originated at a moment when Acton, strongly affected by the Vatican Council, had not yet thought out the implications of his pressure on the minority bishops. One of them retaliated.[57] Bishop Ketteler of Mainz, although his changes of view incensed Acton during the Council, had never disguised the fact that he had joined the opposition not because he was against Infallibility on principle but because he regarded it as inopportune. He rejected being "a representative of a large part of the Catholic world" and the noble lord's expectation that the ideas or opinions of individual bishops of the minority were infallible. These criticisms were directed against the first draft, but not against the definitive proposal when various changes had been made.

Ketteler showed that some of Acton's quotations had been taken out of context and that many of them were directed only against inopportunists. He pointed out that the minority bishops were not a party or a monolithic bloc and were not united by any kind of common bond. They had voiced their misgivings against Infallibility before the decrees but would now accept what the Council had decided. Not they but the Church was infallible. Those who rejected the decrees had no right to appeal to the bishops. They had gone the way of Janus and the Quirinus letters of the *Allgemeine Zeitung,* because they had already refused to subordinate themselves under the bishops but had attempted to use them. Ketteler concluded with a personal challenge: Acton's pamphlet showed the same systematic prejudice against the Council as was to be found in the Quirinus letters. He had hitherto refused to believe that Acton had anything to do with these products because of his high regard for him. He could never believe that Catholics who engaged in hostile acts against the Church were doing so out of a sense of truthfulness. This was a reference to Ketteler's early polemic against the Quirinus letters, made without the knowledge that Acton was Döllinger's main source of information.[58] Acton had first intended to reply to Ketteler's challenge in a preface to the French translation of his *Sendschreiben* but failed to do this during his journey to Rome in October 1870.

A report of Acton's *Sendschreiben* in the *Times* may have been written (Acton speculated) by Malcolm MacColl, an Anglican scholar close to Gladstone, and Gladstone himself might have encouraged publication in the *Times*. The report elicited an anonymous letter by a correspondent signing himself "Fair Play," who compared Acton's and Ketteler's points. Another letter, signed "Vigorniensis," defended Acton and expressed doubt that Ketteler had destroyed Acton's objections.[59]

Acton's *Sendschreiben* was favourably received in the Augsburg *Allgemeine Zeitung,* which even found that "this English lord might add glory and success to a German university chair." But, carried away by nationalist exuberance, the writer thought to see "an immense presumption of Romanism" in Pius IX's declaration of Papal Infallibility, comparing it with the declaration of war that Napoleon III issued against Germany and hoping that just as German arms had defeated the French at Sedan, the Germanic spirit of truthfulness and free scientific enquiry would smash Roman lies and dominance.[60]

After a year's delay, Rome, too, reacted by putting Acton's *Sendschreiben* on the Index of forbidden books, the only product of his pen awarded this distinction.[61] The Continental European perspective was still dominant in the Congregation of the Index, and publications in German and French mattered more to the Jesuit guardians of the faith at Rome than the still relatively insignificant English-speaking Catholics in their diaspora. That explains also why another of Acton's essays, his article on the Vatican Council, escaped the censor's attention when it appeared in an obscure periodical in England, but not when the German version was published in March 1871.[62] In this case Acton, however, was not directly responsible. The translation was made by Professor Wilhelm Reischl, a Munich theologian, but his name was not mentioned so that it looked as though Acton had written it in German. Acton himself, however, was not happy with the translation at all and distanced himself from it, asking Döllinger that it should be made clear, when sending the book out for review, that changes had been made in the text without the author's knowledge or approval.[63] It seems from a comparison of the two texts made by Victor Conzemius that not so much the German translation as its presentation was at fault.[64] Reischl had taken certain quotations from Dupanloup, Schwarzenberg, Strossmayer, and Kenrick out of the appendix into the body of the text, where they appeared italicized, caught the reader's eye, and contributed to the polemical, anti-Roman impression. In fact, Acton's essay, while not so good in the presentation of the theological debates at the Vatican Council, is regarded as one of the best accounts available on the events and currents leading up to it.

When, twenty-five years later, Acton was appointed to the Regius Chair of

Modern History at Cambridge University, his lack of publications was a matter of some concern to the Cambridge authorities. The University Library, however, was able to produce the two German pamphlets, from the first Catholic professor at Cambridge since the Reformation, that Rome had added to its list of forbidden books, and that was more than other loyal Catholics could boast of.

Reviewing Acton's essay on the history of the Vatican Council, the anticlerical Augsburg *Allgemeine Zeitung* concluded with a sharp attack on the bishops of the minority: "Whether they lacked the courage to obey their conscience or the insight to grasp the immense significance of that moment—posterity will say it again and again with all emphasis: Never has a better cause been represented by more spineless men." And the paper felt obliged to rebuke the author for having used a diplomatist's silvery pen rather than the thickest of brush strokes, which would have been more fitting for his theme.[65]

By Christmas 1870 Acton was back at Aldenham. "In England nobody knows anything about the Council beyond what the *Saturday* [*Review*] wrote about it. I must therefore not be silent for long."[66] He told Döllinger of a letter he had received from Bishop James Brown of Shrewsbury, who had said that he "was glad that in Rome all had been united in docile faith." Not wanting to acquiesce in that, Acton replied acidly that "the comments I receive from Rome and from the opposing bishops represent the division in the Church as peremptory and irreparable. I am glad that you have reason to take a more consoling view of the future."[67] Acton was resolved to counter the general impression that the silence of the bishops of the minority was and could be interpreted as acquiescence. But so it was.

For Acton the immediate effect of the ending of the Council was a feeling of emptiness. Whereas the burden of his long mental and physical preoccupation with Papal Infallibility was suddenly lifted, the wounds inflicted by the struggle remained. He experienced a certain aimlessness but also had more time for his family and children. In the summer of 1872, Munich's Ludwig Maximilian University celebrated the four hundredth anniversary of its foundation and bestowed an honorary doctorate of philosophy on its former alumnus. Döllinger told Acton of the award, and Acton wrote back expressing his gratitude for the great honour: "I really must write something so as not to appear too odd a doctor."[68] In his *laudatio*, on 1 August, Friedrich von Giesebrecht, the medieval historian, introduced Acton suitably with the traditional herald's call, *Ist kein Dalberg da?* and said that in his studies in modern history Acton united the scrupulous exactitude of the German scholar and the political acumen of the English statesman.[69] Gladstone, John Stuart Mill, and the Earl of Shaftesbury were among the other foreign recipients of honorary degrees—in their case, doctorates in political science. But the central figure in these events was the rector of the University, Dr. Döllinger. In deliberate response to Rome's excommunication, the highest grade of the Bavarian Order of Merit was bestowed on him by the Bavarian prime minister and he was hailed as a "new Ignatius Loyola," since 31 July, the day of his award, was Ignatius's Saint's Day. Earlier, in May, Döllinger had received an honorary doctorate (D.C.L.) from Oxford University.

In March 1873, Nonna Acton, the eighty-seven-year-old widow of the prime minister of the Two Sicilies, died and was buried at Aldenham. According to Acton's daughter Mamy, her father refused to put up a tablet to her memory because of her indiscretion some time after her arrival in London, more than sixty years before, as a young widow and mother. Her lover was presumed to have been one of the young La Ferronays, the French royalist exiles, brothers of Pauline Craven. The Auguste Ferron de La Ferronays, with their numerous family, had been neighbours of Acton's parents in Naples. Mamy remembered Nonna's ghost haunting their nursery at Aldenham at night. A very small lady in grey silk used to come rustling up to her bed, look down on her, and disappear through the door. But it was said that when a memorial plaque was finally put up after Acton's death by his son Richard, she was not seen again.[70]

While Acton and his wife were on their way to Vienna in April 1873, their baby son John, not even a year old, died of fever. Acton wrote to Marie from Vienna after taking her in her distraught state to her family in Bavaria: "I want you so much in my trouble and have no consolation apart from you except in thinking of Heaven. . . . Heaven seems so much nearer and death seems so much less dreadful now that the dear child I loved is watching and waiting and praying for his father."[71] He himself had a small official assignment in Vienna as a commissary to the World's Fair. The president of Great Britain's contributions to the fair, intended as a major tribute to the industrial age, was the Prince of Wales. He held Acton in high regard and perhaps also had a political interest in wanting to show that he did not share the Queen's dislike of Gladstone and the Liberals.

It was not an onerous job. Acton went round the exhibits with the Prince of Wales, "looked at machinery" and art, and wrote a report. In it he had words of praise for the Prince, a popular figure in Vienna, for the way he handled his task ("a great success with our people, never acting as if he was bored or played a perfunctory part"); he criticized the arts section ("got up in the vulgarest spirit and never promised well").[72] Notwithstanding the recent heartbreak, Acton enjoyed himself in Vienna, working at the Nationalbibliothek for three hours every morning and then dropping in at Demel's for a cup of chocolate; he liked Viennese cuisine and was welcomed back by various "chefs" who knew him as an appreciative guest.

For Vienna's exhibition in the Prater, the city's huge green area by the banks of the Danube, a big building had been put up, then the largest in the world. The central part was formed by the domed Rotunde, eighty-four metres high. The Vienna exhibition had millions more visitors than London's Crystal Palace exhibition had had. Gardens were laid out all round, Acton wrote to Marie, "as large as Regent's Park, . . . beautifully arranged with restaurants, oriental buildings, fountains, etc. I thought I was looking at a fairy scene in an immense theatre. . . . I never saw anything like the festive beauty of the Prater today." The art exhibition contained a new portrait of the Emperor Franz Josef by their Munich friend Franz von Lenbach. "He gives the beauty of the emperor's trousers and vulgarity of his face to perfection," Acton commented, and added that he had converted the Prince of Wales to the Munich school.[73]

Acton's letters are silent on the famous Black Friday, 9 May, when the shares on the Vienna Stock Exchange tumbled disastrously in the big Börsenkrach and thousands lost their savings and their jobs. He only mentioned that his friend, "Natty" [Nathan] Rothschild, had said that he could not afford to come back to Vienna, as they charged him sixty-five florins a day for his apartment! Acton stayed more modestly at the Hotel Munsch (today the Hotel Ambassador), much frequented by the nobility. His first-floor apartment had previously been occupied by the singer Adelina Patti. He dined at the Archduke Rainer's, president of the World's Fair Commission, at the Hotel Sacher, and at the Hohenlohes', bought toys for the children, and "went to the *Burgtheater* for an hour." With his cousin Minnie Throckmorton, still in the employ of Archduchess Valerie, he went to see the famous latest painting of Hans Makart.[74]

This was the huge and panoramic canvas (10.3 × 4 metres) *Caterina Cornaro*, unveiled during the World's Fair in a separate room of the Vienna Künstlerhaus, where the crowds thronged as never before. The room was draped in black cloth, the light from above so arranged that it added to the dramatic effect of the picture. The theme of the historical painting was the return of Caterina Cornaro (1454–1510), widow of James II, King of Cyprus, whom the Venetians forced to surrender her kingdom. She figured frequently as a tragic heroine in the nineteenth-century arts; there were operas about her by Jacques Halévy and Gaetano Donizetti. Makart's rich and pseudo-Baroque painting was the latest Vienna craze. The gigantic and fantastic scene—the painter's wife Amalia had been the model for the Queen—symbolized the showy *Gründerjahre,* the Austro-German equivalent of late Victorian opulence. Acton, too, may have been overcome by Makart's colourful dramatic explosion, but his reaction is not recorded. The picture, which later travelled the world, ended up forgotten in the Austrian State Monuments depot, where it lay rolled up until after World War II, when it was restored and shown on the occasion of the painting's centenary.[75]

GLADSTONE FIGHTS BACK

Back in England, Gladstone suffered defeat in the general election in January 1874 because of his fiscal policies and daring plan to abolish income tax. He also retired from active Liberal leadership but continued as an MP, thus remaining, at sixty-five, an awkward and disturbing element for his party. But at last he was on his own and free to do what his personal and theological interests had warmed him up to do ever since the Vatican Council. He was much exercised over the effects of Infallibility in Church and State and in ecumenical relations and felt deeply for his friend Döllinger, one of the chief victims of "Vaticanism," as Gladstone and also Acton were to call the result of the Vatican Council.

Early in September of that year Gladstone travelled to Munich, mainly to see Döllinger, who, in the middle of that month, was to chair the conference in Bonn on Christian reunion to which the Old Catholics had invited non–Roman Catholic theologians from many parts of the world. Gladstone stopped in Cologne on his outward journey and also on his way back, spending many hours in discussion with his younger sister Helen Jane. Once close to him intellectually, she had been obliged to stay at home to look after their elderly parents and, by way of rebelling against a frustrated life, decided to live in Germany after her conversion to the Roman Catholic Church. This and her subsequent drug addiction—she had always been in bad health and had fallen prey to hysteria and depression, which were then treated with liberal doses of laudanum and alcohol—led to her being practically cut off from her family. Not having seen her since before the Vatican Council, Gladstone was deeply concerned. She had rejected Papal Infallibility and regarded herself as an "old" Catholic, renewing his hopes of persuading her to return to Anglicanism. But it was not to happen on this occasion, and on his return visit to Cologne Gladstone noted in his diary: "She is deeply to be felt for: her mind and soul are in a great strait, but she is striving to battle for the truth and may she be blest."[1]

Gladstone arrived in Munich on 8 September. He was met by the British chargé d'affaires, Robert Morier, and stayed with him. Morier was a friend of Acton and his wife, and through them he met Döllinger, to whom Acton had introduced him as, together with Odo Russell, "one of the best brains among our diplomats . . . also a nephew of Hajji Baba."[2] Apart from some sight-seeing and having his portrait painted by Franz von Lenbach, Döllinger's friend, Gladstone spent most of his four days in Munich in conversation with Döllinger, "who is indeed a most remarkable man," he wrote home, "and it makes my blood run cold to think of *his* being excommunicated in his venerable but, thank God, hale and strong old age. In conversation we have covered a wide field. I know no one with whose mode of viewing and handling religious matters I more cordially agree. . . . He is wonderful, and simple as a child."[3]

Döllinger, too, remembered the visit well: "I think it was in the year 1871 [actually 1874] . . . that I remember his paying me a visit at 6 o'clock in the evening. We began talking on political and theological subjects," he noted, "and became, both of us, so engrossed with the conversation, that it was two o'clock at night when I left the room, to fetch a book from my library, bearing on the matter in hand. I returned with it in a few minutes, and found him deep in a volume he had drawn out of his pocket—true to his principle of never losing time—during my momentary absence."[4] On Gladstone's last day they went for a walk in the Englische Garten. Gladstone later recorded that they came

within near sight of a tall and dignified ecclesiastic—a man of striking presence. . . . As we met, Dr. Döllinger had, as was not unusual with him in walking, his hat in his hands behind him. The dignified personage, on his side, lifted his hat high above his head, but fixed his eyes rigidly straight forward and gave no other sign of recognising the excommunicated professor. "Who," I said to him, "is that dignified ecclesiastic?" "That," he replied, "is the Archbishop of Munich, by whom I was excommunicated." But neither then, nor at any other time, did he, in speech or writing, either towards the Archbishop, towards the Pope, or towards the Latin Church in general, let fall a single word of harshness, or, indeed, of complaint.[5]

To the Englishman Döllinger was the ideal priest of the ideal "Gladstonian Church," and their conversation left a deep impression on Gladstone, further inflaming his mind on the theme of Rome and liberty. It was during that stay in Munich that he added the notorious passage to the proofs on his article on ritualism.[6] This article was intended as an attack on behalf of High Anglicanism on the new ecclesiastical legislation, in particular the law against ritualism in the Church of England, which the Disraeli government proposed to Parliament to counter the Catholic tendencies in the Established Church. To minimize the danger from that quarter, Gladstone attacked the Roman Catholics, saying that it was an "utterly hopeless and visionary effort to Romanise the church and the people of England." At no time since the sanguinary reign of Mary had such a scheme been possible, least of all when "Rome has substituted for the proud boast of *semper eadem* a policy of violence and change of faith," when "no one can become her convert without renouncing his moral and mental freedom, and placing his civil loyalty and duty at the mercy of another, and when she has equally refuted modern thought and ancient history."[7] Naturally there were protests against this intemperate outburst from anti-Catholics as well as from Catholics, and among the Catholic protesters was Lord Ripon, Gladstone's recent cabinet colleague whose conversion to Rome had added to Gladstone's bitter feelings about the Church of Rome.

Soon after Gladstone's return to England came the beginning of Döllinger's Bonn conference, which Gladstone followed from afar. The conference had grown out of a series of lectures on Christian reunion that Döllinger had delivered in 1871, soon after his excommunication.[8] With strong Anglican and Orthodox but practically no Catholic attendance, the conference was intended to be the first reaction of non-Catholic theologians to the shock of Infallibility. When it came to the conference's actual purpose, Döllinger's conciliatory nature overcame many apparently insuperable obstacles, such as the suspicions of the Russian and Greek Orthodox, who were frightened of their own governments at home, and the internal division of the Anglicans. It was "the first Faith and Order Conference of its kind," as Owen Chadwick, with deliberate anachronism, has described that Bonn gathering.[9]

Lady Blennerhassett and Acton considered it necessary to warn Döllinger against the machinations of the Old Catholic organizers of the Bonn conference. "I see you got the Anglicans . . . to drop the little word 'sola' [alone]," Acton wrote.[10] At Bonn the Anglicans were ready to give up "justification by faith alone," the great issue of the Reformation. They also accepted the doctrines of the first six centuries of the history of the Church. But when Döllinger himself rejected the Council of Trent as an ecumenical council, this caused objections among the Catholic-minded Anglican and Orthodox Churches.[11] There were no insuperable problems about assenting to the doctrine of sacrifice in the Eucharist. The Russian Orthodox were opposed, however, to Döllinger's proposal to acknowledge the unbroken episcopal succession in the Church of England—that is, the validity of the Anglican orders—the Russian Orthodox saying that it was an historical question and that on those grounds equal doubt could be cast on the validity of Roman Catholic orders.

Henry Nutcombe Oxenham, the one Roman Catholic convert present, supported by some of the Anglicans, argued for the rejection of the dogma of the Immaculate Conception as distinct from the ancient pious opinion about Our Lady. When Döllinger also rejected this dogma, Acton wrote that the action would widen his breach with Rome. "It may well be possible in future to explain away the Vatican decrees; but a direct retraction such as you postulate in regard to the Immaculate Conception can never be expected. So, at first sight, this does not promote reunion."[12] Moreover, it would be a breach with Döllinger's past if he were no longer to accept, even as a pious opinion, a doctrine of the Church against which he had failed to protest when the dogma was promulgated by Pius IX, in 1854.

Döllinger won the support of the Orthodox theologians by proposing the restoration of the creed to its original form, thus dropping the *filioque* clause introduced by the Western churches into the Nicene Creed. The Anglicans proposed a compromise which argued that while the clause "proceeding from Father and Son" had not been introduced with universal authority, it was faithful both to the New Testament and to the tradition of the early Church. But this proposal was not acceptable to the Orthodox.

By letter from Aldenham, Acton also registered his doubts on the resolutions on private confession, which was held to be permissible rather than binding, thus indicating that forgiveness of sins could be obtained by means not recognized in Catholic theology. Still, the conference was ahead of its day in agreeing that the worship of people should be conducted in the vernacular and that there should be no disagreement whether the Eucharist was administered in one or both kinds. Acton also regretted the absence of German Protestants at Bonn. "It seems to me," he wrote, "that the better men among them are much more serious and profound than the Englishmen. Will you never try to win them over?" He suggested that Döllinger should rather devote himself to a serious historical study showing how the Church had become Ultramontane and infallibilist. "Nobody knows, and not knowing deprives one of finding one's way in the present situation."[13]

It was a first and fundamental disagreement on the religious issues that had been the basis of Acton's and Döllinger's friendship. The Bonn conference bore no immediate fruit. The Bulgarian massacres, followed by the Russo-Turkish War of 1877–78 and various Eastern European tensions, did not mark a propitious time for talks with Eastern theologians. And the pressure put on German Catholics by Bismarck's anti–Roman Catholic legislation was compensated for by their increased loyalty to Rome and the Pope and removed any chances of ecumenical bridge-building by Döllinger or the Old Catholic leaders.

At the end of the conference Döllinger was presented with an illuminated address that recorded "the agreement reached between Old Catholics, Orthodox, Oriental and Anglican Churches to mark the indebtedness for the healing of wounds of God's people and the visible reunion upon earth, under Christ, their head, of His One Catholic Apostolic Church, especially to its originator, Dr. Döllinger." It was signed by 3,838 priests and deacons including 38 bishops, largely from the British Isles, and by 4,170 laity.[14]

One English participant paid tribute to "the extraordinary calmness, fairness and apparent inexhaustible working power" that Döllinger had exercised as president of the conference. "I have never heard him use a bitter word against any opponent," was one judgement. "I have never yet seen him excited or even warm in discussion, never wanting to carry any points of his own strongly, never a partisan of his own strength or clearly held views."[15]

The combined effect of these German events and his visit to Döllinger caused Gladstone to hint to Acton that he might want "to sustain" what he had said in his article on ritualism on the matter of mental freedom and civil loyalty.[16] Acton replied that many Catholics were unsure or inconsistent in their view. "Real Ultramontanism is so serious a matter, so incompatible with Christian morality as well as with civil society, that it ought not to be imputed to men who, if they knew what they were about, would heartily repudiate it."[17] Gladstone, however, felt "drawn onwards. Indeed some of your own words help to draw me. The question with me now is whether I shall or shall not publish a tract which I have written, and of which the title would probably be 'The Vatican Decrees in their bearing on Civil Allegiance: a political Expostulation.' I incline to think that I ought to publish it."[18] And he invited Acton to come over to Hawarden and read the manuscript that was to have the effect of a bombshell, involving Acton and reviving the Infallibility debate, which had already subsided.

Acton spent two days at Hawarden, read Gladstone's manuscript, and was put off by its acrimonious tone. He suggested some corrections in detail, which Gladstone accepted, but also raised the political objection that no other Liberal colleague apart from himself had been consulted. Acton was against publication because the pamphlet would compromise the whole Liberal Party and would also raise a new "no popery" cry, which would harm poorer Catholics rather than their leaders and guilty Ultramontanes or independent-minded Catholics who, like Acton, could take care of themselves. But "to all political, spiritual, and other obvious arguments against publication he was deaf."[19]

Acton left Gladstone in no doubt that because he was one of those Catholics challenged, he would meet the challenge and, deeply upset as he was, answer Gladstone publicly. As there seemed no chance of an early publication, it was agreed that Gladstone would visit Acton at Aldenham, but before this happened Gladstone's pamphlet was published on Guy Fawkes Day, 5 November, an ominous date, and caused the expected sensation.[20] Döllinger knew of the impending publication and surmised that it would cause "a stir, plenty of pronunciamentos, sophistries — and bitterness."[21] Strangely, Gladstone had not mentioned to Döllinger the pamphlet he intended to write, but sent him the proofs, not for criticism but for his opinion. "Had the facts been before me when I was in Munich I should have desired to consult you largely."[22]

But what facts did he mean? The question of civil allegiance had occupied the English bishops of the minority throughout the Vatican Council, as Gladstone knew from Acton's letters. The acrimony that struck Acton may have owed something, as H. C. G. Matthew has suggested, to Gladstone's disappointed hopes in the furtherance of Christian unity through the Council.[23] And there was his rebuff from Lord Clarendon and Odo Russell against an interventionist British policy. Yet Acton felt sure that Gladstone meant to be fair to Roman Catholics. There were presumably also hidden factors — political and emotional — behind Gladstone's sudden anti-Catholic vehemence: various conversions to Rome, such as those that broke off his friendships with Manning and James Hope-Scott; his deep hurt over his sister Helen's Romanism; his defeat by the Irish Catholic bishops and the anti-Catholic nonconformists over his Irish University Bill; his bitterness over the supine reaction of British Roman Catholics to the Vatican decrees; and his regret that Newman had kept his silence about those decrees for so long.

Gladstone had come from Evangelism, but had not, like Newman, arrived at the firm Roman rock of authority, St. Augustine's "Securus iudicat orbis terrarum" (The verdict of the world is final). As an Anglican, Gladstone was in the great central tradition dating from 1662, the position that was neither "high nor low"; reason for him in religion was important, but not too much. The Church, like the State, had to adapt to changing circumstances; the Church had no infallible authority; authority rested in the whole Church, but so long as the Church was divided no formal expression of complete authority was possible; all men were equal in Church and State. Gladstone was driven, as one author has written, by his "burning admiration for the Reformation and the assertion of English nationality which it meant." (His "four doctors," as he called them, were Aristotle, Bishop Joseph Butler, Dante, and St. Augustine.)[24]

Soon 150,000 copies of Gladstone's pamphlet were printed and sold. It caused intense excitement and worldwide debate, and was translated into many languages. The timing, too, helped to revive the Infallibility controversy. The *Kulturkampf* of the Second German Empire was still at its height. In 1872 the Jesuits were expelled first from Prussia and then from all of Germany; in 1873 other religious orders fell under the same ban. The May Laws of 1872, promulgated in Prussia, were designed to undermine papal authority and establish the legality of State authority in ecclesiastical affairs. The Kulturkampf proved to be one of Bismarck's least successful policies, and by 1887 the last of the anti-Church laws had been modified or withdrawn. In Switzerland a similar "struggle" was waged against Catholics. The Kulturkampf remained effective in particular cantons of Switzerland in discriminatory legislation (such as a ban on Jesuits) until far into the twentieth century. Moreover, Bismarck decidedly favoured Tory governments. Disraeli's triumph at the Congress of Berlin in 1878 elicited his famous tribute "Der alte Jude, das ist der Mann" (The old Jew is indeed the man). But the one personal letter Bismarck ever wrote to Gladstone was to congratulate him on his *Vatican Decrees* pamphlet. "It affords me deep and hopeful gratification to see the two nations, which in Europe are the champions of liberty of conscience encountering the same foe, stand henceforth shoulder to shoulder in defending the highest interests of the human race."[25]

The essence of Acton's reply to Gladstone in the *Times* was contained in the following passage:

> The doctrines against which you are contending did not begin with the Vatican Council. At the time when the Catholic oath was repealed the Pope had the same right and power to excommunicate those who denied his authority to depose Princes that he possesses now. The writers most esteemed at Rome held that doctrine as an article of faith; a modern Pontiff had affirmed that it cannot be abandoned without a taint of heresy, and that those who questioned or restricted this authority in temporal matters were worse than those who rejected it in spirituals. . . .
>
> Your indictment would be more just if it were more complete. If you pursue the inquiry further, you will find graver matter than all you have enumerated.

Acton's point was that British Catholics might be honourably trusted whatever the letter and spirit of ecclesiastical law. By hitting the "harmless" Vatican decrees, as Acton now described them, Gladstone had failed to reveal the worse immorality of Ultramontanism itself as it existed in historical facts.

> Pius V, . . . having deprived Elizabeth, commissioned an assassin to take her life; and his next successor, on learning that the Protestants were being massacred in France, pronounced the action glorious and holy. . . . The Irish did not shrink from resisting the arms of Henry II, though two Popes had given him dominion over them. They fought against William III although the Pope had given him sufficient support in his expedition. Even James II, when he could not get a mitre for Petre, reminded Innocent that people could be very good Catholics and yet do without Rome. Philip II was excommunicated and deprived, but he despatched his army against Rome with the full concurrence of the Spanish divines.[26]

On the day—9 November—when Acton's first letter ("Your indictment would be more just if it was more complete") appeared in the *Times,* he and Gladstone and Sir Rowland Blennerhassett travelled from London to Aldenham, where Gladstone was Acton's guest for two nights. Gladstone recorded in his diary: "Much conversation on the way and there." The following day Gladstone noted that he met various local grandees, also in connection with Liberal Party affairs, visited Bridgnorth, the nearest town, and found time to read from Acton's library *A Life of Franz von Baader (1765-1841)*. "Walk and much conversation in this interesting house where time flies at double speed," and the entry for 11 November: "And I reluctantly fly also."[27]

Acton's *Times* letters were an even sharper attack than Gladstone's. Angrily, Catholics challenged him to substantiate his charges. He replied in a second letter, dated 21 November, that covered nearly a page in the *Times* of 24 November and took him three days to write. Then there were two more letters, one written on 29 and published on 30 November, and the last one written from Aldenham on 12 December. What he tried to show with some of his historical revelations, most embarrassing for some defenders of the Church, was that "undogmatic" history need not involve conflict with the teaching authority of the Catholic Church, "whose communion is dearer to me than life." He urged those whose feelings of reverence were wounded to ask themselves whether the laws of the Inquisition were or were not a scandal. "It would be well if men had never fallen into the temptation of suppressing truth and encouraging error for the better security of religion. Our Church stands, and our faith should stand, not on the virtues of men, but on the surer ground of an institution and a guidance that are divine. Therefore I rest unshaken in the belief that nothing which the inmost depth of history shall disclose in time to come can ever bring to Catholics just cause of shame or fear."[28]

These sentiments made a deep impression on a broad public. The *Times* in a leading article commented that Acton either rejected the decrees or treated them "as a nullity."[29] His intention was to do neither but to leave the Council and the decrees out of discussion as "innocuous," irrelevant to the "deeper seat of the evil," which to him was basically the moral question of Ultramontanism, murderous popes, vice in the service of virtue: "Can a Catholic speak the truth or not?"[30] For Acton it was all part of his approach to the Vatican Council. In a letter to Dupanloup, who had asked him what his aims were, he described them in all their simplicity, also quoting them in a letter to his wife: "I am thinking of my children. I want the religion they learn to be pure."[31]

But Catholics were not prepared for Acton's damaging charges, nor were they prepared to say *nostra maxima culpa,* and non-Catholics were bewildered by a defiance of the Papacy that seemed to go further even than Gladstone's. Lady Georgiana Fullerton, Lord Granville's convert sister, wrote to Newman asking him to reply to Gladstone, adding that Catholics were looking to him to do so.[32] Even a friend like Ludovika Brentano Renouf observed that Acton seemed to have been waiting for the opportunity to say disagreeable things about the Vatican and linked him to Manning, who had written to the *Times* in similar fashion about Döllinger.[33] "You seem to be suggesting to the world that you are an infallibilist, and to the Church that you are what she considers a heretic," wrote his friend Wetherell with some truth.[34] But the comment by the *Times* gave Manning the chance of finally dealing with this turbulent layman. And so, three days after Acton's first letter appeared in the *Times,* Manning wrote to him, putting the decisive questions: Had he any heretical intent, and did he accept the Vatican decrees? [35]

Lady Blennerhassett, who was staying with the Actons, described the mood of nervous tension that Gladstone's pamphlet, its repercussions, and Manning's letter evoked at Aldenham. The Irish papers were full of furious attacks on Döllinger and Acton, evidently taking their cue from Manning. The English Catholic papers were less vehement, but the *Tablet* suggested that Lord Acton was one of the "desperately bad Catholics" and "titled apostates" who have been for years out of the pale of the Church, "who do not frequent the sacraments and who are therefore *ipso facto* excommunicate." [36] There were no grounds for this personal attack, but Acton's excommunication seemed to be on the cards. "Even in worldly terms," Lady Blennerhassett wrote to Döllinger, "it is no trifling matter to face such a fate with an entire family. Marie is admirably calm and gentle but prepared for the worst, and if one knew of the anguish with which Lord Acton embarked on the task which he himself called the most difficult and important of his life, one would be surprised by it. But he saw it as his duty in conscience at least to attempt an answer to Gladstone's incontrovertible attack because of the possible damage to the spiritual interests of English Catholics." [37]

The conflict between Manning and Acton, and even more between Manning and Newman, was part of the eternal clash between the doers and thinkers, the active and the contemplative natures. It recalls, particularly within the religious context, the Gospel's parable of Martha and Mary (Luke 10:42) and the question of who was to be regarded as having chosen the "better part," the doers of good works or the advocates of "faith." There is a certain instinctive English partiality for the "activists"—"someone has to do the hostess's chores," "we can't all sit and do nothing," it is said. But Jesus' playful, almost humourous admonition "Martha, Martha, thou art full of care and trouble about many things," seems to be meant less as a condemnation of activists than to suggest that at that particular moment one dish would probably have done to satisfy the needs of hungry travellers, and that Mary's listening and taking-in role was what was required. Manning represents the typical activist, by no means rare among ecclesiastics: Aristotle's "political animal," single-mindedly pursuing his objective, Shakespeare's "tide in the affairs of men, / Which, taken at the flood, leads on to fortune; / Omitted, all the voyage of their life / Is bound in shallows and in miseries" (*Julius Caesar,* 4.3.217). For those happening to be in the way of the activists, this is frequently a trying attitude.

With his undoubted gifts, his advantages of birth and social background, Manning was predestined to succeed wherever he found himself, first as Archdeacon of Chichester in the comfortable trappings of the Anglican establishment, then as a convert sacrificing all in 1851 to join the Catholic Church. Astonishingly soon, and contrary to all expectations, he was unstoppably climbing another ladder of success, as Provost of Westminster, to the Catholic primacy as the aged Cardinal Wiseman's successor. No matter that his rise to power happened in what was as yet England's despised underclass, the Roman Catholic community, "the religion of domestic servants." Manning's contribution was to raise it along with himself as a force of substantial growth to be reckoned with, from the wish to conform and not to offend—the old English Gallicans' ways—to the new Ultramontanist certainty that in their own country English Catholics were really not an oppressed minority but part of a majority, the universal Church.

It was an astonishing feat of ambition that Manning accomplished, and that, according to one-sided biographers like E. S. Purcell and the brilliant Lytton Strachey, forever stained his reputation. They portrayed him as a veritable monster of ecclesiastical and worldly success. More recent biographers, like David Newsome and Robert Gray, have improved the image only slightly by dwelling on his undoubted humanity, instanced in the medal the dead Cardinal was found wearing round his neck, containing a lock of the hair of his wife to whom he was devoted and who had died a lifetime before.[38] There was also his devotion in later life to social causes, to temperance, to the Irish poor, leading to the role he played in settling the London dock strike of 1889. The Cardinal's funeral in 1892 was a memorable event (especially compared with Cardinal Newman's relatively insignificant internment), during which some four hundred thousand people walked past his body. But, considering the decline of Manning's reputation since and the increase of Newman's and Acton's, this ceremony might only confirm the vanity of worldly pomp and success.

Manning's remarkable rise to power was accomplished through both the patronage of Cardinal Wiseman and Pius IX and his cultivation of the conspiratorial schemes of Mgr. George Talbot, his English ally in the Vatican. As the Pope's private secretary for twenty years until his sad demise in a lunatic asylum, this prelate, a younger son of Lord Malahide, served by dropping suitable hints into the papal ear as to who he thought mattered on the British fringes of the Roman world. But Manning principally commended himself to Roman hearts as a political nature first and last, with an English pragmatic bent and a positive mind. As such he was not likely to indulge in dangerous ideas, as that other controversial English convert, Newman, seemed to. As a born administrator Manning also promised to squash the revival of any English independent Gallican—that is, Cisalpine—tendencies. He was of inestimable value to the papal cause at the time of the Vatican Council, helping to carry through Papal Infallibility decisively and, at the same time, pointing the British Catholic body firmly in the Ultramontanist direction.

But Manning was strangely disappointed by the outcome of the Vatican Council. It brought about neither the restoration of the temporal power nor the Infallible Papal Monarchy, as he had wished. In Rome Manning had suspected Acton's secret work on behalf of Döllinger and watched at close quarters what Acton did for the minority. Resenting anyone who got in his way, he minded even more that "left-winger's" influence over his old Oxford friend, Gladstone. What Lord Granville wrote of Manning's feelings about his stepson—"I presume, there is no Protestant or atheist whom he dislikes more than Acton"[39]— summed up exactly what Manning thought of him. As for Acton, it was odd how much he seemed to have been taken in a decade earlier by Manning's flattery and his scattering of banana skins before the footsteps of unwary and innocent potential opponents like himself. But Manning had long been a master of that art, and for him Sir John Acton was then still part of the old English establishment of born Catholics that he must conquer on his way up to succeed the ailing Wiseman. And Acton, in his Catholic enthusiasm and eager to be of service, clearly was gullible, disinclined to recognize what was behind the façade.

Newman, similarly, was in Manning's way, but more as a rival than as a mere irritant to be squashed. He was clearly the superior and more delicate mind, the great thinker, the Romantic visionary, the dreamer and artist. Newman stood for everything that Manning was not, master of the language of the heart in religion, allowing Catholics to benefit from higher education, recognizing the laity as an essential part of the community of the faithful. And Newman, as Manning knew, distrusted the political men in the Church who had made his early life as a convert such a misery, whereas Manning was clearly among his own with the Roman political men like Cardinals Giacomo Antonelli, the Pope's secretary of state, and Alessandro Barnabò, prefect of the Congregation of Propaganda.

Unlike both Manning and Newman, Acton belonged to another generation, distrusted the convert hotheads, and lacked either the Oxford Balliol or the Oriel touch, a common bond between the two converts. Acton, however, at least knew something of the working of politics, although the reason he himself had left that world was his own clear aptitude and preference for the world of ideas and scholarship. He despised Manning's boundless ambition and his use of Machiavellian tactics to achieve his ends. And Newman, with his Tory mind and skill at hedging and sophistry, was certainly Acton's superior when it came to seeing through Manning's diplomatic finesse and cunning. In the end, there was even the double entendre that could be detected in Manning's funeral tribute to the great and difficult Newman, the victor, perhaps, beyond the grave.

Döllinger, from Munich, assured Marie of his sympathies at a time when the condemnation of the Church might fall on her and her husband.[40] Marie's support for her husband was important, particularly against the perspective of later trouble in their marriage. Writing to Lady Blennerhassett after Acton's death, Marie recalled these anxieties of 1874 and emphasized that there was no question of her husband's "submission" in response to Manning. "His full intention remains clear to me to this day. He took back nothing and unsaid nothing." That the Church authorities accepted his declaration had, she believed, two reasons: first, that they wanted to avoid the scandal of the condemnation in the case of a leading English Catholic family; second, that the subtlety of Acton's reply proved an insuperable defence. He was able to evade the issue while remaining true to his conscience. "I cannot accept Döllinger's (later) reproach, that my husband therefore had no right to be so severe on others," Marie Acton wrote. "For if, like Döllinger, he had been categorically confronted with the dogma, there would have been no way out." And she confirmed what remained his standpoint: he was not in opposition to a dogma but to a system that allowed crime, lying, partisanship, corruption of conscience for the greater glory of God. The God of Truth alone mattered to him. He would, for example, never accept Döllinger's forgiving observation made in regard to Dupanloup, that one could defend the *Syllabus* and yet remain "quite a decent fellow."[41]

Manning, in his answer of 16 November, declared himself satisfied with Acton's denial of heretical intent and repudiation of the *Times* commentary, but wanted to know what answer Acton was giving to the second question, "namely whether you adhere to the doctrines defined in the Vatican Council: unless you intend to describe yourself as one of 'those who adopt a less severe and more conciliatory construction' of those decrees."[42] This second letter put Acton in a quandary, and his urgent requests for help by telegram and letters to Simpson showed how much heart-searching went into the draft of his reply and the answer finally sent.[43] The question he asked himself was: Ought he to say he submitted to the decrees? He did not want to do that. So on 18 November he finally wrote what has become a classic in its deliberate ambiguity, yet could be reconciled with what his conscience and faith dictated him to say:

> My dear Lord,—I could not answer your question without seeming to admit that which I was writing expressly to deny, namely, that it could be founded on anything but a misconception of the terms or the spirit of my letter to Mr. Gladstone.
>
> In reply to the question which you put with reference to a passage in my letter of Sunday, I can only say that I have no private gloss or favourite interpretation for the Vatican Decrees. The acts of the Council alone constitute the law which I recognise. I have not felt it my duty as a layman to pursue the comments of divines, still less to attempt to supersede them by private judgments of my own. I am content to rest in absolute reliance on God's providence in His government of the Church.—I remain, my dear Lord, yours faithfully, Acton.[44]

But Manning, still not satisfied and convinced that Acton was being deliberately evasive and obscure, wrote in early December to Bishop Ullathorne, whom he had already consulted over his exchange of letters. "I have had Acton's second letter examined by the most competent person here, and have had a long MS refutation. . . . Can I in conscience allow him to receive Sacraments in London? His scandal was published there. He has caused there the belief that he does not receive the Definitions of the Church Council. I am also of that belief. And he will make neither reparation nor explanation."[45] And in January 1875 he wrote again: "My correspondence with Lord Acton is not satisfactory. I did as you suggested with the Bishop. Then I had a conference here with four of my priests. We unanimously decided that the case ought to be sent to Rome, and I am now doing so."[46]

But in the meantime Manning had sent a third letter to Acton asking whether he "adhered" and repeated his question. Acton courteously replied that he denied the Archbishop's right of exacting any particular explanation on his part, as he had avoided the dogmatic question. As to his own orthodoxy, he would satisfy his diocesan Bishop James Brown of Shrewsbury. Manning had meanwhile written to Bishop Brown to probe about Acton's acceptance of the Vatican decrees. Bishop Brown, angry and upset by Acton's letters to the *Times,* put the question to him.

To his friend Renouf, Acton wrote at about this time:

> I am in hotter water than ever, for my bishop asks angrily at last, whether I accept the decrees or reject them. I think I can fairly say I do not reject them; but I cannot positively say that I accept them unless I say—as the bishops do who are my guides. Kenrick, namely, tells me that they are legally Dogma, but not dogmatically true. Strossmayer lets them be published in his diocese, but agrees with Döllinger. Place does not say a word in their favour. But I don't think that I ought to say anything, as the bishop has admitted that there is nothing heterodox in my public letters, and explains his questions by the nature of my private letters to him which have not alluded to the Vatican Council. He has not a leg to stand upon.

And Acton added: "Dr. Green who, as my confessor here, has a claim to some assurance, writes to a local paper, denying that I have ever virtually attacked the decrees."[47]

To Bishop Brown, Acton replied:

> To your doubt whether I am a real or pretended Catholic I must reply that, believing all the Catholic Church believes, and seeking to occupy myself with no studies that do not help religion, I am, in spite of sins and errors, a true Catholic, and I protest that I have given you no foundation for your doubt. If you speak of the Council because you supposed that I have separated myself in any degree from the Bishops whose friendship I enjoyed at Rome, who opposed the Decrees during the discussion, but accept them now that it is over, you have entirely misapprehended my position. I have yielded obedience to the Apostolic Constitution which embodied those decrees, and I have not transgressed, and certainly do not consciously transgress, obligations imposed under the supreme sanction of the Church. I do not believe that there is a word in my public or private letters that contradicts any doctrine of the Council; but if there is it is not my meaning and I wish to blot it out.[48]

That satisfied his Bishop, and for the time being Acton was safe under his episcopal protection. But he remained in great fear that Manning would not rest until he was excommunicated.

On Sunday, 30 November 1874, Manning's pastoral letter was read out in all the churches of the archdiocese of Westminster, containing a quasi-excommunication of all opponents of the Immaculate Conception and the Vatican decrees, declaring them excluded from the Church. "Some who openly refuse to believe the said doctrines persist, nevertheless, in calling themselves Catholics, and give out that they go to confession and holy communion in the Catholic church."[49]

Acton heard this pastoral letter read out during Mass at the Church of the Jesuit Fathers, Farm Street. It was clearly meant for him, too. "My position is quite clear," he wrote to Döllinger. "There is nothing in my [*Times*] letter on or against the Council. . . . They can hardly get me otherwise than by some formula." But he added that there had been an attempt to withhold absolution when he went to confession, although he escaped that. His "second confessor was thus able only to scold, but had to absolve" him. The passage is interesting in illustrating both the more rigorous ways in which the confessional was then handled by the Catholic clergy and Acton's own devotional practice in evidently going to confession regularly. In the same letter he asserted: "My support in this situation are God and my wife." Marie had insisted that he should make no concession that went beyond his conviction, "and shows a rocklike faith as well as admirable coolness, although particularly she has to cope with the disagreeable consequences."[50]

Acton added that from talking to Gladstone, who had returned from his last visit to Munich deeply impressed by Döllinger, he gathered that the Professor had "less hope for the Church than I have or at least that the hopelessness is more firmly and clearly established for you than for me. I am not saying that you are wrong. *Dans le doute je m'abstiens de désespérer*" (In my doubt I abstain from despairing). As far as Acton was concerned he would have "to see much clearer than I do to give up the Church which I have got to know and love in her greatness precisely through you. . . . I am therefore making it my firm law not to get out or provoke the expulsion, however, if at all possible to put up with being thrown out by men on account of my historical, not my theological, conscience."[51]

Döllinger saw Acton in the role of Mozart's Tamino in *The Magic Flute,* having to undergo the test of fire, "the fire of hierarchical lightning and the water (including the *aquafortis* of falsehood) of Ultramontane journalism." He wished him and his Pamina well. He wondered how Newman would react in his *pronunciamento:* "What he wrote to Acton [about historical truth] *sub sigillo* he would hardly dare say in public. I am curious. Certainly many thousands await a word from him—but if the trumpet gives an uncertain sound?"[52]

Meanwhile Newman, himself under pressure from Bishop Ullathorne to break his silence, was unhappy about Acton's first *Times* letter and told him that he had "gratuitously" introduced the bad popes. Newman's original letter has been lost, but Lady Blennerhassett was shown it when it arrived at Aldenham on 3 December. She wrote to Döllinger that Newman had praised the moderation and form of Acton's second *Times* letter, had strongly criticized those who had reviled him, and that "the truth and the historical facts ought to be told unreservedly."[53]

Acton thanked Newman for his "consoling" letter: "You know, and I need not tell you, what the value of your sympathy has ever been to me, when I could think that I obtained it, and it would never be so valuable as now." He went on to explain his position: that the Vatican decrees were not his problem, but that if he were asked whether to accept them "with a definite understanding and inward conviction of their truth, I can't say yes or no. But this is the question which the Archbishop—taking his letter and his pastoral together—wants an answer to. I certainly cannot satisfy him. I hope you will understand that, in falling under his censures, I act from no spirit of revolt, from no indifference, and from no false shame. But I cannot accept his tests and canons of dogmatic development and interpretation and must decline to give him the only answer that will content him, as it would, in my lips, be a lie."[54] He was sure that he would be excommunicated, and Lady Blennerhassett later recalled that in those days of his correspondence with Manning, Acton had said to her, quite pale with nervous tension: "I would rather die than having to live without the sacraments and to leave the Church."[55]

In January 1875 Newman published his *Letter to His Grace the Duke of Norfolk*. It was a masterly attempt to explain—or, as Acton and Döllinger believed, to explain away—Papal Infallibility. Newman emphasized the limited scope of the new dogma, mocked the intransigence of Pius IX as much as the "chronic extravagance" of certain Catholic extremists on the one side, and on the other the "vehement rhetoric" of Gladstone, which only exacerbated the intense prejudice against Catholics in England. But it had to be admitted that "so religious a mind" as Gladstone's had first been alienated by Catholics themselves, or rather, by those "who had stated truths in the most paradoxical form, and stretched principles till they were close upon snapping; and who at length, having done their best to set the house on fire, leave to others the task of putting out the flame."[56]

Newman clearly distanced himself from Döllinger and the German Catholic scholars who had left the Church, "a tragical event, both for them and for us, that they have left us. It robs us of a great prestige; they have left none to take their place. I think them utterly wrong in what they have done and are doing; and, moreover, I agree as little in their view of history as in their acts. . . . I am denying not their report of facts, but their use of the facts they report. . . . They seem to me to expect from History more than History can furnish." For the Ultramontanes, at the other extreme, history was merely an embarrassing inconvenience. The Church made use of history, as she used Scripture, tradition, and human reason, but her doctrines could not be proved by any of these "informants." She leaves a margin for the exercise of faith so that anyone "who believes the dogmas of the Church only because he has reasoned them out of History, is scarcely a Catholic."[57]

At the heart of Newman's *Letter* is the celebrated passage on the sovereignty of conscience, "the voice of God," but its secularized idea became "the very right and freedom of conscience to dispense with conscience." Conscience cannot come into direct collision with the Church's or the Pope's Infallibility; it is "a practical dictate. . . . A Pope is not infallible in his laws, nor in his commands, nor in his acts of state, nor in his administration, nor in his public policy." St. Peter was not infallible at Antioch. Then, almost casually, Newman concludes with the declaration: "Certainly, if I am obliged to bring religion into after-dinner toasts, (which indeed does not seem quite the thing), I shall drink,—to the Pope, if you please,—still, to Conscience first, and to the Pope afterwards."[58]

The whole tone of the *Letter* can hardly have endeared Newman to Acton, who—this is significant—did not write a line to him either in agreement or disagreement. Acton described the *Letter* as Newman's attempt at rehabilitation, which was achieved only "with quite enormous untruths." The pamphlet had the great significance of indicating "a turning point, a retreat." It did not mean much, but Acton concluded that according to Newman the passage on conscience was meant to be half ironical: "However, it will not be disputed and remains a permissible way of interpretation."[59] And this reluctant concession has since come to the fore in light of Vatican II, sometimes described as Newman's Council.

In her obituary of Lord Acton, written twenty-seven years later, Lady Blennerhassett quoted from a letter Acton had sent to "a friend" (possibly herself), in April 1875, about Newman's pamphlet:

Newman's declaration on the authority of conscience necessarily implies that one may not build up one's system on forgeries, or omission, or forced constructions, and the results that can be obtained subject to this rule are such as none can quarrel about. So that Gladstone's attack has certainly helped to produce a momentary reaction. It may not be voluntary or sincere, or lasting, and it is certainly ambiguous and capable of being explained away, like other things, but it is a sign of what I have always said, that the way out of the scrape will yet be found in insisting on the authority of tradition as the only lawful rule of interpretation.[60]

Outwardly Newman remained well disposed towards Acton, replying severely to an unnamed correspondent who had criticized Acton's letters to Gladstone: "I do not think you should say what you say about Lord Acton. He has ever been a religious, well-conducted, conscientious Catholic from a boy. In saying this, I do not at all imply that I can approve those letters to which you refer. I heartily wish they had never been written."[61]

Lady Blennerhassett reported on the echo of Newman's pamphlet. The British feel good, she observed, when confronted by such an evident literary achievement, which it was: "Achilles has come forth from this tent!" As for her own opinion, she was deeply depressed that the last word of the greatest genius that the Catholic Church had won was after all nothing else but "a useless attempt of wanting to bring into accord what sounds harsh and dissolving contradictions into harmonies. When facts can be explained away so subtly, and, if necessary, even ignored completely, what remains is only blind faith or bitter doubt."[62]

Döllinger, for his part, complimented Gladstone on his pamphlet. It was, he felt, the right word at the right moment, enhanced by Acton's letter published in the *Times* on 9 November. It might have healthy effects in France and Italy. Döllinger found someone to translate Gladstone's pamphlet into German and helped extensively with corrections and suggestions for Gladstone's further pamphlet *Vaticanism*, which dealt with the reactions.[63] On Newman's *Letter to the Duke of Norfolk* he continued: "I can't help wondering about Newman's historical-theological weakness, although in England this is regarded as an enormous strength. . . . N[ewman] is an uncommonly gifted and also deeply religious man, he writes excellently, but his insights into Church history are too scanty, and with his theory of development he transplants Darwinism into religion, except that where Darwin lets the ape develop into Caucasian man, in Newman's case in contrast man gradually degenerates into ape."[64] To Gladstone he wrote that he (Gladstone) treated Newman with too much indulgence: "Whole stretches of Church history and the history of European culture are unknown to him, as the darkest Africa. There is no other way of explaining his naive and daring assertions."[65]

It is an interesting insight into Döllinger's character as a priest that at this time, in August 1875, he visited Gladstone's younger sister Helen Jane in Cologne at her invitation and advised her in her religious scruples to stay in the Church of Rome while rejecting the Vatican decrees, which she felt unable to accept. She feared that she might be refused Communion unless she believed in Infallibility, and thus rather abstained from the Sacraments altogether. Acton and his wife, who had passed through Cologne earlier, in June 1875, also had a conversation with her from which Acton gained the impression that she was hoping for some interpretation that would justify her remaining a Catholic. But when she died, five years later, she was buried with Anglican rites in the Gladstone family vault. Gladstone, who was at her bedside in Cologne before she died, felt entitled to reclaim her for Canterbury. As she had declared herself to be an old Catholic, Gladstone felt "it would have been treason to her memory and wishes to allow her to be buried by a Priest of the actual Roman [Catholic] Church." Gladstone had repeatedly asked her: "Have you anything to say? Have you any wishes? You know how sacred they will be." Her answers were: "Yes, oh yes, I have—if I had the strength," but she was too weak and died. "We have thus cast upon us a difficult and painful duty, through an enigma," her brother wrote. Cologne Catholics accused Gladstone of disregarding her wishes in not having her buried according to Catholic rites. He protested that he would have considered such disregard not only an error but a crime and that he never authorized a statement that she died "a Protestant." This was based on his conviction "that she died in fervent faith and in true penitence, *and* not in the actual Roman Communion. For this is I presume, wholly excluded by her describing herself as 'Altkatholik.'"[66]

Acton did not agree with this interpretation. In his own conversation with Helen Gladstone, she had compared her position to that of men like Bishop Strossmayer and Archbishop Kenrick, who both disbelieved the Vatican decrees and yet remained in the Roman communion. It appeared, Acton recalled, that Miss Gladstone had been given Holy Communion by her Cologne (Roman Catholic) parish priest in her sickroom. Acton's supposition was that she would have preferred to receive absolution and Communion from a priest of the Church of Rome who knew her state of mind rather than from the Bonn

Old Catholics like Reusch or Joseph Langen. "Her declaration that she was Alt Katholik does not appear to me to prove that she was not in the actual Roman Communion. For the term may designate a person who rejects that Communion, or who is rejected by it, who excludes himself or who is excluded by others. I do not understand that she belonged to the first of these categories."[67] Acton's and Gladstone's disagreement on this issue remained unresolved.

For Acton the renewed mental and physical exertions of late 1874 and early 1875 had been an ordeal. His health suffered under the hounding by Manning and the insults heaped upon him by English Catholics, wounded by his cruel way of exposing their historical myths. Moreover, on 21 April 1874, their daughter Elisabeth, called Lily, was born, in a difficult birth for Marie. To help cure the sickly baby they went to live in Torquay, in Devon, for some months, where Acton, cut off from his books, was unable to do much work. Then they moved to Paris, where he worked in the National Library and in the archive of the foreign ministry. In the summer they went back to Tegernsee.

Elizabeth Acton, sister of Lord Acton's father, married Sir Robert Throckmorton, eighth Baronet, heir to one of England's oldest Catholic families. This painting by John Partridge, which hangs at Coughton Court, Warwickshire (the Throckmorton country seat), shows Lady Throckmorton with her eldest daughter, Mary (Minnie), and her son Courtney. Minnie Throckmorton and her younger sister Emily were Acton's favourite cousins, and their ancient stately home became a beloved second home for the young Acton on school holidays from Oscott. Courtesy of Coughton Court.

Anna Marescalchi, Countess Arco, Acton's Italian-born maternal relative. Acton became attached to "la bella Contessa" and her family during his stay with Döllinger in Munich in the early 1850s. Private owner.

Countess Arco with her daughter Marie, whom Acton later married. Private owner.

*The villa at Tizzano, near Bologna, that belonged to Acton's cousins, the Marescalchis.
Private owner.*

Augustus Welby Northmore Pugin (1813–1852), the great champion of the Gothic revival in England, converted to Roman Catholicism in 1835. Among the numerous churches he built was St. George's, Southwark. At the inauguration of what was then London's largest Catholic Church, the architect walked at the head of a long procession of bishops and clergy. At his side was the fourteen-year-old Sir John Acton, the honorary representative of his school, Oscott College, whose duty as acolyte was to swing the censer. Courtesy of the National Portrait Gallery, London.

Cardinal Nicholas Wiseman (1802–1865) was Coadjutor in the Midlands and President of Oscott College, Acton's boarding school, before becoming the first Primate of the restored Hierarchy of England and Wales. He exerted a deep influence on Acton, Newman, and the Oxford converts. A large man of Irish descent and Spanish upbringing, he was fond of wine and a good table, which caused an Irish servant pardonably to address the Cardinal as "Your immense." Portrait by Henry Boyle, courtesy of the National Gallery, London.

*An early drawing of Ignaz von Döl-
linger, Acton's "Professor," by Franz
von Lenbach. Private owner.*

*A photograph of Ignaz von Döllinger
taken shortly before his death in 1890.
Private owner.*

A moving study of two old men—William Ewart Gladstone, then seventy-seven, and Ignaz von Döllinger, eighty-seven—painted by Franz von Lenbach at Tegernsee, Bavaria, in 1886–87, during one of the Gladstones' frequent visits to the Actons. Reprinted by permission of Münchener Staatsgalerie, Munich, on loan to the Embassy of the German Federal Republic, London.

Young Sir John Acton as a Liberal MP and editor of The Rambler *(about 1858). A* carte-de-visite *by P. & D. Colnachi, Scott & Co., London.*

Le Baron d'ECKSTEIN

D'après un crayon d'Alexandre-Evariste Fragonard
daté d'août 1845

(Communiqué par le Comte de Menthon)

The mysterious, probably self-styled "Baron" Ferdinand d'Eckstein (1790–1861), born in Copenhagen to Jewish parents, converted to Protestantism and later to Catholicism. After many adventures, he became one of the pioneers of French liberal Catholicism and was one of the many "false and fallen idols," as Acton later described the heroes of his youth. This sketch is included in an album originally belonging to Countess Alexandre de Menthon, kept in the Château de Saint-Loup, Haute Saône, France. Drawing by Alexandre-Evariste Fragonard, 1845. Private owner.

Antonio Rosmini-Serbati (1797–1855), the Italian philosopher, theologian, and statesman, founded the Institute of Charity, a Catholic missionary congregation also known as the Rosminians. He had the ear of Pope Pius IX in the short-lived early, liberal, and constitutional phase of that pontificate, but he fell into disgrace when the Pope's reactionary advisers gained the upper hand after the Roman Revolution of 1848–49. Private owner.

A Punch *cartoon of Pope Pius IX in his early and idealist phase as a friend of liberty and opponent of the conservative forces of reaction and oppression within the Italian Catholic Church. Private owner.*

Pope Pius IX (1846–1878), at eighty, after Italian troops had occupied Rome as the new capital of united Italy, shortly after the Franco-Prussian War had brought about the premature closure of the First Vatican Council. Private owner.

William Ewart Gladstone (1809–1898) in the early 1870s. Photo by H. J. Whitlock, from the Royal Archives, Windsor Castle, by permission of Her Majesty Queen Elizabeth II, © The Royal Archives.

An early portrait of Charlotte von Leyden (1843–1917), a well-known German liberal Catholic writer. The Bavarian Countess was Döllinger's protegée and Newman's first German biographer. She married Sir Rowland Blennerhassett, the Irish Liberal MP. Private owner.

Félix-Antoine Dupanloup, Bishop of Orléans (1802–1878), the leader of the bishops opposed to Papal Infallibility at the First Vatican Council. The smooth French prelate became famous as confessor of the French Catholic elite, his greatest coup having been the deathbed conversion of Talleyrand. He prided himself on being a "liberal Catholic" but undermined that claim through his support for the notorious Syllabus of Pius IX and for the vanishing temporal power of the Papacy. Private owner.

Bishop Josef Georg Strossmayer (1815–1905), one of the charismatic bishops opposed to Papal Infallibility and Acton's closest friend and ally during the Vatican Council. Strossmayer was denigrated by the Austro-Hungarian government for his Slavic nationalism and his liberal views. His intended elevation as a cardinal under Leo XIII was thus prevented. Private owner.

Giacomo Antonelli (1806–1876), though only a deacon and not a priest, became Cardinal Secretary of State after the Roman Revolution of 1848–49 and the Pope's flight to Gaeta. A crafty Roman and inveterate liar, as Acton described him, Antonelli was at least partly responsible for the Church's intransigent and reactionary diplomacy during the last and longest phase of the pontificate of Pius IX, and for its defence of the temporal power as, at least, a political link to Papal Infallibility. Private owner.

Odo Russell (1829–1884), since 1881 first Baron Ampthill, was British Minister in Rome for twelve years, including the period of the Vatican Council and the fall of the temporal power, when Acton was particularly close to him. Ampthill, a cultured, cosmopolitan English Whig, spent the last fourteen years of his career as first British ambassador to the German Empire. Photo from the London Illustrated News of January 1872, in the archive of the National Portrait Gallery Library, London.

John Henry Newman (1801–1890) at the time of his close but uneasy association with Sir John Acton, his junior by thirty-three years, during Acton's editorship of The Rambler. The photograph, dating from 1861, is probably the first ever taken of Newman for one of the then-fashionable cartes-de-visite. Courtesy of the Fathers of Birmingham Oratory.

John Henry Newman in one of the famous "Spy" cartoons by Sir Leslie Ward (20 January 1877), originally published in Vanity Fair with the caption "Tracts for the times." Courtesy of the Fathers of Birmingham Oratory.

Henry Edward Manning (1808–1892), who succeeded as second Archbishop of Westminster upon Wiseman's death in 1865. He became Acton's fierce persecutor but failed in his attempt to have Acton excommunicated. The remarkable painting by George Frederick Watts shows Manning at the height of his powers. Courtesy of the National Portrait Gallery, London.

Marie Lady Acton, née Countess Arco-Valley (1841–1923), in a pastel drawing by Franz von Lenbach about the time of her marriage to Sir John Acton (1865). Reprinted by permission of Städtische Galerie im Lenbachhaus, Munich.

Marie von Arco-Valley as a fashionable young Munich Comtesse. Private owner.

Lady Acton, the young mother, with her eldest daughter, called Mamy. Private owner.

An early photograph of the two eldest Acton daughters, "Mamy" and Annie (right). Mamy, Acton's favourite, later kept house for him at Cambridge and eventually married Edward Bleidian Herbert. Annie Acton never married; she, more than her younger brother and sisters, shared her father's interest in history and ideas. Private owner.

16

MADONNAS OF THE FUTURE,

FRIENDSHIPS OF THE PAST

Dr. Döllinger had predicted that if Acton had not written a book by the age of forty he would never write one.[1] His fortieth birthday on 10 January 1874 came and went. But the occasion could also be said to separate the "early Acton," who tended to be diffuse and creatively discursive, from the later stern historian and moral critic who could be awesome in his black silences and whose style was almost too concise and loaded with nuances. When, in the summer of 1875, Acton wrote to Döllinger of a new project—to analyse the various "non-theological ailments of the Church" that posed obstacles to any further regeneration—Döllinger took fright. Acton proposed a long list of subjects for which he had collected material and believed could be pressed into some sort of unity: "Reform Attempts before the Reformation; The System of Ideas which caused the Reformation; Indulgences and Dispensation from Sin; Rome's Struggle against Reformation and Attempts to Restore Unity; The Collapse and Abandonment of these Attempts in the Council of Trent; The Roman Inquisition and Development of Toleration; The Index and the System of Mendacity; The Theory and Practice of Assassination for the Glory of God; Rome and England from the Divorce of Henry VIII to the Revolution of 1688; The Catholic Ideal—

which would cover all the better and higher insights since More until your own, in sharp contrast to the preceding Account of the Real State of Things."[2]

To Döllinger it seemed that the plan lacked all coherence and could work only if carried out in the form of individual monographs that might eventually be brought together under some general title. "For heaven's sake, do not wait with publication until you have everything you mentioned (some of it very wide-ranging) ready. Nothing would otherwise come out for ten years. When you are ready with one subject, publish the work right away. That is how most important and lasting books were written."[3] In his reply Acton admitted that he was a slow worker, but he felt that he could write in a concentrated form. He wanted to aim at conciseness, he wrote, and put into footnotes what else was to be added. He was still terrified over the possibility of his excommunication, fearing that he might be asked straight out "Do you believe the doctrine contained in the Vatican decrees?" He would then be able to answer only in the negative and would have to face the consequences.[4]

In December 1875, Marie's father, Maximilian von Arco-Valley, died in Venice. The loss added to Marie's depression after the death of her baby son, and they stayed away from the funeral. Munich mourned the death of Count Arco, a great philanthropist. "When so much is good, the little that is not should be ignored," Dr. Döllinger remarked with regard to the Count's charitable activity and his amorous affairs.[5] Acton had also lost his old friend Richard Simpson, who had died earlier that year in Rome from stomach cancer. They had drifted apart after the *Rambler* years, though not because of disagreement. Simpson had been working on his Shakespeare studies, which, with his biography of Edmund Campion, remain his enduring achievement.

And then, in June 1876, there was a spur to Acton's work in the form of his election, with *magno consensu,* as a foreign member of the Bavarian Academy of Sciences. Döllinger, the president of the Academy, had proposed him. The secretary of the Academy's historical section was Friedrich von Giesebrecht, who was to offer Acton the assignment of writing three volumes of the planned ten-volume *Geschichte von England* (History of England) by Johann Martin Lappenberg, Reinhold Pauli, and Moritz Brosch (Hamburg, 1834–98). Acton was asked to continue Pauli's volumes (3–5) and cover the period 1509 to 1702. An alternative project was Reinhold Pauli's *Geschichte Englands (seit den Friedensschlüssen von 1814–1815)* (History of England [since the Peace Accords of 1814–1815]), based partly on original research (eventually published in Leipzig in three parts and two volumes, 1864–75). Acton was attracted by the idea. There would also be the possibility of an English edition, with more extensive use of his own finds in the Continental archives.

But he feared, as he wrote to Döllinger, that "England's progress from feudal absolutism to modern constitution, and bringing about the richest development of the ideas of the Reformation," could not be covered in less than three volumes. These he was finally offered by Giesebrecht "in order that at least as far as richness of 17th century source materials is concerned one should be able to compete with the best new historians Guizot, Ranke, Macaulay."[6] But Acton was unable to embark on the work until the end of 1878 and wanted three years for it, which Giesebrecht would not concede him. Acton offered to write the volume covering the Reformation years, 1509 to 1562 or 1572, but that plan, too, was abandoned.

The list of Acton's dropped projects was becoming somewhat lengthy: a history of the Popes; the history of liberty; a study of James II and VII, the last Catholic King of England and Scotland; a work on the Reformation based on original documents that would have built on his essays "The Protestant Theory of Persecution," "The Massacre of St. Bartholomew," and "Wolsey and the Divorce of Henry VIII," and on a manuscript Acton had found by the Cambridge theologian Nicholas Harpsfield, "Narration of the Divorce of Henry VIII," which was edited by Nicholas Pocock in 1878 with an extended title.[7] And the list of dropped projects was to grow even further. Mary Gladstone found a name for them. She called Acton's history of liberty the "Madonna of the Future," and it became a kind of private joke between them, but with painful and deeper meaning for him. She castigated him over these projects, which, by the end of Acton's life and the idea of the *Cambridge Modern History,* had become, in his own words, "a whole choir of Madonnas."[8]

The allusion was to one of the early short stories of Henry James, a somewhat macabre tale about an American visitor to Florence who, strolling on the piazza near the Palazzo Vecchio by moonlight, meets a stranger, an impoverished American painter, a fantastic and almost unreal figure, who tells him about the great painting he is working on. The next day they visit the Pitti gallery to see Raphael's *Madonna of the Chair,* the maternal and tender expression of which has captivated the painter. He takes his new friend to the home of the woman who has been the model for his own great work, on which he has been working for twenty years. But the young American sees her as she is—a faded beauty grown stout—and tells the painter so, shattering the illusion the artist had created for himself over the years. The painter falls ill from the shock, his hand is paralysed, and he will never finish his picture. When he dies, the canvas on the easel in his garret is revealed to be "a mere dead blank, cracked and discoloured by time," the "Madonna of the Future" that never was and will never be.[9]

But the Henry James story does not quite fit. Acton was not a would-be Raphael wasting his life in "preparation, transcendent illusions and deplorable failure." His frustration was of a different kind. He was not incapable or lazy, nor was he deceiving himself with self-pity. He did have a masterpiece in him. The reason he did not produce it was partly of his own making. Lionel Kochan has written that Acton had a "lack of courage to affront a hostile world unaided," although surely the answer lies deeper.[10]

It was also the master's faults that the pupil had taken on. He had not been taught self-discipline but had been allowed to spread his interests too widely and to work on too many subjects. Like Döllinger, Acton could not resist the temptation to probe ever further, to go off his course into the byways to find answers to his problems, to exhaust all the material remotely connected with his subject. "I must really get down to writing," Döllinger wrote to him, "and stop collecting, searching, researching any more. But it goes against my nature, *quae, licet expellas, tamen usque recurret*" (You may drive out nature with a pitchfork, but she will constantly come running back). However, the twenty-five books that Döllinger had written made up for this defect. "Each of us must encourage the other by urging him on with *plus ultra*," he added kindly.[11]

To account for his intellectual and spiritual "blockage," Acton wrote: "I never had any contemporaries, but spent years in looking for men wise enough to solve the problems that puzzled me, not in religion or politics so much as along the wavy line between the two. So I was always associated with men a generation older than myself, most of whom died early—for me—and all of whom impressed me with the same moral, that one must do one's learning and thinking for oneself, without expecting short cuts or relying on other men. And that led to the elaborate detachment, the unamiable isolation, the dread of personal influences, which you justly censure."[12] And in another despairing passage written at about the same time, he noted: "The probability of doing good by writings so isolated and repulsive . . . is so small that I have no right to sacrifice to it my own tranquility and my duty of educating my children. My time can be better employed than by waging a hopeless war. And the more my life has been thrown away, the more necessary to turn now and employ better what remains. I am absolutely alone in my ethical position and therefore useless."[13]

Acton always came back to the question of moral judgement in which he was alone among historians, separated from Döllinger after twenty years of loyal discipleship. If he had met with more understanding and sympathy, he would perhaps, as Lady Blennerhassett suggested in one of her obituaries of Acton, "have overcome his natural dislike to limited themes and for composition as circumscribed within the bounds of a book. The incitement was not given, and he followed the natural impulse which prompted him to give the preference to study over production."[14]

In 1877 Acton laid the groundwork for the history of liberty in two lectures that he delivered before members of the Bridgnorth Institute at the Agricultural Hall: the first, on 26 February 1877, dealing with antiquity; the second, on 28 May 1877, dealing with the Christian era. Acton's intellectual contemporaries and later historians have wondered, mockingly, how that Shropshire audience could have followed their demanding lecturer at all for an hour and a half. They "must be above the average provincial intelligence if they encourage their lecturers to maintain such a high level of political reflection. I shall be anxious to know how they followed you," wrote Mark Pattison, the Anglican scholar, Newman's contemporary at Oriel College. But Victorian middle-class audiences were accustomed to substantial fare, both culinary and intellectual. And, according to the *Bridgnorth Journal*'s reports of the first lecture, Acton was interrupted by his listeners "with frequent bursts of applause" and, afterwards, thanked by the chairman for having treated "the history of ancient liberty in so popular a manner." Acton described the debt that English society owed to Greece and Rome and the Middle Ages, telling many anecdotes. He did indulge in his irritating habit of making references to "the most famous authoress of the Continent," "the most renowned logician of the last century," "the most brilliant agitator among Continental socialists," as though even his educated listeners—some local gentry, Anglican parsons, and schoolmasters—would know who was meant.[15]

Acton's lecture took place in the new mood of Empire, inspired by Disraeli's grandiose act, a year earlier, making Queen Victoria Empress of India. As the chairman of Acton's lecture noted, "living under the freest constitution in the world, to anyone in this country the question of freedom must be extremely interesting." Applause followed, and Acton, rising to reply to the vote of thanks at the lecture's end, promised his audience that in his second lecture he would show "how it came to pass, two hundred years ago, that the political development of the Western world seemed doomed to fail, and an invincible despotism was established in almost every country, in the systems of philosophy, and in the selfish aspiration of men." This reference was to Stuart despotism in England and Louis XIV in France, and to the English Revolution of 1688–89 and the defeat of France by its heirs in the eighteenth century. Acton appealed to the national pride of his listeners when he said that it would be his "happier task to tell how, in the midst of universal darkness, a light was kindled in a land encompassed by the inviolate sea which has shone ever since as a beacon to the nations." There could be no doubt about the lecturer's passionate engagement when he defined his subject:

> By liberty I mean the assurance that every man shall be protected in doing what he believes his duty against the influence of authority and majorities, custom and opinion. The State is competent to assign duties and draw the line between good and evil only in its immediate sphere. . . . In ancient times the State absorbed authorities not its own, and intruded on the domain of personal freedom. In the Middle Ages it possessed too little authority, and suffered others to intrude. Modern States fall habitually into both excesses. The most certain test by which we judge whether a country is really free is the amount of security enjoyed by minorities. Liberty, by this definition, is the essential condition and guardian of religion; and it is in the history of the Chosen People, accordingly, that the first illustrations of my subject are obtained. The government of the Israelites was a Federation, held together by no political authority, but by the unity of race and faith, and founded, not on physical force, but on a voluntary covenant.

The brilliance of Acton's ideas made an impact: "The vice of the classic State was that it was both Church and State in one. . . . What the slave was in the hands of his master, the citizen was in the hands of the community. . . . The passengers existed for the sake of the ship. . . . The liberties of the ancient nations were crushed beneath a hopeless and inevitable despotism, and their vitality was spent, when the new power came forth from Galilee, giving what was wanting to the efficacy of human knowledge to redeem societies as well as men."[16]

The second lecture, devoted to freedom in Christianity, continued the story:

> Christianity, which in earlier times had addressed itself to the masses, and relied on the principle of liberty, now made its appeal to the rulers, and threw its mighty influence into the scale of authority. . . . And this doctrine of the divine right of the people to raise up and pull down princes, after obtaining the sanctions of religion, was made to stand on broader grounds, and was strong enough to resist both Church and king. In the struggle between the

House of Bruce and the House of Plantagenet for the possession of Scotland and Ireland, the English claim was backed by the censures of Rome. But the Irish and the Scots refused it, and the address in which the Scottish Parliament informed the Pope of their resolution shows how firmly the popular doctrine had taken root.

This was Acton's distillation of what he called

the sentiments of the most celebrated of the Guelphic writers: "A king who is unfaithful to his duty forfeits his claim to obedience. It is not rebellion to depose him, for he is himself a rebel whom the nation has a right to put down. But it is better to abridge his power, that he may be unable to abuse it. For this purpose, the whole nation ought to have a share in government itself; the Constitution ought to combine a limited and elective monarchy, with an aristocracy of merit, and such an admixture of democracy as shall admit all classes to office, by popular election. No government has a right to levy taxes beyond the limit determined by the people. All political authority is derived from popular suffrage, and all laws must be made by the people or their representatives. There is no security for us as long as we depend on the will of another man." This language, which contains the earliest exposition of the Whig theory of the revolution, is taken from the works of St. Thomas Aquinas. . . . And it is worth while to observe that he wrote at the very moment when Simon de Montfort summoned the Commons.[17]

Acton ended on a patriotic note of Victorian pride, extolling "the same native qualities of perseverance, moderation, individuality, and the manly sense of duty, which give to the English race its supremacy in the stern art of labour, which has enabled it to thrive as no other can on inhospitable shores, and which (although no great people has less of the bloodthirsty craving for glory and an army of 50,000 English soldiers has never been seen in battle) caused Napoleon to exclaim, as he rode away from Waterloo, 'It has always been the same since Crécy.'"[18]

The two lectures were at first intended to be published merely with a supplement of footnotes; it was only later that Acton thought of expanding his theme. That this was never done was owing not to indolence but to his stubborn pursuit of an unrealizable ideal. What he imagined this to be he described one night in his library at Cannes to James Bryce:

He spoke for six or seven minutes only; but he spoke like a man inspired, seeming as if, from some mountain summit high in the air, he saw beneath him the far-winding path of human progress from dim Cimmerian shores of prehistoric shadow into the fuller yet unbroken and fitful light of the modern time. The eloquence was splendid, yet greater than the eloquence was the penetrating vision which discerned through all events and in all ages the play of those moral forces, now creating, now destroying, always transmuting, which had moulded and remoulded institutions, and had given to the human spirit its ceaselessly-changing forms of energy. It was as if the whole landscape of history had been suddenly lit up by a burst of sunlight. I have never heard from any other lips any discourse like this nor from his did I ever hear the like again.[19]

Acton meant the history of liberty to be a philosophy of history. In March 1881 Döllinger, having told Acton of a well-known German jurist about to write a "History of the Freedom of Conscience," implored him to begin at once: "So you must lay siege to a whole series of castles most difficult to conquer, in order to enter into the heavenly Jerusalem, *la città libertà*, so as to be able to say: '*j'y suis, j'y reste*' [this is where I am, this is where I remain]. It frightens me and makes me feel like Moses who also did not live to see the entry into the Promised Land of Liberty."[20]

No response of Acton's exists to this further admonition of Döllinger's, but there are gaps in their surviving correspondence, unfortunate just at this time of their beginning divergences. Yet the Professor's warm regard for him was not diminished, with Döllinger sending his love and good wishes, heartfelt as well as ironic to Acton, who was about to revisit Rome, a "pilgrim *ad limina apostolorum* [to the threshold of the apostles]." But Acton fell ill and was forced to leave Rome after only a week. In a long letter he reported on the changes that he had encountered in the new capital of united Italy:

The old world has disappeared . . . gone the religious semblance. Cardinals ride humbly and in black in their carriages. The flocks of prelates have vanished together with their *raison d'être*. The bigger monasteries have been turned into government offices. . . . When you have last seen Rome at the height of the Council, you cannot observe these tremendous changes without being deeply moved. But to get through to the heart of the capital of Catholicism, you must look behind the facade. All the first places are not taken up by the Italian world. . . . St. Peter's continues to be well maintained. There is even a certain liberality in the Vatican. The remarkable thing is how easily the Church governance has been discarded. It has been done so completely, however, that, understandably, there is deep anger.[21]

Private sorrows much affected the Actons. On 1 October 1881, their seven-year-old daughter Elisabeth, his beloved "Lily," died at Tegernsee after a local outbreak of scarlet fever. The other children had been sent away, but she succumbed to the effects of the illness while Marie was away. She died in Acton's arms. "Be glad, my child, you will soon be with Jesus Christ," were the last words he whispered to her.[22] Their grief was immense. Elisabeth, black-haired like her father, had been born at Tegernsee in the year of Acton's dispute with Gladstone and Manning. He longed for the day when he would be buried in the grave next to her. "Happiness for me . . . ended at Tegernsee in 1881," he wrote in a letter to Annie.[23] And to Mary Gladstone: "She has taken with her one of the strongest links that attached me to this world."[24] Marie did not want to stay on in the house. An undated note among his private papers records his feelings: "What can religion be worth, if there is not more in God to comfort us than there can be in the loss of any, even the dearest and most cherished of his creatures, to distress us."[25]

A poem, written in his hand, recalling "through the mist of tears" the deaths of Lily and, earlier, of little John, ends:

When will our words be stunted,
Our wrong redressed?
Must it be always sickness, sorrow, strife?
Or may we trust with the ancient blest:
"I am the Resurrection and the Life"?[26]

Sometime later, for her gravestone a Latin inscription was devised with Döllinger's help, alluding to the meaning of her name (Elisabeth means "Gift of God"): *Divinitus data, brevi revocata, ad coelestem patriam, aviam praecedens, evolavit* (God, having sent her, recalled her after her short life to her heavenly abode).[27]

Four years later, Acton's mother-in-law, Countess Arco, died at Tegernsee after a long illness, the cancer having been detected too late. "It is the end, though a beautiful and consoling end of a large part of your and my life," he wrote to Döllinger, a strangely detached observation to make, considering Acton's close attachment to her in his Munich years.[28]

The death of Pius IX, in April 1878, had brought hopes to some that his successor, Leo XIII, might be amenable to the idea of a gesture of reconciliation towards the excommunicated Döllinger. An approach was started by the overzealous Lady Renouf (see Chapter 14). Acton wanted no part in it, partly because his own involvement would have been of little help but mainly because he knew that Döllinger did not wish for it.

Years later Acton heard, through his wife, of a private audience that Emmerich Arco, one of her elder brothers, had with Leo XIII. They spoke about Munich welfare matters, in which Count Arco, a lawyer by profession, was involved through his charitable activities. The Pope went on to mention Döllinger; evidently he had been told of the close Arco links with the Professor. He expressed his desire for a rapprochement (*eine Annäherung*). Emmerich asked Marie whether Acton wished to take the matter up; he replied, however, that nothing further need be done. But at the same time Acton informed Döllinger of the Pope's wishes and explained his position: "I wished only to keep such advances from you, unless you want to receive them. In no way do I want, through my interference, either to influence your reaction or intrude with my personal opinion."[29] Döllinger replied cheerfully that the Pope had not only spoken to Emmerich but had also made a similar approach to a Bavarian priest, Alois Rittler, who was a member of the Bavarian Diet and who was coming to interview him. "But in response I have but two words to say: The good Pope has his hands tied—and so have I, though, I must admit, in a totally different way."[30] On this issue, at any rate, teacher and disciple were in total accord.

As far as the new pontificate was concerned, "the tune has changed but not the song." That was the opinion of Acton's wife after she had read the first encyclical of Leo XIII. "I have the good fortune to have a wife with excellent judgement," Acton added. He agreed with Döllinger that Leo XIII was "being guarded and master-minded by Curia and cardinals, morally their prisoner." For Acton, the Pope was "thwarted in his evident goodwill by the College of Cardinals, but allowing himself to be thus easily thwarted. How many men of this sort have there been in the Church! Cervini [the Renaissance scholar-Pope, Marcellus II], [Cardinal Reginald] Pole, men wanting to do good, though not always recognising it . . . well-meaning, but without firmness of purpose, full of good intentions but lacking principle or theory or insight into the truth of opposite standpoints."[31]

The most drastic change in the life of the Actons in those years was undoubtedly their move to the South of France in 1878. It was dictated by the sorry state of Acton's finances as much as by his eldest daughter Mamy's bronchitis, which did not improve in the English climate. The depression in agricultural interests and rising costs depleted the income from the estates at Aldenham and Herrnsheim. Leading a gentleman's life of leisure, even with servants, was then still cheaper on the Riviera than in England. "Between my children and my Shropshire neighbours my choice is indeed decided," he wrote to Mary Gladstone, and the Shropshire neighbours and the climate were certainly no inducement for Marie Acton to remain in England.[32] So they let Aldenham to a Scottish couple, the Starkies, and went to Menton for two winters, spending the summers at Tegernsee and at the Arcos' Austrian Schloss, St. Martin.

In December 1880 the family moved to La Madeleine, Cannes, and about that time also gave up their London residence at 72 Princes Gate. They were delighted with their new abode, with the seemingly eternal summer, roses and violets in all gardens, chimney fires and overcoats being unknown. At the time of their move to the South of France in 1878 there were five Acton children: Mamy, aged twelve; Annie, ten; Richard, eight; the four-year-old Elisabeth (Lily), whose death from scarlet fever was still three years in the future, and, finally, the two-year-old Simmy (Jeanne), who was slightly retarded and who, in her early years, needed particular care. The children soon found friends. "A Frenchman is an exception here. Among the many English there are only enraged landlords. . . . I have been able to study quietly, refreshed by long walks with my wife. . . . Some literature reaches us here."[33] Acton, the proponent of Home Rule, was amused when he was asked to sign a petition against Home Rule for Ireland, beginning, "We, the British people on the Riviera. . . ."[34]

The climate cured Mamy's bronchitis, and the Actons easily became part of the Riviera set. Marie made friends with the Duchess of Vallombrosa, one of their neighbours; the two elder girls had their first parties and, in due course, coming-out dances in the neighbours' villas. As Marie did not go out much because of Simmy, Acton took his daughters to the dances in the neighbourhood. Their Cambridge friend Oscar Browning noted that he "never left till after the cotillon."[35] Russians, even more English, and a Franco-American element lived at Menton, Bordighera, and Alassio; Germans lived at San Remo. It was still an elegant society, which included the heirs to the French monarchy, the Count and Countess of Paris, the Duke and Duchess of Chartres, and exiles like the Casertas from Naples, who no longer called themselves King and Queen of the Two Sicilies because their kingdom had long gone. They were friendly with the Actons, remembering perhaps that loyal prime minister and servant of the Bourbons, Sir John Francis Edward Acton, Lord Acton's grandfather. The Casertas (King Francesco was married to Maria of Bavaria and lived in Bavaria as well as in the South of France) also visited the Actons at Tegernsee and impressed the children in humbly making do with the same felt-mats to put under their beer glasses as everyone else!

Marie von Bunsen, of the well-known Anglo-German family, herself a descendant of the banking Birkbecks and a Prussian diplomat at the Court of St. James's, wrote in her memoirs that Lord Acton, that "international highbrow," gave the "rather too numerous ladies' luncheons and afternoon parties a wide berth, but one met him at times all the same."[36] He was certainly no recluse, as the Actons' stream of visitors showed. And he even joined the Cercle Nautique at Cannes.[37] At the Riviera, royalty abounded. "Have you made the acquaintance of Grand Duke Cyril yet?"—"No, but the Grand Duchess of Mecklenburg nodded to me on the golf course this afternoon." This was one of the snatches of snob-chat that Marie von Bunsen overheard across a tea table at a time when golf was just beginning to challenge tennis as recreation of choice.[38] Pedro II, Emperor of Brazil, was a resident and neighbour, and when Acton's daughter Mamy danced a pavan with the dashing Hungarian Count Vay de Vaga, she finished on top of the Emperor's feet in making her final deep curtsy, because he was standing too close to the dancers. A pony carriage took the Queen of England on outings. Acton saw her again for the first time in five years at Menton and found her "much changed, like an old woman, without distinction but still rather active. She still mourns her empress-maker [Disraeli] and is a constant impediment for his successor [Gladstone]."[39] Meanwhile, at Cannes and Tegernsee subbranches of the Aldenham Library grew.

Back in England, everyone in the late Victorian age had heard of Sir John Lubbock's "Hundred Best Books." The idea of such a guide appealed to the age's unquenchable thirst for knowledge and improvement of the mind, catered for by a bewildering and ever-increasing avalanche of books. Lubbock (1834–1913), a wealthy banker, writer, and prominent Liberal MP, had produced the list, which became a best seller. "He has astonishing attainments, and a power of various work that I always envy," Acton characterized him in a letter to Mary Gladstone. "And he is gentle to the verge of weakness. He has something to learn on the gravest side of human knowledge; apart from that he would execute his own scheme better than almost anybody."[40]

In 1881 Mary Gladstone visited High Elms Down (Kent), where Lubbock was a neighbour of Charles Darwin, who encouraged his enthusiasm for natural history. Their discussion produced the idea of a sort of "Final Count of Selection for the Best Books." Acton, being the acknowledged authority "on the gravest side of human knowledge," was appealed to. He told Mary that there was a Pope who said that fifty books would include every good idea in the world. But literature had doubled since then, and a hundred appeared to be necessary. Lubbock's list stimulated many and infuriated others. He listed

"Shakespeare," "Sir Walter Scott," and so on, as though they were each one book, but the students of the Great Ormond Street Working Men's College could not have found that particularly helpful. The idea that there could be such a definitive list was, of course, impossible; any selection was bound to be subjective, but not necessarily worse for that, given the selector's breadth of mind.

Acton's own list was meant for a different public, "a serious man" who wanted to understand "some twenty or thirty predominant currents of thought or attitudes of mind, or system-bearing principles, which jointly or severally weave the web of human history. . . . All understanding of history depends on one's understanding the forces that make it, of which religious forces are most active, and the most definite. We can't follow all the variations of a human mind, but when we know the religious motive . . . we have the master key."[41] Mary Gladstone was impressed by Acton's list but thought it contained too many books on religion and philosophy and too few on science; moreover, it included no novels at all. Acton, jokingly, excused himself with Dr. Johnson's answer to the question why he defined *pastern* as "the knee of a horse" in his dictionary: "Ignorance, Madam, pure ignorance." Acton compiled two lists, which differ considerably. The earlier one, produced at Cannes in March 1883, included ninety-nine titles.[42] With the exception of Dante's *Divine Comedy,* none of the great works of the literary imagination are included; the *Divine Comedy* was the exception merely because it illustrated "imagination and faith without reasoning faculty." There was no Shakespeare, no Goethe. Some less important books of well-known authors are cited, such as St. Augustine's *Letters* rather than his *Confessions,* Rousseau's *Poland* and *Social Contract* but not his *Confessions,* Coleridge's *Aids to Reflection* rather than his *Poems.* Acton readily admitted that the books that influenced people were likely to be accidental choices.[43]

Acton's list was, as he wrote in an introductory note, to perfect a mind already formed,

> to open windows in every direction, to raise him to the level of his age, so that he may know the (twenty or thirty) forces that have made our world what it is, and still reign over it; to guard him against surprises, and against the constant sources of error within; to supply him both with the strongest stimulants and the surest guides; to give force and fulness and clearness and sincerity and independence and elevation and generosity and serenity to his mind, that he may know the method and law of the process by which error is conquered and truth is won: discerning knowledge from probability and

prejudice from belief; that he may learn to master what he rejects as fully as what he adopts; that he may understand the origin as well as the strength and vitality of systems and the better motives of men who are wrong; to steel him against the charm of literary beauty and talent, so that each book, thoroughly taken in, shall be the beginning of a new life and shall make a new man of him.[44]

Acton's second list, covering ninety-eight "best" books, represented his own subjective idea. It was sent to Mary Gladstone about a year later, at the beginning of February 1884, and was first published only after Mary's death.[45] The list commenced with Plato's *Laws* and Aristotle's *Politics;* many of the other works of ancient writers or representatives of the great non-Christian religions were omitted. There were the foundations of Christian thought—St. Vincent de Lérins's *Commonitorium,* from which the Church's theory of Tradition is derived; Hugo of St. Victor's *De Sacramentis;* St. Bonaventure's *Breviloquium;* St. Thomas Aquinas; Dante; Raymund of Sabunde's *Theologia Naturalis;* Nicholas of Cusa's *Concordantia Catholica* to *La Bible,* the sixteen-volume biblical edition, translation, and commentary by the French Protestant scholar Eduard Reuss (1881); Pascal's *Pensées;* Malebranche's *De la recherche de la vérité*—and a host of books that would have been acknowledged by contemporaries as great philosophy and high thought. Among them was Richard Rothe's *Theologische Ethik,* Acton's favourite, which he recommended when someone wished to convert to Catholicism. This recommendation was bound to surprise, as Rothe was a Protestant scholar.[46]

New to this second list were Newman's *Theory of Development,* Edmond Scherer's *Mélanges de critique religieuse,* Francesco Guicciardini's *Ricordi politici,* Edgar Quinet's *La Révolution française,* Edmund Burke's *Correspondence,* Donoso Cortes's *Ecrits politiques,* John Stuart Mill's *System of Logic,* Baron Alexander von Humboldt's *Kosmos,* and Vincenzo Gioberti's *Pensieri.* There are the great and too-often-forgotten names and works of nineteenth-century scholars: Johann Adam Möhler, Wilhelm Molitor, Bernhard Pünjer, Hans Lassen Martensen, Carl Robert von Hartmann, Ferdinand Christian Baur, Carl Bernhard Hundeshagen. It was typical of Acton to think little of those historians who worked only from printed documents. Accordingly he selected, for example, *Mémorial de Ste. Hélèna* (1832) by Emanuel Augustine Las Cases, the French officer who had shared Napoleon's exile, in preference to countless similar but less authentic compilations, but also in preference to historians like Thucydides and Gibbon.

Drawing up lists of this kind became second nature to Acton. In the Cambridge University Library are his working notes, thousands of slips and cards in black boxes, on which he would transcribe passages from historical works, reflections, and aphorisms of his own and others. Making lists was a useful intellectual exercise, a form of active meditation during which he was constantly turning things over in his mind, making comparisons, reaching new insights. The notes include, for example, the many definitions of liberty, some two hundred. "We can picture his mind as constantly knitting history together," Herbert Butterfield wrote, "and though he failed to produce his *magnum opus,* he left behind in his papers a tremendous intellectual system, which has stimulated many commentators and interpreters in our time." [47]

Their "lean" years, as Mamy Acton called the 1880s, compelled Acton also to sell the Dalberg Schloss, Herrnsheim, linked with the memories of his own youth and with his mother. [48] It had been the scene of the historic meeting before the Vatican Council when Acton, Döllinger, and Dupanloup concerted their campaign; innumerable distinguished visitors had been welcomed there throughout the years. The round tower contained an excellent library. The chapel, very dark, had a Madonna, a clock, and silver lamps and candlesticks. The fine terrace all round the house had black figs growing on its lower wall. Mamy always remembered the huge drawing room that extended the height of two floors, once known as *Conversazions-Saal,* where she had to do her lessons and which in the summer was always plagued by gnats. Herrnsheim was particularly dear to Acton's two Italian grandmothers, though their fondness for the Rhineland never extended to learning the German language.

Lack of proper management and dependence on inefficient and sometimes dishonest stewards mainly contributed to the Actons' encroaching poverty. Money worries seemed ingrained in the family. Even Acton's grandmother, Nonna, who had inherited part of the fortune of the prime minister of the Two Sicilies, was left badly off, for her second son, the Cardinal, was no less extravagant than Acton's father had been. In Cardinal Acton's case the money was at least put to charitable ends, such as helping the poor and building churches, but his debts were notorious. Nonna was obliged to sell her beautiful jewels and got her daughter, Lady Throckmorton, into trouble, too, over a priceless heirloom, a necklace, which was sold to help out the Cardinal, though without her husband's knowledge. The disappearance of the pearls came to light only when the Throckmortons were due to go to a court reception and Lady Elizabeth had nothing to put on her neck. She confessed to her husband what had happened and, according to a family account, Sir Robert went out at once to buy her a replacement.

The Cardinal's nephew was no better, as is shown in Acton's massive correspondence with William Dawes Freshfield, the family's London solicitor, which is preserved among the Cambridge papers. Acton was as good as useless in dealing with business matters. The polite letters and bills from Freshfield suggest growing exasperation:[49]

Not having heard from Your Lordship Making copy of our correspondence	6s 8d
Writing to your Lordship again on subject of investment (shares in the Severn Valley Railway Corporation) concerning sales	5s
Not having received any reply from Your Lordship, making copy of our letter to you of January 16 ulto and writing to you therewith and for reply	7s 6d
16 Oct. 1878 Writing to your Lordship again as to the realisation of Lady Acton's marriage portion and urging that the matter might be completed and the £3,200 paid to the Trustees	5s
Making translation of letter to Herr von Auer at Munich	10s 6d
21 May 1879 Writing to your Lordship for signature by yourself and Lady Acton (balance of Trust Fund having been paid to the Trustees). Preparing authority to the Trustees for investment in Consols	5s
4 June 1879 Not having received any reply writing to you requesting authority	5s

Döllinger warned Acton about a Munich antiques dealer who had apparently been commissioned to sell valuable Dalberg furniture and silver. Everyone except the Actons knew the man to be a crook. The Herrnsheim buyer who paid, for the property and contents (books and paintings excepted), 650,000 marks (£33,000)—almost half went towards debts—was Cornelius Wilhelm Heyl, a local leather manufacturer. He wanted a country seat to go with his new wealth, and three years later was created a baron by the Grand Duke of Hesse. He called himself Heyl zu Herrnsheim, added some of the silver lilies of the Dukes of Dalberg to his coat-of-arms, and adopted, appropriately for the new imperial industrial might of Germany, the motto "*Laboremus*." He was a Lutheran, a proud supporter of Bismarck's unification of Germany. Heyl's rise was symbolic of the transformation from the sleepy Germany of princely states to the self-confident Hohenzollern and "Iron Chancellor" Reich. His leather factory was a model of the new industrialized Germany, with its energetic and disciplined work force, well provided for in Bismarck's welfare state.

In his whole outlook Acton was opposed to the Prussianization of Germany and the exclusion of Austria from the united German Reich. He felt part of the older European order, with family links in four European countries, and he was also a cosmopolitan of the mind whose home was where his books were—and they were movable. So Aldenham and Herrnsheim were consigned to the past. The Actons wanted no truck with the new masters of Herrnsheim. They even left them part of a manuscript by Schiller. The great poet, a protégé of the Duke of Dalberg, was supposed to have written *Die Räuber* in a bower of the garden. Also left behind was a splendid damask tablecloth embroidered with the Dalberg coat of arms encircled by the symbol of the Order of the Holy Ghost. The "patent-leather people" would not know what to do with a tablecloth for sixty guests, the superior Actons said. If indeed the Heyls did not know, they soon learned. The new German establishment took over from the old with ease. The Dalbergs were, anyhow, regarded as traitors to the German national cause because of their dealings with the *Erbfeind* (hereditary enemy), France. Having fought in the Franco-Prussian War, the son and heir of Cornelius von Heyl presently took his seat as Liberal MP (of the German right-wing kind) in the Berlin Diet.[50]

Money worries demanded other economies, for example, curtailing the expensive employment of copyists in many distant archives of the Continent. Towards the end of the 1880s, even the sale of the Aldenham Library had to be faced. The seventy thousand books had to be catalogued (an enormous task with the owner being away) then packed, ready to be sent to London for sale by auction. Gladstone first knew of Acton's plight when the sale was announced by the auctioneers Puttick and Simpson. He wanted to help, knowing how much the books meant to Acton. He found a benefactor in June 1890: Andrew Carnegie, the Scottish-born American steel millionaire whose great charitable bequests included especially libraries, no doubt because he remembered how much he owed to the books he borrowed from a free library in Pittsburgh as a poor telegraph boy. Gladstone approached him privately: "The books have been purchased by him [Acton], purchased, it may be said, one by one," Gladstone wrote, "and there are few amongst them of which he is not believed to have personal knowledge. They might be taken over in the lump with the certainty that no part or no appreciable part of the acquisition would be trash." Gladstone estimated the books to have cost Acton from £25,000 to £30,000. He explained that the majority of them were French, German, and Italian, some in tongues less known, and that it was "in the strictest sense useful— the books may be termed tools of an author and student—there is nothing in the collection to attract the bibliographer or virtuoso. . . . A deplorable necessity due to no dishonourable cause now compels the alienation of this remarkable library."[51] Gladstone suggested a price of four shillings per volume for the estimated seventy thousand books. Carnegie eventually paid less for them, astounding Freshfield by the cheque for £9,000 that arrived in the post without further ado. "I have never heard of anything like it," he wrote to Gladstone.[52]

Carnegie could not have handled the matter with more consideration for the feelings of the beneficiary, whom he had neither seen nor consulted. His one condition, as he put it to Gladstone, was "I wish no one to know about this, not even my wife shall know." For if the news got around, it "must make it somewhat uncomfortable for Lord Acton. I did not expect him ever to know beyond this, that a friend of his and yours had taken the loan and security in place of the Bankers and he should never be disturbed." Carnegie maintained silence for twelve years. Gladstone was less reticent; overjoyed at having encountered such generosity, he told close friends like John Morley. The secret was kept so well, however, that a friend of Carnegie's, Andrew D. White, president of Cornell University, wrote to him after Acton's death suggesting the purchase of the books for presentation to an American university. Carnegie solved the problem eventually by giving the library to John Morley, a friend of his and Acton's, and allowing Morley to decide on their final resting place.[53] Morley, briefly contemplating whether he should keep the books for himself, decided, in July 1902, to present them to Cambridge, the university that had honoured Acton towards the end of this life with the Regius Chair of Modern History, and which diverted a special wing of the University Library to housing the books fittingly.[54]

The saga of Acton's books and Carnegie's rescue requires us to anticipate an important event (see Chapter 18). Dr. Ignaz von Döllinger died, after a brief illness, on 10 January 1890—on Acton's fifty-sixth birthday and shortly before his own ninety-first birthday. Their relationship had cooled, though it was never broken off entirely. But then the need to sort out Döllinger's papers, which included those of Johann Adam Möhler, and the question of Döllinger's biography caused Acton to return to Munich. In the meantime, back in England, Gladstone had immersed himself in the mission of saving the books. Acton, not yet aware of Carnegie's involvement, was grateful to Gladstone for "taking so great an interest in the library I have to part with."[55] But the extraordinary thing about the affair was that it was Gladstone, not Acton, who felt that it was a matter of preventing a deep personal loss. "I feel it is like digging into living flesh," he wrote in sympathy.[56]

Acton, however, seemed not to care what happened to these books that at one time meant so much to him. He now had more pressing things on his mind. The Aldenham Library was far away. Gladstone sent an urgent telegram as well as letters to persuade Acton to return to London. Carnegie, meanwhile, was awaiting a response. "Not having heard from you, I fear my suggestion has not proved acceptable," he wrote to Gladstone from the Hotel Metropole.[57] Whereupon Gladstone sent another impassioned message to Munich: "It is a question of your keeping your library for life, without solicitation, without charge, and with privacy. I cannot doubt that this outline of the matter . . . will bring you here at once. . . . There surely can be nothing in the disposal of Dr. D[öllinger]'s and Professor M[öhler]'s papers, important as it is, which can compare . . . in urgency with the matter which we can only lay before you with the aid of speech, and which is even now placed at some small disadvantage by your absence."[58] That brought Acton back to England. But what astounded everyone was that beyond thanking Gladstone for his success in finding Carnegie, he was no longer committed to these books. They had, as far as he was concerned, served their purpose.

Acton was no longer interested in the sixteenth century and related concerns with the history of liberty and the Church. His books might as well be disposed of or kept—he did not mind which. And thus, when the library was returned to Aldenham by Messrs. Puttick and Simpson, for whom the business of cataloguing and transporting the books to and fro had been a net loss, no one ever bothered to put them back in order. At Cannes and Tegernsee Acton needed other books for work in hand. The Aldenham books were first put in order again by the Cambridge University Library staff after Acton's death.[59] Having been away from Aldenham for so many years, Acton was hard pressed to supply the information wanted by Carnegie and Freshfield, as well as Puttick and Simpson, about what he actually had. It was also unclear which books were in the actual library, which Acton estimated at forty-five thousand to fifty thousand volumes, and which were in other parts of the house at Aldenham, including some fifteen thousand perhaps. Then vast numbers of tracts on the Thirty Years' War, Jansenism, and Church history were found. Perhaps the oddest book in the library was a blank catalogue merely numbered in Acton's hand up to 11,016, another symbolical "Madonna of the Future."[60] Gladstone had to urge him several times to respond at all regarding these particulars. In the end, what Acton had said of Döllinger, that he was greater than the books he had written,[61] also applied to himself, in the sense that he was greater than the books he had collected.

"The question which I now have before me, and which I confess has given me some trouble," wrote Freshfield, "is the mode in which the Library can be secured to Mr. Carnegie. It is quite clear that steps must be taken to put it out of the power of Your Lordship's creditors at any future time, should Your Lordship incur further debts." This, incidentally, was the arrangement Carnegie had suggested.[62] And Freshfield urged to be sent "the very fullest possible list you and Lady Acton can supply of all debts of all kinds and descriptions of what is owing from Your Lordship to creditors. . . . Under no circumstances must anything be kept back. . . . If you have not done so already, please impress upon Lady Acton and your son your present pecuniary position so that they may thoroughly understand that there is nothing to be relied upon except Your Lordship's own pension."[63]

Again there were depressing accounts from the Aldenham estate for the quarter ending June 1890, showing that the expenses more than exhausted the income derived from the property. The family should pay only ready money for everything, Freshfield wrote. The sum that the solicitors had in hand would pay for the next half-year's necessities in advance, in fact, until money came in again. "This would enable you to live (say) a half year without incurring debts." Again the solicitors complained: "Your Lordship's neglect to answer our letters is most embarrassing and we shall, at some inconvenience to ourselves, considering the time of year, and at considerable cost to Your Lordship, have to send Mr. Coulton to see Your Lordship at Tegernsee. It could be very convenient if you could come over and bring the bills which you owe with you. The matter is now really urgent."[64]

In August 1891 the Dalberg and Acton jewels were sold by Messrs. Christie in

London, among them a diamond necklace that fetched £880. Messrs. Garrard, acting for the buyers, paid the Actons £814, having deducted Christie's commission. According to Mamy Acton's recollection, the buyers were the Swaythling family (Lord Montagu).[65]

Acton was certainly aware of his circumstances. In 1889 he wrote to his son Dick at Magdalen College, Oxford, reminding him to be careful over his expenses: "Every shilling wasted is taken away from the girls and compels us to make some deductions from their comforts."[66] They sold other valuables at Christie's: an Elizabethan stoneware jug for £7 8s.; Viennese, Dresden, and Chinese porcelain; and two paintings. The first, "Virgin and Child enthroned in a landscape," by A. Solario, fetched £46 4s.; the second, a grand altarpiece depicting a "Madonna and Child seated on a richly sculptured throne, St. John and St. George standing on either side," by Cesare da Sesto, reached £777.[67]

During the sessions Acton travelled to London to attend the House of Lords and then stayed at the Athenaeum, which became a kind of second home to him. Backed by Lord Granville and Charles Greville, he had "made" the Athenaeum after a brief waiting period as early as 1866, one year after Disraeli, but without having been blackballed in previous attempts as Disraeli, the Tory, had been. In the Athenaeum Acton often worked in the South Library, in a corner close to the English history section, and he used the chair in which Macaulay had often sat. The large armchair in that library was a favoured resting place of Matthew Arnold and Mark Pattison; John Morley came in for a snooze after he had put the *Pall Mall Gazette,* of which he was editor, to bed.[68] Club life suited Acton, who was a member of numerous London clubs. It seemed that the less money he had, the more clubs he joined. He was clearly eminently "clubbable," with the required light touch of playful humour, an appetite for all types of gossip, the ability to make himself agreeable (if he wanted to), and an appreciation of good food and wines. Acton's Pickwickian qualities—kindheartedness, simplicity, and innocent levity—earned him the presidency of the Boz Club, which was set up within the Athenaeum by Dickens fans. Among fellow Pickwickians were Henry Dickens QC, one of the sons of the novelist; Andrew Lang, the historian; and Augustine Birrell, the Liberal MP and author. At the two dinners per year the president sat in Dickens's chair.

Acton easily fulfilled the condition of five hundred miles' travel in order to be accepted as a member of the Travellers Club, apparently also overcoming the resistance of a cantankerous member who had blackballed William Makepeace Thackeray, Cecil Rhodes, Lord Rosebery, and Sir Edwin Landseer. In 1871

Acton joined The Club, founded in 1764 by Joshua Reynolds and Dr. Samuel Johnson. The third member was Edmund Burke. Acton was member number 163. The members used to meet at the Grand Hotel in Northumberland Avenue. When in town, Acton was one of those who regularly attended in the 1880s and 1890s. Others were the Duke of Argyll, Gladstone, the Duke of Daumale, a son of King Louis Philippe of France, the Marquess of Dufferin and Ava, the Marquess of Salisbury, the historian William Edward Hartpole Lecky, Lord Rosebery, Viscount Wolseley, Sir James Paget, Sir George Otto Trevelyan, and there was always that supremo of clubmen, Sir Mountstuart Grant Duff, who was The Club's treasurer, no doubt also collecting material for his diary and playing Boswell to Acton's Johnson. It was "a self-satisfied place," Acton wrote to Mary Gladstone, "good men belong to it, but stay away: Lowe, that he may not meet X, whom he dislikes sober, and detests drunk; the PM, because he too much appreciates the sweetness of home; others, for other futile reasons."[69]

Acton was also a member of Grillion's, the parliamentary dining club founded in 1812, which met at 8 Whitehall Court, where a fine was imposed on him, according to custom, for "letting the side down" when he got married. The spirit of Grillion's was "the belief that private acquaintance and good-fellowship softens the asperity of public conflicts, [and] by a pleasant fiction, no bore is supposed to live." The trouble with this philosophy was, as Gladstone had noted, that people would thus make their opponents like them, and would soften to their opponents in consequence.[70]

Acton was unanimously elected to the Cosmopolitan, a club of exclusive wits, and also to the Dilettanti, London's oldest dining society, probably founded in 1732. One of its rules, before travelling became general, was that new members had to have been personally acquainted with their proposer in Italy. Promoting the fine arts was the Dilettanti's general aim, and leading lights were Charles James Fox, Sir Joshua Reynolds, David Garrick, Sir Joseph Banks, and Lord Palmerston. It was claimed, with exaggeration, that the Dilettanti were responsible for the foundation of the Italian opera in London, the Royal Academy, and the British Museum; its members were certainly involved, directly or indirectly, with all three institutions. They caused much irritation when they opposed Lord Elgin's campaign to rescue from the Acropolis the marbles that bear his name,[71] anticipating thereby the modern controversy of whether these marbles should be regarded as Greece's national heritage and returned, or as properly paid for and saved from environmental destruction in the British Museum.

Towards the end of his life, in 1899, Acton was among the founding members of the Breakfast Club. Other founders were Lord Arthur Russell (brother of Odo, later Lord Ampthill) and Sir James Lacaita, Gladstone's close friend. This club consisted of about a dozen members who, during the London Season, entertained each other in turn once a week in their own houses. Among members were the constitutional jurist Sir Thomas Erskine May, the *Times* correspondent Laurence Oliphant, Sir George Goschen, and the ubiquitous Sir Mountstuart Grant Duff. Only visiting foreigners were admitted as guests, but when a member gave a breakfast, he was allowed to have his son or sons join the table.[72]

"POWER TENDS TO CORRUPT . . . "

Acton's growing severity in his judgement as an historian found telling expression in the charge of moral laxity towards the Papacy that he launched against Mandell Creighton, an Anglican luminary and Fellow of Merton College, Oxford. Creighton was vicar of Embleton, Northumberland, when the first two volumes of his five-volume *History of the Papacy during the Period of the Reformation* were published in 1882. (The second edition, published in 1897, comprised six volumes and had the title *History of the Papacy from the Great Schism to the Sack of Rome*.) Creighton asked Acton to check the proofs for any mistakes and also suggested him as reviewer in the *Academy*, the well-known literary and artistic Victorian monthly. "I wanted to be told my shortcomings by the one Englishman whom I consider capable of doing so," he wrote, and later even thanked Acton for his hatchet-job review, which appeared in December 1882.[1]

Creighton and Acton were to have further dealings. Acton played a leading part in the long-debated founding of the *English Historical Review*. The launch took the form of a dinner given by James Bryce, then Regius Professor for Civil Law at Oxford, at his house in Bryanston Square on 15 July 1885. Also present apart from Acton were Dean Church, one of the main representatives of the High Anglican element; Mandell Creighton; Richard Garnett, librarian and man of letters; Adolphus William Ward, the modern historian; Frederick York Powell, Regius Professor of Modern History at Oxford; and Robertson Smith, the Hebrew and Arabic scholar. They discussed the ways and means of the new journal. Bryce proposed Creighton as editor, and Creighton asked Reginald Lane Poole to be his secretary and assistant editor. Longmans was to be the publisher, and the first issue was to appear in January 1886.[2] Creighton and Acton had already met in person in 1884. "He is a Roman Catholic, and is the most learned Englishman now alive, but he never writes anything," Creighton had noted.[3] Acton described Creighton to Mary Gladstone as "an agreeable and superior man . . . full of general knowledge. But I am afraid you will find his book [*A History of the Papacy during the Period of the Reformation*] a severe study."[4]

For the new *Review* Acton wrote an account of German historical literature emphasizing the value, novelty, and German origin of the science of history. It was a very learned, condensed, allusive contribution, typical of his mature work. "The *Review* is solid, various, comprehensive, very instructive and sufficiently entertaining," Acton wrote, congratulating Creighton on the first issue. "It holds its place worthily between Sybel[5] and the *R[evue] Historique,* and is, in some important respects, superior to them. It is not insular, there is no preference for certain topics and no secret leaning towards any opinions. . . . There is no reason why it should not become, by the end of the year, the best of all historical reviews."[6]

That it was not yet the best was partly Acton's own fault for taking up so many pages. But the *EHR* was not *bahnbrechend* (breaking new ground), he felt; it made no striking discovery, opened no new vistas, produced no new men. He liked the section that dealt with the contents of foreign reviews, but it needed improvement. "A lot of insignificant French periodicals do not make up for the omission of Switzerland, Holland, Belgium, Spain, and Scandinavia, all of which countries possess very good historical reviews. . . . So much depends on awakening men to the fact that the go-ahead work is found in periodicals."[7] About the second issue he wrote: "There is variety, and there is solidity, and there are new lights. But there is not much in the way of stimulus or surprise."[8]

Creighton wrote to Acton on the "German School of History": "Your article fills me, if possible, with greater admiration than before—how can you manage to know so much? You are calculated to reduce ordinary men to despair. Your article will certainly secure the *Historical Review* a respectful attention through-out Europe. Never before has such a conspectus been made, and I do not sup-pose that anyone except yourself could have made it."[9] A tribute for "all-round knowledge and the enlightening illumination arising from it" came from the great German Church historian Adolf von Harnack, who wrote that Acton's article raised the new journal to "a level high above all petty, narrow and limit-ing concerns."[10]

Acton took a close interest in the journal, in the books sent out for review, and, as a former editor himself, in presentation. "Let me beseech you never to say de Tocqueville, von Sybel, von Giesebrecht. Von and de cannot stand un-less there is a name or a title before them. Unless, in French, when the name is a monosyllable, begins with a vowel, or is Belgian or Savoyard."[11] The cir-culation of the *EHR* settled down at about six hundred copies in the second year. "I never was sufficiently sanguine to expect more than a thousand," wrote Creighton.[12] Longmans felt disposed to give it up but was persuaded to con-tinue for a second year.

Creighton was a devoted clergyman whose Englishness, detachment, and optimistic faith in human nature were his outstanding traits. Acton found the *History of the Papacy* infuriating because of Creighton's heavy and sometimes careless approach, his moderate and tentative judgements that always left room for different interpretations, letting the reader make up his own mind. When, in 1887, two further volumes of Creighton's *History of the Papacy* appeared (reach-ing from 1464 to 1517), the author asked Acton again to review them. "I know no one else who would believe me if I told him that I was thankful for criti-cism and really had a very poor opinion of my own productions. . . . So I trust you . . . will knock me about the head as I deserve, believing that I will be the first to acknowledge that I deserved it."[13]

Creighton's humility was astounding, although he wrote to his assistant, Poole, that Acton's review was "the utterance of a man who is in a furious pas-sion, but is incapable of clear expression." Creighton ascribed Acton's opposi-tion to "polemics esoteric to a Liberal Roman who fought against Infallibility. That is all right if he would say so; but he hints and sneers and divagates in a way which seems to me ill-natured."[14] Dr. Döllinger, too, found Creighton's sub-missiveness most strange. "*Qui tacet, consentit* [silence gives consent]," he wrote to Acton. "We shall see the practical effect when in later volumes, if any appear, he gets down to describing the beginnings of the Reformation."[15] The unfortu-nate editor had to print Acton's condemnation in his own review. Because the article provoked the great controversy between the two, some quotations from it seem appropriate.[16]

According to Acton, Creighton "wishes to pass through scenes of raging controversy and passion with a serene curiosity, a suspended judgment, a divided jury and a pair of white gloves" (p. 367). Creighton's sympathy for the pre-Reformation Papacy made him reluctant to admit to any of its scandals, for example the death, probably by poisoning, of Alexander VI. Acton responded, "When three men who had dined together are seized with such illness that the oldest dies, and the youngest is prostrated during the most critical week of his life, we even now suspect verdigris in the saucepan or a toadstool in the mushrooms" (p. 369). Moreover, Acton castigated the future Bishop of London because, while rejecting the claims of the pre-Reformation Popes as theologians, he preferred (as an historian) the Borgias to their adversaries. Creighton had written that the character of Pius III "stood high in all men's estimation, though he was the father of a large family of children. . . . The papacy in the Middle Ages always showed a tolerant spirit in matters of opinion. We cannot think that Roman Inquisitors were likely to err on the side of severity." With cutting irony Acton added that "in varying disinterested history with passages which might be taken from the polemics of Cardinal Newman, Mr. Creighton was not unmindful of the Inquisition" (pp. 372–73).

Acton also took issue with the author's calling Savonarola "the most sincere man amongst the Italians of the time" without seemingly being aware that "an awakened conscience must be traced and proved in public as much as in private life, so that a zealous priest is, normally, a zealous politician. . . . But the man who described in the pulpit his mission from Florence to heaven, and what he heard there, and afterwards explained that this was all a trope, cannot well be pronounced perfectly sincere on any hypothesis of sanity" (pp. 374–75).

Creighton appreciated the humour of printing the article that attacked the editor and resisted the temptation to add: "The editor is not responsible for the opinions expressed in the above article."[17] But to Acton he humbly replied that he respected his views even if he could not share them, and that he admired Acton for remaining true to an unpopular philosophy of history. Acton answered with irony that it was comforting to know that Creighton suffered from his own complaint of not getting people to agree with him.[18]

Part of Acton's disagreement with Creighton concerned the Reformation and Luther's role. But their major difference was on the Inquisition and on whether Creighton could, with historical accuracy, maintain that the later medieval Papacy could be regarded as tolerant and enlightened. Acton wrote to Creighton:

> The system of persecution with its special tribunals, functionaries, and laws meant that a man is hanged not because he can or cannot prove his claim to virtues, but because it can be proved that he has committed a particular crime. That one action overshadows the rest of his career. It is useless to argue that he is a good husband or a good poet. . . . You ignore, you even deny, at least implicitly, the existence of the torture-chamber and the stake. I cannot imagine a more inexplicable error, and I thought I had contrived the gentlest formula of disagreement in coupling you with Cardinal Newman. . . . But if the thing is criminal . . . the person who authorises the act shares the guilt of the person who commits it. . . . Whether Sixtus is infamous or not depends on our view of persecution and absolutism. Whether he is responsible or not depends simply on the ordinary evidence of history. . . . You say that people in authority are not [to] be snubbed or sneezed at from our pinnacle of conscious rectitude. . . . It does not allow of our saying that such a man did not know right from wrong.[19]

Then Acton embarked on the passage since become famous, that he could not accept Creighton's canon that Pope and King should not be judged like other men, but given the benefit of the doubt:

> If there is any presumption it is the other way, against holders of power, increasing as the power increases. Historic responsibility has to make up for the want of legal responsibility. Power tends to corrupt, and absolute power corrupts absolutely. Great men are almost always bad men, even when they exercise influence and not authority: still more when you superadd the tendency or the certainty of corruption by authority. There is no worse heresy than that the office sanctifies the holder of it. . . . You would hang a man of no position, like Ravaillac; but if what one hears is true, then Elizabeth asked the gaoler to murder Mary, and William III ordered his Scots minister to extirpate a clan. Here are the greatest names coupled with the greatest crimes. You would spare these criminals, for some mysterious reason. I would hang them higher than Haman, for reasons of quite obvious justice; still more, still higher, for the sake of historical science.

To Acton, there was no greater error than to lower the standards in consideration of a past age or in deference to station, as the hero worshippers—historians like Froude, Macaulay, and Carlyle—had done. "If we may debase the currency for the sake of genius, or success, or rank, or reputation, we may debase it for the sake of a man's influence, of his religion, of his party, of the good cause which prospers by his credit and suffers by his disgrace. Then History ceases to be a Science, an arbiter of controversy. . . . It serves where it ought to reign; and it serves the worst cause better than the purest."

Returning to Creighton's defence of the Roman system "in its essentials," Acton asked what these essentials were: "Is it essential—for salvation within the communion of Rome—that we should accept what the canonisation of such a Saint implies, or that we should reject it? Does Newman or Manning, when he invokes St. Charles, act in the essential spirit of the Roman system, or in direct contradiction with it? . . . And my dogma is not the special wickedness of my own spiritual Superiors, but the general wickedness of men in authority, of Luther and Zwingli and Calvin and Cranmer and Knox, of Mary Stuart and Henry VIII, of Philip II and Elizabeth, of Cromwell and Louis XIV, James and Charles and William, Bossuet . . ."

Creighton answered disarmingly by accepting gratefully Acton's rigorous lecture and architectural vision of history. Even if he disagreed with Acton on some points, he promised that, if he could, he would mend his ways. However, there were the labours of practical life, he wrote. He had five sermons to preach that week! "Will you not someday write an article in the *His[torical] Rev[iew]* on the Ethics of History? I have no objections to find my place among the shocking examples."[20] It rather seemed as though the lecture Acton gave him had been a waste of effort.

Acton's dispute with Bishop Creighton occurred a few years after his disagreement with Döllinger came to a head in the early 1880s. The matter at issue was the same, only the form was different because of Creighton's Anglican diffidence and Döllinger's reluctance to enter upon what he, too, came to regard as a bee in Acton's bonnet. "Absolute power," Acton wrote to Döllinger in a long letter in June 1882, "is the only reproach I remember on which we differ." He meant Döllinger's "indulgence" for Marcus Aurelius, the thirteenth-century emperor Frederick II, Frederick the Great, and Bismarck, which "a woodenheaded Whig" finds hard to share. Nor could he accept the allowance that Döllinger felt must be made for ignorance. "I have never found that people go wrong from ignorance, but from want of conscientiousness," and in Döllinger's reluctance to condemn, Acton was to diagnose only a wish to be charitable.[21]

Like Creighton, Döllinger wanted to see only the good in people. "You have found out no theologian telling lies," Acton wrote in the same letter, "conniving at murder, praising Borromeo or Pius V, defending Ximenes, esteeming

Philip II, justifying the Inquisition, the Revocation, the Catholic reaction, the Catholic massacres, the Syllabus which covered these things. I have met nothing else wherever I have met Catholics of any distinction." The contradictions Acton discovered in Döllinger differed from those of which he accused the Victorian Bishop, who thought so kindly of the Borgias, in that Döllinger's were more basic.

More than a hundred years after this correspondence, the Acton-Creighton controversy remains unsettled. Herbert Butterfield wrote in 1951:

> The truth was that Creighton could not know enough to exonerate. Neither, on the other hand, did Acton in reality know enough to condemn [Pope Alexander VI] himself. It would have been better to recognize that the historian is not competent to make the necessary calculations, and that he carries the whole issue into a different realm of thought. It is not for him to steal the mantle of the ancient prophets; and it is more fitting that he should keep within the limits that his apparatus and evidence have set for him. Within these limits he has indeed a more important task; for Creighton and Acton had not even said the last word as yet towards the settlement of the question whether Alexander VI had actually committed all the deeds imputed to him.[22]

The century that followed Acton and Creighton has brought such chaos and nightmares to the world that nothing could seem more remote to the concluding twentieth century than Victorian self-confidence and certainties. In their realism, scepticism, and despair today's historians shrink from praise and condemnation and large generalization because they see their calling not in terms of being judge and juror or guide, but as observers, recorders, presenters. They shun the large vistas, preferring to deal with the particular, with the microcosm of human development. And richer as the twentieth century is in its experience of the corrupting effects of absolute power, it has become conscious of the dangers threatening also from the opposite extreme. Men in power tend at least to maintain the semblance of probity, if only to maintain their power. But those who lack power and want it often lack even that restraint.

The greater their gifts and insights are, the more historians will be aware of their own limitations and those of their material and facts. But their seeming greater humility may also disguise merely pride and fear of tackling the fundamental questions, as in the case of the Victorians. Although the goal posts are moved from time to time, the questions remain; the battle between good and evil continues to affect visions of the past, whether the historian sees himself as

God or as the humblest of his creation. And the most chastening aspect of this calling is, perhaps, that the historian never has the last word. There will always be new historians to go over the paths their predecessors have trodden.

Acton appended to his letter to Creighton, already twenty-four pages long, thirty-five "canons" or rules for the historian's craft. They showed that he was well aware of the temptation that threatens the historian from partisanship of country, class, party, religion, and what he called "the authority of talent and the solicitations of friends." The most respectable of these influences were the most dangerous. "Judge not according to the orthodox standard of a system, religious, philosophical, political, but according as things promote or fail to promote the delicate integrity and authority of conscience." But in the end, as Butterfield has pointed out, even the most sensitive historian with all this knowledge, insight, and imaginative power fails "in that innermost region of all, which has to be reached before a personality can be assessed in a moral judgment."[23]

Butterfield has said of Acton that "something in him had been bruised by the spectacles that he had to witness, whether in the past or in the present."[24] It was in that period after the Vatican Council that Acton, then in his early fifties, came to discover a special affinity for George Eliot. The great writer, too, was confronted by a similar problem: "A new code of duty and motive needed to be restored in the midst of the void left by lost sanctions and banished hopes."[25] George Eliot reconstructed for herself, quite independently, without any religious aid, the moral equivalent of a religious faith. Acton had known her in her last years, and his notes, some six thousand cards in boxes kept among his Cambridge papers, show his deep preoccupation with her life and ideas.

"It seems as if the sun had gone out," he wrote to Mary Gladstone after George Eliot's death. "You cannot think how much I owed her. Of eighteen or twenty writers by whom I am conscious that my mind has been formed, she was one. Of course I mean ways, not conclusions. In problems of life and thought, which baffled Shakespeare disgracefully, her touch was unfailing. No writer ever lived who had anything like her power of manifold, but disinterested and impartially observant sympathy."[26] There were common traits: "A spontaneous talent, great natural power to absorb, to think deeply and exactly, to feel. But it was her life that made her, and made her slowly, by learning, and unlearning, by changing her ideas, her gradual separation from friends, reflecting her isolation. . . . Then, at near forty, she suddenly discovered what she was."[27]

George Eliot interested Acton less as a literary genius than as a cultural phenomenon. "That is her infinite merit," he wrote to Döllinger, who needed convincing. "And it seems to me a personal achievement. There was no resonance of her Christian upbringing. . . . It was precisely the morality that she disliked in Christianity. She did not read its more recent literature. She did not sublimate Christian England with its social morality. She stood in open conflict with it. . . . Nothing in the past was sacred to her, she was obedient to no authority. The interest of a bad cause did not force her—to debase the moral currency— to spare reputations."[28]

Impressed though he was by Acton's essay about Eliot's life, which appeared in the *Nineteenth Century* in March 1885, Dr. Döllinger would not agree. He was used to reading novelists "for relaxation" and tended to ignore their philosophical outlook. But in view of the Acton-Döllinger disagreement on moral judgement in history, their exchanges on George Eliot were informative. Gladstone also, like Döllinger, had little time for George Eliot, preferring Scott. And she in turn "disliked and underrated Gladstone, preferring Disraeli," because of Gladstone's ignorance of disbelief and philosophy and his condescension to the popular level. Unlike Gladstone, she could sympathize without acquiescence or agreement.[29]

Acton argued with Döllinger, who thought that George Eliot was simply the product of her unbelieving environment. The undeniable influence of Auguste Comte on her began and remained significant in her novels *Romola* (1863) and *Middlemarch* (1871–1872), then declined. "She read Comte as she read Rousseau, Spinoza, Lessing, Pascal, by searching their ideas with an energy and compass, such as no Englishman had done since Sir William Hamilton. And her purpose was neither aesthetic pleasure or defence of a cause, but practical enlightenment." She was so remarkably free from her environment, Acton told Döllinger, that she was able to translate David Friedrich Strauss's *Life of Jesus* without being in the least attracted by him, never talked with her intimate friend Herbert Spencer about philosophical questions when she found that he was not to be won over to Comte, nor about religion with her partner, George Henry Lewes, as he had no understanding for it. "[Thomas] Carlyle and [John Stuart] Mill were outstanding figures in her circle. Both she found decidedly repulsive. Being so independent is unusual in England. She has drunk from many sources."[30]

The amazing thing for Acton was that George Eliot was not only an unbeliever but an atheist of the extreme kind. There was not a trace of a stoic or pantheist in her. Her great literary talent was in the service of an ideology remote from any moral theory. "It is striking," Acton wrote,

> how much ethics had declined in philosophical thought after the middle of this century. I am thinking of the late Hegelians, Utilitarians, the lack of any ethical school in Positivism, the godless morality of Feuerbach and the materialists. The study of ethics had withdrawn into the spiritualist schools. The prejudice that virtue has no justification without God was everywhere confirmed. . . . The systems which she followed, the circles in which she lived, were helpless in ethics. And yet she created for herself, in the most unfavourable surroundings, under the darkest auspices, such a high, ideal morality that its general influence is elevating and beneficial, and through it atheism competes with theism in the ennoblement of mankind.[31]

And to Lady Blennerhassett he wrote: "The interest lies in the teaching, and in that alone. If her ideas had been common, traditional, Christian, her importance—to me—would have been less. She would have stood in the midst of a very large group, a little above, or a little below many other writers."[32]

Acton went on to note that Eliot's most creative period was between 1840 and 1875, "during the supremacy of atheism and the eclipse of [philosophic] Ethics." In many German universities there were no lectures on ethics in the philosophical faculty. This was to change later in the century, but when George Eliot started, and without aid from philosophers, she contrived to become a great moral teacher. And Acton gloried in what was to him

> one of the most wonderful facts, of the most wonderful feats, in the history of the human mind. Atheism, at the moment of its becoming a permanent and preponderant force. . . . [Atheism] as a teacher of Life, became, roughly speaking, the equal of Christianity in moral dignity when it became its rival in mental power. And all through this one woman who lived among scoffers, professors of impurity, men ignorant of higher things, philosophers destitute of a moral code—a woman who had never read the books that teach the higher virtues to religious men. For these reasons which seem to be too obvious and too certain to be disputed, I would give all the imaginative literature of England since Shakespeare for George Eliot's writings.[33]

Lady Blennerhassett recalled meeting Acton one afternoon in Portman Square on his way to visit George Eliot. He invited her to accompany him to The Priory, St. John's Wood, where George Eliot was then living with George

Lewes, so that he could introduce her. Instead of agreeing at once, the thought of meeting so unexpectedly the famous writer she admired made Lady Blennerhassett hesitate. Acton misunderstood her, thinking she shared the prevailing disapproval for George Eliot's equivocal marital position (she was living with George Lewes while his wife and son and daughter were living in Kensington). Acton made no attempt to help Lady Blennerhassett out of her embarrassment and continued on his way, leaving her for ever after to regret her irresolution. But Acton at least paid her the compliment of calling her "the cleverest woman I ever met out of St. John's Wood."[34]

Mary Gladstone recorded attending a London dinner, in April 1878, at the Tennysons' with her father: in attendance were George Eliot, Lord Acton ("to my delight"), and Miss Thackeray ("oh, how affected she was"). "Mr. Tennyson read *Boadicea*, a good deal of *Maud*, and the *Revenge,* the latter was perfectly splendid. He read it in an ever increasing rush, and shouting out the climax. Enjoyed it beyond all. Lord Acton was really drunk with delight over his dinner, seated next to G. Eliot." Did Mary Gladstone feel a tinge of jealousy upon seeing Acton with that woman with the "repulsively ugly face"? But on a later occasion Mary Gladstone's opinion softened: "Found myself on a sofa talking amicably with George Eliot. . . . Her great strong face (a mixture of Savonarola and Dante) impressed me deeply with the gentleness and earnestness of her manner, both in speaking and listening. There is something a little like affectation sometimes, but I don't expect it's it."[35]

In February 1881 John Walter Cross, the banker who had been managing George Eliot's affairs and whom she married after the death of Lewes when she had only a few more months to live, announced his intention of writing her biography based on her letters and diaries. He probably wanted to forestall another biographer. Spending the best part of a winter in Nice and Grasse, he saw much of Acton and consulted him on literary and other points. Acton revised and corrected, even rewrote whole parts of the three-volume work. Cross accepted Acton's view that to the end of her life George Eliot had been in a state of increasing impartiality and intelligent sympathy towards all forms of religious belief. From her letters one could see that she was not without hope of religion that could be faithfully accepted by the intellect, as well as the emotions, as something in the future not yet realized.[36] Cross expressed his indebtedness to Acton in the foreword of his book.[37]

In his notes Acton summed up what George Eliot meant to him: "She made virtue admirable and attractive, and weakness hateful." She "condemn[s] no man for his opinions. Not even his moral opinions. He is not wrong—only weak, only out of date." "She did not seek her ethics in a system but in mankind." "She had Lessing's idea of religions": China, India, Medina, Egypt, Greece, Rome, all developed the same idea, and the progress of her thought made this deeper. "No thought occurs to her more often than indignation at the persecution of the Jews; but she spares the persecutor." She is so perfectly unprejudiced and detached that she holds up with no insincerity for imitating the things she had spent her life in discarding.[38] Acton's regard for Eliot was clearly a mixture of his taste in idealism and realism.

18

DÖLLINGER'S DEATH

The year 1879 was important for Acton in two respects. It was the beginning of his correspondence with Mary Gladstone and, through that, an intensified friendship also with her father. And, looking back on it in later years, Acton saw 1879 as the beginning, too, of his estrangement from Döllinger. In September the Gladstones came to Tegernsee for an eight-day holiday, and the the lovely Bavarian mountain setting henceforth became a favourite escape for Gladstone. He enjoyed the walks in the forests and mountains, and the sizeable library of some four thousand volumes that Acton had accumulated there. The Arco chalet was beautifully situated on the edge of the clear blue waters of the Tegernsee, twenty-five hundred feet above sea level, with steep and wooded hills rising as though straight out of the lake, six thousand to seven thousand feet high. It was a holiday villa but quite large, with a courtyard and with first-floor balconies opening from all the bedrooms, the windows framed by creepers.

A memorable photograph records the occasion, showing the two families seated near the becreepered terrace of the Villa Arco, which opened into the garden, with the three men forming a kind of triangle. Acton, the bearded host, sits somewhat apart from the others, with legs crossed and a large straw hat on his lap. Next to him is the diminutive, neat figure of Döllinger, almost disappearing into his deck chair, and near him, on a long garden bench, are first a large lady, Leopoldine Arco (known as Tini), then her mother, Acton's mother-in-law, Countess Arco, and finally Mrs. Catherine Gladstone, with a bonnet and fan, keeping a kindly eye on Lily, the second-youngest of the Acton children. Then the lionlike figure of Gladstone, aged seventy, dressed, like Acton, in frock-coat and fawn-coloured trousers with stand-up collar and bow tie, also holding a straw hat in his hands. Standing behind him are the two boys, Herbert Gladstone and the much younger Richard Acton, and on the terrace behind them two ladies with feather hats: Mary Gladstone, looking at an album, and Marie Acton, with her youngest child, Simmy, in her arms. The two other Acton girls are peeping through the greenery. It is a still, late-summer day, and the group seems poignantly captured in time and place.[1]

Döllinger was now in his eightieth year, still with an upright figure and a lively expression on a powerful face. Every morning he took a plunge in the icy waters. "An extraordinary old man indeed," Mary Gladstone noted.[2] And Acton reflected: "Serenity has grown on him with years, although they were years of conflict and of the great grief that men who do not live for themselves can feel for the cause they have lived for. Strength, too, though in less degree, by reason of a vice which besets another great man"—meaning Mary's father. "From a sense of dignity and of charity he refuses to see all the evil there is in men." And he went on to say that this charitable and generous outlook tended to weaken Döllinger's judgement, causing him to look for "the root of differences in speculative systems, in defect of knowledge, in everything but moral causes, and if you had remained with us longer you would have found out that this is a matter on which I am divided from him by a gulf almost too wide for sympathy."[3]

The opening gulf towards Döllinger caused Acton to welcome the sympathy and friendship that Mary Gladstone offered. He was forty-five, she was thirty-two, and she clearly fell in love with him, influenced by the romantic holiday setting. "A sail on the lake," she recorded. "Sat in the garden. How nice a honeymoon wd. be here. A beauteous drive to Kreuth, a fine mixture of a civilized, cultivated land and bold sharp mountains." She and Acton had long talks,

mostly about various people. . . . He has a shrewd eye for character, and yet charitable. Rowed with Herbert to the other end of the lake where we met the others and we drank milk. Papa and Dr. D[öllinger], and Ld. Acton and I walked home at leisurely pace. Lord A. and I in front, lightning came on and storm threatened and we hurried.

He talked to me of Papa and the results of his retirement in '76. He has proved a true prophet. It was deeply interesting. I always sit by him at meals and we have high tea at 8, wh. is delicious, and a long eve. I played for an hour, and from 11 to 1/2 p. 12, when all had gone to bed, talked to Ld. Acton, at least he talked to me, with occasional questions or comments. . . . He told me what he thought of Papa, morally, spiritually, intellectually, of what the judgment of posterity wd. be, of his relations with his colleagues and his party. . . . He said Burke was the only man to whom one cd. compare Papa. Crept up to bed.

Tegernsee, Sat. 20 Sept. . . . Rowed across the lake. H[erbert] and I sat up talking with Ld. A. till 1.15. Majorities and minorities, wh. oftenest right. Birth and cause of intolerance. Influence of great men on age or age on them. Delightful.

Tegernsee, Sunday 21 and Mon. 22 Sept. Service in the drawing room. Mr. Oxenham haunts the place rather. It rained all day. A short sharp walk alone. . . . We only talked till 12.30, about difference of opinion and its effect on friends. Monday, sat out reading *Les Misérables*. Ld A. came and talked for an hour on many things, statesmen and orators chiefly. Talked heaps to him on and off all day. It poured dogs and cats afternoon. Herbert and I in a boat in spite. It was dark and weird and wild. . . .

Tegernsee, Tues. 23 and Wed. 24 and Thurs. 25. A glorious day indeed. . . . Afternoon Herbert and I rowed the gents (Ld. A, the Prof., and Papa) across the lake, delicious. Then we walked right up a mountain gorge high into the hills, talked lots to Ld. A. and joined the carriage ladies and walked down t'other side. . . . H[erbert] and I sat up till 1. Ld A. lectured us on intolerance.[4]

The Gladstones went on to Venice, where they met up again with Acton and family. Acton brought Ruggiero Bonghi and Marco Minghetti to meet Gladstone and talk politics to him in Italian. "Lord A. came and talked to me the whole evening, wh. specially gratified me in being chosen," Mary Gladstone recorded. "Enjoyed it immensely. He thinks me a mystery!" And on their last day at Venice: "He [Lord Acton] gave Herbert and me the History of Liberty, a sketch of it, most interesting. It is extraordinary the way he tingles with it to his fingers' ends and yet can sit patient and quiet over wife and children and wait and wait another year before he writes it. . . . Venice grows in beauty and charm and mystery."[5]

That holiday was the beginning of the celebrated correspondence between Acton and Mary Gladstone; it continued after she was married, in 1886, to Harry Drew, an Anglican clergyman, and went on almost to the end of Acton's life. Her adulation for him was similar to Charlotte Blennerhassett's, who was, however, more on his wave-length about religion. Soon Acton was writing long letters to Mary Gladstone from Menton, Cannes, or Tegernsee, pouring out his historical knowledge and worldly wisdom while she sent him the political news of Gladstone's second administration (1880–85), in which she was given a semiofficial post as a secretary to her father. There was nothing subtle about Acton's admiration of Gladstone, as when he wrote, "You are living the most interesting of lives, by the intensest blaze of light in all the world."[6] When, in 1881, after the tragic death of Acton's daughter Elisabeth she wrote feelingly to express her sympathy, he replied how her death had crushed his spirit, "but I do not follow less keenly the movements of the man who, of all now living, has the greatest power of doing good."[7]

Mary Gladstone grew vexed with Acton about his wasting his years abroad, and about his failure, incomprehensible to her, to apply his genius in some work that she, and others, were convinced he could write. "There is in some quarters a general idea that you do nothing but criticise with folded hands," she wrote of what people in the Liberal Party felt about him, "that you are always negative—that nobody knows anything at all about your real opinions—that you continually pull down and tear to pieces, without raising up or edifying (in the true meaning of the word)."[8] Was he not neglecting his duty as an absentee landlord or, like a clergyman, deserting his parish? she asked after he had spent a few days at Hawarden around New Year in 1882.[9] His excuses were his family, their health, and the never openly admitted state of their finances. There is, he pleaded, in giving up one's home, and country, and friends, and occupations "at least a mixture of good motives with selfish ones, and something sacrificed, if there is also a good deal of calculated pleasure-seeking and ease. If I held an appointment abroad, keeping me permanently away from my—very modest— estate, you would say that the Government was insane to offer it, but you would hardly think it wrong of me to accept it. And the duty I have allowed to precede all other duties is one that possesses a strong, and unmistakable, claim on me. Between my children and my Shropshire neighbours my choice is indeed decided."[10]

But Mary misunderstood the nature of his duties, and because he was not likely to speak openly about his financial straits thought him a deserter, giving vent to her feelings when the Actons were forced to let Aldenham and live the cheaper life at Cannes:

> It seems to me quite dreadfully wicked to entirely foreswear [*sic*] your country and no longer give it any of the benefits which, as a landowner and peer, it has a right to expect from you. It is most cool of me saying this, but I am your country-woman [and] should have some share in those benefits, so I think I may speak. We had a great discussion here the other night . . . on whether "best is the enemy of good," and I could not help thinking sadly of the Madonna of the Future, and that it is indeed not in this world that any mortal man can afford to wait for best. The History of Liberty, when will the time ever arrive here when all the light that can be thrown on a subject has been thrown? Never in this world indeed. . . . Would any great work ever have been done from the beginning if perfection had been waited for? . . . It makes me wretched when I picture to myself the little black leather boxes standing on "my" table, stuffed with notes, the books stuffed with marks and markers, and above all the vast treasure of knowledge and thought that is there, shut up in that person seated at that table, reading and marking those books and writing those notes; and think perhaps we, the hungry and thirsty, may never be fed from those plentyful stores.[11]

That letter stung Acton into an equal outburst (which, however, was omitted from the edition of his letters to Mary Gladstone, edited by Herbert Paul):

> You make writing as difficult as living afar, by your unspeakable goodness, but also by the infusion of the contrary quality. If I promise not to attack the Government, and to believe in Lord Derby, will you agree not to hit me so hard? I cannot well help doing what I do, taking all things into consideration; and as to my tiresome book, please to remember that I can only say things which people do not agree with, that I have neither disciple nor sympathizer, that this is no encouragement to production and confidence, that grizzled men—except [George Otto Trevelyan]—grow appalled at the gaps in their knowledge, and that I have no other gift but that which you so pleasantly describe, of sticking eternal bits of paper into black boxes. There is no help for it. But your reproaches were much more distressing to read than you suppose, and make me think them better to read than to hear.[12]

Acton evidently used Mary Gladstone so that she would convey his views to her father. This connection has been criticized as revealing low motivation on his part, wanting to get at the prime minister through his daughter. But if it is remembered that the friendship between Gladstone and Acton was based on the big issues of life and death and man's purpose in the world, his use of the Machiavellian arts, if such it was, is not so despicable, being intended for a greater good in which he sincerely believed. And she was not unaware of being used. "Somehow I feel as if I had no right to it," she wrote in answer to one of his letters, "and had got it from you on false pretences—that you really wrote it for my father, and I think I ought to confess to you that I am not at all a good pipe or sieve or whatever it should be called, not nearly as good as any one of the secretaries, because neither his eyes or ears are open to me as they are open to them—and it is quite a chance when I can get them for a minute." [13]

Once Mary Gladstone replied to Acton: "I read most of your last letter to my father, he made no remarks, he was lying on the sofa resting, but I could see by his interested face that he drank it all in." [14] She was clearly the best "sieve" available, for Acton's aim was not to fulfil any personal ambition but to be a sort of guardian of Liberalism from his far-away Cannes or Tegernsee hideout, from which he descended occasionally to the Athenaeum in London or to stay with the Gladstones at Hawarden. "Last night a long dispute with Gladstone about Liberalism, of which he seemed to me to understand very little," Acton wrote to his daughter Annie from one of these visits. [15] And as Gladstone grew older and became more anxious to have Acton's advice, Acton in his turn wrote more directly to Mary for Gladstone to hear. Indeed, in the autumn of 1892, at the start of Gladstone's fourth administration and that most dramatic period politically, for Acton, too, he wrote to his daughter Mamy: "I have had to resume the old correspondence with Mrs. Drew. It is a way of conveying some things which I cannot say right off. She was nicer than ever." [16]

Certainly these letters helped to strengthen the friendship between Gladstone and Acton. Even John Morley did not realize how close it was until he discovered the evidence when writing Gladstone's *Life*. In January 1883, for example, Gladstone, aged seventy-four, enjoyed the beauty and comforts of the Wolvertons' Chateau Scott at Cannes and the Actons' La Madeleine, and noted: "Here we fell in with the foreign hours, the snack early, déjeuner at noon, dinner at seven, break-up at ten. . . . I am stunned by the wonderful place, and so vast a change at a moment's notice in the conditions of life." Gladstone's reading included the *Odyssey,* Richard Watson Dixon's *History of the Church of England,* Edmond Scherer's *Miscellanies,* and *The Life of Clerk-Maxwell,* and every day there were "long talks and walks with Lord Acton on themes personal, political

and religious—and we may believe what a restorative he found in communion
with that deep and well-filled mind—that 'most satisfactory mind' as Mr. Gladstone here one day calls it."[17]

But Acton's letters were most important for Mary Gladstone in her own
right, too. They "give me always such splendid confidence," she acknowledged
frankly.[18] In a family centered intensely around that lion figure, her father, she
needed very much to be taken seriously. "If he had the choice between sitting
by the father or sitting by the daughter, he chose the latter, and it was *so* flattering," she wrote, looking back in her old age.[19] And on one of Acton's visits at
Hawarden: "He has a delightful way of realising you, and always listens to the
meanest thing you say."[20] And writing to her friend Lavinia Lyttleton a year
later, she confessed: "Very odd how my greatest friends are all about fifty, Lord
A[cton], Mr. B[urne-Jones] and Sir A. Gordon [later Lord Stanmore]. But it's
a pleasant footing because so delightfully safe." She added in the same letter: "I
think life's a great failure on the whole in spite of there being very jolly things
in it occasionally."[21]

Mary Gladstone's sense of realism and sadness at the world's folly attracted
Acton, with his dislike for the starry-eyed self-confidence of his age, which
he had shared in his own youth, and he felt her expressive appreciation of
his gifts as a conversationalist and letter-writer. Like Charlotte Blennerhassett,
Mary Gladstone had none of Marie's physical attractions. Indeed, his fastidious nature must have been sorely tried by some of her unsavoury habits. As the
Acton family legend has it, she used at dinner to take a piece of bread, dip it
in some piquant sauce that she knew Acton liked, and pass it lovingly to him
in her dirty fingers. He had to accept graciously.[22] But Mary Gladstone—being
an intelligent and sensitive woman, affectionate and generous, and never dull,
though with strong prejudices and not always wise—helped Acton to break
out of his intellectual isolation, which he had considered to be his permanent
condition.

Mary Gladstone also made no bones about her dislike of Acton's provocative
silences and his moods of apparent unapproachability that affected all around
him. In her diary she wrote on his forty-seventh birthday: "Ld. Acton to dinner, fearfully dull."[23] And on Saturday, 31 December, of the same year: "The
last day of 1881 was an interesting day. Ld. A. arrived before 1 o'clock, having
only left Cannes Thurs. aft. and had an evening in the Athenaeum on Friday.
Felt very shy of him. He went on a long walk with Papa. . . . Dinner a marked
failure though we took pains that Ld. A. should be next the PM. . . . The high-

est point to which the conv. ever rose was—'Smuts—Their Cause and Effect.' There was a great deal about *hod men.*"[24]

Gladstone, Mary, and Acton went for a walk through the woods at Hawarden Park in wind and rain, "utterly unenlivened by any spark in the conversation, which was almost entirely topographical, and geological, with a very slight smattering of French politics," she recorded disappointedly afterwards.[25] Acton needed a spark to set him off. In a man of his worldly wisdom his silences were both provocative and constructive, as Morley noted.[26] But it was certainly not his intention that his intimate exchange with Mary Gladstone of ideas and very frank views about well-known contemporaries should ever be published, as he made frequently clear. When, for instance, she asked whether she could show their letters to John Morley, he replied instantly: "Don't show my letters to others—I need to write freely."[27] And again: "I should hardly have resolved to say all this to anybody but yourself, relying on you not to misunderstand the exact and restricted meaning of my letter."[28]

Acton's daughter Mamy remembered how upset he was when, years later, after Gladstone's death, Mary Drew's letter arrived in Cambridge, asking for permission to publish their correspondence. Acton wanted to refuse but felt unable to do so and tried to put her off because of possible clashes with the coming biography of her father. But Mary, convinced of the historical importance of Acton's letters and proud to have been their recipient, was determined to publish, possibly omitting "all the personal bits [which really are the] touch of ill-nature [that] makes the whole world kin."[29] In the course of their further exchanges Acton wrote to her: "Conversations with Morley and Rosebery have made it clearer than ever that those letters cannot be allowed to appear. And even if these were not the decisive reasons, I now see the amount of excision and omission that would have been required would have made them useless."[30] When she sent him the copied letters with certain, but clearly inadequate, omissions, he wrote back: "Pray allow me to keep the type written letters and don't let other copies get about. I don't speak or write as freely as that to anybody now."[31]

Weakly Acton stipulated that in view of Morley's biography the letters should not be published for three years, but by that time Acton was dead and the imprudent Mary Drew was not to be put off anymore. When the letters were published, edited by Herbert Paul, in 1904, and in a slightly fuller version in 1913 but without any further explanation or annotation, they caused a sensation. The historian, known for his carefully weighed views, was suddenly revealed as making some sharp and indiscreet judgements about many people then still living, and about his own Church, that were deeply offensive to devout Catholics, the more so once they were communicated to Gladstone's daughter, a staunch Anglican. Again, Anglicans were hardly amused about various suggestions made by Acton, the Roman Catholic, regarding episcopal appointments in the Established Church. The letters greatly damaged Acton's reputation, and this result was not helped by the fact that Mary Drew, perhaps trying to make amends, dedicated the book to Acton's widow.

Morley, by then embarked on the Gladstone biography and surprised—and impressed—by the extent of Acton's influence on the prime minister, may have contributed to weaken Acton's resistance to Mary Drew's requests for permission to publish. Morley, however, eventually refused to review the Paul edition of Acton's letters, having also tried to dissuade her from publishing. Professor Owen Chadwick provides some interesting finds about omitted passages: an ellipsis after the names Jackson St. George Mivart and Newman, for example, represents the omitted words "two very able and evil men." One also finds that Acton had invested the great W. T. Stead, the Victorian investigative journalist and editor for many years of the influential *Pall Mall Gazette,* with the fitting epithet "the irrepressible Pall Mall bore whom I wish back in his dungeon." Stead had spent three months in Holloway jail for his revelations on the white slave traffic, although these eventually secured the crucial Criminal Law Amendment Act.[32]

Then, on the Gladstones' Tegernsee holiday in 1886, an event of great significance in the Acton-Döllinger relationship occurred. One evening, after a strenuous walk, Döllinger, tired and faint and, for all his sprightliness, perhaps thinking that the end might be near, came into Acton's room and said, very solemnly and kindly, that Acton had been right in their dispute, but that it was hard to adopt and follow lines of thought not one's own. That moment of insight passed, however, and although Döllinger never referred to it again, it remained imprinted on Acton's memory.[33] What had provoked their dispute was, strangely, the death of Bishop Dupanloup, in October 1878. The event in itself had no special significance for Acton; it was part of an almost forgotten past as far as he was concerned. Dupanloup, his first headmaster at Gentilly, his doubtful though major ally among the opposition bishops at the Vatican Council, had, like all the others, made his submission to Pius IX. But then Charlotte Blennerhassett, Acton's and Döllinger's friend and devoted to both, unwittingly lit a match that ignited a tinder-box. She wrote an appreciation of the late Bishop, whom she had long known and admired. To make the piece acceptable to the editor of the *Nineteenth Century,* a letter from Dr. Döllinger was requested, introducing the author (she used the pseudonym C. de Warmont), and this was printed as a prefix to her article. He had known Dupanloup for twenty-five years, Döllinger wrote, and could vouch for the accuracy of the details and the truth of the appreciation. "The author has written with the help of materials inaccessible to others and records events of general interest and importance which are unknown or inaccurately known."[34]

Döllinger, as he later explained to Acton, had no intention of canonizing Bishop Dupanloup. He even told Acton that Lady Blennerhassett had written "a rather interesting article" on Dupanloup, but that it would not have been published without a recommending letter from him to the editor.[35] Döllinger insisted that he did not care one way or the other about Dupanloup, but that the Bishop had always had a strong fascination for women, Lady B. in particular. When she pestered him about a recommendation for the *Nineteenth Century,* Döllinger had found the matter disagreeable. "But you know how this woman can get what she wants and how difficult it is . . . to refuse her." So he gave in and assumed that the article would be an admirer's harmless effusion. He had not even bothered to read the piece before or after it was published. "When you now blame me for having in this affair behaved weakly, frivolously, thoughtlessly, I must agree," Döllinger wrote to Acton in 1886. "It is unfortunately not the only such weakness of which I have carelessly been guilty in my life. But there can obviously be no question of any principle whatsoever that might have come into question in that."[36] But this explanation came from an exasperated Döllinger only seven years after the Dupanloup article—or rather, Döllinger's approval of it—had first roused in Acton the suspicion that the Professor had, all along, basically misunderstood him. The gist of the Blennerhassett article—and for Acton this was the crux of the matter—was that an eminent and enthusiastic admirer and defender of the Papacy like Dupanloup could be regarded as a man of honour who, even if he was wrong, was without blemish. And here was the excommunicated Döllinger, bestowing his blessing on an appreciation of Dupanloup as an enlightened Christian!

Acton wrote at once to Lady Blennerhassett: "You have often told me that I am naive, but that is what I recognise in the way you have written of the bishop." Her long friendship with Dupanloup had presumably prevented her from saying what "pitiless history" would say. Ironically, Acton likened her to Duc Etienne Pasquier, elected in Dupanloup's place to the Académie Française, who would soon laud his predecessor, as was customary. The worst blow to Acton, however, was that the professor, in praising this defender of the Papacy, the *Syllabus Errorum,* and the temporal power, had opened up "unforeseen horizons."[37]

And to Döllinger Acton wrote:

The ground was thus cut from under my feet. It was as if I had never known your basic principles: my whole accord with you was based on an illusion. From that moment on I no longer knew where I was with you. If Dupanloup, with his justification of the papacy, was a worthy, devout, sincerely religious Christian, then why not also Hefele [who praised the Grand Inquisitor], Ximenes, Falloux with Pius V [who demanded that the Huguenot prisoners should be put to death], Newman with Charles Borromeo [who approved the murdering of Protestants by private individuals]. . . . We should have to make our peace with these people and concentrate our artillery on Darwin, Renan, Kuenen. This inevitably means that the higher ecclesiastical end justifies bad means; sin ceases to be sin for the sake of the faith.[38]

Acton had also used these much-disputed examples of "bad Popes" in his letter published in the *Times* on 9 November 1874.

Lady Blennerhassett went straight to Döllinger with Acton's letter and recorded the Professor's reactions. "No one in the whole world knows me better than Acton and knows more about me," he told her. "But the difference between us is that I am tolerant towards people while he is an absolutist in judging them and is totally intolerant." When someone had a point of view that Acton regarded as wrong, he would be rejected and that was the end of it. That is what probably happened in the case of the Dupanloup article. Acton might have glanced at it, seen something he disliked, and stopped reading. "There is nobody like Acton for telling half-truths!" When, a few days later, Lady Blennerhassett saw Döllinger again, he was still deeply disturbed and told her that he had thought much about the affair, that he and Acton, knowing each other so well, were transparent to each other. Acton was intolerant towards anyone he suspected of denying the truth against his better knowledge, whereas he, Döllinger, accepted mitigating circumstances, excuses that one had to recognize in all moral failings. As far as Dupanloup was concerned, Döllinger went on, no denial of the truth was involved. The Bishop was simply ignorant on many matters and would have had no time to arrive at a firm position during the Council. "Surely, you can defend the Pope, the *Syllabus* and much else besides and yet be quite a good and useful fellow." All that Dupanloup was guilty of was "some tight-rope walking" around the *Syllabus*.[39]

Dupanloup—quite a good and useful fellow! To Acton it was the most wounding of insults. Was Döllinger merely insensitive, as he, Acton, had sometimes shown himself to be? What was really at the bottom of this crisis of misunderstanding that was breaking out between them? Clearly it was to do with the Vatican Council and Infallibility, although the Blennerhassett article dealt with neither subject. But the article served to bring these differences into the open. The point was that for Acton, Papal Infallibility had all along not been the main issue, as it had been for Döllinger and the bishops at the Council. For Acton, Infallibility was only a symptom of a larger disease, namely, Ultramontanism, the doctrine that anything was allowed if the interest of the Church was at stake. That teaching had existed before the Council and seemed to Acton, if possible, more unpardonable after 1870 than it was before.

Acton, the Catholic layman, saw the problem primarily in moral terms. To him there was behind the dogma of Infallibility an immoral state of mind, a kind of theological Machiavellianism. Döllinger, however, saw Infallibility as based on dogmatic-historical grounds. This difference also explains the tortuous efforts Acton made to arrive at some interpretation of the dogma that would at least reconcile his conscience, if not appease Manning, and allow him to remain in the Church. To repeat his lines to the Archbishop in 1874: "I can only say that I have no private gloss. . . . I am content to rest in absolute reliance on God's providence in His government of the Church."[40] And this strategy worked as long as Manning failed to pin him down in the way that Döllinger, the priest, had been pinned down by his superiors. There was a radical theological difference between them on Infallibility, which caused Döllinger to interpret his break with the Church as a sad but inevitable necessity but a lesser evil, whereas Acton could never have faced this Ultramontane sacrifice, because membership in the Catholic Church was dearer to him than life,[41] meaning that it could not be separated from his love of goodness and truth.

Acton's disillusion with the Church was in a sense greater than Döllinger's but also less, for Acton at least entertained the thought that the dogma of Infallibility might one day be "explained away" or, as Catholics of the Vatican II generation might say, placed in its theological context, whereas Döllinger hoped for a retraction, which Rome would never make. Acton and Döllinger were agreed that there existed among Catholics an attitude towards religion that was immoral. "This immorality consists in the belief that sin ceases to be sin when it is committed for the sake of the Church. Robbery is not robbery, lying is not lying, murder not murder, when sanctioned by religious interests or authorities."[42]

For Acton it was not a matter concerning heretics or sceptics but something worse. Unbelievers or Protestants could have the strictest moral code. But this mentality that historically had grown and been strengthened by the Papacy allowed for a deadly double standard that enabled its adherents to lead exemplary private lives, but when it came to Church affairs, it became a matter of "my Church—right or wrong." The Papacy was not rejected by him, Acton wrote, just as Louis XV did not spoil the monarchy for him, or Marat the republic.

Trying to answer Acton's moral arguments, Döllinger sought to explain them at first by citing the age and social difference between him and Acton. Before congratulating Acton on his forty-seventh birthday he wrote that forty years ago he, too, had been a harsher judge of people and their actions than later, and had even had the nickname "the iron ruler." Then there were their completely different lives: "You—you are born with a silver spoon in the mouth—highly placed, enjoying every freedom, a citizen of the mightiest empire, able to develop your convictions and attitudes without prejudice or any sort of intellectual pressures. How very different from my own upbringing in a narrow-minded, small country, and then because of my choice of career bound by the straight-jacket of a hierarchical system, even if that, sixty years ago, was not as strait-laced and oppressive as it has become under Pius IX."[43]

But Acton would not accept that he was motivated by immature zeal that "you yourself used to share at one time." For him metaphysical or purely theological doctrines had never been causes for blame and prejudice, Acton wrote. As far as he was concerned the same standards applied whether one was a Jew, pagan, Christian, unbeliever, Jansenist, Jesuit, Catholic, or Protestant. He reminded Döllinger how they had disagreed in the past on many of Döllinger's own judgements, for example, on the German biblical scholar Ferdinand Christian Baur, on Savonarola, on Erasmus, on Thomas More's accusations against Luther, Bossuet's against Fénelon, Leibniz's against Descartes. "The reason why I drop people, as you would say, is not because of untruth but because of untruthfulness, not because of erring conscience but lack of conscience. . . . The charge is therefore not of too great or too general severity but of severity in the wrong place in too concentrated a form. That is very different from [the rigidity of] an 'iron ruler.'"[44]

His defects, Acton admitted, came from "banal enthusiasm rather than recklessness." He had long been blinded by his early heroes, by Josef von Görres, Johann Möhler, Franz von Baader, Ernst von Lasaulx, Joseph de Maistre, Baron Ferdinand d'Eckstein, Donoso Cortes, Joseph Maria von Radowitz, Friedrich Julius Stahl, John Henry Newman, Orestes Brownson, Gioacchino Ventura Di Raulico, Alexandre Vinet, Richard Rothe. It had cost him a lot to overcome the influence of Edmund Burke, Thomas Babington Macaulay, Johannes and Adam Müller, Georg Friedrich Creuzer, and Heinrich Leo. Liberation and independence had come to him through years of studying the sources. Slowly and unwillingly these early rulers were deposed. Politics with a religious slant had always attracted him. With a heavy heart he had then entered upon "the solitude of autonomy. [Because] I lacked altogether the fighting spirit, the awareness of my own ability, the sharpness of the skilled public speaker, . . . I sought out the most talented men of my time: [William Ewart] Gladstone, [Charles Forbes] Montalembert, [John Henry] Newman, [James Robert] Hope[-Scott], [Ferdinand] Eckstein, [Alphonse] Gratry, [August Friedrich] Gförer, [Count Joseph von] Eichendorff, [Wilhelm] Roscher, to be saved from the need of thinking and researching for myself. I was captured by naive trust rather than by iconoclasm. I have the letters in which Simpson scorned me for still believing in Newman. Only in 1863—I still remember the day—did I give up Montalembert."[45]

Could they not agree to differ, Döllinger proposed, tired of the dispute. But Acton would not hear of it and countered with the example of Martin Luther as illustrating their differences. "To weigh good and evil, as you say, and see which predominates is precisely what in the case of Luther I cannot do," Acton wrote. "All the qualities of Kempis and Shakespeare united weigh nothing against a single crime." And to justify his persistence, for which he apologized, he ended that letter on a note of sorrow: "After sitting at your feet for a life time, that a mysterious chasm separates us and that I am constrained to follow a path which is opposite to your own."[46]

Their differences on Luther were not on dogmatic grounds. Döllinger, particularly, anticipating modern Roman Catholic scholarship, saw Luther in a more favourable light. For Acton the moral point of view mattered more. He condemned Luther for sacrificing monogamy for the benefit of two rulers— Henry VIII, who wanted to divorce his Queen in 1528 and marry another wife, and Philipp von Hessen. To both he conceded the royal privilege of bigamy. Besides, Luther had preached freedom, established the doctrine of passive obedience, but then handed the Church over to the civil power and allowed princes to be absolute rulers. "At first he advocates freedom of conscience, then compulsion of conscience—wants the peasants to be treated even worse than Marat [in the French Revolution] wanted to treat the rich. But it seems to me, on the whole, that the peasants had right on their side, more at any rate than the French nobility, and it is thus only with the darkest colours at my command that I can paint this absolutist, this brutal tyrant who sacrificed principles to interest and morality to power."[47]

Luther touched a sore point in Döllinger's German patriotism. Acton's letter about Luther's double morality and the moral ambiguity of the German hero worship of the early Romantic school of Goethe, Frederick II, and Frederick the Great, raised the question of whether Luther must not be regarded as suspect. Döllinger retaliated in exasperation that Acton was being disrespectful to the nation that made Luther its leader.[48] Acton replied with the question, What would one think if "like a good Whig, I sought to palliate the massacre of Glencoe, or if, as an Englishman, a Catholic, a Liberal, I refrained from admitting the brutal ferocity of Sir Thomas More, the glory of Englishmen, Liberals and Catholics?"[49]

Luther's popularity in Germany despite his cruelty and disregard for human life seemed to Acton as disgraceful as the French worship of Voltaire and Napoleon, the Irish and Italians' hailing O'Connell and Cavour, Presbyterian reverence for John Knox, or Catholic devotion to Borromeo. The consequence of such popularity was a condemnation of the nations concerned. "But I do not draw up an indictment against a nation, any more than I excuse a man by reason of his nationality." Annoyed about Acton's "moral death sentences," Döllinger answered: "We must agree to differ."[50] But Acton persisted: "Unfortunately it is not a question on which one can agree to differ. Historical science does not tolerate such differences. . . . As long as history cannot attain to such certainties as compels the assent of honest men, it is worthless as an arbiter of controversy and a teacher of nations."[51]

Döllinger, in his old age, was becoming more charitable, his student more unbending: "I find that I have misunderstood the very teaching from which I started," wrote Acton, "and that my canons have become inconsistent with yours. Apart from dogma, I should feel myself, at heart, nearer to Rothe or Vinet or [Hans Lassen] Martensen or [Heinrich] Thiersch than to a Church in which nobody agrees with me in the fundamental question of the conditions of Grace."[52]

Acton tried to probe into their dispute. But he had the feeling that the Professor put him off or regarded his points not as the result of long study but as a hasty paradox or prejudice not worthy of serious treatment. "At last, in 1883, he made it very clear that it was time for our conversations to cease, for this world."[53] The whole thing had become distasteful to Döllinger. "He thinks an Ultr[amontane] can be saved. He thinks they have a right to toleration. He thinks they carry with them, weakened, and impaired, but still efficacious, the sacramental gifts. His obj[ection] w[ould] be the same, if [there were] no Inq[uisition], no Casuists, no tyrannicide. To me they are in religion what Jacobins and Communards are in politics. I w[ould] never call by the name of Ultr[amontane] a man in a state of grace. I do not waste on blunderers or inconsistency, or ignorance, the powder destined for Guy Fawkes and Ravaillac."[54]

Therefore, Acton continued,

so far as I can see, I have thoroughly misunderstood the Prof[essor], have been in opp[osition] when I thought mys[elf] his disciple, and have had to spend five years in trying to find out his real sentiments. . . . I have renounced public life, and a pos[ition] fa[vourable] to infl[uence] my own country, to pursue an object I cannot attain. I am absolutely alone in my essential ethical position, and therefore useless. . . . No other person can ever be so fav[ourably] situated as the Prof[essor]. He seeks nothing, knows more, and had, assuredly, a prejudice in my favour.[55]

Döllinger's rebuff seemed to Acton to make his isolation complete.

As the years passed, the acrimony with Döllinger cooled. When, on 28 February 1889, the Professor celebrated his ninetieth birthday, Acton failed to send a message of congratulation but finally explained, writing in March, that he had been persistently if not seriously unwell for several months, and had been prevented from writing.[56] Full of his old concern, Döllinger replied: "You ought to consider very carefully whether there is anything injurious in your diet (taken in the widest sense). I have often found that what physicians consider to be harmless is in reality the opposite."[57] Their correspondence had slowed down but never broken off, and the warmth with which the Actons received one of Döllinger's nieces at Cannes also indicated that their friendship was never totally broken.

Their last letters concerned uncontroversial matters of mutual interest. Acton told Döllinger what a loss the death, at Versailles, of Edmond Scherer had been to him.[58] Scherer was a friend to Alexandre Vinet, the Lausanne reformed theo-

logian, known as "the Swiss Pascal," and both of them had had a strong influence on Acton in his middle age: he did not take over their views, he used to
say, but their friendship meant much to him. Scherer had been an "excellent
whetstone" for him in all French affairs. Like Acton, he had lost all faith in
absolute authority. Acton also told Döllinger about his son's studies. Döllinger
wrote back: "What I would wish for your son at Oxford is that he should in
time choose a preferred subject and make it the centre of his studies. The way
we went, you and I, is not the *regia via,* we are exceptions to the rule." And he
signed his very last letter to him in his old way, "totus tuus—J. Döllinger."[59]

Acton visited Döllinger for the last time in October 1889, finding him, as he
wrote to Gladstone, "well in health, and in mind, too, when talking German
and at close quarters; but deafness and bodily weakness have increased seriously
during the last few months."[60] On New Year's Day, Döllinger caught a chill and
had to stay in bed for a week, but his irrepressible energy did not keep him away
from his desk. In the early evening of 9 January 1890, after he had gone to bed,
he had a stroke and died the following evening, having only partially regained
consciousness. In the morning of that 10 January—the birthday of Acton, who
was in Rome—Johann Friedrich, the theologian, who had been excommunicated with Döllinger and who was active in the Old Catholic movement, came
to administer the Sacrament for the Dying to him. It was done in accordance
with Döllinger's wishes.

"And so, on my birthday, came the end of our forty years unbroken friendship," Acton wrote to Mamy from Rome:

> And it has been more than that; for of all the many priests and prelates I have
> known in many countries the Professor, now lying dead in the rooms where
> I was educated, was the one who took the deepest and the most earnest view
> of Religion. He did not agree with me in many things, and sometimes he
> was angry with me; but to talk to him was altogether different from talk on
> such matters with any other man. The void, for me, is a very great one; for I
> always knew that he knew more than I. . . . What makes me sorry now is not
> his death, at such an age and with such work done, but the sense that he never
> really understood me and my ways, though I am sure he liked me better,
> at one time, than anyone else. On that account he was not always a good
> adviser, and he felt sometimes unpleasantly, that there was a gap between us.

Acton recalled the Tegernsee holiday of 1886 and Döllinger's apparent admission of guilt after an exhausting walk. "Perhaps, if I had taken the other route
from Geneva, he would have given me the consolation of saying so once more

on his deathbed." Guessing what her husband must have felt at not being in Munich at that time, Marie had sent him a message of sympathy, and he added, "Thank mother a million times for the reassuring telegram I received in the middle of this letter."[61]

Döllinger had been "the best, the most wonderful and most patient of friends," Acton wrote in his letter of condolence to Döllinger's niece, Jeanette. But his greatest sadness was "to think of the way I have lost him," of the grief he had caused him lately, and the weariness over sustained long discussions that the Professor resented. He had finally and visibly evaded tiring conversations. "I shall regret not to have been there," Acton wrote.[62] He was aware of having caused pain by not going to Munich. "No doubt, I made a tremendous mistake, but it was not my fault," he wrote to Annie.[63] To Gladstone he explained the circumstances of what had happened: how he had started for Italy when he heard of the Professor's serious illness from the newspapers. He had arranged to go at first only to Genoa and to have telegrams sent on to him. But at Genoa he heard from Döllinger's nieces that the Professor seemed out of danger. "So I turned South for a few days, and so missed his last hours."[64] To Mamy again he wrote about the deepening realization of the void in his life: "He was a tremendous background. Now, when I don't understand, there is nobody to go to."[65]

Gladstone had written at once to Acton on the death "of the great and dear Professor." He expressed "astonishment that (if Wemyss Reid speaks the truth) you had prompted him to desire me to write something in the Speaker. . . . And this without any time to learn from you whether, and how far and why you meant it. . . . But (if there be truth in Wemyss Reid) you have brought it upon yourself."[66]

Gladstone wrote two articles for the *Speaker* (edited by Reid, a shared friend and prominent Liberal), both moving and light-hearted, based upon his "friendship over forty-five years." He described how he had "walked seven miles with the eighty-seven year old Döllinger across the hill which separates the Tegernsee from the next valley to the eastward," and how, when Döllinger had sleepless nights, he found an antidote by "memorising the three first books of the Odyssey." He noted Döllinger's spiritual bonds with Pusey and Newman. "In the true sense of that term more horribly abused than any other, [Döllinger] was a free thinker absolutely without a theological prejudice, properly so called." No one was more qualified to write his life than Lord Acton, and it "would be a fraud upon mankind" if the story of such a life was not rightly told. Later, reviewing Döllinger's posthumously published *Academi-*

cal Addresses, Gladstone singled out "The Jews in Europe," written in the late 1880s. Prophetically (as it might seem more than a hundred years later), he noted that it had originated "at a time when the anti-semitic movement raged in Germany, and evidently with the purpose of making it ashamed of itself." Döllinger "knew, as other men did not, the almost incredible sufferings of that race which dishonour Europe much as the sufferings of Ireland have dishonoured England; and his historic conscience and sense of justice were offended by the threatened infliction of new injuries."[67]

In a later exchange, Gladstone wrote to accept Acton's proposition that Döllinger's "attitude of mind was more historical than theological"; that after their first mainly theological conversation in 1845, Döllinger had told him in 1874 how much the Vatican decrees had caused him to "reperuse and retry the whole circle of his thought" away from post-Trentine Catholicism and that, finally, the Bonn conferences on Christian reunion of 1874–75 "appeared to show him nearly at the standing point of Anglican theology. I thought him more Liberal as a theologian than as a politician." Gladstone had earlier signified his intention of contributing towards a memorial "as an acknowledgment, not in any degree a liquidation of, what I owe to Dr. Döllinger, most of all perhaps for his conversation in 1845." Soon after Döllinger's death, Gladstone acquired in London, for fifty pounds, a portrait of him, which he offered to Acton "unless you prefer your living inward recollections."[68]

Lady Blennerhassett had been so close to Döllinger for twenty-five years that friends wrote to her expressing sympathy as though she were a member of his family. Among these tributes was one from an English friend, Henry Cadogan, who with Franz von Lenbach, the painter, had gone to see the dead Döllinger laid out in a little room next to his study, "not out of mere curiosity, but because I knew his face, always so spiritual, could only gain in grandeur by the quiet of death. He was lying, so peacefully and as it were unostentatiously . . . —his beautiful long thin hands clasping a wooden crucifix—his frail little body appeared to be just covered by his black cloak, and his neck and breast decked with the brilliant-coloured ribbons of his various orders. The head was inexpressively noble, and the action of death—in these few hours gentle—only threw his forehead and nose into higher relief—altogether the noblest sight I have ever seen." Like others, Cadogan noted "the great likeness with Dante" and also "in the lower lip and jaw with Savonarola—but without the narrow, fanatical look of the latter."[69]

Franz Xavier Kraus, the distinguished German priest-scholar, another of

Lady Blennerhassett's clerical friends and correspondents, was moved to write mournfully: "There he lies, as a corpse, but how much more seems to lie there, equally shattered and destroyed! Gone another bit of the nineteenth century world in the shape of its first and better half! How deeply I feel what this great man's loss means to you." And to his diary Kraus confided, "Next to Döllinger's there lies another, bigger corpse, which is that of our Catholic theology."[70]

Lady Blennerhassett's friendship with Döllinger survived his excommunication. Remaining a loyal Catholic, she was unable to follow him into his isolation from their Church. As a member of the laity, she was of course far less subject to the Church's sanctions, which Döllinger once described as "sweeties kept in reserve by the Curia for priests."[71] Her contacts with Döllinger were, if anything, closer in his last years. Their correspondence ceased, but there was no need for letters, because in 1885 she moved back to Munich with her three children to live in her mother's townhouse after the death of her father, the Count von Leyden. Economic circumstances enforced this breakup of the Blennerhassett London home. Sir Rowland Blennerhassett lost his Commons seat in 1880. It was cheaper to split up and for the children to be taught privately by their mother until they were old enough to be sent to boarding schools. Encouraged by her husband and Döllinger, her mentor, Charlotte Blennerhassett resolved to become a professional writer. The success of her first book, a monumental three-volume biography of Madame de Staël, subsequently translated into English and French, established her on this road.[72]

Lady Blennerhassett would have liked to write Döllinger's biography but would not enter into rivalry with Acton. She confined herself to commemorating her friend on the occasion of his hundredth birthday with some personal recollections, in which she stressed that the longing for Christian reunion had throughout his life marked his priesthood. His academic life had been dominated by polemics, owing to inauspicious circumstances of the times rather than to his choice; his adversaries changed, but never what he cared for most of all—truth.[73] Like Acton, she disapproved of Döllinger's all-too-tolerant acceptance of his Old Catholic following.

But Lady Blennerhassett's relations with Acton, too, cooled somewhat, because of Acton's growing closeness to Gladstone, "that despicable hypocrite," as she called him, reflecting the common Tory view.[74] Her first "distinctly negative impression," upon meeting him after her arrival in London in 1871, was later changed by his "seductive charm," but she came to distrust him on account of his "political and religious ambiguities," his "Anti-Germanism," and above all, his "divine mission"—his Irish policy—which caused his portrait as the "Friend of Ireland" to adorn the walls of thousands of peasant hovels. As a staunch Liberal, that party was Sir Rowland Blennerhassett's political home, as it was for most Irish Catholics, indebted to the Whigs for Catholic Emancipation. But Blennerhassett, too, became critical when Gladstone's Irish Land Acts limited the previously absolute power of the landowning class, to which Blennerhassett belonged. Whereas the big landlords were able to escape the negative side-effects of the long-overdue reforms, the Blennerhassetts, owning a medium-sized estate near Killarney, County Kerry, were facing economic ruin. A hundred of the Blennerhassett tenants refused to pay rents that had not been increased for half a century. The Blennerhassetts were thus caught between the growing agitation against the injustices of the traditional Irish system of land tenure and the concessions wrung from the Gladstone government in London. It gave way finally to the Irish Land League and terrorist outrages to grant the famous "Three Fs"—Fair Rent, Fixity of Tenure, and Free Sale.

On the eve of World War I, Lady Blennerhassett published a series of her personal recollections of Victorian England.[75] Writing as a German admirer as well as a critic of England, she mentioned how, in 1886, she was invited to the Villa Arco at Tegernsee. Gladstone would be there, as well as the two men she most admired, Acton and Döllinger. "It cost me a tremendous effort not to go." Acton, she knew, was rather bored by her type of liberal and emancipated views, but worse would be conservative Döllinger's presence, with his Anglophile views. "If one knew of any weakness in him, it was his partiality for the English in general, which sometimes, to one's tacit delight, deceived him over the merits of particular individuals: he regarded them all as equally charming."

Upon Döllinger's death, his nieces received numerous telegrams of condolence. There were large wreaths from the Arcos, the Empress Frederick, Gladstone, the Bavarian regent, the universities of Europe. Acton, still in Rome, wrote movingly to Marie: Jeanette Döllinger "has well understood the friendship you had for the Professor and that, with reason, it should not be confounded with mine. It was all the more precious for that, and you alone perhaps may say to yourself that you have done nothing but good to him in the solemn decline of his life."[76]

On the controversial question of Friedrich's administering the Sacrament for the Dying to Döllinger, Acton wrote that if he had regained consciousness, they would have asked him whether he wanted to die in the faith in which he had been raised and he would have said simply and without entering into discussions what he wanted. Döllinger told Acton some time before that he was counting on Friedrich to come to him in the hour of his death. It was said that they had not been so close lately. Acton knew nothing of that, but he had noted that Döllinger had drawn away further from Rome. He had looked back on his excommunication as "a misfortune for religion . . . though a deliverance for himself."[77] Döllinger would not perhaps have refused to receive Communion from a Roman Catholic priest. But the studies and meditations of these last years had deepened his separation. Acton believed that the Professor would have accepted Communion from a Greek-Orthodox priest or even, under certain conditions, from an Anglican. He would certainly have disapproved of a civil funeral.

Friedrich, in his biography of Döllinger, recorded that he had been called by the two nieces, Jeanette and Elise, on the morning of 10 January and had found Döllinger already unconscious and death evidently approaching. In agreement with the two women, and in accordance with Döllinger's wish earlier expressed, Friedrich administered the Sacrament for the Dying and then, having notified friends living in the neighbourhood, awaited Döllinger's death. All those present in the room joined in saying a prayer. Death occurred at a quarter to nine in the evening. Friedrich also conducted the funeral service, which took place on the afternoon of 13 January with great participation of the people of Munich, but without Roman Catholic clergy. Döllinger was laid to rest in a grave next to his parents and brothers and sisters in Munich's Southern Cemetery. An Old Catholic service of commemoration was held on 16 January.

There was some attempt to reclaim Döllinger for the Catholic Church. When he fell ill, the parish priest of the St. Ludwig Church offered his services but was told he was not wanted. Friedrich noted that Jeanette had exclaimed: "Now they come after having ill-treated him in every possible manner throughout all these years. They shall not be allowed near him." Various rumours circulated in the press, for example, that close Catholic friends had been forcibly prevented from visiting the dying Döllinger. One Catholic paper in Mainz wrote that Döllinger had to share "the sad fate of all heresiarchs, to die without spiritual assistance, and that he was found dead in the lavatory." The Munich director of police, Ludwig August von Müller, was told that the Old Catholic Bishop Reinkens and Professor Reusch planned to lead an Old Catholic funeral procession through the city, and went to Professor Berchtold to prevent it. All these reports, however, turned out to be without foundation.[78]

Everybody expected Acton to write the Professor's biography. Acton was attracted by the idea, but he was not interested in an "official biography" and declined the offer politely in a letter to Jeanette Döllinger. A long-winded work was not in his line, he wrote. "I was neither an Ultramontane nor an Old Catholic, but a Catholic liberal. That is a different point of view in regard to many issues where political and moral motivations matter more than pure theology." People in Munich, Bonn, and Rome would say that Acton was not an initiate, not even a confidant. The biography should be written by someone who, having been an Ultramontane like Döllinger and, like him, an Old Catholic, "knew and felt" the reasons for both, but not by that person among his friends who was neither one nor the other.[79]

So the choice eventually had to be Friedrich, although he was remote from Döllinger on both the human and spiritual levels and lacked the imagination to understand him. Books like those of Johannes Nepomuk Huber and Friedrich, Acton had written to Döllinger in the course of their controversy, "seem to me weapons borrowed from the enemy's arsenal," meaning that the enemies of the Ultramontanes were sometimes not much better than what they attacked.[80] For all that, Friedrich's three-volume biography (1899–1901) remains the only full treatment of Döllinger's life and covers at least most of the relevant facts. Privately Acton got down to collecting voluminous notes, making excerpts from some eight hundred books, as he told Gladstone in October 1891: "I propose so to write the life of the Professor as to give a substantive chapter dealing with each of the matters that engaged him."[81] But after having spent two years on the project, he gave it up.

Acton's essay "Döllinger's Historical Work" gave an indication of what he might have produced and how much indeed they were alike:

> Everybody has felt that his power was out of proportion to his work, and that he knew too much to write. It was so much better to hear him than to read all his books, that the memory of what he was will pass away with the children whom he loved. . . . Throughout the measureless distance which he traversed, his movement was against his wishes, in pursuit of no purpose, in obedience to no theory, under no attraction but historical research alone. It was given to him to form his philosophy of history on the largest induction ever available to man; and whilst he owed more to divinity than any other historian, he owed more to history than any other divine.[82]

It was typical of the clinical approach of the author to his subject that he should write forty pages without giving so much as a hint that he had stood side by

side with Döllinger in the greatest battle of their lives during the Vatican Council. But the "Roman interlude" in Döllinger's life was, strictly speaking, outside
Acton's theme: the evaluation of Döllinger the historian.

In August of that year, 1890, Cardinal Newman died, and the following April
there was another death, that of Lord Granville, which cut deep into Acton's
own life. And it was another funeral from which Acton stayed away, confess-
ing later that he was ashamed of himself for having missed it. "Your best friend
and mine," he called Granville in the cable sent to Gladstone from Cannes.[83] It
does not sound quite sincere, but Acton had that extraordinary and cool objec-
tivity that enabled him to abstract his own feelings for his stepfather. He knew
the Gladstone-Granville relationship from the inside and wrote to Gladstone:
"There was an admirable fitness in your union; and I had been able to watch
how it became closer and easier, in spite of so much to separate you, in mental
habits, in early affinities and even in the form of fundamental convictions, since
he came home from your first budget, overwhelmed, thirty-eight years ago. I
saw all the connexions which had their root in social habit fade before the one
which took its rise from public life and proved more firm and more enduring
than the rest."[84] What separated Gladstone and Granville was hardly less than
the gulf between the young Acton and his mother's second husband.

Acton had seen little of his stepfather after Granville's second marriage, which
he and Marie attended. Holding the office of the Lord Warden of the Cinque
Ports and not having a country place of his own, Granville lived, with his young
family, in the windblown residence accompanying that office, Walmer Castle,
on the Kent coast. The new Lady Granville was deeply hurt when Acton's letters to Mary Gladstone were published and revealed him as thinking little of
her husband's capabilities and regard for Gladstone. The second Lady Granville
was jealous, too, of her husband's abiding devotion both to his first wife and to
Acton's daughter Mamy because she reminded Granville of Marie.[85]

Acton had known Granville for forty years, and his own early and tense links
with his stepfather were certainly not improved by the uncomfortable relationship he knew existed between Granville and his hero, Gladstone. Lord Granville had wielded great influence as a politician, always at the top of the Liberal
governments. His tenure of the Foreign Office from 1870 to 1874 and 1880 to
1885, however, did not place him among the great statesmen of the century.
What Acton thought of him was expressed in a letter to his friend and one-
time fellow-editor Thomas Wetherell, whom he had helped into the position
of Granville's private secretary. "He has very little real knowledge of foreign

countries. . . . [He] does not understand the point about the Pope, and has not got the landlord prejudices because his wealth is underground. [This referred to the Granville family's investments — ultimately disastrous — in iron foundries and coal mines.] . . . He has a habit of discussing most men in the category of bores or nonentities, chiefly because they don't amuse him at dinner. If a man be called droll, he is safe."[86] It was a harsh, if perhaps understandable, judgement on the man who, the fatherless schoolboy had felt, had married and stolen his mother.

19

GLADSTONE'S FRIEND AND

THE QUEEN'S LORD

From his Riviera and Bavarian hideouts, Acton remained in close touch with affairs at home. He regularly read the main British newspapers, also *Le temps* and German newspapers, as well as weeklies and monthlies. A stream of visiting British friends kept him au courant about events and the latest political gossip. He also conducted a voluminous correspondence with the Gladstones.

Acton's friendship with Gladstone, which dated back to 1859, had always been grounded in wide-ranging interests—religious, intellectual, and political. In the earlier years Gladstone had virtually begged Acton to become more involved in English public life. When he proposed Acton for the peerage, Gladstone was motivated, at least in part, by his desire to see his friend become active in the House of Lords. But this was not to be. Parliament bored Acton, and he soon came to believe that he was too much alone in his views to be effective there. Then, largely for familial and financial reasons, Acton chose to spend much, if not most, of his time in the South of France and in Germany. But the fundamental reality was that up to the great divide in Acton's life, the Vatican Council, his sights were set on making his mark as an intellectual in the Catholic world. Although Gladstone regularly pleaded with the "exile" to return home, their relationship was not then essentially political. In the 1880s and 1890s, how-ever, Acton found himself more directly involved in Gladstone's political world and much closer to Gladstone personally and to his family. Eventually, he also found himself in pursuit of office, for he needed an income.

Acton's perception of this experience, revealed especially in his letters to his daughters, was that Gladstone came to depend upon him more and more, that he was a central (if not the determining) influence at certain points in the devel-opment of Gladstone's Home Rule policy. On occasion Acton saw himself as a pivotal figure in several areas of Liberal policy development and in behind-the-scenes political maneuverings. That Acton relished seeing himself at the center of power is underscored time and again in his letters. Regardless of what schol-ars say about the extent to which Acton influenced Gladstone on Irish Home Rule or other issues, this friendship profoundly shaped Acton's perception of himself during these years.

It was at Cannes in May 1882 that Acton heard the awful news of the assas-sination in Phoenix Park, Dublin, of Lord Frederick Cavendish, chief secretary of the Lord Lieutenant of Ireland, and his permanent undersecretary, Thomas Burke. It was a devastating family tragedy for the Gladstones, for Lady Fred-erick Cavendish was the beautiful and beloved Lucy, the favorite niece of both Gladstones. Moreover, it had been Mr. Gladstone who had appointed Caven-dish to the Irish post.[1] Knowing that Gladstone would blame himself, Acton immediately wired Mary Gladstone: "Do not let him lose confidence in him-self." He then wrote immediately: "It must have been a dreadful blow in your home." He also feared, rightly, that those in the cabinet who had so reluctantly supported Gladstone's "heroic policy" for the pacification and self-government of Ireland "will either forsake him or urge him to forsake his own ideal lines. . . . It seems to me that much ground must inevitably be lost, and that the true moral of this catastrophe can never be made visible to the average English-man."[2]

Gladstone's introduction of Home Rule for Ireland, and, overseas, the rising of the Mahdi, the death of General Charles George Gordon, and the fall of Khartoum dominated the eclipse of his second administration in 1885, and his short-lived third government, in 1886, perhaps the stormiest two years in his life. When his retirement was discussed in the family, Acton advised against it, "because nobody stands as you do between the old order of things and the new."[3]

Early in 1886, the Home Rule debate began in Westminster. Acton saw it as

Gladstone's "great and perhaps final crisis," hoping that he would view it from the position of the Irish, and with their historic eyes. "I know neither how to resist the claim of the Irish nation to govern themselves nor even their claim to possess the land," he wrote to Mary Gladstone.[4]

But the Home Rule Bill was defeated and followed by the fall of the government. The exhausted Gladstone went to Tegernsee, in the late summer of 1886, to recuperate. Only his second daughter, Helen, accompanied him. More than ever he needed the haven of peace and trust that the philosophic onlooker and friend was able to provide. Acton instituted a ban on all politics, leading Gladstone "in the direction of little French novels from his library,"[5] and, as Acton put it in a letter to John Morley, "away from the tragedy of existence."[6] Gladstone entered in his diary: "Conversations daily with Lord Acton and the professor," and "walk with Dr. D. and Lord A. It is wonderful to hear them pour forth their learning in two great streams."[7] Their daily walks were something of a trial for the two British visitors, used to taking their exercises briskly. But Lady Acton liked walking slowly; her sister, the large "Tini" Arco, even wore a long dress with a train. Dr. Döllinger walked slowly, too, and he had the additional habit of stopping altogether when he spoke. So progress was extremely slow.

Upon Gladstone's return to England, his need for Acton's counsel seemed to increase. "Come early to England—& stay long. We will try what we can to bind you," he wrote in January 1887. And three months later: "I do not like to let too long a time elapse without some note of intercourse, even though that season approaches, which brings you back to the shores of your country. Were you here, I should have much to say, on many things." A week later: "When do you *repatriate?*"[8]

There was worse trouble in store for Gladstone following the break in 1890 with the Irish nationalist leader, Charles Parnell. When Parnell was cited as co-respondent in a divorce action brought by Captain O'Shea against his wife, Acton, watching matters from abroad, thought at first, wrongly, that too much was made of this scandal in Anglo-Irish politics. He would not send another morale-boosting telegram to her father as after the Phoenix Park murders, he wrote to Mrs. Drew, because he felt that in the case of Parnell, Gladstone had made no miscalculation and had resisted calls to set himself up as a judge of Parnell's moral fitness to be a leader of the Irish party.[9] But Acton underestimated the effect that the Parnell affair would have on the British Liberal electorate, as he admitted in a later letter to Gladstone.[10]

If the election, in the summer of 1892, had taken place before the Parnell case came to court, Gladstone would probably have had the hoped-for landslide victory for his fourth government. As it was, the Liberals won with a majority of barely forty seats, which included the Irish nationalist vote. Gladstone's own majority in Midlothian fell from five thousand to less than seven hundred. Liberal support was virtually reduced to England's Celtic fringe. The "Grand Old Man" was eighty-three, handicapped by deafness, with a progressive worsening of the cataract in one eye, and frequently indisposed, an increasing liability to his colleagues. It was the sad beginning of his final chapter.

Acton, in Munich, had sensed the atmosphere at the centre of Liberal politics. "As the plot thickens, it draws me strongly homewards," he wrote to his friend James Bryce as elections neared.[11] He arrived in England on 14 June, stayed with the Bryces, and helped Gladstone to draft the Liberal manifesto. In July he accompanied the Gladstones to Dalmeny, Lord Rosebery's seat near Edinburgh, convenient for Gladstone's Midlothian election campaign. Rosebery was, with John Morley, closest to the Liberal leader. He had Gladstone's personal confidence at a time when everybody was asking how much longer the Grand Old Man could hold on to power, and who was to succeed him.

A general jockeying for position was beginning in Gladstone's immediate circle. It was a fascinating spectacle for an historian. Until then, Acton had had no driving political ambitions of his own except for the the desire to see Liberalism triumph. He had advised against Gladstone's retirement and was anxious for the promised second attempt at Home Rule to succeed. He had used up his capital, needed money, and would have been glad for some employment in a diplomatic post. But he had read enough history to know how uncertain it was to need to depend on men of power. He also realized that the more Gladstone wanted his company and advice, the more Acton was deemed suspicious by the senior ministers.

The mood among the Liberal leaders was depressing, in contrast with the triumphant atmosphere of Gladstone's Midlothian victory of 1880. Gladstone's daughter Helen, writing to her sister Mary, noted that this second time it "had a feeling of such crushing finality about it, and a pathos simply beyond words and almost beyond thought with regard to Father." The daughters felt the stress much more than their old father. They had to join in the artificial gaiety of election campaigning, pretending to be sure of victory, smiling and waving to the crowds of faithful followers. They needed, Helen felt, someone to give them moral support, but Sir Algernon West and Acton could not be with them all the time. Acton copied Helen Gladstone's letter to send to his own daughters.[12] These letters to Annie and Mamy, who were with their mother at Tegernsee, and to his son Richard, then in his final year at Magdalen College, Oxford, served Acton increasingly as a kind of diary of tense developments. When Acton returned to Dalmeny, the election results of the counties were beginning to come in. Helen continued her account to Mary: "Words can't say what a help in every possible way Lord A. has been and is—such very very strong sympathy, and making one feel such absolute confidence in him. . . . Every person in the house is continually getting hold of him for private interviews, so, what a blessing he is so entirely trustworthy." [13]

After the depressing election results were out, in the second half of July, the Gladstones went to the Highlands to stay at the house of the faithful George Armitstead, in the hope that the clear air would improve Gladstone's health. There he began to form his cabinet. Acton came, too. Gladstone was now suddenly realizing the extent of the Rosebery problem, which had become important to Acton before the election. At that time Rosebery, the most intimate of Gladstone's friends, was turning away from him. At one point Gladstone had asked Acton, "Do you really think him fit to be Premier?" and Acton had bluntly said that nobody else was.[14] Gladstone had shown Rosebery, as far as he could remember, a cabinet list with Rosebery's name as foreign secretary on it. Rosebery had made no objection but had not formally accepted it either. Thus Gladstone felt committed yet knew from Acton's conversation with Rosebery that he was playing for higher stakes. Being more defence- and empire-minded than other Gladstonians, Rosebery wanted control of foreign affairs. This desire was to open up the possibility of future divergences, which actually caused the collapse of Gladstone's fourth government.

In sudden doubt that Rosebery might thwart his strategy, Gladstone asked Acton to write to him to find out his intentions. No answer came for ten days. Acton was asked to write again, but then Gladstone, beside himself with worry, took the letter, wanting to write himself instead. "I drop without scruple the part of an impartial . . . and comparatively discreet observer," Acton wrote to Rosebery, "to tell you what I think: you cannot mean to leave suspended and unanswered such an offer as Gladstone made to you, or to deposit a quicksand under the foundation while he is building up his cabinet. The second course cannot be laid before the first. . . . The future of the party as well as its immediate fate, and the last scene of a prodigious drama depend mainly on your reply." [15]

Rosebery, continuing to pretend indifference, replied to Acton that Gladstone had not made him an offer of any kind at Dalmeny and that there had been no commitment on his part. To Gladstone on 31 July he sent a refusal, saying that he wished to retire and proposing Earl Kimberley as foreign secretary.[16] Acton recognized the danger of his own position, "appearing as a busybody and doing more harm than good." He wrote to Bryce, who had been undersecretary for foreign affairs under Rosebery in the last Gladstone government, saying that Morley thought he himself had intervened too much with Rosebery. "All that one can say has been said to R. I know not yet with what effect. Having no authority from you, I have always spoken only in a general way on the assumption that, if he comes in, you would not accept your ancient office. Every list places you elsewhere. If you see John Morley say as little as possible about R. and what we have said about that affair."[17]

Acton was in a dilemma. No one liked his intimacy with Gladstone, but he had failed in his mission and feared that people would say he had purposely mismanaged it because getting rid of one peer might make room for himself in the cabinet. To his son, Richard, he wrote that Gladstone was not well: "He looked very haggard, and said R[osebery] had made him suffer tortures. . . . I saw signs of fever, and he looked very like the pictures of the Ancient Mariner. I must add that there was not a word of reproach for my failure, and he ended by saying that Morley and I were the only men he entirely trusted."[18]

It was only on 15 August, when Gladstone had just arrived at Osborne House on the Isle of Wight for his royal audience as prime minister, that he received Rosebery's telegram in which he consented to join the government. What had caused the change? Rosebery was a man of strange moods. Acton—writing to Richard from Rosebery's house, the Durdans, near Epsom, where he was staying a week later—explained that Morley had almost quarrelled with him because of his intervention to get Rosebery to accept office. "It might have spread to Rosebery himself. . . . He attributes to me the efforts Gladstone made to secure him and is grateful now." Rosebery showed him the beautiful, immensely valuable crucifix hanging in his bedroom. It had been carved by Michelangelo on the order of Pope Pius III, from some ebony and ivory presented to him by missionaries. Rosebery told Acton that the Pope was more important to Britain than the Kingdom of Italy. "Possibly this is one of the reasons of his newborn intimacy with me," Acton wrote to his son.[19]

But Acton's mere presence close to Gladstone during the last weeks caused bad blood all round. Acton had to tell the touchy Morley, who wanted to be foreign secretary, that this was not to be and thus caused even more resentment. Edward Hamilton, Gladstone's former private secretary, talked to Sir William Harcourt, who was to be the new chancellor of the exchequer, of "the meddlesomeness of Lord Acton."[20] Regarding Rosebery's claim to the Gladstone succession, Acton said to his son that his only doubt was that people said he prepared his speeches with great care and could not make them off the cuff. "He answered at once, quite warmly, that he never prepared at all. Then, I said, you had better consider the question settled."[21]

To his daughter Mamy, Acton wrote: "You are clever enough to understand that people will say that I had an unparalleled opportunity of earwigging the coming Prime Minister, and poisoning his mind; and those who are disappointed will lay the blame on my innocent shoulders. At this moment a quarrel rages with Morley and perhaps with Rosebery; and I have had to request Gladstone not to discuss the Rosebery problem whilst Morley and I are together at dinner tomorrow. This makes it difficult for me to take office myself."[22]

From Braemar, Gladstone, thinking of a cabinet post for Acton, had written to Morley, the incoming chief secretary for Ireland: "Acton is here with me. In some way he ought to be brought into the circle."[23] No reply came, but the fury Morley felt at the mere suggestion is shown in a comment elsewhere. After a London dinner party, Sir William Harcourt recorded that Morley had told him that he could hardly contain himself listening to Gladstone telling Acton "all his inmost thoughts on men and things."[24] The previous evening, when most of the incoming ministers were also present, Acton and Lord Spencer (First Lord of the Admiralty) had had a wide-ranging conversation that Acton mentioned to Mamy, but evidently without realizing the effect it had had on Spencer, who, the following day, went to Gladstone to say that Acton was impossible as a member of the cabinet because he was politically unknown and had no official experience.[25]

There was mention of a cabinet post for Acton as Chancellor of the Duchy of Lancaster. But this position involved the dispensing of Anglican benefices and was not suitable for a Roman Catholic. And with one member of that faith, Lord Ripon, already in the cabinet, Gladstone was not in a position to risk further affront to English Protestant opinion, which had been upset by the Irish policy. For a number of ministers it was the decisive point, quite apart from the consideration that Gladstone would have been favouring a private friend. This was the feeling in particular of Sir William Harcourt, the rising strong man in the House of Commons, who represented Protestant opposition.

Acton's success in bringing Rosebery "into the circle" had in fact blocked his own chance. "You were kind enough to intimate," he wrote to Gladstone as late as 23 August, "that, if one of the Five Peers had been out of the way, you would have regarded me as standing next to the Five as one who might possibly be made useful. I hope you will still look upon me as occupying that rank, if changes should occur."[26] The letter caused Acton to be regarded as grovelling for office. The five peers he referred to were Lord Herschell, the Lord Chancellor; Earl Kimberley, the President of the Council and Indian secretary; Earl Spencer, First Lord of the Admiralty; Lord Ripon, colonial secretary; and Lord Rosebery, foreign secretary. Acton's financial state was such that any salaried position would be better than none. So he grasped the straws held out to him, only too aware of Gladstone's difficulties in fitting him in anywhere.

Rightly or wrongly, Acton viewed John Morley, the supposed friend and an admirer of Acton's mind, as the principal critic in this matter. But Morley's admiration indeed seemed to be laced with paranoiac jealousy: "Morley frightfully jealous of my influence with G."[27] Morley suspected intrigues. Acton, for his part, resented the low motives and personal ambitions that Morley seemed to impute to him and doubted Morley's basic devotion to Gladstone. In 1886 he had written to Mary Drew: "John Morley's importance is excessive. No, I do not trust him. I think that he has not the serene superiority needed. He is, at bottom, a fanatic, full of Jacobinical possibilities, and therefore, as I think, without ethical basis. Sooner or later I shall expect a fiasco, or at least a breach."[28]

In early 1893 Acton called Morley "much my enemy during the last summer," although he had written to Mamy: "You will like John Morley. He is not, in the supreme sense of the term, quite a gentleman. There are some refinements he is not prepared for. He was very angry with me for interfering in the making of the Ministry, because he has a careful game to play, to find himself, with Rosebery, ruling the party in the time to come."[29] This antagonism between them remained till Gladstone's death, when the discussion over his biography brought them together and the work on that and his reading of Acton's letters to Gladstone gave Morley cause for self-examination. He discovered for the first time how large a part Acton had played in Gladstone's life, and told him that he was rather ashamed of his opposition to him and his influence in 1892.[30] At the time, however, there was a basic clash between these two opposed political types. "He sees nothing in politics but higher expediency and no large principles. As there are, for him, no rights of God, there are no rights of man—the consequence, on earth, of obligations in Heaven."[31]

Morley was also prejudiced against Roman Catholicism. He told Acton that his stepdaughter had become a Catholic very much against his wish. Although he had said nothing and assured her that it would make no difference, he felt that "there is an enemy in my house, and I always see the Pope's eye peeping through the key hole."[32] It was typical of the anti-Catholic feeling prevalent at the time.

In the end there was no cabinet post for Acton. Gladstone did not have the heart to tell him; Sir Algernon West was dispatched to do it and, finding him at the Senior United Services Club, broke it to him "as well as I could." Acton "took it beautifully."[33] When Mary Drew commiserated with Acton, he told her that his main concern was not political power but the "very sordid reason" of an income that would have been satisfactory for his family. The sale or letting of Aldenham for which he had given instructions depended on that. "You must not think of me as a person deserving sympathy on account of claims unacknowledged, any more than of services unrewarded. . . . Nor had I the slightest right to dream dreams, but what your father intimated once to me at a time when I was trying to fix the errant Rosebery." He evidently felt some shame about his place in power politics. "If I had been more prescient instead of thinking selfishly of myself, I would have tried to get a private secretaryship for my son, as it would be a good introduction to the science of affairs."[34] Regardless, his one serious attempt to obtain office had failed.

It was not the least of many ironies in Acton's life that, in the end, it was to Rosebery, Gladstone's successor, he owed a congenial reward—the Cambridge appointment he had never sought. Whether a ministerial post or indeed the ambassadorship dangled before him would have brought greater fulfilment and happiness may be doubted. Acton was a sower of ideas; the harvesting needed other hands.

Acton had travelled down to Windsor with the old prime minister and his wife for the customary kissing of hands, his fourth in twelve years, on 15 August 1892. Gladstone's audience with the Queen had been as anticipated, "like Marie Antoinette meeting the executioner."[35] Queen Victoria found it altogether difficult to accept "this iniquitous government."[36] She regretted that, as she told Lord Lansdowne, according to the rule of constitutional monarchy the majority had decided against the government she approved of and replaced it with another with only a small majority.[37] She had her revenge by announcing Lord Salisbury's resignation as prime minister "with much regret."[38] Now she had to entrust the Empire "to the shaking hand of an old, wild and incomprehensible man of eighty-two and a half," her only consolation being that "England is sound" and that the new government could not last long.[39] Later, when Acton was Lord-in-Waiting, he confided to Annie: "She treats him like a caretaker waiting for the lawful owner."[40] On the day of the audience, each of them using a cane, she said to him: "You and I, Mr. Gladstone, are more lame than we were." In her journal she wrote: "I found him greatly altered and changed, not only much aged and walking rather bent with a stick, but altogether; his face shrunk, deadly pale, with a weird look in his eyes, a feeble expression about the mouth, and the voice altered." Discussing the Queen's Household officers, Gladstone mentioned Acton as a possibility, and she noted that she thought Lord Granville's stepson "a very clever charming person."[41]

Acton's court appointment in 1892 was, on the face of it, a meagre consolation prize for his behind-the-scenes endeavours on Gladstone's behalf, but there was a political consideration linked with it all the same. The cosmopolitan Acton might, it was hoped, exert his charms on the old Queen, as the late Lord Beaconsfield had done so successfully a little more than a decade ago, and convert her, if not to Irish Home Rule or to Liberalism, at least to a more kindly view of what was to her an unwelcome new government. At first it was proposed that Acton should play the role of the Queen's *charmeur* as a Captain of the Yeoman of the Guard, which would have obliged him, portly as he was, to make his appearance at Court in Gilbert-and-Sullivan-style uniform, with plumed brass helmet. Because Acton's peerage was not particularly elevated and he had not distinguished himself in Parliament, this function was considered fitting. And because he needed the money, he was ready to "accept it, cheerfully and gratefully," as he wrote to Gladstone in a pathetic letter, thanking him "for keeping me in your thoughts, and offering me the appointment which West and Morley tell me of. . . . Rosebery assures me that you would prefer it, and that there is no other opening to employment at present."[42]

The incongruous position was then withdrawn at the wish of the Queen, who, having already agreed to it, had changed her mind. In a remark clearly intended for the prime minister, Queen Victoria told Sir Henry Ponsonby that she would be very glad if Lord Acton was appointed to a place where she would "encounter him and be able to talk to him. Lord-in-Waiting is the only one; it is really very important, as much as chamberlain."[43] The change of the royal mind was brought about by Acton's staunch friend, the Empress Frederick (the Queen's eldest daughter, Victoria), who was as much in favour of Gladstone as the Queen was against him. From Bad Homburg she wrote to her "beloved Mama" that she should keep in mind for a position in her household "Lord Granville's stepson, Lord Acton. He is such a cultured man and in spite of being terribly shy so agreeable! He is so highly respected and so much thought of—in France, Germany and Italy—that I fancy he would be a most valuable acquisition! He has a nice wife whom I know, and charming daughters. What a resource it would be to have so cultured, I may say, learned a person at Court. They are very poor and from that point of view I should be very glad for them." [44]

Answering Sir Henry Ponsonby, Gladstone corrected the Empress's observation: Acton "is not at all shy, he is as modest as he is learned and requires drawing out. He knows much of the world without living in it and has a notable insight into character." [45] To Acton he wrote: "If you agree, it is a costly compliment, but it is a compliment from the Queen herself. You would I have no doubt have a term at Windsor (a month?) and I think would not dislike it." [46] Acton's appointment was tied to government duties as "junior whip" in the House of Lords, seconding John Morley, the secretary of state for Ireland, on the Home Rule Bill. It drew a small government salary that allowed him to put off the sale of Aldenham. When, three years later, he was appointed Cambridge Regius Professor of Modern History, he was able to shelve that plan for good. Aldenham thus remained in the hands of the Acton family until after World War II.

Mary Drew, referring to Acton's rotund shape, wrote that his appointment would give a "totally new aspect" to the term "Court Circular." Mrs. Drew, who had given Acton secret papers concerning the details of Gladstone's disastrous relationship with the Queen, wrote to Acton that "the PM trusts your judgement absolutely." [47] But realistically Acton had not much confidence that he would effect any change in the Queen's political attitude. To Annie he wrote: "It is beginning to be whispered that the History of England will have to be written from the correspondence between the Queen's own courtier and certain privileged young ladies away in the Alps." [48] And again, "I am expected of having powers to charm ladies of a certain rank and age. The funny thing that Mr. G. insists upon is not that I know certain books and foreign countries and can talk small talk—in other tongues—but that since the secession of Argyll I am left *le plus grand seigneur du parti liberal*. On the strength of this I shall at once order a new suit of clothes." [49]

At Osborne, on 30 November, Queen Victoria recorded in her private journal: "Lord Acton, stepson of Ld. Granville, a very clever, well-informed man, one of the new Lords-in-Waiting, was presented by Sir Henry Ponsonby."[50] It was not a difficult office, Acton told Bryce; until one dined with the Queen there was nothing to do but "to cajole your friends, the maids-of-honour."[51] One of them instructed the new Lord-in-Waiting in the finer points of etiquette: "Avoid three things: Never say it is cold. Never say that anyone is old (for then she says: 'No, I think you must be wrong. We were born in the same year'). Never object to a marriage of cousins." All this was faithfully reported to the family at Tegernsee, avid for news of English royalty. Acton also told the family that the Queen had said he was "the only man who can go to foreign courts and condole with my relations in their own languages, in case of funerals," and he added: "Expect to hear of my being sent wherever there is a gap in the Gotha." This letter contained some news that was more important to him: "I have this day received some public money, for the first time in my life, for my office."[52]

Acton got on well with the Queen, as her occasional references to him in her journal show: "Talked for some time to Lord Acton whom I found most agreeable, sensible and clever." A year later: "Lord Acton is a charming person with the most pleasant manners (rather foreign), very like his mother, the late Lady Granville (a widow, daughter of the last duc de Dalberg) who was so agreeable and clever."[53] In December 1892 Acton had his first "turn" at Windsor, spending many days in the library to the amusement of everybody, especially the Queen, he told his fellow-scholar James Bryce. But when one day he was looking for a passage in Schiller and could find no copy, he judged: "This is not an intellectual place" and "I have found much good literature, but a very bad library."[54]

Dinners with the Queen were "slightly stiff, on the whole there was no hitch or awkwardness," he told his girls, except once or twice when he directed royal dinner guests to the wrong places. He jested with her on the last day of his December turn of duty: "Ma'm, you really ought to send me away." The Queen often discussed the Catholic religion with him; they had long conversations about Germany, the Emperor, the two Empresses, the House of Wittelsbach, Lord Granville, Carlyle, and Tennyson. "I saw her trying to approach the topics she wanted to discuss (the ministry and the [Poet] Laureate [to succeed Tennyson]), but I have escaped, and she must see, now, that I mean to escape until challenged distinctly. But I make her laugh immoderately."[55]

The death of Tennyson, on 6 October 1892, was one of the events that tolled the death knell of the Victorian age. Acton went to Westminster Abbey for the funeral; an immense gathering was there, representing all the great and good in British society. The Balaclava veterans of the Charge of the Light Brigade, whom Tennyson had immortalized, formed the guard of honour. Verses from "In Memoriam" were read by distinguished mourners, and "Crossing the Bar" and "Silent Voices," set to music by Lady Tennyson, were sung. "The dead poet lay with the British flag over him," Acton recorded the scene for Mamy, "surrounded by some of the greatest living Englishmen, not one of whom will be buried with so much pomp and feeling. . . . When he was laid in his grave I was just standing under the bust of Longfellow with Milton facing me. The whole ceremony was even too splendid. Perhaps there was an undercurrent of anti-Gladstonianism in it."[56]

The Tennysons had stayed for two days with the Actons at Tegernsee in the summer of 1880. The poet was widely known in Germany, where *Enoch Arden* was a great success. Tennyson was popular with Acton's wife and children because of his generous manner and because

> he told us lots of good stories. . . . There was a shell to crack, but I got at the kernel, chiefly at night, when everybody was in bed. His want of reality, his habit of walking on the clouds, the airiness of his metaphysics, the indefiniteness of his knowledge, his neglect of transitions, the looseness of his political reasonings — all this made an alarming *cheval de frise* [set of obstacles].
>
> But then there was a gladness — not quickness — in taking a joke or story . . . a grave groping for religious certainty, and a generosity in the treatment of rivals — of Browning and Swinburne, though not of Taylor.[57]

Still, after the "lofty heights that surround Tennyson even when he butters toast," there followed an earthly search for a successor.[58]

Acton was involved in the consultations, enjoying, as he wrote to his daughter Mamy, "my first appearance as leader of opinion in poetry."[59] The Prince of Wales led the lobby for Algernon Charles Swinburne, but Gladstone had reservations, which Acton shared on account of the sensuality of Swinburne's poetry. Gladstone found the *Poems and Ballads* (1866) "both bad and terrible." He asked Acton if they had been revised or dropped in a later edition. "If they have is it a reparation. Wordsworth and Tennyson have made the place great. They have also made it extremely clean."[60]

Acton replied at once that the objectionable poems had not been dropped in the 1871 edition, the fourth, which he possessed. "I am forced to testify against him, whilst I am dazzled by the splendour of his better passages, and believe that no rival approaches him as a writer of verse."[61] Acton's objections to Swinburne were not based on morals alone. Worse were Swinburne's opinions on tyrannicide in his later work *Notes by an English Republican,* and Acton regarded it "an offence to the Queen to select for the special honour of being her Poet the one English poet who is ostentatiously vicious, and who proclaims himself a Republican; as well as an offence to Her Majesty's Imperial Brother and ally to place in office, involving appearance at Court, a man, who clamours to have him murdered, and whose plea for Tyrannicide is not remote, or obscure or unnoticed . . . , but is only two years old, is almost the last thing he published, and has had the attention of Parliament drawn to it, within recent memory."[62] Gladstone nevertheless tried hard for Swinburne. Acton warned him again, pointing out that Tennyson had made very little money until he became Laureate, after which he became rapidly rich—he left a fortune of more than £57,000—and the appointment of Swinburne "would stimulate the circulation of the offending volume (and condone it)."[63] That decided Gladstone on the absolute "impossibility" of Swinburne. "Mr. G. is in great trouble about his Laurel Crown," Acton told his daughter Annie. "The first poet in England is Swinburne. But he is a man of the worst character."[64]

Acton came up with another suggestion, John Ruskin, who eventually had to be ruled out on account of his deteriorating mental condition. William Morris, "shopkeeper and socialist, in the opinion of many people the next best," as Acton described him to Annie, was the next candidate to be considered and was particularly favored by James Bryce.[65] Bryce reported that Morris had declined his private approach by writing, "I am a sincere republican, and therefore could not accept a post which would give me even the appearance of serving a court for complaisance sake."[66] Others tried and dropped were William Watson, Lewis Morris, and Sir Theodore Martin, author of the five-volume *Life of the Prince Consort,* also of ballads and translations of Heine and Goethe, but the Queen did not seem to have backed him.

There were voices in favour of abolishing the royal office altogether. Others, such as Rosebery, Morley, and Augustine Birrell, the essayist and politician, wanted merely to leave it vacant.[67] Acton disagreed with this view, "as if nobody could wear the armour of Achilles"; it would merely leave "the matter in the hands of another Prime Minister, after an interval of intrigue."[68] This is roughly what happened. Gladstone told the Queen on 4 November that he "did not at present see his way to making an unexceptionable recommendation." This advice was backed by Bryce's memorandum, according to which "there is precedent for declining to abolish [the office], but letting it remain vacant until there arises a poet conspicuously worthy to fill it."[69] This vacancy was agreed to by the Queen. Rosebery, who succeeded Gladstone, made no appointment. His Tory successor, Lord Salisbury, appointed the Conservative Alfred Austin in 1896. Acton knew him from his Vatican Council days, when Austin was the Rome correspondent of the *London Standard* and secured a scoop for his paper, a copy of Newman's famous letter to Bishop Ullathorne deploring the activities of the "aggressive insolent faction" and pushing the Council in the direction of extreme Ultramontanism.[70]

This ended Acton's interlude of literary politics. He felt satisfied with the impression he was making at court. In the spring of 1893 he dined with the Queen almost every day. His small talk and "frequency of chaff" were well received. But it "gives me no hope of doing good."[71]

"Cellar excellent, kitchen less good," was the *bon viveur* Acton's opinion of the royal establishment at Sandringham, the Prince of Wales's residence. In July 1893 the King of Denmark, the Princess of Wales's father, Charles IX, came on a visit. "Bertie" was an excellent host, made everything easy and pleasant, but the household was decidedly lowbrow. "They say that the princess is too Danish, too anti-German to mix with the rest of the family, and there is much isolation if not actual friction. . . . As to the [Prince's] suite, they are not immensely intellectual but faithful, well-meaning and much less envious and quarrelsome than the Windsor household."[72] The Sandringham Library was put at his disposal as a matter of course; there were delightful strolls in the grounds, "the princesses—distinctly amiable and easy, if not exactly remarkable. The level of intellectual ideas is a low one in this family. The Prince of Wales is wide awake, immensely on his guard, and the favour he shows to that grave person, your papa, is a sign of his endeavour to prepare for the coming responsibilities."[73]

At Windsor, the King of Denmark engaged Acton in a political conversation, professing admiration for the Tsarevich Nicholas and alarm at the Home Rule Bill. "I got out of that as well as I could, and when I was gone he said to Oxholm: *Der Acton ist doch ein ganz charmanter Mensch!*" (That Acton is quite a charming fellow!). The King told Acton that he wanted to give him the Grand Cross of the Dannebrog. Acton had to decline, but accepted a hideous snuff-box set in diamonds with the King's portrait, to the immense amusement of Lord Carrington, the Lord Chamberlain, who detected it in his pocket in the House of Lords. Seeing the Danish guests off at Tilbury, Acton chatted on the way back with Sir Francis Knollys, the Prince's private secretary, who told him that the Princess of Wales was entirely Russian in her sympathies. All the German element was odious to her, and she had no feeling for English institutions. Acton ended his account for his daughter Annie: "Some day this will be difficult and I shall not always be there to write their speeches."[74]

Acton was at Osborne in the summer of 1893. "It is pleasant here, if not exactly comfortable. The house is half a mile from the sea, on a low hill. An Italian terrace and gardens lead down." The Queen remained most of the day out of doors; breakfast was served under trees or in tents. Osborne House had "pervading galleries, open porticoes in the cool Italian style, with good works of art; and some rooms are handsome. The grand dining room is richly decorated in pure Indian white, the electric light, unseen, is reflected from the creamy walls." Describing the place for the benefit of his daughters, Acton concluded: "All this only lately finished, and one wonders at the enterprise of old ladies. . . . I fancy that you have made out that this place is not quite royal. . . . Having Windsor, this place seems unnecessary, only it helps the royal family to predominate and be a centre in the yachting season, and to complete the leadership of society."[75]

Politics obtruded on the courtier's life. In November 1892 Acton went with Bryce, his best friend in the cabinet, to the Inter-University Club dinner at Cambridge. "Things are not going on well here," he wrote to Annie about Gladstone's reluctance to face Irish Home Rule. At last the second Home Rule Bill, drawn up chiefly by Bryce, was introduced in cabinet. "It looks as if he [Gladstone] means to keep it in his own hands to resist interposition, and to carry his plan with a rush. He has lost precious time."[76] Acton assisted Earl Spencer, who was in charge of the Irish business in the Lords. The Bill that was to decide the government's fate was confronted by a huge Unionist majority. In the Commons the prime minister, eighty-three years old, amid cheers and a standing ovation from his supporters, introduced the measure on 13 February, speaking for two and a half hours. The Home Rule debate lasted for several months. Acton claimed a proprietary interest in Irish Home Rule. He believed that he and John Morley, Irish secretary in the 1886 and 1892 Gladstone governments, had decisively influenced Gladstone to take up the cause. Morley denied this claim so far as he was concerned. In his biography of Gladstone he wrote: "As for the story of my being concerned in Mr. Gladstone's conversion to home rule, it is, of course, pure moonshine."[77]

Morley repeated this denial to Acton personally, who concluded from it, as he wrote to his daughter Mamy, "that I remain the one decisive author of the policy."[78] Mary Gladstone shared that view. After Acton's death and during the controversial rush into publication of his letters and recollections, both by her and others, she wrote in a letter to Sir Mountstuart Grant Duff: "It may interest you to know that instead of following my father at the time of the great Home Rule Bill split it would be truer still to have said that Lord Acton led my father into Home Rule."[79] The question of the extent of Acton's influence on Gladstone's Home Rule policy remains a fascinating one.[80]

The role of the anonymous adviser behind the scenes, which Acton cherished, involved renunciation of responsibility for particular policies. In the realm of Liberal ideas Acton had laid the groundwork in Gladstone's mind on many basic issues of justice, freedom, and morals. It could be left to others to construct the actual policies, whether on Ireland or reform. But the professionals disliked his influence on Gladstone and denigrated it readily. Gladstone's last eighteen months in office were also the time when Acton was closest to him in matters of major and minor concern: "My enjoyment has been disturbed by Gladstone consulting me about everything."[81] The reference here was to the first Oxford "Romanes Lecture," on which Acton had helped Gladstone extensively, relishing his role as ghostwriter. The theme was Oxford's greatness, but it was really the speaker who mattered. Acton described the historic occasion: "Gladstone wore his crimson gown, and was splendid. Once the spoilt child and favourite of the university, then contumeliously ejected, he now returns, in the glory of his final triumph to be very handsomely and warmly received. The lecture itself was quite superfluous, and only a text for opinions."[82]

The continuing Home Rule debate led to frantic reactions among Ulster Protestants, who prepared to arm themselves and expel Catholic workers from the region. Lord Salisbury was about to go over to incite and organize them, Acton believed, in the hope that the Bill would be defeated in the House of Commons and the Lords would not incur all the blame of rejection. Moreover, a defeat in the Lords would not injure the ministry. "Gladstone wants me to represent these things to the Queen—wrongfully, since he does not do it himself. . . . I am not here, strictly, as a political personage, and this intervention will rather injure my position. This, however, is a favoured one."[83] The government had been losing ground since the beginning of the session because of weak tactics. In the Bill, Gladstone had failed to show his old mastery of finance. There was a severe fight over the second reading. Were they right, Acton asked in a letter to Annie, to go on, knowing that the measure would not be carried in the Lords and that we "do it only to redeem our pledges? Of course we cannot admit that we have no hope of success."[84]

On 27 July 1893, at ten in the evening, the committee sessions of the Home Rule Bill reached their closure. Joseph Chamberlain, who had broken with Gladstone and the Liberal Party over Home Rule in 1886, was speaking in the crowded chamber. He made a strong attack on the Bill and compared Gladstone to Herod. The Irish members responded with cries of "Judas." A scene of confusion followed, and the chairman lost control.

> One intemperate Irishman—it was just after dinner—took [A. J.] Balfour's seat [a former Tory secretary for Ireland], gesticulating. A Tory took him by the scruff of his neck and cast him out. Then there was a rush in the Tory gangway, a very dangerous one it seemed, and I saw one man go down, one strike another in the face, and a dozen pummelling each other and shouting furiously. In the gallery behind me the spectators rose to their feet and hissed, most properly. Tremendous agitation and shrieks in the crowded Ladies' Gallery. At the end of ten terrible minutes I saw [Edward] Majoribanks [the Liberal chief whip] standing alone at the top of the gangway—how he got there, heaven knows—having separated the combatants and made peace. . . . Mr. G[ladstone] who, in 60 years, had seen nothing like it, spoke very feebly, and without influencing the mob of members. After that the Bill got through the Committee with an average majority of about thirty-three.[85]

But the Commons majority was a Pyrrhic victory. A week later, the Lords defeated the Bill with no fewer than 419 against 49 votes. Gladstone's immediate reaction was to dissolve Parliament and to appeal to the country on the "People versus Peers" issue, but the cabinet refused to follow him. Undaunted, he announced that he would bring back the Bill in the next session, but before he could do so, the smouldering effect between the two groups in the cabinet came to a head over the matter of naval expenditure and led to his resignation.

The end of Home Rule seemed the right moment to Acton to ask the prime minister to release him from his duties in the House of Lords so that he could devote himself to the projected biography of Döllinger. "As long as I have constant occupation at the Irish Office—consequent on my native ignorance of the subjects to be prepared—the main employment of my life has to be indefinitely suspended. . . . And if Rosebery sends me to Munich, I have hopes of seeing certain correspondence which the government there would not disclose to anyone less important."[86]

The reference to Munich concerned the hopes for a diplomatic post for Acton, sustained by Gladstone and Rosebery, who wanted to do something for him but did not quite know where and how to fit him in. In the 1880s there had been the idea of sending him to Berlin, "the only place where I could hope to be of any special use." The embassy in Berlin he recognized as "the best prize of a profession not my own," but he also knew that it would be "so exorbitant a preference of private friendship over public service" that it could only be justly and wisely resented.[87] When Acton's friend Lord Ampthill (Odo Russell) died in 1884, last having served as ambassador in Berlin for thirteen years, the matter came up again. The Empress Frederick warmly supported Acton and assured her mother, Queen Victoria, that because there was no obvious candidate among the available diplomats, the choice could only be between Acton and Ampthill's elder brother, Lord Arthur Russell, then Liberal MP for Tavistock. The Crown Princess "would prefer Acton," Lord Granville commented from Osborne, "but I told her that it would be for me impossible, and, I believed, almost equally for a person unconnected with him to put him over the heads of the whole Corps Diplomatique." Acton might possibly be as good as Ampthill, Granville said, but he had never done any official business and had "neglected to distinguish himself in Parliament."[88] Sir Henry Ponsonby wrote from Balmoral to Gladstone's secretary, Horace Seymour: "The question you ask about Berlin is one that perplexes us all here and the Crown Princess talks of nothing else. Naturally, as it is of momentous interest to her. She wants Lord Acton. I don't know him, Lord Granville will never propose him, but I don't think he would do very well. So the Crown Princess says she would propose him. I only observe that for one Protestant state to send to another Protestant state a Roman Catholic is peculiar, and as he has a tiresome wife—no advantage is gained."[89]

Ponsonby's unfavourable opinion of Lady Acton was based not so much on the fact that she was German and not fluent in English, which then was not an obstacle, but on the fact that Marie Acton had made no bones about how little she cared for life in England, either at Aldenham or in London, or for the climate. She had lost one son in England, and one of her daughters needed special care. Lady Acton was disdainful of English high society, which Acton's mother had conquered with such ease. All this had been noted with due disapproval. Marie clearly preferred life at Cannes or Tegernsee. Sir Edward Malet, then minister at Brussels, was in a different category altogether—persona grata with Bismarck, which Acton was not, and just married to Lady Ermyntrude Russell, the Duke of Bedford's daughter and a niece of Lord Ampthill. So Berlin it was for Malet, and for many years. Whether Acton would have been the right man for Berlin is questionable. Acton's sympathies were for Austria and the German

South rather than for the new German nationalism that found its backbone in Prussia. He would have been out of sympathy with the martial imperialism and strident nationalism of the new German Reich, and powerless to influence the course of events launched in 1888 when Frederick III, Germany's "liberal" Emperor for only ninety-nine days, died of cancer. At the time of Frederick III's death Acton said that "no public event since Gordon's death has affected me so deeply."[90] The accession of William II meant the end of his English mother's influence. Anglo-German naval rivalry intensified after Bismarck himself was dismissed by the young Emperor, who did everything he could to blot out what few memories the Germans had of his parents.

In August 1892, just at the time when Acton was closest to Gladstone, the matter of the Munich legation came up. It was Rosebery, the foreign secretary, who had proposed an "incentive," an honour perhaps, to induce the current minister, Victor Drummond, or rather his American wife, to accept "promotion" to a post in South America. Acton did not turn down the idea of achieving a desirable end with questionable means. It was not he who had suggested the move. So he wrote to Gladstone: "If you approved of his [Drummond's] promotion, and of my appointment, I may, of course, fairly say that there are no complications between this country and Bavaria that would give me any opportunity for mismanagement; and I not only know Germany pretty well, but I enjoy a measure of favour with the Royal family. You will laugh, but it is a fact, due to family and social connexions."[91]

Only at Munich perhaps would Acton be a round peg in a round hole, Rosebery had said.[92] "Whisper to your mother," Acton wrote to his daughter, "that I beg the most absolute discretion and secrecy about Drummond and Rosebery, even with Auntie [Countess Arco]."[93] When Rosebery succeeded Gladstone, the retiring prime minister wrote to the new foreign secretary, Lord Kimberley, about the possibility of a diplomatic post for Acton. Lord Kimberley replied noncommittally, but pointed out: "You know how much jealousy there is in the service of outsiders, and such appointments you would I am sure agree with me must be sparingly made."[94] Kimberley was not really disposed to do much for Acton. To Rosebery he wrote: "Acton is an excellent good fellow, and has high literary attainment, but he has made no mark whatever in public life, and if he gets an appointment, it can only be because he is poor and one of our few supporters in the Lords."[95] In the Foreign Office, the mere idea of choosing an outsider like Acton over men of approved diplomatic standing would have been felt as an insult.

Meanwhile, Gladstone's retirement was fast approaching on account of his age, failing eyesight, and loss of control over government problems and the cabinet. After the exertions over Irish Home Rule, he went to Biarritz in January 1894, accompanied by his two daughters, Mary Drew and Helen. Acton, on the Gladstones' insistence, had to go, too, although he wanted to go to Tegernsee, hating to be kept at hotels day after day with nothing to do.

Acton and Gladstone disagreed on the way the resignation was to be carried out and collided unpleasantly over Ireland and the proposed rise in the naval estimates, the two matters that brought about the end of the government. Gladstone felt that because he had not resigned over the Lords' defeat of Home Rule but had given in and stayed on, he was destroying his party. Acton's view was that the Home Rule case was hopeless because of the government's small majority and that the prime minister must accept the inevitable and come to terms with the Unionists. As for increased naval expenditure, Gladstone thought he was being untrue to himself and his customary political economy by giving way, which Acton urged him to do.

In a letter to Gladstone, Acton had argued: "Great and sudden increase in expenditure on armaments is a thing that has been done twice within my memory and before my eyes, twice by yourself, each time with an eye to France alone with no other complications. In 1860 nothing was urged by Palmerston in behalf of his fortifications but the danger from France. In 1859, the admiralty spoke vaguely of Russia, but the real consideration was the rapid triumph over Austria, and the state of the French fleet. That fleet was not then so near an equality with our own as it is today."[96] With reference to this letter, Gladstone's daughter had written to her father: "He has always agreed with you until now. Is not his judgement on this point likely to be more important than even yours?"[97]

As he wrote to Bryce, Acton found Gladstone "generally . . . wild, violent, inaccurate, sophistical, evidently governed by resentment. Now and then, for a moment, he collected himself and was full of force, but never full of light and able to see any argument but his own."[98] Annoyed that the Grand Old Man was so difficult to reason with, Acton told Gladstone that he thought him a little below his own level and left crossly for Madrid. He had accepted an invitation by Sir Henry Drummond Wolff, the British ambassador. It was Acton's first visit to Spain, and from Madrid Acton wrote to his daughter Annie, giving her his impressions of the country: "The people are more religious than the Italians and more energetic; but yet they are indolent, listless, without the notion of progress. . . . The clergy denounce the bullfights, always in vain." He lived in the palace that had belonged to the great Cardinal Ximenes, who was both the leader of reform in the Spanish Church and the Grand Inquisitor. "The old Inquisition is across the street, the windows confined by the same bars that existed when every Protestant and every Jew was tortured and burnt. There is an underground passage under the street, and there are bones in it. It is like living in the worn out gates of Hell."[99]

Back in England for Windsor duties, Acton witnessed the sensation caused by Gladstone's resignation after sixty-one years at Westminster on Saturday, 3 March 1894. On the announcement in Parliament on Thursday, there followed the famous last "blubbering cabinet," as Gladstone called it because of the tearful farewells of the ministers.[100] On Friday the Gladstones went to Windsor for the last audience with the Queen and the presentation of his letter of resignation prepared at Biarritz, the text of which Acton was shown.[101]

There was a dinner with the Queen. Gladstone, looking weak, led in the Queen's granddaughter, the fair-haired Alix of Hesse-Darmstadt ("Alicky"), who was about to be engaged to the future Tsar and who, a quarter of a century later, would be killed along with him by the Bolsheviks. After the Queen had retired, Gladstone sat with Acton, who then walked down the long corridor with him. The next morning they had an early talk during which Gladstone said that he would prefer Rosebery for prime minister and Morley for foreign office, and he liked to think of his son Herbert in Morley's place.[102] Acton's version is contradicted by Morley's, who wrote that, if asked, Gladstone would have suggested Lord Spencer as his successor.[103] But the Queen dispensed with the duty to consult the outgoing prime minister and sent for Rosebery after she had ascertained, through Ponsonby, that the Liberal Party in general had declared for him against Harcourt, whom she disliked. Acton, writing to his daughter after a conversation with Harcourt's son, noted that Harcourt insisted on his claim to the succession while knowing quite well that it would not be successful, because he wanted to avoid Rosebery and accept Spencer. "No doubt the elevation of Rosebery is a proof of the general dislike of Harcourt," Acton reported.[104]

Acton again had been at the centre of events. The atmosphere was like that of 1892, with all the politicians pursuing their own ambitions. As he saw it, "Rosebery is far the ablest but he has enemies, and he is indifferent to the Irish cause. Morley, however, undertakes to keep the Irish vote. Harcourt and Rosebery are not friends, Harcourt is impossible [as] Premier, but he is the first man in the Commons. That is why Morley and others would prefer Spencer, a perfect gentleman, a man without reproach, but also without any kind of talent."[105]

At Windsor a Council was held on the morning of Saturday, 3 March, to which five ministers, apart from Gladstone, were summoned from London: Lord Kimberley, Lord President of the Council; Lord Rosebery, Secretary of State for Foreign Affairs, Sir William Harcourt, Chancellor of the Exchequer; Lord Ripon, Secretary of State for the Colonies; and Lord Spencer, First Lord of the Admiralty. Acton's task as Lord-in-Waiting was to show the ministers into one of the drawing rooms, with the Queen waiting next door where the Council was to be held, and to hand the box containing Gladstone's letter of resignation to the Queen. After the Council the Queen asked Gladstone to remain for his last audience while the others went away to lunch. Acton waited outside. After a time, as though by chance, the Empress Frederick appeared at the end of the corridor, on her way to lunch. Acton disappeared in a doorway, but she had seen him and came up. As there might be servants about, some of them German, she asked him in Italian whether it was all over, whether Gladstone's eyes were going, and praised him for choosing the right moment. Acton answered, indeed, it was high time. Then Gladstone came out. The Queen could not have been very amiable, Acton noted, for he seemed not moved at all. But the Empress turned so tenderly to Gladstone and spoke so kindly that "he went down on one old knee as he kissed her hand and thanked her."[106]

Then Acton went in and found the Queen "pretty jolly," with the letter of resignation on the table. He then took Gladstone to lunch, where there were twenty people. Afterwards he saw Mrs. Gladstone to her carriage, and her last whispered question was "Faut-il donner quelque chose?" (Should I leave a tip?). She had had an audience with the Queen in the morning and had assured her that Gladstone's aim had always been to preserve the Crown and constitution. "I was always sure of it," the Queen had said, taking pity on her. Acton wrote to Annie: "That is the *fiche de consolation* she carries away for her descendants. . . . As he said nothing when I put them into the royal carriage, I fancy, the historic solemnity of the moment did, at that parting, come over him. And that was the last, last end of the Gladstonian greatness, and the extinction of the brightest light in our history."[107]

Acton was pleased that at least he had been there to lighten Gladstone's ordeal. The Queen wrote to Gladstone the same day, saying merely that he was quite right to go and save his eyes; she hoped he would, with Mrs. Gladstone, have many years of enjoyment of life, and added that she would have been very glad to have offered him a peerage had she not been sure he would have refused it. "And this," said Gladstone with a sigh, "is the only record that will remain of fifty-one years as Privy Councillor." [108]

Acton went on in his account to his daughter Annie: "I was summoned to Ponsonby's room to learn that Rosebery had accepted. Gladstone had ostensibly not been asked by the queen for his advice. The secret as to whom she had selected to succeed him from the candidates—Rosebery, Harcourt, Kimberley, Spencer—was so well kept that only Rosebery knew." And so "a jolly row," as Acton described it, ensued. "For, at one moment of the audiences today, Sir William Harcourt walked into the Royal Closet alone, saying he believed he had been sent for. 'No,' said the queen, 'I asked for Mr. G.' She now wants to know how the mistake arose, and thought I could tell." Not aware of the incident, Acton thought that Harcourt might have slipped in behind him in an effort to surprise the Queen. He had had a lot of champagne at lunch, as one of the Ladies-in-Waiting who sat next to him told Acton. The Queen saw the incident from the comic side. But because no one ought to be introduced except by Acton, it showed "either looseness on my part, or very sharp practice indeed on his" and the making of a future legend: after the Privy Council, Lord Acton introduced Harcourt to the Queen as prime minister, to the detriment of Rosebery! [109]

After Gladstone's resignation, Acton was involved in an official visit by the Empress Frederick. Following a dinner at Lion Mansions, the Gladstones' London residence, the Empress took him into a corner to talk politics, he reported to Annie. "She poses as a special adherent of mine, as a liberal of the right sort," and she expressed her hatred for Rosebery "because he was a friend of Bismarck's son Herbert." [110] He accompanied the Empress to Flushing and, on her yacht, to Germany, and accepted a "lift" on her train as far as Cologne. This trip confirmed his impression, as he reported home, that what had been widely rumoured about a secret marriage between the widowed Empress and Count Götz von Seckendorff, her chamberlain, was in fact true. The count, two years younger than she was, had been in her service all along, when she was Crown Princess, Empress, and throughout the long years of her widowhood. He was very much the experienced and relaxed courtier and liked playing the part of the sporting English country gentleman. "I have no more doubt about the Seckendorffs!" Acton wrote to his daughter. [111]

Acton was on waiting duty at Coburg, accompanying the Queen to the wedding of Princess Victoria Melitta of Coburg, known as "Ducky," and Ernst of Hesse (Ernie). The Queen, with her great talent for changing her mind, made clear by her attendance that she was delighted rather than displeased with a marriage between cousins. The Prince of Wales was there, and the Empress and Emperor William II were received with military display. "This evening all the crowned heads are together, there will be presentations, and perhaps some indication of politics. The place is crowded with reporters, especially French, perturbed at the manifest conjunction of Russia and Germany."[112]

Acton went on to visit the Empress Frederick at Schloss Friedrichshof, near Kronberg, on the southern edge of the beautiful Taunus forest. It was more like an immense villa than a great country seat, bearing the efficient touch of Queen Victoria's eldest daughter. Acton wrote for his daughter's benefit:

> Electric light all over. My very toilette lights, electric; and this morning a luxurious warm bath. She certainly likes having me about her; and was excessively kind and nice, and showing confidence, even indiscretion. She has an easy way of uttering her dislikes. . . . The empress is as simple, as unpretentious, as can be; and dresses cheaply. But last night she put on about £12,000 of pearls in my honour. I was dreadfully tired; but I find that my discourse on Napoleon opened their eyes rather. There is a good amount of *Bildung,* but not of a very high order. . . . [It is all very] conventional and obvious, and Seck[endorff] is not likely to raise the level. He so coolly expressed a hope that I would find my way there again, that I forgot that he was not the master of the house. . . . In her isolation and friendlessness, with uninteresting daughters and sons-in-law, this poor woman, whose memory will seem so tragic to posterity, tried to cultivate her friendships as a sort of international person, *de plus,* the faithful servant of her mother.[113]

Back in London, Acton became aware of Gladstone's rapid decline. He had received a letter from Sir George Murray, his former private secretary, who had stayed on with Rosebery, asking him to give up certain keys by which he made his own way into the House of Commons. Gladstone, startled as if he had been stung, exclaimed: "Won't they even leave me that?" Acton commented: "This was pathetic, in the role of Lear; but not in taste or keeping. Mrs. Drew at once wrote an angry and wounded letter to Murray, stimulated by Armitstead. It would have been deplorable and a false note. So I caused it to be torn up." The business was left to Acton to sort out.[114]

The government fared worse once Gladstone had retired. It was not only the loss of his great name and authority without any adequate successor, but the ministry became divided by the rivalry between Harcourt, "the strong commoner," and Rosebery, "the ornamental peer." Rosebery had tried to prevent Gladstone from taking office in 1892 and yet began by refusing to serve himself. "All this was disgraceful, worse even than appears in my letters at the time," Acton wrote on the day after the Liberal government fell in June 1895.[115]

The "extreme" Irish MPs, some of the eighty who had been given voting rights on all except exclusively British affairs in order to get the Irish Bill through, had turned against the government, which had done nothing for them, and thus reduced its majority. While the moderate Irish had remained supportive, the English constituencies "gave us up, the Irish enemy had no part in the final defeat." "One reason why the country people turned," Acton explained to Mamy, "is our Bill for enabling parishes to restrict public houses. It is a good Bill, and another instance of immorality on the part of our adversaries. But that does not make our case better. We have richly deserved our inglorious fall; and your father's Home Rule policy is dead."[116]

Another contributory factor, Acton suggested in his letter, was the affair concerning Cromwell's statue in which the Liberal prime minister had clashed with the Queen, which showed also that the English struggle between Roundheads and Cavaliers remained endemic. The statue, commissioned in 1899 for the tercentenary celebrations of Cromwell's birthday, was originally intended to stand in the Central Lobby of the Houses of Parliament, but the Tories objected to the expenditure of taxpayers' money to honour the man who had murdered King Charles I. They had the support of the Queen, because she shared their view about her ancestor and also because of the constitution. Westminster was, after all, a "royal palace" where she reigned as "the Queen in Parliament." Eventually a compromise was reached: the Liberals decided to put up the monument outside Westminster Hall, where it still stands, and Rosebery advanced the money for it. As Acton explained to his daughter: "You know that the Presbyterian majority in parliament was against bringing Charles to trial—a trial which could only end in one way, as the tribunal would be named by the same enemies who insisted on the trial. So an officer of Cromwell's army arrested the members of the majority, until so many were locked up that the minority became the majority, and voted away the King's head. I hold this, which Cromwell approved, but did not do, an act of murder; and I do not envy Rosebery his interview with the queen."[117]

Towards the end of November 1897, the Gladstones went once more to Cannes, to stay at Stuart Rendel's Chateau de Thoreno. The Grand Old Man talked with his usual force with his host and visitors, but was mostly lying or sitting half asleep, depressed. Helen Gladstone wrote to Acton and implored him to come.[118] He came in January with his daughter Mamy, who sang to Gladstone, which greatly delighted him. On Acton's last day, he and Gladstone went for a long drive and had a conversation in which Gladstone said "everything that could prove sympathy and friendship" and which was for Acton a testament of their closeness.[119]

Back in England, Gladstone went into a slow decline. On 17 May 1898, Herbert Gladstone wrote to Acton that the doctors expected him to die at any moment. They had found signs of a cancer that was beginning to affect the brain. "He understands some things that are said to him, but I don't think he can recognise us. My mother holds up bravely."[120] Two days later, on Ascension Day 1898, Herbert Gladstone's telegram arrived at the Athenaeum Club, where Acton was staying: "My father passed away peacefully at five this morning."[121] To Annie, Acton wrote on that day: "His death makes a great change to me as there is no one left that I really look up to or should care to consult."[122] And to Mary Drew: "I wish I could feel sure that your father knew how I felt, what his friendship was to me during more than thirty years. But I do think you know it."[123]

Acton's own splendid obituary of Mary Gladstone Drew's father had already been delivered to her verbally one night at Tegernsee almost twenty years before, when the Gladstones were visiting Bavaria and Acton and Mary were talking alone. It was a monologue, sparked by a visionary flash such as sometimes fired Acton in the presence of a receptive listener. Deeply moved by that moment and the impact of his words in the beautiful setting of a still summer's evening in the Bavarian Alps, she was emotionally overcome and had merely recorded: "Crept up to bed."[124] Afterwards Mary Gladstone had asked Acton to write down this "Judgment of Posterity on Mr. Gladstone." Acton wrote:

When our descendants shall stand before the slab that is not yet laid among the monuments of famous Englishmen, they will say that Chatham knew how to inspire a nation with his energy, but was poorly furnished with knowledge and ideas; that the capacity of Fox was never proved in office, though he was the first of the debaters; that Pitt, the strongest of ministers, was among the weakest of legislators; that no Foreign Secretary has equalled Canning, but that he showed no other administrative ability; that Peel, who excelled as an administrator, a debater, and a tactician, fell everywhere short of genius; and that the highest merits of the five without their drawbacks were united in Mr. Gladstone. Possibly they may remember that his only rival in depth, and wealth, and force of mind was neither admitted to the Cabinet, nor buried in the Abbey. They will not say of him, as of Burke, that his writing equalled his speaking, or surpassed it like Macaulay's. . . . But that illustrious chain of English eloquence that begins in the Walpolean battles, ends with Mr. Gladstone.[125]

Acton's regard for Gladstone had almost a mystical quality. That makes it difficult to understand for a later generation tempted to gloss over it as sycophantic adulation, which it was not. It was meant for a statesman with whom he felt at one in fundamentals, both religious and moral—for, as he said, for him the Liberal Party had always had the status of a dogma, even a Church. Actually, there were aspects in which what Gladstone owed to Acton was more important than what Acton owed to him. It was through Acton's influence that Gladstone, the original Tory who described himself as a Liberal-Conservative, had come to an understanding of Liberalism. And, however scholars weigh the other factors that brought Gladstone to support Home Rule for Ireland, there is no doubt that Acton's relentless questioning and prodding on this issue were vital. And through Acton and Döllinger, the High Anglican Gladstone had reached a deeper understanding of Catholicism. In an undated letter, which Acton wrote to his wife from a visit to the Gladstones, probably in the early 1880s, he noted: "He might one day become a Catholic, is however highly paradox and extravagant." This was after the two had had a private conversation lasting two hours.[126]

Acton did not share Gladstone's many insular prejudices, or indeed his Homeric theories. When friction increased between Britain and Germany over the consequences of Disraeli's imperialist policies, Acton tried to interpret to Döllinger the Gladstonian policy. Gladstone had become prime minister for the second time in April 1880, and at once Anglo-German clashes of interest emerged in regard to Russia and Egypt. Russia wanted to regain what it had lost as a result of the Russo-Turkish War and the settlement reached at the Peace of San Stefano.[127] But with Egypt coming under British influence after the murder of General Gordon at Khartoum, the British were constrained in their own criticism of Russia's imperialism. Great Britain became "perfidious Albion" in German eyes. German colonial expansion started in 1882 with acquisitions in Africa and an expansionist German policy in southeastern Europe and the Middle East arising from the Triple Alliance of the German and Austro-Hungarian empires and Italy (1883). This pattern was designed by Bismarck to forestall a combined attack of France and Russia, with British control of Egypt and the Suez Canal matched by German Middle East expansion through the building of the Bagdad railway and the eventual German alliance with Turkey in World War I. Behind Anglo-German imperialist rivalry was the fact that Britain was then governed by the Gladstonian administration, which in Germany was doubly unpopular because, as Acton put it to Döllinger, no educated German would want to be associated with what he would regard as a morally and intellectually inferior system. Gladstone was aware of the German rejection of his Weltanschauung and what he valued most—his High Church view and his beliefs in political and economic freedom. Knowing little of Germany himself, Gladstone responded with a lack of interest.[128]

In a later letter Acton returned to his theme of explaining Gladstone, "the one-time supporter of intolerance and West Indian slavery" who had embarked on a long and still developing path of political conversions. Odd sympathies, indeed convictions, survived: his evident regard for Queen Elizabeth, Archbishop Laud, Robert Peel, and John Henry Newman, and an outright distaste for the spirit of French and German learning. Radical Liberalism of the Gladstonian kind was, being on the left, sympathizing with John Bright and Charles Dilke rather than with those on the side of the Duke of Argyll, the Earl of Selborne, Viscount Goschen, or the Holland House Whigs of the school of Charles James Fox and Lord Grey. Contemporary Continental Liberals like Adolphe Thiers, Camillo Cavour, and Francis Deak would be, in Gladstone's eyes, akin to Tories. Gladstonian ideas would in Germany have been considered extremely liberal, if not revolutionary. They involved "wanting the Bourbons thrown out of Naples, the Austrians out of Italy, the Turks out of Europe, introducing secret ballots, leaving the colonies to themselves, the Imperial frontiers to be restricted, reducing the army to the extent of the Indian garrison, so that waging war from political calculations would become impossible." Acton's catalogue of Gladstonian aims included abolishing the rule of the landed gentry in the army, in Ireland, and in the counties, and doing away with the political preferment of, and tutelage by, the Established Church. The franchise was to be given not only to townspeople but also to agricultural labourers, and Ireland—had not the assassination of its chief secretary in Phoenix Park, Dublin, in May 1882, forestalled this aim—was to be governed by its own MPs.[129]

Gladstonian government was to be through the masses of the people, not through the opinion of the better-educated sections expressed by the media, that is, by the London newspapers. Gladstone, Acton concluded, would want legislation to be decided by those among the masses whose very existence depended on good or bad laws, and whom he would regard as representing virtually the whole nation. Acton told Döllinger, who was deeply impressed by Gladstone's Christian statesmanship, of his friend's increasing repugnance for the Church of England in her relations with the State, as he thought that the Church was constantly conceding ground in matters of faith, allowing unbelievers and rationalists too much influence. Instead the nonconformist churches became much closer to the Catholic tradition in developing greater devoutness and activity. The British educated classes had, for thirty years, been dominated by intellectuals like Thomas Carlyle, Jeremy Bentham, James Mill and John Stuart Mill, George Grote, Henry Thomas Buckle, Charles Darwin, Thomas H. Huxley, John Morley, and George Eliot and had given up their religious belief under that influence. Gladstone trusted the masses more than the intellectuals. "For him the internal struggle in the Church against what is contrary to the Church and, outside the Church, against unbelief is everything, apart from the fulfilment he finds in politics."[130]

Comparing his own political convictions to Gladstone's, Acton wrote that he was "less orthodox in economic theory and less frightened than Gladstone was by the disastrous impact of biblical criticism." Politically Gladstone would have been sympathetic to the democratic institutions in some of the North American states and would have felt more at home in Gambetta's France than in Bismarck's Prussia.

With thousands of others, Acton went to Westminster Hall to view his old friend lying in state on the catafalque. There were six great candles burning, a cross at his head, and a black cloth with the words "Requiescat in Pace" embroidered on it, symbolical of the mixture of Catholicism and Protestantism in his Anglican faith.[131] The funeral, at which the two royal princes, the future Edward VII and George V, were among the pall-bearers, was in Acton's words "the burial of the greatest figure in parliamentary history."[132]

Even before Gladstone's death the family had consulted Acton about a biography. "There is one biographer whom I feel we should all prefer, were he not too deliberate an historian to perform the nimble task," wrote Mary Drew. Morley, too, proposed Acton at first, but they all knew that this, like others of his great projects, if accepted, would never be realized. Morley, an experienced biographer, was the obvious alternative, but he declined and proposed Herbert Paul.[133] Acton, rightly, did not think much of the idea and wrote to his daughter Mamy that he had suggested James Bryce, who, he thought, would do it as well as Morley.[134] Acton's third candidate was Sir George Otto Trevelyan, cabinet minister under Gladstone and biographer of both his uncle, Macaulay, and of Charles James Fox.[135]

In the event, in July 1898 Acton replied to specific questions Herbert Gladstone had put to him. First, he suggested the priority to be a political biography in two or three volumes, with the author being given full access to all the papers he might want. A second author should be chosen to compile a documentary volume, but this work was to be subordinate to the first. As it was less urgent, its author should be "sacrificed" to the main biographer, whose work was "to meet the public expectation and the commercial demand." The biography was more important, too, from the point of view of "the party and also the family interest." Acton added, "I should dread the consequences of giving the two works to one writer, because the biography cannot appear too soon." The other volume would not be read "by the man in the street or sold on stations or multiplied in cheap editions." Having evidently Morley in mind, Acton added that men competent in literary talent and political knowledge ought not to be excluded by want of sympathy with Gladstone's inner, religious life: "They are difficult enough to find as it is." And he emphasized the urgency of a political biography, the statesman's—Gladstone's public—life, which should also be indicated in the title. His advice to the family, tactfully put, was that "other things cannot be excluded, but they must not be treated in a way to satisfy the demands of those mainly interested in the religious, the ecclesiastical, the theological part of his life and career." It would depend on the nature of the material whether this should be the topic of a separate work, or whether what related to it could be included in the documentary publication.[136]

Acton's preference was clearly for Morley, as he explained to Mary Drew: "Morley is the one who knew him best, and had most of his confidence, both as to men and things. . . . Trevelyan knew him much less intimately; but he lives for Parliamentary history, and has shown himself capable of writing a biography which is one of the best in the language." His advantage was that he was out of public life and would not have to weigh every word he said about colleagues like Harcourt. Acton's third candidate, Bryce, had the advantage of having "greater knowledge of politics than anybody, and proved his power of appreciating your father by what he said at the time."[137] But when asked, Bryce expressed his misgivings about writing contemporary history.

That Morley had no interest in the religious side of Gladstone's nature, so important to many others of the time, and, moreover, as he told Acton, that he did not really like Gladstone as a man, were not seen as obstacles. Morley was an obvious choice if Acton was not to do it.[138] And so it was that, in October 1898, Morley accepted the commission and got down to his mammoth task. *The Life of William Ewart Gladstone,* in three volumes, was published in 1903 and proved to be one of the great biographies of, and an epitaph on, the Victorian age. In a way it was also Acton's last service to his friend.

The Gladstones on their visit to the Acton chalet at Tegernsee in 1879. To the right of Mrs. Gladstone (with fan) are Lady Arco-Valley, Acton's mother-in-law; her daughter, nick-named Tini; Dr. Döllinger, aged eighty, almost disappearing into his deck chair; and Lord Acton. Lily (Elisabeth) Acton sits next to Gladstone, and standing behind him are his son Herbert and Acton's son Richard. Behind them on the terrace are Mary Gladstone, Lady Acton (holding her daughter Simmy), and Lady Blennerhassett. Private owner.

An engraving of Aldenham, Shropshire, before Acton's library was built at the side of the house. Acton's seventy thousand books are now housed in the Cambridge University Library. Not a trace remains of the library addition, a monstrosity of iron stacks and walkways. Private owner.

The Acton villa at Tegernsee in its present incarnation as a health spa. Private owner.

Gladstone's house at 11 Carlton House Terrace, London, scene of many famous breakfasts with Acton, as well as the endpoint of Gladstone's nightly walks to try and "rescue" the prostitutes at nearby Haymarket. Here the drawing room is shown with its original furniture. Courtesy of the Foreign Press Association, London (the present occupant of the house).

The Princess Royal (Vicky), Queen Victoria's eldest daughter (1840–1901), who married the liberal German Crown Prince, later Emperor Frederick III. She almost pursued Acton with her friendship and regard for him. She considered herself indeed to be a "fellow liberal"— relative to her mother's Toryism. Private owner.

Queen Victoria at the time of her Diamond Jubilee in 1897, when she conferred on Acton the Knight Commander of the Victorian Order. Gladstone had appointed Acton in 1892 as her Lord-in-Waiting, hoping that he might persuade the Tory-minded Queen to think better of the Liberal prime minister she hated. As the Queen recorded in her diaries, however, Acton succeeded in captivating her in every respect but that. Photo by W. and D. Dawney, courtesy of the National Portrait Gallery, London.

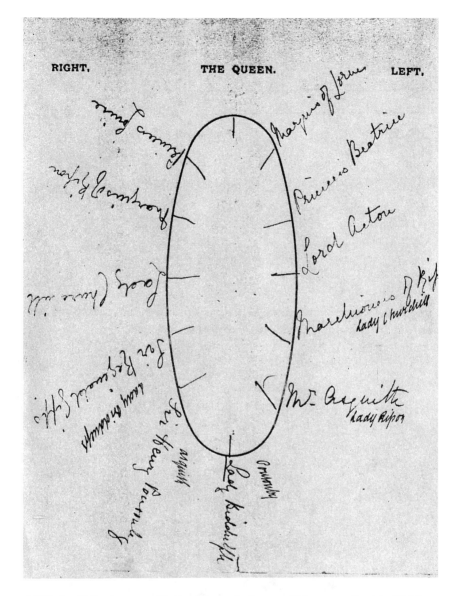

A Windsor Table plan as used by Lord Acton during one of his turns as Lord-in-Waiting. He confessed sometimes to have made rather a "hash" of directing the Queen's royal guests to their dinner places, but his lapses were graciously forgiven because the Queen appreciated his value as an entertaining table companion. Courtesy of Cambridge University Library.

Herbert Gladstone's telegram informing Acton that his father, W. E. Gladstone, had died on 19 May 1898. Courtesy of Cambridge University Library.

The house at 6 Chaucer Road, Cambridge, which Acton acquired about 1896 but where he lived for not even two years before his final illness necessitated his return to the better climate of Tegernsee. The house was built by a previous owner in the opulent late Victorian style. This drawing is by Andrew Coburn, a former research architect of the Martin Centre for Architecture (part of Cambridge University), which occupies the building today. Courtesy of Andrew Coburn.

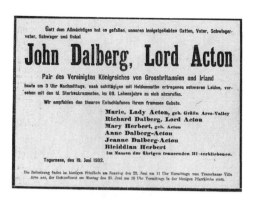

The announcement of Lord Acton's death on 19 June 1902, from the Tegernsee local paper. The German text reads: "It has pleased Almighty God to call to Himself our beloved husband, father, father-in-law, and uncle, John Dalberg, Lord Acton, peer of the United Kingdom of Great Britain and Ireland, today at 3 in the afternoon after eight days of severe suffering borne heroically, furnished with the holy sacrament for the dying, in his 69th year. We recommend our beloved departed to your devoted prayers." Private owner.

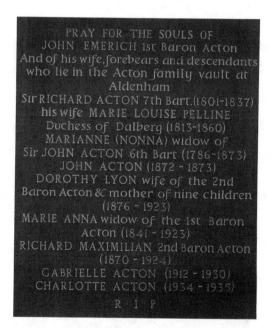

A commemorative plaque in the church of St. John the Evangelist, Bridgnorth, Shropshire, for the members of the Acton family buried in the vault of the former Aldenham chapel. The name of the first Lord Acton is mistakenly included. Acton was buried at Tegernsee, Bavaria, and the family's intention to have his remains brought to England was never realized. Private owner.

The Acton coat of arms originally consisted of two lions over six fleurs-de-lis. After Sir Edward Acton was wounded in the thigh in the Battle of Worcester in 1651, he adopted as his crest a man's leg encased in armour, amputated at mid-thigh, surrounded by a scarf of red and gold. The family motto has remained Deo adjuvante (with God's help), although during the Great Rebellion (1628–49) Sir Edward Acton temporarily substituted Pereant discrimina (Let differences perish) as a counsel of the times.

Queen Victoria, Prince Albert, and their five eldest children, painted in 1846 by Franz Xavier Winterhalter (1807–1872). Albert, wearing the Garter, sits next to the enthroned Queen, her arm round her heir, the Prince of Wales, symbolizing dynastic continuity. The more domestic element is provided by the two girls and the baby, with the young Prince Alfred toddling across the scene. Photo from the Royal Archives, Windsor Castle, reprinted by permission of Her Majesty Queen Elizabeth II, © The Royal Archives.

20

REGIUS PROFESSOR

The last and probably happiest part of John Acton's life had begun earlier, in February 1895, with his appointment to the Regius Professorship of Modern History at Cambridge. Strangely, he owed the appointment not, as might be expected, to Gladstone but to his successor as prime minister, Rosebery. The Queen's approval was needed, and she gave it after some hesitation. Thus Acton's duties as Lord-in-Waiting ended in the summer of 1895. By then he was "dining with the Royalties for the sixth day running, to the disgust of everybody," as he wrote to Annie.[1] The Queen had told him that she hoped the professor of history would not obstruct the Lord-in-Waiting. And he had replied, in his courtier's manner, elegant as well as light-hearted, that what made her gracious approval so valuable to him was the fact that he would not have to relinquish her service. When he left, she gave him an engraving of herself as a remembrance and through her Lady-in-Waiting requested a photograph of him for her "Memories book."[2]

Earlier Acton had written home about the anticipated end of the Rosebery ministry: "The Queen will be sorrier to lose me than anyone else. She will not live to see another Liberal ministry."[3] In June 1895 it was to be succeeded by a

Salisbury ministry including Joseph Chamberlain and the Duke of Devonshire (formerly Lord Hartington), who had broken with the Gladstonian Liberals and now called themselves Liberal-Unionists. During his brief premiership and in the exercise of the then widespread ministerial patronage, Rosebery made two interesting university appointments. They suggested his wide, unpolitical interests in history and literature (apart, of course, from the turf). In December 1894 he nominated Frederick York Powell to succeed the late J. A. Froude as Regius Professor of Modern History at Oxford. There had been some expectation that Acton might be chosen. But Rosebery had already earmarked him for Cambridge. "It is strange," he wrote to John Morley, "that our party choice should lie between a Papist and a Comtist."[4] John Robert Seeley, then Regius Professor at Cambridge, was gravely ill; he died in January 1895. As early as October 1894 Rosebery had written to Gladstone "in strict secrecy" that "the name of Acton smiles upon me" for one of the professorships of history that were likely to become vacant soon.[5] He had long had Acton's interests at heart. Acton's great learning was not in doubt, but: "1. he is a Roman Catholic. 2. I do not feel sure from his writings that he would find it easy to impart his knowledge to others—to be in short a good lecturer. 3. I do not think that he was at Oxford or Cambridge. No. 1 is the crucial objection. Acton is eminently antipapal, but Great Britain on these points is eminently suspicious. . . . I do not the least know if Acton would entertain the idea. But I like to write to ask your guidance."

Gladstone agreed with Rosebery on the difficulties. Although he believed that Acton's lecturing would be more effective than his writing, he feared that Acton "would be attacked as R.C. for party reasons: and the R.C.s might be found very shy of defending him. . . . The storm would be from without." Acton wanted a chair, Gladstone added, but his limited means and continued wish for a diplomatic position might deter him from accepting it. "My general feeling is against my wishes," Gladstone concluded. "It is that difficulty preponderates; but the matter is worth a very thorough probing."

Among other candidates were George Walter Prothero, formerly of King's College, Cambridge, who had, however, recently been appointed to the Edinburgh chair and could hardly be moved again. Frederick Pollock, the Oxford professor of jurisprudence, recommended Paul Vinogradoff of Moscow University, the great Russian authority on English medieval history. Rosebery replied that he "could hardly carry the Entente Cordiale so far as to appoint a Russian professor of modern history at Cambridge." Vinogradoff eventually came to England in 1901 and succeeded in Pollock's chair in 1903. George Otto Trevelyan, Rosebery's cabinet colleague, suggested Frederic William Maitland, then only forty-five, who had held the Downing Chair of the Laws of England since 1888, adding that he acted on information "taken on the spot" by his son, George Macaulay Trevelyan, an undergraduate at Trinity College, a former secretary of the University Liberal Association, who had ascertained that Maitland was "a Unionist" with Liberal views but no strong opinions and regarded in Cambridge history circles as "no partisan."

Acton's backers were Henry Sidgwick, the moral philosopher at Trinity College, Cambridge, and, surprisingly, Bishop Mandell Creighton, with whom Acton had so savagely dealt because of his mild attitude towards the Renaissance Popes. According to H. A. L. Fisher, Creighton described Acton as "the dark horse"[6] and said (to Sir Edward Hamilton, the former Treasury secretary, who passed this on to Rosebery) that he believed him to be "the man who would be best received—as perhaps the most learned Englishman."[7]

The appointment went quietly ahead. There was some uncertainty whether old statutes might require the professor to have a degree, but high-level discussions between the vice-chancellor and Rosebery's secretary, Sir George Murray, proved this to be unnecessary and confirmed Acton's eligibility.[8] The statute that the professor had to be a Cambridge graduate had been repealed in 1861.

"Supposing what seems absurd should occur," Acton wrote to his friend James Bryce most confidentially, "and that I shall have to consider the matter we discussed with Creighton—can you tell me anything about the conditions, the role as to time and work?"[9] Bryce replied that residence amounted to six weeks each in two terms and less in the third. The stipend was likely to be £800 a year, but might be only £700 (the equivalent of between £35,000 and £31,000 today). "In the interests of history I cannot but feel anxious you should accept. Your presence would be an immense stimulus to the study in Cambridge."[10]

Acton formally accepted the chair on 15 February 1895. His nomination was then laid before the Queen, who, before approving, raised the chief obstacle once more. Would Acton as "a good and firm, though very liberal-minded Catholic . . . not cause some difficulty to himself and the University? The universities are generally strong in their orthodox views and might render it difficult for Lord Acton, of whose efficiency there can be no doubt."[11] Rosebery, "frightened" by the Queen, sent for Acton to come and supply an answer, but the message did not reach Acton until it was too late and the Queen had given her consent, satisfied by Rosebery's reply quoting what Acton had written in response to a previous letter: "My reply to the religious scruple would then have been that, when Creighton became Bishop of Peterborough, he wished me to succeed him as Dixie Professor of Ecclesiastical History, although, or because, I had cut his book to pieces in his own *Review*."[12] After the announcement was made, Queen Victoria recorded: "Lord Rosebery told me that the people of the University of Cambridge were highly pleased with Lord Acton being appointed professor of history there."[13]

There was a somewhat comic side-line to these events, and it concerned the indefatigable and eccentric Oscar Browning, formerly a Master at Eton (which he left under a cloud because of his homosexuality) and now a Fellow of King's College, Cambridge. He wrote a long letter to Rosebery, his fellow-Etonian, on the day after the vice-chancellor's notification of the vacancy. In retrospect it is strange to think of Acton and the clownish Browning, an historian without great claim to scholarship but a prominent Cambridge busybody, as rivals in the race, but Acton had known Browning long enough to know that he had to be handled with care.

Warnings poured in to 10 Downing Street from the historians Henry Melvill Gwatkin, Maitland, and Creighton, just in case Rosebery might be tempted by the pull of the old school tie to favour Browning, also a fellow-Liberal. "As to the most notorious candidate, well, I need not tell a fellow-Etonian that O.B. is about the only person who takes himself seriously," wrote Sir Frederick Pollock. Just how seriously is shown in the way Browning wrote to the prime minister in January, immediately after Seeley's death: "The post [Seeley] held should be occupied by a man of genius, and I know of no man of genius to fill it. Having been, as you are probably aware, engaged in the College and University teaching of history for many years back, it has been suggested to me that I might have some claim to succeed to the Regius Professorship which is in your gift, and I have also been told that if I wished to be considered a candidate, I ought to write to you and say so." He warned Rosebery that his appointment would not be acceptable "to a certain section at Cambridge," where anti-Liberal prejudice had "injuriously affected" his position.[14]

But Rosebery knew his man and answered blandly: "I . . . take note of the wish you express in so modest and friendly a spirit," but in fact he took no notice of it. In the end Oscar Browning graciously congratulated Rosebery for an appointment that "does equal credit to the donor and the recipient. My only doubt is whether he is not too good for such a poor lot as our Cambridge historians are at this moment."[15]

Acton, who, as a letter to his daughter Annie shows, knew that Browning had been turned down for the professorship at Glasgow but was still hoping to succeed at Cambridge,[16] wrote to him to inform him of "the very strange and unexpected news" of his appointment: "Of course, I at once told him [Rosebery] that I could not entertain or consider the proposal if it was to stand in your way, but I learned that he had been advised to prefer several other candidates in case of my refusal and that there was no chance that the offer would be made to you." And he concluded that the Queen's pleasure had not yet been taken, and if any hitch should occur by which an opening was yet to be made for Browning, he would feel "that a great master of the art of teaching history has been preferred to the most inexperienced and untrained of imaginable professors."[17] In the face of such flattery even Browning must have felt obliged to bow to the inevitable.

Browning had known the Actons for many years, having visited them at Cannes, Tegernsee, and St. Martin during his vacations in the 1880s. He would have liked nothing better than to have taken Acton under his wing, more so Acton's good-looking undergraduate son, Richard, to whom he showed much kindness. But Acton was adept in keeping just the right distance. In 1888, for instance, Browning issued an invitation to all the Actons to stay with him during May Week. Acton accepted a day's invitation for himself, his daughter Mamy, and Richard, so that they would take in a garden party and then return to London the same evening.

When Cambridge awarded Acton an honorary doctorate of law, in July 1888, he and Rosebery, the two Liberal recipients, were put up by Browning, their fellow-Liberal, and Acton reported to Mary Gladstone Drew: "Rosebery stood very generously and manfully the touch of ridicule which attaches to guests of Oscar Browning."[18] When Acton's letters to Mary Gladstone Drew were published by her after his death, his son Richard apologized to Browning for that remark; it had not been omitted, as intended, through an oversight, adding that he regarded Browning's friendship as "one of the most treasured legacies bequested by my father."[19]

At the Cambridge awards of the honorary degrees, Acton's fellow-recipients apart from Rosebery were Lord Randolph Churchill, the first Earl of Selborne, a former Lord Chancellor; and the Liberal politician George Goschen, who, according to Acton's description of the ceremony to Mamy, was "the only one of us who was nervous at hearing himself praised in Latin before all men. I must confess I did not much like it." They sat opposite the Prince of Wales and his three little daughters. "The Duke of Devonshire (chancellor of the university) forgot so much of his Latin that I am not sure whether I have my degree after all. . . . Enough of my life as an LL.D. at Cambridge."[20]

Browning had also busied himself, in 1891, over the possibility of Acton's succeeding to the Dixie Chair of Ecclesiastical History when Mandell Creighton became Bishop of Peterborough.[21] Acton thanked him but declined, because he felt that he would "not satisfy requirements as a teacher of Protestant divines."[22] He had been offered a fellowship at King's College, Cambridge, simultaneously with an honorary one for All Souls, Oxford, which would involve occasional residence in Oxford. Acton accepted the latter. Another offer of a King's fellowship was made to him after he became a Regius Professor, which he then accepted.

Acton was flattered to be so much sought after. In his speech at All Souls he described himself as belonging to "the last of many generations excluded from academic joys," not mentioning that it had been done for reasons of religious discrimination. His Oxford audience gave him a long ovation. All were conscious of an historic occasion: Acton was the first Catholic in three hundred years to receive the honour.[23] Moreover, he shared the honour of the All Souls fellowship with Gladstone. Thus the ground was prepared for the Cambridge chair.

The country was "ringing with my appointment," Acton wrote to his daughter Mamy when the chair was finally his. It was "the highest post open to a literary man, pure and simple, and a great platform for exercising influence." Macaulay had been offered it after the appearance of his *History,* "as a fit acknowledgment of his unique position." But as no history of Acton had appeared, "I am rewarded for my silence as others are for their writings." Given that the last Catholic to hold a professorship at Cambridge or at Oxford lived under James II, and that Acton was not a Cambridge man, the chair was an unexampled honour. "I must now produce the harvest of a lifetime of private study."[24]

Letters of congratulations poured in. Bishop Creighton was delighted. "In Oxford everyone wanted to know what party you belonged to—political, ecclesiastical, social, journalistic. In Cambridge people only wanted to know if you were in earnest about your subject, and they appraised you accordingly and gave you a free hand to do what you liked."[25] Acton's friend Reginald Lane Poole, the Oxford historian, pupil of William Stubbs and assistant editor of the *English Historical Review* since its foundation, congratulated him. "I am far from being an enthusiastic admirer of the Modern History school here, but by the honourable admission of Cambridge it has much greater vitality and attracts far better material than the Historical Tripos does. . . . The very fact that Cambridge has hitherto been backward in historical study enhances the sanguine anticipations with which those who wish well to it must welcome the news of your appointment."[26] A particularly warm welcome came from Gladstone's second daughter, Helen, the vice-principal of Newnham Hall, Cambridge, for the Higher Education of Women, who also offered Acton help with finding a house. She was delighted at his appointment, she wrote, because a large number of the Newnham students worked at history, but of the four best historians at Cambridge in recent years—Sir John Robert Seeley, Creighton, Gwatkin, and Sir George Walter Prothero—only Gwatkin was left. "I felt that we were rather badly off so you see, you are doubly welcome."[27]

Acton was anxious to find out more about the work of his predecessor in the Cambridge Chair, John Robert Seeley. Originally a classicist and professor of Latin at University College, London University, Seeley had been elected at Cambridge to succeed Charles Kingsley largely on the strength of his fame as the author of the widely read and controversial *Ecce Homo,* a life of Christ, whose divinity he denied. When his *Short History of Napoleon the First* came out, first written for the *Encyclopaedia Britannica,* Acton, reviewing it in the *English Historical Review,* gave a long list of his inaccuracies and, while admiring his literary power and stimulating thought, described Seeley as the "philosopher of national greatness."[28]

Writing to Gladstone, who had appointed Seeley, Acton pointedly observed that there was "no great school of history there [at Cambridge], and not much studious curiosity about it." And if Seeley did not awaken it, "there is no chance of my doing much. . . . He was full of literary power, never oppressed with raw material, and not above the employment of stirring paradox. In all these respects," Acton went on, flatteringly—he was, after all, Rosebery's appointee— "he justified your selection, and did far more than his predecessors." Clearly Acton differed from Seeley considerably, not least in his view that "teachable history does not include the living generation and the questions of the day, as Seeley maintained that it does." Because of this disagreement, Acton felt, as he wrote earlier in the same letter, that in his own Inaugural Lecture there would be "some delicate ground to traverse at first, in the endeavour not to clash too rudely with so considerable a writer. I shall have to avoid his special topics."[29]

Seeley, in his own Inaugural Lecture (1869), had answered the question why history should be studied: "Because it is the school of statesmanship. . . . Our university is and must be a great seminary of politicians. Without at least a little knowledge of history no man can take a rational interest in politics, and no man can form a rational judgment about them without a good deal."[30] Moreover, Seeley opposed the common notion that history dealt with the remote past, not least because he wanted it to attract the young men who would become the legislators and statesmen of the future. He felt, as G. P. Gooch mentions, a hearty contempt for the purveyor of the picturesque and infuriated the youthful George Trevelyan by dismissing Trevelyan's uncle, Macaulay, and Carlyle as charlatans. It was said that he approached history and facts like a lawyer, making the lines of his argument converge on a single point. His conclusions, hammered into the minds of his students, were neither misunderstood nor forgotten. History possessed a meaning and taught lessons that it was the main duty of the historian to discover.

It was Seeley's direct reference to the problems of the day that helped to win for the *Expansion of England* its phenomenal success and for its author a knighthood in recognition for his services to the Empire in his writings. When in 1870, together with Henry Sidgwick, he had established the Historical Tripos (final examination for the honours degree at Cambridge), he claimed a leading place in it for political science. Seeley regarded himself as a political historian of the school of Ranke, to whom he owed most, and saw the significance of political history in the relation between historical facts, that is, in purely pragmatic terms. For him the diplomatic world was very much like a chessboard, governed by rules devoid of emotion. Political science—together with political economy, jurisprudence, and international law—was the backbone of history. Seeley's concept could not have been more remote from Acton's vision of universal history, in which "needless utterance of opinion, and the service of a cause" (such as politics or the Empire) were to be avoided, as was contemporary history, because it was insufficiently known. And he did not wish all history to be reduced "to a mere narrative of political transactions." Acton wanted his history to be "aloof from speculation and system" and to show convincing reason "for our impartial reserve."[31]

Nevertheless, as Helen Gladstone told him, Seeley's work with students had been impressive. Unlike others who look on history as a collection of facts, "he didn't end with paradoxes and leave you in a puzzle, he generally hurled them at you at the beginning, and then worked round and showed you what he meant." Seeley had even broken the mould and instituted a conversation class "for women students" (besides one for men) and did extremely valuable work in political science, raising difficulties and disposing of them, destroying the commonplace and stirring their minds. "I believe," Helen Gladstone wrote, "the 'conversation' was almost wholly on his part, as it was a most formidable matter to join in and if anyone ventured to uphold a different view to Prof. Seeley's, he (or she) was led on by insidious questions, till he had committed himself thoroughly and was neatly turned on his back." What she valued in Seeley's teaching above all was that "he *made them think*."[32]

Among the congratulations that Acton received upon his appointment to succeed Seeley, especially gratifying were those from Cardinal Herbert Vaughan, "the kindest and most touching letter that it has ever been my happy fortune to possess," as he put in his reply.[33] The Cardinal, Manning's successor, as a conciliator, had written to Acton from Rome. An attack on Acton in the *Irish Catholic,* which the Cambridge appointment had provoked, gave Vaughan the opportunity of distancing himself from it and saying how much "I rejoice in your nomination to the distinguished post, and how confident I feel in your goodness and fidelity to the Church. I know and understand something of the awful trials you must have gone through in years past, and I cannot but thank God that you are what I believe you to be—faithful and loyal to God and to his Church, though perhaps, by your great learning and knowledge of the human in this same Church, tried beyond other men."[34]

Acton responded gladly: "If I was not afraid of being presumptuous, I would in reply assure you that you have judged me rightly as well as most graciously, and I beg that you will believe in my sincere gratitude for all you say." And he added that his new position full of promising opportunities was "almost more a platform before the country than a *cathedra* with serious students under it."[35] The Vaughans of Courtfield in Herefordshire and the Actons of Aldenham were socially close, fellow-owners of Catholic estates. The Cardinal, Acton's senior by a year and a half, and Acton had known each other as boys. The Cardinal was also within the cousinage of the Herberts of Llanarth, the old Catholic family in Monmouthshire into which Acton's daughter Mamy was to marry.[36] The reconciliation was sealed by the special invitation that the Cardinal extended to Acton as a leading Catholic layman to the ceremony of the laying of the foundation-stone of Westminster Cathedral, in July 1895. At the lunch that followed it, Acton proposed the toast to "the Founders," after a list of those who had given money was read out.[37]

Earlier, Acton had actually been able to anticipate his official "re-admission" to the fold by doing a little service to the Cardinal in a matter of rank and dress and precedence, which exercised Roman Catholics of that generation after their transition from an oppressed to a tolerated though still denigrated minority. Having found the ancient sees occupied by the national Church, and having to appear under new territorial titles, the bishops of the restored hierarchy regarded the assertion of their position as of considerable importance for the dignity of the Church and more than a mere matter of etiquette. The Cardinal thus liked to put on his purple, which in Protestant England was then considered a provocative act. The Prince of Wales, who had already encountered trouble some years earlier for allowing Cardinal Manning to take precedence before other dignitaries, remarked to Acton on Vaughan's preference for "striking colours." He feared, he said, that it might be imprudent and might some day lead to some impertinence or protest or unpleasant demonstration.

Acton passed the royal hint on to Thomas Stonor, his friend and ally in Rome during the Vatican Council, now back in London as Archbishop of Trebizond, adding that the Prince had spoken as *amicus Curiae*. This hint was duly passed on to the Cardinal, who, thanking Acton, saw the point and proposed a compromise, writing that he had thought it "more respectful" to appear in the evening dress always worn by Cardinals on the Continent, even in Protestant Prussia, "than to suppose the continuance of such prejudice and sensitiveness in English society as to require some disguise." However, he proposed to meet the difficulty by going to Catholic houses in his proper Cardinal's evening dress, and to non-Catholic parties in "what may be called a semi-dress—black coat, red stockings and zuchetto, unless the host or hostess should express a preference for the full dress."[38] Having informally told the Prince of Wales "of the distinction which Your Eminence means to draw," Acton wrote back to the Cardinal that the Prince had found the Cardinal's decision "in point of caution the right one."[39]

Acton's duties as Lord-in-Waiting ended in August. But at Windsor he was able to shut himself away in his room to work on his Inaugural Lecture. The Queen was told about his writing by one of her Maids-of-Honour, and after a long talk with her he wrote to Annie that "the queen's partiality *finit par déborder* [overshoots the mark]. She did not like [Sir George Otto] Trevelyan [secretary for Scotland in Gladstone's last cabinet], whom she had seen for the first time, and she did not much like his famous uncle [Macaulay], whose praises, however, I resolutely proclaimed." That opening led him to say how kindly he had been received at Cambridge and how no shadow of enmity appeared. "She answered: What a happy change there has been! — All due, Ma'm, to Your Majesty's reign. And so on, *au grand détriment des autres* [to the great detriment of others], until the hour for retiring."[40]

Acton was sixty-one years old when the Cambridge appointment was made. He had only seven more years to live, but they were at least on a par with the happy first years of his marriage, when he enjoyed his freedom after having been an MP and a Catholic editor harassed by his Church. In Cambridge he finally came into his own. To Gladstone he wrote: "It is a most interesting enterprise, to me." And he added: "The appointment, I am glad to think, did no harm to Rosebery. I was received at Cambridge, not exactly with warmth, but with as friendly a welcome as I could have hoped for. But then I had already many good friends there, as you know better than any one. A tendency towards garrulity seems a natural consequence of having such a platform to speak from."[41]

Early in May 1895, Acton's Cambridge initiation took place in the form of a short ceremony of admission. He was made a Master of Arts and a member of the Senate, appointments that gave him various privileges regarding the University Library. He ordered an expensive silk Master of Arts gown, and when he was measured for the cap it was found that his head was the largest on record. "If Browning finds it out," he wrote to Mamy, "he will put it in the papers; but he did not turn up." The Registrar of the University charged him £17 5s. for the cost of his complete degree of LL.D., including five guineas in consideration of the Orator's speech.[42] In the evening there was a "grand feast" at St. John's, where "I held a sort of levée, as Americans call it," with the classical scholar Sir John Sandys, the Master, introducing him to everybody: heads of houses, professors, notables. It was a kind of homecoming for Acton, and when, some time later, the Master of Magdalene College invited him to dinner, he was shown the entry of his father and uncle in the books, in 1819, and, as he told his daughter, his host was "perturbed" when Acton told him that Magdalene would not have him in 1849.[43]

Acton was generally received with every courtesy, kindness, and distinction, but he was under no illusion about what this treatment meant. "I am too strange to them, too much off the line, for it to be more warm and cordial than just what I have described. It is a triumph that there should have been no *Misston* [false note] and no blunder."[44] Trinity College offered him a set of rooms in Nevile's Court, staircase 2, A1, on the first floor, and later added on next door to it when his library there, too, grew to overflowing. This was the college hallowed by Francis Bacon and Isaac Newton, Lord Byron and Thomas

Babington Macaulay, William Makepeace Thackeray and Alfred, Lord Tennyson, the prime ministers Spencer Perceval, Lord Grey, Lord Melbourne, Arthur James Balfour, Sir Henry Campbell-Bannermann, and Stanley Baldwin. For Acton it meant "interesting company and a good table," and he managed to decline the fellowship offered him by Trinity Hall, whose master, his close friend Sir Henry Maine, Regius Professor for Civil Law, had just died. He was put up at Trinity Lodge as the guest of Henry Montagu Butler, the Master of Trinity College, and royally treated. His host, Dr. Butler, he reported to Annie, was almost too gushing. "His son, a clerk in the House of Lords, (son of a first wife), arrived after us and the father kissed him as if they had not met three days ago. . . . He says my dear wife, my dear wife's dear old father in Scotland, our dear servants. . . . OB [Oscar Browning] came to dinner (he is called 'dear OB,' like everybody else here)." On Sunday morning, Acton went to early Mass at the Church of Our Lady and the English Martyrs in Hills Road, newly built in the Pugin manner, consecrated only five years earlier, "one of the finest we have in England," he wrote to Annie. "There were near a dozen undergraduates at Communion."[45]

In May Acton had his first meeting of the committee that regulated historical studies, where he met Frederic William Maitland, who, as he knew, had also been considered for his chair. The brilliant legal historian admired Acton, who told his daughter that he laid the foundation of "good fellowship." Shortly afterwards Acton was sent an essay, "which they want the University to print, and which is medieval—and consequently in Maitland's department. He is in favour of it. I have had to report adversely."[46] Human relations at Cambridge, he was discovering, had to be treated with circumspection.

Acton delivered his Inaugural Lecture on Tuesday, 11 June 1895, not, as customary for Regius Professors, at the Senate House, but at the Divinity Library Lecture Rooms. This smaller place was thought to be less of a strain for the speaker's voice. It was filled to overflowing on the stairs, and many turned disappointedly away. Cambridge's leading lights were there, Henry Sidgwick the philosopher among them, as well as many elegant women, as were always attracted to Acton, among them the two Gladstone daughters, Helen, vice-principal of Newnham College, and Mary Drew, the eldest, his special friend. Silence fell over the audience when Acton entered, a sturdy and imposing figure, his huge head held erect, the once black beard now greying, still with piercing blue eyes. The Continental nobleman showed in his appearance; he wore his new silk gown, his "drapery," as he called it. His opening sentences touched his listeners. He told them that as a young man, he had set his heart on coming to Cambridge, but that, "as things then were," he was denied admittance at three colleges. He refrained from saying that it was done for reasons of religious discrimination, but mentioned that his hopes, "in an happier hour, after five and forty years, . . . are at last fulfilled."[47]

The theme of his lecture was the Unity of Modern History. He gently distanced himself from Seeley's notion of history as little more than a handmaiden of politics or as including contemporary history. In a fine passage Acton said that for him history is "one consistent epic," in which mind and ideas matter: "A speech of Antigone, a single sentence of Socrates, a few lines that were inscribed on an Indian rock before the Second Punic War, the footsteps of a silent yet prophetic people who dwelt by the Dead Sea, and perished in the fall of Jerusalem, come nearer to our lives than the ancestral wisdom of barbarians who fed their swine on the Hercynian acorns." Modern history begins "unheralded" in the fifteenth century, with the new order of the world marked by investigation, discovery, and independence and founded by Columbus, Machiavelli, Erasmus, Luther, and Copernicus (2:506–7). What previously was done by authority, outward discipline, and organized violence was now done by division of power and the conscience of free men. Toleration became a political, moral, and theological dogma, a question of conscience in the seventeenth century (2:516–17).

Acton referred to those of his own generation, among them Ranke, Comte, Newman, and Carlyle, who rejected the idea of progress towards freedom, power balanced and cancelled rather than power concentrated, and who held that the Whig theory that authority is legitimate only by virtue of its checks is rebellion against the divine will. Against that he put forward his own view that the action of Christ, who redeemed humanity, appears not in the perfection but the improvement of the world. But what do people mean, he asked, who proclaim liberty as the ultimate prize, seeing that it is an idea of which there are two hundred definitions? Was it French democracy, American federalism, Italian independence, the reign of the fittest as in Germany? The tests he applied were certain outward signs like representation, the extinction of slavery, free speech, the security enjoyed by weaker, indeed unpopular groups in society: "The liberty of conscience which, effectually secured, secures the rest" (2:519–25).

Acton's message was that solidity of criticism matters more than plenitude of erudition: sources, authorities, testimony must be thoroughly tested, characters and motives examined. "The maxim that a man must be presumed to be innocent until his guilt is proved, was not made for him" (the historian) (2:529). The historian's dogma is rigorous impartiality. "Ideas which, in religion and in politics, are truths, in history are forces. They must be respected; they must not be affirmed" (2:530). Acton said that even the impartial Ranke had slipped: when Ranke described how William III had a Catholic clan murdered at Glencoe, he found the excuses of William's defenders to be untenable. However, when he came to evaluate William's character, that moral judgement was forgotten over Ranke's hero-worship (2:548). "Never debase the moral currency or . . . lower the standard of rectitude," Acton exhorted his audience, but he felt contemporary opinion to be against him. "At every step we are met by arguments which go to excuse, to palliate, to confound right and wrong, and reduce the just man to the level of the reprobate." He castigated the current fluidity of moral notions, the historians' refusal to accept a common code in their wish to make distant times and deeds intelligible and acceptable to modern society. "It became a rule of policy to praise the spirit when you could not defend the deed. . . . You must consider the times, the class from which men sprang, the surrounding influences, . . . until responsibility is merged in numbers and not a culprit is left for execution." With irony Acton seemed to anticipate a society used to trials for war crimes: "A murderer was no criminal if he followed local custom, if neighbours approved, if he was encouraged by official advisers or prompted by just authority, if he acted for the reason of state or the pure love of religion or if he sheltered himself behind the complicity of the Law" (2:546-47).

Acton quoted Edmund Burke, "who, when true to himself, is the most intelligent of our instructors: 'My principles enable me to form my judgement upon men and actions in history, just as they do in common life; and are not formed out of events and characters, either present or past. History is the preceptor of prudence, not of principles. The principles of true politics are those of morality enlarged; and I neither now do, nor ever will admit of any other.'" Modern historians have the power to be more "rigidly impersonal," and "to learn from undisguised and genuine records to look with remorse upon the past, and to the future with assured hope of better things; bearing this in mind, that if we lower our standard in history, we cannot uphold it in Church and State" (2:551-52).

There was warm applause led by the Master of Trinity, Henry Montagu Butler and his wife, Acton reported to his son. He had carried Richard's letter with good wishes as an amulet in the pocket of his gown, he wrote. Some ladies had left quite early and he was told that they were "merely bored generally and not offended at anything in particular I had said." His own impression was that it had gone quite well. He had spoken for just an hour (which, if true, must have been taxing for his listeners). "Sometimes I had a sense of it not being a very intelligent audience and some points were lost. . . . All wished to read it at their ease, hinting that it would take as much digesting as a dressed crab. . . . There was certainly some bewilderment. More, I think, because it was unexpected than because it was obscure. But whatever drawbacks, I have clearly established my position here."[48]

The Inaugural survives as one of the finest and most polished in the history of the Regius Professors. On the whole, praise outweighed criticism in the widespread press reactions. The *Times* devoted a leading article to the "unusual interest" that "the appointment of a distinguished, if very independent, Roman Catholic as the chief representative of the teaching of modern history has drawn to Lord Acton's address." It paid him the compliment of showing "no theological bias whatever" and "absolute impartiality," and presenting "a conception of history" that "is pregnant and stimulating." Disagreeing with Acton's view that the immense multiplication of new material would encourage independence of judgement either in writers or in readers of history, the *Times* found that some of his statements "have the delusive precision which at once attracts and repels us in the historical speculations of Frenchmen." Lord Acton would "have to guard against a tendency to paradox and exaggeration if he is to use his ample stores of erudition and reflection to the best advantage of the great University . . . in which he now worthily occupies a place of influence, dignity, and honour."[49]

Like the *Times,* the *Spectator* concurred "heartily" with Acton's appeal "never to debase the moral currency" and applauded "a very successful performance full of thought and epigram" and "showing no sign of religious partiality." However, "it is possible for a historian to know too much, and, if we wished to be bitter, we might say that Lord Acton was himself a living example of the new trouble, mass of materials. The single defect of his lecture is that he is overwhelmed by the multitude of his own thinking and leaves on the mind a less definite impression than many a teacher without half his wide wisdom or a tenth of his accumulated learning."[50]

The vigorous *Saturday Review,* a favourite journal among the more literate Tory squires, revised its first impression of "confused thinking" on rereading the text and perceiving "that much of his apparent incoherence and inconsequence proceeds from a difficulty of expression, partly due to a lax grasp on the immense mass of materials with which he endeavours to deal, and partly due to the laboured and pretentious style, in which he has chosen to muffle his expression." He had evidently never learned to write English. It was "not to be endured" that "the well digested knowledge and unfailing lucidity of Seeley or even the brilliant historical imagination and splendid prose of his predecessor, Kingsley, should be succeeded by . . . the Batavian splutterings of Lord Acton's awkward pen." And the *Saturday Review* hoped that, unless in succeeding lectures the new professor could match his reputed learning with greater lucidity, he would resign his post.[51] Both these aforementioned censures could probably also be explained as coming from traditionally xenophobic Tory circles, for whom Acton was damned as a Gladstonian Liberal. But the Liberal *Guardian*, too, reviewing the published Inaugural, found it "surcharged with matter to overflowing and the style—weighty, concise and occasionally epigrammatic—is not such as to aid a listener in the ready comprehension of it; it must have been extremely difficult to follow in delivery." Nevertheless, the University of Cambridge was to be congratulated "on the acquisition of a professor who adds to profundity a lofty and unyielding morality."[52]

H. A. L. Fisher, the historian and Liberal MP who reviewed the Inaugural and *Lectures on Modern History* after Acton's death, judged him to have been "a brilliant success" at Cambridge but questioned his absolutist moral standard. Allowances for environment had to be made, because there have been, for example, societies in which theft was regarded as an honourable accomplishment. Acton, "like all good historians," in practice applied a double standard, "denouncing murder and cruelty wherever he finds it, but at the same time he is careful to exhibit the texture of a society, in which murder is promoted and persecution enforced, not that he may weaken the abhorrence felt by good men for crime, but in order that his readers should understand how certain states of society are less favourable than others to the practice of virtue." And on Acton's view of the process by which political liberty grew out of the claim for religious toleration, which was in turn the creation of sectaries who dissented from dissenters, Fisher concluded that the principle that he holds to be of the most transcendent value in human affairs was in fact "the result of the fissiparous tendencies of the Reformation, of that anarchy of opinion which it is the aim and function of the papacy to correct."[53]

Acton found more support in J. L. Hammond, the journalist and social writer and Gladstonian sympathizer. "When the men who are competent to hold the scales of history are few," he observed, "it is unfortunate that one of them should have been so reluctant to let the world know his conclusions, without letting it know also the processes by which he had reached them." He went on:

Few men give justice the first place in politics, though almost every one gives it the second. Most men think vaguely or certainly that the maintenance of established interests in some category is the sovereign end, and as far as morality is friendly or neutral, they are glad enough to patronise it or they think that morality is not meant for slippery times, though it does well enough for tranquil and comfortable days. Lord Acton gave morality itself pre-eminence; and he allowed no boisterous storm of temptation or disorder to excuse men for declining on some other standard. If he had never carried out his great dream, he would have traced the slow growth of the sense of morality between States and nations. He lived very close to what he once called "the wavy line between religion and politics."[54]

Two adverse criticisms came from abroad. Henry Charles Lea, an American medievalist and historian of the Inquisition, wrote: "The historian who becomes an advocate or a prosecutor instead of a judge forfeits his title to confidence, and, if he aspires to be a judge, he should not try a case by a code unknown to the defendants."[55] That was unfair, as Acton's point, of course, was that the moral law was universal and independent of time and place. But Lea may have wanted revenge for Acton's review of his *History of the Inquisition of the Middle Ages,* which, though generous in praise of the author's knowledge and scholarship, found it to be "inadequate" as a philosophy of religious persecution. Acton's main criticism was of Lea's view that the thinking of the Middle Ages was sophistry and its belief superstitious. "Mr Lea is not under compulsion to that rigid liberalism, which . . . converts history into a frightful monument of sin. . . . He does not sentence the heretic, but he will not protect him from his doom. He does not care for the inquisitor, but he will not resist him in the discharge of his duty."[56] That cannot have endeared Acton to the author.

Both critical and hostile was the Marburg historian Karl Lamprecht (1856–1915), head of the Leipzig Institute for Culture and Universal History. He judged the authorized German translation as "excellent." It cannot have been that, however, on the mere basis of the extracts he quoted. Oddly, Lamprecht discerned "the Utilitarianism of his people running deeply in the noble Lord's veins." Wrongly he ascribed to Acton Seeley's view of history "as the handmaiden of diplomacy, politics and pedagogy." Acton had explicitly distanced himself from it. Lamprecht also condemned Acton for rejecting "a scientific view of history" and having recourse to "the corrective of a safety valve, a motive power of thought, unstable in itself, and therefore dangerous, namely the demand for certain supreme and stable ethical principles in history."[57]

The young George Macaulay Trevelyan—eventually to become Master of Trinity College, Cambridge, and to follow Acton as Regius Professor of Modern History—was probably the informed source of his father's letter to Rosebery in November 1895:

> You may care to know, what perhaps you may have heard from other quarters, what an immense success Acton is at Cambridge. At least two hundred people came to his first lecture, and quite as many attend every one of them since: whereas I am told that even a famous Regius Professor thinks himself happy if he can draw one freshman, and three or four young women. It is not only undergraduates of both sexes: but the cleverest and most fastidious of the young historical specialists, who themselves are lecturing and writing, are always there. He is regarded distinctly as a great man, and the younger people pay him the unusual compliment of thinking him a great deal younger than he is. The feeling is that the lectures which he is delivering are literature of a very high order. Altogether, it has been a tremendous hit.[58]

Rosebery, who had resigned his position as prime minister in June of that year, had no reason to regret Acton's appointment. And G. M. Trevelyan, a former student of Seeley's, remembered Acton in his own Inaugural as Regius Professor more than thirty years later: "His incomparable learning, his cosmopolitan outlook, and his moral and philosophical power made us feel that we had found a master who soon proved to be a friend."[59]

Summing up all these reactions, Acton wrote to Annie: "Think how unsympathetic my teaching must be to the philistine, the sordid, the technical, the faddist, the coward, the man of prejudice and passion, the zealot, etc. This makes much more than half the world. So I am always surprised at praise, and only wonder at blame, and especially misapprehension in particular places."[60]

Cambridge, rather than Aldenham or Tegernsee, may today be said to have become Acton's permanent home, considering that his library and extensive archives also found their final resting place in the Cambridge University Library. The man who was instrumental in securing them there was Owen Chadwick, who had sat at the feet of Trevelyan and others who had studied under Acton, who has also followed him in the Regius Professorship (1968–83), and who has long commanded familiarity with all aspects of Acton's life and thought. In his

1995 address on the centennial of Acton's coming to Cambridge, Chadwick referred to the "reverence" for one of the great minds of the nineteenth century, which scholars from all over the world developed when working among those books and notes. "In a sense Acton is the poet of history." "He made liberty not just a political expedient but a moral right; and he had a mystical sense that this moral right would slowly conquer the world." "He saw corruption and slavery and crime and yet could exult in what whole societies had achieved." And Chadwick portrayed Acton as one who established history as a respected discipline at Cambridge, "a genius . . . when he spoke about history," with a wonderful ability to make narrative history exciting and colourful.[61]

In the autumn of 1895 Acton began his first course of lectures; thirty-two on the French Revolution were delivered over the two academic years 1895–96 and 1896–97, and repeated over the subsequent two years, 1897–98 and 1898–99, fitting in with the Historical Tripos, which had the French Revolution in those years as one of its special subjects and determined the scope of the course. A second course on modern history covered nineteen lectures over two years from 1899, concentrating on European history and ending with the American Revolution. Both lecture courses were published, after Acton's death, by Macmillan: first the European history, and then the lectures on the French Revolution, which appeared without the apparatus of notes Acton provided for the Inaugural Lecture. The needed revision and expansion of the other lectures were left undone.[62]

Acton's lectures were held in a room under the Trinity College Library. Remembering Helen Gladstone's praise of the usefulness of Seeley's conversation class, Acton started one in October, held on Monday afternoons in the Divinity Library Lecture Rooms (in the same building in which the Inaugural Lecture was delivered), and women students also came. Because the room under the Trinity Library held only 150 people and there were rumours of a large attendance, particularly women, it was decided—much against Acton's will—to exclude the general public by charging a heavy fee. Oscar Browning, the misogynist, complained: "Seeley found it necessary to charge a fee to all who are not members of the University. I am told that you let in Newnham and Girton students free—Seeley did not—they all had to pay, and it made a considerable addition to his income. I would suppose that you should either impose the fee, or give the women a separate lecture by themselves."[63] But Acton did not accept that advice.

Most of Acton's lectures were crowded, always attracting great curiosity and

not serious students only. He wrote out every word of his beautifully composed text, but reading it verbatim must have harmed the delivery, especially
because of his intricate thought and style, which, even in the published version, require concentrated attention. Having a sweet tooth, he liked nibbling
biscuits, or preferably his favourite marshmallows, even during his lectures and
while working.

Acton's ready help to women students brought him an invitation from Helen
Gladstone and the principal of Newnham College, Eleanor (Nora) Sidgwick
(wife of his friend Henry Sidgwick, who had done so much to set up Newnham College), to become an honorary member and join its Council. He took
part in the campaign, fought through many years, to grant degrees to women.
They had been allowed to share the men's studies, and to compete in examinations (for instance, in the Historical Tripos) since 1881, but not to get their
degrees. Acton signed a memorial—whose supporters included two-thirds of
the professors, the Archbishop,and many bishops—to correct the injustice. But
student opposition was the main obstacle. "Our undergraduates are foolish,"
he wrote to his daughter Mamy before another University vote on the issue;
"they are all against them, and the boys at several Public Schools have made a
pact not to go to what they call a girls' school, but only to Oxford. The feelings are evidently excited, and we shall be well beaten."[64] And they were, despite some two thousand signatures, remarkable, as Helen Gladstone told him,
for the strong ecclesiastical element, including the Archbishop of Canterbury,
the bishops of English sees, Arthur James Balfour, Sir George Otto Trevelyan,
and Hugh Culling Childers, the former cabinet minister.[65] The universities of
Oxford and Cambridge continued to refuse women the B.A. degree, Oxford
until after World War I, Cambridge until after World War II.

It is strange that Acton seems not to have encouraged either of his daughters
to study at a university; Annie certainly had the required intellect. But sending his son to Oxford put a financial restraint on the education of the girls.[66]
In regard to women's suffrage, his feelings were eminently Victorian, as a letter
to Gladstone showed. He opted to take "the side preferred by Cato," he wrote,
an allusion to the elder Cato's uncompromising reaction to the women's movement of his day. Gladstone had asked Acton about giving women the vote, and
he answered that it ought to be decided by expediency. Because women were
likely to vote Tory, he did not see why the Liberals should sacrifice their interests. If it could be shown that a majority of women would vote Liberal or divide
equally, "the balance is, very slightly, in favour of giving them votes."[67]

In October 1896 Acton received his first American degree, the honorary doctorate of law from Princeton University, but he was unable to travel to the United States for it. In the following year he went to St. Andrew's to collect another honorary doctorate of law, and the Rector, John Patrick, third Marquess of Bute and a fellow-Catholic, whom Acton had met in Rome at the time of the Vatican Council, sent him his gown as a gift. The moral philosopher Henry Sidgwick, a dominant personality in the University, invited Acton to join the Eranus Society in Cambridge. It had only a dozen members, among them some of the top brains of the University, such as Henry Jackson, professor of Greek; F. W. Maitland, Downing Professor of English Law; the physicist and mathematician Sir George Darwin (one of Charles Darwin's sons); the modern historian Adolphus William Ward; and the Regius Professor of Physic Sir Thomas Allbutt. The Eranus had been founded in 1872 by Brooke Foss Westcott, Joseph Barber Lightfoot, and Fenton John Anthony Hort but was not intended to be specifically theological. The aim was to give scholars of different subjects a regular opportunity for a more serious and methodical exchange of ideas than ordinary social gatherings allowed. They met five times a year at the home of each member in turn, who read a paper on the subject selected by himself, which was then formally debated. Acton's first meeting was at Darwin's house, Newnham Grange.

In May 1897 it was Acton's turn to receive his fellow-members in his rooms at Trinity, and he read to them a paper, kept in a lighter vein but profound, on his adventures and researches in some forty Continental archives in the early 1860s and what the implications were for the historian's task. "I think very few [of my listeners] had any idea before what I meant by history, and the work it involves," he wrote to Annie afterwards.[68] The opening of archives in Acton's lifetime was the great fact for historical studies, and his paper reflected his enthusiasm in these discoveries: "By going on from book to manuscript and from library to archive we exchange doubt for certainty, and become our own masters. We explore a new heaven and a new earth, and at each step forward the world moves with us."[69] But against the optimism of his Eranus Society talk was the doubt expressed in his private notes that documents, too, could lie, because they are themselves selected and must be distributed, because there are gaps, because "Papier ist geduldig" (paper is patient [or gullible, that is, one can do, or prove, anything on paper]). "What people conceal is not their best deeds and motives, but their worst. What archives reveal is the wickedness of Man. It destroys idols and scatters theories."[70]

Acton's mind and ideas came across at their best not in his lectures but in his contacts with small groups of students. He was always patient, ready with advice and encouragement. Unmitigated praise was rare and given for genuine qualities: effort, sincerity, large-mindedness. His rebukes were rare, too, but could be stinging. "I don't like clever young men," he is reported to have said, meaning not, of course, that he disliked cleverness, but the display of it, perhaps in remembrance of his own early cleverness with which it had been so easy for him to deceive older contemporaries and disguise his immaturity. "It is a great demerit not to know Italian," he said to one undergraduate who was airily excusing his ignorance of that language. His students took to his irony—it was not of the wounding, ridiculing sort. John Pollock told of a pupil reading a paper before him on Austrian policy during the year 1815. It was a careful piece of work, largely based on the *Memoirs of Fouché*. Acton analysed and corrected it, pointed out weaknesses, and finally, as if in an afterthought, remarked: "I think you made some use of Fouché's *Memoirs*. I suppose you know they are not authentic?"[71] In his rooms in Nevile's Court he was at all times accessible to great scholars as well as humble undergraduates. He sat at his desk behind shelves that he had put up to hold the books for work in hand, each volume with oblong slips of newspaper—he had little piles of these cut up in readiness— sticking out from the pages to mark passages of importance.

Acton liked in his lectures to bring out the melodrama of history. He described to his daughter Annie, with evident enjoyment, how he managed to make his lecture audience "very miserable" about a courageous young woman being carted slowly through the streets of Paris in a tumbrel, painting one of the grand tableaux of the French Revolution in starkest colours; how the young woman hoped "that the quiet people of Paris, once they saw her head on the pike, would remember that for them her young life was given. And, as the cart moved slowly through the shrieking crowd, and Samson [the executioner], said: 'You must find this takes a long time,' she answered: 'Oh, I am not afraid of being late.' The terrible episode ended with those words and the effect seemed to me deeper than any other has been." And he had added as in a throwaway sentence: "I forgot to say how I told the maiden's name: 'She was the daughter of M. d'Armont, but in the immortality of history she bears the name of Charlotte Corday.'" And hoping for approval from beyond the Bavarian Alps, he asked: "Comment trouvez-vous cela?" (How do you find that?).[72]

A fortnight later he reported that some old dons in the audience hid their faces in their hands and shook with sobs as he described the flight of the King and Queen to Varennes: "I was delayed by Oscar Browning to write the fall of Danton. It was not one of my better lectures. But Lady Alwyn [Compton], the wife of the bishop of Ely, was quite dissolved. I look forward to Thermidor next week. . . . Marie Antoinette was executed today, with unbending severity. . . . I find my voice improving greatly—with the help of an egg in Martini—and I am also better heard. A cheque for nineteen guineas arrived for my lectures before Easter which is very pleasant."[73]

Acton liked historical riddles, the knotty problems of history; he was forever making his lists of analogous cases and names that enabled him to bring out crucial comparisons. He enjoyed setting historical puzzles like: "How often has England been saved by changes in the wind?" Answer: "1588, 1688, 1788, 1798, 1805." "Where should we all have been if the geese of the Forum had not called and roused Manlius, if the parrot had not diverted Columbus, if Caesar had read the warning message, if the walls of Hougoumont [near Waterloo] had fallen, if the Chinese missionaries had pushed on to Rome, if the nose of Cleopatra had been longer, if Hannibal had not marched against Rome, or Lee against Washington?"[74] General Robert E. Lee was his favourite military commander, and thirty years earlier and despite the immorality of slavery he had supported Lee's cause against the North in the American Civil War. "You were fighting the battles of our liberty, our progress and our civilization," he wrote to him at the time of Lee's defeat, "and I mourn for the stake which was lost at Richmond more deeply than I rejoice over that which was saved at Waterloo."[75]

Dr. Henry Jackson, professor of Greek at Cambridge, Acton's fellow-student in Nevile's Court, Trinity, recalled:

"I suppose, Lord Acton," said some one interrogatively, "that So-and-so's book is a very good one?" "Yes," was the reply, "perhaps five per cent less good than the public thinks it." But a casual question not seldom drew from him an acute comment, an interesting reminiscence, or a significant fact. "When was London in the greatest danger?" asked some one rather vaguely. "In 1803," was the immediate answer, "when Fulton proposed to put the French army across the Channel in steamboats, and Napoleon rejected the scheme."[76]

Acton had an insatiable appetite for curiosities as well as the "backstairs" of history, noting, for instance, that the name of Ipswich could be spelled in fifty-seven different ways, or that, in 1805, one Captain Franks struck a whale in Davis Street, which was later killed near Spitzbergen by his son, who found his father's name on an harpoon sticking in its belly. He liked telling the story of the young married couple, friends of his, on their honeymoon on the Spanish Atlantic coast. A huge wave swept the husband out to sea, but when his wife had already given him up for dead, he was carried back by a later wave to the same spot, alive. Acton tried to impress upon his children the complexities that lessons of history contain. "Try to understand," he wrote to Annie, "that the right is not all on one side, that good men are often wrong, and that wicked men sometimes accomplish what is necessary for the welfare of nations. History only teaches us to nurse and encourage our passions, if we do not learn to look at it with divided sympathies."[77]

Closer contact with his pupils led Acton, in December 1896, to found the Trinity Historical Society, which still flourishes. There were around a dozen members including all the Trinity history dons, and he presided at most of their meetings. They met once a month in his rooms and once elsewhere for reading papers and discussing them. "It will be very useful to them and no great bore to me," he wrote to Annie.[78] He led off the first meeting with a lecture that produced an animated discussion. The undergraduates took to him, and outsiders from other colleges were eager to join. He checked the "insular and provincial tendencies" of the Cambridge historians who looked upon Stubbs's Select Charters to 1307 (1870) as "the Bible of the history school."[79]

To the students, Acton was the scholar-statesman, not a mere theoretician. He had been involved in the world of politics. They were, of course, impressed by his immense knowledge, viewing him as a kind of walking dictionary of dates and sources. They liked his foreignness and his interest in scandal. He was "at home," as Maitland put it, "no doubt, upon the frontstairs, but supreme upon the backstairs, and (as he once said) getting his meals in the kitchen: acquainted with the use of cupboards and with the skeletons that lie therein; especially familiar with the laundry where the dirty linen is washed; an analyst of all the various soaps that have been employed for that purpose in all ages and all climes."[80] Manuscript work attracted him because of the scientific detection it involved, the knowledge of detail it required, because it penetrated to "the pourquoi du pourquoi."[81]

If one could catch him at the right time and in the right mood, he lived up to his great reputation and let loose a flood of illuminating knowledge. But when he was in one of his black moods or in ungenial company, his silence could be deafening. The Cambridge historian Thomas Thornely, who often sat with Acton on the History Board, noted that he always refused to preside and "could hardly be persuaded to open his lips, unless directly appealed to, and even then, if the question admitted of a monosyllabic answer, that was the form it took."[82]

Acton could speak straight from the heart and head. "Age, experience and erudition had not taught him to minish and mince," wrote F. W. Maitland, who thought that there was some justice in Manning's old accusation that Acton and Simpson, as young Catholic editors, indulged in "the ruthless talk of under-graduates." But according to Maitland, behind the occasional irony and rail-lery there was always an acute, "an almost overwhelming sense of the gravity, the sanctity of history." Acton's daily reading consumption was "one German octavo." Mastering that, however, was for Acton not a matter of sitting idly in an easy chair, but a serious task requiring a table, pencil, pen, and abundant pieces of paper and total application to his task.[83]

There is the famous story told by James Bryce about a dinner in the late 1880s, when apart from Acton his guests were Mandell Creighton, the histo-rian of the Renaissance Popes, and Robertson Smith, the historian of Semitic religion. When Creighton talked of Pope Leo X, Acton could easily cap his evidence, which was not surprising. But when Robertson Smith talked of Old Testament history, Acton was also more than able to hold his own.[84] And in this conversation among friends it was not a matter of scoring points. Acton was amazingly knowledgeable, for example, about the new biblical scholarship that, in his time, was advancing so fast, and the shelves of his library bore out this particular interest.

In Cambridge Acton fought in vain for his young friend George Peabody Gooch, a scholar after his heart, whom he regarded as a promising historian but whose prize essay met with much disapproving criticism. The questions for the Trinity fellowship examination in 1897 were set by Acton, the subject being Barbarossa. But Gooch, then twenty-four years old, failed to win the fel-lowship, though years later, as a renowned historian, he was elected honorary fellow of his college.[85]

"There is some mild complaint of my too great popularity with the students, especially with the ladies of whom twenty-five are regular attendants," Acton wrote to his daughter Mamy.[86] There was a collision with his friends Sidgwick and Browning at the Board of Studies meeting. Acton wanted his course to be general European history. They moved an amendment, a course on the devel-opment of a European polity, which, to him, meant that "history is nothing but politics, and that, if told plainly, it means nothing." So, unusually, he broke his silence and declared that it cut at the root of history proper and that he must protest. "There was almost a scene." Alfred Marshall, the professor of political economy who had proposed the motion, assured him that he would not act against his wishes, so Acton prevailed.[87]

Acton returned to Windsor during the year of Queen Victoria's Diamond Jubilee, in 1897. "Was very glad to see Lord Acton again and had some conversation with him. He is very happy lecturing at Cambridge on the French Revolution," the Queen recorded in her journal.[88] The occasion was a visit of her daughter, the Empress Frederick. At dinner Acton sat next to her, while she was placed at the Queen's right. The Queen was unable to stand and could only walk a few steps with the greatest difficulty, supported by an Indian attendant. Her eyes were failing, but she was well and lively, Acton reported home. On the day of the Jubilee, 22 June, he received her *Hausorden,* as he described the Knight Commander of the Victorian Order, given only to relations and people in her personal service. He thanked her, writing on the same day of the Jubilee that "the honour associated the distinction conferred upon him with the most striking and most touching scene he has ever beheld."[89]

The scene moved all Britain and the Empire: Victoria's historic journey through jubilant London, where 5 million thronged to see her attend the *Te Deum* celebrated outside St. Paul's. She remained sitting in the state carriage, and her daughter Vicky rode in the next coach; they did not allow her to sit in the Queen's, as Empress Vicky could not sit with her back to the horses and the Queen could not have anyone next to her. Acton, attending in his levée uniform, described the festive occasion for his daughters. He had a grandstand view of the procession from the balcony of Lord Beaumont's house near Hyde Park Corner, with a crowd of thousands below. "There has been a thrill of loyalty, and of imperialism, and perhaps not more militarism than the love of gaudy uniforms in the fearful drab of London life. I am not quite sure. . . . [The Queen] looked well when we saw her, but in St. James's Street the thing began to tell upon her nerves and they saw her drop her parasol. . . . At St. Paul's she gave way to emotion, and the Prince of Wales, as if he began to realise what his inheritance will be, was as white as a sheet."[90]

Liberal friends such as Henry Sidgwick, whom Acton later met in the street, were depressed by the military display, noticing that the artillery met with a cool reception "as if the masses were sick of mere force." After the troops came the royal procession, led by a group of aides-de-camp, last of all, in gorgeous raiment, Pertab Sinha, the Rajpur chief, followed by the special envoys, among them the papal ambassador, with the Chinese sitting opposite, then the Queen's grandchildren, the German Empress in great magnificence, and last the Queen, with Field Marshall Viscount Garnet Joseph Wolseley, Commander in Chief of the Forces, riding before her.[91] As with the century itself, Acton's as yet unburdened years at Cambridge drew to a close.

21

LAST YEARS

In March 1896 Richard Wright, secretary of the Syndics of the Cambridge University Press, first approached Acton asking whether he would consider the general direction of a monumental history of the world, if such a plan were desirable and feasible also on financial grounds. Acton's faith in the new scientific history, as he had expanded on it in his Inaugural Lecture, had made an impression in Cambridge. It coincided with the growing general interest in the study of history in English universities, which stimulated interest in the schools as well as the demand for historical books and for new kinds of historical books. Acton agreed to entertain the idea but pointed out that it would be taxing the capacity of any man to undertake such a task, and he asked whether "a serious compilation or an original work" was wanted. The Syndics wanted an original work. By May they had modified their scheme to cover "Modern History only, beginning with the Renaissance," and asked Acton to join the undertaking.[1]

It was a temptation that Acton could not resist, although the work involved was to curtail his life and prevent him from writing anything else. He replied: "I do not hesitate as much as I ought to do on account of the difficulty, because my office makes it a duty not to be declined, and because such an opportunity of promoting his own ideas for the treatment of history has seldom been given to any man."[2] He was asked to make a more detailed plan of the work for the Syndics' meeting in October and was told that they hoped he would reconsider his refusal to write any part of the work himself. "The Syndics on the contrary hope that you will yourself write as considerable a portion as you find practicable." In fact, they wanted him to write the first part of the first volume because, as Wright put it, "this would give the thing a start and materially increase its prospect of success."[3] They clearly wanted to sell Acton as well as his great history.

A subsyndicate was appointed, consisting of F. W. Maitland and Leonard Whibley, to confer with Acton on how to further the great project.[4] Given the right assistants, Acton clearly thought he could cope, and, being an experienced editor, he might have done had he been a younger man. He envisaged his editorial task as "to piece the whole thing together, to worry writers, and to supervise their work so as to bring unity and harmony into the whole, but not to write myself."[5] But his friends were soon wondering whether, at sixty-two, he could stand the pace. Early in 1896 he had one of his throat infections and had to put off his lecture for ten days. In winter he often had to sit in his cold room at Trinity College, a blanket over his shoulders. The rich fare served at the College High Table dinners, to which he went increasingly, and his lack of exercise did him no good. And with his sweet tooth he was unlikely to be sensible: "I have just had an exquisite lunch: nectarines, gingersnaps, sherry, coffee, liqueur," read a later unashamed boast to Annie.[6]

Before returning to Bavaria for an Easter vacation in 1897, Acton wrote to Marie: "You'll find me a bit aged. Life here is very agreeable, but by dint of neglecting the world and its pomps. My days are always satisfying and without a hitch, but in the evening I am often tired and short of breath. What matters most is the friendship I find everywhere."[7] Relations with Marie were on an even keel again. It seems from the tone of later letters to Munich that he had forgiven her. They were accepting each other with that mutual fondness that had always been there, regardless of whether it could be called love. In general, the family was concerned over his health. That winter he kept off influenza, to which he was prone, by taking quinine pills. In the meantime another tempting offer, by the American publisher Appleton combining with the British firm of John Murray, was made for Acton to direct a kind of *Kulturgeschichte,* a history of civilization, which would not clash with the Cambridge plan but which, however, he felt he had to decline.[8]

The governing idea of the *Cambridge Modern History* was, as Acton told Wright:

> Universal history is not the sum of particular histories, which are subordinate, and may or may not contribute to it. That we ought to consider, first, that which is general: Renaissance, Reformation, Wars of Religion, absolutism, Revolution etc., and to distribute our topics accordingly. The history of particular countries, off the line, must not suffer. It must be told as accurately as if the whole was divided into annals. But attention ought not to be dispersed, as it would be by dealing with Portugal and Transylvania side by side with France and Germany. . . . I propose to group them in another connection, not in strict chronological order.

For instance, there would be no Russian chapter until Russia became an active agent under Peter the Great, and in dealing with that there would be a retrospective treatment; so with Prussia, Sweden, and so forth. Similarly, Venice, after a season of renewed importance early in the seventeenth century, vanished from the scene. So he would wind up with a "retrospective sketch." In this way, Acton thought, a country's history would appear as connected by cause and effect, "not side by side, that is, with no real connection at all." He wanted to get away from the idea of history as a chronicle, though that meant that the ignorant reader would not know "where to look for little things."[9]

Over the summer, at Tegernsee, Acton prepared his plan, which the Syndics accepted.[10] They wanted Acton as general editor or nothing else, though not at any price. They offered him as payment the sum of £300 in respect of his preliminary work and a further sum of £100 for each of the twelve volumes contemplated on publication, contributors to be paid the meagre sum of 10s. per page of 550 words. For an assistant, Stanley Mordaunt Leathes of Trinity College, the sum of £75 "might suffice," the Syndics considered.[11] They even agreed that Acton should have the assistant editor he wanted, Professor Adolphus William Ward, head of Owens College, Manchester, but they would not pay him more than £75. "The sum of money may seem a small one," Wright observed, "but it was felt that in view of the very large total expense of the book more could not be afforded, nor did it seem out of proportion when compared with the rate of payment to the writers themselves."[12]

There was disagreeable haggling. Acton supported Ward's wishes for increased remuneration, for which he was even prepared to have his own payment reduced, and for recognition of his valuable assistance. Ward was a great-nephew of Thomas Arnold of Rugby. He had been partly brought up in Germany, where his father was a diplomat, and had acquired German habits of efficiency and organization. Acton could not have done without him. But the close-fisted Syndics would not allow his name to be associated with Acton's as editor and even let him drop out altogether until they were forced to recall him when Acton's health broke down under the burden of the task. "Silly old OB," Annie Acton wrote of Browning's objections to Acton's taking on the gigantic and basically unrealizable enterprise, but at least in that OB was not wrong.[13]

The Acton Papers in the Cambridge University Library contain what is evidently a draft of an undated letter that Acton wrote from Tegernsee, probably in 1897, to his friend Baron Nathan Rothschild, to ask for support of his "vast" undertaking so as to enable him to improve on "the niggardly offer of ten shillings a page," which the university wanted him to make to his writers and which was much less than they could get elsewhere. Rothschild was the son of the Liberal MP for the City of London who was to have been raised to the peerage with Acton in 1869 but whose name was later withdrawn; his son received the honour in 1885. Acton was a frequent guest of the "Rothschildren," as he called them, at Tring. In reply to Rothschild's encouraging response Acton wrote that if he could offer his contributors a guinea instead, it might "make the difference between a good book and a great book, for which the university makes virtually no allowance." He wanted an endowment of between £1,000 and £1,250 a year for eight years. "I shall be delighted to come to Cambridge on 4 November, if I can be of use to my old university," was Rothschild's answer, but the records are silent on whether Acton's expectations were fulfilled.[14] A useful contribution to Acton's welfare at Cambridge was one of the new "electric reading lamps, equal to sixteen candles, a present from Lady Rothschild."[15]

Defining the aim of his noble enterprise, Acton wrote: "We are established, not under the meridian of Greenwich, but in longitude 30 West."[16] The Waterloo of the *Cambridge Modern History* must be one to satisfy French and English, Germans and Dutch. And nobody ought to be able to say, "without examining the list of authors, where the Bishop of Oxford [Stubbs] laid down the pen, and whether Fairbairn or Gasquet, Liebermann or Harrison took it up." It was a unique opportunity of recording, in the way most useful to the greatest number, "the fulness of the knowledge which the nineteenth century is about to bequeath." Acton's report to the Syndics, marked "strictly private and confidential," was submitted in October 1896. It had been written at Tegernsee over the summer and covered twenty-seven pages. Apart from the difficulties on the material and financial side, there were the disappointments that the editor had to face when nearly one-third of more than a hundred writers he was hoping to get declined to contribute, "some, because they have no time, some on account of old age which is the same thing, and others because the particular topic proposed to them did not suit."[17] For example, of the five names quoted above as representing five different religious denominations, only the Rev. Andrew Martin Fairbairn came in. Mandell Creighton intended to write but could not find the time. James Bryce refused the chapter on the Emperor Maximilian and the German sixteenth century because, as he said, he had not written any history for thirty years and was out of touch with recent German research.[18] Reginald Lane Poole turned down the offer to write on the Reformation. Refusals came from Rosebery (whom Acton had earmarked for Napoleon), G. M. Trevelyan, Edward James Stephens Dicey, Goldwin Smith, Max Müller, and Cecil Rhodes. Acton's idea was to get "English, American, colonial pens. But in an emergency we must take a capable foreigner rather than an inferior countryman."[19]

The Syndics agreed to pay "special fees" (ten guineas) to certain contributors, among them Acton's friend Field Marshal Lord Wolseley, the Commander in Chief whom he wanted to write on Bonaparte in Egypt, and four colonels he had suggested, but nothing more was heard of them, perhaps because they were otherwise engaged in the Boer War.[20] Nor did Acton secure the planned collaboration of Henri de Blowitz, the Paris correspondent of the *Times,* the "prince of journalists," a pompous figure of Bohemian origin who knew all the leading statesmen of his time. At the Congress of Berlin in 1878, he had obtained a long interview with Bismarck as well as the text of the Berlin Treaty ahead of anybody else. What Acton had in common with Blowitz was a curiosity in what went on behind the corridors of power.

The first volume of the *Cambridge Modern History* was published in September 1902, in an edition of two thousand at a price of 15s. per volume, yielding the publishers 8s. per volume. Their costs amounted to £948 11s. 4d.[21] The editor did not live to see the appearance of that last "Madonna of the Future," perhaps fortunately, because she, too, was not what he wanted her to be. Acton had great visions for the *Cambridge Modern History* as a stepping-stone to definitive history, a summing up of the historical research of preceding generations and his own, and as an abstract of all knowledge of the modern period. The venture hardly lived up to the high hopes. For many years afterwards, generations of English students had to plough through the massive twelve volumes that were completed under different hands. The planning was vitiated by a positivist and atomistic approach to the subjects, and the contributions were unequal in value.

Even Acton's own assignments were bedevilled in that he could not make his contributors do what he wanted and had, for example, to give up John Morley as contributor to the volume on the French Revolution because he expected the great historian and Bishop of Oxford, Stubbs, to object, and he had to do without Henry Morse Stephens because of objections from the Syndics. Also Acton's own contribution, the introductory chapter of the first volume, covering the medieval roots of modern history in fifty pages, which Bishop Creighton was unable to take on, remained unwritten. In the end, Richard Acton, on behalf of his father, who had fallen ill, had to inform the Syndics on 19 July 1901 of Lord Acton's resignation from his project. It was completed by three editors—Dr. Ward, who had meanwhile become Master of Peterhouse, Dr. Prothero, and Dr. Leathes—and Acton's assistant, W. A. J. Archbold.[22]

Notwithstanding his frustrations, Acton loved these last years at Cambridge. He liked everything about the place, the old colleges, the treasures of the libraries, the "deadly dons and their even deadlier wives," the crowded dinner parties in tiny rooms and bad food with very few exceptions. "Last night I dined with Maitland, whom I consider the ablest man in Cambridge. [It was] the worst dinner I ever had here. His wife is a handsome person, with expressive eyes, but a little nervous and spoilt. She loves a monkey who came into the drawing room. Her husband justly called him a revolting beast."[23] Acton and Maitland had become close over their work on the *Cambridge Modern History* project, as is reflected in the glowing tribute Maitland paid to Acton a few months after his death. Referring to the Inaugural Lecture, at which he was present, Maitland wrote that contrition for past intolerance must also have caused his listeners to ask themselves whether, had Cambridge received him earlier, he would have been—even after a similar, distinguished academic career—quite such "a master of contemporary history, quite such an impartial judge of modern England, so European, so supranational, so catholic, so liberal, so wise, so Olympian, so serene."[24]

Acton engaged a servant, Charles Erroll Andrews, for £60 a year; "my man," as he called him, an ex-soldier with a moustache, was kept busy packing and unpacking parcels of books, arranging them on shelves as instructed, or taking them to the post. For the first time in years Acton's finances were in better shape, and he wrote to Mamy in a generous mood to tell her mother: "I am good for, say, five hundred marks for this occasion."[25] His solicitors, Freshfields, watchful as ever, were not so content and disapproved, because of the expense, of his idea of acquiring Birnam, a house in Chaucer Road, near Trumpington Road, "the most civilised road here," as he described it, whence a footpath led across the river and the fields to Trinity College.[26]

The house, standing in two acres of grounds and gardens, was irregularly built and quite large, with four big bedrooms and two smaller rooms upstairs, and five servants' bedrooms on the top floor. It had a good kitchen, a large basement room—suitable for billiards, he reported to the family—servants' hall, pantry, "dinner admitted through the wall," stabling, and a conservatory kept in order by an aged gardener. Though ugly outside, it was convenient inside. It was partly furnished. "Ask mother whether she would like me to wait until you have seen it in Easter week—if there is any other alternative. If not, and they agree to do what we want, I would not wait."[27] He arranged to have it redecorated: the floors stained darkest oak, the dining room terra-cotta, the morning room woodwork white with yellow wallpaper. Curtains, furniture, and a few thousand favourite books were sent down from Aldenham.

Mamy and Annie came over in November 1899 to keep house for their father while their mother remained in Munich to look after Simmy, who was not thought up to the move. Mamy Acton recalled "an eerie experience" when they were unpacking the cases sent from Aldenham. Among them one got left to the last as it was very heavy. It contained some of the black cloth panels that were hung up at the Aldenham chapel for the family funerals, and they felt it to be a portent of their father's last illness and death. Birnam was also bound to remind them of the ominous prophecy "till the wood / of Birnam rise and our high-plac'd Macbeth / shall live the lease of nature, pay his breath / to time and mortal custom" (*Macbeth* 4.1.96–99).

Acton's children made the house habitable with furniture, drapes, baize curtains to keep the draught out of the bedrooms, pictures, heavy curtains. There were coal fires in every room, bookshelves, and a piano in the living room. Andrews was kept busy in the basement polishing silver and glass. Two carved Dalberg saints guarded the entrance hall. The German Emperor and, separately, Acton's devoted friend the Empress Frederick, came on official visits when Acton did the honours of the University, guided the distinguished guests on *Blitz* tours, and introduced them to the leading lights.

In November 1900 Acton accepted an invitation from Oxford University to deliver the Romanes Lecture for June 1901. The lecture founded by George John Romanes, the Cambridge biologist and friend of Charles Darwin's, was given annually by an eminent personality on a literary or scientific topic. The founder's widow, Mrs. Ethel Romanes, wrote to Acton warmly to say how glad she was that he would be giving it.[28] His predecessors were Gladstone, Morley, Thomas Huxley, Creighton, and the classical scholar Richard Claverhouse Jebb. The event would take place in the Sheldonian Theatre where Acton had received his D.C.L. "So it is a great honour," he wrote to Annie. The prestige was greater than the fee, which was £25.[29] However, the breakdown of his health forced Acton to withdraw and lay down his pen forever in the spring of 1901. He had already made numerous notes for the lecture (three boxes with 383 cards altogether, which are kept among the Acton Papers at the Cambridge University Library). His theme was a striking one—history in the new century, the history of modern history—and he wanted to give the latest views on various crucial issues, as the following selection may indicate:[30]

How much a man is the product of time and place and race: culture emancipates him—gives him the world to choose from for his governing ideas. By the predominance of mind over matter releases him from his nation in the past, and by the predominance of moral over intellectual motives, releases him from his countrymen at the present.

[History has done harm by promoting war by the] excuses for the great—unholy dread of injuring a cause by exposing its champion to damaging truth by speaking truth. . . . H[istory] has done much to encourage the delight in war. The motive has been to make men willing to fight, and to dissimulate the discouraging facts: the night after the battle, the scenes in the hospital, the horrible wounds, the ruined homes, the devastation, the suffering and misery, the terrors of sudden death, all kept out of sight, the horrors of captured towns.

The faults of historians: too many needless opinions. All this divides instead of uniting. [It] prevents history instead of causing it to prevail.

The materialistic socialist will improve h[istory] for the poor. Their best writer, Engels, made known the errors and horrors of our factory system.

Tendency is towards sociology. Reduction of the personal element and the range of providence. So, against religion.

H[istory] deals mainly with results—that is, with the world as it is, the making of it, the direction in which it has been moving. [There is] no presumption in favour of that which endures or prevails.

For centuries, h[istory] was national. People were curious about their own country—ignorant and indifferent about others. There was the difficulty of language. This had begun to give way to a larger view.

History had depended on theology, jurisprudence, philology. [It] has out-
grown them. No further troubles of that kind, [but it is] still much interfered
with by politics. . . . The history of ideas undermines national treatment—
ideas are not national, like laws and customs.

H[istory] is an iconoclast, not a school of reverence. . . . By an honest historian we mean one who pleads no cause, who keeps no shelter for a friend,
no pillory for a foe—who does the same justice to that which he loathes as
to that which he loves.

Acton clearly contradicted the usual wisdom that allowed for radicalism in
youth, mellowing into sensible conservatism in old age. His development had
taken quite the opposite course, from the opinionated and arrogant youth at
Oscott, Munich, and Aldenham to the professor of youthful ideas at sixty-six.

Acton was looking forward to enlarged horizons, to a grand unity of history.
Liberty was the force that overcame modern absolutism, although its roots
reached back to the days of Samuel and to an age before the first slave, the theme
of his Bridgnorth lecture "The History of Freedom in Antiquity" thirty years
earlier. When Queen Victoria died, on 22 January 1901, and all felt it to be the
death of an era, he, that apparent pillar of Victorianism, wrote to his wife that
what had died was "the England of tradition. I am not weeping over it."[31] Mary
Gladstone Drew was even angrier about the military character of the funeral,
"distasteful beyond words." The "idea of that little body, all that remained of a
great good Queen, laid on the top of a gun, and the gun carriage newly painted
khaki just now, when our chief peril is militarism—it seemed the last thing to
be accentuated."[32]

But it was their own age that was passing with the old Queen. Only six
months later, on 5 August 1901, Victoria's daughter, Acton's friend the Empress
Frederick, died after a long illness, "the last champion of a lost cause, the partnership of a liberal Britain and a liberal Germany."[33] Acton took his oath to
King Edward VII and signed the Rolls. The new King's name had a medieval as
well as a Reformation ring. Acton wrote to Annie: "I don't suppose the Scots
will like it, who have no Edward except Edward I, who conquered them."[34]

Shortly before Easter in the same year, 1901, Acton had the breakdown that
virtually put an end to his active Cambridge life. The medical diagnosis was
a strong gouty tendency that had gone into the whole system, aggravated by
overwork and no exercise. He was looked after by his daughters. "He is very
good and patient in doing all he is told," Mamy wrote to Lady Blennerhassett.
"His nights are very poor and his appetite is better than the amount he gets

to satisfy it."[35] He got up for several hours every day and read Max Müller's biography. They were hoping that he would be well enough to go abroad for a cure. He had to ask for a leave of absence for the summer term, but in fact all his literary work ceased.

At Tegernsee Acton seemed to recover somewhat over the summer months. In October 1901 the marriage of his eldest daughter, Mamy, took place. The family did not allow him to go to the church, so Richard Acton gave the bride away. The wedding and reception afterwards at their house were naturally a cause for excitement that Acton had to avoid. Mamy married Lieutenant Colonel Edward Bleiddian Herbert, of the Seventeenth Lancers, the third son of John Herbert of Llanarth, the diplomat, a Catholic who had also been a student of Dr. Döllinger's in Munich. The Herberts of Monmouthshire were connected to the Earls of Pembroke. The departure of his beloved Mamy and her "Blei" was upsetting for Acton, but they came to visit him at Merano, where he was taken to spend the winter months. In February he was well enough to write to Reginald Vere Laurence at Trinity College, to ask him and another of his pupils, John Pollock, to supervise the sending of his books from Nevile's Court to Merano. "Some days I am a bit weary. There are ups and downs," he wrote to Dick, who was at his diplomatic post at the Berlin embassy. "The last thing was sciatica which lamed me."[36]

Acton's immaculate handwriting deteriorated. That handwriting, rare among his great contemporaries in its rounded regularity and legibility, had hardly changed from the age of twenty. It seemed to reflect an inward equanimity and spiritual beauty. But it had changed markedly by the time he had to write his letter of resignation to the vice-chancellor of Cambridge University. In the spring of 1902 they brought him back, quite hopefully, from Merano to Tegernsee, but on 11 June he suffered a severe stroke followed by great pain, while the paralysis affected his internal organs. From the second day the doctors had no hope of saving him. Marie, apparently the last to realize it, sat up with him day and night until the end. Annie telegraphed Dick and Mamy to come home and was terrified that they might arrive too late.

Acton died at three in the afternoon on 20 June 1902 in Marie's arms, as her mother had died in his arms in the same house in 1885. He had received the Sacrament for the Dying from the Benedictine priest Odilo Rottmanner, a friend of the family. "Religion alone makes a good death," read one of the many aphorisms Acton recorded, of which it is difficult to say whether they were his own or not. But this one was fitting for him, and so was the afterthought:

"Religion alone cannot make a good life."[37] They laid him out in state in his Cambridge crimson robes. "He looked more beautiful in the majesty of death than anyone who didn't see him can imagine," Annie wrote to Acton's cousin Minnie Dease (née Throckmorton), who had loved him throughout her life. "Mother is very tired now and lies down a great deal. . . . We love talking about him and recalling all the dear kind ways and his noble life. It is something to have had such a father and to be able to look up [to him] unreservedly and to cherish his loved memory."[38]

The funeral took place in the morning of 22 June, with a long procession of family and friends walking, while the church bells tolled, from the Villa Arco to the little Tegernsee cemetery at the lakeside, overshadowed by weeping willows and the Wallberg mountain, with its rounded top reaching into the clouds. Monsignor Georg Dannerbeck, the parish priest, spoke feelingly of Acton as one of the greatest scholars of the time, who—equipped with a marvellous memory, good schooling, and great strength of will—had dedicated his life to historical research. His incomparable library was built up in the time that others use to enjoy and distract themselves; he had collected books and documents from all over Europe and copied documents in many archives, and always generously and readily allowed those who wished it to share in the enjoyment of these treasures. Among Acton's ancestors, the Bavarian priest mentioned "the great Gibbon," and as a descendant of the German Dalbergs he had turned their sword into a weapon of the mind and always used it honourably. His widow, his children, and friends knew only too well that he was, above all, a man of Christ. And the priest recalled that when Acton's little daughter, Elisabeth, had died, her father had closed her eyes with the words: "Be glad, my child, you will soon be with Jesus Christ," and they should use these words also as their farewell to him.[39]

Acton was buried, as he had wished, by the side of his child. The intention of bringing their remains over to England to be interred with the other dead of the family in the Aldenham chapel crypt was never realized, and today time and neglect have made it difficult even to find their resting place. The simple marble cross with the inscription "Ave Crux Spes Unica" (Hail, holy cross, our only hope) has long since disappeared.[40] Marie received tributes from all over the world, telegrams of condolence from King Edward VII, from Lord Lansdowne, the foreign secretary (he was one of the Joseph Chamberlain Liberals to break with his party over Irish Home Rule), from members of the House of Hohenzollern, and from the Bavarian regent. In Cambridge, a Requiem Mass was celebrated at the Church of Our Lady and the English Martyrs, on 26 June. The vice-chancellor-elect, Dr. F. H. Chase, and the Master of Trinity, Dr. Henry Montagu Butler, were among the congregation.

The three celebrants of that Mass—Mgr. Christopher Scott, Mgr. Edmund Nolan, and Dom Cuthbert Butler, O.S.B.—were all linked to Acton through their friendship, to which they later independently testified in the columns of the *Tablet*. The occasion was the publication, in 1904, of Acton's intimate correspondence with Mary Gladstone, which caused widespread indignation in Catholic circles because of his frank opinions, which had never been intended for publication. The protests were led by the well-known Jesuit controversialist Herbert Thurston. Accustomed to enter the lists on the lines of "my Church, right or wrong," he remonstrated against the *Tablet* editor's view that Acton "was a great asset," that "no man of his time and place served the Church with a deeper love and with a more selfless devotion, and that Cardinal Vaughan had been right to drop the veil of charity over whatever faults and words that may have been written earlier in a time of irritation and unrest."[41] This commentary was a kind of belated *amende honourable* for the paper's past attacks on Acton. Unhappily, as it turned out, it seized on Abbot Gasquet's one-sided selection of Acton's early letters to his fellow-editor Richard Simpson to make that point. Fr. Thurston, suspecting Gasquet's whitewashing attempt but unable to prove it, concentrated instead on Acton's religious views expressed in the letters to Gladstone's daughter and pointed out that no link could be made between Gasquet's Acton, the earlier champion of the Church, and the post–Vatican Council Acton who embarrassed the Church and Catholics by describing St. Charles Borromeo and St. Pius V as assassins. In the light of the Drew letters, Fr. Thurston wrote, "It is impossible to maintain that Lord Acton remained consistently a loyal son of the Church so long as we understand plain words in the plain and ordinary meaning." In the ensuing lengthy correspondence, Fr. Thurston seemed to have much support among the journal's readers, although he felt eventually persuaded "to withdraw from the unequal contest" after disclaiming his intention to describe Acton as a heretic. His review of Abbot Gasquet's *Lord Acton and His Circle* in the *Month,* published by the Jesuits, was clearer on that score, however. "Whatever view may be taken of Lord Acton's orthodoxy or lack of orthodoxy . . . ," it began.[42]

Those who came to Acton's defence were unanimous in their tribute to his deep spirit of devotion. Mgr. Scott, who had himself doubted Acton's orthodoxy before he became parish priest in Cambridge, revealed that he had written to Cardinal Vaughan for advice on how to treat Acton and was told that he was, of course, to treat him as a thoroughly practising Catholic. He told how Acton came to pay his respects to his pastor, how he was invited by Mgr. Scott to carry one of the poles of the canopy of the Blessed Sacrament publicly and in full academicals, and how punctual and regular he was in attending Mass every Sunday. When, during his final illness, Mgr. Scott came at his request to bring him the viaticum, he sprang up, although the doctor had ordered him not to move, and knelt to receive it. "I was not only satisfied, but consoled and edified by his demeanour and resignation."[43] Two other letters deserve to be mentioned. Mgr. Edmund Nolan, another University chaplain who had known Acton for several years, wrote that he had never heard him say one word that might be construed as disloyalty to the Church. Taking up the question asked by one of Acton's attackers, "What did he ever do for Catholics?" a nun from Nazareth House answered: "There is one thing he did, he was always kind to the poor of Nazareth House, and if charity covers a multitude of faults, it should also obtain many other blessings for us."[44]

Baron Anatole von Hügel, director of the Museum of Ethnography and Archaeology at Cambridge, the less gifted but more orthodox brother of Friedrich, the religious philosopher, was a close friend of Acton's and paid his tribute to him. While Friedrich von Hügel, himself suspected of modernism, had told Mary Gladstone Drew that he found Acton's "direct and absorbing anti-Ultramontanism" no less disagreeable than Ultramontanism itself,[45] Anatole von Hügel wrote to express a different view: what Acton wrote to Mary Gladstone Drew may not have been edifying, yet it was the outpouring of a holy wrath and did not contradict the reality of Acton's devout spirit. "Surely a man who is known to have habitually recited the 'Jesus Psalter' on every Friday of the year, and who expressed his delight when informed that it had been composed in a room at Queens', . . . and whose devoutness in life stood him in such good stead in death, should need no further exoneration from the charge of double-facedness and of want of loyalty to Mother Church."[46]

The Jesus Psalter is usually attributed to Richard Whytford, a Bridgetine monk who was a prolific devotional writer and became a Fellow of Queens' in 1495, though modern scholars doubt it was composed in a room there. Like the rosary, the Jesus Psalter was made up of 150 parts or petitions, divided into fifteen groupings, so that, being rather long, it would be said either on three successive days or, as by Acton, at one go. It was a penitential devotion to the Holy Name of Jesus, with refrains like "Mercy" or long petitions. The prayer was naturally discarded by Protestants but remained a staple of English Catholic piety from the seventeenth to the early twentieth centuries.[47]

Acton also had a great devotion to another fifteenth-century work, the *Imitation of Christ* by Thomas à Kempis, which he looked upon as "the most perfectly normal expression of Catholic thought, as it bears the least qualifying impress of time and place."[48] Throughout the ages it had an immense and universal appeal, particularly in the nineteenth century, and to non-Christians and Christians alike. George Eliot and Marco Minghetti, for example, were devotees, and Acton tried to persuade Oscar Browning to adopt Kempis in place of Dante as an ideal Christian, precisely because "he was not a discoverer, an anticipator, a universal thinker, but a Catholic and nothing else."[49]

What may have added to the *Imitation*'s attraction for Acton was that touch of late medieval resignation reflected in the neo-Gothic nostalgia of nineteenth-century Catholicism. The trials that he had to face in his own life influenced his religious outlook and made it more doom-laden. The *Imitation*, which combined simple faith with humility and mystical elements in fine literary presentation — as did also the *Fioretti*, the Little Flowers of St. Francis of Assisi — satisfied Acton's thirst for the essence of Catholic spirituality. Strange though it seems, we must think of this man of great learning on his knees before some Puginesque neo-Gothic altar, in devotions that would have satisfied very ordinary Catholics much less versed than he was in what the Gothic "ages of faith" were really like. "Remember that one's destiny is settled in Heaven," he wrote to Annie. "Remember to be always on the side of too much kindness, rather than that of dignity and self-respect. There is nothing more dignified than to be humble or more self-respecting, than respect for others."[50] Some entries in a little personal notebook read: "Nobody to help in danger or in death — we are alone with God. Practise being alone with him. Depend on oneself alone, trustful only." And "To return hatred, scorn, mockery is to deserve it."[51] These were some of the lessons of his own sombre and simple faith.

The key to understanding Acton is his childlike faith. It was and is a scandal to many of his critics, especially those who would pride themselves upon either their religious indifference or religious tolerance. His faith bore the imprint of his mother, with her French upbringing and sympathy for *bien pensant* Catholicism rather than any liberal variety. This inheritance produced nonetheless a religious practice that was lasting, simple though not superficial, and satisfying to his spirit. Very different was the converts' experience of their Roman Catholic faith that was so significant for many of Acton's and Newman's generation.

They came to their new faith at an intellectually and emotionally more advanced age. Acton was a "cradle Catholic," and his experience stood him in good stead when he had to instruct his own children in their religion, which he was able to do in simple language and biblical forms that they could understand.

Much has been made of a statement by M. E. Mountstuart Grant Duff, Acton's early fellow MP and friend, who recorded being told by him before 1865, at the time of Acton's clashes with the English Catholic hierarchy over the *Home and Foreign Review:* "I am not conscious that I ever in my life had the slightest shadow of doubt about any dogma of the Catholic church."[52] To a non-Catholic admirer of Acton's mind who was quite ready to admit that he understood only a small part of that mind, this statement added not a little puzzlement regarding Acton's religious convictions. However, Acton made much the same remark some forty years later, to Oscar Browning at Cambridge, when the great struggle of the Vatican Council, which caused such an upheaval in his life, was long past.[53]

In a remarkable document found among his papers after his death, Acton left to posterity, in an imaginative form, a tempting insight into the sensitivities of his complex mind: He

> said things that were at first sight grossly inconsistent, without attempting to reconcile them. He was reserved about himself, and gave no explanations, so that he was constantly misunderstood. . . .
>
> He respected other men's opinions . . . and when forced to defend his own he felt bound to assume that every one would look sincerely for the truth, and would gladly recognise it. . . . Being quite sincere, he was quite impartial, and pleaded with equal zeal for what seemed true, whether it was on one side or on the other. He would have felt dishonest if he had unduly favoured people of his own country, his own religion, or his own party, or if he had entertained the shadow of a prejudice against those who were against them, and when he was asked why he did not try to clear himself from misrepresentation, he said that he was silent both from humility and pride.
>
> At last I understood that what we had disliked in him was his virtue itself.[54]

The sincerity he mentioned in that reflection was an essential ingredient of Acton's religion. "I think that faith implies sincerity, that it is a gift that does not dwell in dishonest minds," he wrote to Mary Gladstone, well aware that she might think it either bad dogma or psychology. For "there is much more danger for a high-principled man of doing injustice to the adherent of false doctrine, of judging with undeserved sympathy the conspicuous adherent of true doctrine, than of hating a Frenchman or loving a member of Brooks's." And it was the honesty that helped Acton to hold on to his faith, which to him was "dearer than life itself," when some of its intellectual supporters were badly shaken under the impact of the Vatican Council and Cardinal Manning's persecution.[55]

In a way, the tragedy of Acton's life is embedded in the two dominant currents of his generation, the spiritual-religious and the political-material. From the prostration of the Church everywhere in the eighteenth century at the mercy of absolutist sovereigns or an absolutist State, Catholicism arose again but itself became increasingly absolutist in the process that culminated in the Vatican Council. The initial revival of spiritual-religious values after the setback of the Age of Enlightenment, the shock of the French Revolution and its wars, was, however, not sustained in the nineteenth century as it had been in the seventeenth through the Counter-Reformation or the Lutheran-nonconformist revival. The nineteenth century triumphed in the secularization of modern society and its divorce from traditional religious and moral values.

The heritage of eighteenth-century rationalism, however, together with the anti-religious or atheist element of the French Revolution, survived in the development of Continental liberalism and the centralized modern national state. Belief reigned in the unstoppable advance of science, in Darwinism, modern technology, economics, capitalism. The educated elite and the working classes constituting a new urban proletariat became increasingly divorced from religious influences. Politics and economics mattered as never before; political passions replaced the religious zeal of old.

As for the religious rebirth, it became entangled at first with Romanticism, with the age of restoration and early conservative (de Maistre) and liberal Catholic (Lamennais) ideological reaction. But the Catholic Church, too, though weakened by the eighteenth century's onslaught on religion, survived it with strengthened authoritarian power and growing dependence of weakened episcopates on the Papacy. In her structures the Church followed the centralized system of modern governments, in her teaching, the theological trend of traditionalism and Neo-Scholasticism. Her dalliance with conservative and liberal ideas and the shock of the liberal-leftist revolutions of 1848 confirmed Church and Papacy in the authoritarian conservative camp of reaction against the equally jejune forces of democracy and socialism.

The dominance of these political struggles in changing European societies led everywhere to the entrenchment of the religious forces fearing the victory of science, the increasing hostility or indifference to religious or moral values. To themselves they seemed like the last defenders of the faith, rejecting everything the modern world stood for; seen from their uprooted followers or outsiders they seemed a reactionary and increasingly irrelevant element. And everywhere in the late nineteenth century there was a hardening of the ideological fronts, of Catholics, Protestants, agnostics, atheists, socialists, conservatives, and so forth. A Catholic scholar like Döllinger (who found good things to say of Luther and who felt that the Pope should not be a temporal ruler) or an English Liberal like Acton (who saw through the illiberal partisanship of Continental liberals and nationalists and who sensed the corrupting effects of absolute power in Church or State) seemed like traitors to their side, as well as hopelessly out of tune with their age. But, like Newman, they were really in advance of it.

It is interesting to note that modern historians like Aubert, seeing the Vatican Council with the benefit of hindsight after Vatican II, and with a more dispassionate view owing to the passage of time, have provided something of a vindication for the anti-infallibilists or "inopportunists" like Newman. The latest historian of Vatican I, the German Jesuit Klaus Schatz, points to the extreme partisanship of all the protagonists, infallibilists and their opponents, as the key to the understanding of the Council. This includes the role of Pius IX, not least in his famous and hitherto much denied remark "La tradizione sono io" (It is I who am the tradition). According to Schatz, and confirming Acton, the whole development of the nineteenth-century Papacy leads almost in a straight line towards the proclamation of Infallibility in 1870.[56] The basis for this development is the Napoleonic Concordat of 1801, in which Pius VII, soon to be Napoleon's prisoner as his predecessor, Pius VI, had been, managed, with the skilful Ercole Consalvi at his side, to secure most important concessions for the Church. These were the deposition of all French bishops, including those legitimately appointed during the Revolution. This fundamental reform of the French Church was soon repeated in Germany.

Such a display of papal power served as an enormous precedent enhancing the dependence of bishops on Rome, especially when it is remembered that this occurred at a time of the Papacy's extreme weakness. And this was followed in the 1830s by the Jesuit-led reform of theological teaching, the cleansing of Roman seminaries of rationalist influences, and the establishment of the ahistorical, Neo-Scholastic traditionalist school of theology. When Pius IX was forced by the violent Roman Revolution of 1849 to flee to Gaeta, the Pope himself experienced a conversion of great bearing for his future pontificate, that is, from his early idealist enthusiasm for the Italian liberal and national cause to the opposite end of the spectrum, the extreme reaction represented by Cardinal Antonelli and his Jesuit advisers. The direct line leads on to 1854, when the Immaculate Conception was proclaimed a dogma of the faith merely by polling the bishops of the world but without calling an ecumenical Council, regarded as necessary for ex cathedra pronouncement on doctrine. This was taken as another victory of the Pope—and, particularly, of the Jesuits, his zealous defenders—over the Dominicans, who for centuries had contested that particular doctrine of the Church. Then, finally, in 1864 Pius IX issued the encyclical and *Syllabus* condemning eighty "Errors of the Age," which, apart from preparing for the Council, added fuel to the controversy of whether the *Syllabus* was to be regarded as an infallible pronouncement.

The crux of Vatican I, according to Schatz, who used a term of the post–Vatican II Church that was hardly to be found at the time of Vatican I, was "the lack of a genuine dialogue among the opposing parties." This concept of dialogue, one of the most significant innovations of Vatican II, is a form of "conversing with the world"—with Christian believers in other churches, with Jews, and even with unbelievers. Schatz emphasizes how infallibilists, anti-infallibilists, or inopportunists—including the increasingly impatient Pius IX—became more and more entrenched in their standpoints despite far-reaching agreement, for instance, between moderate infallibilists and moderate opponents. Confirming the Ultramontanist course and its confusion with political and other factors that led the nineteenth-century Church towards Papal Infallibility, Schatz concludes his work by defining the leitmotiv of Vatican I as a strengthening of authority against the modern trend of disintegration, securing the faith as such rather than a particular doctrine, the universal Church insofar as the Church finds her identity in her link with the Pope. The cause of the infallible Pope thus became identified with a titanic struggle to safeguard faith in modern society. What seemed at stake was less a particular dogma than the survival of faith itself. And its defenders were deeply divided into intolerantly opposed camps, in which Acton's and Döllinger's role on behalf of the minority and the losers is that of precursors of a greater truth.

Acton's life was sadly littered with all sorts of disappointments and ambitious projects unrealized. All the strands of his life seemed to have dissolved in his hands by the time he was forty: his revered teacher condemned, the link between historical truth and Catholicism apparently broken, and his own rift with Döllinger on the horizon. It was then that he began the process, forced upon him, to unlearn and relearn many of his early lessons. With the fragments of his ideals and dreams, he struggled to become the sage of his later years. It is not easy to follow the transition from the early to the late Acton. He found a substitute Infallibility in the inner voice of conscience, the "voice of God that never misleads or fails, and that ought to be obeyed always, whether enlightened or darkened, right or wrong."[57] But his understanding of conscience was very different from the modern idea of conscience, as a substitute for religion. He was impressed by the example of George Eliot, who had constructed herself a belief out of unbelief. As if for the first time, George Eliot and the Swiss Protestant Alexandre Vinet were then demonstrating to Acton, the late developer, the force of modern secular humanism and atheism as rivals to Catholicism.

Acton may have left little in the way of finished books or a system of ideas. His written work is nonetheless substantial and impressive. And it is not paradoxical to admire him for books he never wrote or for what he tried to do rather than for what he succeeded in achieving. Unlike other great Victorians, his influence has increased rather than diminished in the century following his death. His ideas and jottings, like Blaise Pascal's *Pensées* not ordered by the author himself, continue to attract attention because of their enigmatic character. The very failures of his own life's struggles seem lessons to be learned from one of humanity's great teachers of freedom. Perhaps after the horrors of Auschwitz and the Gulag we feel that they might have been lessened if in his own and subsequent times more attention had been paid to freedom as the moral and religious end of society and as the absolute value, the reign of conscience, to which Acton wished to hold all those who would wield power.

Acton foresaw the destructive power that nationalism and socialism would manifest in the twentieth-century amalgam produced in Germany. While nationalism raised the valid concept of national independence to an idolatry, socialism was "the worst of all enemies of freedom because, if it could fulfil what it promises, it would render such a service to the world that the interests of freedom would pale, and mankind would carry over its allegiance to the benefactor who had a higher claim on its gratitude."[58] But socialism, having developed from the notion of equality, at least tried to save the individual from the misery and starvation that modern society heaps upon labour. It was a revolt against the economic autocracy of feudalism and acceptable if—this was his big proviso—it tackled the ills of society with sound economics and without totalitarian means. But it "can only be realised by a tremendous despotism."[59]

Acton noted the compatibility of Christianity with socialism; his strictures were clearly directed against totalitarian socialism, not against its liberal form, and he told Mary Gladstone that he quite agreed "with [Joseph] Chamberlain, that there is latent Socialism in the Gladstonian philosophy."[60]

In Acton's changing evaluation of socialism he realized, according to G. E. Fasnacht, that private enterprise had failed to solve the problem of distribution, that what the poor needed before they could make their potential effective was comfort and security, that division of power is the condition of liberty, and that the right of self-government is inherent in all corporations and associations. Acton's criteria were always: "Is it just? Is it in accordance with the permanent will of the community? Is it practicable? Will it be efficient? Will it increase or diminish real freedom?"[61] Fasnacht has shown how thoroughly Acton studied economics and socialism. In 1873 he wrote to Gladstone about Karl Marx's "remarkable book, as the Koran of the new socialists. Have you not had time to look at it?"[62] Acton was referring to the completely revised second edition of the first volume of *Das Kapital,* which he had apparently compared with the original edition, published six years earlier. There is no evidence that Gladstone followed Acton's suggestion. Reviewing Sir Erskine May's *Democracy in Europe* in 1878, Acton well expressed his passionate feelings on the subject of social justice:

> For the old notions of civil liberty and of social order did not benefit the masses of the people. Wealth increased, without relieving their wants. The progress of knowledge left them in abject ignorance. Religion flourished, but failed to reach them. Society, whose laws were made by the upper class alone, announced that the best thing for the poor is not to be born, and the next best, to die in childhood, and suffered them to live in misery and crime and pain. As surely as the long reign of the rich has been employed in promoting the accumulation of wealth, the advent of the poor to power will be followed by schemes for diffusing it.[63]

But nationalism did not have the saving utopian grace of socialism; it

> does not aim either at liberty or prosperity, both of which it sacrifices to the imperative necessity of making the nation the mould and measure of the State. Its course will be marked with material as well as moral ruin, in order that a new invention may prevail over the works of God and the interests of mankind. . . . It is a confutation of democracy, because it sets limits to the exercise of the popular will. . . . Thus, after surrendering the individual

to the collective will, the revolutionary system makes the collective will subject to conditions which are independent of it, and rejects all law, only to be controlled by an accident.[64]

Acton wrote his essay "Nationality" when he was twenty-eight years old, two years after Italy had won its independence by force of arms as well as by wielding the art of diplomacy as practised by the liberal Cavour. Acton was in sympathy with Austria as having first realized the liberal and federal principle, but at that time his "Austricism" made him conscious of being "a partisan of sinking ships."[65] Never was a liberal more isolated than Acton from the principles of his age, which applauded the victories that nationalism achieved all over Europe and influenced the enthusiasm of the London crowds who applauded Garibaldi.

In the ancient world idolatry and nationality went together, Acton noted, and the same term is applied in Scripture to both. Christianity imposed a new principle of self-government, and a nation became a moral and political being, developed in the course of history by the action of the State. The modern theory of nationality was awakened by the partition of Poland, the most blatant act of the age of absolutism. "For the first time in modern history a great State was suppressed, and a whole nation divided among its enemies," and it was successfully asserted in consequence of the revolutionary and Napoleonic Wars. Thenceforwards, Acton commented, "there was a nation demanding to be united in a State,—a soul, as it were, wandering in search of a body in which to begin life over again." The co-existence of several nations under the same State "is a test, as well as the best security of its freedom. It is also one of the chief instruments of civilisation; and, as such, it is in the natural and providential order, and indicates a state of greater advancement than the national unity which is the ideal of modern liberalism."[66] But the contrast between the ideal and the reality could not have been greater. Virtually alone among the liberals of his age, Acton saw where its obsessions with class, race, and nationality would lead in the twentieth century and what would happen to humanity when it lost sight "of the concept of man as created in the image of God and sharing in the salvation offered it by Christ." As an historian he found the racial idea a convenient tool, while rejecting the racialist philosophy that was developed then by contemporaries like Houston Stewart Chamberlain (1855–1927) and Comte Arthur Gobineau (1816–1882). Their racialist theories, which ultimately inspired Hitler, were, to Acton, "one of the many schemes to deny free will, responsibility, and guilt, and to supplant moral by physical forces."[67]

But the theory of nationality is a retrograde step in history. Making the State and the nation commensurate with each other in theory practically reduces to a subject condition all other nationalities within the frontiers. "It is in general a necessary condition of free institutions, that the boundaries of governments should coincide in the main with those of nationalities," Acton quoted John Stuart Mill.[68] This very idea was realized fifty-seven years later in Woodrow Wilson's peace settlement of 1919, with the disastrous results remembered by the generation that witnessed Hitler's occupation of Austria and dismemberment of Czechoslovakia. German reunification, the collapse of the Soviet empire, and war in the former Yugoslavia in the 1980s and 1990s only underlined the significance and accuracy of Acton's insight. "What he said was always interesting, but sometimes strange," wrote G. M. Trevelyan. "I remember, for instance, his saying to me that States based on the unity of a single race, like modern Italy and Germany, would prove a danger to liberty; I did not see what he meant at the time, but I do now!"[69]

In the German and Italian national movements of his time, as Acton knew from personal experience, the threat to liberty arose, paradoxically, with strong support from the Italian Liberals and the equally right-wing German National-Liberals who advocated centralized state power, protectionism, and imperialism. A new era dawned for Machiavelli, "the earliest conscious and articulate exponent of certain living forces in the present world. Religion, progressive enlightenment, the perpetual vigilance of public opinion, have not reduced his empire, or disproved the justice of his conception of mankind. . . . And he is more rationally intelligible when illustrated by lights falling not only from the century he wrote in, but from our own, which has seen the course of its history twenty-five times diverted by actual or attempted crime."[70]

Acton's calculation at least shows—with the hindsight of the more violent twentieth century—the Victorians to have been morally and materially relatively well behaved. He demonstrated that when religion declined in influence, as in the sixteenth century, naked power reasserted the supremacy it had in antiquity, and unlimited expansion of power became the "law of the modern world."[71] The restraining forces of the Church, of the moral law, and of the individual were in retreat everywhere. It was symbolic that the first celebratory act of united Italy was the Florentine government's publication at public expense of the collected works of Niccolò Machiavelli.[72] Acton had studied him as well as his followers, especially his English disciple Francis Bacon, and was conscious of the link with the controversial "Jesuit principle" of "the end justifies the means." There were more than forty editions of *Il principe* in Acton's library, and in his own introduction to L. A. Burd's new English edition of *Il principe* he assembled an impressive catalogue of quotations to show that "the authentic interpreter of Machiavelli . . . is the whole later history."[73]

The list of Machiavelli's interpreters comprises all the great and representative European minds from Francis Bacon and Thomas Hobbes to Gottfried Wilhelm Leibniz, Johann Gottfried von Herder, Johann Gottlieb Fichte, Georg Wilhelm Friedrich Hegel, Leopold von Ranke, Henrich von Sybel, Heinrich von Treitschke, Theodor Mommsen, and Thomas Carlyle, and Acton went on to illustrate Machiavelli's continuing pervasive influence: "When we say that public life is not an affair of morality, that there is no available rule of right and wrong, that men must be judged by their age, that the code shifts with the longitude, that the wisdom which governs the event is superior to our own, we carry obscurely tribute to the system which bears so odious a name." And the more nationalistic politics became, so much more Machiavelli was praised as "a faithful observer of facts," who "discovered" the law of future society, a patriot, a republican, a Liberal, but "above all this, a man sagacious enough to know that politics is an inductive science."[74]

Acton's words echo the lessons of his life as an historian, a Catholic, and a Liberal, and particularly the long disagreement with Döllinger. It is fitting that Acton's name should remain popularly identified with the much-misquoted "Power corrupts . . ."[75] and also with his call, made in his Cambridge Inaugural Lecture, to "suspect power more than vice."[76] His conclusion was that the expansion of absolute power must be shunned at all costs, as it was in the late Middle Ages when it was "deemed more intolerable and more criminal than slavery."[77] The medieval theory of politics restrained the State, as Acton interpreted it: "Laws are made for the public good, and, for the public good, they may be suspended. The public good is not to be considered, if it is purchased at the expense of an individual. Authorities are legitimate if they govern well. Whether they do govern well those whom they govern must decide."[78] That conviction had produced Acton's empathy with the friar of Naples, his "fellow-countryman," St. Thomas Aquinas, whom he hailed as the earliest exponent of the "Whig theory of revolution," politically centuries ahead of St. Thomas's contemporary Simon de Montfort, who summoned and thus founded Westminster's Commons.

In the century of the Reformation, its religious supporters and opponents alike served to reinforce the royal absolutism with doctrines such as those of divine right and passive obedience. "When the last of the reformers died, religion, instead of emancipating the nations, had become an excuse for the criminal acts of despots. Calvin preached and Bellarmine lectured, but Machiavelli reigned."[79] Similarly, in the nineteenth century, Ultramontanism became one of religion's political props or substitutes in the struggle between Church and State, with the same detrimental effect on religion as Gallicanism.

The problems that puzzled Acton, he once told Mary Gladstone, were "not in religion or politics so much as along the wavy line between the two."[80] In politics he inclined, near the end of his life, towards the federal system as offering "the true natural check on absolute democracy," limiting the "central government by the powers reserved, and the state governments by the power they have ceded. It is the one immortal tribute of America to political science, for state rights are at the same time the consummation and the guard of democracy."[81] Acton was writing at a time when federalism, because of its association with slavery and feudalism, had fallen into disrepute and given way everywhere to centralism. Nevertheless, he concluded: "It is the only method of curbing not only the majority but the power of the whole people, and it affords the strongest basis for a second chamber, which has been found the essential security for freedom in every genuine democracy."[82]

When Acton died, the *Times,* in the imperialist climate of the age, felt obliged to charge him with a "want of national fibre,"[83] and it is true that he seems to have been less than enthusiastic for the arms race in the 1880s and 1890s, when Great Britain was no less involved than Germany. His attitude towards British policy was quite unambiguous. "In judging our national merits," he wrote, "we must allow much for our national hypocrisy. Wherever we went, we were the best colonists in the world, but we exterminated the natives wherever we went. We despised conquests, but we annexed with the greed of Russia."[84] Acton's support for Gladstone's Home Rule for Ireland was motivated by no more than a wish to remedy a plain injustice of centuries. He was under no illusion that this political solution would make any difference to the love-hate relationship that fate had bequeathed to Britain and Ireland by placing the smaller island at the geographical mercy of its bigger neighbour. Similarly, Acton was opposed to British injustice in India and Africa. He rejoiced at Gladstone's moderate peace terms negotiated with the Boers in 1881 "in defiance of military indignation" and "after disasters unavenged."[85] He instilled these international lessons in his own children by emphasizing that "right is not all on one side, that good men are often wrong, and that wicked men sometimes accomplish what is necessary."[86] This, too, entitled him at the end of his own century and the beginning of the twentieth, to be remembered as first among English Europeans as well as the last great liberal.

Being the Catholic that he was, as well as opposed to Prussian militarism and sympathizing with Austria, Acton would certainly have been a diplomatic misfit in the Kaiser's Berlin in those final decades of Anglo-German rivalry before the Great War. He had the advantage over other historians in having some personal experience of politics as a member of both Houses of Parliament and through his extensive family connections in Great Britain, Italy, France, and the German-speaking world—just as being an English Catholic with a German-trained mind added another dimension to the way he was able to marshal his vast knowledge and Weltanschauung. "No priest, accustomed to the Confessional," he once noted, "and a fortiori, no historian, thinks well of human nature."[87] That perspective made him a sad but never lachrymose analyst of human affairs. But it was the grandeur and loftiness of Acton's liberal and Catholic vision that elevated it beyond his own time. When he was forty-five, he confided to Lady Blennerhassett the innermost core of his conscience, that his was

> the story of a man who started in life believing himself a sincere Catholic and a sincere Liberal; who therefore renounced everything in Catholicism which was not compatible with Liberty, and everything in Politics which was not compatible with Catholicity.
>
> I carried farther than others the Doctrinaire belief in mere Liberalism, identifying it altogether with morality, and holding the ethical standard and purpose to be supreme and sovereign.
>
> I carried this principle into the study of history. . . .
>
> That is my entire Capital.[88]

NOTES

The following abbreviations are used in the notes:

Briefwechsel   *Ignaz von Döllinger Briefwechsel,* vols. 1–3, *Mit Lord Acton, 1850–1890;*
                 vol. 4, *Briefwechsel mit Lady Blennerhassett, 1865–1886,* ed. Victor Con-
                 zemius (Munich, 1963–81).

CUL   Cambridge University Library, Cambridge

PRO   Public Record Office, London

Chapter 1: Birth in Naples

1. Corpo della Citta di Napoli, Sezione Chiaja, 10 January 1834, CUL Add. 8121/4/
   380. On the birth certificate the baby's name is given as Giovanni Emerico Odoardo
   Carlo.

2. Henry Edward Fox, journal, 23 October 1828, *The Journal of the Hon. Henry Edward
   Fox, 1818–1830, afterwards Fourth Lord Holland,* ed. Earl of Ilchester (London, 1923),
   328.

3. Elizabeth Acton to Sir Ferdinand Richard Acton, 16 June 1826, CUL Add. 8121/4/
   311/1.

418 NOTES TO PAGES 2-5

4. Lady (Nonna) Acton to Elizabeth Acton Throckmorton, 21 July [1829], Throck-morton Papers, Warwickshire County Record Office, Warwick, CR1998, "smaller veneered box," no. 4 [French]. Unless otherwise noted, all translations are my own.

5. Sir Richard Acton to Lady (Nonna) Acton, 15 July 1824, CUL Add. 8121/3/313 [French].

6. Cardinal Charles Januarius Acton (1803–1847), first English cardinal of the Roman Curia since the Reformation, Cardinal (1839), a special protégé of Gregory XVI and sternly conservative, spent his short ecclesiastical career in the Church's diplomatic service, in the Roman ecclesiastical courts, and as vice-legate in Bologna. Involved with the preparations for the restoration of the English hierarchy, he expressed reservations, considering the British prelates of the time as deficient in the necessary qualities. See Joseph Gillow, ed., *Bibliographical Dictionary of the English Catholics* (London, 1885–95), 1:3–6; *Dictionary of National Biography* (London, 1884–1950), 1:65.

7. Charles Acton was devoted to the patron saint and martyr of Naples, whose body is preserved in the cathedral. Two phials of the blood of Saint Januarius are shown annually on his feast (19 September) and on other occasions, when the phenomenon of the liquefaction of his blood occurs (since 1389). See *Encyclopaedia Britannica*, 11th ed. (1910–11), s.v. "Januarius."

8. Sir Harold Acton, *The Bourbons of Naples (1734–1825)* (London, 1956), and *The Last Bourbons of Naples (1825–1861)* (London, 1961).

9. Sir Richard Acton to Lady (Nonna) Acton, 23 January 1834, CUL Add. 8121/1/150 [French].

10. Lady Marie Dalberg-Acton to Lady (Nonna) Acton, 25 January 1834, CUL Add. 8121/2/70 [French].

11. Lady Marie Dalberg-Acton to Lady (Nonna) Acton, 30 January 1834, CUL Add. 8121/2/71 [French].

12. Lady Marie Dalberg-Acton to Lady (Nonna) Acton, 1 February 1834, CUL Add. 8121/2/72 [French].

13. Lady Marie Dalberg-Acton to Lady (Nonna) Acton, 6 February 1834, CUL Add. 8121/2/73 [French].

14. Sir Richard Acton to Lady (Nonna) Acton, 13 and 20 February 1834, CUL Add. 8121/1/152, 153.

15. John Orlando Parry, diary, 1 March 1834, *Victorian Swandown: The Early Travel Diaries of John Orlando Parry,* ed. Cyril Andrews and J. A. Orr-Oriving (London, 1935), 196–97.

16. Ibid., 197.

17. Sir Richard Acton to Lady (Nonna) Acton, 4 March 1834, CUL Add. 8121/1/154.

Chapter 2: A Cosmopolitan Background

1. Acton to Mary Gladstone, 1 September 1883, *Letters of Lord Acton to Mary, Daughter of the Right Hon. W. E. Gladstone,* ed. Herbert Paul, 2d rev. ed. (London, 1913), 137.

2. Even the author's name conveyed the message of her Bourbon royalism: Pauline-Marie-Amande-Aglae de La Ferronays. The eldest of eleven children, she was born in 1808 in London, to which her parents, both members of historic families, had immigrated in 1805. The family returned to France in 1827, when her father joined the royalist government; resigning on grounds of ill health, he accepted instead the position of Charles X's ambassador to the Pope. He resigned again after the July 1830 Revolution and settled in comparative poverty at Castellamare, Naples, in a house near the Villa Acton. *Récit d'une soeur* took twelve years to write and was not published in Paris until 1867, after a private edition was circulated in 1865. It was an instant literary success in France, being "crowned" by the Académie Française. The book initiated a then-new literary genre, a "real-life documentary," the main theme of which was the love and religious conversion of Pauline's brother, Albert de La Ferronays, and Alexandrine d'Alopeus, and their tragic early deaths. The story was told by means of letters, the author acting merely as editor and providing a linking commentary. The La Ferronays-Acton-Naples link was echoed by another, a love affair between one of the La Ferronays brothers in London and Lady (Nonna) Acton, then a twenty-six-year-old widow who had gone from Naples to London after her husband's death to look after the English education of her three children. The result of their indiscretion was a child who was brought up by foster parents and who later took the name of Burnell (from the place-name Acton Burnell), becoming a colonel in the Belgian army.

3. Duke of Dalberg to Sir Richard Acton, n.d. [ca. 1830], CUL Add. 8121/2/21–28. See also H. J. St. John to Sir Richard Acton, n.d. [ca. 1830], CUL Add. 8121/2/8.

4. Charles Greville, C.F., journal, 24 May 1830, *The Greville Memoirs: A Journal of the Reigns of King George IV, King William IV and Queen Victoria,* ed. Henry Reeve (London, 1888), 1:380.

5. Henry Edward Fox, journal, 18 June 1821, *The Journal of the Hon. Henry Edward Fox, 1818–1830, afterwards Fourth Lord Holland,* ed. Earl of Ilchester (London, 1923), 74.

6. Lady Harriet Granville to Lady Georgiana Morpeth, 18 December 1824, *The Letters of Harriet, Countess Granville, 1810–1845,* ed. F. Leveson Gower (London, 1894), 1:326.

7. Charles Greville, journal, 3 May 1830, *Greville Memoirs,* 1:361.

8. Edward Gibbon, *The Autobiographies of Edward Gibbon,* ed. Oliphant Smeater (London, 1932), 372–74.

9. G. Nuzzo, entry on Sir John Francis Edward Acton (1736–1811), *Dizionario Biografico degli Italiani* (Rome: Istituto della Enciclopedia Italiana, 1960–   ), 1:206–10. This entry presents the more favourable view of modern Italian historians towards Acton's grandfather. It discounts as untenable the old but still prevailing view of him as a "foreign adventurer," hostile towards the Neapolitan nobility, and the Queen's lover. See also Joseph Alexander von Helfert, *Maria Karolina von Österreich, 1790–1814* (Vienna, 1884), a biography that received the special praise of Professor Ignaz von Döllinger. It exonerated, according to him, "this most calumniated queen" as well as [in German] "your grandfather who extended his influence over the whole of southern Italy and safeguarded the interests and the honour of his adopted country." Döllinger to Acton, 13 September 1876, *Briefwechsel,* 3:168. For the occasion of the centenary of General Acton's death, Acton's second daughter, Annie, wrote a biography of her great-grandfather, which was never published. In her preface she wrote with reference to the biography of Queen Marie Caroline by André Bonnefous, who had described the Queen's minister as "un aventurier anglais" (an English adventurer) and "cet être étrangé" (this unlikely foreigner), that the word *étrangé* had, in this case, an unmerited negative interpretation, "for although Acton was in a sense a soldier of fortune, we should bear in mind that, as a Catholic, he was debarred from all chance of a career in England, whilst in France he could scarcely have preserved his nationality in identifying himself with the fortunes of that country. And had he succeeded then in overcoming the grand duke's opposition to the extent of taking service in France, it is doubtful whether without him King Ferdinand could have held Sicily against Napoleon." Annie, who researched her biography in the state archives of Naples, continued: "While condoning none of his faults, nor attempting to palliate that ambition which undoubtedly was the *Leitmotiv* of his life, it will be possible to demonstrate an integrity of purpose, a steadfast attachment to the varying fortunes of his royal master, with the fearless assumption of the responsibilities frequently forced upon him by the queen against his better judgement. How it was largely due to Acton's diplomatic resource that Nelson lent the protection of his fleet to sorely pressed Naples, and how he combined faithful and devoted service to his adopted sovereigns with unswerving loyalty to his own country, I have endeavoured to relate." Annie Acton, "Sir John Francis Edward Acton," unpublished manuscript, CUL Add. 8121/10/211–59.

10. Lord Nelson to Admiral Samuel Goodall, 11 March 1800, *Letters from Lord Nelson,* comp. Geoffrey Rawson (London, 1949), 280. Acton was actually sixty-four.

11. Lord Nelson to Earl Spencer, First Lord of the Admiralty, 13 July 1799, *Letters from Lord Nelson,* 242.

12. Mamy Acton, "Notes Taken from Memory, 1866–1936," 7, CUL Add. 8119/9/427.

13. Emily Dease to Annie Acton, 23 February 1909, CUL Add. 8121/10/214/1–2.

14. Various letters to Lady (Nonna) Acton, CUL Add. 8121/3, 4.

15. W. Casey to Charles Williams Wynn, 15 October [1813?], CUL Add. 8121/1/100. Casey was the headmaster of Westminster School, and Wynn was Acton's lawyer.

16. W. Williams Wynn to the Rev. Matthew Jones, 2 October 1819, CUL Add. 8121/5/ 147.

17. Sir Richard Acton to Lady (Nonna) Acton, 10 January [1835], CUL Add. 8121/4/ 270 [French].

18. *Le moniteur universel* (Paris), 7 February 1837.

19. Sheridan Gilley, *Newman and His Age* (London, 1990), 220.

20. "Acton's Naturalisation Act Amendment," CUL Add. 8121/3/491. See also "An Act for Naturalising Dame Marie L. P. de Dalberg and Sir John E E Dalberg Acton, Bart.," 21–22.Vic.c.11 (private act, not printed) and "Acton Nationality Act of 1911," 1–2.G.5 (not printed or numbered).

Chapter 3: Onwards to Oscott

1. Lady Harriet Granville to Lady Carlisle, 26 June 1838, *The Letters of Harriet, Countess Granville, 1810–1845,* ed. F. Leveson Gower (London, 1894), 2:260.

2. Lady Georgiana Fullerton to Mlle. Eward, 18 July 1840, quoted in Mrs. Augustus Craven, *Life of Lady Georgiana Fullerton,* trans. H. J. Coleridge (London, 1888), 105–6. Lady Fullerton was received into the Catholic Church in Rome in 1846.

3. Lady Harriet Granville to Mrs. Hamilton Hamilton, 5 November 1840, *Letters of Harriet, Countess Granville,* 2:312–13.

4. Lady (Nonna) Acton to Elizabeth Throckmorton, 6 January 1846, Throckmorton Papers, Warwickshire County Record Office, 1998/P. 121, "smaller veneered box," no. 158 [French].

5. Lady (Nonna) Acton to Elizabeth Throckmorton, 7 [July 1837], Throckmorton Papers, Warwickshire County Record Office, 1998/P. 121, "smaller veneered box," no. 12 [French].

6. Lady (Nonna) Acton to Elizabeth Throckmorton, 2 February 1846, Throckmorton Papers, Warwickshire County Record Office, 1998/P. 121, "smaller veneered box," no. 162 [French].

7. Félix Dupanloup to Lady Leveson, 7 September 1842, CUL Add. 8121/6/19 [French]. For a detailed treatment of Acton's education, see James C. Holland, "The Education of Lord Acton" (Ph.D. diss., Catholic University of America, Washington, D.C., 1968).

8. A note from Acton is based on what he had heard from Ernest Renan and Dupanloup, in CUL Add 8119/8/558. For an account of Talleyrand's submission, see Duff Cooper, *Talleyrand* (London, 1937), 362–74.

9. Acton to Lady Leveson, 23 January 1842, CUL Add. 8121/6/8.

10. Acton to Lady Leveson, 12 September 1842, CUL Add. 8121/7/451.

11. Acton to Lady Leveson, 8 December 1842, CUL Add. 8121/7/452.

12. Acton to Lady Leveson, 11 May 1843, CUL Add. 8121/7/453.

13. Acton to Lady Leveson, 12 August 1843, CUL Add. 8121/7/454.

14. Acton to Lady Leveson, 15 February 1844, CUL Add. 8121/7/456.

15. Acton to Lady Leveson, 12 February [1844], CUL Add. 8121/7/470.

16. Acton, quoted in Wilfrid Ward, *The Life and Times of Cardinal Wiseman* (London, 1897), 1:348–49.

17. Acton to Wilfrid Ward, 15 August 1895, St. Andrew's University Library, Fife, Scotland, Manuscript Department.

18. Acton to Lady Leveson, dated "Tuesday," CUL Add. 8121/7/478.

19. Acton to Wilfrid Ward, 14 April 1895, St. Andrew's University Library, Manuscript Department.

20. Acton to Lord Leveson, 23 January 1844, CUL Add. 8121/7/478.

21. Acton to Lady Leveson, 27 January 1844, CUL Add. 8121/7/464.

22. Acton to Lady Leveson, 21 February 1844, CUL Add. 8121/7/457.

23. Acton to Lady Leveson, 3 June 1846, CUL Add. 8121/7/463.

24. Lady (Nonna) Acton to Elizabeth Throckmorton, 6 January 1846, Throckmorton Papers, Warwickshire County Record Office, 1998/P. 121, "smaller veneered box," no. 158 [French].

25. Acton to Lady Leveson, dated "Samedi" [1848], CUL Add. 8121/7/488 [French].

26. Acton to Lady Leveson, 14 April and 21 May [1848], CUL Add. 8121/7/490, 494.

27. Acton to Lady Leveson, dated "Lundi" [1848], CUL Add. 8121/7/495 [French].

28. Acton to Lady Leveson, 21 May [1848], CUL Add. 8121/7/494.

29. Acton, note, CUL Add. 4905/212.

30. Acton to Mary Gladstone, 1 September 1883, *Letters of Lord Acton to Mary, Daughter of the Right Hon. W. E. Gladstone,* ed. Herbert Paul, 2d rev. ed. (London, 1913), 139.

31. Sir Mountstuart E. Grant Duff, *Out of the Past: Some Biographical Essays* (London, 1903), 2:190.

32. Acton to Lord Granville, dated "Edinburgh, Wednesday" [1849], CUL Add. 8121/7/1093.

33. Acton to Lady Granville, dated "Mardi" [1850], CUL Add. 8121/7/499 [French].

Chapter 4: Dr. Döllinger's Apprentice

1. Ignaz von Döllinger to Lady Granville, 12 August 1850, *Briefwechsel,* 1:3–4.

2. Acton to Lady Granville, dated "Monday" [August 1850], CUL Add. 8121/7/506 [French]. This letter must have been written about the same time as Dr. Döllinger's letter to Lady Granville cited above.

3. Acton to Lord Granville, n.d. [ca. mid-August 1850], *Selections from the Correspondence of the First Lord Acton,* ed. John Neville Figgis and Reginald Vere Laurence (London, 1917), 7. The editors wrongly estimate the date to be 1848.

4. Döllinger to Anna Gramich, [22 May 1864], *Ignaz Döllingers Briefe an eine junge Freundin,* ed. Heinrich Schrörs (Kempten, Germany, 1914), 163 [German].

5. Acton to Lord Granville, n.d. [ca. mid-August 1850], *Selections from the Correspondence,* 7.

6. Ibid., 8.

7. Acton, note, CUL Add. 5609/66–67.

8. Acton to Lord Granville, n.d. [ca. mid-August 1850], *Selections from the Correspondence,* 8.

9. Acton, note, CUL Add. 4909/268.

10. Acton to Minnie Throckmorton, 19 August 1850, Throckmorton Papers, Warwickshire County Record Office, "Tribune," part 2, bundle 31, no. 6.

11. Acton to Lady Granville, dated "Monday" [August 1850], CUL Add. 8121/18.

12. Döllinger to Lady Granville, 12 August 1850, *Briefwechsel,* 1:4.

13. Döllinger to Lady Granville, 12 December 1850, *Briefwechsel,* 1:7 [French].

14. Acton, note, CUL Add. 5671/22.

15. Louise von Kobell, *Conversations of Dr. Döllinger,* trans. Katherine Gould (London, 1892), 38–41.

16. Acton, note, CUL Add. 4913/65.

17. The portrait is in the possession of the fourth Baron Acton. It is pictured on the dustcover of this book.

18. Acton to Döllinger, 18 March [1853], *Briefwechsel,* 1:13 [German].

19. Acton to Annie Acton, 12 April 1896, CUL Add. 8121/9/126. The letter summarized Acton's view of the history of Venice.

20. See Acton's paper on Rawdon Lubbock Brown's work in the archives, "Notes on Archival Researches, 1864–1868," read to the Eranus Society at Trinity College, Cambridge, May 1897, published in *Lord Acton: The Decisive Decade, 1864–1874: Essays and Documents,* ed. Damian McElrath, James Holland, Ward White, and Sue Katzman (Louvain, Belgium, 1970), 127–40; Acton to Annie Acton, 7 May 1897, CUL Add. 8121/9/134.

21. Acton, note, CUL Add. 4971, various cards. See also Stefan Lösch, *Döllinger und Frankreich: Eine geistige Allianz, 1823–1871* (Munich, 1955), 176–208; and the biography by Nicholas Burtin, *Un semeur d'idées au temps de la Restauration: Le Baron d'Eckstein* (Paris, 1931).

22. Acton to Döllinger, n.d. [probably May 1881 or 1882], *Briefwechsel,* 3:260 [German].

23. Charlotte Blennerhassett, "Lord Acton," *Deutsche Rundschau* 122 (1905): 68 [German].

24. Acton, note, CUL Add. 4973/151. One of similar statements that abound in Acton's Cambridge notes reads: "D[öllinger] never was a Liberal, and was not influenced by the problems which arise when a Whig politician is a religious Catholic. He much preferred liberty to oppression. He admitted that men must claim for others what they claim for themselves. But though a liberal government was better, a conservative gov[ernment] was good, was legitimate." Acton, note, CUL Add. 4909/196. See also Acton to W. E. Gladstone, 22 March 1891, *Selections from the Correspondence,* 69–70.

25. Acton, note, CUL Add. 4915/14–15; see also CUL Add. 4914/21.

26. Acton, "Döllinger's Historical Work," *English Historical Review* 5 (1890): 700–44, reprinted in *Selected Writings of Lord Acton,* ed. J. Rufus Fears (Indianapolis, 1984–88), 2:412.

27. Ibid., 422.

28. Acton to Döllinger, 25 November 1858, *Briefwechsel,* 1:156 [German]. Of course, Acton meant "Anglo-Catholic" to apply to English Catholics, not to indicate, as in the modern sense, the High Church wing of the Established Church.

29. W. E. Gladstone to Catherine Gladstone, 30 September 1845, quoted in John Morley, *The Life of William Ewart Gladstone* (London, 1903), 1:318–19.

Chapter 5: The Newfound Family

1. Although the Arcos were in fact his cousins, Acton at once addressed them as uncle and aunt, and soon began calling the Countess "mother." These were terms of endearment not to be confused with actual genealogy. Throughout this book I have let his usage prevail without correction, although I have attempted in the narrative to be faithful with regard to their cousinhood.

2. Emmerich Arco to Acton, 15 October 1874, CUL Add. 8121/7/233 [German].

3. Acton to Minnie Throckmorton, 11 January 1853, Throckmorton Papers, Warwickshire County Record Office, "Tribune," part 2, bundle 31, no. 7.

4. Acton to Countess Arco, 25 November 1857, CUL Add. 8121/7/691 [German].

5. Acton to Countess Arco, 16 September 1857, CUL Add. 8121/7/686 [French].

6. Acton to Countess Arco, 31 December 1858/1 January 1859, CUL Add. 8121/7/697.

7. Lord Granville to Acton, 21 July 1852, CUL Add. 8121/6/67/1.

8. Acton, note, CUL Add. 4914/227.

9. Hyazinth Holland, *Lebenserinnerungen eines neunzig-jährigen Alt-Münchners* (Munich, 1921), 40. Holland (1827–1918), who wrote under the pen name Reding von Bibereg, was a student of Johann Joseph von Görres and became well known as a writer and art historian, one of the last literary figures of Munich's late Romantic period. See Wilhelm Kösch, *Das Katholische Deutschland* (Augsburg, Germany, 1933–39), 1:1048.

10. Acton, "Döllinger's Historical Work," *English Historical Review* 5 (1890): 700–44, reprinted in *Selected Writings of Lord Acton,* ed. J. Rufus Fears (Indianapolis, 1984–88), 2:436.
11. For Peter Ernst von Lasaulx (1805–1861), German historian of religion, see Josef Höfer and Karl Rahner, eds., *Lexikon für Theologie und Kirche,* 2d rev. ed. (Freiburg, Germany, 1957–65), 6:802. See also James C. Holland, *The Legacy of an Education,* intro. Stephen J. Tonsor (Grand Rapids, Mich., 1997).
12. W. E. Gladstone to Catherine Gladstone, 20 October 1845, quoted in John Morley, *The Life of William Ewart Gladstone* (London, 1903), 1:320. On Johann Joseph von Görres (1776–1848), German writer and politician, intellectual leader of the Catholic revolutionary movement in the early nineteenth century, and professor in Munich from 1827, see *Staatslexikon* (Freiburg, Germany, 1889), 6th ed. (1956 et seq.), 2:1082.
13. Acton, note, CUL Add. 4909/103, 291. For the Görres circle in Munich, see Franz Schnabel, *Deutsche Geschichte im neunzehnten Jahrhundert,* 2d ed. (Freiburg, Germany, 1951), 4:164–202.
14. Acton, note, CUL Add. 5478/54.
15. Madame de Staël (Germaine Necker) *Corinne; ou, l'Italie* (Paris, 1807). The original of the much misquoted saying is: "Tout comprendre rend très indulgent" (To understand all is to be very lenient).
16. Acton, note, CUL Add. 5609/27.
17. Acton, note, CUL Add. 4909/174.
18. Acton, note, CUL Add. 4909/169.
19. Acton, note, CUL Add. 5394/46.
20. Acton, note, CUL Add. 4909/289.
21. Acton, note, CUL Add. 4909/291.
22. Acton, note, CUL Add. 4909/65.
23. Acton to Countess Arco, dated "Mardi: soir" [22 August 1854?], CUL Add. 8121/7/660 [French].
24. Annecy was the home of the de Menthon family, friends of Dr. Döllinger and Acton and Baron d'Eckstein, whom they also met there in the late summer of 1854.
25. Countess Arco to Acton, Herrnsheim, 24 August [1854?], CUL Add. 8121/7/114 [French].
26. Acton to Countess Arco, dated "Mardi: soir" [22 August 1854?], CUL Add. 8121/7/660 [French].

Chapter 6: The Squire

1. Acton to Döllinger, 4 December [1854], *Briefwechsel,* 1:42 [German].
2. Lord Granville to Lord Canning, 4 September 1859, quoted in Lord Edmund Fitz-

maurice, *The Life of Granville George Leveson Gower, Second Earl Granville,* 2d ed. (London, 1905), 1:358.

3. Acton to Döllinger, 18 January 1855, *Briefwechsel,* 1:52 [German].

4. Acton to Countess Arco, 11 January [1855], CUL Add. 8121/7/655/1 [French].

5. The Acton family's dealings with Freshfield's firm of solicitors in the City of London seems to have begun with Acton's grandfather, the general and prime minister of the Kingdom of the Two Sicilies, and continued with his widow, Lady (Nonna) Acton, when she came to London in 1811 for the education of her three children; the association lasted throughout the century. The firm with the name of Freshfield, founded probably in 1743, was first headed by James William Freshfield (1775–1864). He was a dissenter, close to William Wilberforce, the antislavery campaigner; he was a Tory MP for Penryn but lost his seat in the Reform election of 1832, was reelected in 1835, and retired from Parliament in 1857. His eldest son, also named James William Freshfield, born in 1801, was a partner until his sudden death in 1857. And until 1927 the partners of the firm, now at 67 Fleet Street, London EC4, at all times included one or more members of the Freshfield family, among them Charles Kaye Freshfield (1835–1870), Henry Ray Freshfield (1839–1877), William Dawes Freshfield (1858–1903), and Edwin Freshfield (1858–1918). Among their prominent clients were W. E. Gladstone, Sir Robert Peel, Nathan Meyer Rothschild (founder of the English house of Rothschild), the first and second Lord Carrington (of the banking house founded by Robert Smith), and the Bank of England. See Judy Slinn, *A History of Freshfields* (London, 1983), published by Freshfields.

6. A draft of Acton's letter is at Cambridge, n.d., CUL Add. 8121/7/1099; the original is in the Granville Papers, PRO, 29/30, nos. 18–19.

7. Lord Granville to Lord Canning, 25 March 1856, quoted in Fitzmaurice, *Life of the Second Earl Granville,* 1:173–74.

8. Newman to Acton, 7 January 1855, *Letters and Diaries of John Henry Newman,* ed. C. S. Dessain et al. (Oxford, 1961–84), 16:344.

9. Acton to Lord Granville, 27 October 1853, CUL Add. 8121/7/1098.

10. Archivio Storico, Propaganda Fide Archives, Rome, *Scritti Referiti, Inghilterra 1870,* no. 1375.

11. Canon John Brande Morris to Sir John Acton, 6 and 22 October 1855, Shropshire County Council Record Office, Shrewsbury, 1903/461, 464. The quotation from the letter of 6 October 1855 omits Morris's various Greek interjections.

12. F. W. Faber to Canon John Brande Morris, 15 December 1846, Brompton Oratory, London, MSS, fol. 119.

13. F. W. Faber to Canon John Brande Morris, 4 June 1847, Brompton Oratory, MSS, fol. 114.

14. Acton to Döllinger, 15 December 1855, *Briefwechsel,* 1:86–87 [German].

15. Acton to Bishop James Brown, 22 May 1862, Shrewsbury Diocesan Archives, Shrewsbury.

16. Acton to Richard Simpson, 13 November 1858, *The Correspondence of Lord Acton and Richard Simpson,* ed. Josef L. Altholz, Damien McElrath, and James C. Holland (Cambridge, England, 1971–75), 1:84.

17. See three articles relating to Aldenham Park, Salop, by Gervase Jackson-Stops, in *Country Life* (London), 23 and 30 June and 7 July 1977.

18. Elizabeth Throckmorton to Richard Acton, 30 June 1826, CUL Add. 8121/4/310.

19. Acton to Döllinger, 14 August 1863, *Briefwechsel,* 1:319 [German].

20. See Johann Friedrich, *Ignaz von Döllinger* (Munich, 1899–1901), 3:134.

21. Acton to Döllinger, 3 July [1855], *Briefwechsel,* 1:76 [German].

22. Lord Granville to Lord Canning, 4 September 1859, quoted in Fitzmaurice, *Life of the Second Earl Granville,* 1:358.

23. W. E. Gladstone to Acton, 28 April 1889, BL, London, Add. 44094/53–55; Acton to W. E. Gladstone, 7 May 1889, BL Add. 44094/56–57.

24. John H. Bohn to Acton, 15 September 1868, Shropshire County Council Record Office, 1093/508.

25. Döllinger to Acton, 3 September 1877, *Briefwechsel,* 3:183 [German].

26. Acton, note, CUL Add. 4905/89.

27. Owen Chadwick, "The Challenge of Acton," *Tablet,* 28 January 1984, 77–78.

28. Reinhold Pauli to his wife, 9 September 1877, *Lebenserinnerungen nach Briefen und Tagebüchern zusammengestellt,* ed. Elizabeth Pauli (Halle, Germany, 1895), 319–22 [German].

29. Ibid.

Chapter 7: Three Journeys

1. Acton to Countess Arco, n.d., CUL Add. 8121(7)/647 [French].

2. "Lord Acton's American Diaries," printed in *Fortnightly Review* 110 (November 1921):727–42, (December 1921):917–34, (January 1922):63–83; reprinted as *Acton in America: The American Journal of Sir John Acton, 1853,* ed. S. W. Jackman (Shepherdstown, W.Va., 1979).

3. Acton to Döllinger, 22 June [1853], *Briefwechsel,* 1:26.

4. Acton, American diary, 15 June 1853, *Acton in America,* 45.

5. Acton, American diary, 10 June 1853, *Acton in America,* 15–16, 18.

6. Acton to Döllinger, 22 June [1853], *Briefwechsel,* 1:27–29.

7. Ibid., 1:29–30.

8. Acton, "The American Revolution," chap. 19 of Acton, *Lectures on Modern History,* ed. John Neville Figgis and Reginald Vere Laurence (London, 1906), reprinted in *Selected Writings of Lord Acton,* ed. J. Rufus Fears (Indianapolis, 1984–88), 1:197.

428 NOTES TO PAGES 66–70

9. Acton to Döllinger, 21 July [1853], *Briefwechsel,* 1:32, 34, 36 [German]. These letters show how impressed Acton was by Brownson. The letters also contain an account of Brownson's life (1803–1876) and of his spiritual odyssey. He grew up an unbeliever, converted to Presbyterianism when he was nineteen, became a rationalist and, through his acquaintance with Robert Owen, a radical Socialist. He told Acton that he had also been a Unitarian, a Deist, a Freemason, and close to the Mormons, but that "there was method" in his religious straying. In 1840, under the influence of Aristotle, Brownson deepened his supranatural and metaphysical interests and, in 1844, entered the Catholic Church. John Bernard Fitzpatrick (1812–1866), Bishop of Boston, one of the most learned American prelates, held Brownson, according to Acton, in higher regard than Newman. Acton, who spent four days with Brownson at Emmitsburg, described him as having "an extremely high forehead and small eyes," and remarked that "he is very dirty." Brownson published the *Boston Quarterly Review* (1838–42) and *Brownson's Quarterly Review* (1844–64, 1873–75). Twenty volumes of his collected writings (1882–87) were published by Brownson's third son, Henry Francis (1835–1913), who was Döllinger's student for a year in Munich and became a lawyer. See *National Cyclopaedia of American Biography* (New York, 1918), 16:436; W. Romig, *Josephine Van Dyke Brownson* (Detroit, 1955), 11–13, 17, 25, 39–41. For Orestes Brownson, see *The Catholic Encyclopaedia* (New York, 1907–12), 3:1ff.

10. Acton, American diary, 7 July 1853, *Acton in America,* 87–88.

11. Acton to Döllinger, 6 September [1853], *Briefwechsel,* 1:38.

12. The essay, privately printed in London in 1863, is reprinted in *Selected Writings,* 3:395–442.

13. Acton to Döllinger, 20 May [1856], *Briefwechsel,* 1:109 [German].

14. Acton to Döllinger, 6 June [1856], *Briefwechsel,* 1:112 [German].

15. Lord Granville to Acton, [5 September 1856], CUL Add. 8121/6/71a/1–2.

16. Lord Granville to Acton, 18 June 1856, CUL Add. 8121/6/70b.

17. Acton to Lord Granville, 12 and 16 June 1856, CUL Add. 8121/7/1101/1, 1102/1.

18. Acton to Lady Granville, 13 June 1856, CUL Add. 8121/7/582 [French].

19. Acton, Moscow Functions Book, CUL Add. 4872. Several of these notations are not in Acton's hand.

20. Acton to Lord Granville, 16 June 1856, CUL Add. 8121/18.

21. Lord Granville to Lord Canning, 7 September 1856, quoted in Lord Edmund Fitzmaurice, *The Life of Granville George Leveson Gower, Second Earl Granville,* 2d ed. (London, 1905), 1:200–201.

22. Lord Granville to Lord Canning, 2 September 1856, quoted in Fitzmaurice, *Life of the Second Earl Granville,* 1:198.

23. Lord Granville to Lord Canning, 9 September 1856, quoted in Fitzmaurice, *Life of the Second Earl Granville,* 1:205.

24. Acton to Döllinger, 27 November 1856, *Briefwechsel*, 1:116. "The Influence of the Reformation on Morality" appeared in the *Weekly Register*, 29 November 1856, 6; "The Political Working of the Austrian Concordat" appeared in the *Weekly Register*, 6 December 1856, 8.

25. Acton to Döllinger, 4 December 1856, *Briefwechsel*, 1:117 [German].

26. Acton proposed for the inspectorate Edward Herbert (formerly Jones) of Llanarth, from one of the old families of Monmouth squires who were Aldenham neighbours; Herbert had also been Döllinger's pupil in Munich. Acton's advice was, however, not taken. Instead Scott Nasmyth Stokes (1821–1891), a scholar, barrister, and convert, was appointed, as well as William Marshall (1818–1877), an Anglican clergyman and Tractarian who was compelled to give up the post when he converted to Roman Catholicism. "I became aware of the lack of deeper political education among Catholics only now that Stokes and Marshall defend the introduction of conscription in England," Acton wrote on 17 February 1858 to Döllinger (*Briefwechsel*, 1:131–32 [German]).

27. Acton to Döllinger, 29 January 1857, *Briefwechsel*, 1:119.

28. Two issues of the *Rambler* (October and November 1856) were reviewed and attacked by Cardinal Nicholas Wiseman: "The Present Catholic Dangers," *Dublin Review* 41 (1856): 441–70, to which the *Rambler* replied in February 1857, 140–44, and in turn Wiseman responded in *Dublin Review* 42 (1857): 245–48. What Wiseman attacked ostensibly was what he regarded as the *Rambler*'s attempt at sowing disunity in the English Catholic body and denigrating his own optimistic view of the Catholic future in Great Britain. For this controversy, see also Wilfrid Ward, *William George Ward and the Catholic Revival* (London, 1893), chap. 10.

29. Acton's Rome journal was edited and published by Herbert Butterfield in the *Cambridge Historical Journal* 8 (1946):186–204 (hereafter *Cambridge Historical Journal*). This particular quotation is from Acton, Rome journal, 12 May 1857, *Cambridge Historical Journal*, 194.

30. Acton, notes, CUL Add. 4905/131, 4903/144, 4905/72.

31. Acton, "Döllinger's Historical Work," in *Selected Writings*, 2:441.

32. Döllinger to Charlotte von Leyden, n.d. [21 January 1870], *Briefwechsel*, 4:454 [German], also CUL Add. 4911.

33. Acton, note, CUL Add. 4804; see also Acton, note, CUL Add. 5644/71: "1857 made him indifferent to Roman literature."

34. Acton, Rome journal, 22 June 1857, *Cambridge Historical Journal*, 201. Ultramontanism and Gallicanism are discussed in detail in Chapter 9 of this book.

35. Acton to Döllinger, 5 February 1865 and 31 January [1867], *Briefwechsel*, 1:384, 469 [both German].

36. Acton, note, CUL Add. 4912/52.

37. Clemens Wenzel Lothar, Fürst von Metternich to Count Rudolf Apponyi, 7 Octo-

ber 1847, and Metternich to Count Karl Ludwig von Ficquelmont, 9 December 1847, *Mémoires of Prince Metternich* (Paris, 1880–84), 7:342–43, 443.

38. Acton, Rome journal, [27] April 1857, *Cambridge Historical Journal*, 192.

39. Acton to Döllinger, n.d. [September–October 1878], *Briefwechsel*, 3:207 [German].

40. Acton, note, CUL Add. 4999/164.

41. The books were *Delle cinque piaghe della Santa Chiesa* (1848) and *La Costituzione civile secondo la giustizia sociale* (1848), in which Antonio Rosmini-Serbati defended the doctrine of natural right. Both condemnations were clearly politically motivated. So was the condemnation, long after Rosmini's death, of forty propositions taken from Rosmini's philosophical writings. See articles on Rosmini in *Encyclopaedia Britannica*, 14th. ed. (1972), 10:188; and Josef Höfer and Karl Rahner, eds., *Lexikon für Theologie und Kirche*, 2d rev. ed. (Freiburg, Germany, 1957–65), 9:54–55; also Claude Leetham, *Rosmini: Priest, Philosopher and Patriot* (London, 1957).

42. Acton, notes, CUL Add. 4999/149, 164.

43. Acton, note, CUL Add. 5641/70/71.

44. Acton, note, CUL Add. 5643/21.

45. Acton to Döllinger, n.d. [September–October 1878], *Briefwechsel*, 3:207 [German].

46. Acton, Rome journal, n.d. [20 June 1857], *Cambridge Historical Journal*, 200.

47. Acton, note, CUL Add. 5001/188.

48. Acton, Rome journal, 12 May 1857, *Cambridge Historical Journal*, 194.

49. Acton, Rome journal, 3 May 1857, *Cambridge Historical Journal*, 192.

50. Acton, Rome journal, [27] April 1857, *Cambridge Historical Journal*, 190.

51. Acton, Rome journal, 3 May 1857, *Cambridge Historical Journal*, 192–93. Archbishop Flavio Prince Chigi (1810–1885), later Cardinal, was nuncio in Munich from 1861 to 1873 and papal ambassador at the coronation of Tsar Alexander II of Russia.

52. Acton, Rome journal, 12 June 1857, *Cambridge Historical Journal*, 199.

Chapter 8: Pleasing Lord Granville and Mama

1. Lord Granville to Lord Canning, 10 March 1857, quoted in Lord Edmund Fitzmaurice, *The Life of Granville George Leveson Gower, Second Earl Granville*, 2d ed. (London, 1905), 1:227.

2. Lord Granville to Lord Canning, 24 October 1857, quoted in Fitzmaurice, *Life of the Second Earl Granville*, 1:262.

3. Acton to Lord Granville, dated "Tuesday" [1857], CUL Add. 8121/7/1103/1.

4. Acton to Countess Arco, 2 April [1857], CUL Add. 8121/7/683 [French].

5. Archbishop Paul Cullen to Acton, 21 November 1857, CUL Add. 8119/I/C326.

6. Cardinal Nicholas Wiseman to Acton, 27 November 1857, *Selections from the Correspondence of the First Lord Acton*, ed. John Neville Figgis and Reginald Vere Laurence (London, 1917), 29–30.

7. Acton to Simpson, 5 April 1859, *The Correspondence of Lord Acton and Richard Simpson,* ed. Josef L. Altholz, Damien McElrath, and James C. Holland (Cambridge, England, 1971–75), 1:166.

8. Lord Granville to Acton, 20 April 1859, CUL Add. 8121/6/79.

9. James J. Auchmuty, "Acton's Election as an Irish Member of Parliament," *English Historical Review* 61, no. 241 (1946): 398.

10. Lord Granville to Acton, 9 May 1859, CUL Add. 8121/6/82.

11. Döllinger to Anna Gramich, 20 August 1863, *Ignaz Döllingers Briefe an eine junge Freundin,* ed. Heinrich Schrörs (Kempten, Germany, 1914), 155. Döllinger was referring to Acton's frequent throat trouble.

12. Acton to Simpson, 8 May 1859, *Acton-Simpson Correspondence,* 1:178.

13. Acton to Fr. Maher, 8 May 1859, published in the *Times,* 17 May 1859.

14. *Times,* 18 May 1859.

15. Auchmuty, "Acton's Election," 401.

16. Fr. Maher to Acton, 26 June 1859, CUL Add. 8119/I/M46.

17. Acton to Countess Arco, dated "Carlow, Saturday" [4 June 1859], CUL Add. 8121/7/797.

18. *Freeman's Journal,* 9 June 1859, quoted in Auchmuty, "Acton's Election," 404.

19. *Carlow Post,* 11 June 1859, quoted in Auchmuty, "Acton's Election," 404.

20. Roman Catholic Relief Act, 1829, 10 Geo. 4. c. 7, *Statutes of the United Kingdom,* 3d ed., vol. 3. The text of the Oath of Supremacy as given in the 1829 Emancipation Act appears in Bernard Ward, *The Eve of Catholic Emancipation* (1911–12; reprint, London, 1970), 3:362.

21. Lord Granville to Lord Canning, 4 September 1859, quoted in Fitzmaurice, *Life of the Second Earl Granville,* 1:358.

22. W. E. Gladstone to Catherine Gladstone, 9 April 1859, St. Deiniol's Archives, Hawarden, B2.

23. Acton, Rome journal, 12 June 1857, in *Cambridge Historical Journal,* 199.

24. Acton to Simpson, 23 August 1859, *Acton-Simpson Correspondence,* 1:210; "Contemporary Events," the *Rambler,* n.s., 24, pt. 3 (September 1859): 406–7.

25. Acton to Simpson, 26 August 1859, *Acton-Simpson Correspondence,* 1:215.

26. Acton, note, CUL Add. 5528/203.

27. There are many examples of invitations sent by W. E. Gladstone to Acton in CUL Add. 8119/9.

28. Acton to Döllinger, [July 1860], *Briefwechsel,* 1:179 [German].

29. W. E. Gladstone, *Studies on Homer and the Homeric Age* (Oxford, 1858).

30. Acton to Döllinger, 14 June 1858, *Briefwechsel,* 1:146 [German].

31. Acton to Döllinger, 30 June 1863, *Briefwechsel,* 1:316 [German].

32. W. E. Gladstone to Acton, 8 May 1861, *Selections from the Correspondence,* 158, also BL Add. 44093/7. See Acton, "Political Causes of the American Revolution," *The*

Rambler, n.s., 28, pt. 3 (May 1861): 17–61, reprinted in *Selected Writings of Lord Acton,* ed. J. Rufus Fears (Indianapolis, 1984–88), 1:216–62.

33. Acton, "Political Causes of the American Revolution," *Selected Writings,* 1:219.

34. Ibid., 259.

35. "The Civil War in America: Its Place in History," *Bridgnorth Journal,* 20 January 1866, reprinted in *Selected Writings,* 1:263–79.

36. Ibid., 273, 277.

37. Acton to Döllinger, November 1865, *Briefwechsel,* 1:416 [German].

38. H. C. G. Matthew, *Gladstone, 1809–1874* (Oxford, 1986), 89–95. See also W. E. Gladstone, *The Gladstone Diaries,* ed. M. R. D. Foot and H. C. G. Matthew (London, 1968–94), 3:xlv–xlix.

39. Acton to Döllinger, 2 December 1863, *Briefwechsel,* 1:329 [German].

40. Acton to Döllinger, 29 September 1859, *Briefwechsel,* 1:165.

41. Lord Granville to Lord Canning, 4 August 1860, quoted in Fitzmaurice, *Life of the Second Earl Granville,* 1:387.

42. Sir Mountstuart E. Grant Duff, *Out of the Past: Some Biographical Essays* (London, 1903), 2:192; the date given is "about 1863."

43. Henry Edward Manning, *Sermons on Ecclesiastical Subjects* (London, 1873), 3:7. In *The Temporal Sovereignty of the Popes* (London, 1860), his first publication as a Catholic, the future Archbishop of Westminster had made extravagant claims for the temporal power, that is, that it would be defined as a dogma of faith. These early lectures, translated into Italian, were too much even for Roman tastes and came close to being censored, although Pius IX, according to Edmund Sheridan Purcell (*Life of Cardinal Manning* [London, 1896], 2:153), expressed his approval. Manning later somewhat modified his extremist view but still claimed that "the temporal power of the popes is as manifestly and as fully ordained of God as the power of Queen Victoria." He went on to write that besides, with the Pope's royal sovereignty, the Papal State was endowed "with the justice, clemency and mercy which have marked its administration through the course of ages" (*Sermons on Ecclesiastical Subjects,* 2:21–22).

44. Acton to Simpson, 7 December 1859, *Acton-Simpson Correspondence,* 2:37.

45. *Hansard Parliamentary Debates,* 3d ser. (1860), 4 May 1860, 158:679–81.

46. Lord Granville to Countess Arco, 5 May 1860, Shropshire County Council Record Office, 1093/487.

47. Acton to Simpson, 6 December 1860, *Acton-Simpson Correspondence,* 2:98.

48. Acton to Simpson, 9 July 1860, *Acton-Simpson Correspondence,* 2:78–79.

49. Acton to Döllinger, 25 February 1861, *Briefwechsel,* 1:196 [German].

50. Acton to Simpson, 7 May 1862, *Acton-Simpson Correspondence,* 2:300.

51. Acton to Döllinger, [20 December 1861], *Briefwechsel* 1:239 [German].

52. Lord Granville to Acton, 6 March 1861, Granville Papers, PRO, 29/30, 24, pt. 2.

53. Lord Granville to Acton, 30 August 1861, CUL Add. 8121/6/113.

54. Acton to Döllinger, 4 April 1864, *Briefwechsel,* 1:344–45 [German].

55. Quoted in Herbert Butterfield, "Lord Acton," *Cambridge Journal* 6 (May 1953): 478.

56. W. E. Gladstone, diary, 4 April 1864, *Gladstone Diaries,* 6:267.

57. The story is found in Grant Duff, *Out of the Past,* 1:192.

58. Acton to Marie Arco (later Acton), July [1865], CUL Add. 8121/18; see also Acton to Marie, dated "Aldenham, Tuesday," CUL Add. 8121/7/883.

59. Acton to Marie, n.d., CUL Add. 8121/18.

60. "Appeal to the Working Electors of Bridgnorth," CUL Add. 8119/8/551.

61. *Times,* 14 July 1865.

62. Newman to Acton, 21 July 1865, *Letters and Diaries of John Henry Newman,* ed. C. S. Dessain et al. (Oxford, 1961–84), 22:15.

63. Acton to Marie, n.d., CUL Add. 8121/7/926.

64. *Spectator,* 18 July 1868, 383.

65. Acton to Döllinger, 5 September [1868], *Briefwechsel,* 1:518 [German, English].

66. Lord Granville to Acton, 19 November 1868, CUL Add. 8121(6)/165.

67. Simpson to Acton, 19 November 1868, *Acton-Simpson Correspondence,* 3:258.

68. Acton to Marie, dated "Friday," CUL Add. 8121/7/851.

69. Acton, "My Mother's Wishes," dated "Thursday morning, 27 October 1859," CUL Add. 4862/1–4.

70. Acton to Marie, 18 November 1859, Shropshire County Council Record Office, 1093/551 [French].

71. Acton to Marie, 26 November 1859, Shropshire County Council Record Office, 1093/552 [French].

72. Acton to Marie, 18 November 1859, Shropshire County Council Record Office, 1093/551 [French].

73. Lord Granville to Queen Victoria, 20 November 1859, Royal Archives, Windsor Castle, Berkshire, B18/46.

74. Acton to Countess Arco, 22 February [1860], CUL Add. 8121/7/708 [French].

75. Acton to Countess Arco, [14 March 1860], CUL Add. 8121/7/711/1–2.

76. Countess Arco to Acton, telegram, 20 March 1860, CUL Add. 8121/7/54.

77. Acton, "My Mother's Wishes," CUL Add. 4862/1.

78. Lord Granville to Lord Canning, 23 March 1860, quoted in Fitzmaurice, *Life of the Second Earl Granville,* 1:370–71.

79. Jean Lemoine, in *Le journal des débats* (March 1860).

80. Lord Granville to Acton, 25 September 1860, CUL Add. 8121/6/99.

81. Lord Granville to Marie, 22 May 1860, CUL Add. 8121/6/564; see also Lord Granville to Marie, 19 August 1861, CUL Add. 8121/6/570.

82. Acton to Simpson, 7 October 1859, *Acton-Simpson Correspondence,* 2:11.

83. Acton to Döllinger, 2 December 1863, *Briefwechsel*, 1:327 [German].

84. James J. Auchmuty, "Acton: The Youthful Parliamentarian," *Historical Studies of Australia and New Zealand* 9, no. 34 (May 1960): 135.

85. Bishop James Brown of Shrewsbury to Acton, 24 February 1860, CUL Add. 8119/I/G133.

86. Acton to Döllinger, 6 December 1861, *Briefwechsel*, 1:229 [German].

87. Acton to Döllinger, 14 March [1855], *Briefwechsel*, 1:56–57 [German].

88. Acton to Döllinger, 6 December 1861, *Briefwechsel*, 1:229 [German].

89. Acton, "Döllinger's Historical Work," in *Selected Writings*, 2:429.

90. Acton to Döllinger, 23 June 1865, *Briefwechsel*, 1:411 [German].

91. Acton, note, CUL Add. 5528/191–92.

92. Acton, review of *English History*, by Leopold von Ranke, *Home and Foreign Review* (April 1864): 715, reprinted in Acton, *Essays on Church and State*, ed. Douglas Woodruff (London, 1952), 425–26.

93. Acton to Marie, 10 July 1877, *Briefwechsel*, 3:179–180; Acton, "A Study of History," Inaugural Lecture at Cambridge, reprinted in *Selected Writings*, 2:533. See also Leopold von Ranke, *Das Briefwerk*, ed. W. P. Fuchs (Hamburg, 1949), 421, with a reference to the meeting with Acton and Macaulay in London.

94. See the vivid account of Garibaldi's visit in its political and popular aspects in Derek Beales, "Garibaldi in England: The Politics of Enthusiasm," in *Society and Politics in the Age of Risorgimento: Essays in Honour of Denis Mack Smith*, ed. John A. Davis and Paul Ginsborg (Cambridge, England, 1991), 184–216.

95. *The Scotsman*, 19 April 1864.

96. Lord Granville to Queen Victoria, 21 April 1864, *The Letters of Queen Victoria . . . between the Years 1862 and 1878*, ed. G. E. Buckle (London, 1926), 1:175–76.

97. Acton to Döllinger, 3 June 1864, *Briefwechsel*, 1:361.

98. Pauline Craven to Acton, dated "Paris, Monday 25th," CUL Add. 8119/I/C240.

Chapter 9: Editor in Chains

1. W. F. Poole, quoted in *Wellesley Index to Victorian Periodicals, 1824–1900*, ed. Walter E. Houghton (Toronto, 1966–89), 1:xv.

2. John Morley, "Anonymous Journalism," *Fortnightly Review*, n.s., 2 (September 1867): 293.

3. Gertrude Himmelfarb, *Essays on Politics and Culture: John Stuart Mill* (New York, 1962), quoted by Walter E. Houghton in "Periodical Literature and the Articulate Classes," in *The Victorian Periodical Press: Samplings and Soundings*, ed. Joanne Shattock and Michael Wolff (Leicester, 1982), 9. Houghton adds: "In this light, to talk of instruction or guidance is to belittle the periodical achievement. It conferred, in addition, 'that large-mindedness and general breadth of view which are

so constantly found missing in deeply-read theologians, in erudite philologists, and profound philosophers'" *Literary Gazette,* 5 May 1860, 555.

4. Matthew Arnold, *Essays in Criticism,* 1st ser. (London, 1902), 37.

5. Ibid., 19–20.

6. Quoted in Francis Williams, *Dangerous Estate: The Anatomy of Newspapers* (London, 1957), 111.

7. Ibid., 108–9.

8. Elie Halévy, *Histoire du peuple anglais au XIX siècle* (Paris, 1947), 4:357. It is interesting to note Halévy's use of the more modern term "inner emigration" as applying to those Germans opposed to the Nazi regime who failed to express their opposition by emigrating abroad but regarded themselves justified by describing their stance as one of inner emigration, that is, rightly or wrongly, they felt themselves practically excluded from their country because of their general Weltanschauung, the public and professional expression of which was banned.

9. On the Catholic press in England, see the following: Josef L. Altholz, *The Liberal Catholic Movement in England: The Rambler and Its Contributors, 1848–1864* (London, 1962) and *The Religious Press in Britain, 1760–1900* (New York, 1989); J. J. Dwyer, "The Catholic Press, 1850–1950," in *The English Catholics, 1850–1950,* ed. George Andrew Beck (London, 1950), 475–514; Philip Hughes, "The Coming Century," in *English Catholics,* ed. Beck, 1–41; Michael Walsh, *The Tablet, 1840–1990: A Commemorative History* (London, 1990); John R. Fletcher, "Early Catholic Periodicals in England," *Dublin Review* 198, nos. 396–97 (January–June 1936): 284–310; Denis Gwynn, "The Dublin Review and the Catholic Press," ibid, 311–21; Adrian Hastings, *Bishops and Writers* (London, 1977); J. Derek Holmes, *More Roman than Rome* (London, 1978); Douglas Woodruff, "Catholic Press, World Survey 9, England," in *New Catholic Encyclopedia* (New York, 1967), 3:294–96. Mary Griset Holland offers many insightful observations on the comings and goings of English Catholic journalism in her published doctoral dissertation, *The British Catholic Press and the Educational Controversy, 1847–1865* (New York, 1987).

10. Alfred, Lord Tennyson, "To W. G. Ward In Memoriam," in *Tennyson and His Friends,* ed. Hallam, Lord Tennyson (London, 1911), 171.

11. John Henry Newman, *The Letter to the Duke of Norfolk,* chap. 9 in *Certain Difficulties Felt by Anglicans in Catholic Teaching* (London, 1850; 2d ed., 1876), 2:321. The "tyrannous ipsedixits" are meant to refer to Ward, Herbert Vaughan, and other members of the *Dublin Review–Tablet* mafia who had become vociferously aggressive in their Ultramontanism. The same reference to the "aggressive and insolent faction" occurred in Newman's letter to Bishop Ullathorne, 28 January 1870, *Letters and Diaries of John Henry Newman,* ed. Charles Stephen Dessain et al. (Oxford, 1961–84), 25:19, which was leaked to the *Standard* of 6 April 1870.

12. See Walsh, *The Tablet.*

13. Ibid., 13.

14. Acton to Döllinger, 29 January 1857, *Briefwechsel*, 1:119 [German].

15. See the excellent pioneering study by Josef L. Altholz, *The Liberal Catholic Movement in England* (London, 1962).

16. Acton to Döllinger, 20 March [1858], *Briefwechsel*, 1:135 [German]. For an appreciation of Simpson, see Damian McElrath, *Richard Simpson, 1820–1876* (Louvain, Belgium, 1972).

17. Simpson to his wife, Elizabeth Mary, 22 September 1862, Richard Simpson Papers, Mitcham Public Library, quoted in *The Correspondence of Lord Acton and Richard Simpson,* ed. Josef L. Altholz, Damien McElrath, and James C. Holland (Cambridge, England, 1971–75), 1:xvii.

18. See Hugh A. MacDougall, *The Acton-Newman Relations: The Dilemma of Christian Liberalism* (New York, 1962).

19. J. H. Newman, *The Idea of a University* (1873), ed. I. T. Ker (Oxford, 1976), 94, 198.

20. Acton to Simpson, 22 January 1859, *Acton-Simpson Correspondence*, 1:141.

21. Acton to Döllinger, 29 January 1857, *Briefwechsel*, 1:121 [German].

22. Edward Serjeant Bellasis, *Memorials of Mr. Serjeant Bellasis (1800–1873)* (London, 1893), 162–64; Beck, *The English Catholics,* passim.

23. Sir Peter le Page Renouf (1822–1897), of an old Guernsey family, was an Egyptologist, Oriental scholar, theologian, and a man of polemical temperament. He went up to Pembroke College, Oxford, in 1842, where he was much influenced by Newman. He was received into the Catholic Church at Easter 1842 at Oscott, where Wiseman employed him as a professor, and he also studied for ordination. But having decided not to be a priest, he became tutor to the son of the Marquis de Vaulchier, travelling with the family and continuing his studies. Newman invited Renouf to Dublin in 1854, to be professor of ancient history and geography. In 1855–56 Renouf went to Germany, where he met Acton and Döllinger, with whom he sympathized, in Munich. In 1857 Renouf married Ludovika von Brentano la Roche, a daughter of the Catholic writer Christian von Brentano and niece of Clemens von Brentano, the leading poet of the Heidelberg Romantics; another uncle was Friedrich Karl von Savigny, the jurist. They had one son and one daughter. Because of their close friendship with Döllinger, Renouf's wife tried to bring Döllinger back into communion with Rome under Leo XIII. In 1866 Renouf became inspector of Catholic schools in England and held this position for twenty years. Acton had helped him with this appointment and also, in 1885, to obtain a position much more suited to a scholar of his calibre as keeper of the Egyptian and Assyrian antiquities in the British Museum. Because of internal intrigues at the museum, Renouf was forced to retire at the age of seventy, in 1891. He was engaged in the controversies on Papal Infallibility (on Döllinger's side) but did not break with the Church. He wrote a pamphlet in 1868 accusing Pope Honorius of being a

Monothelitic heretic; the pamphlet was put on the Index. In 1896, in an act of belated rehabilitation, Renouf was knighted for his services to the British Museum.
There is an anonymous biography, possibly written by Sir Rowland Blennerhassett, in Renouf, *The Egyptian Book of the Dead,* trans. and commentary by Peter le
Page Renouf, continued and completed by Edouard Naville (London, 1902–7),
4:iii–cxxxiii; see also *Dictionary of National Biography Supplement,* vol. 22 (Oxford,
1917), 3:294–95.

24. Acton to Peter le Page Renouf, April 1863, quoted in Renouf, *Egyptian Book of the
Dead,* 4:lxiii.

25. Newman to Edward Bellasis, 6 April 1858, *Letters and Diaries,* 18:314–15.

26. Newman, journal, 8 January 1860 and 21 January 1863, *John Henry Newman: Autobiographical Writings,* ed. Henry Tristram (London, 1956), 251–57.

27. Acton to Döllinger, 29 January 1857, *Briefwechsel,* 1:124 [German].

28. Acton to Döllinger, 17 February 1858, *Briefwechsel,* 1:128 [English, German].

29. Ibid.

30. Ibid., 129.

31. Quoted in Simpson to Acton, 16 February 1858, *Acton-Simpson Correspondence,* 1:3.

32. Acton to Simpson, 16 February 1858, *Acton-Simpson Correspondence,* 1:5.

33. W. G. Ward, quoted in Wilfrid Ward, *William George Ward and the Catholic Revival*
(London, 1893), 140.

34. Acton to Döllinger, 20 March [1858], *Briefwechsel,* 1:136 [German].

35. Acton to Döllinger, 25 July 1858, *Briefwechsel,* 1:153.

36. Newman to Acton, 27 July 1858, *Letters and Diaries,* 18:427–28.

37. Acton to Döllinger, 25 November 1858, *Briefwechsel,* 1:157.

38. Newman to William Kirby Sullivan, 30 November 1858, *Letters and Diaries,* 18:521.

39. Acton to Döllinger, 20 March [1858], *Briefwechsel,* 1:134–35. Acton refers to Edward Lowth Badeley (died 1868), the Oxford barrister who had converted to
Catholicism in 1851 with Manning; and to James Hope-Scott (1812–73), a leading figure of the Oxford converts from the family of the Earls of Hopetown, who
knew Gladstone and Döllinger and advised Acton on property matters after his
return to Aldenham.

40. Ibid.

41. Acton to Simpson, 16 February 1858, *Acton-Simpson Correspondence,* 1:7.

42. Lord Granville to W. E. Gladstone, 10 November 1874, *The Political Correspondence
of Mr. Gladstone and Lord Granville, 1868–1876,* ed. Agatha Ramm (London, 1952),
1:458.

43. Acton to Simpson, 22 January 1859, *Acton-Simpson Correspondence,* 1:142. "Eppur
si muove" (But it does move) was Galileo's reputed protest when he was forced
to recant. Newman's essay that, according to Acton's standards, qualified as "a bit
of theology" was "On the Formula μία φύσις τοῦ θεοῦ λογοῦ σεσαρκωμένη," *Atlan-*

tis 1 (July 1858): 330–61, reprinted in *Tracts Theological and Ecclesiastical* (London, 1874).

44. Acton, "The Catholic Press," *Rambler*, n.s., 11 (February 1859): 73–90, reprinted in *Selected Writings of Lord Acton,* ed. J. Rufus Fears (Indianapolis, 1984–88), 3:37–54, also in *Essays on Church and State,* ed. Douglas Woodruff (London, 1952), 260–78. The final quotation is from *Selected Writings,* 3:53–54.

45. The article on Jacques Bénigne Bossuet in the *Rambler* (n.s., 9 [June 1858]: 388) was wrongly attributed to Acton, and extracts from it are included in *Essays on Church and State,* 230–45. See Altholz, *Liberal Catholic Movement in England,* 77; Simpson to Acton, 25 August 1858, *Acton-Simpson Correspondence,* 1:74.

46. Acton, review of *Marie Stuart et Catherine de Medici,* by A. Chéruel, in *Rambler,* n.s., 10 (August 1858): 134–36, reprinted in *Selected Writings,* 2:35.

47. Charles Meynell to Acton, December 1858, CUL Add. 8119/I/M172.

48. Döllinger, letter on the paternity of Jansenism, *Rambler,* n.s., 10 (December 1858): 361–73.

49. Acton to Simpson, 14 December 1858, *Acton-Simpson Correspondence,* 1:105.

50. Acton to Simpson, 15 and 18 November 1858, *Acton-Simpson Correspondence,* 1:85, 91; see also Simpson to Acton, 23 December 1858 and 20 February 1859, *Acton-Simpson Correspondence,* 1:111, 154.

51. This was the term used by Acton and Simpson with both affection and irritation for the decidedly awkward Newman and his Oxford ways. I am indebted to the invaluable archivist of the Birmingham Oratory for discovering the allusion: It was derived from Newman Noggs, the clerk of that name to Ralph Nickleby in *Nicholas Nickleby* by Charles Dickens, first published in 1837.

52. Acton to Simpson, 1 January 1859, *Acton-Simpson Correspondence,* 1:116.

53. Newman to Acton, 31 December 1858, *Letters and Diaries,* 18:559–62.

54. Acton to Simpson, 21 April 1859, *Acton-Simpson Correspondence,* 1:175.

55. John Henry Newman, "On Consulting the Faithful in Matters of Doctrine," *Rambler,* 3d ser., 1 (July 1859): 198–230, also published as *On Consulting the Faithful in Matters of Doctrine,* ed. John Coulson (London, 1961).

56. Ibid., Coulson ed., 54–55.

57. Ibid., 63.

58. Ibid., 75–76, 106.

59. Archivio Storico, Propaganda Fide Archives, Scritti Referiti 1858–60, Anglia 15/1802, 30 October 1859. Bishop Thomas Joseph Brown (1798–1880), an old Catholic and Benedictine from Downside, is not to be confused with Acton's diocesan bishop of Shrewsbury, James Brown (1812–1881).

60. Newman, "On Consulting," Coulson ed., 72.

61. For the retraction, see Acton, note, CUL Add. 4990/75, also in Newman to Acton, 31 July 1859, *Letters and Diaries,* 19:185–86.

62. Newman to Acton, 20 June 1860, *Letters and Diaries,* 19:372.

63. [John Henry Newman], "The Mission of the Isles of the North," *Rambler,* 3d ser., 1 (May, July 1859): 1–22, 170–85, reprinted as "The Northmen and Normans in England and Ireland," in John Henry Newman, *Historical Sketches* (London, 1872), 255–312.

64. Newman to Emily Bowles, 19 May 1863, *Letters and Diaries,* 20:445–48. Acton had copied this letter and kept it among his collection of Newmania, regarding it as providing an important insight into Newman's character.

65. Döllinger's Odeon Lectures on the Temporal Power were published as Ignaz von Döllinger, *Kirche und Kirchen, Papstthum und Kirchenstaat: Historisch-politische Betrachtungen* (Munich, 1861). An English translation came out the following year: *The Church and the Churches; or, The Papacy and the Temporal Power,* trans. W. B. MacCabe (London, 1862). The *Saturday Review* commented on "the remarkable reaction within the pale of the Church against identifying temporal and spiritual authority, and exposing the Papacy in its ecclesiastical character to be dragged down in the wake of the sinking fortunes of the States of the Church." Dr. Döllinger's lecture "startled his audience by the crushing indictment of the Pontifical Government. Its worst enemy never would have composed a more overwhelming indictment, or a more hopeless horoscope for its future than has been done by this reverend gentleman, a sincere and enthusiastic servant of the Church." The journal coupled Döllinger's with the recent similar criticism by the Italian priest-philosopher and founder of the Institute of Charity, Antonio Rosmini-Serbati. "The Ecclesiastical Reaction against the Pope's Temporal Power," *Saturday Review,* no. 288 (4 May 1861): 443–44. See also "Döllinger on the Temporal Power," *Edinburgh Review* 116 (1862): 261–93; "Döllinger and the Temporal Power of the Popes," *Dublin Review* (1861): 195–234.

66. Acton to Countess Arco, fragment of letter, n.d. [1859 or 1860?], CUL Add. 8121/7/840.

67. Acton, note, CUL Add. 5666/25.

68. Acton, note, CUL Add. 4987/17.

69. Acton, note, CUL Add. 4988/300; John Henry Newman, *Apologia pro Vita Sua,* new ed. (London, 1902), 204.

70. Acton, note, CUL Add. 4990/279–80, 284–85.

71. Acton to Simpson, 14 June 1862, *Acton-Simpson Correspondence,* 2:326.

72. Acton, note, CUL Add. 4990/62.

73. Quoted in A. W. Hutton, "Personal Reminiscence of Cardinal Newman," *Expositor,* 4th ser., 2 (1890): 228.

74. Acton, note, CUL Add. 4987, quoted in ibid. Arthur William Hutton, the author of this article, was an Anglican clergyman received by Newman into the Church and, soon afterwards, in 1876, into the Congregation of the Oratorian Fathers,

which he left in 1883 under a cloud. Apparently he lost his faith, married one of the Oratory Parish teachers, and returned to the ranks of the Anglican clergy. His reminiscences, spiteful and bitter and compounded by his own experiences, seem to have been shaped by the adulation sweeping the English press when Newman died in 1890. See Meriol Trevor, *Newman*, vol. 2, *Light in Winter* (London, 1962), 2:594–99.

75. Acton to Döllinger, 28 February [1868], *Briefwechsel*, 1:502 [German].

76. Acton, note, CUL Add. 4915/71.

77. Acton, note, CUL Add. 5704/76.

78. Acton to W. E. Gladstone, 14 August 1890, *Selections from the Correspondence of the First Lord Acton*, ed. John Neville Figgis and Reginald Vere Laurence (London, 1917), 59.

79. Acton to W. E. Gladstone, 12 April 1896, *Selections from the Correspondence*, 227.

80. Acton to W. E. Gladstone, 28 January 1895, BL Add. 44094.

81. Acton, note, CUL Add. 4914/280.

82. Newman to Acton, 7 June 1861, *Letters and Diaries*, 19:506.

83. Acton to Döllinger, 16 June 1882, *Briefwechsel*, 3:284–85.

84. "Current Events," *Rambler*, 3d ser., 5 (May 1861): 138.

85. Newman to Acton, 7 June 1861, *Letters and Diaries*, 19:509.

86. Döllinger, *Kirche und Kirchen, Papstthum und Kirchenstaat*; Acton, "Döllinger on the Temporal Power," *Rambler*, 3d ser., 4 (November 1861): 1–62, reprinted in Acton, *The History of Freedom and Other Essays*, ed. John Neville Figgis and Reginald Vere Laurence (London, 1907), 301–74, and in *Selected Writings*, 3:67–127.

87. F. W. Faber, *Devotion to the Church* (London, 1861), 27–28. Extracts were published in the *Weekly Review*, 1 June 1861, and the *Tablet*, 1 June 1861.

88. Acton to Döllinger, 4 July 1861, *Briefwechsel*, 1:215 [German].

89. Acton to Newman, 19 June 1861, *Letters and Diaries*, 19:517.

90. Newman to Acton, 30 June 1861, *Letters and Diaries*, 19:523.

91. Simpson to Acton, 7 October 1861, *Acton-Simpson Correspondence*, 2:181; "To Readers and Correspondents," *Rambler*, n.s., 6 (November 1861): 147–48: "The Conductors of the Rambler having found it necessary to change the publishers, contemplate no further alterations in the existing arrangements. It will be their aim, as it has ever been, to combine devotion to the Church with discrimination and candour in the treatment of her opponents, to reconcile freedom of thought with implicit faith, to discountenance what is untenable and unreal, without forgetting the tenderness due to the weak and the reverence rightly claimed for what is sacred; and to encourage a manly investigation of subjects of public interests under a deep sense of the prerogatives of ecclesiastical authority."

92. Acton to Simpson, 10 October 1861, *Acton-Simpson Correspondence*, 2:186.

93. Simpson to Acton, 30 June 1858, *Acton-Simpson Correspondence*, 1:40; Acton to Döllinger, 17 February 1858, *Briefwechsel*, 1:130 [German].

94. Simpson to Acton, 17 May 1861, *Acton-Simpson Correspondence,* 2:147.

95. Acton, "The Catholic Academy," *Rambler,* 3d ser., 5 (September 1861): 261–302, reprinted in *Essays on Church and State,* 279–90.

96. Cardinal Nicholas Wiseman, Pastoral Letter, 17 December 1861, printed in *Weekly Register,* 21 December 1861, 2.

97. Archivio Storico, Propaganda Fide Archives, Scritti Referiti, 1861–62, Anglia, 16/208–12, 8 July 1861.

98. Bishop William Bernard Ullathorne to Cardinal Alessandro Barnabò, 8 July 1861, Archivio Storico, Propaganda Fide Archives, Scritti Referiti, 1861–62, Anglia 16/208–12, 8 July 1861.

99. Richard Simpson, *Edmund Campion: A Biography* (London, 1867), 63–64. Simpson's biography of Edmund Campion was serialized in the *Rambler* (January, March, May, July, and September 1861; January, March, and May 1862) but was discontinued when the *Rambler* ceased. It did not appear in book form until 1867, when Williams and Norgate published it. It remains the authoritative life based on original sources, along with Evelyn Waugh, *Edmund Campion* (London, 1935).

100. Acton, "Nationality," *Home and Foreign Review* 1 (July 1862): 1–25, reprinted in *History of Freedom,* 270–300, in *Essays on Freedom and Power,* ed. Gertrude Himmelfarb (Boston, 1948), 166–95, and in *Selected Writings,* 2:409–33; Acton, "The Secret History of Charles II," *Home and Foreign Review* 1 (July 1862): 146–74, reprinted in *Selected Writings,* 2:132–62, in *Historical Essays and Studies,* ed. John Neville Figgis and Reginald Vere Laurence (London, 1907), 85–122, and in *Essays in the Liberal Interpretation of History,* ed. William H. McNeill (Chicago, 1967), 95–130.

101. Acton to Peter le Page Renouf, 26 March 1862, CUL Add. 8119/8/515. The original Acton-Renouf correspondence is kept at Pembroke College, Oxford, but a transcript exists in Cambridge and is cited here.

102. Acton to Döllinger, 1 November [1862], *Briefwechsel,* 1:283 [German].

103. Acton to W. E. Gladstone, 30 June [1862], BL Add. 44093/8.

104. Acton to Peter le Page Renouf, n.d. [October 1863], CUL Add. 8119/8/515.

105. *National Review* (London) 16 (January–April 1863); *Home and Foreign Review* 1–2 (1863): 264–66. Reviewing the second number of the *Home and Foreign Review,* the *Universal News,* a London Irish Catholic weekly newspaper, paid tribute to the new journal's "talent and consistency," recalling that its predecessor, the *Rambler,* had "offended Catholic opinion on a variety of delicate points." In the matter of Cardinal Wiseman's "remarkable language" used in his grave rebuke to the journal on his return from Rome in his "Reply to the Address of the Clergy," the *Home and Foreign Review* was showing "a spirit of dignified submissiveness." But turning away "with pleasure" from the controversy between the Cardinal and the *Review* on the matter of the Church's acceptance or not of scientific truths in apparent opposition to her own dogmas, it welcomed the "sensible" and "non-English" view expressed in the review of the Abbé Adolphe Perraud's work on Ireland, especially the *Re-*

view's "audacity" in stating, in complete antagonism to the expressed opinion of the Irish Church: "Education—thanks to the National system, one of the greatest blessings ever bestowed upon a country—has become almost universal." And after discussing various other articles in eulogistic terms, the writer concluded that the *Home and Foreign Review*, "as a literary organ, stands without exaggeration at the head of the contemporaries." *Universal News* (London), 25 October 1862.

106. Richard Simpson, *Bishop Ullathorne and the Rambler: A Reply to Criticisms Contained in a Letter on the Rambler and Home and Foreign Review by Bishop Ullathorne*, appeared in pamphlet form (London, 1862). A second edition of the forty-page pamphlet, published in the same year, contains a postscript.

107. Acton to Döllinger, 7 January 1863, *Briefwechsel*, 1:288 [German].

108. Ibid., 1:289, 290 [German].

109. Nicholas Wiseman, *Rome and the Catholic Episcopate: Reply of His Eminence Cardinal Wiseman to an Address Presented by the Clergy, Secular and Regular, of the Archdiocese of Westminster* (London, 1862), 27.

110. [Acton, assisted by Richard Simpson and Thomas Frederick Wetherell], "Cardinal Wiseman and the Home and Foreign Review," *Home and Foreign Review* 1 (October 1862): 501–20, reprinted in *History of Freedom*, 436–60, and in *Selected Writings*, 3:128–48, esp. 139, 147–48.

111. Acton to Döllinger, 10 October 1862, *Briefwechsel*, 1:279 [German].

112. Ibid., 1:278–79 [German].

113. Ibid., 1:280 [German].

114. Simpson to Acton, 3 September 1862, *Acton-Simpson Correspondence*, 3:15.

115. Acton, "Ultramontanism," *Home and Foreign Review* 3 (July 1863): 162–206, reprinted in *Essays on Church and State*, 37–86, and in *Selected Writings*, 3:149–94.

116. Jansenism was the name of a complex seventeenth-century theological movement with moral and political implications and divergent national (Belgian, Dutch, and French [Port Royal]) varieties. Originally an attempt to reform post-Tridentine theology, it encountered papal opposition and thereafter became allied with the Gallican and Josephinist opposition to Roman centralism and was chiefly opposed by the Jesuits. Its founder was the Dutch Louvain theologian Cornelius Jansen (Jansenius) (1585–1638). Febronianism was a powerful eighteenth-century movement and constitutional Church system restricting the papal power and aiming at independence of national churches. It was named after the pseudonym Justinus Febronius of the German Auxiliary Bishop and canon lawyer Johann von Hontheim (1701–1790).

117. See Franz Schnabel's excellent and detailed description of the German Catholic religious situation in *Deutsche Geschichte im Neunzehnten Jahrhundert* (Freiburg, Germany, 1951), 4:3–276.

118. John Henry Newman, *Difficulties of Anglicans* (London, 1868), 2:207.

119. David Mathew, *Catholicism in England* (London, 1936), 147–48.

120. Acton, "Ultramontanism," *Home and Foreign Review* (July 1863), reprinted in *Selected Writings*, 3:153.

121. Klaus Schatz, *Vaticanum I, 1860–1870*, vol. 1, *Before the Opening of the Vatican Council* (Paderborn, Germany, 1992), 1–29.

122. Acton, "Ultramontanism," *Selected Writings*, 3:179–80.

123. Ibid., 3:180, 191–94.

124. Acton to Döllinger, 14 August 1863, *Briefwechsel*, 1:318–19 [German].

125. Acton to Döllinger, 23 February 1864, *Briefwechsel*, 1:331–32 [German]. The letter continues about Gladstone: "He likes talking to me about the most secret state matters, and will do that certainly even more when the government is beaten."

126. Acton to Döllinger, 13 November 1863, *Briefwechsel*, 1:326 [German].

127. Acton, "The Munich Congress," *Home and Foreign Review* 4 (January 1864): 209–44, reprinted in *Essays on Church and State*, 159–99, and in *Selected Writings*, 3:195–233.

128. Ibid., *Selected Writings*, 3:223.

129. *Tuas libenter*, 21 December 1863, in Heinrich Joseph Denzinger and Clement Bathworth, S.J., eds., *Enchiridion Symbolorum Definitionum et Declarationum*, 6th ed. (Freiburg, Germany, 1928), 454–57.

130. Acton to Döllinger, 9 March 1864, *Briefwechsel*, 1:335–36 [German].

131. Newman to Acton, 18 March 1864, *Letters and Diaries*, 21:83–84.

132. Charles Kingsley, *What, Then, Does Dr. Newman Mean?* published 20 March 1864 and reprinted in Appendix B (356–84) of Cardinal John Henry Newman, *Apologia pro Vita Sua: Being a History of His Religious Opinions*, ed. Martin J. Svaglic (Oxford, 1967). Charles Kingsley (1819–1875), clergyman and novelist, Vicar at Cambridge (1860), represented an aggressive blend of English Victorian jingoism, liberal Protestantism, and anti-Popery. In the January 1864 issue of *Macmillan's Magazine* he had written, "Truth, for its own sake, had never been a virtue with the Roman clergy. Father Newman informs us that it need not, and, on the whole ought not to be; that cunning is the weapon which Heaven has given to the saints wherewith to withstand the brute male force of the wicked world which marries and is given in marriage." Kingsley's attack, in response to Newman's pamphlet *Mr. Kingsley and Dr. Newman: A Correspondence on the Question Whether Dr. Newman Teaches That Truth Is No Virtue* (London, 1864), was more against the casuistry of Catholic morality, in particular St. Alphonsus of Liguori, than against Newman himself. Frederick Meyrick (1827–1906), "But Isn't Kingsley Right After All? A Letter to Dr. Newman, dated 18 March 1864," excused Newman of untruthfulness but maintained that he was committed to it owing to the teaching of St. Alphonsus. Meyrick was an Anglican theologian, fellow of Trinity College, Oxford, and secretary of the Anglican Society for the Support of the Anglican Idea on the European Con-

tinent. He was also friends with Dr. Döllinger, whose Bonn reunion conferences he attended in 1874–75.

133. Acton to Newman, 10 April 1864, *Letters and Diaries*, 21:94.

134. Newman to Acton, 15 April 1864, *Letters and Diaries*, 21:94.

135. Newman, *Apologia pro Vita Sua* (1902), 270–71.

136. Ibid., 244, 248.

137. Acton to Simpson, 8 March 1864, *Acton-Simpson Correspondence*, 3:185.

138. Acton to Döllinger, [27 March] 1864, *Briefwechsel*, 1:339 [German].

139. Acton to Döllinger, 18 April [1864], *Briefwechsel*, 1:347–48 [German].

140. Acton, "Conflicts with Rome," *Home and Foreign Review* 4 (April 1864): 667–96, reprinted in *History of Freedom*, 461–91, and in *Selected Writings*, 3:234–59.

141. Ibid., *Selected Writings*, 256, 257.

142. Ibid., 258, 259. See also James Whisenant, "Lord Acton's Responses to the Hierarchy in the Controversies of 1858–1864," *Downside Review* 1071 (1989): 34–48. The author suggests in justification of Acton's submission that whereas in his previous controversies Acton was able to argue validly that the bishops were interfering in disputed matters of historical or political controversy, the Pope had now decided to draw his own demarcation line, which left Acton no ground outside theology to make his stand. His liberal philosophy was judged to be incompatible with the Church. This was emphasized eight months later in 1864, in the *Syllabus Errorum* of Pius IX, in which the last of the condemned errors of the age was said to be the suggestion that "the Roman Pontiff can and should reconcile himself to progress, liberalism and the modern civilization." Denzinger and Bannwarth, *Enchiridion Symbolorum Definitionum et Declarationum*, 465–73.

143. Cardinal Nicholas Wiseman, *Words of Peace and Justice Addressed to the Catholic Clergy and Laity of the London District on the Subject of Diplomatic Relations with the Holy See* (London, 1848), 15–16. I am indebted to Father Philip Jebb, OSB, of Downside Abbey for tracing this passage quoted in Francis Aiden Gasquet, ed., *Lord Acton and His Circle* (London, 1906), xxvii.

144. Matthew Arnold, *Essays in Criticism,* 1st ser., ed. Sister Marion Hoctor (Chicago, 1964), 19.

145. Acton to Döllinger, 6 May 1864, *Briefwechsel*, 1:352 [German].

146. Guy A. Ryan, OFM, "The Acton Circle, 1864–1871: The Chronicle and the North British Review" (Ph.D. diss., University of Notre Dame, South Bend, Ind., 1969). This dissertation exhaustively covers the last phase of Acton's periodical journalism. A summary is published in the *Victorian Periodicals Newsletter* 7, no. 2 (June 1974): 10–24.

147. Acton to W. E. Gladstone, 1 January 1867, BL Add. 44093/55.

148. Acton to Thomas Frederick Wetherell, 27 March 1867, CUL Add. 8119/8/3.

149. Acton to W. E. Gladstone, 11 February 1868, BL Add. 44093.

150. Ryan, "Acton Circle," 236–37.

151. Acton, "The Massacre of St. Bartholemew," *North British Review* 51 (October 1869): 30–70, reprinted in *Selected Writings*, 2:198–240; Acton, "The Pope and the Council," *North British Review* 51 (October 1869): 127–35, reprinted in *Selected Writings*, 3:280–89; Acton, "The Vatican Council," *North British Review* 53 (October 1870): 183–229, reprinted in *Selected Writings*, 3:290–338; Acton, "The Borgias and Their Latest Historian," *North British Review* 53 (January 1871): 351–67, reprinted in *Selected Writings*, 2:241–58.

152. Paulus Lauxtermann, *Constantin Frantz: Romantik und Realismus im Werke eines politischen Aussenseiters* (Groningen, Germany, 1978); Manfred Ehmer, *Constantin Frantz: Die politische Gedankenwelt eines Klassikers des Föderalismus* (Rheinfelden, Germany, 1988).

153. Altholz, *Liberal Catholic Movement in England*, 239.

Chapter 10: Marie Consents

1. Acton to Marie, 18 October [1860], Shropshire County Council Record Office, 1093/587 [French].

2. Döllinger to Acton, June 1863, *Briefwechsel*, 1:317 [German]. Only a fragment of this letter has been found.

3. Acton to Döllinger, 28 January 1864, *Briefwechsel*, 1:329 [German and French]. *Hors de jeu* means "outside the game," that is, free to act.

4. Acton to Marie, 23 November [1861], Shropshire County Council Record Office, 1093/589 [French].

5. Acton to Döllinger, 29 March 1862 and 1 November [1862], *Briefwechsel*, 1:256 [German], 284 [German].

6. Acton to Marie, 25 December 1861, Shropshire County Council Record Office, 1093/563 [French].

7. Marie to Acton, n.d., CUL Add. 8121/8/11–14 [French].

8. Acton to Marie, n.d., Shropshire County Council Record Office, 1093/569 [French].

9. Acton to Marie, 23 January 1863, Shropshire County Council Record Office, 1093/567 [French].

10. Papal dispensation, CUL Add. 8119/2/556. This document is kept among the Acton Family Papers in the Cambridge University Library; it is dated 22 June 1863 and was signed by Bishop James Brown of Shrewsbury and Thomas Green, Acton's chaplain.

11. Acton to Döllinger, 14 October 1864, *Briefwechsel*, 1:368.

12. Döllinger to Anna Gramich, 8 February 1865, *Ignaz Döllingers Briefe an eine junge Freundin*, ed. Heinrich Schrörs (Kempten, Germany, 1914), 198–99.

13. Lady Walpurga Paget, *Embassies of Other Days and Further Recollections* (London, 1923), 1:226–28. The author, born a Hohenthal, wife of the British minister accredited to the Italian government, described Laura Acton in her somewhat catty memoirs: "Her mother was French, and this element was strongly blended in her nature. I met her for the first time at an evening party at the Belgian Legation. She wore a cream-coloured satin dress, with creamy coloured lace about it, out of which her beautiful creamy shoulders did more than peep. Her eyes and hair were jet-black, her face very long and narrow in shape and colouring like that of a Byzantine saint, in expression more French than Italian. I instinctively felt that she took my measure as we met, and that she did not find the result quite satisfactory. . . . Her genius lay in her unrivalled powers of adapting herself to the person she happened to be with. People left her with the impression that they were forever enthroned in her heart, when she had not even taken the trouble to find out their names. She was very calculating and ambitious, and it was a severe blow to her when Minghetti was hurled from his post of Prime Minister, ten days after their marriage."

14. The quotation was a later judgement expressed by Acton to Mary Gladstone Drew, 14 April 1886, *Letters of Lord Acton to Mary, Daughter of the Right Hon. W. E. Gladstone,* ed. Herbert Paul, 2d rev. ed. (London, 1913), 176.

15. Acton to Newman, 26 March 1867, *Letters and Diaries of John Henry Newman,* ed. Charles Stephen Dessain et al. (Oxford, 1961–84), 23:80.

16. Acton to Döllinger, dated "Rome Piazza di Spagna, Sunday," 5 February 1865, *Briefwechsel,* 1:380 [German].

17. Acton to Döllinger, dated "Geneva," 4 December 1864, *Briefwechsel,* 1:380 [German].

18. Acton to Döllinger, 23 November 1864, *Briefwechsel,* 1:372–73 [German].

19. Acton to Marie, dated "Bologna, Saturday night" [1865], CUL Add. 8121/7/820.

20. Acton to Marie, dated "Florence, Friday" [1865], CUL Add. 8121/7/819.

21. Acton to Marie, dated "Munich, Saturday" [1865], CUL Add. 8121/7/825.

22. Acton to Marie, dated "Munich, Sunday" [1865], CUL Add. 8121/7/826.

23. Acton to Marie, dated "London, Friday" [1865], CUL Add. 8121/7/830.

24. Acton to Marie, 20 April 1865, CUL Add. 8121/7/836.

25. Simpson to Acton, 1 March 1865, *The Correspondence of Lord Acton and Richard Simpson,* ed. Josef L. Altholz, Damien McElrath, and James C. Holland (Cambridge, England, 1971–75), 3:203.

26. Acton to Marie, dated "Monday" [1865], CUL Add. 8121/7/865.

27. Acton to Marie, 28 April 1865, CUL Add. 8121/7/843/1.

28. Acton to Marie, dated "Aldenham, Monday" [Easter Monday, 1865], CUL Add. 8121/7/832.

29. Acton to Döllinger, 23 June 1865, *Briefwechsel,* 1:413 [German].

30. Acton to Marie, dated "Friday" [May 1865], CUL Add. 8121/7/855.

31. Acton to Marie, dated "Aldenham, Tuesday" [1865], CUL Add. 8121/7/833.

32. Acton, passport, 24 July 1865, CUL Add. 8119/9/418.

33. Marie to Acton, 3 February 1866, CUL Add. 8121/8/16/4.

34. Acton to Döllinger, 20 August [1866], *Briefwechsel*, 1:443 [German].

35. Marie to Acton, 28 September 1866, CUL Add. 8121/8/16/2.

36. Henry Manning to Acton, dated "12th" [October 1866], CUL Add. 8119/I/M122.

37. Döllinger to Anna Gramich, July 1866, *Döllingers Briefe an eine junge Freundin*, 198–99.

38. Acton to Döllinger, 21 March 1872, *Briefwechsel*, 3:60 [German].

39. Acton to Marie, dated "Vienna, Tuesday" [1873], CUL Add. 8121/7/983.

40. Acton to Marie, dated "Hesleyside, Tuesday," CUL Add. 8121/7/930.

41. Acton to Döllinger, 24 May 1878, *Briefwechsel*, 3:202 [German].

42. Acton to Marie, n.d. [1869?], CUL Add. 8121/7/1084.

43. Döllinger to Acton, 27 September 1882, *Briefwechsel*, 3:314.

44. Mamy Acton, "Notes Taken from Memory, 1866–1936" 11, CUL Add. 8119/9/427.

45. Acton to Richard Acton, 14 January 1890, CUL Add. 8121/10/126.

46. Mamy Acton, "Notes Taken from Memory," 6, CUL Add. 8119/9/427.

47. Ibid., 20.

48. Ibid., 21.

49. Conversation with Lord Acton's granddaughter, the Hon. Mrs. Mia Woodruff, 2 February 1990.

50. Acton to Mary Gladstone, 18 December 1884, *Letters to Mary Gladstone*, 158.

51. Marie to Acton, 3 May [1893 or 1894], CUL Add. 8121/8/34 [French]. The reference to Cambridge visits was evidently made before Acton's appointment to the Regius Chair in 1895; he was made Hon. LL.D., Cambridge, in 1888.

52. Marie to Acton, 17 May [1893], CUL Add 8121/8/35 [French].

53. Marie to Acton, 22 May [1893], CUL Add 8121/8/36 [French].

54. Marie to Acton, 24 June [1893], CUL Add. 8121/8/38/1–2 [French].

55. Acton to Mamy Acton, 6 August 1893, CUL Add. 7956/115.

56. Mamy Acton, "Notes Taken from Memory," 20, CUL Add. 8119/9/427.

57. Marie to Acton, 10 November 1897, CUL Add. 8121/8/112 [French].

Chapter 11: Roman Courtesies

1. Acton to Döllinger, 4 December 1864, *Briefwechsel*, 1:378 [German].

2. The French government's ban was contained in a circular letter of the French minister for religious affairs, Pierre Jules Baroche, of 1 January 1865. Roger Aubert, *Le pontificat de Pie IX (1846–1878)* (Paris, 1952), 256.

3. Acton to Döllinger, 5 February 1865, *Briefwechsel*, 1:390 [German].

4. Ibid., 391.

5. Cardinal Giacomo Antonelli to Acton, January 1865, CUL Add. 8121/1/5.

6. Kurd von Schlözer, 22 January 1865, in his posthumously published *Letzte Römische Briefe, 1882–1894* (Stuttgart, 1924).

7. Acton to Döllinger, 5 February 1865, *Briefwechsel,* 1:394 [German].

8. Ibid. François Xavier de Mérode (1820–1874) was a Belgian bishop and papal minister of war (1860–65) who, because of clashes with Antonelli, had to resign his office. He was an "inopportunist" during the Vatican Council.

9. Acton to Minnie Throckmorton, 28 May [1865], Throckmorton Papers, Warwickshire County Record Office, "Tribune," part 2, bundle 31, no. 28.

10. Acton to Marie, n.d., CUL Add. 8121/7/844.

11. Acton to Döllinger, 5 February 1865, *Briefwechsel,* 1:396–98 [German].

12. Ibid., 397. Mgr. George Talbot (1816–1886), fifth son of the third Baron Talbot of Malahide, was received into the Church by Wiseman in 1842, was appointed a canon of St. Peter's and a papal chamberlain, and played a prominent role in English affairs while in Rome; he was also a friend of Pius IX's. In 1868 he was removed to a mental asylum at Passy, near Paris. *Tablet,* 23 October 1886; Frederick Boase, *Modern English Biography* (Truro, England, 1892–1921), 6:658.

13. Acton to Döllinger, 5 February 1865, *Briefwechsel,* 1:399–401 [German].

14. Acton to Marie, dated "Naples, Sunday," CUL Add. 8121/7/814.

15. Acton to Döllinger, 5 February 1865, *Briefwechsel,* 1:403 [German].

16. Acton to Marie, dated "Naples, Tuesday" [31 January 1865], CUL Add. 8121/7/815.

17. Acton to Döllinger, 5 February 1865, *Briefwechsel,* 1:404 [German].

18. Girolamo Marchese d'Andrea (1812–1868) became Archbishop of Mytilene in 1841 and a Cardinal in 1852. As Prefect of the Index Congregation he encountered the hostility of the Jesuits because of his support for the Italian national cause. Refusing to sign a decree condemning the book *Il Papato* (Florence, 1861) by the Roman theologian Mgr. Francesco Liverani, which aimed at the papal surrender of the temporal power and reconciliation with the Italian government, he resigned and retired to Naples. He had his Cardinal's salary and administrative function stopped; when he submitted to the Church shortly before his death, his title and salary, but not his office, were restored to him.

19. Acton to Döllinger, 5 February 1865, *Briefwechsel,* 1:403 [German].

20. Acton to Marie, 1 February 1865, CUL Add. 8121(7)/816.

21. Alfonso Capecelatro del Castelpagano (1824–1912), from one of the princely Neapolitan families who reorganized the Oratorian house at Naples, was a writer who became Cardinal in 1865 and was much criticized by the Ultramontanists in the Curia because of his links with the Italian royal family and the liberals.

22. Acton to Döllinger, 5 February 1865, *Briefwechsel,* 1:401–402 [German].

23. Acton's lecture to the Eranus Society at Trinity College, Cambridge, May 1897, on

his archival researches is published as "Notes on Archival Researches, 1864–1868," in *Lord Acton: The Decisive Decade, 1864–1874: Essays and Documents,* ed. Damian McElrath, James Holland, Ward White, and Sue Katzman (Louvain, Belgium, 1970), with introduction remarks by James Clarence Holland, 121–40, quotations on 133–34. Acton also described Theiner as "the most singular figure I encountered in my long pilgrimage."

24. The story of Augustin Theiner as a double agent has not been confirmed by other sources. A vivid account of Theiner is given in Owen Chadwick, *Catholicism and History: The Opening of the Vatican Archives* (Cambridge, England, 1978), 32–45.

25. Acton, Eranus Society Lecture, *Decisive Decade,* 134.

26. Chadwick, *Catholicism and History,* 50.

27. Acton, review of *Documents inédits relatifs aux Affaires réligieuses de la France (1790 à 1800),* by Augustin Theiner, *Rambler* 10 (October 1858): 265–67.

28. Acton, Eranus Society lecture, *Decisive Decade,* 135.

29. Acton to Döllinger, 5 February 1865, *Briefwechsel,* 1:407 [German].

30. Acton to Döllinger, 25 April 1863, *Briefwechsel,* 1:304 [German].

31. Augustin Theiner to Acton, 31 October 1865, CUL Add. 8120/1/646 [German].

32. Acton to Simpson, 6 December 1866, *The Correspondence of Lord Acton and Richard Simpson,* ed. Josef L. Altholz, Damien McElrath, and James C. Holland (Cambridge, 1971–75), 3:226.

33. Döllinger to Anna Gramich, 7 April 1865, *Ignaz Döllingers Briefe an eine junge Freundin,* ed. Heinrich Schrörs (Kempten, Germany, 1914), 204.

34. Acton to Döllinger, November 1865, *Briefwechsel,* 1:421 [German].

35. Acton, "Fra Paolo Sarpi," *Chronicle,* 30 March 1867, 14–17, reprinted in *Essays on Church and State,* ed. Douglas Woodruff (London, 1952), 251–59, passage referred to on 258–59.

36. Newman to Thomas Wetherell, 2, 4, and 9 April 1867, *Letters and Diaries of John Henry Newman,* ed. Charles Stephen Dessain et al. (Oxford, 1961–84), 23:122–23, 125–26, 136.

37. Acton to Thomas Wetherell, dated "Friday" [March/April 1869], CUL Add. 8119/8/341.

38. Acton to Thomas Wetherell, [13 May 1867], CUL Add. 8119/8/346.

39. Guy A. Ryan, OFM, "The Acton Circle, 1864–1871: The Chronicle and the North British Review" (Ph.D. diss., University of Notre Dame, South Bend, Ind., 1969), 242–45; Herbert Butterfield, *Man on His Past* (Cambridge, England, 1955), 171–201.

40. Herbert Butterfield, "Lord Acton," *Cambridge Journal* 6 (May 1953): 480.

41. Acton to Döllinger, 17 December 1865, *Briefwechsel,* 1:428 [German].

42. Acton, Eranus Society Lecture, *Decisive Decade,* 139–40.

43. Butterfield, *Man on His Past,* 81.

44. Acton to Lord Romilly, 2 October 1866, published in *Decisive Decade*, 68–70.

45. The quotation is from Simpson to Acton, 11 November 1866, *Acton-Simpson Correspondence*, 3:221.

46. Acton, Eranus Society lecture, *Decisive Decade*, 135.

47. Mary Gladstone Drew, diary, 28 October and 2 November 1866, *Mary Gladstone (Mrs. Drew): Her Diaries and Letters*, ed. Lucy Masterman (London, 1930), 33–34.

48. W. E. Gladstone to Acton, 11 September 1866, quoted in John Morley, *The Life of William Ewart Gladstone* (London, 1903), 2:214.

49. Acton to Marie, 21 November 1866, CUL Add. 8121 /71174 [French]. Acton explained that the Holy Office that sent them there, however, "does not inform the authorities sometimes of the nature of the crimes these priests have committed. Some are there for life. Otherwise remissions of punishment for good conduct are possible after a certain time." He added that the Holy Office's action was actually intended to prevent any shameful effect on the priesthood from having priests treated as common criminals for crimes against canon law.

50. *Baiocco* refers to a former papal coin, worth 1/2d., hence the Italian phrase "Non volare un baiocco" (It isn't worth a ha'penny).

51. Acton to Cardinal Giacomo Antonelli, 23 November 1866, Archivio Segreto Vaticano, Rome, Segretario di Stato, 1866, Rubrica 204.

52. Ibid.

53. Döllinger to Acton, 19 February [18]67, *Briefwechsel*, 1:476 [German].

54. "Correspondence de France," *Civiltà Cattolica*, 7th ser., 5 (6 February 1869). Cf. Aubert, *Le pontificat de Pie IX*, 316.

55. Döllinger to Acton, 23 July [18]69, *Briefwechsel*, 1:567 [German].

56. Acton to Marie, n.d. [10 September 1869], CUL Add. 8121/7/933.

57. Acton, review of *The Life of Fra Paolo Sarpi*, by Arabella G. Campbell, *North British Review* 51 (October 1869): 238–39.

58. Acton, "Pope and Council," *Selected Writings of Lord Acton*, ed. J. Rufus Fears (Indianapolis, 1984–88), 3:280–89; Acton, "Massacre of St. Bartholomew," *Selected Writings*, 2:198–240.

59. Acton, "Pope and Council," *Selected Writings*, 3:280.

60. Ibid., 282.

61. Acton to Döllinger, 15 June 1869, *Briefwechsel*, 1:566 [German].

62. Acton to Marie, dated "Saturday" [May 1865], CUL Add. 8121/7/850.

63. Acton to Peter le Page Renouf, 2 September 1869, CUL Add. 8119/8/515/13.

64. Acton to Marie, n.d. [9 September 1869], CUL Add. 8121/7/934 [German]. The Bavarian Cardinal Karl August von Reisach, Prefect of the Congregation of Studies, who presided over one of the preparatory Council commissions for the Council, might have played an important role in the Council but for his death, in December

1869. He was close to Pius IX, a supporter of Archbishop Manning, and known to be much opposed to Döllinger and his English pupil.

65. Acton to Peter le Page Renouf, 18 September 1869, CUL Add. 8119/8/515/14.

66. Acton to Peter le Page Renouf, 25 September 1869, CUL Add. 8119/8/515/15.

67. The German bishops' private letter to the Pope, dated 4 September 1869, sent with the official Fulda pastoral letter, is published in Jesuits of Maria Laach, eds., *Acta et Decreta Sacrorum Conciliorum Recensiorum: Collectio Lacensis* (Freiburg, Germany, 1870–90), 7:1196a.

Chapter 12: The Unbidden Guest

1. W. E. Gladstone to Queen Victoria, 11 August 1869, Royal Archives, Windsor, RA51/4, published in John Morley, *The Life of William Ewart Gladstone* (London, 1903), 2:430.

2. Lord Granville to Queen Victoria, 23 August 1869, quoted in Lord Edmund Fitzmaurice, *The Life of Granville George Leveson Gower, Second Earl Granville,* 2d ed. (London, 1905), 2:17.

3. W. E. Gladstone to Acton, 6 November 1869, BL Add. 44093/87.

4. Acton to W. E. Gladstone, 11 November 1869, BL Add. 44093/89.

5. Acton to W. E. Gladstone, 23 November 1869, BL Add. 44093/91. The hereditary ducal title of Dalberg passed in 1859 to Charles Tascher de la Pagerie, a descendant of a niece of the last Duke, Acton's father-in-law. The last holder of the title was Robert duc Tascher de la Pagerie (1840–1910). See Joseph Valynseele, *Les princes et ducs du Premier Empire non maréchaux* (Paris, 1959), 54.

6. W. E. Gladstone to Acton, 1 December 1869, BL Add. 44093/96–99.

7. Acton to Döllinger, 22 November 1869, *Briefwechsel,* 2:17 [German].

8. Acton to Marco Minghetti, 29 October 1869, Minghetti Papers, Biblioteca Communale dell'Archiginnasio Bologna, 13.

9. Acton to Marie, 4 November [1869], CUL Add. 8121/7/941.

10. Acton, journal, CUL Add. 7727, 7728. There are at Cambridge two exercise books in Acton's hand that cover the period from 22 November to 27 December 1869 and, with fewer entries, up to 24 January 1870. These have been edited with an introduction by Edmund Campion under the title *Lord Acton and the First Vatican Council: A Journal,* published by the Catholic Theological Faculty (Sydney, 1975). Among the vast literature concerning the First Vatican Council the following works are important and relevant: Edward Cuthbert Butler, *The Vatican Council: The Story Told from Inside in Bishop Ullathorne's Letters,* 2 vols. (London, 1930; abbreviated edition, London, 1962); Roger Aubert, *Le pontificat de Pie IX* (Paris, 1963); Roger Aubert, *Vatican I,* ed. Gervaise Demeige, S.J. (Paris, 1964);

Klaus Schatz, *Vaticanum I, 1869-1870,* 3 vols. (Paderborn, Germany, 1992–94); James J. Hennesey, *The First Council of the Vatican: The American Experience* (New York, 1963); Odo Russell, *The Roman Question: Extracts from the Dispatches of Odo Russell from Rome, 1858-1870,* ed. Noel Blakiston (London, 1962); Owen Chadwick, *Catholicism and History: The Opening of the Vatican Archives* (Cambridge, England, 1978); *Lord Acton: The Decisive Decade, 1864-1874: Essays and Documents,* ed. Damian McElrath, James Holland, Ward White, and Sue Katzman (Louvain, Belgium, 1970).

11. Acton to Döllinger, 6/7 January 1870, *Briefwechsel,* 2:67 [German].

12. Isaac Thomas Hecker (1819–1888), the New York–born son of German Protestants, became a Catholic under Orestes Brownson's influence, in 1844. After studies for the priesthood in Belgium and England, he joined the Redemptorists and was ordained by Archbishop Wiseman in 1849. He was a successful missionary in New York, but when, under his own auspices in 1857, he went to see the Redemptorist General to submit his ideas for the American mission and a distinctive American presentation of Catholicism, he was dismissed from the Redemptorists and founded his own Missionary Society of St. Paul (1858) with the support of Pius IX, acting as its first General from 1858 to 1871. From early on he recognized the importance of ecumenical ideas with a view to a Catholic-Protestant rapprochement and emphasis on the freedom of the individual and on the working of the Holy Spirit rather than the Church's authoritarian system. See Walter Elliott, *The Life of Father Hecker* (New York, 1898).

13. Döllinger to Acton, 22 November 1869, *Briefwechsel,* 2:8 [German].

14. Acton to Döllinger, 6/7 and 22 January 1870, *Briefwechsel,* 2:67 [German], 101 [German]. On the U.S. bishops, see Giovanni Domenico Mansi, ed., *Sacrorum Conciliorum, nova et amplissima collectio* (Graz, Austria, 1901–27), vol. 51, cols. 650–57; see also Hennesey, *First Council of the Vatican,* 57. Hennesey notes that there was no discernible "American policy" and that even if at times individual bishops gave signs of a distinctively American approach to particular conciliar problems, they never voted as a bloc.

15. This was Count Karl Tauffkirchen-Guttenburg, minister in St. Petersburg, who had recently married a relation of the Arcos, a useful circumstance for Acton. Acton's Roman-Bavarian links were, of course, close because of the liberal Hohenlohe government and the support of Louis Arco, his brother-in-law, a young attaché at the Bavarian legation since 1869, which enabled Acton to use the diplomatic bag for the communications with Döllinger.

16. Acton to Lord Granville, 17 February 1870, CUL Add. 8121/7/1107/1.

17. Louis Arco to Acton, 10 June 1869, CUL Add. 8121/6/483/1 [German].

18. Acton to Döllinger, [28 November 1869], *Briefwechsel,* 2:20 [German].

19. Acton to W. E. Gladstone, 1 January 1870, BL Add. 44093/102–9, published in

Decisive Decade, 170, and in *Selected Writings of Lord Acton,* ed. J. Rufus Fears (Indianapolis, 1984–88), 3:344.

20. Acton to Countess Arco, 23 November [1869], CUL Add. 8121/7/729 [French].

21. Acton to W. E. Gladstone, 24 November 1869, *Selections from the Correspondence of the First Lord Acton,* ed. John Neville Figgis and Reginald Vere Laurence (London, 1917), 85, and in *Decisive Decade,* 163.

22. Acton, journal, 14 December 1869, *First Vatican Council Journal,* 44–45.

23. Acton to Döllinger, [10 June 1870], *Briefwechsel,* 2:422 [German].

24. Acton to Döllinger, 10 January [1870], *Briefwechsel,* 2:82 [German].

25. Neptune shouted, "I'll show you," thus calming the winds, in Vergil's *Aeneid* 1:135.

26. Acton to Döllinger, 4 January 1870, *Briefwechsel,* 2:58 [German].

27. Acton to Döllinger, 6/7 January 1870, *Briefwechsel,* 2:65 [German].

28. Acton to Döllinger, n.d. [19 January 1870], *Briefwechsel,* 2:99 [German]. Darboy's speech is printed in Mansi, ed., *Sacrorum Conciliorum,* vol. 50, cols. 400–406, and in Butler, *Vatican Council,* 190–91.

29. Acton, "The Next General Council," *Chronicle,* 13 July 1867, 368–70, reprinted in *Selected Writings,* 3:263–68, quotation on 267.

30. Acton to W. E. Gladstone, 1 January 1870, BL Add. 44093/102–9, published in *Decisive Decade,* 170.

31. The declaration of the English Catholic bishops that Acton had particularly in mind is referred to in Bernard Ward, *The Eve of Catholic Emancipation* (1911–12; reprint, London, 1970), 3:169–70. Ward writes that the text was prepared by Dr. William Poynter as "a simple and straightforward statement of Catholic doctrine, free from the Gallican or any other controversial tendencies which disfigured the 'Protestation and Declaration' of 1789, and written in a style well calculated to remove Protestant prejudice." An edition of one hundred thousand copies of the *Declaration of the Catholic Bishops, the Vicar Apostolics and the Coadjutors in Great Britain* [in Latin] (London, 1826) was distributed. It was signed by all the bishops of England and Scotland. I am indebted for the English translation of the relevant passages of the official Latin texts to J. W. Hooker, late of Birmingham University, and Terence Weiler. In the *Declaration,* the bishops disclaimed any "pretended right to the property of the Established Church in England." And they went on to declare that "neither the pope nor anyone who holds an office nor any religious functionary of the Roman Catholic Church have any right by reason of their spiritual and ecclesiastical office to claim for themselves, either directly or through others, any civil or temporal jurisdiction, power, sovereignty or authority in this kingdom; and that it is not lawful for them, either through their own efforts or with the help of others, to become involved in matters which concern the civil government of the United Kingdom or any part of it. [English Catholics] believe that they are bound by the law of conscience to obey the secular power in this estate in

everything which has been laid down by legislation and the common law; and they would have no regard for any dispensation for acting contrary to any law or edict which may have been given by the Pope or any authority in the Roman Church whatsoever." The more explicit text of the declaration of the Irish hierarchy stated that Irish Catholics do not believe in, and solemnly declare that they abominate and regard as wicked and completely incompatible with Christian teaching, the proposition that "it is lawful to murder or destroy any person or group of persons on the ground of their heresy." In the same way they abominate the view that "an understanding given to heretics does not have to be kept." They further assert on their solemn oath their belief that "no conduct which is unjust, dishonourable or civil by its nature can in any way be justified or excused on the pretext or false premise that it was carried out for the benefit of the Church or under the law of obedience to any ecclesiastical power whatsoever." They further believe that "it is not an article of faith nor are they in any way bound to believe that the Pope is infallible" and that they are not constrained by any duty "to obey an order which is in its nature shameful notwithstanding that the Pope or any holder of an office in the Church has given such an order. On the contrary to attribute any authority or proffer obedience to such an order is disgraceful." See "Address of the Catholics of Ireland to the People of England," *Times* (London) 21 December 1826, 3, cols. 2–3; and "Correspondence," *Times* (London), 29 December 1826, 3, col. 6.

32. Acton to W. E. Gladstone, 24 November [1869], BL Add. 44093/92–94, published in *Decisive Decade,* 163. Manning, as the supreme and fanatical advocate of Papal Infallibility, was involved in a controversy with Dupanloup before the Vatican Council began. In his pastoral letter *The Ecumenical Council and Infallibility,* published in March 1870, Manning had claimed, according to Dupanloup, that the Pope was infallible *apart* (*seorsum*) from the Church. Manning answered that Dupanloup, not understanding English, had been misled by a faulty translation. Dupanloup retorted that the translation was done "by your friend and henchman, M. Veuillot, in the *Univers*" and reiterated the charge of theological error. Manning dropped the controversy; being, at the time, in the Council, he objected to carrying on the discussion. See Edmund Sheridan Purcell, *Life of Cardinal Manning* (London, 1896), 2:425.

33. W. E. Gladstone to Odo Russell, telegram n.d. [ca. 1 December 1869], BL Add. 44093/95, published in *Decisive Decade,* 164. Gladstone's undated telegram was communicated to Acton by Russell on 6 December 1869.

34. Quoted in Purcell, *Life of Cardinal Manning,* 2:434.

35. Odo Russell to Lord Clarendon, 22 December 1869, *Roman Question,* 375.

36. Acton to Döllinger, 1 April [1870], *Briefwechsel,* 2:277 [German]: "Liszt to depart tomorrow for Munich and will take my letter."

37. Acton to Döllinger, 12 December 1869, *Briefwechsel,* 2:33.

38. Acton, notes, CUL Add. 5542/71.

39. Bishop Josef Strossmayer wrote to Döllinger on 10 June 1871: "There have been all sorts of attempts to intimidate me. Rumours were spread that I was the most frivolous and unworthy of men, and that an investigation was initiated by a certain tribunal. The Austrian embassy allowed itself to be used by someone called Palombo, a member of the embassy staff. One day Archbishop Haynald came to see me to say that he had been unable to sleep all night because the previous evening Palombo had told him the most awful scandals about me. He thought that could only have the effect of compromising the opposition in the eyes of the world. I calmed my friend, saying that it was all dastardly calumnies and an unworthy attempt at intimidation tried also in the case of others. . . . My position in my own country is a very delicate one. I am close to the Church and the political affairs of my nation. The poor South Slavs are to the highest degree ill-treated by the governments of Vienna and Budapest. I am a thorn in their side and for years they have looked for some excuse to remove and silence me." This letter was published in Dr. Johann Friedrich von Schulte, *Der Altkatholizismus* (Giessen, Germany, 1887), a history of the Old Catholic movement's development, its formation, and its legal position in Germany, by its chief organizer. The Old Catholics clearly exerted pressure on Bishop Strossmayer to join their ranks. Theodor Granderath, S.J., in his famous *Geschichte des Vatikanischen Konzils von seiner ersten Ankündigung bis zu seiner Vertagung: Nach den authentischen Dokumenten,* ed. Konrad Kirch (Freiburg, Germany, 1903–6), made much of Strossmayer's alleged contacts with the German Catholic dissenters, but no evidence has been produced to undermine Strossmayer's repeated assurance never to separate himself from Rome. See Ivo Sivric, OFM, *Bishop J. G. Strossmayer, New Light on Vatican I* (Rome, 1975), 245; Johann Friedrich, *Geschichte des Vatikanischen Konzils* (Bonn, 1877–87), 3:393–94.

40. Quirinus [Acton, Johann Friedrich, and Ignaz von Döllinger], *Römische Briefe vom Conzil, des Quirinus* (Munich, 1870).

41. Acton to Döllinger, 6/7 January 1870, *Briefwechsel,* 2:67 [German].

42. Acton to Döllinger, n.d. [13 February 1870], *Briefwechsel,* 2:163 [German].

43. Odo Russell to Lord Clarendon, 22 December 1869, Clarendon Papers, Bodleian Library, Oxford, 487. Russell wrote again on 1 January 1870: "The newspapers are not to be trusted—the correspondents are misleading the public—there is a regular manufacture of false reports and canards in Rome which the correspondents serve up with a sensational 'sauce piquante' that fills me with surprise whenever I take up a newspaper." And on 5 January 1870: "The sensationalism of the press with regard to the Council is doing more harm than good I think. Most of the anecdotes of the correspondents' Letters are unfounded and even such powerful minds as Lord Acton are more credulous than the true state of affairs appears to warrant."

44. Augsburg *Allgemeine Zeitung,* 21 February 1870, 795, quoted in Acton to Döllinger, n.d. [24 February 1870], *Briefwechsel,* 2:167 [German].

45. Victor Conzemius, "Die Verfasser der 'Römischen Briefe vom Konzil' des 'Quirinus,'" in *Festschrift für Hans Förster: Freiburger Geschichtsblätter* 52 (1963–64): 229–56.

46. Tauffkirchen complained about the letters in a letter dated 26 January 1870 to the Bavarian Prime Minister Prince Chlodwig Hohenlohe-Schillingsfürst. Döllinger to Acton, 8 February 1870, *Briefwechsel,* 2:138 [German]. He was encountering a lessening of the confidence he had previously enjoyed in his Roman contact, Tauffkirchen wrote, because persons close to the legation like Professor Friedrich, Count Arco, and Lord Acton were suspected as being among the informants of Quirinus.

47. Shane Leslie, *Henry Edward Manning,* 2d ed. rev. (London, 1921), 219.

48. Acton to Döllinger, 8 February [1870], *Briefwechsel,* 2:142 [German].

49. Quoted in Acton to Döllinger, 16/17 March [1870], *Briefwechsel,* 2:228 [German].

50. Acton, quoting the Pope, to Döllinger, [14 March 1870], *Briefwechsel,* 2:221 [German]. See also Emile Ollivier, *L'église et l'état au Concile du Vatican,* 2 vols. (Paris, 1879; reprint, 1900, 1909), 1:449–58, 2:49–52, 63. On the award of the Patricius Romanus, see also Edouard Lecanuet, *Montalembert* (Paris, 1895–1902), 2:503.

51. Montalembert's letter was published on 7 March 1870 in the *Gazette de France,* reprinted in Lecanuet, *Montalembert,* 3:406–69.

52. Acton to Döllinger, 16/17 March [1870], *Briefwechsel,* 2:229 [German].

53. Gertrude Himmelfarb, *Lord Acton: A Study in Conscience and Politics* (London, 1952), 106. See also Leslie, *Henry Edward Manning,* 220. Acton's eldest daughter, Mamy, wrote in her "Notes Taken from Memory," 17: "One of my earliest recollections was when I was about 3 or 4 in Rome and we children, Annie and myself and the nurses were being driven round the Pincio when suddenly we were told that His Holiness Pope Pius IX was also driving round and our carriage stopping, we all got out and kneeling on the road were blest by the Pope." CUL Add. 8119/9/427.

54. Albert du Boys, *Ses souvenirs du Vatican, 1869–1870* (Louvain, Belgium, 1968), 105.

55. Acton, journal, 13 December 1869, *First Vatican Council Journal,* 39 n. 167.

56. Charlotte von Leyden to Döllinger, 10 February 1870, *Briefwechsel,* 4:460 [German].

57. Quoted in Campion, introd. to Acton, *First Vatican Council Journal,* ix–x.

58. Charlotte von Leyden to Döllinger, 27 January 1870, *Briefwechsel,* 4:456 [German].

59. Döllinger to Charlotte von Leyden, 14 February 1870, *Briefwechsel,* 4:460 [German].

60. Charlotte von Leyden to Döllinger, [20 February 1870], *Briefwechsel,* 4:462 [German].

61. Ibid.

62. The message sent by Barkis, the carrier, through David Copperfield to old Miss Peggotty, David's nurse and friend, indicating willingness to marry her, has passed into proverbial usage, meaning consent. Charles Dickens, *David Copperfield* (London, 1907), 60–61. See also Mamy Acton, "Notes Taken from Memory," 16, CUL Add. 8119/9/427.

63. Charlotte von Leyden to Döllinger, 6 March 1870, *Briefwechsel,* 4:467 [German].

64. Raffaele de Cesare, in *Roma e lo Stato del Papa dal ritorno di Pio IX* (Rome, 1907), 2:35, mentions that Russell was much appreciated on account of his wit, but more so for presenting the Roman ladies with the latest in hats sent out by his order from London. Russell, according to this author, was mad about music, sang tenor roles in Roman amateur opera productions such as Donizetti's *Lucrezia Borgia,* and had a passion for snakes. He kept many in his home, but had to give them up when he got married. *The Last Days of Papal Rome, 1850–70,* trans. Helen Zimmern, intro. G. M. Trevelyan (London, 1909), 82.

65. Acton, Council journal, 7 December 1869, *First Vatican Council Journal,* 26.

66. Acton to W. E. Gladstone, 1 January 1870, *Selections from the Correspondence,* 96.

67. W. E. Gladstone to Lord Clarendon, 13 January 1870, Clarendon Papers, Bodleian Library, 498. See also H.C.G. Matthew, "Gladstone, Vaticanism and the Question of the East," *Studies in Church History* 15 (1978): 417–42, esp. 432, where the author emphasizes the "acute sense of frustration" arising from Gladstone's exchanges with the foreign secretary. "It is by threats and threats alone that the court of Rome as to its Roman and Church policy is influenced: its whole policy is based on the rejection of reason." Gladstone's frustration was "increased by relations with the Irish, for the more the Liberals conciliated the Irish Catholics, the more they found themselves limited by Irish constraints." The fact that Gladstone found himself prevented from taking any effective government action during the Vatican Council worked on his emotions to such an extent, according to Matthew, that the built-up resentment over the affront "to his religious nationality" burst out four years later in his pamphlet *The Vatican Decrees in Their Bearing on Civil Allegiance: A Political Expostulation* (London, 1874). This was written when he was free from the restraints of government and able as "a betrayed Anglican," rather than prime minister of England, to attack Ultramontanism as striking at the roots of his political and religious conviction of toleration and freedom. The vehemence of that outburst astonished Acton, who reacted with his celebrated letters to the *Times* (see Chapter 15).

68. Odo Russell to Lord Clarendon, 24 January 1870, *Roman Question,* 385–86.

69. Odo Russell to Lord Clarendon, 24 February 1870, *Roman Question,* 396–97.

70. Lord Clarendon to Odo Russell, 1 March 1870, *Roman Question,* 398.

71. Ibid., 399.

458 NOTES TO PAGES 208-12

72. Odo Russell to Lord Clarendon, 9 March 1870, *Roman Question,* 408.

73. The Duchess of Dalberg passed this compliment on to Döllinger, telling him how the Bishop still remembered Döllinger's devout expression when saying Mass and that this had remained imprinted on his mind. See Johann Friedrich, *Ignaz von Döllinger* (Munich, 1899–1901), 2:122–30.

74. Jacob Speigl, *Traditionslehre und Traditionsbeweise in der historischen Theologie Ignaz von Döllingers* (Essen, Germany, 1964).

75. Acton to Sir Rowland Blennerhassett, dated "Saturday" [1872], published in *Decisive Decade,* 110–11.

76. Acton to Döllinger, 6/7 January 1870, *Briefwechsel,* 2:66 [German].

77. Wilhelm Emmanuel von Ketteler, *Die Unwahrheiten der Römischen Briefe vom Konzil in der Allgemeinen Zeitung* (Mainz, Germany, 1870).

78. Victor Conzemius, "Acton, Döllinger und Ketteler: Zum Verständnis des Ketteler-Bildes in den Quirinusbriefen und zur Kritik an Vigeners Darstellung Kettelers auf dem Vatikanum I," *Archiv für Mittelrheinische Kirchengeschichte* 14 (1962): 194–238; Victor Conzemius, "Die Minorität auf den Ersten Vatikanischen Konzil: Vorhut des Zweiten Vatikanums," *Theologie und Philosophie* 45 (1970): 409–34.

79. Rapporti sul Concilio Vaticano, Archivio Storico del Ministero degli Esteri, Roma, 20 Gennaio–25 Luglio 1870, 302–3; lettere particolari di Emerico Tkalac al Ministero degli Esteri, E. Visconti Venosta, Archivio del Gabinetto (1861–70), Concilio Ecumenico, Busta 209, facs. 4, Rome, 1966, in Angelo Tamborra, *Imbro I. Tkalac and l'Italia* (Rome, 1966); see also Sivric, *Bishop J. G. Strossmayer,* 193.

80. Ferdinand Gregorovius, journal, 19 June 1870, *The Roman Journals of Ferdinand Gregorovius, 1852-1874,* ed. Friedrich Althaus, trans. G. W. Hamilton (London, 1911), 367–68.

81. Acton to Döllinger, [5 June 1870], *Briefwechsel,* 2:410–11 [German].

82. Letter 44, 13 May 1870, *Römische Briefe vom Conzil,* 398. Conzemius refers to Acton's deep-seated suspicion of Ketteler bordering on unfairness in "Acton, Döllinger und Ketteler," 230. Whether the Bishop of Mainz's alleged denunciation of Acton to the Jesuits, which was thought to have caused Theiner's dismissal, was actually ever made has not been established.

Chapter 13: Papal Infallibility and Beyond

1. Acton to W. E. Gladstone, 16 February 1870, BL Add. 44093/117–20, published in *Lord Acton: The Decisive Decade, 1864-1874: Essays and Documents,* ed. Damian McElrath, James Holland, Ward White, and Sue Katzman (Louvain, Belgium, 1970), 174–76, and *Selections from the Correspondence of the First Lord Acton,* ed. John Neville Figgis and Reginald Vere Laurence (London, 1917), 102–5.

2. Acton to W. E. Gladstone, 10 March 1870, BL Add. 44093/123–26, published in *Decisive Decade*, 177–78, and in *Selections from the Correspondence*, 106–9.

3. Acton to Döllinger, [9 March 1870], *Briefwechsel*, 2:204 [German].

4. Odo Russell to Lord Clarendon, 1 March 1870, *The Roman Question: Extracts from the Dispatches of Odo Russell from Rome, 1858–1870*, ed. Noel Blakiston (London, 1962), 398.

5. Lord Clarendon to Odo Russell, 1 March 1870, *Roman Question*, 399.

6. Lord Clarendon to W. E. Gladstone, 23 March 1870, BL Add. 44134 /169, published in *Briefwechsel*, 2:243–44 n. 2.

7. Acton to W. E. Gladstone, 15 March [1870], BL Add. 44093/129–30, published in *Decisive Decade*, 180; also Acton to Döllinger, [14 March 1870], *Briefwechsel*, 2:218 [German]. See also Odo Russell's telegram to Lord Clarendon, 17 March 1870, *Roman Question*: "Acton wishes you to know that some English bishops will found their protest against Infallibility on the repudiation of that doctrine by their predecessors at the time of the Emancipation Act" (409).

8. On the attitude of the Austrian minister during the Council, see Friedrich Engel-Jánosi, "Die Österreichische Berichterstattung über das Vatikanische Konzil, 1869–1870," *Mitteilungen des Instituts für Österreichische Geschichtsforschung* 62 (1953): 595–615.

9. Otto von Bismarck's instructions to Count Arnim, 5 January 1870, in *Gesammelte Werke*, ed. Friedrich Thimme (Berlin, 1951), 6B:197.

10. Cf. Erika Weinzierl-Fischer, "Bismarck's Haltung zum Vatikanum und der Beginn des Kulturkampfes nach den Österreichischen diplomatischen Berichten aus Berlin 1869–1871," *Mitteilungen des Österreichischen Staatsarchivs* 10 (1957): 302–31. The author assumes that Bismarck's change of mind relates to his ambassador Bernstorff's meeting with Lord Clarendon on 9 March 1870. *Gesammelte Werke*, 1869–70, 293, no. 1534.

11. Odo Russell to Lord Clarendon, 9 March 1870, Clarendon Papers, Bodleian Library, 487. Only the part of this long letter referring to the steps Russell had taken in Rome to protect Lord Acton is published in *Roman Question*, 408.

12. Rudolf Lill, *Die ersten deutschen Bischofskonferenzen* (Freiburg, Germany, 1964), 81.

13. Acton to Döllinger, 20 March [1870], *Briefwechsel*, 2:240 [German].

14. Reported in Odo Russell to Lord Clarendon, 7 March 1870, *Roman Question*, 406–7.

15. Acton to Mary Gladstone, 10 February 1881, *Letters of Lord Acton to Mary, Daughter of the Right Hon. W. E. Gladstone*, ed. Herbert Paul, 2d rev. ed. (London, 1913), 53.

16. Acton to Döllinger, [24 February 1870], *Briefwechsel*, 2:171 [German].

17. Ibid., 2:167 [German].

18. Ibid., 2:172 [German]. The quotation is in French.

19. Acton to Döllinger, [9 March 1870], *Briefwechsel,* 2:206 [German].

20. Acton to Döllinger, 4 January 1870, *Briefwechsel,* 2:59–60 [German]. Strossmayer was born in 1815 at Osijek in Slovenia, then part of the Austrian Empire. He was ordained at Diacovo, Croatia, there appointed professor of theology, and then sent to Vienna as chaplain to the Imperial Court. He became Bishop of Diacovo in 1849, and later Apostolic Administrator for Serbia. A charismatic, active, and reforming Bishop, he founded schools and religious houses, financed his cathedral at Diacovo out of his own pocket, and was instrumental in the founding of the Croatian Academy of Sciences (1867) and the University (1874) at Zagreb (then Agram). He was an advocate of the Union of Churches and supported the Old Slavonic liturgical movement, establishing close links with the like-minded Vladimir Solov'ëv (1853–1900), the Russian philosopher and poet. Strossmayer aimed at first at a federal reform of the Habsburg Empire, then took up the Pan-Slav cause (see note 25). Fêted as *Pater patriae* (Father of the Fatherland) for his Croatian patriotism, he was nominated under Leo XIII to be made a Cardinal. The Imperial Government in Vienna, however, blocked his elevation. See Josef Höfer and Karl Rahner, eds., *Lexikon für Theologie und Kirche,* 2d rev. ed., 10 vols. (Freiburg, Germany, 1957–65), 9:1114.

21. Acton to Döllinger, 4 January 1870, *Briefwechsel,* 2:60.

22. Strossmayer's speech of 22 March is in Giovanni Domenico Mansi, ed., *Sacrorum Conciliorum, et amplissima collectio* (Graz, Austria, 1901–27), vol. 51, cols. 72–77. For its effect, see Edward Cuthbert Butler, *The Vatican Council: The Story Told from Inside in Bishop Ullathorne's Letters,* 2 vols. (London, 1930; abbreviated edition, 1962), 236–38. Acton's account is in Acton to Döllinger [27–28 March 1870], *Briefwechsel,* 2:258 [German], which mentions that Strossmayer had told him afterwards "It was like in Ephesus" and that, fearing for his life, his Croat servants had tried to get near the platform to protect him.

23. Acton to Döllinger, n.d. [27–28 March 1870], *Briefwechsel,* 2:259 [German].

24. Quoted in Shane Leslie, *Henry Edward Manning,* 2d ed. rev. (London, 1921)@, 227.

25. Strossmayer was a Slavophile of a special kind, "not akin to the Russian Slavophils. While the Russian Slavophils strongly believed in the power and orthodoxy of their common people (*muzhiks*), Strossmayer opined that the people should move ahead and become ennobled by enlightenment, Christianity and modern achievements.... While the Russian Slavophils were inimical to anything Western, he was a strong advocate of westernising the Slavs and still preserving their Slav identity." Ivo Sivric, OFM, *Bishop J. G. Strossmayer, New Light on Vatican I* (Rome, 1975), 272. See also R. W. Seton-Watson, *The Southern Slav Question and the Habsburg Monarchy* (London, 1911), 128–29: "In the true political significance of the

word, [Strossmayer] was anything but Pan-Slav. Like Franz Palacky [Czech historian and the Bishop's friend] and many other distinguished Slavs in the Habsburg Monarchy, he believed in the mission of Austria, and desired to see her great and prosperous." With these qualifications in mind, it is worth noting the inevitable collapse of Strossmayer's reputation in the course of the modern disintegration of Communist Yugoslavia, Croatia having been the first victim of that failed attempt at realising a form of Pan-Slavism.

26. Josef Strossmayer to W. E. Gladstone, 13 March 1879, BL Add. 44459/183–90 [German], published in *Briefwechsel,* 2:59–60.

27. Acton to Döllinger, 13 April 1870, *Briefwechsel,* 2:314–16 [German].

28. *North British Review* 51 (October 1869): 30–70, reprinted in *Selected Writings of Lord Acton,* ed. J. Rufus Fears (Indianapolis, 1984–88), 2:198–240.

29. F.A.P. de Falloux, *Histoire de Saint Pie V: Pape de l'ordre des frères prêcheurs* (Paris, 1844). Comte Falloux (1811–1885), a royalist politician and historian who supported the Revolution of 1848, was Minister of Education (1849–50) and responsible for the Loi Falloux, which secured for the clergy great influence in the French educational establishments.

30. Acton to Döllinger, 13 April 1870, *Briefwechsel,* 2:315, editor's note 5.

31. Butler, *Vatican Council,* 1962 ed., 303.

32. Acton to Döllinger, 15 May [1870], *Briefwechsel,* 2:354–55 [German].

33. Archbishop Luigi Natoli's address is in Mansi, ed., *Sacrorum Conciliorum,* vol. 52, cols. 45–46; Acton to Döllinger, 15 May [1870], *Briefwechsel,* 2:352–53. See also Theodor Granderath, S.J., *Geschichte des Vatikanischen Konzils von seiner ersten Ankündigung bis zu seiner Vertagung: Nach den authentischen Dokumenten,* ed. Konrad Kirch (Freiburg, Germany, 1903–6). The author of this history, with strong Ultramontane bias, not very aptly used this true incident to illustrate the "mendaciousness of the Munich story-teller" (2:583–85).

34. Acton to Döllinger, [25 May 1870], *Briefwechsel,* 2:377 [German]. See also Butler, *Vatican Council,* 1962 ed., 311. Bishop Clifford's speech, recorded in Mansi, ed., *Sacrorum Conciliorum,* vol. 52, cols. 274–84, showed an appreciation, rare at the time, of the Anglican Protestant attitude towards the Catholic Church.

35. Count Tauffkirchen's report to King Louis II is in Bayrisches Geheimes Staatsarchiv, Munich, MA I, 639.

36. Acton to Döllinger, [10 June 1870], *Briefwechsel,* 2:422 [German].

37. Odo Russell to Lord Clarendon, 9 June 1870, *Roman Question,* 441.

38. Earl Clarendon to Lord Lyons, ambassador in Paris, 15 June 1870, *Roman Question,* 445.

39. Odo Russell to Lord Clarendon, 18 June 1870, *Roman Question,* 446.

40. Henry Edward Manning to W. E. Gladstone, n.d., and reply, 12 November 1870. Both quoted in Leslie, *Henry Edward Manning,* 231.

41. Henry Manning to W. E. Gladstone, 15 November 1870, BL Add. 44249/241.

42. Lord Granville to W. E. Gladstone, 18 November 1870, BL Add. 44167/175–76. See also Lord Edmund Fitzmaurice, *The Life of Granville George Leveson Gower, Second Earl Granville,* 2d ed. (London, 1905), 2:136.

43. Lord Granville to Acton, 16 December 1870, CUL Add. 8121/6/178, writing from Windsor and adding: "The Queen did not know you were in England or she would have asked you to come with me here."

44. Mansi, ed., *Sacrorum Conciliorum,* vol. 53, cols. 1242–43, supplies the full list of votes.

45. Quoted in Leslie, *Henry Edward Manning,* 230, 233.

46. Acton to Döllinger, n.d. [14 July 1870], *Briefwechsel,* 2:428 [German].

47. Acton to Döllinger, 21 July 1870, *Briefwechsel,* 2:434 [German].

48. Döllinger to Acton, 23 July 1870, *Briefwechsel,* 2:436 [German].

49. Quoted in Butler, *Vatican Council,* 1962 ed., 116–19. See also the moving account in Emile Ollivier, *L'église et l'état au Concile du Vatican,* 2 vols. (Paris, 1879; reprint, 1900, 1909), 1:416ff., by the French premier during the Council.

50. Acton to Marie, dated "Munich, Saturday" [27 May 1871], CUL Add. 8121/7/959.

51. The Declaration of 30 August 1870, signed by only nine of the twenty-four German bishops, is published in *Briefwechsel,* 3:12–13 n. 4.

52. Döllinger to Acton, 27 November 1872, *Briefwechsel,* 3:95–96 [German], with the text of Hefele's declaration.

Chapter 14: A Misfortune for Religion

1. Quoted in Johann Friedrich, *Ignaz von Döllinger* (Munich, 1899–1901), 3:347–58.

2. Döllinger to Acton, 23 July 1870, *Briefwechsel,* 2:436 [German].

3. Augsburg *Allgemeine Zeitung,* no. 22, January 1871; see also Friedrich, *Ignaz von Döllinger,* 3:561ff.

4. Augsburg *Allgemeine Zeitung,* special supplement 90, 31 March 1871.

5. Archbishop Scherr, pastoral letter, 2 April 1871, published as *Hirtenbrief Seiner Exzellenz Gregorius Erzbischof von München und Freising* (Munich, 1871).

6. Segretario di Stato to Nunzio Apostolico Baviera, 5 April 1871, Archivio Segreto Vaticano, 1441; Friedrich, *Ignaz von Döllinger,* 3:578–79.

7. *Stenographischer Bericht über die Verhandlungen des Katholiken Congresses, abgehalten vom 2. bis 24. September 1871 in München* (Munich, 1871), 108ff.; Friedrich, *Ignaz von Döllinger,* 3:612–13.

8. By the Bull *Unigenitus* of 8 September 1731, Clement IX condemned Jansenism. Döllinger's letter to Oxenham of 22 August 1870 (in German) is quoted in Victor Conzemius, "Aspects ecclésiologiques de l'évolution de Döllinger et du vieux catholicisme," *Revue des sciences réligieuses* 34 (1960): 247–79.

9. Lady Charlotte Blennerhassett to Acton, dated "Mardi," 22 August 1890, CUL Add. 8119/7608/1. This letter forms part of fourteen letters written by her to Acton between 1885 and 1890. The typed manuscript copies, approved by her, were given by Lady Blennerhassett on 29 March 1914 to the second Lord Acton with authorization for publication, which may not have occurred. The letter concerns Döllinger and replies to Acton's criticisms of her books.

10. Sir Rowland Blennerhassett's letter to the *Times* of 19 June 1871, 12: "Sir, Several newspapers give among the signatures to the Declaration of the German Catholics who lately met at Munich the names of 'Lord Acton-Dalberg' and 'Sir Blenner-Hassett.' It is needless to say that these are not authentic signatures, but it may be necessary to add that what purports to be my name has been affixed as mere conjecture and that authority to fix it was never asked nor given."

11. Lady Blennerhassett to Döllinger, n.d. [end of June] 1871, *Briefwechsel*, 4:504 [German].

12. The Declaration was published in *Rheinischer Merkur*, 13 June 1871, 238–40, and supp. to the Augsburg *Allgemeine Zeitung*, 13 June 1871, 164:28–29, also in Johann Friedrich von Schulte, *Der Altkatholizismus* (Giessen, Germany, 1887), 16–22.

13. Gertrude Himmelfarb, *Lord Acton: A Study in Conscience and Politics* (London, 1952), 114–16.

14. Professor Josef Berchtold, in his letter published in the *Allgemeine Zeitung* of 19 July 1871 (no. 3585), intended as an answer to Blennerhassett's letter to the *Times,* admitted that Lord Acton's authority to use his name had not been sought. "But Lord Acton will not deny us our testimony that, far from acting in bad faith towards him, we were entitled to consider his full consent to the content of the declaration to be beyond doubt." Reprinted in von Schulte, *Der Altkatholizismus,* 339 n.

15. Acton to Döllinger, 19 August 1871, *Briefwechsel*, 3:24 [German].

16. Döllinger to Acton, 26 June and 24 August 1871, *Briefwechsel*, 3:20, 27 [both German].

17. Acton to Döllinger, 19 August and 15 September 1871, *Briefwechsel*, 3:24–25, 32 [both German].

18. Lady Blennerhassett diary, 26 September 1871, *Briefwechsel*, 4:117 [German].

19. Döllinger to Acton, 19 September 1871, *Briefwechsel*, 3:36–37 [German].

20. Acton to Döllinger, 5 September 1871, *Briefwechsel*, 3:28 [German].

21. Lady Blennerhassett diary, 27 August 1871, *Briefwechsel*, 4:714–715 [German].

22. Döllinger's excommunication, quoted in Friedrich, *Ignaz von Döllinger*, 3:578–79.

23. Acton to Döllinger, n.d. [23 April 1878], *Briefwechsel*, 3:184 [German]. See also Jean Bowes Gwatkin, "Döllinger, the Renoufs and Rome," *Tablet* 222, no. 6661 (January 1968): 54–55. This article is based on the biographical essay in volume 4 of Renouf, *The Egyptian Book of the Dead,* trans. and commentary by Peter le Page

Renouf, continued and completed by Edouard Naville (London, 1902–7); and on Renouf's letters deposited at Pembroke College, Oxford.

24. Edward Cuthbert Butler, *The Vatican Council: The Story Told from Inside in Bishop Ullathorne's Letters*, 2 vols., (London, 1930; abbreviated edition, 1962); Roger Aubert, *Vatican I*, ed. Gervaise Demeige, S.J. (Paris, 1964). See also Augustin Fliche and Victor Martin, eds., *Histoire de l'Eglise depuis les origines jusqu'à nos jours*, vol. 21 (Paris, 1963); Klaus Schatz, *Vaticanum I, 1869–1870* (Paderborn, Germany, 1993).

25. Döllinger's statement of 8 March 1871 is included in the collection of documents with these signatures. See von Schulte, *Der Altkatholizismus*, 205.

26. Ibid., 206.

27. Newman to Döllinger, 9 April 1871, Döllingeriana, Bayrisches Geheimes Staatsarchiv, Munich. This archive contains a number of personal letters of Newman's, like the one of 9 April 1871, not included in the English edition of Newman's *Letters and Diaries*.

28. Döllinger to Newman, 19 March 1870, *Letters and Diaries of John Henry Newman*, ed. C. S. Dessain et al. (Oxford, 1961–84), 25:84.

29. Newman to Döllinger, 9 April 1870, *Letters and Diaries*, 25:85.

30. Sir Rowland Blennerhassett to Acton, 10 April 1871, CUL Add. 4989/193.

31. Lady Blennerhassett to Döllinger, 19 May 1874, *Briefwechsel*, 4:561 [German]. "He has something monastic about him," she wrote, "a devout poetic gaze, but his other traits do not quite correspond to the way he looks, however genial and strange. He is very well, walks vigorously. . . . He appears very melancholy though his frequently recurring subtle and serene smile seems to change him totally in this respect. . . . He asked us to come and see him in Birmingham. . . . But I doubt whether he would give or express himself more openly. It seems as though he had said to himself: *A te fia bello averti fatta parte per te stesso* (So 'twill be well for thee to have made a part for thyself alone), quoting Dante, *Paradiso*, canto 17, lines 68–69.

32. Döllinger to Lady Blennerhassett, 4 June 1874, *Briefwechsel*, 4:563 [German].

33. Acton to Döllinger, 17 June [1872], *Briefwechsel*, 3:71–72 [German].

34. Acton to Marie, n.d. [24 June 1870?], CUL Add. 8121/7/946.

35. Acton, note, 7 August 1870, Shropshire County Council Record Office, 1093/602.

36. Döllinger to Acton, 8 August 1870, *Briefwechsel*, 3:418 [German].

37. Acton to Marie, Salzburg, [October 1870], CUL Add. 8121/7/1030.

38. See Acton's own paper "The Causes of the Franco-Prussian War," read by him in 1899 at the Eranus Society at Trinity College and the St. Catharine's College Historical Society, published in Acton, *Historical Essays and Studies*, ed. John Neville Figgis and Reginald Vere Laurence (London, 1907), 204–25. The British historian Harold Temperley commented on Acton's essay: "Lord Acton was the first to supply real evidence to the effect that the Empress Eugénie was an ardent advocate

of war—and to prove that the British Cabinet expected France to win. His views on the actions of Bernhardi in Spain and the evidence as to his bribery of Spaniards are extremely valuable. He supplied new and extremely important evidences as to the bellicosity of Bismarck on the 13 July, the force of which is not even yet appreciated by historians. . . . In every direction except one [Lord Acton assumed on the strength of a dispatch by Lord Loftus that Austria was on the side of France] Acton's evidence anticipated the results of later researches." Harold Temperley, "Lord Acton on the Origins of the War of 1870, with Some Unpublished Letters from the British and Viennese Archives," *Cambridge Historical Journal* 2 (1926): 68–82. Acton's Cambridge paper was preceded by a lecture titled "The War of 1870," delivered at the Bridgnorth Literary and Scientific Institution on 25 April 1871, published in Acton, *Historical Essays and Studies,* 226–72.

39. Acton to Marie, dated "October," Vienna, CUL Add. 8121/7/1030. Louis Adolphe Thiers (1797–1877) was a French historian who came to the fore as the spokesman of the anti-imperialist party. He was president of the Third Republic (1871–73).

40. Theodor von Sickel, *Römische Erinnerungen,* ed. L. Santifaller (Vienna, 1947), 135–36, 169–70. See also Herbert Butterfield, *Man on His Past* (Cambridge, England, 1955), 81–82; Butterfield, review of *Lord Acton: The Decisive Decade,* ed. Damian McElrath, James Holland, Ward White, and Sue Katzman, *Historical Journal* 15 (1972): 825–26. This episode is vividly described also by Owen Chadwick in *Catholicism and History: The Opening of the Vatican Archives* (Cambridge, England, 1978), 72–109.

41. Sickel, *Römische Erinnerungen,* 135–36; Butterfield, *Man on His Past,* 81–82. The *Liber Diurnus* was an early manuscript of the Papal Chancery, used between 750 and 1050, with models and formularies for certain recurring events such as changes of Popes, consecration of bishops, and so on. In the debate over papal authority during the Vatican Council it became prominent, because Formulary 84 contained a profession of faith in which the Popes accepted the Sixth General Council and condemned Pope Honorius I. The case of Honorius I had important bearings on Infallibility. Honorius was Pope from 625 to 638. He is supposed to have supported the Monothelite Heresy, although that is disputed. What was more important, he was condemned at the Council of Constantinople in 680. In the oath taken by every new Pope from the eighth to the eleventh centuries he was anathematized. A full history of the *Liber Diurnus* is in Hans Foerster, ed., *Liber Diurnus Romanorum Pontificum* (Bern, Switzerland, 1958). What involved debate at the Vatican Council was the question whether the Roman Curia had for centuries suppressed the edition produced by Lucas Holste in 1650. The fear appears to have been that it might become known as a precedent that a newly elected Pope, in his profession of faith, was made to condemn one of his predecessors because of heresy, and this quite apart from the dispute over whether or not Honorius I was really

guilty of heresy. On the First Vatican Council controversy, see A. Hager, "Hefele und das Vatikanische Konzil," *Tübinger Theologische Quartalschrift* 123 (1942): 223–52; Peter le Page Renouf, *The Case of Pope Honorius, Reconsidered with Reference to Recent Apologies* (London, 1869); also C. de Hefele, *Causa Honorii papae* (Naples, 1870).

42. Acton's archival tour and his Eranus Society Lecture are in *Lord Acton: The Decisive Decade, 1864–1874: Essays and Documents,* ed. Damian McElrath, James Holland, Ward White, and Sue Katzman (Louvain, Belgium, 1970), 121–40.

43. Sickel, *Römische Erinnerungen,* 136.

44. Marco Minghetti to Acton, 23 September 1870 [French]; Minghetti to Emilio Visconti-Venosta, 11 October 1870 [Italian]; Minghetti to Visconti-Venosta, 12 October 1870 [Italian], all in *Documenti Diplomatici Italiani,* 2d serv., 1870–96, vol. 1 (Rome: Ministero degli Affari Esteri, La Libreria dello Stato, 1960).

45. Acton to Marie, dated "Florence, Saturday" [October 1870], CUL Add. 8121/7/952, published in *Decisive Decade,* 101–2.

46. Lady Walpurga Paget was author of gossipy memoirs about being an ambassador's wife, *Embassies of Other Days* and *The Linings of Life* (London, 1928), in which Acton and the Minghettis figure.

47. Acton to Marie, 17 October 1870 [French], published as "Une lettre de Lord Acton sur la fin du pouvoir temporel du pape," ed. Damian McElrath, *Revue d'histoire ecclésiastique* 65 (1970): 86–113.

48. Chadwick, *Catholicism and History,* 75–76, 66.

49. Ivo Sivric, OFM, *Bishop J. G. Strossmayer, New Light on Vatican I* (Rome, 1975), 190–200.

50. "Lord Acton on the Roman Question: Report of a Speech of Acton in the Kidderminster Shuttle," 4 February 1871, 4, *Decisive Decade,* 240–45. The speech was given at a Catholic meeting attended on the platform by the mayor of Kidderminster, the local MP, and clergy of the Church of England, with some six hundred people in the audience.

51. Charles Loyson (1872–1912) was first ordained a secular priest (1851), taught philosophy and dogmatics, then entered the Dominicans (1859), taking the name Père Hyacinthe. He later joined the Discalced Carmelites and became a notable preacher at Notre Dame. His reformist ideas led to his excommunication before the Vatican Council. In 1872 he married and joined the Old Catholics briefly as their pastor in Geneva but was soon alienated by them. In 1879 he founded his own "Gallican Church of Paris," which did not take root.

52. Charles Loyson to Acton, 20 February 1871, CUL Add. 8120/1/460 [French], quoted in Damian McElrath, "An Essay on Acton's Critical Decade," *Decisive Decade,* 34.

53. Marco Minghetti to Acton, 7 June 1871, published in *Decisive Decade,* 35.

54. Acton, *Sendschreiben: An einen deutschen Bischof des Vatikanischen Concils,* dated 30 August 1870 (Nördlingen, Germany, 1870), reprinted in *Decisive Decade,* 228–39.

55. Acton to Döllinger, 15 September 1871, *Briefwechsel,* 3:32–33 [German].

56. The speculation is found in Himmelfarb, *Lord Acton,* 111.

57. Wilhelm Emmanuel von Ketteler, Bishop of Mainz, *Die Minorität auf dem Concil: Antwort auf Lord Acton's Sendschreiben: An einen deutschen Bischof des Vaticanischen Concils* (Mainz, Germany, 1870).

58. Ketteler, *Die Unwahrheiten der Römischen Briefe vom Konzil.* Copies of this pamphlet as well as of Acton's *Sendschreiben* are among the Acton Papers, CUL Add. 7731/1.

59. Acton to Döllinger, 23 December 1870, *Briefwechsel,* 2:459 [German]. See also the *Times,* 11 November 1870, 10a, and 30 November 1870, 4e.

60. Augsburg *Allgemeine Zeitung,* no. 262, 19 September 1870.

61. By decree of the Holy Office, dated 20 September 1871.

62. Acton, "The Vatican Council," *North British Review* 53 (October 1870): 183–229, reprinted in *Selected Writings of Lord Acton,* ed. J. Rufus Fears (Indianapolis, 1984–88), 3:290–338.

63. Acton to Döllinger, 5 March 1871, *Briefwechsel,* 3:14–15 [German].

64. See *Briefwechsel,* 3:35 n. 4, for a comparison of the German and English versions by Conzemius.

65. Review of "Zur Geschichte des Vaticanischen Concil" by Lord Acton, Augsburg *Allgemeine Zeitung,* supp. no. 94, 4 April 1871, and supp. no. 95, 5 April 1871.

66. Acton to Döllinger, 23 December 1870, *Briefwechsel,* 2:459 [German].

67. The letter from Bishop James Brown and Acton's answer are quoted in ibid.

68. Acton to Döllinger, 12 July 1872, *Briefwechsel,* 3:84 [German].

69. *Chronik der Ludwig Maximilian Universität München für das Jahr 1871–1872* (Munich, 1872), 40ff.

70. The child born of the liaison between La Ferronays and the widowed Lady Marie Anne (Nonna) Acton was, according to Acton and Throckmorton family tradition, brought up by foster parents, educated in England under the name of Burnell (from one of the Acton family derivatives, Acton Burnell), and then lived in Belgium, where, as Colonel de Brunell, he became aide-de-camp to King Leopold II. Whenever one of the Actons or Throckmortons stopped in Brussels, the Colonel, being a gentleman, invariably called and left a card. During World War I he came back to England as one of the Belgian refugees, a sick old man, and was sent to a hospital near Shrewsbury, where he died, curiously within the shadow of the home of the Actons, where his mother was buried. A member of the Dease family—into which Acton's cousin Emily Throckmorton had married—used to go to the hospital to read the *Revue des deux mondes* to the Colonel, but learned only after his

death that de Brunell was Nonna's illegitimate son. Apparently Earl Fortescue had wished to marry Nonna Acton, but feeling that she might have to confess to that little episode in her past, she foolishly refused him, badly off though she was (Cardinal Acton, her son, had spent a great deal of money on various charities and she was obliged to sell her jewelry to get the Cardinal out of his difficulties). Mamy Acton, "Notes Taken from Memory," 8, CUL Add. 8119/9/427.

71. Acton to Marie, n.d. [April 1873], CUL Add. 8121/7/981.

72. Acton to Prince of Wales, Vienna, 19 May 1873, Royal Archives, Windsor, Prince of Wales, vol. 9, November 1871–June 1873, Z 451/163.

73. Acton to Marie, n.d. [15 May 1873], CUL Add. 81217/979.

74. Ibid.

75. This information is from the Österreichische Galerie, Vienna.

Chapter 15: Gladstone Fights Back

1. W. E. Gladstone, diary, 24 September 1874, *The Gladstone Diaries,* ed. M. R. D. Foot and H. C. G. Matthew (London, 1968–94), 8:528.

2. Acton to Döllinger, 5 March [1872], *Briefwechsel,* 3:52 [German]. Morier's uncle was James Justinian Morier, the travel writer and author of the popular *Adventures of Hajji Baba of Isphahan* (London, 1924). Morier was a Germanophile who held diplomatic posts in Berlin, Frankfurt, and Stuttgart; in 1866 he was British minister at Darmstadt. He was, like Acton, among the friends of Queen Victoria's Vicky, the liberal Princess Royal and future Empress Frederick of Germany. His major, and indeed most disastrous, contribution to history was to have found, in 1866, Georg Hintzpeter as tutor to the then six-year-old future Kaiser, who had suffered mental and physical damage during his difficult birth. Hintzpeter, a Calvinist doctor of philosophy and classical philology, Spartan, idealist, well-meaning, and totally insensitive, proved the worst possible influence, in a rigid age and environment, for that royal heir. John C. G. Röhl, *The Kaiser and His Court: Wilhelm II and the Government of Germany* (Cambridge, England, 1996); Hannah Pakula, *An Uncommon Woman: The Empress Frederick* (London, 1996). Because Morier was known to be close to Acton and Döllinger, he was involved in controversy with Cardinal Manning over a series of articles on State-Church relations and the *Kulturkampf* in Germany, published in 1874 in *Macmillan's Magazine,* which showed Morier's hostility to Bismarck: "The Settlement of the Peace of Westphalia" (30:464–72); "The Relations between Church and State in Prussia up to 1859 (30:559–68); "Prussia and the Vatican" (31:72–88); and "The Prussian and the German Legislation to Which the Vatican Decrees Gave Rise" (31:261–80). See also Cardinal Manning's letter to the editor, "Prussia and the Vatican" (31:259–60), and Morier's reply (31:373–75). And see Lady Victoria, Hester Wemyss, ed., *Mem-*

oirs and Letters of the Right Hon. Sir Robert Morier G.C.B., from 1826-1876 (London, 1911), 2:305–6, 312.

3. W. E. Gladstone to Catherine Gladstone, 12 September 1874, quoted in John Morley, *The Life of William Ewart Gladstone* (London, 1903), 2:513–15.

4. Louise von Kobell, *Conversations of Dr. Döllinger,* trans. Katherine Gould (London, 1892), 100.

5. W. E. Gladstone, "The Right Rev. Dr. von Döllinger," *Speaker* (London), 18 January 1890, 57–60.

6. W. E. Gladstone, diary, 13 September 1874, *Gladstone Diaries,* 8:525.

7. W. E. Gladstone, "Ritual and Ritualism," *Contemporary Review* 24 (1874): 663–81, quotation on 674.

8. The seven lectures delivered at Munich in 1871 were published as Ignaz von Döllinger, *Über die Wiedervereinigung der christlichen Kirchen* (Nördlingen, Germany, 1888).

9. Owen Chadwick, "Döllinger and Reunion," in *Christian Authority: Essays in Honour of Henry Chadwick,* ed. G. R. Evans (Oxford, 1987), 296–334. See also Clément Lialine, "Vieux-catholiques et Orthodoxes: Enquête d'union depuis trois quarts de siècle," *Istina* 5 (1958): 22. The "Faith and Order Conference" is part of the international conferences occasioned by meetings of the World Council of Churches in Geneva. The Bonn conference is inadequately covered by the minutes kept in German by F. H. Reusch, rector of Bonn University and one of the Old Catholic leaders, and published as *Bericht über die Unionskonferenz von Bonn* (Bonn, 1874–75). An English version, translated from German, based on Reusch's notes, was published with an introduction by Canon Henry Parry Liddon (most of the papers were originally read in English) as *Report of the Proceedings of the Reunion Conference Held at Bonn on September 14, 15, and 16, 1874* (London, 1875). See also Frederick Meyrick, ed., *Correspondence between the Anglo-Continental Society and the Secretaries of the Friends of Spiritual Enlightenment in St. Petersburg Concerning Statements on the Validity of Anglican Orders* (London, 1874); Meyrick, ed., *Correspondence between Members of the Anglo-Continental Society and the Old Catholics* (pt. 1), *Oriental Churchmen* (pt. 2) (London, 1874–77); and Meyrick and Edward Bickersteth, *Two Papers on the Old Catholic Movement and the Bonn Conference* (London, 1877). The general background is well described in one of the few modern studies, P. Neuner, *Döllinger als Theologe der Ökumene: Beiträge zur ökumenischen Theologie,* ed. H. Fries (Paderborn, Germany, 1979); also Christian Oeyen, "Die Entstehung der Bonner Unions-Konferenzen im Jahr 1874" (Ph.D. diss., Old Catholic Theological Faculty, University of Bern, 1971). On the dispute on the doctrine of the Immaculate Conception, see the fierce *Times* attack on Liddon, 30 September 1874, and Liddon's reply in the *Times,* 2 October 1874. Full press reports on the conference include the *Saturday Review,* 21 August 1875; *Times,* 19 August 1875; *Pall Mall*

Gazette, 20 August 1875; *Daily Telegraph,* 21 August 1875; *Spectator,* 21 August 1875; *Times,* 21 August 1875; *Tablet,* 21 August 1875; and Liddon's letter in the *Spectator,* 4 September 1875. See also J. O. Johnston, *Henry Parry Liddon* (London, 1904), 186ff.; also Henry Parry Liddon, *Life of Edward Bouverie Pusey* (London, 1897), 4:294ff.

10. Lady Blennerhassett to Döllinger, 24 October 1874, *Briefwechsel,* 4:575–76 [German]; Acton to Döllinger, 19 September 1874, *Briefwechsel,* 3:124 [German]. Acton's pessimism about Döllinger's ecumenical endeavours was increased by the recently published *Correspondence of Leibniz and the Princess Sophie, Electress of Brunswick (1680–1714),* mainly based on the Leibniz Papers in the Royal Library at Hanover, edited by Onno Klopp (Hanover, Germany, 1873).

11. See P. G. Florovsky, "L'oecumenisme au XIXe siècle," *Irénikon* 27 (1954): 443.

12. Acton to Döllinger, 19 September 1874, *Briefwechsel,* 3:125 [German].

13. Ibid., 124–25.

14. The illuminated address, beautifully bound in red velvet and presented to Döllinger at the Bonn conference in August 1875, is kept in the Döllingeriana Collection of the Bayrisches Geheimes Staatsarchiv.

15. R. J. Nevin, in a letter to the Anglican journal the *Churchman* (London), 14 October 1874.

16. W. E. Gladstone to Acton, 19 October 1874, BL Add. 44093/154–55, published in *Selections from the Correspondence of the First Lord Acton,* ed. John Neville Figgis and Reginald Vere Laurence (London, 1917), 44–45.

17. Acton to W. E. Gladstone, 21 October 1874, BL Add. 44093/156–57, published in *Selections from the Correspondence,* 46–47.

18. W. E. Gladstone to Acton, 26 October 1874, BL Add. 44093/158–59, published in *The Correspondence of Lord Acton and Richard Simpson,* ed. Josef L. Altholz, Damien McElrath, and James C. Holland (Cambridge, England, 1971–75), 47–48.

19. Acton to Simpson, 4 November 1874, *Acton-Simpson Correspondence,* 3:319. Confirmation of Acton's account is in *The Political Correspondence of Mr. Gladstone and Lord Granville, 1868–1876,* ed. Agatha Ramm (London, 1952), 2:458.

20. W. E. Gladstone, *The Vatican Decrees in Their Bearing on Civil Allegiance: A Political Expostulation* (London, 1874).

21. Döllinger to Acton, 7 November 1874, *Briefwechsel,* 3:127 [German].

22. Gladstone to Döllinger, 1 November 1874, BL Add. 44140/310–13.

23. H.C.G. Matthew, "Gladstone, Vaticanism and the Question of the East," *Studies in Church History* 15 (1978), esp. 417.

24. Agatha Ramm, "Gladstone's Religion," *Historical Journal* 28, no. 2 (1985): 327–40, esp. 335, 339. For St. Augustine, see *Contra epistolam Parmeniani,* 3.24.

25. Otto von Bismarck to W. E. Gladstone, 1 March 1875, BL Add. 44446/293. Bismarck's famous phrase applied to Disraeli, "Der alte Jude, das ist der Mann," appar-

ently was expressed in a conversation Bismarck had with Count Louis Arco-Valley, the German diplomat, Acton's brother-in-law, who passed it on to the family. Mary Gladstone recorded the words, having heard them from Acton during the Gladstones' Tegernsee visit in 1879: "Ld. Salisbury is a pettyfogging country attorney. The Old Jew is quite a different fellow." Mary Gladstone, diary, 21–22 September 1879, *Mary Gladstone (Mrs. Drew): Her Diaries and Letters*, ed. Lucy Masterman (London, 1930), 167. Being an experienced diplomat, Bismarck no doubt would also have told others what he wanted the world to know.

26. Acton's first letter to the *Times*, dated 8 November 1874, published 9 November 1874, reprinted in *Lord Acton: The Decisive Decade, 1864–1874: Essays and Documents*, ed. Damian McElrath, James Holland, Ward White, and Sue Katzman (Louvain, Belgium, 1970), 246–49; in *Selections from the Correspondence*, 121–24; and in *Selected Writings of Lord Acton*, ed. J. Rufus Fears (Indianapolis, 1984–88), 3: 363–67. Sir Edward Petre, a Jesuit priest, was a close counsellor of King James II.

27. W. E. Gladstone, diary, 9, 10, and 11 November 1874, *Gladstone Diaries*, 8:542. Franz von Baader was the philosopher and theosoph of the Munich Romanticist circle to which Döllinger and Görres also belonged. Baader advocated the union of the Western and Eastern churches and was an early opponent of Papal Infallibility but died reconciled with the Catholic Church. He had a considerable influence in German philosophy. His main work, *Fermenta cognitionis* (1822–25), deals with the relationship of religion and philosophy. See D. Baumgardt, *Franz von Baader und die philosophische Romantik* (Halle, Germany, 1927); and E. Susini, *Franz von Baader et le romantisme mystique* (Paris, 1942). Susini also edited three volumes of Baader's letters (Paris, 1942).

28. Acton's second letter to the *Times*, dated 21 November 1874, published 24 November 1874, reprinted in *Decisive Decade*, 249–57, in *Selections from the Correspondence*, 125, and in *Selected Writings*, 3: 367–79.

29. *Times*, 9 November 1874.

30. Acton to W. E. Gladstone, 19–20 December 1874, *Selections from the Correspondence*, 147.

31. Acton to Marie, n.d. [May 1870?], CUL Add. 8121/7/944 [French].

32. Georgiana Fullerton to Newman, 9 November 1874, *Letters and Diaries of John Henry Newman*, ed. Charles Stephen Dessain et al. (Oxford, 1961–84), 27:155.

33. Henry Edward Manning, letter, *Times*, 9 November 1874, 9. Manning described Döllinger as "the author of this national evil" (the *Kulturkampf*).

34. Thomas Frederick Wetherell to Acton, 10 November 1874, CUL Add. 8119/8/234/1.

35. Manning's first letter of 12 November is not extant, nor is Acton's reply sent on 15 November. But from Manning's answer of 16 November 1874 (*Selections from the Correspondence*, 151–52), it can be deduced what they contained.

36. *Tablet* 44 (28 November 1874): 674.

37. Lady Blennerhassett to Döllinger, 16 November 1874, *Briefwechsel*, 4:578–79 [German].

38. David Newsome, *The Parting of Friends* (London, 1966); Robert Gray, *Cardinal Manning: A Biography* (London, 1985).

39. Lord Granville to W. E. Gladstone, 18 November 1870, BL Add. 44167/175/176. See also Lord Edmund Fitzmaurice, *The Life of Granville George Leveson Gower, Second Earl Granville*, 2d ed. (London, 1905), 2:136.

40. Döllinger to Lady Acton, 23 November 1874, *Briefwechsel*, 3:132 [German].

41. Marie Acton to Lady Blennerhassett, n.d. [1902], CUL Add. 8121/8/230/1.

42. Henry Edward Manning to Acton, 16 November 1874, *Selections from the Correspondence*, 152.

43. Acton to Simpson, 17 November amd 3 December 1874, and Simpson's reply, 17 November and 3 December 1874, *Acton-Simpson Correspondence*, 3:320–23.

44. Acton to Henry Edward Manning, 18 November 1874, *Selections from the Correspondence*, 152–53.

45. Henry Edward Manning to William Bernard Ullathorne, 7 December 1874, quoted in Shane Leslie, *Henry Edward Manning*, 2d ed. rev. (London, 1921), 232.

46. Henry Edward Manning to William Bernard Ullathorne, 2 January 1875, quoted in Leslie, *Henry Edward Manning*, 230.

47. Acton to Peter le Page Renouf, n.d., Renouf Papers, Pembroke College, Oxford, 63/9/4/52. Charles Philippe Place (1814–1893), then Bishop of Marseilles, later Archbishop of Rennes and Cardinal, was a firm opponent of Infallibility. Disregarding this circumstance, the clergy of his diocese wrote to the Pope during the Council to express their devotion also in the matter of Infallibility, for which they were praised by Pius IX while the Bishop complained; he nevertheless published the Council Decrees on 4 August 1870. *Enciclopedia Cattolica* (Rome, 1948–54), 9:1956.

48. Acton to Bishop James Brown of Shrewsbury, 16 December 1874, quoted in Leslie, *Henry Edward Manning*, 233.

49. Henry Edward Manning, Advent pastoral letter, *Tablet* 44 (5 December 1874): 726.

50. Acton to Döllinger, 25 November 1874, *Briefwechsel*, 3:134 [German].

51. Ibid., 135.

52. Döllinger to Lady Blennerhassett, 10 December 1874, *Briefwechsel*, 4:585–586 [German, Latin, English].

53. Lady Blennerhassett to Döllinger, 3 December 1874, *Briefwechsel*, 4:583–584 [German].

54. Acton to Newman, 4 December 1874, *Letters and Diaries*, 27:165–67.

55. Lady Blennerhassett recording a conversation with Döllinger on 23 February 1879, in which she recalled what Acton had said to her while she and her husband were staying with the Actons at Aldenham in November and December during the crisis days of his correspondence with Manning. CUL Add. 8120/2 [German].

56. John Henry Newman, *A Letter to His Grace the Duke of Norfolk on Occasion of Mr. Gladstone's Recent Expostulation* (London, 1875), reprinted in J. H. Newman, *Certain Difficulties Felt by Anglicans in Catholic Teaching* (London, 1876), 2:175–378, quotation on 176–77.

57. Ibid., 309, 311–12.

58. Ibid., 247–57, 261.

59. Acton to Döllinger, Paris, 28 May 1875, *Briefwechsel,* 3:142 [German].

60. Quoted in Charlotte Blennerhassett, "The Late Lord Acton," *Edinburgh Review* 197 (1903): 527–28.

61. Newman to a lady, 13 April 1875, *Letters and Diaries,* 27:276–77.

62. Lady Blennerhassett to Döllinger, n.d. [mid-January 1875], *Briefwechsel,* 4:591 [German].

63. W. E. Gladstone, *Vaticanism: An Answer to "Reproofs and Replies"* (London, 1875).

64. Döllinger to Lady Blennerhassett, 20 February 1875, *Briefwechsel,* 4:597–98 [German].

65. Döllinger to W. E. Gladstone, 17 February 1875, BL Add. 44140/348–49 [German].

66. W. E. Gladstone to Acton, 26 January 1880, BL Add. 44093/209–14; also W. E. Gladstone to Acton, 6 March 1880, BL Add. 44093/215/218.

67. Acton to W. E. Gladstone, 11 March 1880, BL Add. 44093/219–20.

Chapter 16: Madonnas of the Future, Friendships of the Past

1. James Bryce, *Studies in Contemporary Biography* (London, 1903), 392.

2. Acton to Döllinger, 9 June 1875, *Briefwechsel,* 3:144 [German].

3. Döllinger to Acton, 12 June 1875, *Briefwechsel,* 3:145 [German].

4. Acton to Döllinger, 18 June 1875, *Briefwechsel,* 3:146–47 [German].

5. Döllinger to Acton, 17 January 1876, *Briefwechsel,* 3:157 [German, Latin].

6. Acton to Döllinger, 30 May 1878, *Briefwechsel,* 3:205 [German].

7. Acton, "The Protestant Theory of Persecution," *Rambler,* n.s., 6 (March 1862): 318–51, reprinted in *Selected Writings of Lord Acton,* ed. J. Rufus Fears (Indianapolis, 1984–88), 2:98–131; Acton, "Massacre of St. Bartholemew," *Selected Writings,* 2:198–240; Acton, "Wolsey and the Divorce of Henry VIII," *Quarterly Review* 143 (January 1877): 1–51, reprinted in *Selected Writings,* 2:259–311; Nicholas Harpsfield (1519–75), *A Treatise of the Pretended Divorce between Henry VIII and Catherine of Aragon . . . Now First Printed from a Collation of Four Manuscripts,* ed. Nicholas Pocock (London: Camden Society, 1878).

8. Acton to Mary Gladstone Drew, 23 December 1896, *Letters of Lord Acton to Mary, Daughter of the Right Hon. W. E. Gladstone,* ed. Herbert Paul, 2d rev. ed. (London, 1913), 197.

9. "The Madonna of the Future," first published in the periodical *Atlantic Diary,*

March 1873, then in *A Passionate Pilgrim and Other Tales* (Boston, 1875), and in further editions of Henry James's collected works.

10. The quotation is from Lionel Kochan, *Acton on History* (London, 1954), 33.

11. Döllinger to Acton, 29 December 1872, *Briefwechsel*, 3:101 [German, Latin]. Döllinger quotes Horace, *Letters* 10:24.

12. Acton to Mary Gladstone, 3 June 1881, *Letters to Mary Gladstone*, 83.

13. Acton, note, CUL Add. 5403.

14. Charlotte Blennerhassett, "The Late Lord Acton," *Edinburgh Review* 197 (1903): 531.

15. Acton's "The History of Freedom in Antiquity" and "The History of Freedom in Christianity" were published verbatim in the *Bridgnorth Journal*, March and June 1877, and in two three-penny pamphlets by C. Edkins, Printers, Bridgnorth, 1877, reprinted in *The History of Freedom and Other Essays*, ed. John Neville Figgis and Reginald Vere Laurence (London, 1907), 1–60, and in *Selected Writings*, 1:5–53. See also *Lord Acton's History of Liberty* by George Watson (Aldershot, England, 1994), who has made a study of Acton's unpublished notes to "The History of Liberty," CUL Add. 4938–4955; most date from 1877 to 1883. Finally, see Mark Pattison to Acton, 11 March 1877, Shropshire County Council Record Office, 1093/781a.

16. Acton, "History of Freedom in Antiquity," *Selected Writings*, 1:7, 17–18, 27.

17. Acton, "History of Freedom in Christianity," *Selected Writings*, 1:32–34.

18. Ibid., 34, 53.

19. Bryce, *Studies in Contemporary Biography*, 396–97.

20. Döllinger to Acton, 4 March 1881, *Briefwechsel*, 3:241 [German, Italian, French].

21. Acton to Döllinger, [end of March 1881], *Briefwechsel*, 3:242–43 [German].

22. Quoted in Charlotte Blennerhassett, "Late Lord Acton," 534.

23. Acton to Annie Acton, dated "December 4 Thursday" [1885?], CUL Add. 8121/9/169.

24. Acton to Mary Gladstone, 15 October 1881, *Letters to Mary Gladstone*, 83.

25. Acton, note, CUL Add. 5548/10. The passage was quite possibly copied by Acton from an unknown source.

26. Acton, note, CUL Add. 8122/2.

27. Döllinger to Acton, 24 August 1885, *Briefwechsel*, 3:351.

28. Acton to Döllinger, 22 July 1885, *Briefwechsel*, 3:351 [German].

29. Acton to Döllinger, early May 1886, *Briefwechsel*, 3:352 [German].

30. Döllinger to Acton, 7 May 1886, *Briefwechsel*, 3:354 [German].

31. Acton to Döllinger, 30 April 1878, *Briefwechsel*, 3:186–87 [German]. For more on Döllinger's opinion of Leo XIII, see his letter to Acton, 4 March 1881, *Briefwechsel*, 3:240 [German]; and for Acton's opinion, see his letter to Döllinger, n.d. [end of March 1881], *Briefwechsel*, 3:243 [German]. To Mary Gladstone, Acton wrote on 25 March 1881: "I think he is the first Pope who has been wise enough to de-

spair, and has felt that he must begin a new part, and steer by strange stars over an unknown sea." *Letters to Mary Gladstone,* 80. The first encyclical of Leo XIII was *Inscrutabili Dei Consilio,* of 21 April 1878, concerning an understanding between the Church and modern culture.

32. The quotation is from Acton to Mary Gladstone, 25 February 1882, *Letters to Mary Gladstone,* 99.

33. Acton to Döllinger, 30 December 1880, *Briefwechsel,* 3:218 [German].

34. Acton to James Bryce, 29 March 1886, James Bryce Papers, Bodleian Library, 1/24.

35. Oscar Browning, "Personal Recollections of Sir John Seeley and Lord Acton," *Albany Review* 2 (1908): 553.

36. Marie von Bunsen, *The World I Used to Know, 1860–1912,* ed. and trans. Oakley Williams (London, 1930), 161.

37. Lord Acton's membership card, "Cercle Nautique," Cannes, CUL Add. 8120/1.

38. Bunsen, *World I Used to Know,* 163–64.

39. Acton to Döllinger, 5 May 1882, *Briefwechsel,* 3:255 [German].

40. Acton to Mary Gladstone, 10 February 1881, *Letters to Mary Gladstone,* 54.

41. Acton to Mary Gladstone, 31 March 1885, *Letters to Mary Gladstone,* 134.

42. This list was originally written on two different pages of Mrs. Drew's diary and circulated among friends such as Sir Mountstuart Grant Duff (1829–1906), then lieutenant governor of Madras. It was first published in *Some Hawarden Letters, 1878–1913, Written by Mary Drew,* ed. Lisle March-Phillips and Bertram Christian (London, 1917), 187–91.

43. Acton to Mary Gladstone, 10 February 1881, *Letters to Mary Gladstone,* 54.

44. Drew, *Some Hawarden Letters,* 155–56.

45. Clement Shorter, "Lord Acton's Hundred Best Books," *Pall Mall Magazine* 36, no. 147 (July 1905): 3–10.

46. Sir Mountstuart E. Grant Duff, *Out of the Past: Some Biographical Essays* (London, 1903), 2:195.

47. Herbert Butterfield, "Acton: His Training, Methods and Intellectual System," in *Studies in Diplomatic History and Historiography in Honour of G. P. Gooch, C.H.,* ed. A. O. Sarkissian (London, 1961), 169–98, quotation on 195.

48. Mamy Acton, "Notes Taken from Memory," 10–11, CUL Add. 8119/9/427.

49. William Dawes Freshfield to Lord Acton, 5 September 1878, CUL Add. 8119/IF80 onward.

50. Cf. L. C. Freiherr von Heyl zu Herrnsheim, "Cornelius Wilhelm Freiherr von Heyl zu Herrnsheim und seine Familie," *Herrnsheim, 771–1971: Festbuch zur 1200. Jahrfeier,* ed. Otto Bardong (Worms, Germany, 1971), 156–66; see also essays on the Acton ancestors, the Dalbergs (116–27), and the history of the Schloss Herrnsheim (105–16), and a contribution by Victor Conzemius on Lord Acton and free speech in the Church (145–55).

51. W. E. Gladstone, memorandum for Andrew Carnegie, 9 June [1890], BL 44773/ 182–86.

52. William Dawes Freshfield to W. E. Gladstone, 13 June 1890, BL 44510/93, 94, 104, 117, 119.

53. Andrew Carnegie to W. E. Gladstone, 13 June 1890, quoted in Burton J. Hendrick, *The Life of Andrew Carnegie* (London, 1933), 308, 310.

54. CUL Add. 7732 (miscellaneous papers). The Congregation of Cambridge University resolved, on 3 October 1902, to accept the books of the late Professor Lord Acton and convey the thanks of the University to Mr. Morley for his magnificent gift. The acceptance of the books cost the University Library altogether £7,600. The sum was made up as follows: costs of removal from Aldenham, £400; making alterations and bookshelves, £2,300; cataloguing staff, £2,800; printing catalogue, £1,000; binding, £1,000; incidentals, £100.

55. Acton to W. E. Gladstone, 7 May 1890, BL 44094/80.

56. W. E. Gladstone to Acton, 10 May 1890, CUL Add. 8119/9/70.

57. Andrew Carnegie to W. E. Gladstone, 12 June 1890, BL 44510/89.

58. W. E. Gladstone to Acton, 13 June 1890, CUL Add. 8119/9.

59. Various papers, CUL Add. 7732/2.

60. See H. R. Tedder, "Lord Acton as a Book Collector," *Proceedings of the British Academy* 1 (1903–4): 285–88.

61. Acton, note, CUL Add. 5696/12.

62. William Dawes Freshfield to W. E. Gladstone, 9 July 1890, BL 44510/157: "You may imagine, it is somewhat difficult both to arrange that Lord Acton shall have the use of the Library to the fullest extent and still to make it safe from future creditors. . . . Of course, Mr. Carnegie must rely to a very large extent upon Lord Acton doing no act which shall jeopardise the Library in any way by making it liable to his creditors." Cf. Judy Slinn, *A History of Freshfields* (London, 1983), 125–26; also William Dawes Freshfield to Acton, 10 July 1890, CUL Add. 8119/I/F113.

63. William Dawes Freshfield to Acton, 10 July 1890, CUL Add. 8119/I/F113.

64. William Dawes Freshfield to Acton, 29 July 1890, CUL Add. 8119/I/F114.

65. William Dawes Freshfield to Acton, 28 August 1891, CUL Add. 4855/101; Mamy Acton, "Notes Taken from Memory," 11, CUL Add. 8119/9/427.

66. Acton to Richard Acton, 28 November 1889, CUL Add. 8121/10/122.

67. Christie's auction on 8 July 1890, the picture sale on 20 June 1896, Christie's Archives, King Street, London SW1.

68. Henry R. Tedder, "The Athenaeum: A Centenary Record," *Times,* 16 February 1924. Henry R. Tedder was the club's secretary and also Acton's own one-time librarian at Aldenham.

69. Acton to Mary Gladstone, 14 December 1880, *Letters to Mary Gladstone,* 38.

70. Acton to Mary Gladstone, 2 April 1881, *Letters to Mary Gladstone,* 66–67.

71. Grant Duff, *Out of the Past,* 1:156–166.

72. On Acton's club activities see various mentions, especially in the later volumes, in Sir Mountstuart Grant Duff, *Notes from a Diary, 1851–1901* (London, 1905), and *Out of the Past.*

Chapter 17: "Power Tends to Corrupt . . . "

1. Mandell Creighton to Acton, 9 December 1882, CUL Add. 6871/1–2; Acton, review of *A History of the Papacy during the Period of the Reformation,* by Mandell Creighton, vols. 1 and 2, *Academy* 22 (1882): 407–9.

2. Louise Creighton, *Life and Letters of Mandell Creighton* (London, 1904), 1:333–54.

3. Mandell Creighton to Dorothy Widdrington, 2 December 1884, quoted in Louise Creighton, *Life and Letters of Mandell Creighton,* 1:275.

4. Acton to Mary Gladstone, 9 December 1884, *Letters of Lord Acton to Mary, Daughter of the Right Hon. W. E. Gladstone,* ed. Herbert Paul, 2d rev. ed. (London, 1913), 156–57.

5. Heinrich von Sybel (1817–95), German historian and founder of the *Historische Zeitschrift* in 1859.

6. Acton to Mandell Creighton, 19 January 1886, CUL Add. 6871/35.

7. Ibid., 35–36.

8. Acton to Mandell Creighton, 18 April 1886, CUL Add. 6871/39.

9. Mandell Creighton to Acton, 23 December 1885, CUL Add. 8119/I/C250.

10. Adolf von Harnack to Acton, 20 January 1886, CUL Add. 8120/I/308.

11. Acton to Mandell Creighton, 19 January 1886, CUL Add. 6871/37.

12. Mandell Creighton to Acton, 24 January 1887, CUL Add. 8119/I/C255.

13. Ibid.

14. Mandell Creighton to Reginald Lane Poole, 29 March 1887, quoted in Louise Creighton, *Life and Letters of Mandell Creighton,* 1:369.

15. Döllinger to Acton, 25 April 1887, *Briefwechsel,* 3:368 [German].

16. Acton, review of *A History of the Papacy during the Period of the Reformation,* by Mandell Creighton, vols. 3 and 4, *English Historical Review* 2 (1877): 571–81, reprinted in *Historical Essays and Studies,* ed. John Neville Figgis and Reginald Vere Laurence (London, 1907), 426–41, and in *Selected Writings of Lord Acton,* ed. J. Rufus Fears (Indianapolis, 1984–88), 2:365–77, from which the following quotations are taken.

17. Mandell Creighton to Reginald Lane Poole, 29 March 1887, quoted in Louise Creighton, *Life and Letters of Mandell Creighton,* 1:370.

18. Acton to Mandell Creighton, 29 March 1887, CUL Add. 6871/51.

19. Acton to Mandell Creighton, 5 April 1887, CUL Add. 6871/53–62. The following quotations are also from this letter. The famous passage was first published in *Historical Essays and Studies,* 504, reprinted in *Selected Writings,* 2:383–84. The Acton-Creighton correspondence has been reprinted in its entirety in *Selected Writings,* 2:378–91.

20. Mandell Creighton to Acton, April 1887, CUL Add. 6871/65–71.

21. Acton to Döllinger, 16 June 1882, *Briefwechsel,* 3:289.

22. Herbert Butterfield, *History and Human Relations* (London, 1951), 119.

23. Ibid., 117. Acton's "canons" have been reprinted in *Selected Writings,* 2:386–88.

24. Herbert Butterfield, *Lord Acton* (London, 1948), 9.

25. Acton, review of *Life of George Eliot,* by J. W. Cross, *Nineteenth Century* 17 (March 1885): 464–85, reprinted as "George Eliot's Life" in Acton, *Historical Essays and Studies,* 273–304, and in *Selected Writings,* 3:460–85.

26. Acton to Mary Gladstone, 27 December 1880, *Letters to Mary Gladstone,* 43–44.

27. Acton, note, CUL Add. 5019/180, 342.

28. Acton to Döllinger, n.d. [end of May/beginning of June 1885], *Briefwechsel,* 3:348 [German].

29. Acton, note, CUL Add. 5019/575.

30. Acton to Döllinger, n.d. [end of May/beginning of June 1885], *Briefwechsel,* 3:349 [German].

31. Ibid., 3:347 [German].

32. Acton to Lady Blennerhassett, 9 July 1885, *Selections from the Correspondence of the First Lord Acton,* ed. John Neville Figgis and Reginald Vere Laurence (London, 1917), 289.

33. Ibid., 291–92.

34. Acton to Mary Gladstone, 14 December 1880, *Letters to Mary Gladstone,* 33.

35. Mary Gladstone, diary, 18 May 1877, 28 March and 8 April 1878, *Mary Gladstone (Mrs. Drew): Her Diaries and Letters,* ed. Lucy Masterman (London, 1930), 124, 134–35, 136–37.

36. Acton, various notes, CUL Add. 5019. Acton's notes on George Eliot (CUL Add. 5019–21, 5627–28) indicate how much reflection he devoted to her life and work. Although he shunned the approach of her literary critics, modern Eliot scholars have found Acton's insights, which were greatly condensed and only partly made use of in his essay published in the *Nineteenth Century,* invaluable. See, e.g., Gordon S. Haight, *George Eliot: A Biography* (Oxford, 1968).

37. John Walter Cross to Acton, 12 May 1883, 26 April 1884, and 3 March 1895, CUL Add. 8119/I/C293, C299, C314.

38. Acton, notes, CUL Add. 5019/1273, 1404, 1419, 1421, 1486.

Chapter 18: Döllinger's Death

1. The photograph was first published in *Letters of Lord Acton to Mary, Daughter of the Right Hon. W. E. Gladstone,* ed. Herbert Paul, 2d rev. ed. (London, 1913), facing 1.

2. Mary Gladstone, diary, 16–17 September 1879, *Mary Gladstone (Mrs. Drew): Her Diaries and Letters,* ed. Lucy Masterman (London, 1930), 166.

3. Acton to Mary Gladstone, 31 October 1879, *Letters to Mary Gladstone,* 2.

4. Mary Gladstone, diary, 18–25 September 1879, *Mary Gladstone, Her Diaries and Letters,* 166–68.

5. Mary Gladstone, diary, 7–8 October 1879, *Mary Gladstone, Her Diaries and Letters,* 172–73.

6. Acton to Mary Gladstone, 1 July 1880, *Letters to Mary Gladstone,* 18.

7. Acton to Mary Gladstone, 15 October 1881, *Letters to Mary Gladstone,* 83.

8. Mary Gladstone to Acton, 20 June 1880, CUL Add. 8119/9/118.

9. Mary Gladstone to Acton, 10 January 1882, CUL Add. 8119/9/171/1.

10. Acton to Mary Gladstone, 25 February 1882, *Letters to Mary Gladstone,* 99.

11. Mary Gladstone to Acton, January 1884, CUL Add. 8119/9/208/1.

12. See Acton to Mary Gladstone, 9 February 1884, *Letters to Mary Gladstone.* This passage, on 140, was omitted in the published edition but is quoted from the original in Owen Chadwick, *Acton and Gladstone* (London, 1976), 23.

13. Mary Gladstone to Acton, 30 September 1880, CUL Add. 8119/9/128, in answer to his letter of 27 September 1880, *Letters to Mary Gladstone,* 28–31.

14. Mary Gladstone to Acton, n.d. [26 June 1880], CUL Add. 8119/9/119.

15. Acton to Annie Acton, n.d. [12 June 1888], CUL Add. 8121/9/13.

16. Acton to Mamy Acton, 31 October 1892, CUL Add. 7956/90.

17. John Morley, *The Life of William Ewart Gladstone* (London, 1903), 3:103.

18. Mary Gladstone to Acton, 7 October 1881, CUL Add. 8119, box 9.

19. Mary Gladstone Drew to Mrs. Lavinia Talbot [née Lyttleton], n.d., *Mary Gladstone, Her Diaries and Letters,* 48.

20. Mary Gladstone, diary, 12 January 1878, *Mary Gladstone, Her Diaries and Letters,* 129.

21. Mary Gladstone to Lavinia Lyttleton, n.d. [1879], *Mary Gladstone, Her Diaries and Letters,* 144.

22. This is part of the Acton family's oral recollections, for which I am indebted to the late Hon. Mia Woodruff, Lord Acton's granddaughter. She knew Mary Drew (née Gladstone) and remembered a tea party at Aldenham when the old lady bit into a sandwich with her very own false teeth, then replaced it on the platter, exclaiming, "I don't like that!" But her off-putting habits were more than made up for by the great kindness and thoughtfulness which she showed Acton's granddaughter after the death of her parents. The Gladstones evidently inhabited a world of ideas,

where material things were of little importance. At Tegernsee the British prime minister once had spilled thick brown soup down his starched dress shirt front on the first day of his visit, and appeared again with the brown stains at four consecutive dinners. At the Gladstones' residence at Hawarden, Acton also recalled that hosts and guests, after arrival from long journeys, used to be sustained by hot soup kept in stoneware hot-water bottles normally used as warming pans for cold beds. And the irreverent Acton children held much in awe the air-cushion filled with the "Grand Old Man's" sacred breath, which, however, they had seen one of the servants blow up in the morning.

23. Mary Gladstone, diary, 9 January 1881, *Mary Gladstone, Her Diaries and Letters*, 214.

24. Mary Gladstone, diary, 31 December 1881, *Mary Gladstone, Her Diaries and Letters*, 237–38. "Hod men" was a term contemptuously applied to literary hacks.

25. Mary Gladstone, diary, 2 January 1882, BL Add. 46259/118.

26. John Morley, *Recollections* (London, 1917), 1:230.

27. Acton to Mary Gladstone, 3 October 1880, BL Add. 46240/42–43, this part omitted from *Letters to Mary Gladstone*, 31.

28. Acton to Mary Gladstone, 19 June 1884, BL Add. 46239/202–203, also in *Letters to Mary Gladstone*, 149.

29. Mary Gladstone Drew to Acton, 21 July [1898], CUL Add. 8119/9/305, quoting a phrase Acton had used in Acton to Mary Gladstone, 8 August 1880, *Letters to Mary Gladstone*, 24.

30. Acton to Mary Gladstone Drew, 25 October 1898, BL Add. 46239/333–334.

31. Acton to Mary Gladstone Drew, 29 November 1898, BL Add. 46239/335.

32. Chadwick, *Acton and Gladstone*, 50–55. The Criminal Law Amendment Act of 1885 raised the age of consent to thirteen.

33. Acton recorded this important episode in August 1886 in a note, CUL Add. 4914/38. He also mentioned it in his letter to Gladstone, 22 March 1891, *Selections from the Correspondence of the First Lord Acton*, ed. John Neville Figgis and Reginald Vere Laurence (London, 1917), 70: "It was when you were at Tegernsee last, on the day after your expedition. He had had a seizure, and he came into my room, and spoke some very solemn words which I have never repeated." In an earlier letter to Gladstone, written from Rome on 18 January 1890, shortly before Döllinger's death, Acton mentioned the incident as the only time that he succeeded in making Döllinger understand what he meant, but later realized that Döllinger had not really agreed with him. BL 44094/72–73.

34. C. de Warmont [Lady Blennerhassett], "Félix-Antoine Dupanloup, Bishop of Orleans," *Nineteenth Century* 5 (February 1879): 219–46.

35. Döllinger to Acton, 19 January 1879, *Briefwechsel*, 3:209 [German].

36. Döllinger to Acton, 7 May 1886, *Briefwechsel*, 3:355 [German].

37. Acton to Lady Blennerhassett, 17 February 1879, CUL Add. 8120/2 [French].

38. Acton to Döllinger, n.d. [1881/1882], *Briefwechsel,* 3:262–63 [German]. Abraham Kuenen (1821–1891) was a Dutch Protestant theologian and biblical scholar; he lectured in England in 1882.

39. Lady Blennerhassett in a personal memoir recorded these meetings, realising their importance for Döllinger and Acton, 23 February 1879, CUL Add. 8120/2.

40. Acton to Cardinal Henry Edward Manning, 18 November 1874, *Selections from the Correspondence,* 153.

41. Acton's second letter to the *Times,* dated 21 November 1874, reprinted in *Lord Acton: The Decisive Decade, 1864–1874: Essays and Documents,* ed. Damian McElrath, James Holland, Ward White, and Sue Katzman (Louvain, Belgium, 1970), 249, in *Selections from the Correspondence,* 125, and in *Selected Writings of Lord Acton,* ed. J. Rufus Fears (Indianapolis, 1984–88), 3:368.

42. Acton to Döllinger, n.d. [1879/1880], *Briefwechsel,* 3:212 [German].

43. Döllinger to Acton, 11 January 1881, *Briefwechsel,* 3:223 [German, English].

44. Acton to Döllinger, n.d. [1881/1882], *Briefwechsel,* 3:258–60 [German].

45. Ibid., 3:260–61 [German].

46. Acton to Döllinger, n.d. [end of September 1882], *Briefwechsel,* 3:315–16.

47. Acton to Döllinger, n.d. [middle of September 1882], *Briefwechsel,* 3:303 [German].

48. Döllinger to Acton, 21 September 1882, *Briefwechsel,* 3:305–6 [German].

49. Acton to Döllinger, 22 September 1882, *Briefwechsel,* 3:307.

50. Döllinger to Acton, 27 September 1882, *Briefwechsel,* 3:308, 312 [German, English].

51. Acton to Döllinger, n.d. [end of September 1882], *Briefwechsel,* 3:315.

52. Acton to Döllinger, 16 June 1882, *Briefwechsel,* 3:291.

53. Acton, note, CUL Add. 5403/25.

54. Acton, note, CUL Add. 5403/29. François Ravaillac (1587–1610), expelled from the monastery, murdered Henry IV, instigated by pamphlets recommending tyrannicide. See also Acton to Lady Blennerhassett, CUL Add. 5403, published in part in *Selections from the Correspondence,* 53–57, but dated incorrectly.

55. Acton, note, CUL Add. 5403/20, 21. Himmelfarb has published the draft of this letter to Lady Blennerhassett in her *Lord Acton: A Study in Conscience and Politics* (London, 1952), in what appears the correct order of notes, 150–55. In the Cambridge papers there are notes on cards included in a file labelled "D. Table Talk" and numbered, probably by a Cambridge University librarian. The proper order should be 29, 26, 25, 24, 21, 20, 10. The letter retaining the wrong date of "February 1879" from *Selections from the Correspondence,* 53–57, has been reprinted in *Selected Writings,* 3:657–59.

56. Acton to Döllinger, 28 March 1889, *Briefwechsel,* 3:400 [German].

57. Döllinger to Acton, 6 April 1889, *Briefwechsel,* 3:403 [German].

58. Acton to Döllinger, 28 March 1889, *Briefwechsel,* 3:402 [German]. Edmond Henri

Adolphe Scherer (1805–1889) was a French Protestant theologian who, after teaching at Geneva, lived in Paris and became a Hegelian and an agnostic.

59. Döllinger to Acton, 6 April 1889, *Briefwechsel*, 3:404 [German].

60. Acton to Gladstone, 12 October 1889, BL 44094/65–66.

61. Acton to Mamy Acton, 11 January 1890, CUL Add. 7956/40.

62. Acton to Jeanette Döllinger, Rome, 11 January 1890, CUL Add. 8121/6/636 [French].

63. Acton to Annie Acton, 15 January 1890, CUL Add. 8121/9/18/1–2.

64. Acton to W. E. Gladstone, 17 January 1890, CUL Add. 8119/9/104.

65. Acton to Mamy Acton, 27 January 1890, CUL Add. 7956/45.

66. W. E. Gladstone to Acton, 13 January 1890, Shropshire County Council Record Office, 1093/812. Sir Thomas Wemyss Reid (1842–1905) was a prominent Liberal author. The *Speaker* was founded in London in 1890 to support the extreme radical wing of the Liberal Party; it was later absorbed by the political weekly *New Statesman and Nation*.

67. W. E. Gladstone's tributes are: "The Right Rev. Dr. Von Döllinger," *Speaker*, 18 January 1890, 57–60, and "Dr. Döllinger's Posthumous Remains," *Speaker*, 30 August 1890, 231–33. These articles were republished in W. E. Gladstone, *The Impregnable Rock of Holy Scripture* (London, 1890).

68. W. E. Gladstone to Acton, 26 March 1891, *Selections from the Correspondence*, 71. See also Acton's letters from Munich to W. E. Gladstone, 1 and 9 February 1892, relating to Gladstone's cheque of £20 towards a Döllinger memorial. *Selections from the Correspondence*, 74, 75. What was then a substantial contribution was handed by Acton to Professor Hermann von Sicherer, late Rector of Munich University and chairman of the Committee of Old Catholics organising the Döllinger monument. The Döllinger portrait mentioned by W. E. Gladstone in his letter to Acton (4 March 1890, *Selections from the Correspondence*, 241) remained in possession of the Gladstone family and hangs at St. Deiniol's Library, Hawarden, which preserves the Glynne-Gladstone Papers.

69. Henry Cadogan to Lady Blennerhassett, 12 January 1890, Blennerhassett Papers, CUL Add. 7486. Victor Conzemius published this and other letters collected by Lady Blennerhassett in "Der Tod Ignaz von Döllingers in den Briefen der Freunde," *Kurtrierisches Jahrbuch* 8 (1968): 300–316, quotation on 301.

70. Franz Xavier Kraus to Charlotte Blennerhassett, 12 January 1890, in Conzemius, "Der Tod Döllingers," 303–4. The diary quotation is from Franz Xavier Kraus, *Tagebücher*, ed. H. Schiel (Cologne, 1957), 562. Kraus (1840–1901), one of the most eminent German Catholic nineteenth-century scholars, was professor of Christian archaeology and history of art at Strasbourg (from 1872) and professor of Church history at Freiburg im Breisgau (from 1878). As a liberal Catholic he was opposed to the trend towards extreme Ultramontanism and centralization in the Church

and fought for the conciliation of Church and State and contemporary culture. See Josef Höfer and Karl Rahner, eds., *Lexikon für Theologie und Kirche*, 2d rev. ed. (Freiburg, Germany, 1957–65), 6:596.

71. Quoted in Conzemius's introduction to *Briefwechsel*, 4:xix.

72. Charlotte Blennerhassett, *Frau von Staël, ihre Freunde und ihre Bedeutung in Politik und Literatur*, 3 vols. (Berlin, 1887–89). Other biographical studies followed: *Talleyrand* (1894), *Gabriele D'Annunzio* (1901), *Chateaubriand* (1903), *John Henry Newman* (1904), *Joan of Arc* (1906), *Mary Queen of Scots* (1907). Lady Blennerhassett was a regular contributor to the *Spectator, Fortnightly Review,* and *Nineteenth Century*. Two of her essays, commissioned by Lord Acton, were published in the *Cambridge Modern History,* and she was among the first writers for the renowned *Hochland,* the German Catholic journal founded by Karl Muth in 1903. As a British citizen, she was cut off in Munich from her children by the outbreak of World War I, her husband having died in his last position as president of Queen's College, Cork, in 1909. Charlotte Lady Blennerhassett died, aged seventy-four, on 11 February 1917, in Munich. In her last will, she requested a simple burial, that the artery of her right hand be severed before she was laid in her coffin, and that three Masses be said for her. "In the name of the Father, the Son and the Holy Spirit, I die in the faith of the Holy Catholic Church whose means of grace have accompanied me throughout my life and all its trials." After a number of bequests she concluded with what she described as her mother's favourite principle, taken from St. Augustine's Confessions and surely summing up her own life's meaning: "Thou hast created us for Thyself and our heart is restless until it rests in Thee." *Briefwechsel,* 4:721–23. The introduction to this volume (ix–xxxii) contains a sensitive account by Victor Conzemius of Lady Charlotte Blennerhassett's life and work, and there is a full bibliography (xxxiii–xlv). No biography of Lady Blennerhassett exists apart from an unpublished dissertation by Edith Schuhmann, "Charlotte Lady Blennerhassett als Historikerin und Essayistin" (subtitled "A Contribution to the History of Ideas at the Turn of the Century"), University of Mainz, 1955 (214 pp.).

73. Charlotte Blennerhassett, "In Memoriam I. von Döllinger—28 Februar 1799—10 Januar 1890," *Deutsche Rundschau* 25 (1899): 459–63.

74. Quoted by Schuhmann, "Charlotte Blennerhassett," 36 n. 125.

75. The quoted passages in the preceding and this paragraph are from Charlotte Blennerhassett, "Das Viktorianische England," *Deutsche Rundschau* 157 (1913): 383–405; 158 (1914): 269–93; 159 (1914): 220–44; 160 (1914): 220–36; 161 (1914): 376–96.

76. Copy of a letter from Acton to Marie, n.d., CUL Add. 8121/6/550 [French].

77. Ibid.

78. Friedrich, *Ignaz von Döllinger* (Munich, 1899–1901), 3:708–11 and endnotes 5, 6, and 7.

79. Acton to Jeanette Döllinger, Rome, 1 February 1890, CUL Add. 8121/6/637 [French].

80. Acton to Döllinger, 16 June 1882, *Briefwechsel,* 3:287, reprinted in *Selected Writings,* 3:668. Johannes Nepomuk Huber (1830–1879) and Johann Friedrich were Döllinger's collaborators on Janus, *Der Papst und das Concil* (Leipzig, Germany, 1869). Both joined the Old Catholics. Huber's *Die Philosophie der Kirchenväter* was put on the Index because of the author's rejection of scholasticism and "Jesuitism." He refused to submit to Rome and died unreconciled with the Catholic Church.

81. Acton to Gladstone, 28 October 1891, BL 44094/183. See also Acton to Gladstone, 1 December 1891, BL Add. 44094/185.

82. Acton, "Döllinger's Historical Work," in *The History of Freedom and Other Essays,* ed. John Neville Figgis and Reginald Vere Laurence (London, 1907), and in *Selected Writings,* 2:412–61. Apart from this article there are the Acton-Döllinger correspondence, edited by Dr. Victor Conzemius in three volumes, and forty-three boxes crammed with notes by Acton in the Cambridge University Library, material for a many-volume biography, the fruits of Acton's lifelong preoccupation with his teacher.

83. Acton to Gladstone, telegram, 1 April 1891, BL 44094/162.

84. Acton to Gladstone, 20 April 1891, BL 44094/163–164, published in *Selections from the Correspondence,* 205.

85. Mamy Acton, "Notes Taken from Memory," 25, CUL Add. 8119/9/427; also Walpurga Paget, *The Linings of Life* (London, 1928), 56.

86. Acton to Thomas Wetherell, 2 April 1871, CUL Add. 8119/8/471.

Chapter 19: Gladstone's Friend and the Queen's Lord

1. Lady Frederick Cavendish was the daughter of Catherine Gladstone's only sister, Mary, who married Gladstone's close friend, Lord George Lyttleton. The sisters were practically inseparable until Mary's death in 1857. Lucy soon became the person closest to Catherine—and to William Gladstone. See Joyce Marlow, *The Oak and the Ivy* (New York, 1977), 94–95. Her marriage, marked by extraordinary mutual devotion, brought Lady Cavendish into the circle of Lord Hartington (later eighth Duke of Devonshire), who ranked next to Gladstone in the Liberal Party leadership. Despite family ties, Lady Cavendish did not always agree with the Gladstones when tensions arose between Gladstone and Hartington.

2. Acton to Mary Gladstone, 8 and 9 May 1882, telegram and letter, *Letters of Lord Acton to Mary, Daughter of the Right Hon. W. E. Gladstone,* ed. Herbert Paul, 2d rev. ed. (London, 1913), 124–25.

3. Acton to W. E. Gladstone, 2 February 1885, quoted in John Morley, *The Life of William Ewart Gladstone* (London, 1903), 3:172. These three events—the assassi-

nation in Phoenix Park in May 1882, the assassination by the Mahdi's followers of the popular General Charles Gordon at Khartoum, and the arrival of the scouts of the relief expedition only to find that the city had fallen and that its heroic defender was slain (1884–85)—combined to deal the death blow to Gladstone's second administration. Gladstone suffered from his handling of the repercussions of Gordon's death, which was a deep shock to the British public when the news finally reached it. Gladstone's great majority in the 1880 election vote was spirited away in the February election of 1885, when he was deserted by members of the Irish Party, who for the first time allied themselves with the Conservatives, and by six Liberals, with another seventy of them, mainly Radicals, abstaining.

4. Acton to Mary Gladstone, 1 January 1886, *Letters to Mary Gladstone,* 172.

5. W. E. Gladstone, who had the habit of meticulously recording daily what he did, whom he wrote to, and what he read, noted, apart from Dante and religious and philosophical books, the following contemporary works: G. V. E. Augier, *Les effrontés, Comédie en cinq acts* (1861); V. Sardou, *Daniel Rochat* (1880); G. V. E. Augier, *Fils du Giboyer* (1861); E. Pailleron, *Le monde où on s'ennuye* (1881); A. Dumas fils, *Ami des femmes* (1864); George Sand, *La marc au diable* (1864); A. Daudet, *Lettres du mon moulin* (1869); O. Feuillet, *Le roman d'un jeune homme pauvre* (1858). See W. E. Gladstone, diary, 31 August–13 September 1886, *The Gladstone Diaries,* ed. M. R. D. Foot and H. C. G. Matthew (London, 1968–94), 11:608–12.

6. Acton to John Morley, 7 September 1886, quoted in Morley, *Life of Gladstone,* 3:351.

7. W. E. Gladstone, diary, 6 September 1886, *Gladstone Diaries,* 11:608–12. The Gladstones stayed at Tegernsee beginning on 27 August, then went on to St. Martin, the Arco castle in Austria, and began their return journey to England on 17 September 1886, after: "Walk in the woods. Olympian conversation with Acton. Farewell to this most kind house."

8. W. E. Gladstone to Acton, 13 January 1887, 1 and 8 April 1888, and 13 May 1888, quoted in Morley, *Life of Gladstone,* 3:356–60.

9. Acton to Mary Gladstone Drew, 7 December 1890, *Letters to Mary Gladstone,* 189–90.

10. Acton to W. E. Gladstone, 22 March 1891, *Selections from the Correspondence of the First Lord Acton,* ed. John Neville Figgis and Reginald Vere Laurence (London, 1917), 70.

11. Acton to James Bryce, 20 May 1892, Bryce Papers, Bodleian Library, 1/58.

12. Extract by Lord Acton of a letter from Helen Gladstone to Mary Gladstone Drew, Dalmeny, 11 July 1892, CUL Add. 8121/9/376. Sir Algernon West, a former chairman of the Inland Revenue Board, had lately come back to serve his old chief unofficially as secretary and companion.

13. Ibid.

14. Quoted in Owen Chadwick, *Acton and Gladstone* (London, 1976), 33.

15. Acton to Lord Rosebery, 18 July 1892, National Library of Scotland, 10090ff. 100–1; this letter is fully quoted in Chadwick, *Acton and Gladstone,* 36; a draft is in the Acton Papers, CUL Add. 4863/62–65.

16. Rosebery to Acton, 29 July 1892, quoted in Chadwick, *Acton and Gladstone,* 36; Rosebery to Gladstone, 31 July 1892, BL 44289/157–59.

17. Acton to James Bryce, 23 June 1892, Bryce Papers, Bodleian Library, 1/68.

18. Acton to Richard Acton, 1 August 1892, CUL Add. 8121/10/155.

19. Acton to Richard Acton, 23 August 1892, CUL Add. 8121/10/156.

20. Chadwick, *Acton and Gladstone,* 38.

21. Acton to Richard Acton, 23 August 1892, CUL Add. 8121/10/156.

22. Acton to Mamy Acton, 26 July 1892, CUL Add. 7956/75.

23. W. E. Gladstone to John Morley, 17 July 1892, BL Add. 44256/215.

24. Sir William Harcourt, diary, 27 July 1892, Bodleian Library, quoted in Chadwick, *Acton and Gladstone,* 39.

25. Algernon West, diary, n.d., *The Private Diaries of the Rt. Hon. Sir Algernon West,* ed. Horace G. Hutchinson (London, 1922), 38.

26. Acton to W. E. Gladstone, 23 August 1892, BL Add. 44094/205.

27. Acton to Annie Acton, October 1892, CUL Add. 8121/9/40.

28. Chadwick has published the full version of this passage, of which Herbert Paul printed only the first sentence. Acton to Mary Gladstone Drew, 31 March 1886, in Chadwick, *Acton and Gladstone,* 41, and in part in *Letters to Mary Gladstone,* 176.

29. Acton to Mamy Acton, 16 February 1893 and 3 November 1892, CUL Add. 7956/104, 91.

30. Chadwick, *Acton and Gladstone,* 41.

31. Acton to Mary Gladstone Drew, 8 October 1887, *Letters to Mary Gladstone,* 179.

32. Acton reported this incident to his son as characterising Morley. Acton to Richard Acton, 5 March 1893, CUL Add. 8121/10/168.

33. West, diary, n.d., *Private Diaries,* 40.

34. Acton to Mary Gladstone Drew, 11 August 1892, quoted in Chadwick, *Acton and Gladstone,* 43.

35. Acton to Annie Acton, 21 August 1892, CUL Add. 8121/9/36.

36. Queen Victoria to the Prince of Wales, 13 August 1892, *The Letters of Queen Victoria,* 3d ser., 1886–1901, ed. G. E. Buckle (London, 1930), 2:143.

37. Lord Newton, *Life of Lord Lansdowne* (London, 1929), 100. The fifth Marquess of Lansdowne (1845–1929) was one of the Liberal members of the government who had broken with Gladstone over Home Rule.

38. *Times,* 15 August 1892.

39. Lord Newton, *Life of Lord Lansdowne,* 100.

40. Acton to Annie Acton, 21 February 1893, CUL Add. 8121/9/59.

41. Queen Victoria, journal, 15 August 1892, in *Letters of Queen Victoria,* 3d ser., 2:145–46.

42. Acton to W. E. Gladstone, 23 August 1892, BL Add. 44094/205.

43. Sir Henry Ponsonby to Queen Victoria, 25 August 1892, Royal Archives, Windsor, C 39/138; this letter informs the Queen of the change in Acton's employment.

44. Empress Frederick (Victoria) to Queen Victoria, 20 August 1892, Royal Archives, Windsor, Z53/26.

45. W. E. Gladstone to Sir Henry Ponsonby, 25 August 1892, Royal Archives, Windsor, 39/138.

46. W. E. Gladstone to Acton, 24 August 1892, CUL Add. 8119/9/83.

47. Mary Gladstone Drew to Acton, 1 December 1892, CUL Add. 8119/9/281.

48. Acton to Annie Acton, 9 October 1892, CUL Add. 8121/9/40.

49. Acton to Annie Acton, 14 October 1892, CUL Add. 8121/9/41.

50. Queen Victoria, journal, 30 November 1892, Royal Archives, Windsor, 39/138.

51. Acton to James Bryce, 5 December 1892, Bryce Papers, Bodleian Library, 1/73.

52. Acton to Annie Acton, 28 October 1892, CUL Add. 8121/9/41.

53. Queen Victoria, journal, 8 December 1892, 1 December 1893, Royal Archives, Windsor, 39/138.

54. Acton to James Bryce, 5 and 11 December 1892, Bryce Papers, Bodleian Library, 1/74, 76.

55. Acton to Annie Acton, 11–12 December 1892, CUL Add. 8121/9/54/1.

56. Acton to Mamy Acton, 12 October 1892, CUL Add. 7956/75.

57. Acton to Mary Gladstone, 21 June 1880, *Letters to Mary Gladstone,* 16–17.

58. Acton to Mary Gladstone, 27 December 1880, *Letters to Mary Gladstone,* 42.

59. Acton to Mamy Acton, n.d. [7 October 1892], CUL Add. 7956/84.

60. W. E. Gladstone to Acton, n.d. [7 October 1892], BL Add. 44094/212–213.

61. Acton to W. E. Gladstone, 18 October 1892, BL Add. 44094/221–222.

62. Ibid.

63. Acton to W. E. Gladstone, 8 and 9 October 1892, BL Add. 44094/221–22 and 216.

64. Acton to Annie Acton, 9 October 1892, CUL Add. 8121/9/40.

65. The quotation is from Acton to Annie Acton, 29 October 1892, CUL Add. 8121/9/45.

66. William Morris quoted by James Bryce in Alan Bell, "Gladstone Looks for a Poet Laureate," *Times Literary Supplement,* 21 July 1972, 847.

67. Bell, "Gladstone Looks for a Poet Laureate."

68. Acton to W. E. Gladstone, 9 October 1892, BL Add. 44094/216.

69. Bell, "Gladstone Looks for a Poet Laureate."

70. The letter was published in the *London Standard,* 14 March 1870, reprinted in *Letters and Diaries of John Henry Newman,* ed. C. S. Dessain et al. (Oxford, 1961–84), 25:18–20, quotation on 19.

71. Acton to Annie Acton, 22 March 1893, CUL Add. 8121/9/63.

72. Acton to Annie Acton, 28 July 1893, CUL Add. 8121/9/66, also 23 July 1893, 8121/9/67.

73. Acton to Mamy Acton, 29 July 1893, CUL Add. 7956/114.

74. Acton to Annie Acton, 28 July 1893, CUL Add. 8121/9/66.

75. Acton to Mamy Acton, 18 August 1893, CUL Add. 7956/116.

76. Acton to Annie Acton, 13 November 1892, CUL Add. 8121/9/48.

77. Morley, *Life of Gladstone*, 3:296 n. 1.

78. Acton to Mamy Acton, 14 November 1898, CUL Add. 7956/224.

79. Mary Gladstone Drew to Sir Mountstuart Grant Duff, 13 August 1902, CUL Add. 8119/8/543.

80. Chadwick argues: "If Acton advised that something should happen, and then the something happened, Acton assumed that it happened because he advised. Other sources show that it often happened by more compelling reasons. We shall not be far wrong if we think of him more as the intangible aura of a wind and spirit than the definable stimulus of a statesman who understands how votes are caught and policy executed." Chadwick, *Acton and Gladstone*, 31.

81. Acton to Mamy Acton, 25 October 1892, CUL Add. 7956/88.

82. Acton to Richard Acton, n.d. [24 October 1892], CUL Add. 8121/10/157.

83. Acton to Annie Acton, 14 March 1893, CUL Add. 8121/9/62.

84. Acton to Annie Acton, 22 March 1893, CUL Add. 8121/9/63.

85. Acton to Annie Acton, 28 July 1893, CUL Add. 8121/9/66.

86. Acton to W. E. Gladstone, 10 December 1893, BL Add. 44094/242–43, printed only with the omission of the last sentence in *Selections from the Correspondence,* 172.

87. Acton to W. E. Gladstone, 31 May 1880, *Selections from the Correspondence,* 171.

88. Lord Granville to W. E. Gladstone, 26 August 1884, *The Political Correspondence of Mr. Gladstone and Lord Granville, 1876–1886,* ed. Agatha Ramm (London, 1962), 2:236.

89. Sir Henry Ponsonby to Horace Seymour, 7 September 1884, Royal Archives, Windsor, Vic. Add., A/12, 2225.

90. Acton to Mamy Acton, 15 June 1888, CUL Add. 7956/19.

91. Acton to W. E. Gladstone, 12 October 1892, BL Add. 44094/218–19.

92. Alan Bell, "Lord Acton Gets His Chair," *Times Literary Supplement,* 8 February 1974, 137, quoting from the Rosebery Papers in the National Library of Scotland.

93. Acton to Annie Acton, 14 July 1893, CUL Add. 8121/9/65.

94. Lord Kimberley to Gladstone, 10 May 1894, BL Add. 44229/222.

95. Quoted in Alan Bell, "Lord Acton Gets His Chair."

96. Acton to W. E. Gladstone, 31 January 1894, BL Add. 44094/249–252.

97. Mary Gladstone Drew to Gladstone, 25 January 1894, St. Deiniol's Archives, C3.

98. Acton to James Bryce, 7 February 1894, Bryce Papers, Bodleian Library, 1/83.

99. Acton to Annie Acton, 22 January 1894, CUL Add. 8121/9/78.

100. Fifth Earl of Rosebery, "Mr. Gladstone's Last Cabinet," *History Today* (January 1952): 17.

101. Gladstone's letter of resignation, published in Morley, *Life of Gladstone,* 3:514–15.

102. Acton to Annie Acton, 3/4 March 1894, CUL Add. 8121/9/82/1.

103. Morley, *Life of Gladstone,* 3:512.

104. Acton to Annie Acton, 3/4 March 1894, CUL Add. 8121/9/82/1.

105. Acton to Annie Acton, Athenaeum, 14 March 1894, CUL Add. 8121/9/833/4.

106. Acton to Annie Acton, 3/4 March 1894, CUL Add. 8121/9/82/1–2.

107. Ibid.

108. Quoted in West, diary, 4 March 1894, *Private Diaries,* 289.

109. Acton to Annie Acton, 3/4 March 1894, CUL Add. 8121/9/82/2.

110. Acton to Annie Acton, 14 March 1894, CUL Add. 8121/9/84.

111. Acton to Annie Acton, 16 March 1894, CUL Add. 8121/9/85.

112. Acton to Annie Acton, 18 April 1894, CUL Add. 8121/9/87.

113. Acton to Annie Acton, 8 May 1894, CUL Add. 8121/9/88.

114. Acton to Annie Acton, 16 March 1894, CUL Add. 8121/9/85.

115. Acton to Mamy Acton, 24 June 1895, CUL Add. 7956/163.

116. Ibid.

117. Ibid.

118. Helen Gladstone to Acton, 10 December 1897, CUL Add. 8119/9/399.

119. Acton to Annie Acton, 19 May 1898, CUL Add. 8121/9/141/1. See also Acton to Annie Acton, 12 January 1898, CUL Add. 8121/9/140.

120. Herbert Gladstone to Acton, 17 May 1898, CUL Add. 8119/9/407.

121. Herbert Gladstone to Acton, telegram, 19 May 1898, CUL Add. 8121/9/141/2.

122. Acton to Annie Acton, 19 May 1898, CUL Add. 8121/9/141/1.

123. Acton to Mary Gladstone Drew, n.d., CUL Add. 8119/9/371.

124. Mary Gladstone, diary, 19 September 1879, *Mary Gladstone (Mrs. Drew): Her Diaries and Letters,* ed. Lucy Masterman (London, 1930), 166–67.

125. Acton to Mary Gladstone, 14 December 1880, *Letters to Mary Gladstone,* 34, 36.

126. Acton to Marie, dated "Hawarden Castle, Monday evening," CUL Add. 8121/7/1021 [German].

127. The preliminaries of the treaty of peace concluding the eleven-month war between Russia and Turkey were signed on 3 March 1878 at San Stefano, the Turkish resort near Istanbul. From the defeated Ottoman Empire arose Greater Bulgaria, an enlarged Serbia and Montenegro, but above all an increased Russian sphere of influence, which caused the concern of Great Britain and Austria. At the Congress of Berlin (13 June–13 July 1878) Disraeli's achievement was to modify the settlement of San Stefano and to curtail Russia's gains, which won him international praise expressed in Bismarck's famous words: "Der alte Jude, das ist der Mann" (The old Jew is indeed the man). See Robert Blake, *Disraeli* (London, 1966), 629–54.

128. Acton to Döllinger, 30 August 1882, *Briefwechsel,* 3:295–96 [German].

129. Acton to Döllinger, n.d. [middle of September 1882], *Briefwechsel,* 3:298–300 [German].
130. Ibid., 3:302–3.
131. Acton to Mamy Acton, 27 May 1898, CUL Add. 7956/212.
132. Acton to Mamy Acton, 31 May 1898, CUL Add. 7956/213.
133. Herbert Woodfield Paul (1853–1935) was to edit the controversial *Letters to Mary Gladstone,* the preface of which showed his appreciation of Acton as a fellow Liberal and Gladstonian, though not of Acton's religious ideas.
134. Acton to Mamy Acton, 31 May 1898, CUL Add. 7956/213.
135. Acton to Mary Gladstone Drew, 13 August 1898, *Letters to Mary Gladstone,* 201.
136. Acton to Herbert Gladstone, July 1898, CUL Add. 8119/9.
137. Acton to Mary Gladstone Drew, 13 August 1898, *Letters to Mary Gladstone,* 201.
138. Chadwick, *Acton and Gladstone,* 56.

Chapter 20: Regius Professor

1. Acton to Annie Acton, 20 May 1895, CUL Add. 8121/9/105.
2. Lady Harriet Phipps to Acton, 30 July 1895, CUL Add. 8119/I/P83.
3. Acton to Mamy Acton, 16 February 1895, CUL Add. 7956/154.
4. Quoted by G. N. Clark, "The Origin of the Cambridge Modern History," *Cambridge Historical Journal* 8 (1945): 57–64, quotation on 59 n. 5.
5. This and the following quotations are from the Rosebery Papers, National Library of Scotland, quoted in Alan Bell, "Lord Acton Gets His Chair," *Times Literary Supplement,* 8 February 1974.
6. H. A. L. Fisher, "Lord Acton's Lectures," *Independent Review* 11 (1906): 224–28.
7. Quoted in Alan Bell, "Lord Acton Gets His Chair." Owen Chadwick, in his centenary commemoration of Acton's appointment, succinctly gave the following reasons for it: "(1) S. R. Gardiner wanted to write his book; (2) Mandell Creighton had gone away to be a bishop; (3) Thomas Hodgkin had no desire to work in a university and wanted to finish his book; (4) the prime minister was liberal and so was Acton; (5) Acton needed paid work, not so easy for a peer in those days; (6) since an unlearned person inside the university [Oscar Browning] had certain claims even though he had earned some contempt, it was absolutely necessary to bring in a very learned person from outside the university; and (7) it was possible to appoint a Roman Catholic for the first time because the liberal governments had slowly opened public offices to members of every denomination; and this particular Roman Catholic was acceptable to Protestants because on his record he was thought to be not at all in favour of popes." Chadwick, *Professor Lord Acton: The Regius Chair of Modern History at Cambridge* (Grand Rapids, Mich., 1995), 7.
8. Sir George Murray to Acton, 13 February 1895, CUL Add. 8119/I/M 357.

9. Acton to James Bryce, 6 February 1895, Bryce Papers, Bodleian Library, 1/86.

10. James Bryce to Acton, 8 February 1895, CUL Add. 8119/I/B240.

11. Queen Victoria, journal, 18 February 1895, Royal Archives, Windsor, 39/138.

12. Quoted in Alan Bell, "Lord Acton Gets His Chair."

13. Queen Victoria, journal, 18 February 1895, Royal Archives, Windsor, 39/138.

14. Both quoted in Alan Bell, "Lord Acton Gets His Chair."

15. Ibid.

16. Acton to Annie Acton, 5 July 1894, CUL Add. 8121/9/96.

17. Acton to Oscar Browning, 18 February 1895, Oscar Browning Papers, King's College, Cambridge. In his centennial lecture on Acton's Cambridge appointment, Owen Chadwick described Oscar Browning as "the most inaccurate man ever to hold a Cambridge lectureship in history. The apocryphal story about him was that he wrote a book on Frederick the Great of Prussia and everybody was surprised to find him devoting so much military history to the conquest of Siberia; and that afterwards the book had an erratum slip: wherever Siberia comes please read Silesia." Chadwick, *Professor Lord Acton*, 4–5.

18. Acton to Mary Gladstone Drew, 2 July 1888, *Letters of Lord Acton to Mary, Daughter of the Right Hon. W. E. Gladstone,* ed. Herbert Paul, 2d rev. ed. (London, 1913), 186.

19. The second Lord Acton to Oscar Browning, 13 February 1913, Oscar Browning Papers, King's College, Cambridge.

20. Acton to Mamy Acton, 10 June 1888, CUL Add. 7956/16.

21. Oscar Browning to Acton, 4 March 1891, CUL Add. 8119/I/B163.

22. Acton to Oscar Browning, 6 March 1891, Oscar Browning Papers, King's College, Cambridge.

23. Acton to Annie Acton, 3 November 1891, CUL Add. 8121/9/28.

24. Acton to Mamy Acton, 19 February 1895, CUL Add. 7956/155.

25. Mandell Creighton to Acton, 21 February 1895, CUL Add. 8119/I/C282.

26. R. L. Poole to Acton, 19 February 1895, CUL Add. 8119/I/P129.

27. Helen Gladstone to Acton, 19 February 1895, CUL 8119/9/394.

28. John Robert Seeley, *Ecce Homo,* published anonymously, 1865. His *A Short History of Napoleon the First* (1885) was reviewed by Acton in the *English Historical Review,* vol. 2 (1887), reprinted in *Historical Essays and Studies,* ed. John Neville Figgis and Reginald Vere Laurence (London, 1907), 442–58, quotation on 450. Seeley's *Expansion of England* (London, 1883) became "the bible of British Imperialists," although he held no "unrestrained enthusiasm for empire." See G. P. Gooch, *History and Historians in the Nineteenth Century* (1913; 2d rev. ed., London, 1952), 347.

29. Acton to Gladstone, Munich, Easter Sunday, 1895, BL Add. 44094, 267–68.

30. Quoted in Gooch, *History and Historians in the Nineteenth Century,* 345.

31. Some points mentioned in Lord Acton, *The Cambridge Modern History,* the plan

as submitted to the Syndycs of the Cambridge University Press, published in 1969 in facsimile edition by the Cambridge University Press under the title *Longitude 30 West,* reprinted in *Selected Writings of Lord Acton,* ed. J. Rufus Fears (Indianapolis, 1984–88), 3:675–86.

32. Helen Gladstone to Acton, 26 February 1895, CUL Add. 8119/9/395.

33. Acton to Cardinal Herbert Vaughan, 30 April 1895, quoted in J. G. Snead-Cox, *The Life of Cardinal Vaughan* (London, 1910), 2:299.

34. Cardinal Herbert Vaughan to Acton, 27 February 1895, CUL Add. 8119/I/V4.

35. Acton to Cardinal Herbert Vaughan, 30 April 1895, quoted in Snead-Cox, *The Life of Cardinal Vaughan,* 2:229.

36. See David Mathew, *Catholicism in England* (1936; 3d ed., London, 1955), 219–20.

37. "The New Cathedral," *Tablet,* 6 July 1895, 50.

38. Cardinal Herbert Vaughan to Acton, 4 February 1894, Westminster Diocesan Archives, London.

39. Acton to Cardinal Herbert Vaughan, 10 February 1894, Westminster Diocesan Archives. Altogether some six letters were exchanged between Acton, Archbishop Thomas Stonor, and the Cardinal on this matter between 24 July 1893 and 10 February 1894.

40. Acton to Annie Acton, 20 May 1895, CUL Add. 8121/9/105.

41. Acton to W. E. Gladstone, Easter Sunday 1895, BL Add. 44094/267–68, published in *Selections from the Correspondence of the First Lord Acton,* ed. John Neville Figgis and Reginald Vere Laurence (London, 1917), 172–73.

42. J. W. Clark (Registrar of Cambridge University) to Acton, 28 May 1895, CUL Add. 8119/C/132. These charges have since been abolished. Acton's enormous head measurements recall the Cambridge experiments in 1888 of Sir Francis Galton, the anthropologist, a cousin of Darwin. Galton lined up a group of graduates and measured their heads. He found, and psychologists have argued for and against the theory ever since, that the size of a man's head was correlated to his intellectual eminence. Acton seemed to have thought little of the discovery.

43. Acton to Mamy Acton, 17 February 1897, CUL Add. 7956/183.

44. Acton to Mamy Acton, 8 May 1895, CUL Add. 7956/158.

45. Acton to Annie Acton, 12 May 1895, CUL Add. 8121/9/103.

46. Acton to Mamy Acton, 8 May 1895, CUL Add. 7956/158.

47. Lord Acton, *A Lecture on the Study of History Delivered at Cambridge, June 11, 1895* (London, 1896), reprinted in *Selected Writings,* 2:504–52, quotation on 504. Subsequent quotations are taken from this excellent edition.

48. Acton to Richard Acton, n.d. [12 June 1895], CUL Add. 8121/10/185.

49. *Times,* 12 June 1895.

50. "Lord Acton's First Lecture," *Spectator* 74 (15 June 1895): 807, 814–15.

51. *Saturday Review* 79 (22 June 1895): 821–22.

52. *Guardian,* 6 November 1895, 1729. This was a London church newspaper with no connection to the *Manchester Guardian,* today the *Guardian.*

53. H. A. L. Fisher, "Lord Acton's Lectures," *Independent Review* 11 (1906): 224–28.

54. J. L. Hammond, "Lord Acton's Liberalism," *Independent Review* 2 (May 1904): 651–56.

55. Henry C. Lea, "Ethical Values in History," in *Minor Historical Writings,* ed. A. C. Howland (Philadelphia, 1942), 60.

56. Acton's review of Lea's three-volume *History* was published in the *English Historical Review* 3 (1888): 773–88, reprinted in *Selected Writings,* 2:392–411, quotations on 411, 406, 410. In letters to Döllinger Acton admitted to a "fiasco" inasmuch as only his criticism of Lea was published. A separate article setting out his own views on the Inquisition, which he was asked to write, was never published. Acton to Döllinger, 21 September 1888 and 28 March 1889, *Briefwechsel,* 3:398, 401 [German]. Lea apparently found Acton's review "exceedingly gratifying," admitting the "force of much that he says." Acton to Döllinger, 20 November 1888, *Briefwechsel,* 3:400 [German and English]. A more favourable view of Lea's *History* was taken in Germany by the Catholic theologian Franz Heinrich Reusch in *Theologische Literaturzeitung* 23 (1888): cols. 564–65. While correcting some of Lea's errors, Reusch found his book to be "essentially objective" and shared the American author's view, expressed in his preface, that the morality of the subject "ought to develop in the reader's mind without being imposed upon it." Reusch (1825–1900), who, because of his opposition to Infallibility, was excommunicated in 1872, joined the Old Catholics as their first Vicar-General. He became increasingly disillusioned with them, in particular with their abandonment of Catholic beliefs and practices like celibacy, and resigned his offices in 1878. He died unreconciled with the Catholic Church. Josef Höfer and Karl Rahner, eds., *Lexikon für Theologie und Kirche,* 2d rev. ed. (Freiburg, Germany, 1957–65), 8:855.

57. Karl Lamprecht, "Lord Acton, *Über das Studium der Geschichte,* Eröffnungsvorlesung, gehalten zu Cambridge am 11. Juni 1895. Rechtmäßige Übersetzung von I. Immelmann, Berlin 1897," in *Deutsche Zeitschrift für Geschichtswissenschaft, 1897–1898* (Freiburg, Germany, 1898), 212–14. The same translator and publisher (Gärtner Verlag, H. Heyfelder, Berlin) were also responsible for the publication in German of Acton's major essay "German Schools of History," published in the first issue of the *English Historical Review* 1 (1886): 7–42, reprinted in *Selected Writings,* 2:325–64.

58. G. O. Trevelyan to Rosebery, quoted in Alan Bell, "Lord Acton Gets His Chair."

59. G. M. Trevelyan, *The Present Position of History: An Inaugural Lecture* (Cambridge, 1927), 3.

60. Acton to Annie Acton, 30 October 1895, CUL Add. 8121(9)111/1.

61. Chadwick, *Professor Lord Acton,* 33, 15, 23, 24, 33.

62. Acton, *Lectures on Modern History*, ed. John Neville Figgis and Reginald Vere Laurence (London, 1906); Acton, *Lectures on the French Revolution*, ed. Figgis and Laurence (London, 1910).

63. Oscar Browning to Acton, 16 October 1895, CUL Add. 8119/I/B170.

64. Acton to Mamy Acton, 20 May 1897, CUL Add. 7956/167.

65. Helen Gladstone to Acton, 27 January 1896, CUL Add. 8119/9/397.

66. Acton to Annie Acton, 19 June 1890, CUL Add. 8121/9/19: "He has also learnt all about money and economy," Acton wrote to his daughter Annie about Richard, "and has spent £20 less [in his last year at Magdalene College]. I saw with just pride that he travels third class. All the best men do that."

67. Acton to W. E. Gladstone, 26 April 1891, BL Add. 44094/167–68. The allusion was to Cato's opposition when he was consul, in 195 B.C., and when a great issue was made of the repeal of the Oppian law. He once said bitterly: "All men rule their wives, we rule all men—and who rules us? Our wives?" Plutarch, *Cato major* 8.4. See also J. P. V. D. Balsdon, *Roman Women* (London, 1962).

68. Acton to Annie Acton, 7 May 1897, CUL Add. 8121/9/134.

69. Acton's Eranus Society Lecture, *Lord Acton: The Decisive Decade, 1864–1874: Essays and Documents,* ed. Damian McElrath, James Holland, Ward White, and Sue Katzman (Louvain, Belgium, 1970), 140.

70. Acton's notes kept in the Cambridge University Library reflected his preoccupation with the problem: CUL Add. 4929/121, 4931/52, 4931/206. CUL Add. 5397/36 reads: "Expose my canons of history: no private life, no religious, political, national tests, moral tests applied strictly, impartially, universally. Defend as long as you can. No case sure until you know the worst."

71. John Pollock, "Lord Acton at Cambridge," *Independent Review* 2 (1904): 371, 372.

72. Acton to Annie Acton, 4 May 1896, CUL Add. 8121/9127.

73. Acton to Annie Acton, 18 May 1896, CUL Add. 8121/9/128. See also Acton, *Lectures on the French Revolution,* 179, 188, 266.

74. Acton, notes, CUL Add. 5647/18, 5688.

75. Acton to Robert E. Lee, 4 November 1866, *Selected Writings,* 1:363. The Acton-Lee correspondence is reprinted on 361–67.

76. Quoted in Paul, "Introductory Memoir," *Letters to Mary Gladstone,* lxii. I am indebted to Owen Chadwick for pointing out that Fulton had no viable steamboat in 1803.

77. Acton to Annie Acton, 10 July 1884, CUL Add. 8121/9/5.

78. Acton to Annie Acton, 6 December 1896, CUL Add. 8121/9/129.

79. Reginald Vere Laurence, Acton's brilliant history student and later editor of his published papers, wrote in "Acton as a Teacher," *Cambridge Review,* 23 October 1902, 23–34: "Lord Acton checked this provincial and insular tendency and reminded us that the history of Western Europe has a unity of its own which it is

necessary to remember if we are to understand aright the history of our country and the part which it has played in the world's drama. The history of ideas was to him more important than the history of institutions, as being the history of the forces which give institutions their life and make them effective." Stubbs's *Select Charters to 1307* (London, 1870) became a kind of symbol for the German method of scientific history, which William Stubbs (1825–1901), following the model of Georg Waitz, introduced in Oxford in 1866, when he became Regius Professor of Modern History. Stubbs was Bishop of Chester and Oxford successively. Acton had a high regard for his knowledge of documents and theology. He "is one of the most agreeable, friendly men I know. But he has little political understanding, few ideas and no fervour. His lecture room at Oxford became deserted," he wrote to Döllinger, 13 June 1884, *Briefwechsel,* 3:331 [German].

80. F. W. Maitland, "The Late Lord Acton," *Cambridge Review,* 16 October 1902, 8.

81. "Savoir le pourquoi du pourquoi" (knowing the why of the why) was one of Acton's favourite sayings. He apparently derived it from the Electress Sophie of Hanover (1630–1714), the mother of King George I of England. This was noted by Lady Blennerhassett in her obituary of Lord Acton in *Biographisches Jarhbuch und deutscher Nekrolog* 7 (1902): 17.

82. Thomas Thornely, *Cambridge Memories* (London, 1936), 117.

83. Maitland, "Late Lord Acton," 8.

84. James Bryce, *Studies in Contemporary Biography* (London, 1903), 387.

85. J. B. Mullinger to Acton, 29 October 1897, CUL Add. 8119/I/M328. J. B. Mullinger was a member of the University's History Board and wrote to Acton on the subject of Gooch's failure. "It is not simply that I regret that a man of so many admirable qualities and such high character should have missed the recognition to which, by general consent, his many attainments entitled him, but I look upon it as really serious for the prospects of historical studies in his college and the university. I can with difficulty conceive any candidate presenting himself with better credentials, especially when the knowledge of German and French literature, and to some extent of Italian, which he has acquired since the Tripos, is taken into consideration. What the decision of the electors practically amounts to is this—that no amount of academic distinction in history shall be deemed to have much weight when compared with mathematical or scientific attainments. If this is really to be the case, students in history who mean to do thorough and systematic work and have the legitimate reward of such labour in view, will certainly elect to go to Oxford, and it would be difficult for a conscientious advisor not to recommend them to go."

86. Acton to Mamy Acton, 10 February 1897, CUL Add. 7956/182.

87. Acton to Annie Acton, 28 February 1896, CUL Add. 8121/9/121.

88. Queen Victoria, journal, 22 February 1897, Royal Archives, Windsor, 39/138.

89. Acton to Queen Victoria, 22 June 1897, Royal Archives, Windsor, 54/110.

90. Acton to Annie Acton, 22 June 1897, CUL Add. 8121/9/138.

91. Ibid.

Chapter 21: Last Years

1. The first entry in the minutes of the Syndics of the University Press is dated 13 March 1896 and is a resolution that Acton should be approached. See R. T. Wright, *The Cambridge Modern History: An Account of Its Origin, Authorship and Production* (Cambridge, England, 1907). Acton's involvement in the project is covered by some sixteen boxes in the Cambridge University Library. See G. N. Clark, "The Origin of the Cambridge Modern History," *Cambridge Historical Journal* 8 (1945): 57–64; M. H. Black, *Cambridge University Press, 1584-1984* (Cambridge, England, 1984).

2. Acton to R. T. Wright, 21 May 1896, CUL Add. 8119/8/490.

3. R. T. Wright to Acton, 23 May 1896, CUL Add. 8119/I/W305.

4. R. T. Wright to Acton, 14 May 1896, CUL Add. 8119/I/W 304.

5. Acton to R. T. Wright, 21 May 1896, CUL Add. 8119/8/490.

6. Acton to Annie Acton, 14 August 1900, CUL Add. 8121/9/152.

7. Acton to Marie Acton, 2 March 1897, CUL Add. 8121/8.

8. Acton to Annie Acton, 18 May 1896, CUL Add. 8121/9/128.

9. Acton to R. T. Wright, 14 July 1896, CUL Add. 8119/8/492.

10. See R. T. Wright to Acton, 20 October 1896, CUL Add. 8119/I/W307. This letter thanks Lord Acton on behalf of the Syndics for his scheme, which they approved.

11. R. T. Wright to Acton, 9 November 1896, CUL Add. 8119/I/W309. W. Stanley Mordaunt Leathes (1861–1901) was at Trinity College and was secretary of the General Board of Studies at Cambridge. To convert the sums of money to today's value, multiply by 44.30.

12. R. T. Wright to Acton, 5 June 1897, CUL Add. 8119/I/W315.

13. Annie Acton to Acton, 31 October 1896, CUL Add. 8121/9/216.

14. Acton to first Baron Rothschild of Tring, draft, n.d. [1897?], CUL Add. 8119/I/R150. Rothschild left instructions that all his private papers, which included trunks of letters from Benjamin Disraeli and Lord Rosebery, were to be destroyed. His wife, Emma Louise (1844–1935), insisted that these instructions be carried out by the executors. I am indebted to the late Hon. Mrs. Miriam Rothschild for this information. See her life of the naturalist Lionel Walter Rothschild of Tring (1868–1937): *Dear Lord Rothschild: Birds, Butterflies and History* (Philadelphia, 1983), 296–97.

15. Acton to Mamy Acton, 26 January 1897, CUL Add. 7956/180. The letter was written after Acton had spent a pleasant weekend at Tring, the Rothschilds' country house.

16. A facsimile edition of Acton's Report to the Syndics was published by Cambridge University Press under the title *Longitude 30 West* (Cambridge, England, 1969), and is reprinted in *Selected Writings of Lord Acton,* ed. J. Rufus Fears (Indianapolis, 1984–88), 3:675–86. Some of his views on universal history were also expressed in the letter sent out to the contributors, published in *Lectures on Modern History,* ed. John Neville Figgis and Reginald Vere Laurence (London, 1906), 315–18, for example: "By universal history I understand that which is distinct from the Cambridge History of all centuries, which is not a rope of sand but a continuous development, and is not a burden on the memory, but an illumination of the soul. It moved in a succession to which the nations are subsidiary. Their story will be told, not for their own sake, but for reference and subordination to a higher series according to the time and degree in which they contribute to the common fortunes of mankind."

17. CUL, Cambridge University Press: *Cambridge Modern History.* The date on which Acton sent out this letter to contributors—12 March 1898—symbolized to the British historian Professor Max (now Lord) Beloff "the beginning of the decadence of English historical writing," because specialization, the idolization of technique, and "concentration upon the materials of history themselves rather than the great concerns of mankind [became] the business of the historian." "A Challenge to Historians," *Listener,* 10 November 1949, 816–17. But it seems unjust to castigate Acton as the villain in the development of modern historical writing. The *Cambridge Modern History* as published was not what Acton had intended, unrealisable as his aim was. See also Gertrude Himmelfarb, "Lord Acton, the Historian as Moralist," in *Victorian Minds* (London, 1968), 172–74.

18. Acton to James Bryce, 28 March 1899, Bryce Papers, Bodleian Library, 1/107. Acton first offered Bryce "Rome under Sixtus V" (22 January 1897), then, on 28 March 1899: "I have carved out a chapter, a short chapter, which fits you like a glove. It is one on the Empire down to the election of Charles V—that is, during the reign of Maximilian." But Bryce declined.

19. Acton, *Longitude 30 West,* in *Selected Writings,* 3:681.

20. Minutes of the Cambridge University Press, 27 November 1896 and 12 February 1897, Cambridge University Press, Cambridge.

21. Accounts of the Cambridge University Press for 1902, CUL PRV 10/81.

22. Richard Acton to the Syndics of Cambridge University Press, 19 July 1901. The Syndics, according to their minutes of 19 April, 14 June, 19 July, and 8 November, made their alternative decision, which was to appoint A. W. Ward, G. W. Prothero, and Stanley Leathes as editors. Clark, "Origin of the Cambridge Modern History," 64.

23. Acton to Mamy Acton, 20 November 1896, CUL Add. 7956/177.

24. F. W. Maitland, "The Late Lord Acton," *Cambridge Review,* 16 October 1902, 9.

25. Acton to Mamy Acton, 29 October 1896, CUL Add. 7956/174.

26. The quotation is from Acton to Mamy Acton, 23 February 1899, CUL Add. 7956/235. Birnam House, now Number 6 Chaucer Road and containing the University of Cambridge's Martin Centre of Architectural and Urban Studies, was then still on a private road with a gate across the front. The house was built on agricultural land owned by the University that was originally part of the Pembroke estate. From 1880 onwards a ninety-nine-year lease was granted to the dons who bought or built houses on the land. Acton acquired the house from the zoologist Richard Assheton but lived there only briefly before his breakdown in the spring of 1901. I am indebted to the architect Andrew Coburn of the Cambridge Eden Centre for permission to use his fine pen drawing of the house, which has remained largely as it was in Acton's day.

27. Ibid.

28. Mrs. Ethel Romanes to Acton, 17 December 1900, CUL Add. 7731/42.

29. Acton to Annie Acton, Trinity college, 5 December [1900], CUL Add. 8121/9/64.

30. CUL Add. 4981, 5002; the following quotations are from notes in CUL Add. 4981/23, 27, 64, 66, 56, 50, 133, 139, 74, 75, 107, 192. See also G. E. Fasnacht, "Acton's Notes for a Romanes Lecture," *Contemporary Review* 182 (December 1952): 348–53.

31. Acton to Marie, 23 January 1901, CUL Add. 8121/7/1015 [French].

32. Mary Gladstone Drew to Acton, February 20 [1901], CUL Add. 8119/9/310.

33. Alan Palmer, *Crowned Cousins* (London, 1985), 197.

34. Acton to Annie Acton, 24 January 1901, CUL Add. 8121/9/165.

35. Mamy Acton to Lady Blennerhassett, dated "Easter Sunday," 1901, CUL Add. 7956.

36. Acton to Richard Acton, [n.d.], CUL Add. 5526, not foliated.

37. Acton, note, CUL Add. 5684/93.

38. Annie Acton to her aunt Minnie Dease (née Throckmorton), 25 June [1902], Throckmorton Papers, Warwickshire County Record Office, bundle 37, not foliated.

39. An account of the funeral appeared in the *Münchener Neueste Nachrichten,* 23 June 1902.

40. The place where Lord Acton was buried at the Tegernsee cemetery has been altered. The marble headstone cross with the inscription "Ave Crux Spes Unica" was preserved through World War II. Today, however, nothing indicates the location of Acton's grave or that of his daughter Elisabeth, nor of the neighbouring Acton family vault. Nevertheless, the site has not been used again and is considered by the Tegernsee cemetery authorities as an "open area." No exhumation has taken place of Acton's mortal remains. Acton scholars and others in the German-speaking countries, in Britain, and in the United States have expressed an interest in restoring the headstone or putting up a plaque dedicated to his memory.

41. *Tablet,* 22 September 1906, 448.

42. Herbert Thurston, S.J., review of *Lord Acton and His Circle,* in the *Month* 509 (November 1906): 547-49; "The Late Lord Acton and the 'Cambridge Modern History,'" *Tablet,* 15 July 1905; Thurston, "The Late Lord Acton," *Catholic World* 84 (1906): 357-72. See also further letters to the *Tablet* (15 October 1906): 576-77; (20 October): 616-17; (27 October): 656-58; (3 November): 696-98; (10 November): 736-37; (17 November): 775-76; (24 November): 816.

43. Letter from Mgr. Christopher Scott, *Tablet,* 27 October 1906, 656.

44. Letter from Mgr. Edmund Nolan, *Tablet,* 27 October 1906, 657. The letter from the nun of Nazareth House was merely signed "R," *Tablet,* 10 November 1906, 737.

45. Friedrich von Hügel to Mary Gladstone Drew, 4 June 1904, in *Selected Letters of von Hügel, 1896-1924,* ed. Bernard Holland (London, 1927), 127.

46. Letter from Anatole von Hügel, *Tablet,* 10 November 1906, 736-37.

47. I am indebted for information on the Jesus Psalter to the Reverend Jonathan Holmes, Chaplain and Acting Dean of Queens' College, Cambridge; Dr. Eamon Duffy, Magdalene College, Cambridge; and Mr. Harvey Porter.

48. Acton, "George Eliot's Life," *Historical Essays and Studies,* ed. John Neville Figgis and Reginald Vere Laurence (London, 1907), 301.

49. Acton to Oscar Browning, [late 1880?], Browning Papers, King's College, Cambridge.

50. Acton to Annie Acton, Rome, 15 January 1890, CUL Add. 8121/9/18. This was written just after Acton had received the news of Döllinger's death.

51. Acton, notebook, CUL Add. 8119/423.

52. Quoted in Sir Mountstuart E. Grant Duff, *Out of the Past: Some Biographical Essays* (London, 1903), 2:195.

53. Oscar Browning, *Memories of Sixty Years at Eton, Cambridge and Elsewhere* (London, 1910), 16.

54. This document is quoted by Figgis and Laurence in the introduction to Acton, *The History of Freedom and Other Essays,* ed. John Neville Figgis and Reginald Vere Laurence (London, 1907), xxxviii-xxxix.

55. Acton to Mary Gladstone, 31 March 1883, *Letters of Lord Acton to Mary, Daughter of the Right Hon. W. E. Gladstone,* ed. Herbert Paul, 2d rev. ed. (London, 1913), 134-35. That Acton found it difficult to love a member of Brooks's, that great and elegant Regency club, has less to do with its members' proclivity for reckless gambling in the tradition of Charles James Fox than it has to do with the polemical storm caused by Gladstone's Home Rule Bill. In an orgy of mutual blackballing, the club's Whig membership was split into opposing camps until Lord Granville urged peace, saying, according to Anthony Lejeune, that "there should be one place left in London where animosities could be set aside and friends could meet." Anthony Lejeune, *The Gentlemen's Clubs of London* (London, 1979), 68. The phrase

that communion with the Church "is dearer to me than life" occurs in Acton's second letter to the *Times*, 21 November 1874, reprinted in *Selected Writings*, 3:368.

56. Klaus Schatz, S.J., *Vaticanum I, 1869–1870* (Paderborn, Germany, 1992–94), 3:305–7. As for the controversial remark of Pius IX, "La tradizione sono io," this is now shown to have been made on 18 June 1870 to Cardinal Guidi, according to the testimony of Cardinal Vincenzo Tizzani (1802–92), an Italian member of the Curia who during the Council was on the side of the inopportunists, in his recently discovered and published diaries and papers. L. Pásztor, "Il Concilio Vaticano I: Diario di Vincenzo Tizzani (1869–70)," in *Päpste und Papsttum* 25 (Stuttgart, 1991).

57. Acton, *Lectures on Modern History*, 31.

58. Acton, note, CUL Add. 5487/39.

59. Acton, note, CUL Add. 5487, esp. 45, 55, 58.

60. Acton to Mary Gladstone, 11 November 1885, *Letters to Mary Gladstone*, 169. See also the excellent analysis in G. E. Fasnacht, *Acton's Political Philosophy* (London, 1952), 117–25.

61. Fasnacht, *Acton's Political Philosophy*, 124.

62. Acton to W. E. Gladstone, 17 November 1873, BL Add. 44093/150–151.

63. Acton, review of *Democracy in Europe*, by Sir Erskine May, *Quarterly Review* 145 (January 1878): 112–14, reprinted in *Selected Writings*, 1:54–85, quotation on 81.

64. Acton, "Nationality," *Home and Foreign Review* 1 (July 1862): 1–25, reprinted in *Selected Writings*, 1:409–33, quotation on 433.

65. Acton to Simpson, 7 December 1859, *The Correspondence of Lord Acton and Richard Simpson*, ed. Josef L. Altholz, Damien McElrath, and James C. Holland (Cambridge, England, 1971–75), 2:37.

66. Acton, "Nationality," in *Selected Writings*, 1: 429, 413, 425.

67. Acton, note, CUL Add. 4940/81.

68. John Stuart Mill, *Considerations on Representative Government* (London, 1861), quoted in Acton, "Nationality," *Selected Writings*, 422.

69. G. M. Trevelyan, *An Autobiography and Other Essays* (London, 1949), 18.

70. Acton, introduction to L. A. Burd's edition of Machiavelli, *Il principe* (Oxford, 1891), reprinted in *History of Freedom*, 212–31, and in *Selected Writings*, 2:479–95, quotation on 494–95.

71. Acton, *Lectures on Modern History*, 51; "The History of Freedom in Christianity," reprinted in *Selected Writings*, 1:37.

72. G. E. Fasnacht, *Acton's Political Philosophy*, 126–39.

73. Acton, introduction to Burd's edition of Machiavelli, *Il principe*, in *Selected Writings*, 2:479.

74. Ibid., 485, 490.

75. Acton to Mandell Creighton, published first in *Historical Essays and Studies*, 504,

fully reprinted in *Selected Writings*, 2:378–91, quotation on 383. The actual quotation begins, of course, "Power tends to corrupt . . . ."

76. Acton, "A Study of History," reprinted in *Selected Writings*, 2:545.

77. Acton, "History of Freedom in Christianity," *History of Freedom*, 39, also *Selected Writings*, 1:36.

78. Acton, "The Renaissance," in *Lectures on Modern History*, 80.

79. Acton, "History of Freedom in Christianity," *Selected Writings*, 1:40.

80. Acton to Mary Gladstone, 3 June 1881, *Letters to Mary Gladstone*, 83.

81. Acton, "The Influence of America," in *Lectures on the French Revolution*, ed. John Neville Figgis and Reginald Vere Laurence (London, 1910), 20–38, reprinted in *Selected Writings*, 1:198–212, quotation on 211.

82. Acton, review of May's *Democracy in Europe*, in *Selected Writings*, 1:84.

83. Obituary of Lord Acton, *Times*, 20 June 1902.

84. Acton, note, CUL Add. 4954/23.

85. Acton to Mary Gladstone, 25 March 1881, *Letters to Mary Gladstone*, 63.

86. Acton to Annie Acton, 10 July [1888?], CUL Add. 8121/9/5.

87. Acton, note, CUL Add. 4908/55.

88. Acton to Lady Blennerhassett, February 1879, *Selections from the Correspondence of the First Lord Acton*, ed. John Neville Figgis and Reginald Vere Laurence (London, 1917), 54–56.

SELECT BIBLIOGRAPHY

Unpublished Sources

Archivio Segreto Vaticano, Rome.

The Vatican Archive contains some Acton letters, mainly his correspondence with Cardinal Antonelli and Augustus Theiner; the Döllinger material is more extensive, especially in the reports of the Munich Apostolic Nuncios. Yet some of this Döllinger material is still, even after nearly 130 years, withheld from scholars by order of the Holy Office.

Bayrisches Geheimes Staatsarchiv, Munich.

The extensive Döllingeriana (MAI 631, 633, 635, 636–639, 641, 642) contains, among numerous letters written to and from Döllinger, a few from Acton and Newman.

Biblioteca Communale dell'Archiginnasio, Bologna.

This archive preserves correspondence and documents relating to the Bolognese statesman Marco Minghetti, second husband of Lord Acton's cousin Laura Acton. There are some twenty letters of Acton to Minghetti and ten of Minghetti to Acton.

Bodleian Library, Oxford.

Among the Clarendon Papers are private letters from Odo Russell to his father-in-law, Lord Clarendon, the Foreign Secretary before and during the First Vatican Council. The Bodleian also preserves letters from Acton to James Bryce (Bryce Papers).

British Library, Additional Manuscripts, London.

The Gladstone Papers, collected in some 750 bound volumes and excellently catalogued, include correspondence with Acton and Döllinger.

Brompton Oratory, London.

A large collection of letters of Newman, Faber, and the early Oratorian Fathers is housed here. There is also a well-stocked library.

Cambridge University Library, Cambridge.

The Cambridge Acton collection comprises Acton's personal library and his working notes as well as a voluminous family correspondence bearing directly on the life and ancestry of the historian. There are also additional letters, notes, and manuscripts, all of which the University Library in Cambridge has acquired by gift and purchase. The papers relating to Acton's life and ancestry include correspondence with Döllinger, Newman, Gladstone, Mary Gladstone, Lord Granville, Mandell Creighton, the Empress Frederick, and Charlotte Lady Blennerhassett, as well as with his mother-in-law, his wife, and their children. After Acton's death, these papers remained in the possession of the Acton family at Aldenham, Shropshire. When, in 1947, the Acton family emigrated to Africa and Aldenham was sold, the Acton papers were removed to Marcham Priory, Berkshire, the residence of Douglas Woodruff, who, with his wife, the Hon. Mia Woodruff, granddaughter of Lord Acton, continued to make these papers accessible to various Acton scholars. Negotiations for the acquisition of these papers from their legal owner, the Honourable Richard Acton, now the fourth Lord Acton, were started on behalf of the Cambridge University Library by the Keeper of Manuscripts, Mr. A. E. B. Owen, in 1971 and completed in 1973. In June 1973 this material was transported to Cambridge. With some smaller groups of later acquisitions, the Cambridge University Library is now custodian of the most comprehensive source for materials of the first Lord Acton. The extensive task of cataloguing these Acton papers has been accomplished by Mr. John Wells.

Kings College, Cambridge.

A number of letters and postcards from Acton written in the late 1880s and early 1890s, when he was still resident at Cannes, are included in the Oscar Browning Papers.

Pembroke College, Oxford.

The Peter le Page Renouf Papers include correspondence with Acton.

Propaganda Fide Archives, Rome.

The Archivio Storico Propaganda Fide at Piazza di Spagna contains the correspondence of the English bishops with the Vatican. Especially relevant is the correspondence from the period of Acton's editorship of the *Rambler* and the *Home and Foreign Review* (1858–64), which also illuminates the negative attitude of some of the English bishops towards Newman.

Public Record Office, London.

The diplomatic papers, such as Odo Russell's reports on the First Vatican Council and the papers of Lord Granville, are kept at the PRO.

Royal Archives, Windsor Castle, Berkshire, England.

There are frequent references to Acton during his periods as Lord-in-Waiting and as Regius Professor of Modern History, Cambridge, in the letters and journal of Queen Victoria.

Shrewsbury Diocesan Archives, Shrewsbury, England.

An extensive collection of correspondence, papers, and books covers the history of the diocese, founded in 1850.

Shropshire County Council Record Office, Shrewsbury, England.

More than a thousand Acton family letters, also estate papers, came into the possession of the County Record Office and have been catalogued.

St. Andrew's University Library, Fife, Scotland.

The Library houses the Friedrich von Hügel Papers, and there are also some Acton letters: one from Newman in 1859, during the *Rambler* period; some concerning the award of the honorary degree of Lord Acton in 1895; and a few letters to Acton from Wilfrid Ward, as well as some concerning the abortive project of an Acton biography by Ward.

St. Deiniol's Archives, Hawarden, Wales.

The library founded by W. E. Gladstone preserves his books as well as the Glynne-Gladstone Family Papers.

Warwickshire County Record Office, Warwick, England.

The Throckmorton Papers are kept here, including several letters of the young Acton to his cousins.

Westminster Diocesan Archives, London.

These archives contain the papers relating to the archbishops of Westminster (with the exception of the bulk of the Manning Papers, which were scattered) and the documents relating to the English Catholic mission from 1688 to the end of the Apostolic vicars in 1829. Expectations that the Manning papers would eventually be housed in the Westminster Diocesan Archives have been disappointed, and their fate is a sorry tale. They were badly neglected by the Oblates of St. Charles in their Bayswater College, originally funded by Manning. After World War II the papers were rescued by a French priest, Alphonse Chapeau. He catalogued them and used the material for his own doctoral thesis at the Sorbonne but restricted access to it by almost everyone else. After Chapeau's death the papers were dispersed to Oxford and

Angers, France; they now seem to have been sold to Emory University in Atlanta, Georgia.

Published Sources

Acton, Ferdinando, and Francesco Acton. *Genealogia degli Acton*. Naples, 1969.

Acton, Harold. *The Bourbons of Naples (1734–1825)*. London, 1956.

———. *The Last Bourbons of Naples (1825–1861)*. London, 1961.

Acton, John Emerich Edward Dalberg, First Baron. *Acton in America: The American Journal of Sir John Acton, 1853*. Edited by S. W. Jackman. Shepherdstown, W. Va., 1979.

———. *The Correspondence of Lord Acton and Richard Simpson*. Edited by Josef L. Altholz, Damian McElrath, and James C. Holland. 3 vols. Cambridge, England, 1971–1975.

———. *Essays on Church and State*. Edited by Douglas Woodruff. London, 1952.

———. *Essays on Freedom and Power*. Edited by Gertrude Himmelfarb. Boston, 1948.

———. *Essays in the Liberal Interpretation of History*. Edited by William H. McNeill. Chicago, 1967.

———. *Historical Essays and Studies*. Edited by John Neville Figgis and Reginald Vere Laurence. London, 1907.

———. *The History of Freedom and Other Essays*. Edited by John Neville Figgis and Reginald Vere Laurence. London, 1907.

———. "Journal of Lord Acton: Rome, 1857," edited by Herbert Butterfield. *Cambridge Historical Journal* 8 (1946): 186–204.

———. *Lectures on the French Revolution*. Edited by John Neville Figgis and Reginald Vere Laurence. London, 1910.

———. *Lectures on Modern History*. Edited by John Neville Figgis and Reginald Vere Laurence. London, 1906.

———. *Letters of Lord Acton to Mary, Daughter of the Right Hon. W. E. Gladstone*. Edited by Herbert Paul. London, 1904. 2d rev. ed. London, 1913.

———. "Une lettre de Lord Acton sur la fin du pouvoir temporal du pape," edited by Damian McElrath. *Revue d'histoire ecclésiastique* 65 (1970): 86–113.

———. *Longitude 30 West*. Cambridge, England, 1969.

———. *Lord Acton: The Decisive Decade, 1864–1874, Essays and Documents*. Edited by Damian McElrath, James Holland, Ward White, and Sue Katzman. Louvain, Belgium, 1970.

———. *Lord Acton and His Circle*. Edited by Abbot Gasquet. London, 1906.

———. *Lord Acton and the First Vatican Council: A Journal*. Edited by Edmund Campion. Sydney, 1975.

———. *Selected Writings of Lord Acton*. Edited by J. Rufus Fears. 3 vols. Indianapolis, 1984–88.

———. *Selections from the Correspondence of the First Lord Acton*. Edited by John Neville Figgis and Reginald Vere Laurence. London, 1917.

———. *Sendschreiben: An einen deutschen Bischof des Vaticanischen Concils*. Nördlingen, Germany, 1870.

———. *See also* Quirinus.

Acton, Richard Maximilian Dalberg, Second Baron. Letter to the editor. *Times* (London), 28 October 1906.

Altholz, Josef L. *The Conscience of Lord Acton*. Houston, 1970.

———. *The Liberal Catholic Movement in England: The Rambler and Its Contributors, 1848–1864*. London, 1962.

Arnold, Matthew. *Essays in Criticism*. 1st ser. (London, 1902). Edited by Sister Marion Hoctor. Chicago, 1964.

Aubert, Roger. *Le pontificat de Pie IX (1846–1878)*. Paris, 1963.

———. *Vatican I*. Edited by Gervaise Dumeige, S.J. Paris, 1964.

Auchmuty, James J. "Acton: The Youthful Parliamentarian." *Historical Studies of Australia and New Zealand* 9, no. 34 (May 1960): 131–39.

———. "Acton's Election as an Irish Member of Parliament." *English Historical Review* 61, no. 241 (1946): 394–405.

Bardong, Otto, ed. *Herrnsheim, 771–1971: Festbuch zur 1200. Jahrfeier*. Worms, Germany, 1971.

Baumgardt, D. *Franz von Baader und die philosophische Romantik*. Halle, Germany, 1927.

Beales, Derek. "Garibaldi in England: The Politics of Enthusiasm." In *Society and Politics in the Age of Risorgimento: Essays in Honour of Denis Mack Smith,* edited by John A. Davis and Paul Ginsborg, 184–216. Cambridge, England, 1991.

Beck, George Andrew, ed. *The English Catholics, 1850–1950*. London, 1950.

Bell, Alan. "Gladstone Looks for a Poet Laureate." *Times Literary Supplement,* 21 July 1972, 847.

———. "Lord Acton Gets His Chair." *Times Literary Supplement,* 8 February 1974, 137.

Bellasis, Edward Serjeant. *Memorials of Mr. Serjeant Bellasis (1800–1873)*. London, 1893.

Beloff, Max. "A Challenge to Historians." *Listener,* 10 November 1949, 816–817.

Biehl, Vincent. "Newman, the Bishops and the *Rambler*." *Downside Review,* no. 90 (1972): 20–40.

———. "Newman's Delation: Some Hitherto Unpublished Letters." *Dublin Review* 204 (1960–61): 296–305.

Bishop, Maria Catherine. *A Memoir of Mrs. Augustus Craven*. 2 vols. London, 1894.

Bismarck, Otto von. *Gesammelte Werke*. Edited by Friedrich Thimme. 15 vols. Berlin, 1951.

Black, M. H. *Cambridge University Press, 1584–1984*. Cambridge, England, 1984.

Blake, Robert. *Disraeli*. London, 1966.

Blennerhassett, Charlotte. "Acton." *Biographisches Jahrbuch und deutscher Nekrolog* 7 (1902): 16–22.

———. "The Late Lord Acton." *Edinburgh Review* 197 (1903): 501–34.

———. "Lord Acton." *Deutsche Rundschau* 122 (1905): 64–92.

———. "In Memoriam I. von Döllinger—28 Februar 1799–10 Januar 1890." *Deutsche Rundschau* 25 (1899): 459–63.

———. "Das Viktorianische England." *Deutsche Rundschau* 157–61 (1913–14).

——— [C. de Warmont, pseud.]. "Félix-Antoine Dupanloup, Bishop of Orleans." *Nineteenth Century* 5 (February 1879): 219–46.

Blennerhassett, W. L. "Acton: 1834–1902." *Dublin Review* 194 (1934): 169–88.

Boase, Frederick. *Modern English Biography.* 6 vols. Truro, 1892–1921.

Bonnefons, André. *Une ennemie de la révolution et de Napoléon: Marie-Caroline, reine des Deux-Siciles, 1748–1814.* Paris, 1905.

Bossy, John. *The English Catholic Community, 1570–1850.* London, 1975.

Bowle, John. *Politics and Opinion in the Nineteenth Century.* London, 1954.

Brooke, Christopher. *A History of the University of Cambridge.* Vol. 4, *1870–1990.* Cambridge, England, 1993.

Browning, Oscar. *Memories of Later Years.* London, 1923.

———. *Memories of Sixty Years at Eton, Cambridge and Elsewhere.* London, 1910.

———. "Personal Recollections of Sir John Seeley and Lord Acton." *Albany Review* 2 (1908): 548–56.

Brownson, Orestes. *Conversations on Liberalism and the Church.* New York, 1904.

Bryce, James. "The Letters of Lord Acton." *North American Review* 178 (1904): 698–710.

———. "Lord Acton." *Proceedings of the British Academy* 1 (1903–4): 277–82.

———. *Studies in Contemporary Biography.* London, 1903.

Bunsen, Marie von. *The World I Used to Know, 1860–1912.* Edited and translated by Oakley Williams. London, 1930.

Burtin, Nicholas. *Un semeur d'idées au temps de la Restauration: Le Baron d'Eckstein.* Paris, 1931.

Butler, Edward Cuthbert. *The Life and Times of Bishop Ullathorne.* 2 vols. London, 1926.

———. *The Vatican Council: The Story Told from Inside in Bishop Ullathorne's Letters.* 2 vols. London, 1930. Abbreviated edition, London, 1962.

Butterfield, Herbert. "Acton: His Training, Methods and Intellectual System." In *Studies in Diplomatic History and Historiography in Honour of G. P. Gooch, C.H.,* edited by A. O. Sarkissian, 169–98. London, 1961.

———. *Cambridge Modern History: An Account of Its Origin, Authorship and Production.* Cambridge, England, 1967.

———. *History and Human Relations.* London, 1951

————. *Lord Acton*. London, 1948.

————. "Lord Acton." *Cambridge Journal* 6 (May 1953): 475–85.

————. *Man on His Past*. Cambridge, England, 1955.

————. Review of *Acton: The Formative Years*, by David Mathew. *English Historical Review* 61 (1946): 414.

————. Review of *Lord Acton: The Decisive Decade*, ed. Damian McElrath, James Holland, Ward White, and Sue Katzman. *Historical Journal* 15 (1972): 825–26.

————. *The Whig Interpretation of History*. London, 1931.

Cannadine, David. *The Decline and Fall of the British Aristocracy*. New Haven, 1990.

————. *G. M. Trevelyan: A Life in History*. London, 1992.

The Catholic Encyclopedia. 15 vols. plus index. New York, 1907–12.

Cesare, Raffaele de. *The Last Days of Papal Rome, 1850–1870*. Translated by Helen Zimmer, with an introduction by G. M. Trevelyan. London, 1909.

————. *Roma e lo Stato del Papa dal ritorno di Pio IX*. 3 vols. Rome, 1907.

Chadwick, Owen. "Acton and Butterfield." *Journal of Ecclesiastical History* 38, no. 3 (July 1987): 386–405.

————. *Acton and Gladstone*. London, 1976.

————. *Acton, Döllinger and History*. The 1986 Annual Lecture, German Historical Institute. London, 1987

————. *Catholicism and History: The Opening of the Vatican Archives. Herbert Henson Lectures in the University of Oxford*. Cambridge, England, 1978.

————. "The Challenge of Acton." *Tablet*, 28 January 1984, 77–78.

————. "Döllinger and Reunion." In *Christian Authority: Essays in Honour of Henry Chadwick*, edited by G. R. Evans, 296–334. Oxford, 1987.

————. *From Bossuet to Newman*. Cambridge, England, 1957.

————. "Lord Acton at the First Vatican Council." *Journal of Theological Studies*, no. 28 (1977): 465–97.

————. *Newman*. Oxford, 1983.

————. *Professor Lord Acton: The Regius Chair of Modern History at Cambridge, 1895–1902*. Foreword by Robert A. Sirico. Introduction by James C. Holland. Grand Rapids, Mich., 1995.

Chapman, Ronald. *Father Faber*. London, 1961.

Chronik der Ludwig Maximilian Universität München für das Jahr 1871–1872. Munich, 1872.

Clark, G. N. "The Origin of the Cambridge Modern History." *Cambridge Historical Journal* 8 (1945): 57–64.

Conzemius, Victor. "Acton, Döllinger and Gladstone: A Strange Variety of Anti-Infallibilists." In *Newman and Gladstone Centennial Essays*, edited by J. Bastable, 39–56. Dublin, 1978.

————. "Acton, Döllinger und Ketteler: Zum Verständnis des Ketteler-Bildes in den

Quirinusbriefen und zur Kritik an Vigeners Darstellung Kettelers auf dem Vatikanum I." *Archiv für Mittelrheinische Kirchengeschichte* 14 (1962): 194–238.

———. "Aspects ecclésiologiques de l'évolution de Döllinger et du vieux catholicisme," *Revue des sciences réligieuses* 34 (1960): 247–79.

———. "Ignaz von Döllinger. Zum 100, Todestag." *Neue Zürcher Zeitung,* 6–7 January 1990, 65.

———. "Katholizismus und moderne liberales: Katholizismus als Versuch der Aussöhnung." *Stimmen der Zeit* (Freiburg, Germany) 3 (1996): 173–185.

———. "Lord Acton and the First Vatican Council." *Journal of Ecclesiastical History* 20 (October 1969): 267–294.

———. "Die Minorität auf dem Ersten Vatikanischen Konzil: Vorhut des Zweiten Vatikanums." *Theologie und Philosophie* 45 (1970): 409–34.

———. *Propheten und Vorläufer: Wegbereiter des neuzeitlichen Katholizismus.* Zurich, 1972.

———. "Römische Briefe vom Konzil." *Theologische Quartalschrift* 140 (1960): 427–462.

———. "Die Römischen Briefe vom Konzil: Eine entstehungsgeschichtliche und quellenkritische Untersuchung zum Konzilsjournalismus Ignaz von Döllingers und Lord Actons." *Römische Quartalschrift für christliche Altertumskunde und Kirchengeschichte* 59 (1964): 186–229; and 60 (1965): 76–119.

———. "Die Verfasser der 'Römischen Briefe vom Konzil' des 'Quirinus.'" *Freiburger Geschichtsblätter: Festschrift für Hans Förster* 52 (1963–64): 229–256.

———. "Zwischen Rom, Canterbury und Konstantinopel: Der Altkatholizismus in römisch-katholischer Sicht." *Theologische Quartalschrift* 145 (1965): 188–234.

Conzemius, Victor, ed. "Der Tod Ignaz von Döllingers in den Briefen der Freunde." *Kurtrierisches Jahrbuch* 8 (1968): 300–316.

Cooper, Duff. *Talleyrand.* London, 1937.

Cowling, Maurice. "Mr. Woodruff's Acton." *Cambridge Journal* 6 (December 1952).

Craven, Mrs. Augustus. *Life of Lady Georgiana Fullerton.* Translated by H. J. Coleridge. London, 1888.

———. *Récit d'une sœur.* 2 vols. Paris, 1867. Translated by E. Bowles as *The Story of a Sister.* London, 1875.

Creighton, Louise. *Life and Letters of Mandell Creighton.* 2 vols. London, 1904.

Creighton, Mandell. *A History of the Papacy during the Period of the Reformation.* 5 vols. London, 1882–94.

Cwiekowski, Frederick J. *The English Bishops and the First Vatican Council.* Louvain, Belgium, 1971.

Declaration of the Catholic Bishops, the Vicar Apostolics and the Coadjutors in Great Britain. London, 1826 [Latin].

Denzinger, Heinrich Joseph, and Clement Bannwarth, S.J., eds. *Enchiridion Symbolorum Definitionum et Declarationum.* Würzburg, Germany, 1854. 37th ed., edited by Peter Hünermann. Freiburg, Germany, 1991.

Denzler, Georg, and Ernst Ludwig Grasmück, eds. *Geschichtlichkeit und Glaube.* Gedenkschrift zum 100. Todestag von Ignaz von Döllinger. Munich, 1990.

Dictionary of National Biography. Edited by Leslie Stephen and Sidney Lee. 65 vols. London, 1884–1950. Edited (since 1992) by H. C. G. Matthew.

Dizionario Biografico degli Italiani. Rome, 1960– .

Documenti Diplomatici Italiani. 2d ser., 1870–96. Vol. 1. Rome, 1960.

Döllinger, Ignaz von. *Akademische Vorträge.* 3 vols. Nördlingen, Germany, 1888–1891.

———. *Briefe und Erklärungen über die Vaticanischen Decrete, 1869–1887.* Munich, 1890; reprint, 1968.

———. *The Church and the Churches; or, The Papacy and the Temporal Power.* Translated by W. B. MacCabe. London, 1862.

———. *Declarations and Letters on the Vatican Decrees, 1869–1887.* Edited by F. H. Reusch. Edinburgh, 1891.

———. *Die Reformation: ihre innere Entwicklung und ihre Wirkungen im Umfange des lutherischen Bekenntnisses.* 3 vols. Regensburg, Germany, 1846–48.

———. *Ignaz Döllingers Briefe an eine junge Freundin.* Edited by Heinrich Schrörs. Kempten, Germany, 1914.

———. *Ignaz von Döllinger Briefwechsel.* Vols. 1–3, *Mit Lord Acton, 1850–1890;* Vol. 4, *Briefwechsel mit Lady Blennerhassett, 1865–1886.* Edited by Victor Conzemius. Munich, 1963–81.

———. *Kirche und Kirchen, Papstthum und Kirchenstaat, Historisch-politische Betrachtungen.* Munich, 1861.

———. *Kleinere Schriften.* Stuttgart, 1890.

———. *Lectures on the Reunion of the Churches.* Translated by H. N. Oxenham. London, 1872.

———. *Über die Wiedervereinigung der christlichen Kirchen.* Nördlingen, Germany, 1888.

Drew, Mary Gladstone. *Acton, Gladstone and Others.* London, 1924.

———. *Mary Gladstone (Mrs. Drew): Her Diaries and Letters.* Edited by Lucy Masterman. London, 1930.

———. *Some Hawarden Letters, 1878–1913, Written by Mary Drew.* Edited by Lisle March-Phillips and Bertram Christian. London, 1917.

Du Boys, Albert. *Ses souvenirs du Vatican, 1869–1870.* Louvain, Belgium, 1968.

Ehmer, Manfred. *Constantin Frantz: Die politische Gedankenwelt eines Klassikers des Föderalismus.* Rheinfelden, Germany, 1988.

Elliott, Walter. *The Life of Father Hecker.* New York, 1898.

Enciclopedia Cattolica. 12 vols. Rome, 1948–54.

Engel-Jánosi, Friedrich. "The Correspondence between Lord Acton and Bishop Creighton." *Cambridge Historical Journal* 6 (1940): 307–21.

———. "Die Österreichische Berichterstattung über das Vatikanische Konzil, 1869–1870." *Mitteilungen des Instituts für Österreichische Geschichtsforschung* 62 (1953): 595–615.

Engel-Jánosi, Friedrich, ed. *Österreich und der Vatikan, 1846–1918.* 2 vols. Graz, Austria, 1958–60.

Faber, F. W. *Devotion to the Church.* London, 1861.

Falloux, F. A. P. de. *Histoire de Saint Pie V: Pape de l'ordre des frères prêcheurs.* Paris, 1844.

Fasnacht, G. E. "Acton's Notes for a Romanes Lecture." *Contemporary Review* 182 (December 1952): 348–53.

———. *Acton's Political Philosophy.* London, 1952.

Finer, Herman. "Acton as Historian and Political Scientist." *Journal of Politics* 10 (1948): 603–35.

Finsterhölzl, Johann. *Ignaz von Döllinger.* Graz, Austria, 1969.

Fisher, H. A. L. *James Bryce.* 2 vols. London, 1927.

———. "Lord Acton's Lectures." *Independent Review* 11 (1906): 224–28.

———. *Studies in History and Politics.* Oxford, 1920.

Fitzmaurice, Edmond. *The Life of Granville George Leveson Gower, Second Earl Granville.* 2d ed. 2 vols. London, 1905.

Fliche, Augustin, and Victor Martin, eds. *Histoire de l'Eglise depuis les origines jusqu'à nos jours.* Vol. 21. Paris, 1963.

Florovsky, P. G. "L'oecumenisme au XIXe siècle." *Irénikon* 27 (1954): 443.

Foerster, Hans, ed. *Liber Diurnus Romanorum Pontificum.* Bern, Switzerland, 1958.

Fox, Henry Edward. *The Journal of the Hon. Henry Edward Fox, 1818–1830, afterwards Fourth Lord Holland.* Edited by the Earl of Ilchester. London, 1923.

Frederick, Empress. *Letters of the Empress Frederick.* Edited by F. Ponsonby. London, 1929.

Friedrich, Johann. *Geschichte des vatikanischen Konzils.* 3 vols. Bonn, 1877–1887.

———. *Ignaz von Döllinger.* 3 vols. Munich, 1899–1901.

———. *See also* Janus.

Fries, H. "J. H. Newman. Ein Wegbereiter des Zweiten Vatikanischen Konzils." *Newman Studien* 7 (1978): 281–91.

Fulford, Roger, ed. *Letters Between Queen Victoria and Her Daughter Victoria* (title varies), *1858–71.* London, 1964–71.

Gibbon, Edward. *The Autobiographies of Edward Gibbon.* Edited by Oliphant Smeater. London, 1932.

Gilley, Sheridan. *Newman and His Age.* London, 1990.

Gillow, Joseph, ed. *Bibliographical Dictionary of the English Catholics.* 5 vols. London, 1885–95.

Gladstone, Mary. *See* Drew, Mary Gladstone.

Gladstone, William Ewart. "Dr. Döllinger's Posthumous Remains." *Speaker* (London), 30 August 1890, 231–33.

———. *The Gladstone Diaries.* Edited by M. R. D. Foot and H. C. G. Matthew. 14 vols. Oxford, 1968–94.

———. *The Impregnable Rock of Holy Scripture.* London, 1890.

———. *Later Gleanings.* London, 1898.

———. *The Political Correspondence of Mr. Gladstone and Lord Granville, 1868–1876.* Edited by Agatha Ramm. 2 vols. London, 1952.

———. *The Political Correspondence of Mr. Gladstone and Lord Granville, 1876–1886.* Edited by Agatha Ramm. 2 vols. London, 1962.

———. "The Right Rev. Dr. von Döllinger." *Speaker* (London), 18 January 1890, 57–60.

———. "Ritualism and Ritual." *Contemporary Review* 24 (1874): 663–81.

———. "Robert Elsmere, the Battle of Belief." *Nineteenth Century* 23 (1888): 766–88.

———. *Studies on Homer and the Homeric Age.* 3 vols. Oxford, 1858.

———. *The Vatican Decrees in Their Bearing on Civil Allegiance: A Political Expostulation.* London, 1874.

———. *Vaticanism: An Answer to "Reproofs and Replies."* London, 1875.

Gooch, George P. *History and Historians in the Nineteenth Century.* London, 1913; 2d rev. ed., 1952.

———. "Lord Acton: Apostle of Liberty." *Foreign Affairs* 25 (July 1947): 629–42.

———. *Under Six Reigns.* London, 1958.

Granderath, Theodor, S.J. *Geschichte des Vatikanischen Konzils von seiner ersten Ankündigung bis zu seiner Vertagung: Nach den authentischen Dokumenten.* Edited by Konrad Kirch. 3 vols. Freiburg, Germany, 1903–6.

Grant Duff, Mountstuart E. "Lord Acton's Letters." *Nineteenth Century and After* 55 (1904): 765–75.

———. *Notes from a Diary, 1851–1901.* 14 vols. London, 1897–1905.

———. *Out of the Past: Some Biographical Essays.* 2 vols. London, 1903.

Granville, Harriet. *The Letters of Harriet, Countess Granville, 1810–1845.* Edited by F. Leveson Gower. 2 vols. London, 1894.

Gray, Robert. *Cardinal Manning: A Biography.* London, 1985.

Gréard, Octave. *Edmond Scherer.* Paris, 1890.

Gregorovius, Ferdinand. *The Roman Journals of Ferdinand Gregorovius, 1852–1874.* Edited by Friedrich Althaus, translated by G. W. Hamilton. London, 1911.

Greville, Charles, C.F. *The Greville Memoirs: A Journal of the Reigns of King George IV, King William IV and Queen Victoria.* Edited by Henry Reeve. 8 vols. London, 1888.

Gunn, Peter. *The Actons*. London, 1978.

Gwatkin, Jean Bowes. "Döllinger, the Renoufs and Rome." *Tablet* 222, no. 6661 (January 1968): 54–55.

Gwynn, Denis. *A Hundred Years of Catholic Emancipation*. London, 1929.

———. *Lord Shrewsbury, Pugin and the Catholic Revival*. London, 1946.

Hacker, Rupert. *Ludwig II von Bayern in Augenzeugenberichten*. Düsseldorf, 1966.

Hager, A. "Hefele und das Vatikanische Konzil." *Tübinger Theologische Quartalschrift* 124 (1942): 223–52.

Haight, Gordon S. *George Eliot: A Biography*. Oxford, 1968.

Hales, E. E. Y. *Pio Nono*. 2d ed. London, 1956.

Hammond, J. L. "Lord Acton's Liberalism." *Independent Review* 2 (May 1904): 651–56.

Hansard Parliamentary Debates. 3d ser., vols. 158–66, 1860–62; 4th ser., vols. 346–51, 1890–97.

Hart, Joseph A. "Lord Acton and the First Vatican Council: A View of Infallibility from His Writings and Unpublished Manuscripts." Doctoral diss., Theological Faculty in the Pontifical Gregorian University, Rome, 1994.

Hefele, C. de. *Causa Honorii papae*. Naples, 1870.

Helfert, Joseph Alexander von. *Maria Karolina von Österreich, 1790–1814*. Vienna, 1884.

Hendrick, Burton J. *The Life of Andrew Carnegie*. London, 1933.

Hennesey, James J. *The First Council of the Vatican: The American Experience*. New York, 1963.

Himmelfarb, Gertrude. "The American Revolution in the Political Theory of Lord Acton." *Journal of Modern History* 21 (1949): 293–312.

———. *Lord Acton: A Study in Conscience and Politics*. London, 1952.

———. *Marriage and Morals among the Victorians and Other Essays*. London, 1986.

———. *Victorian Minds*. London, 1968.

Höfer, Josef, and Karl Rahner, eds. *Lexikon für Theologie und Kirche*. 2d rev. ed. 10 vols. Freiburg, Germany, 1957–65; 3d ed., 1993–   .

Holland, Hyazinth. *Lebenserinnerungen eines neunzig-jährigen Alt-Münchners*. Munich, 1921.

Holland, James C. "The Education of Lord Acton." Ph.D. diss., Catholic University of America, Washington, D.C., 1968.

———. *The Legacy of an Education*. Introduction by Stephen J. Tonsor. Grand Rapids, Mich., 1997.

Holland, Mary Griset. *The British Catholic Press and the Educational Controversy, 1847–1865*. New York, 1987.

Holmes, J. D. *More Roman Than Rome: English Catholicism in the Nineteenth Century*. London, 1978.

———. "Newman's Attitude towards the Definition of Papal Infallibility Illustrating the Significance of History in Christian Belief." *Newman Studien* 9 (1974): 119–35.

Houghton, Walter E., ed. *The Wellesley Index to Victorian Periodicals, 1824–1900*. 5 vols. Toronto, 1966–89.

Howland, A. C., ed. *Minor Historical Writings*. Philadelphia, 1942.

Huber, Johannes Nepomuk. *See* Janus.

Hügel, Friedrich von. *Selected Letters*. Edited by Bernard Holland. London, 1927.

Hutton, A. W. "Personal Reminiscense of Cardinal Newman." *Expositor*, 4th ser., 2 (1890): September, 223–40; October, 304–20; November, 336–50.

Hyde, H. Montgomery. *Henry James at Home*. London, 1969.

Jackson-Stops, Gervase. Several articles relating to Aldenham Park. *Country Life* (London), 23 and 30 June and 7 July 1977.

Jagger, Peter J., ed. *Gladstone, Politics and Religion: A Collection of Founder's Day Lectures Delivered at St. Deiniol's Library, Hawarden, 1967–83*. London, 1985.

Janus [Ignaz von Döllinger, Johann Friedrich, and Johannes Nepomuk Huber]. *Der Papst und das Concil*. Leipzig, Germany, 1869. Published in English as *The Pope and the Council*. London, 1869.

Jenkins, Roy. *Gladstone*. London, 1995.

Jesuits of Maria Laach, eds. *Acta et Decreta Sacrorum Conciliorum Recensiorum, Collectio Lacensis* (Collection of Vatican Council Acts and Decrees). 7 vols. Freiburg, Germany, 1870–90.

Johnston, J. O. *Henry Parry Liddon*. London, 1904.

Jörg, Edmund. "Döllinger." *Historisch-Politische Blätter* 105 (1890): 237–48, 248–62.

Keenan, Stephen. *Controversial Catechism; or, Protestantism Refuted and Catholicism Established*. 3d ed. Edinburgh, 1854.

Kenrick, Peter Richard. *An Inside View of the Vatican Council*. Edited by Leonard W. Bacon. New York, 1872.

Kenyon, John. "'Absolute Power Corrupts . . .': The Great Historians—Lord Acton." *Observer Magazine* (London), 5 December 1976, 25–33.

Ker, Ian. *John Henry Newman: A Biography*. Oxford, 1988.

Ketteler, Wilhelm Emmanuel von. *Die Minorität auf dem Concil: Antwort auf Lord Actons Sendschreiben: An einen deutschen Bischof des Vaticanischen Concils*. Mainz, Germany, 1870.

———. *Die Unwahrheiten der Römischen Briefe vom Konzil in der Allgemeinen Zeitung*. Mainz, Germany, 1870.

Kettenacker, Lothar. "Lord Acton: Wegbereiter der deutschen historischen Schule und Kritiker des Historismus." In *Kirche, Staat und Gesellschaft im 19. Jahrhundert: Ein deutsch-englischer Vergleich*, edited by Adolf M. Birke and Kurt Kluxen, 99–120. Prinz Albert Studienband 2. Munich, 1984.

———. "Lord Acton und Ignaz von Döllinger." Ph.D. diss., Oxford University, 1971.

Klausnitzer, Wolfgang. *Päpstliche Unfehlbarkeit bei Newman und Döllinger: Ein historisch-systematischer Vergleich*. Innsbruck, Austria, 1980.

Kobell, Louise von. *Conversations of Dr. Döllinger.* Translated by Katherine Gould. London, 1892.

Kochan, Lionel. *Acton on History.* London, 1954.

Kösch, Wilhelm. *Das Katholische Deutschland: Biographisch-bibliophiles Lexikon.* 3 vols. Augsburg, Germany, 1933–1939.

Kraus, Franz Xavier. *Tagebücher.* Edited by H. Schiel. Cologne, 1957.

Kremser, H. "Die Bedeutung des Vinzenz von Lerinum für die römisch-katholische Wertung der Tradition." Ph.D. diss., University of Hamburg, 1959.

Lally, F.E. *As Lord Acton Says.* Newport, R.I., 1942.

Lamprecht, Karl. "Lord Acton, Über das Studium der Geschichte, Eröffnungsvorlesung, gehalten zu Cambridge am 11. Juni 1895. Rechtmäßige Übersetzung von I. Immelmann, Berlin 1897." *Deutsche Zeitschrift für Geschichtswissenschaft, 1897–1898.* Freiburg, Germany, 1898, 212–214.

Lappenberg, Johann Martin, Reinhold Pauli, and Moritz Brosch. *Geschichte von England.* 10 vols. Hamburg, 1834–98.

Laurence, R. V. "Acton as a Teacher." *Cambridge Review,* 23 October 1902, 23–24.

Lauxtermann, Paulus. *Constantin Frantz: Romantik und Realismus im Werke eine politischen Aussenseiters.* Groningen, Germany, 1978.

Lecanuet, Edouard. *Montalembert.* 3 vols. Paris, 1895–1902.

Leetham, Claude. *Rosmini: Priest, Philosopher and Patriot.* London, 1957.

Leibniz, Gottfried Wilhelm von. *Correspondence of Leibniz and the Princess Sophie, Electress of Brunswick (1680–1714).* Edited by Onno Klopp. Hanover, Germany, 1873.

Lejeune, Anthony. *The Gentlemen's Clubs of London.* London, 1979.

Leslie, Shane. *Henry Edward Manning.* 2d ed. rev. London, 1921.

Leveson-Gower, George. *Years of Endeavour.* London, 1942.

Lialine, Clément. "Vieux-catholiques et Orthodoxes Enquête d'union depuis trois quarts de siècle." *Istina* 5 (1958): 22.

Liddon, Henry Parry. *Life of Edward Bouverie Pusey.* 4 vols. London, 1897.

———. *Report of the Proceedings of the Reunion Conference Held at Bonn on September 14, 15, and 16, 1874.* London, 1875.

Lill, Rudolf. *Die ersten deutschen Bischofskonferenzen.* Freiburg, Germany, 1964.

Lösch, Stefan. *Döllinger und Frankreich: Eine geistige Allianz, 1823–1871.* Munich, 1955.

Loyoz, Eduard. *Essai sur Edmond Scherer, théologien.* Paris, 1890.

MacDougall, Hugh A. *The Acton-Newman Relations: The Dilemma of Christian Liberalism.* New York, 1962.

Mackay, James. *Little Boss: A Life of Andrew Carnegie.* London, 1997.

Maioli, Giovanni. *Marco Minghetti.* Bologna, 1926.

Maitland, Frederick William. *Collected Papers.* Edited by H. A. L. Fisher. 3 vols. Cambridge, England, 1911.

———. "The Late Lord Acton." *Cambridge Review,* 16 October 1902, 7–9.

Mann, Golo. *Geschichte und Geschichten*. Frankfurt, 1961.

Manning, Henry Edward. Advent pastoral letter. *Tablet* 44 (5 December 1874): 726.

———. *Caesarism and Ultramontanism*. London, 1874.

———. *The Ecumenical Council and Infallibility*. Pastoral letter. March 1870.

———. Letter to the editor. *Times*, 9 November 1874, 9.

———. "Prussia and the Vatican." *Macmillan's Magazine* 31 (1874): 259–60.

———. *Sermons on Ecclesiastical Subjects*. London, 1873.

———. *The Temporal Power of the Vicar of Jesus Christ*. 2d ed. London, 1862.

———. *The Temporal Sovereignty of the Popes*. London, 1860.

———. "The True Story of the Vatican Council." *Nineteenth Century* 1 (1877): 122–40, 177–97, 479–503, 596–610, 790–808.

Mansi, Giovanni Domenico, ed. *Sacrorum Conciliorum, nova et amplissima collectio*. 55 vols. *Oecumenia Concilii Vaticani*. Graz, Austria, 1901–27. Edition of Microcard Foundation. Washington, 1961

Mathew, David. *Acton: The Formative Years*. London, 1946.

———. *Catholicism in England*. London, 1936. 3d rev. ed., London, 1955.

———. *Lord Acton and His Times*. London, 1968.

Matthew, H. C. G. *Gladstone, 1809–1874*. Oxford, 1986.

———. *Gladstone, 1875–1898*. Oxford, 1995.

———. "Gladstone, Vaticanism and the Question of the East." *Studies in Church History* 15 (1978): 417–42.

McElrath, Damian. *Richard Simpson, 1820–1876*. Louvain, Belgium, 1972.

———. "Richard Simpson and John Henry Newman: *The Rambler*, Layman and Theology." *Catholic Historical Review* 52, no. 4 (January 1967): 509–33.

———. *The "Syllabus" of Pius IX: Some Reactions in England*. Louvain, Belgium, 1964.

Metternich, Clemens Wenzel Lothar, Fürst von. *Mémoires of Prince Metternich*. 8 vols. Paris, 1880–84.

Meyer, Bernhard von. *Erlebnisse*. 2 vols. Vienna, 1875.

Meyrick, Frederick, ed. *Correspondence between the Anglo-Continental Society and the Secretaries of the Friends of Spiritual Enlightenment in St. Petersburg Concerning Statements on the Validity of Anglican Orders*. London, 1874.

———. *Correspondence between Members of the Anglo-Continental Society and the Old Catholics* (pt. 1); *Correspondence between Members of the Anglo-Continental Society and the Oriental Churchmen* (pt. 2). London, 1874–77.

———. *Memoirs of Life at Oxford, and Experiences in Italy, Greece, Turkey, Germany, Spain and Elsewhere*. London, 1905.

Meyrick, Frederick, and Edward Bickersteth. *Two Papers on the Old Catholic Movement and the Bonn Conference*. London, 1877.

Mill, John Stuart. *Considerations on Representative Government*. London, 1861.

Morier, Robert. "Prussia and the Vatican." *Macmillan's Magazine* 31 (1874): 72–88. Cardinal Manning's letter of protest on pp. 259–60 and Morier's reply on pp. 373–75.

———. "The Prussian and the German Legislation to Which the Vatican Decrees Gave Rise." *Macmillan's Magazine* 31 (1874): 261–80.

———. "The Relations between Church and State in Prussia up to 1859." *Macmillan's Magazine* 30 (1874): 559–68.

———. "The Settlement of the Peace of Westphalia," *Macmillan's Magazine* 30 (1874): 464–472.

Morley, John. *The Life of William Ewart Gladstone.* 3 vols. London, 1903.

———. *Recollections.* 2 vols. London, 1917.

Moss, C. B. *The Old Catholic Movement: Its Origins and History.* 2d ed. London, 1964.

Mozley, Thomas. *Letters from Rome on the Occasion of the Oecumenical Council.* 2 vols. London, 1891.

Nelson, Lord. *Letters from Lord Nelson.* Compiled by Geoffrey Rawson. London, 1949.

Neuner, P. *Döllinger als Theologe der Ökumene: Beiträge zur ökumenischen Theologie.* Edited by H. Fries. Paderborn, Germany, 1979.

Nevin, R. J. Letter to the editor. *Churchman* (London), 14 October 1874.

Newman, E. R. "Cardinal Manning and the Temporal Power." In *History, Society and the Churches: Essays in Honour of Owen Chadwick,* edited by Derek Beales and Geoffrey Best. Cambridge, England, 1985.

Newman, John Henry. *Apologia pro Vita Sua.* New ed. London, 1902.

———. *Apologia pro Vita Sua: Being a History of His Religious Opinions.* Edited by Martin J. Svaglic. Oxford, 1967.

———. *Certain Difficulties Felt by Anglicans in Catholic Teaching.* 2 vols. London, 1850; 2d ed., London, 1876.

———. *Historical Sketches.* London, 1872.

———. *The Idea of a University.* 1873. Edited by I. T. Ker. Oxford, 1976.

———. *John Henry Newman: Autobiographical Writings.* Edited by Henry Tristram. London, 1956.

———. *Letters and Diaries of John Henry Newman.* Edited by Charles Stephen Dessain, Vincent Ferrer Blehl, S.J., Edward E. Kelley, S.J., Thomas Gornall, S.J., Ian Ker, and Gerard Tracey. 31 vols. planned, 27 published to date. Vols. 1–6, Oxford, 1978–84; vols. 11-22, London, 1961–72; vols. 23–31, Oxford, 1973–77.

———. *Mr. Kingsley and Dr. Newman: A Correspondence on the Question Whether Dr. Newman Teaches That Truth Is No Virtue.* London, 1864.

———. *On Consulting the Faithful in Matters of Doctrine.* Edited by John Coulson. London, 1961. First published in *Rambler*, 3d ser., 1 (July 1859): 198–230.

———. *Tracts Theological and Ecclesiastical.* London, 1874.

Newsome, David. *The Parting of Friends: A Study of the Wilberforces and Henry Manning.* London, 1966.

Newton, Lord. *Life of Lord Lansdowne*. London, 1929.

Noack, Ulrich. *Geschichtswissenschaft und Wahrheit: Nach den Schriften von John Dalberg Acton*. Frankfurt, 1935.

——. *Katholizität und Geistesfreiheit: Nach den Schriften von John Dalberg Acton*. Frankfurt, 1936.

——. *Politik als Sicherung der Freiheit: Nach den Schriften von John Dalberg Acton*. Frankfurt, 1947.

Norman, Edward. *Anti-Catholicism in Victorian England*. London, 1968.

——. *Roman Catholicism in England from the Elizabethan Settlement to the Second Vatican Council*. Oxford, 1985.

Nurser, John. *The Reign of Conscience: Individual, Church and State in Lord Acton's History of Liberty*. New York, 1987.

Oeyen, Christian. "Die Entstehung der Bonner Unions-Konferenzen im Jahr 1874." Ph.D. diss., Old Catholic Theological Faculty, University of Bern, 1971.

Ollivier, Emile. *L'Eglise et l'état au Concile du Vatican*. 2 vols. Paris, 1879.

Paget, Walpurga. *Embassies of Other Days and Further Recollections*. London, 1923.

——. *The Linings of Life*. 2 vols. London, 1928.

Pakula, Hannah. *An Uncommon Woman: The Empress Frederick*. London, 1996.

Palmer, Alan. *Crowned Cousins*. London, 1985.

Parry, John Orlando. *Victorian Swandown: The Early Travel Diaries of John Orlando Parry*. Edited by Cyril Andrews and J. A. Orr-Oriving. London, 1935.

Pásztor, L. "Il Concilio Vaticano I: Diario di Vincenzo Tizzani, 1869–1870." In *Päpste und Papsttum* 25. Stuttgart, 1991.

Pauli, Reinhold. *Geschichte Englands seit den Friedensschlässen von 1814 und 1815*. 3 vols. Leipzig, Germany, 1864–75.

——. *Lebenserinnerungen nach Briefen und Tagebüchern zusammengestellt*. Edited by Elizabeth Pauli. Halle, Germany, 1895.

Pezzimenti, Rocco. *Il pensiero politico di Lord Acton: I cattolici Inglesi dell'Ottocento*. Rome, 1992.

Plummer, Alfred. "Recollections of Dr. Döllinger." *Expositor,* 4th ser., 1 (1980): 212–25, 270–84, 422–35.

Pollock, John. "Lord Acton at Cambridge." *Independent Review* 2 (1904): 360–78.

Poole, R. L. "John Emerich Lord Acton." *English Historical Review* 17 (1902): 692–99.

Purcell, Edmund Sheridan. *Life of Cardinal Manning*. 2 vols. London, 1896.

Quirinus [John Emerich Edward Dalberg Acton, Johann Friedrich, and Ignaz von Döllinger]. *Römische Briefe vom Concil des Quirinus*. Munich, 1870. Published in English as *Letters from Rome on the Council,* translated by Henry Nutcombe Oxenham, London, 1870. Republished in 2 vols., New York, 1973.

Ramm, Agatha, ed. "Gladstone's Religion." *Historical Journal* 28, no. 2 (1985): 327–40.

————. *Sir Robert Morier: Envoy and Ambassador in the Age of Imperialism, 1876–1893*. Oxford, 1973.

Ranke, Leopold von. *Das Briefwerk*. Edited by W. P. Fuchs. Hamburg, 1949.

————. *Leopold von Ranke: Neue Briefe*. Edited by Bernhard Höft, and after his death by Hans Herzfeld. Hamburg, 1949.

Renan, Ernest. *Recollections of My Youth*. Edited by G. G. Coulton. London, 1929.

Renouf, Peter le Page. *The Case of Pope Honorius, Reconsidered with Reference to Recent Apologies*. London, 1869.

Renouf, Peter le Page, trans. *The Egyptian Book of the Dead*. Continued and completed by Edouard Naville with a short introduction on the life and work of Sir Peter le Page Renouf. London, 1902–7.

Report of the Proceedings of the Reunion Conference Held at Bonn on September 14, 15, and 16, 1875. London, 1875.

Reusch, F. G. *Bericht über die Unionskonferenz von Bonn*. Bonn, 1874–75.

Reynolds, E. E. *Three Cardinals: Newman—Wiseman—Manning*. London, 1958.

Roberts, Andrew. *Salisbury, Victorian Titan*. London, 1999.

Röhl, John C. G. *The Kaiser and His Court: Wilhelm II and the Government of Germany*. Cambridge, England, 1996.

Romig, W. *Josephine Van Dyke Brownson*. Detroit, 1955.

Rosebery, Fifth Earl of. "Mr. Gladstone's Last Cabinet." *History Today* (January 1951): 17.

Roskell, M. F. *Memoirs of Francis Kerril Amherst*. London, 1903.

Rosmini-Serbati, Antonio. *Delle cinque piaghe della Santa Chiesa . . .* Perugia, Italy, 1849.

————. *La Costituzione secondo la giustizia sociale*. Milan, 1848.

Rothschild, Miriam. *Dear Lord Rothschild: Birds, Butterflies and History*. Philadelphia, 1983.

Russell, Odo. *The Roman Question: Extracts from the Dispatches of Odo Russell from Rome, 1858–1870*. Edited by Noel Blakiston. London, 1962.

Ryan, Guy A. "The Acton Circle, 1864–1871: The *Chronicle* and the *North British Review*." Ph.D. diss., University of Notre Dame, South Bend, Ind., 1969.

————. "The Acton Circle and the *Chronicle*, 1867–1868." *Victorian Periodicals Newsletter* 7, no. 2 (June 1974): 10–24.

Schatz, Klaus, S.J. "Kirchenbild und päpstliche Unfehlbarkeit bei den deutschsprachigen Minoritätsbischöfen auf dem 1. Vaticanum." Doctoral diss., Università Gregoriana Editrice, Rome, 1975.

————. *Vaticanum I, 1869–1870*. 3 vols. Paderborn, Germany, 1992–94.

Scherer, Edmond Henri Adolphe. *Mélanges de l'histoire religieuse*. Paris, 1864.

Scherr, Archbishop Gregor von. *Hirtenbrief Seiner Exzellenz Gregorius Erzbischof von München und Freising*. Pastoral letter, 2 April 1871. Munich, 1871.

Schlözer, Kurd von. *Letzte Römische Briefe, 1882–1894*. Stuttgart, 1924.

————. *Römische Briefe, 1864–1869*. Stuttgart, 1913.

Schnabel, Franz. *Deutsche Geschichte im neunzehnten Jahrhundert.* 2d ed. 4 vols. Freiburg, Germany, 1951.

Schuhmann, Edith. "Charlotte Lady Blennerhassett als Historikerin und Essayistin: Ein Beitrag zur Geistesgeschichte um die Jahrhundertwende." Ph.D. diss., University of Mainz, 1955.

Schulte, Johann Friedrich von. *Der Altkatholizismus.* Giessen, Germany, 1887.

Seeley, John Robert. *Ecce Homo: A Survey of the Life and Work of Jesus Christ.* London, 1876.

————. *The Expansion of England: Two Courses of Lectures.* London, 1883.

————. *Life and Times of Stein; or Germany and Prussia in the Napoleonic Age.* 3 vols. Cambridge, England, 1878.

————. *A Short History of Napoleon the First.* London, 1886.

Seton-Watson, R. W. *The Southern Slav Question and the Habsburg Monarchy.* London, 1911.

Shattock, Joanne, and Michael Wolff, eds. *The Victorian Periodical Press: Samplings and Soundings.* Leicester, England, 1982.

Shorter, Clement. "Lord Acton's Hundred Best Books." *Pall Mall Magazine* 36, no. 147 (1905): 3–10.

Sickel, Theodor von. *Römische Erinnerungen.* Edited by L. Santifaller. Vienna, 1947.

Simpson, Richard. *Bishop Ullathorne and the Rambler: A Reply to Criticisms Contained in a Letter on the Rambler and Home and Foreign Review by Bishop Ullathorne.* London, 1862.

————. *Edmund Campion: A Biography.* London, 1867.

Sivric, Ivo, OFM. *Bishop J. G. Strossmayer: New Light on Vatican I.* Rome, 1975.

Slinn, Judy. *A History of Freshfields.* London, 1983.

Smith, R. A. L. "Acton." *New Statesman,* 27 May 1944, 355.

Snead-Cox, J. G. *The Life of Cardinal Vaughan.* 2 vols. London, 1910.

Speigl, Jacob. *Traditionslehre und Traditionsbeweise in der historischen Theologie Ignaz von Döllingers.* Essen, Germany, 1964.

Staatslexikon. Freiburg, Germany, 1889. 6th ed., 1956–   .

Staël, Madame de [Germaine Necker]. *Corinne; ou, l'Italie.* 2 vols. Paris, 1807. Reprint, 1841–42.

Stenographischer Bericht über die Verhandlungen des Katholiken Congresses, abgehalten vom 2. bis 24. September 1871 in München. Munich, 1871. Copy in Bayerisches Geheimes Staatsarchive, Munich, Döllingeriana.

Strachey, Lytton. *Eminent Victorians.* London, 1918.

Susini, E. *Franz von Baader et le romantisme mystique.* Paris, 1942.

Tamborra, Angelo. *Imbro I. Tkalac and l'Italia.* Rome, 1966.

Tedder, Henry R. *The Athenaeum, 1824–1924.* London, 1924.

———. "The Athenaeum: A Centenary Record." *Times,* 16 February 1924.

———. "Lord Acton and His Circle." *Month* 509 (November 1906): 547–49.

———. "Lord Acton as a Book Collector." *Proceedings of the British Academy* 1 (1903–4): 285–88.

Temperley, Harold. "Lord Acton on the Origins of the War of 1870, with Some Unpublished Letters from the British and Viennese Archives." *Cambridge Historical Journal* 2 (1926): 68–82.

Tennyson, Hallam Tennyson, Baron. *Tennyson and His Friends.* London, 1911.

Thornely, Thomas. *Cambridge Memories.* London, 1936.

Thurston, Herbert. "The Late Lord Acton." *Catholic World* 84 (1906): 357–72.

———. "The Late Lord Acton and the 'Cambridge Modern History.'" *Tablet,* 15 July 1905, 88–90.

———. "Lord Acton and His Circle." *Month* 509 (November, 1906), 547–49.

Trevelyan, G. M. *An Autobiography and Other Essays.* London, 1949.

———. *The Present Position of History: An Inaugural Lecture.* Cambridge, England, 1927.

Trevor, Meriol. *Newman.* Vol. 1, *The Pillar of the Cloud;* Vol. 2, *Light in Winter.* London, 1962.

Tulloch, Hugh. *Acton.* London, 1988.

Ullathorne, William Bernard. *From Cabin-Boy to Archbishop: The Autobiography of Archbishop Ullathorne.* Edited by Shane Leslie. London, 1941.

———. *A Letter on the "Rambler" and the "Home and Foreign Review."* London, 1862.

Valynseele, Joseph. *Les princes et ducs du Premier Empire non maréchaux.* Paris, 1959.

Veuillot, Eugène, and François Veuillot. *Louis Veuillot.* 4 vols. Paris, 1902–13.

Veuillot, Louis. *Rome pendant le Concile.* 2 vols. Paris, 1872.

Victoria, Queen of Great Britain. *The Letters of Queen Victoria.* 2d ser., *A Selection from Her Majesty's Correspondence and Journal between the Years 1862 and 1878.* Edited by G. E. Buckle. 3 vols. London, 1926. 3d ser., *1886–1901.* Edited by G. E. Buckle. 3 vols. London, 1930.

Walsh, Michael. *The Tablet, 1840–1990: A Commemorative History.* London, 1990.

Ward, Bernard. *The Eve of Catholic Emancipation.* 3 vols. 1911–1912. Reprint, London, 1970.

Ward, Maisie. *The Wilfrid Wards and the Transition.* 2 vols. London, 1934.

Ward, Wilfrid. *The Life and Times of Cardinal Wiseman.* 2 vols. London, 1897.

———. *The Life of John Henry Newman.* 2 vols. London, 1912.

———. *William George Ward and the Catholic Revival.* London, 1893.

Watkin, Edward Ingram. *Roman Catholicism in England from the Reformation to 1950.* London, 1957.

Watson, George. *The English Ideology: Studies in the Language of Victorian Politics.* London, 1973.

———. *Lord Acton's History of Liberty*. Aldershot, England, 1994.

———. *Politics and Literature in Modern Britain*. London, 1977.

Watt, E. D. "Rome and Lord Acton: A Reinterpretation." *Review of Politics* 28, no. 4 (October 1966): 493–507.

Weinzierl-Fischer, Erika. "Bismarcks Haltung zum Vatikanum und der Beginn des Kulturkampfes nach den Österreichischen diplomatischen Berichten aus Berlin 1869–1871." *Mitteilungen des Österreichischen Staatsarchivs* 10 (1957): 302–31.

Wemyss, Lady Hester. *Memoirs and Letters of the Right Hon. Sir Robert Morier, G.C.B., from 1826 to 1876*. London, 1911.

West, Algernon. *The Private Diaries of the Rt. Hon. Sir Algernon West*. Edited by Horace G. Hutchinson. London, 1922.

———. *Recollections: 1832–1886*. 2d ed. 2 vols. London, 1899.

Whisenant, James. "Lord Acton's Responses to the Hierarchy in the Controversies of 1858–1864." *Downside Review* 1071 (1989): 34–48.

White, William Ward. "Acton and Gladstone: Their Friendship and Mutual Influence." Ph.D. diss., Catholic University of America, Washington, D.C., 1972.

Williams, Francis. *Dangerous Estate: The Anatomy of Newspapers*. London, 1957.

Wilson, A. N. *Eminent Victorians*. London, 1989.

Wiseman, Nicholas. *Essays on Various Subjects*. 3 vols. London, 1853.

———. *Rome and the Catholic Episcopate: Reply of His Eminence Cardinal Wiseman to an Address Presented by the Clergy, Secular and Regular, of the Archdiocese of Westminster*. London, 1862.

———. *Words of Peace and Justice Addressed to the Catholic Clergy and Laity of the London District on the Subject of Diplomatic Relations with the Holy See*. London, 1848.

Woodward, E. L. *The Age of Reform, 1815–1870*. Rev. ed. Oxford, 1958.

———. "The Place of Lord Acton in the Liberal Movement of the Nineteenth Century." *Politica* 4 (September 1939): 248–65.

Wright, R. T. *The Cambridge Modern History: An Account of Its Origin, Authorship and Production*. Cambridge, England, 1907.

INDEX

Academia dei Lincei, 174

Academical Addresses (Döllinger), 325–26

Acta Genuina Concilii Tridentini (Theiner), 241

Acton, Anne Cathérine Loys, 10

Acton, Anne Mary Catherine Georgiana, "Annie" (daughter), 12, 130, 172, 236, 283, 384, 420n.9; in Cambridge house, 398; correspondence with father, 313, 325, 342, 343, 346, 348, 355, 356, 359, 369, 374, 376, 382, 386, 388, 393, 400; death of father, 401, 402; relationship with father, 167; in Rome, 204, 456n.53

Acton, Carlo Giuseppe, 6

Acton, Charles, Cardinal, 2–3, 13, 15, 18, 44, 79, 82, 179, 287, 418n.6, 468n.70

Acton, Edward (Dr.), xx, 9–10, 11

Acton, Sir Edward, 3d Baronet, 10, 57

Acton, Elisabeth, "Lily" (daughter), 169, 272, 281, 283, 309, 311, 402

Acton, Elizabeth. *See* Throckmorton, Elizabeth Acton

Acton, Elizabeth Gibbon, 10, 57

Acton, Sir Ferdinand Richard, 7th Baronet (father), xxi, 1, 3, 4, 5, 57; character and appearance of, 13–14; death of, 14; marriage to Marie Dalberg, 7–9

Acton, Giuseppe Eduardo, 11

Acton, Sir Harold Mario, 3

Acton, Jeanne, "Simmy" (daughter), 168–69, 170, 283, 309, 398

Acton, John (Commodore), xx, 11

Acton, John (son), 169, 249, 281

Acton, Sir John Emerich Edward Dalberg, 8th Baronet, 1st Baron: Aldenham estate of (*see* Aldenham); in America, 63–67; on American Civil War, 87–88, 387; and Arco family, xxi, 27, 40–44, 47–49, 424n.1; background of Acton family, xx–xxi, 2–3, 9–15; background of Dalberg family, 7–8, 9, 42; in Berlin, 103; best-book lists of, 284–87; birth and christening of, 1; Bridgnorth lectures of, 277–80; and *Cambridge Modern History,* 392–97; and Cambridge University (*see* Cambridge University); characterized, xix, 169, 170, 293, 388–89; and Charlotte Blennerhassett, 205–6, 311, 327; clubs of, 293–95; contemporary influence of, 410–16; on corrupting nature of power, xxiv, 300, 413–14; courtship of Marie Arco, 43–44, 53, 97–100, 101–2, 157–60, 161–64; and Creighton controversy, 296, 298–301, 302–3; death and burial of, 401–3, 498n.40; and death of Döllinger, 324–25, 328–29; death of father, 14–15; death of mother, 97, 100–101; deaths of children, 249, 281, 311; defiance of Vatican decrees, 259–61, 264–66, 272; diplomatic post sought by, 350–52; -Döllinger estrangement, 33, 170, 232, 256, 301–2, 308, 309, 316–24, 409–10; on Döllinger's scholarship, 329–31; -Döllinger travels, 33–34, 42–43, 50, 72–74, 78–80, 159; early life in Naples, 3–4, 6; education at Gentilly, 19–20; education at Oscott, 18–19, 20–22, 24, 55; education in Edinburgh, 24–25; education in Munich, xxi, 25–33, 44–47, 108; elections to Parliament, 82–85, 94–97; and *English Historical Review,* 296–98; and excommunication threat,

261, 263–66, 267, 268, 274; as father, 166–69, 235–36, 249, 272, 281, 283, 384, 388; on federalism, 415; finances of, 53–54, 282, 287–93, 397–98; on freedom, xix, 278–79; on Garibaldi, 106–7; and George Eliot, 303–7; in Gladstone biographer selection, 362–64; -Gladstone friendship, 86–87, 89, 94, 223, 308–9, 312–14, 332–33, 335; and Gladstone's retirement, 354–56; Gladstone tribute by, 359–60; on Gladstonian policy, 360–62, 411; and Granville, 22–23, 26, 29, 44, 53, 108, 331–32; health of, 393, 395, 397, 400–401; honours and awards to, 248–49, 274, 369–70, 385, 390; in House of Commons, 85–87, 90–92, 102–3, 107; in House of Lords, 235, 293, 343; intellectual influences on, 25, 31, 34–35, 45–47, 303, 321; journalism of, 71, 97, 102–3, 108, 114, 154–56, 189–90 (*see also Home and Foreign Review, The; Rambler, The*); liberalism of, 74, 219–20, 330, 360, 415–16; as Lord-in-Waiting, 342–48, 356–57, 374; maiden speech in Parliament, 91–92; marriage of, 97, 164–66, 168–72, 183, 393; and Mary Gladstone Drew, 309–16; and moral judgements in history, 46, 301–2, 320–22, 380–81, 410; and mother's remarriage, 18; in Naples, 178–80; on nationalism, 410, 411–13; naturalization of, 15; on Newman's sovereignty of conscience, 269–70; and Old Catholic movement, 229–31; papal audience of, 78–80, 182–83; on Papal Infallibility, 197–99, 209, 220, 232, 319; peerage of, 192–93, 235, 332, 342; physical appearance of, xix; on Pius IX, 75, 77, 158, 176; and Poet Laureate appointment, 345–47; and political ambition,

81–82, 336; political influence on Gladstone, 334, 336–41, 348–49, 353, 360; posthumous defence of, 403–5; priests' penitentiary visit of, 187–88; at Queen Victoria's Diamond Jubilee, 390–91; and Ranke, 103–5; religious faith of, 405–7; religious influences on, 6, 7, 24, 115–16, 128–31, 404–5; research in Italian archives, 33, 72, 174–75, 179, 180–83, 185–86, 210–11; Riviera residence of, 282–84, 311–12, 332; Romanes Lecture of, 398–400; on Roman question, 242–43; in Rome, 72–80, 174–78, 180–83, 186–88, 193–222, 237–42, 280; in Russia, 67–70; on St. Bartholomew Massacre, 184–85; on Sarpi, 183–84; on slavery, 88–89; on socialism, 410–11; in Spain, 353–54; and Vatican Archives, 180, 185, 186, 209–10, 237–38, 240–41; and Vatican Council (*see* Vatican Council of *1870*); at Vienna World's Fair, 249–51; on women's suffrage, 384; written work of, 183–85, 273–77, 362, 410

Acton, General Sir John Francis Edward, 6th Baronet (grandfather), xx, xxi, 11–13, 167, 283, 420n.9, 426n.5

Acton, Marie Elisabeth Anna, "Mamy" (daughter), 168, 235–36, 249, 287, 315, 359, 369, 373, 384; birth of, 165; in Cambridge house, 398, 400–401; correspondence with father, 313, 324, 325, 337, 339, 345, 348, 362, 370, 389, 397; and Granville, 331; marriage of, 401; relationship with father, 166–67, 169, 172; on Riviera, 282, 283, 284; in Rome, 204, 456n.53

Acton, Marie Louisa von Dalberg, Lady (mother). *See* Granville, Marie Louisa Dalberg-Acton, Countess

Acton, Marie von Arco-Valley, Lady (wife), 184, 235, 401, 402; birth of children, 166, 167, 168, 169, 235, 249, 272; characterized, 99; correspondence with Acton, 95, 96, 97, 99–100, 105, 158, 159, 166, 170–72, 178, 179, 180, 189, 190, 193, 194, 240, 249, 250, 325, 360; courtship of, 43–44, 53, 98–100, 101–2, 157–60; death of father, 274; engagement of, 97, 159, 161–64; in England, 165–66, 351; and excommunication threat, 261, 264, 267; on Leo XIII, 282; and marital relations, 166, 168–72, 393; papal blessing on marriage, 158, 177; physical appearance of, 165; on Riviera, 283; in Rome, 195, 196, 206, 221; wedding of, 164–65, 183

Acton, Mary Anne, "Nonna," Lady (grandmother), 4, 6, 52, 179, 195, 236–37; and Acton's upbringing, 18–19, 23–24; death of, 249; in England, 13, 419n.2, 426n.5; financial problems of, 287; illegitimate son of, 419n.2, 467–68n.70; lover of, 249, 419n.2; marriage of, 11–13; papal audience of, 79

Acton, Sir Richard, 5th Baronet, xx–xxi, 11

Acton, Sir Richard Maximilian, "Dick," 9th Baronet, 2d Baron (son), 249, 283, 309, 338, 378, 397, 401; birth of, 167, 235–36; at Oxford, 293, 324, 337, 369; relationship with father, 167–68, 172

Acton, Sir Walter, 2d Baronet, 10

Acton, Sir Whitmore, 4th Baronet, 10, 57

Acton, Sir William, 10

Agassiz, Jean Louis, 65

Albert, Prince Consort of Queen Victoria, 66–67, 93

Aldenham, 343; chapel at, xx, 14–15, 57–58; chaplain at, 54–55; decision

Aldenham (continued)
to remain master of, 51–53; family life at, 165–66, 169; finances of, 53–54, 292–93; Gladstone's visit to, 259; inheritance of, 11, 15; as intellectual centre, 61; letting of, 283, 341; library at, 29, 57, 59–62, 117, 168, 185, 289–92; liturgical and devotional practices at, 58–59; neglect of, 2; *Rambler* meeting at, 120–21; renovation of, 51, 56–58; twenty-first birthday celebration at, 53
Alexander, John, 82–83, 84
Alexander II, Tsar, 67, 68
Alexander VI, Pope, 299, 302
Alix of Hesse-Darmstadt, 354
Allbutt, Sir Thomas, 385
Allgemeine Zeitung, 200–202, 217, 227, 247, 248
Allies, Thomas William, 120, 139
Altholz, Josef L., 156
Ampthill, Lord. *See* Russell, Odo William Leopold
Andrea, Girolamo Marchese d', Cardinal, 179, 180, 203, 448n.18
Andrews, Charles Erroll, 397
Angelica library, 174
Anglicans. *See* Church of England
Antonelli, Giacomo, Cardinal, 132, 173, 174, 177, 238, 241, 263; archival access given by, 175, 186, 210; career of, 175–76; and Döllinger's excommunication, 228; influence on Pius IX, 77, 78, 176; and priests' penitentiary, 187, 188; and Vatican Council, 189, 207, 214, 216
Apologia pro Vita Sua (Newman), 150, 443n.132
Apponyi, Rudolf, 75
Aquinas, St. Thomas, 73, 286, 414
Arbues, Pedro de, 188
Archbold, W. A. J., 397
Arco, Louis, 189, 195, 202, 452n.15

Arco-Valley, Anna Marescalchi von, Countess, 25, 40, 52, 53, 63, 195, 221, 222, 309; children of, 41; death of, 281; marriage of, 42; relationship with Acton, xxi, 42–43, 44, 48–49, 70, 101
Arco-Valley, Emmerich, 282
Arco-Valley, Leopoldine, "Tini," von, 41, 309
Arco-Valley, Marie von. *See* Acton, Marie von Arco-Valley, Lady
Arco-Valley, Max, 235
Arco-Valley, Maximilian von, 40, 41–42, 43, 176, 177, 178, 274
Arco-Valley, Toni von, 43, 235
Arco-Valley family, 40–42, 235, 424n.1
Argyll, George Douglas Campbell, 8th Duke of, 294
Aristotle, 286
Armitstead, George, 337
Arneth, Alfred von, 236
Arnim-Suckow, Harry von, 178, 206, 215
Arnold, Matthew, 110–11, 153–54, 293
Arnold, Thomas, 395
Artom, Isaac, 240
Athenaeum, 293
Atlantis, 136
Aubert, Roger, 233, 408
Augusta, Queen of Prussia, 100, 103
Augustinian-Jansenist controversy, 123–24
Austria-Hungary, and Vatican Council, 214, 215
Avenir, 145

Baader, Franz von, 45, 321
Bach, Alexander von, 178
Bacon, Francis, 413, 414
Balfour, Arthur James, 1st Earl of, 384
Balmès, Jaime, 135, 145
Banks, Sir Joseph, 294
Banneville, Gaston-Robert Morin, 214

Barclay, John, 167
Barclay, William, 167
Barnabò, Alessandro, Cardinal, 134, 263
Barnes, Thomas, 112
Baronius, Caesar, 197
Bastard, Edward Rodney Pollexfen, 55
Bath, John Alexander, 4th Marquess of, 106
Baur, Ferdinand Christian, 286
Bautain, Louis-Eugène-Marie, 145
Beccadelli di Bologna, Prince Paul (Camporeale), 160–61
Bellarmine, Robert, Cardinal, 123, 197
Bellasis, Serjeant Edward, 117
Beloff, Max, 497n.17
Benedict XIV, Pope, 174
Berchtold, Josef, 230–31
Berghe von Tripps, Maria Eleanora, Countess, 6, 12
Bernetti, Thomas, Cardinal, 181
Bernstorff, Albrecht von, Count, 215
Beust, Ferdinand von, 214
Bevilaqua, Carlo, 78, 92
Birmingham Oratory, 117
Birnam House, 398, 498n.26
Birrell, Augustine, 293, 346
Bismarck, Prince Otto von, 93, 135, 155, 396; dismissal of, 352; on Disraeli, 470–71n.25, 489n.127; and Franco-Prussian War, 465n.38; *Kulturkampf* policy of, 225, 258; and Vatican Council, 215, 225
Blackwood's Magazine, 154
Blennerhassett, Charlotte, Countess von Leyden, xix, 230, 261, 268, 269–70, 305–6; and Acton, 205–6, 311, 327; death of, 483n.72; and Döllinger, 36–37, 38, 205, 229, 326–27; Dupanloup article of, 316–18; on Gladstone, 327–28
Blennerhassett, Rose, 38

Blennerhassett, Sir Rowland, 129–30, 154, 155, 166, 206, 230, 234, 259, 327, 328
Blowitz, Henri de, 396
Boero, Giuseppe, 175
Bohn, John H., 60
Bonald, Louis-Gabriel-Ambroise, Vicomte de, 45
Bonaventure, St., 286
Bonetty, Augustin, 145
Bonghi, Ruggiero, 310
Borch, Count, 68
Borghese, Prince Camillo, 205
Borghese, Princess, 205
Borromeo, St. Charles, 174, 184, 220, 403
Bossuet, Jacques Bénigne, Bishop, 31
Bouillerie, François Alexandre de la, Bishop, 203
Bourdaloue, Louis, 31
Bowles, Emily, 126
Boys, Albert du, 204
Boz Club, 293
Brancaccia, Francesco Maria, Cardinal, 179
Bray, Otto von, Count, 239
Breakfast Club, 295
Brewer, John Sherren, 26, 135
Bridgnorth, Member of Parliament for, 94–97
Bridgnorth lectures, 277–80
Bright, John, 112, 113, 166
Brignole-Sale, Antonio, Marchese di Groppoli, 33
Brignole-Sale, Maria, 4
Brignole-Sale family, 9, 42, 78
British Museum, 70
British Nationality Act of *1772,* 15
British Quarterly Review, 110
Brooks's club, 499n.55
Brown, James, Bishop, 54, 56, 248, 265–66
Brown, Rawdon Lubbock, 34

Brown, Thomas Joseph, Bishop, 126, 147

Browning, Oscar, 283, 368–69, 375, 376, 383, 389, 395, 405, 406, 491n.17

Brownson, Henry Francis, 428n.9

Brownson, Orestes, 65–66, 428n.9, 452n.12, 321

Brunell, Colonel de, 419n.2, 467–68n.70

Bryce, James, Viscount, 279, 296, 336, 338, 344, 346–47, 362–63, 367, 389, 396

Buddeus, Aurelio, 155

Bülow, Bernhard von, 161

Bülow, Maria von, 161

Bunsen, Marie, Freiherrin von, 283–84

Buoncompagni, Angela Brignole-Sale, 42

Burd, L. Arthur, 414

Burghersh, Lord, 67

Burke, Edmund, 25, 286, 321, 378

Burke, Thomas, 334

Burnell, Colonel, 419n.2, 467–68n.70

Burns, James (publisher), 132, 133

Buss, Franz Joseph von, 49

Bute, John Patrick Crichton-Stuart, 3d Marquess of, 205, 385

Butler, Edward Cuthbert, Abbot, 233, 403

Butler, Henry Montagu, 376, 378, 403

Butterfield, Sir Herbert, 94, 184–85, 237, 302, 303

Byng, George, 67

Cadogan, Henry, 326

Cadorna, Raffaele, 236

Caetani, Michelangelo. See Sermoneta, Michail Angelo Caetani, Duke of

Cagiano de Azevedo, Antonio, Bishop, 178

Cajazzo, Luigi Riccio, Bishop, 224

Callista (Newman), 70

Calvin, John, 73

Cambridge Modern History, 275, 392–97, 483n.72

Cambridge University: Acton's predecessor in Regius Chair at, 371–73; appointment to Regius Chair at, xxiv, 247–48, 341, 343, 365–68, 370–71, 490n.7; Chadwick's centennial address on Acton at, 382–83; denial of admission to, 25, 375, 377; Eranus Society Lecture at, 181, 182, 385; house at, 398, 498n.26; Inaugural Lecture at, xxiv, 374, 376–82, 392, 397, 414; lecture courses at, 383–84, 386–90; relations with students at, 386, 388, 389, 494–95n.79; rooms at, 375–76; Trinity Historical Society, 388; and women's education at, 384

Cambridge University Library: Acton Papers in, 395, 399; Aldenham Library donated to, 290, 291, 382

Cambridge University Press, 392, 394, 395

Campbell, Arabella G., 189–90

Campbell, Frederic, 183

Campion, Edmund, 134

Camporeale, Prince. See Beccadelli di Bologna, Prince Paul

Canestrini, Giuseppe, 240

Canning, Charles John, 2d Viscount, 52, 59, 101

Canning, George, 63

Cantù, Cesare, 42, 184

Capalti, Annibale, 217, 218–19

Capecelatro del Castelpagano, Alfonso, Cardinal, 180, 448n.21

Capes, John Moore, 114, 115, 120–21, 123

Cardoni, Giuseppe, Archbishop, 210

Carlow (Ireland), 82–85, 94

Carlow Post, 85

Carlyle, Thomas, 163, 304, 372, 377, 414

Carnegie, Andrew, 168, 289–90, 291, 292

Caroline, Queen of the Two Sicilies (Queen to Ferdinand II), 3, 4

Carrington, Charles Robert Wynn-, 3d Baron and 1st Marquess of Lincolnshire, 347

Caserta family, 283

Caterini, Prospero, Cardinal, 178

Catholic Church: authoritarian reaction in, 407–9; Creighton's history of the papacy, 296, 298–301; and Döllinger's excommunication, 226–28, 229, 233–35; and Gallicanism, 140–41; and Italian independence, 75–76, 91–92; and Jansenism, 123–24, 140, 442n.116; Lateran Treaty of *1929*, 242; loss of temporal power, 143–44, 236, 238–43; and Marian devotions, 58; priests' penitentiary of, 187–88; and Scholasticism, 73; and temporal power of papacy, 127, 131, 132–33, 143, 432n.43; universalization of, 219; Vatican Archives, 74, 180, 185, 186, 209–10, 237–38, 240–41. *See also* Jesuits; Papal Infallibility; Pius IX, Pope; Ultramontanism; Vatican Council of *1870; specific countries* (e.g., English Catholicism)

"Catholic Press, The" (Acton), 123

Catholic Relief Bill of *1829,* 141

Catholic Standard, 114

Cavendish, Lord Frederick Charles, 67, 334

Cavendish, Lucy Caroline Lyttleton, Lady, 334, 484n.1

Cavour, Camillo Benso di, Count, 93, 132, 143, 160, 238, 240, 361, 412

Chadwick, Owen, 254, 316, 382–83, 490n.7, 491n.17

Chamberlain, Houston Stewart, 412

Chamberlain, Joseph, 86, 350, 366, 411

Chambers Journal, 111

Charles I, King of England, and Spanish marriage negotiations, 181–82

Charles IX, King of Denmark, 347

Chase, F. H., 403

Chigi, Prince Flavio, 127, 158, 189

Childers, Hugh Culling, 384

Christina, Queen of Sweden, 185

Chronicle, The, 154–55, 184, 189

Churchill, Randolph Henry Spencer, Lord Randolph, 369

Churchill, Sir Winston Leonard Spencer, 20

Church of England: and Bonn conference, 255; central tradition in, 258; Gladstone's criticism of, 362; Oxford Movement in, 21; Tractarians in, 21, 39, 119

Cisalpines, 141–42, 198–99

Civiltà Cattolica, 77–78, 188–89

Civil War (U.S.), 87–88, 387

Clarendon, George William Frederick Villiers, 8th Earl of, 103, 199, 201, 206, 207, 208, 213–14, 222–23, 236, 257

Clement XI, Pope, 33

Clement XIV, Pope, 181

Clifford, William J. H., Bishop, 139, 214, 221–22, 244

Club, The, 294

Cobden, Richard, 112, 166

Coleridge, Samuel Taylor, 285

Coligny, Gaspard de, 185

Comte, Auguste, 304, 377

Concordat of *1801,* 143, 408

Congress of Berlin, 489n.127

Consalvi, Ercole, 143, 408

Conzemius, Victor, 36, 202, 209, 220

Cornaro, Caterina, 250–51

Cornthwaite, Robert, Bishop, 137, 214

Corsiniana library, 174

Cortes, J. Donoso, 145, 286, 321

Cosmopolitan club, 294

Council of Trent, 255

Craven, Augustus, 7, 203

Craven, Pauline de la Ferronays, 7, 107, 203, 249, 419n.2

Creighton, Mandell, Bishop, 389, 396, 399; and Acton's Cambridge appointment, 367, 368, 370, 490n.7; dispute with Acton, 296–301, 302, 303

Creuzer, George Friedrich, 321

Cromwell, Oliver, statue of, 358

Cross, John Walter, 306

Cullen, Paul, Cardinal, 82, 83, 121, 126, 147

Dalberg, Carl Theodor von, Archbishop Elector of Mainz and Worms, 9, 140, 198

Dalberg, Emmerich Josef, Duke of, 7–8

Dalberg, Marie Louisa von. See Granville, Marie Louisa Dalberg-Acton

Dalberg, Maria Pellina T. C. de Brignole-Sale, Duchess of, 7, 15, 16, 18, 42, 183, 208

Dalberg family, 9, 289

Dalgairns, John, 116, 122

Dalkeith, William Henry Walter, 6th Duke of Buccleuch, styled Earl of, 67

Dannerbeck, Georg, 402

Dante Alighieri, 34, 285, 286, 326

Darboy, Georges, Archbishop: death of, 225; at Vatican Council, 195, 196–97, 217, 222, 244

Darnell, Nicholas, 117, 160

Daru, Napoleon, Comte, 214

Darwin, Charles, 284, 398

Darwin, Sir George, 385

Das Kapital (Marx), 411

Daumale, Duke of, 294

Deak, Francis, 361

Dease, Emily Throckmorton, 12–13, 102, 467–68n.70, 402

Dease, Sir Gerald, 102

Dechosal, Anne, 205

Delane, John Thaddeus, 112

Democracy in Europe (May), 411

Denbigh, Rudolph W. B., Baron Feilding, 8th Earl of, 205

Derby, Edward George Geoffrey Smith Stanley, 14th Earl of, 83, 86, 87, 106, 166

Devonshire, Spencer Compton Cavendish, Marquess of Hartington and 8th Duke of, 366

Devonshire, William George Spencer Cavendish, 6th Duke of, 67, 68

Dicey, Edward James Stephens, 396

Dickens, Charles, 166, 293

Dickens, Henry, 293

Dilettanti club, 294

Di Pietro, Camillo, Cardinal, 221

Disraeli, Benjamin, Earl of Beaconsfield, 87, 96, 114, 166, 205, 254, 258, 277, 304, 360, 470–71n.25, 489n.127

Divine Comedy (Dante), 285

Dixon, Richard Watson, 313

Döllinger, Elise, 329

Döllinger, Ignaz Christoph von, 36, 38

Döllinger, Ignaz von: -Acton estrangement, 170, 232, 256, 301–2, 308, 309, 316–24, 409–10; on Acton's scholarly projects, 273, 274, 280; Acton's studies with, 22, 27–28, 29–33, 45; Acton's travels with, 33–34, 42–43, 50, 72–74, 78–80, 159; Acton's wedding performed by, 164; at Aldenham, 61, 120; on Arbues canonization, 188; and Arco-Valley family, 41, 157–58, 235; on Augustinian-Jansenist controversy, 124; biography of, 329–31; career of, 35–36, 37; and Catholic scholars' congress, 148; characterized, 28–29, 36–37, 38; and Charlotte Blennerhassett, 36–37, 38, 205, 229, 326–27; and Christian reunion conference,

254–56, 326, 469n.9; correspondence with Acton, 56, 64, 65, 67, 70, 75, 77, 87, 89, 96, 102, 103, 118, 119, 137, 139, 147, 154, 167, 175, 176, 177, 179, 180, 193, 199, 200, 220, 245–46, 248, 267, 273, 275, 281, 304; on Creighton, 298; death of, 290–91, 324–29; early life of, 36; and English Catholics, 25–26, 39; excommunication of, 226–28, 229, 233–35; on George Eliot, 304; and Gladstone, 86, 213, 252, 253–54, 267, 270–71, 325–26; and historical method, 47; on *Home and Foreign Review* suspension, 151; honours and awards to, 249; household of, 29, 32–33; and inopportunists, 208–9, 264; as "Janus," 190, 205, 211, 484n.80; and Leo XIII, 281–82; library of, 29, 60; on Marian devotion, 58; and Newman, 39, 128–29; and Old Catholics, 228–29, 230, 231–32, 255, 271; on Papal Infallibility, 188, 189, 190; and Pius IX, 127, 173–74, 182–83; posthumous tributes to, 325–27; on Ranke, 104; and Romantic School, 46, 322; in Rome, 72–80; scholarship of, 37–38, 276, 301–2, 330; on temporal power, 127, 131, 143–44, 181, 439n.65; and Ultramontanism, 36, 38–39, 127, 145; Vatican Council reports of, xxiii, 200–202, 217, 221, 224

Döllinger, Jeanette, 325, 328, 329, 330

Dönhoff, Karl von, 161

Donizetti, Gaetano, 251

Doria-Pamphili-Landi, Prince Filippo, 177

Dormer, John, 205

Drew, Harry, 311

Drew, Mary Gladstone, xix, 275, 281, 294, 308, 334, 340, 353, 359, 362, 363, 376, 404, 406, 411, 415, 479n.22; on Acton's court appointment, 343; on Acton's political influence, 348–49; and best-book lists, 284–85; friendship with Acton, 309–15; on George Eliot, 306; publication of Acton correspondence, 315–16, 331, 369, 403; on Queen Victoria's funeral, 400; in Rome, 186–87

Drummond, Victor, 352

Dublin Review, 112–13, 119, 120, 133, 136, 138, 147

Dufferin and Ava, Frederick Temple Hamilton-Blackwood, 1st Marquess of, 294

Dunraven, Edwin Richard Windham Wyndham-Quin, 3d Earl of, 154

Dupanloup, Félix, Bishop, 38, 66, 220, 264; Acton-Döllinger dispute over, 316–19; and Acton-Leveson marriage, 17; background of, 205; headmaster at Gentilly, 19, 21; as inopportunist, 209, 264; at Vatican Council, 189, 190, 195, 199, 202, 203, 204, 217, 218, 244

Ecce Homo (Seeley), 371

Eckstein, Ferdinand, Baron, 34–35, 128, 321

Economist, 111

Edinburgh Review, 110, 111, 112, 136, 155

Edward VII, King (Prince of Wales), 249–50, 347, 357, 369–70, 374, 402

Elgin, Thomas Bruce, 7th Earl of, 294

Eliot, George (Mary Ann Evans), 303–7, 405, 410

Ellesmere, Francis Leveson-Gower Egerton, 1st Earl of, 63, 64, 66

Ellesmere, Lady, 63, 64

Ellis, Augustus Frederic, 102

Emancipation Act of *1829,* 85

English Catholicism: and Catholic Emancipation, 141, 198, 214; conversion of Acton family, xx, 10; defence of Acton, 403–5; dissension within,

English Catholicism (continued)
116–19, 121; Döllinger's links to, 25–
26, 29, 39; and Erastianism, 141;
and excommunication threat, 266–
67; growth of, 54–55; journals of,
112–14 (see also Home and Foreign
Review, The; Rambler, The); and
Manning's rise to power, 261–63;
members of parliament, 95–96; and
national loyalty, 198–99, 453–54n.31;
and oath for officeholders, 85, 90;
Old Catholics (Cisalpines), 109–
10, 141–42, 198–99; opening of St.
George's Cathedral, 24; opposition
to Acton, 116–17, 118–19, 261, 263–
66, 272, 403; Oxford converts, xxii,
21, 109; partisan nature of, 153; and
Quanta Cura encyclical, 176–77;
Queen Victoria's attitude towards,
53; Romanization of, 110; schools
of, 20–22, 117; and Vatican Council,
199, 200, 205, 207, 213–14
English Historical Review, 296–97, 370,
371
English History (Ranke), 104
Eranus Society, 181, 182, 385
Erastianism, 141
Errington, George, Bishop, 22, 214
Estées, César d', Cardinal, 185
Everett, Edward, 65
Examiner, 111
Expansion of England (Seeley), 372
Express, 111

Faber, Frederick William, 55, 56, 116,
118, 121, 122, 124, 131, 139
Fairbairn, Andrew Martin, 396
Falloux, Alfred, Comte de, 33, 220
Farrell, John Arthur, 205
Fasnacht, George E., 411
Febronianism, 140, 442n.116
Fénelon, François de Salignac de la
Mothe, Bishop, 31, 38

Ferdinand I, King of the Two Sicilies,
xx, 2, 3, 11, 420n.9
Ferdinand II, King of the Two
Sicilies, 2
Ferronays, Auguste Ferron de la, 249
Ferronays, Pauline de la. See Craven,
Pauline de la Ferronays
Fichte, Johann Gottlieb, 414
Ficquelmont, Karl Ludwig von, 75
Fischer, Kuno, 66
Fisher, Herbert Albert Laurens, 367,
380
Fitzalan-Howard, Edward, 192
Fitzgerald, Edward, Bishop, 224
Fitzpatrick, John Bernard, 428n.9
Förster, Heinrich, Archbishop, 222
Fox, Charles James, 294, 363
Fox, Henry Edward, 4th Lord Hol-
land, 2, 8
France: and Vatican Council, 212, 214.
See also French Catholicism
Franco-Prussian War, 224–25, 235, 236,
464–65n.38
Frantz, Constantin, 135, 155–56
Franz Josef I, Emperor, 76
Frederick, Empress, 103, 342–43, 351,
355, 357, 390, 400, 468n.2
Frederick III, Emperor of Germany,
352
French Catholicism: death of Darboy,
225; death of Montalembert, 203–4;
and Döllinger, 38; and Gallicanism,
141; minority bishops at Vatican
Council, 194, 196–97, 212, 214; and
Quanta Cura encyclical, 174; Revi-
val, 45; and Ultramontanism, 143,
144–45, 189
French Revolution lectures, 383, 386–87
Freshfield, James William, 52, 426n.5
Freshfield, William Dawes, 288, 290,
292, 426n.5
Freshfield solicitors, 398–99, 426n.5
Friedrich, Johann, 87, 190, 199, 202,

230, 324; biography of Döllinger, 329, 330

Frohschammer, Jakob, 78, 148, 149, 152

Froude, James Anthony, 71, 366

Fullerton, Georgiana Charlotte, Lady, 17, 260

Gallicanism, 140–41

Galton, Sir Francis, 492n.42

Garibaldi, Giuseppe, 105–7, 239, 412

Garnett, Richard, 297

Garrick, David, 294

Gasquet, Francis Aidan, Cardinal (Abbot), 403

Gayangos y Arcre, Pascual de, 236

German Catholicism: Bavarian, 30; and Christian reunion, 254–56, 326, 469n.9; and congress of Catholic scholars, 148; and Döllinger's excommunication, 226–28, 229, 233–35; minority bishops at Vatican Council, 190–91, 194, 210, 215, 217; and national Church, 9, 140–41, 198; Odeon lectures on temporal power, 127; Old Catholic movement in, 228–33, 252, 253, 255, 271–72, 455n.39; Renewal, 50, 141; and submission to Vatican decrees, 225, 226–28, 233–34, 268–69; and Ultramontanism, 36, 38–39, 145

Germany: colonial expansion of, 360–61; Franco-Prussian War, 224–25, 235, 236, 464–65n.38; Kulturkampf policy, 225, 258, 468n.2; nationalism in, 410, 413; Prussianization of, 289, 352. See also German Catholicism; Munich; Prussia

Geschichte Englands (seit den Friedensschlüssen von 1814–1815) (Pauli), 274

Geschichte von England (Lappenberg, Pauli, and Brosch), 274

Gibbon, Edward, 9

Gibbon, Edward (historian), xx, 10

Giesebrecht, Friedrich von, 248–49, 274, 275

Gioberti, Vincenzo, 76, 77, 112, 135, 145, 178, 286

Gladstone, Catherine, 89, 90, 309

Gladstone, Helen, 335, 336–37, 353, 359; at Cambridge University, 371, 372–73, 376, 383, 384

Gladstone, Helen Jane, 252–53, 258, 271–72

Gladstone, Herbert, 309, 310, 354, 359, 363

Gladstone, Mary. See Drew, Mary Gladstone

Gladstone, William Ewart, 3, 7, 26, 32, 60, 97, 106, 147, 166, 183, 219, 247, 249, 294, 304, 399; -Acton friendship, 86–87, 89, 94, 223, 312–14, 332–33, 335, 359; and Acton's Cambridge appointment, 366; Acton's obituary of, 359–60; and Acton's peerage, 192–93; Acton's political influence on, 334, 336–41, 348–49, 353, 360; and Aldenham Library sale, 289–90, 291, 292; biographer of, 362–64; and Chronicle, 154–55; death of, 359; and Döllinger, 46, 86, 213, 252, 253–54, 267, 270–71, 325–26; election of 1885, 485n.3; election of 1892, 336–37; funeral of, 362; and Granville, 331; Irish policy of, 206, 328, 334–35, 348–50, 353, 415, 457n.67; in papal audience, 186–87; personal habits of, 480n.22; Pius IX on, 79–80; and Poet Laureate appointment, 345–46; political aims of, 94, 360–62; Queen Victoria's attitude towards, 249, 341–42, 343; rescue work among prostitutes, 89–90; retirement of, 352, 353, 354–56, 357–58; Romanes Lecture of, 349; at Tegernsee, 308–9, 316, 325, 328, 335; and Vatican Council, 198, 199, 207,

Gladstone, William Ewart (continued)
212–14, 252; Vatican decrees attacked
by, 254, 257–58, 259, 270–72
Gladstone Diaries, The, 89
Globe, 111
Glyn, George Grenfell, 2d Baron
Wolverton, 155
Gobineau, Arthur, 412
Goethe, Johann Wolfgang von, 63, 145
Gonzales, Thyrsus, 32
Gooch, George Peabody, 372, 389,
495n.85
Gordon, Charles, 360, 485n.3
Görres, Johann Joseph von, 25–26, 36,
45, 46, 64, 112, 145, 147, 321
Goschen, George Joachim, 1st Vis-
count, 295, 369
Gramich, Anna, 28, 166
Grant, Thomas, Bishop, 139
Grant Duff, Sir Mountstuart E., 25, 90,
155, 294, 295, 349, 406
Granville, Castalia Rosalind Campbell,
Countess, 183, 331
Granville, Granville George Leveson-
Gower, 2d Earl, 59, 63, 66, 98, 159,
160, 164, 194, 208, 263, 293, 351,
499n.55; and Acton-Arco engage-
ment, 100, 101–2; and Acton's politi-
cal career, 81, 82, 83, 86, 90, 91–92,
97, 223, 235; and Aldenham estate,
51–53; and Catholic peers, 192; death
of, 331; as Foreign Secretary, 236;
on Garibaldi, 106; and Gladstone,
331; marriage to Castalia Campbell,
183, 331; marriage to Marie Dalberg-
Acton, 16–18; relationship with
Acton, 22–23, 24, 26, 29, 44, 53,
108, 331–32; in Russia, 67–68, 70; on
Turnbull affair, 93–94
Granville, Harriet, 8
Granville, Lady (mother of George
Leveson-Gower), 17–18
Granville, Marie Louisa Dalberg-

Acton, Countess (mother): and
Acton-Arco engagement, 98–99,
100; and Aldenham estate, 51–53, 54,
56, 57–58, 66, 91; birth and infancy
of son, 1, 3–4; Catholicism of, 6, 58;
death of, 97, 100–101; and death of
Richard Acton, 14–15; marriage to
Richard Acton, 7–9, 42; in Naples,
4–5, 6–7; naturalization of, 15;
physical appearance of, 17; Queen
Victoria on, 344; relationship with
son, 40, 44, 98; remarriage of, 16–18,
23; in Russia, 67, 70
Gratry, Alphonse, 38, 190, 204
Gray, Robert, 262
Great Britain: fall of Palmerston, 92–
93; formation of Gladstone cabinet
(*1892*), 336–41; -Germany rivalry,
360–61; Irish policy in, 94, 96–97,
206, 328, 334–35, 348–50, 353, 415,
457n.67; and Italian nationalism,
90–92, 93; successor to Gladstone,
354–56, 357–58; and Vatican Coun-
cil, 198, 199, 207–8, 212–14
Green, Thomas Louis, 56, 163
Gregoriana, 73
Gregorovius, Ferdinand, 174, 210
Gregory VII, Pope, 142
Gregory XIII, Pope, 42
Gregory XVI, Pope, 3, 145
Greville, Charles, 8, 63, 293
Grillon's dining club, 294
Grote, George, 103
Guardian, 380
Guasti, Cesare, 240
Guéranger, Prosper, 145
Guicciardini, Francesco, 286
Guizot, François, 218, 275
Guyon, Jeanne Bouviér de la Motte, 38
Gwatkin, Henry Melvill, 368, 371

Halévy, Elie, 112, 435n.8
Halévy, Jacques, 251

Hamilton, Sir Edward, 367

Hamilton, Emma, Lady, 12

Hamilton, Sir William, 12, 304

Hammond, J. L., 380–81

Harcourt, Sir William, 339, 354–55, 356, 358

Harpsfield, Nicholas, 275

Hartmann, Carl Robert von, 286

Harvard University, 65

Haynald, Ludwig, Bishop, 203, 217, 232, 244

Hecker, Isaac Thomas, 194, 452n.12

Hefele, Karl Josef von, Bishop, 191, 196, 198, 216, 222, 225, 232, 244

Hegel, Georg Wilhelm Friedrich, 47, 414

Herbert, Edward Bleiddian, 401, 429n.26

Herbert, John, 401

Herbert, Marie. *See* Acton, Marie Elisabeth Anna, "Mamy"

Herberts of Llanarth, 373, 401

Herder, Benjamin, 34, 49

Herder, Johann Gottfried von, 414

Herder, Karl Raffael, 34

Herrnsheim Schloss, 33, 48, 58–59, 62, 98, 189, 208, 224, 232, 287, 288–89

Herschell, Ferrer, 1st Baron, 340

Heyl, Cornelius Wilhelm, 288–89

Himmelfarb, Gertrude, 110, 230

Hintzpeter, Georg, 468n.2

Hirscher, Johann Baptist von, 49

Historische-politishche Blätter, 45

History of England (Macaulay), 25

History of England from the Fall of Wolsey to the Defeat of the Spanish Armada (Froude), 71

History of the Inquisition of the Middle Ages (Lea), 381

History of the Papacy during the Period of the Reformation (Creighton), 296, 297, 298–301

History of the Papacy from the Great Schism to the Sack of Rome (Creighton), 296

Hobbes, Thomas, 414

Hochland, 483n.72

Hogarth, William, Bishop, 139

Hohenlohe, Prince Gustav-Adolf, Cardinal, 186, 194, 199, 201, 202, 214

Holland, Hyazinth, 45, 424n.9

Home and Foreign Review, The, 115; editors of, 136; English hierarchy's opposition to, 137–39, 151; extinction of, 149, 151–53; reception of, 136–37, 153–54, 441–42n.105; and Roman censorship, 147–49, 151, 152; Ultramontanism article in, 139–47; writers for, 135–36. *See also Rambler, The*

Honorius I, Pope, 465–66n.41

Hope-Scott, James Robert, 154, 258

Hort, Fenton John Anthony, 385

Huber, Johannes Nepomuk, 190

Hügel, Anatole von, 404

Hügel, Friedrich von, 404

Hughes, John Joseph, 65

Hugo of St. Victor, 286

Humboldt, Alexander von, 286

Hundeshagen, Carl Bernhard, 286

Hutton, Arthur William, 439–40n.74

Huxley, Thomas Henry, 113, 399

Illustrated London News, 111

Il principe (Machiavelli), 414

Imitation of Christ (Kempis), 405

Immaculate Conception, 73, 143, 255, 266

Inaugural Lecture, xxiv, 374, 376–82, 392, 397, 414

Infallibilism. *See* Papal Infallibility

Innocent III, Pope, 142

Institute of Charity, 76

Ireland: Acton's parliamentary seat for Carlow, 82–85, 94; and Disestablishment, 94, 96–97; and Home

Ireland (continued)
Rule, 206, 334–35, 348–50, 353, 415; Phoenix Park murders, 334, 335, 361
Irish Catholic, 373
Irish Catholicism, 82, 83, 141, 198, 454n.31; and Infallibility, 214, 215
Irish Universal News, The, 136
Italy: and independence movement, 75–76, 91–92, 105–7, 143; negotiations with Pope, 240, 241; occupation of Rome, 236–40; Papal relations with, 178–79; and Vatican Council, 215–16

Jackson, Henry, 385
James, Henry, 275–76
Jansen, Cornelius, 442n.116
Jansenism, 123–24, 140, 442n.116
Jebb, Richard Claverhouse, 399
Jenner, Sir William, 168–69
Jervoise, Harry, 241
Jesuits, 139, 175; expulsion from Germany, 258; and Gallicanism, 140; persecution of Passaglia, 73–74; and Pius IX, 77, 180, 181, 197, 409
Jesus Psalter, 404–5
Johnson, Samuel, 294
Jörg, Josef Edmund, 37, 148
Joseph II, Emperor, 140
Josephinism, 140
Journals, English: Catholic, 71, 112–14 (*see also names of specific journals*); place in intellectual life, 109, 110–11; taxes on, 111–12
Jowett, Benjamin, 166
Juárez, Benito Pablo, 166
Julius II, Pope, 32

Keble, John, 115
Kempis, Thomas à, 405
Kenrick, Francis Patrick, Archbishop, 118, 194, 196, 203, 222, 232, 244, 271

Kerrill, Francis, Bishop, 205
Ketteler, Wilhelm Emmanuel von, Bishop, 191, 208–9, 217, 218, 244, 246
Kimberley, John, 3d Baron and 1st Earl of, 338, 340, 352, 355
Kingsley, Charles, 150, 371, 443n.132
Kirchenlexikon, 58
Kleutgen, Josef, 73
Knollys, Sir Francis, 347–48
Kobell, Louise von, 32
Kochan, Lionel, 276
Kraus, Franz Xavier, 326–27, 482–83n.70

Lacaita, Sir James, 295
Lacordaire, Jean-Baptiste-Henri, 34, 120, 145
Lake-Fox, George, 205
Lallemand, Paule de, 204
Lambruschini, Luigi, 2
Lamennais, Félicité Robert de, 38, 112, 144–45, 152, 407
Lamprecht, Karl, 381–82
Lang, Andrew, 293
Lansdowne, Henry Keith Petty-Fitzmaurice, 5th Marquess of, 341, 402
La patrie, 137
Lasaulx, Ernst von, 45, 46, 87, 321
Las Casas, Emanuel Augustine, 286
Lateran Treaty of *1929,* 242
Lathbury, Daniel Connor, 136
Lathbury, George, 154
Launoy, Jean de, 32
Laurence, Reginald Vere, 401, 494–95n.79
Lea, Henry Charles, 381
Leathes, Stanley Mordaunt, 394, 397
Le catholique, 35
Lecky, Edward Hartpole, 294
Le correspondent, 35
Lectures on Modern History (Acton), 380

Lee, Robert E., 387
Leibniz, Gottfried Wilhelm von, 218, 414
Lemoine, Jean, 101
Lenbach, Franz von, 33, 165, 253, 326
Leo, Heinrich, 104, 321
Leo IV, Pope, 238
Leo X, Pope, 32, 389
Leo XIII, Pope, 49, 233, 281–82
Lerchenfeld, Ludwig Heinrich von, 157
Lérins, St. Vincent de, 286
Letter to His Grace the Duke of Norfolk (Newman), 268–69, 270
Leveson-Gower, Edward Frederick, "Freddy," 67
Leveson-Gower, Granville George. *See* Granville, Granville George Leveson-Gower, 2d Earl
Leveson-Gower, Margaret, 67
Leveson-Gower, Marie. *See* Granville, Marie Louisa Dalberg-Acton, Countess
Lewes, George Henry, 304, 305–6
Lewis, David, 139
Leyden, Charlotte, Countess von. *See* Blennerhassett, Charlotte
Liber Diurnus, 465n.41
Lichfield, Thomas George, 2d Earl of, 67
Life of William Ewart Gladstone, The (Morley), 364
Lightfoot, Joseph Barber, 385
Liguori, St. Alfonso Maria di, 150–51
Lincoln, Abraham, 163
Lincoln, Henry Pelham Alexander Pelham-Clinton, Earl of, 67
Lister, Lord, 67
Liszt, Franz von, 199
Liverani, Francesco, 448n.18
Logan, Henry John Charles, 24, 25
Longfellow, Henry Wadsworth, 65
Lord Acton and His Circle (Gasquet), 403

Love Me Little, Love Me Long (Reade), 99
Loyson, Charles, 243, 466n.51
Lubbock, Sir John, 4th Baronet and 1st Baron Avebury, 284–85
Luca, Antonino de, Cardinal, 203
Lucas, Frederick, 71, 113–14
Ludwig I, King of Bavaria, 30, 37, 41, 45
Lugo, Juan de, 56
L'univers, 33–34, 114
Luther, Martin, 30, 38, 73, 321–22, 408
Lyell, Sir Charles, 64
Lyons, Richard Bickerton Pemell, 2d Baron and 1st Earl, 91, 92
Lyttleton, Lavinia, 314

Mabillon, Jean, 33
Macaulay, Thomas Babington, 1st Baron, 25, 103, 105, 275, 293, 321, 363, 370, 372, 374
MacColl, Malcolm, 247
Machiavelli, Niccolò, 413–14, 415
MacMahon, Patrice Maurice de, 235
Macmullen, Richard, 120, 133
Maher, James, 83, 84, 85
Maine, Sir Henry, 376
Maistre, Joseph de, 33, 45, 130–31, 135, 144, 321, 407
Maitland, Frederic William, 367, 368, 376, 385, 388, 389, 393, 397
Makart, Hans, 250, 250–51
Malebranche, Nicolas, 286
Malet, Sir Edward Baldwin, 4th Baronet, 351
Malmesbury, James Howard, 3d Earl of, 106
Manning, Henry Edward, Cardinal Archibishop of Westminster, 91, 113, 126, 138, 142, 165, 182, 257; dislike of Acton, 223, 263; and excommunication threat, 264–67; on Papal Infallibility, 220, 454n.32; and

Manning, Henry Edward (continued)
  Rambler, 132–33, 389; rise to power,
  261–63; rivalry with Newman, 263,
  264; Roman Academia centre of,
  133; successor to Wiseman, 177; on
  temporal power, 432n.43; at Vatican
  Council, 195, 196–97, 199, 200, 203,
  207, 214, 217, 219, 224, 263
Manzoni, Alessandro, 76
Marcellus II, Pope, 282
Marciano archives, 34, 161
Marescalchi, Anna, Countess. See Arco-
  Valley, Anna Marescalchi von
Marescalchi, Antonio, 235
Marescalchi, Caterina Brignole-Sale,
  Contessa, 42
Marescalchi, Ferdinando, Conte, 183
Maret, Henri Louis Charles, 38, 216
Marie Caroline, Queen of the Two
  Sicilies (Queen to Ferdinand I), xx,
  2, 3, 11, 12, 13, 420n.9
Marie Nicolaievna, Grand Duchess, 70
Marshall, William, 429n.26
Martensen, Hans Lassen, 286
Martin, Sir Theodore, 346
Marx, Karl, 411
Massari, Giuseppe, 240
Massillon, Jean-Baptiste, 31
Massimo, Prince Camillo Vittorio
  Emmanuele, 177
Mastai, Giovannia Maria. See Pius IX,
  Pope
Mathew, David, Archibishop, 142
Matthew, H. C. G., 89, 257
Maximilian, Archduke Ferdinand,
  Emperor of Mexico, 166
May, Sir Thomas Erskine, Baron
  Farnborough, 295, 411
Mazzini, Giuseppe, 239
Meglia, Francesco, 215, 228
Meiderlin, Peter, 114–15
Meignan, Guillaume-René, 38
Melchers, Paul, Archbishop, 245

Mermillod, Gaspard, 49, 173, 195, 196,
  203
Mérode, François Xavier, 178, 203
Metternich, Prince Clemens Wenzel
  Nepomuk Lothar, 46–47, 74–75
Meynell, Charles, 119, 123–24
Meynell, Wilfrid, 114
Meyrick, Frederick, 150, 443–44n.132
Middlemarch (Eliot), 304
Mill, John Stuart, 166, 249, 286, 304,
  413
Milnes, Richard Monckton, 1st Baron
  Houghton, 89, 163
Minghetti, Laura Acton, 160, 161, 236,
  238, 446n.13
Minghetti, Marco, 160–61, 193, 236,
  237, 238, 239, 310, 405
Mirari Vos, 145
Missionary Society of St. Paul, 452n.12
Mission of the Isles of the North, The
  (Newman), 126
Mivart, Jackson St. George, 316
Mocenigo, Foscarina Rosa, 34
Modena, Angelo Vincenzo, 78
Möhler, Johann Adam, 25, 37, 286, 291,
  321
Molitor, Wilhelm, 286
Mommsen, Theodor, 414
Monsell, William, 90, 154
Montalembert, Charles Forbes-René,
  Comte de, 17, 33, 34, 35, 38, 61, 112,
  120, 141, 145, 220, 321; death of,
  203–4; and Quanta Cura encyclical,
  174
Monteith, Joseph, 205
Montez, Lola, 37
Montfauçon, Bernard de, 33
Montfort, Simon de, 414
Moriarty, David, Bishop, 154, 214
Morier, James Justinian, 468n.2
Morier, Robert, 253
Morley, John, 1st Viscount Morley of
  Blackburn, 110, 290, 293, 313, 315,

399; and Aldenham library, 168; anti-Catholicism of, 341; biographer of Gladstone, 362–64; in Gladstone government, 336, 338, 340, 343, 346; and Home Rule, 348

Morning Advertiser, 111

Morning Chronicle, 111

Morning Herald, 111

Morning Post, 111

Morris, John Brande, 55–56, 121, 122, 124

Morris, Lewis, 346

Morris, William, 346

Mostyn, George Charles of Kiddington, 6th Lord Vaux of Harrowden, 177

Mount St. Mary's College, 66

Moy de Sons, Karl Ernst, 230

Müller, Adam, 321

Müller, Johannes, 321

Müller, Ludwig August von, 329

Müller, Max, 396, 401

Mullinger, J. B., 495n.85

Munich (Germany), 26, 29–30; as Catholic centre, 30; Catholic scholars' congress in, 148; intellectual life in, 30–31, 45–46, 108; Odeon lectures on temporal power, 127, 439n.65; Old Catholics conference in, 229–31; Romantic School of, 45, 46–47

Munich, University of, 29, 35, 37, 45

Munich Declaration of Whitsuntide, 230–31

Murray, Sir George, 357, 367

Nägelsbach, Carl Wilhelm Friedrich, 87

Naples (Italy), Villa Acton in, 1–2, 4–5, 7

Napoleon I, 8, 11, 30, 143, 144, 408

Napoleon III, 75, 93, 128, 196, 204

Nardi, Francesco, 158

Nationalism, 411–13

"Nationality" (Acton), 135, 412

National Review, 136–37

Natoli, Luigi, Archbishop, 221

Nelson, Horatio Nelson, Viscount, 12

Newman, John Henry, Cardinal, 1, 26, 53, 96, 113, 145, 166, 184, 286, 331, 347, 377; conversion to Catholicism, 21; and Döllinger, 39, 128–29; and Döllinger's excommunication, 234; on *Home and Foreign Review,* 149; influence on Acton, 115–16, 128–31, 321; Manning's rivalry with, 263; on Papal Infallibility, 128, 234–35, 268–71; as *Rambler* editor, 125, 132; on Roman censorship, 150; scholarly method of, 122; school and Catholic university schemes of, 117–18, 121; on sovereignty of conscience, 269–70; in theological controversies, 118, 121, 124–27; in truthfulness controversy, 150–51, 143–44n.132; and Wilberforce, 70

Newnham College, 371, 384

Newsome, David, 262

Niccolini, Antonio, 2

Nicene Creed, 255

Nicholas of Cusa, 286

Nineteenth Century, 317

Nolan, Edmund, 403, 404

North British Review, 97, 155, 189–90

Notes by an English Republican (Swinburne), 346

O'Connell, Daniel, 112, 113, 141, 198

O'Farrell, Richard More, 90

O'Hagan, Thomas, Lord O'Hagan of Tullalogue, 90, 154, 155, 235

Old Catholic movement, 228–33, 252, 253, 255, 271–72, 455n.39

Oliphant, Laurence, 295

"On Consulting the Faithful in Matters of Doctrine" (Newman), 125–26, 127

O'Reilly, John, 22, 24
Owen, Robert, 428n.9
Oxenham, Henry Nutcombe, 200, 229, 255
Oxford Movement, 21, 109
Oxford University, Romanes Lecture, 349, 398–400

Pacca, Bartolomeo, Cardinal, 79, 176
Paget, Sir Augustus Berkeley, 240
Paget, Sir James, 1st Baronet, 294
Paget, Walpurga, 446n.13
Pall Mall Gazette, 293, 316
Palmerston, Henry John Temple, 3d Viscount, 81, 86, 90, 92, 94, 100, 166, 176, 183, 294; anti-Catholicism of, 79, 93; and Garibaldi, 105, 106
Panizzi, Sir Anthony, 60, 147
Papal Infallibility, 49, 73, 78, 113; Acton's position on, 197–99, 209, 220, 232, 319; and Church-State relations, 198–99, 212; Gladstone's attack on, 257–58; Ketteler's position on, 209; Newman's position on, 128, 234–35, 268–71; and submission to Council dogma, 225, 226–35, 259–61, 264–72; and Ultramontanism, 144–45, 188–89, 319. *See also* Vatican Council of *1870*
Parnell, Charles Stewart, 206, 335
Paroles d'un croyant (Lamennais), 145
Parry, John Orlando, 4–5
Pascal, Blaise, 286
Pasquier, Etienne, 317
Passaglia, Carlo, 73–74, 119
Pattison, Mark, 277, 293
Paul, Herbert, 315, 362
Paul III, Pope, 134–35
Paul V, Pope, 183
Pauli, Reinhold, 61–62
Pearson, Charles Henry, 135
Pecci, Vincenzo Giocchino, Cardinal, 233
Pedro II, Emperor, 284

Peel, Sir Robert, 63, 67, 86
Perfall, Karl von, 230
Perrone, Giovanni, 73
Petre, Sir Edward, 182
Petre, William Bernard, 12th Baron, 154
Phillips, George, 49–50
Phoenix Park murders, 334, 335, 361
Pietro, Camillo di, Cardinal, 203
Pius III, Pope, 299
Pius IV, Pope, 184
Pius V, Pope, 134–35, 184, 198, 220, 259, 403
Pius VII, Pope, 143, 408
Pius IX, Pope: Acton's audience with, 78–80, 87, 182–83; Antonelli's influence on, 77, 78, 176; background of, 75; characterized by Acton, 176; and death of Darboy, 225; and death of Montalembert, 203–4; death of, 281; and Döllinger, 127, 173–74, 182–83; entourage of, 178; Gladstone's audience with, 186–87; and Italian independence, 76, 91; and Jesuits, 77, 180, 181, 197, 409; liberal opposition to, 78; liberal phase of, 75–76, 197, 408–9; loss of temporal power, 127, 143–44, 236, 238–43; marriage blessing to Marie Arco, 158, 177; Metternich on, 74–75; Munich Brief of, 148–49, 151, 152; negotiations with Italian government, 240, 241; *Quanta Cura* encyclical, 143, 174, 176–77, 409; *Syllabus Errorum,* 113, 143, 174, 189, 190, 409; Theiner's dismissal by, 210–11, 241; and Ultramontanism, 77. *See also* Vatican Council of *1870*
Place, Charles Philippe, Bishop, 218, 472n.47
Plato, 286
Pole, Reginald, Cardinal, 174, 185, 282
Pollock, Sir Frederick, 3d Baronet, 366, 368
Pollock, John, 386

Ponsonby, Gerald, 67
Ponsonby, Sir Henry Frederick, 342, 343, 344, 351, 354
Poole, Reginald Lane, 297, 370–71, 396
Poole, William Frederick, 109
Pope and Council (Der Papst und das Konzil) (Döllinger), 190, 205
Portugal, and Vatican Council, 215
Powell, Frederick York, 297, 366
Poynter, William, Bishop, 453n.31
Preysing, Johann Konrad, 210
Probabilism, 32
Prothero, George Walter, 366, 371, 397
Prussia: coronation of William I, 103; and Vatican Council, 215, 225. *See also* Germany
Pugin, Augustus Welby Northmore, 24
Punch, 111
Pünjer, Bernhard, 286
Purcell, Edmund Sheridan, Archbishop, 244, 262, 432n.43
Pusey, Edward, 21, 26, 39
Puttick and Simpson, 291, 292

Quanta Cura, 143, 174, 176–77, 409
Quarterly Review, The, 110, 111, 112, 155
Quin, Michael J., 112
Quinet, Edgar, 286
Quirinus letters, 200–202, 209, 217, 221, 224, 246

Raby, Richard, 25
Racialist theory, 412
Radowitz, Joseph Maria von, 321
Rambler, The, 35, 72, 87, 91; and Aldenham meeting, 120–21; changeover to *Home and Foreign Review,* 135, 136; circulation of, 121–22; editors of, 119–20; English hierarchy's criticism of, 120, 123, 124, 133–35, 137, 429n.28; Manning's interference with, 132–33, 389; motto of, 114–15, 122; Newman's connection to, 125, 132; and Oratory school scheme,

117; scholarly method in, 122–23; Simpson's role in, 115, 119, 120; and temporal power issue, 131–32; in theological controversies, 123–27, 131, 137
Rampolla del Tindaro, Mariano, Cardinal, 233
Ranke, Leopold von, 25, 61, 103–5, 185, 236, 237, 275, 372, 377, 378, 414
Raulico, Gioacchino Ventura di, 321
Rauscher, Joseph Othmar Ritter von, Cardinal, 210, 244
Raymund of Sabunde, 286
Reade, Charles, 99
Récit d'une soeur (Craven), 7, 419n.2
Redemptorists, 452n.12
Reform Act of *1867,* 96
Reform Bill, 83, 154
Reid, Sir Thomas Wemyss, 325
Reinkens, Josef Hubert, Bishop, 227, 230, 234, 329
Reisach, Karl August von, Cardinal, 73, 177, 178
Reischl, Wilhelm, 247
Renouf, Ludovika Brentano, 233, 260, 281, 436n.23
Renouf, Sir Peter le Page, 117, 135–36, 190, 233, 266, 436–37n.23
Rerum Novarum, 49
Reusch, Franz Heinrich, 227, 329
Reuss, Eduard, 286
Revue des deux mondes, 110
Reynolds, Sir Joshua, 294
Rheinischer Merkur, 45
Rhodes, Cecil, 396
Ringseis, Johann Nepomuk von, 42–43, 148
Ripon, George Frederick Samuel Robinson, 1st Marquess of, 254, 339, 340, 355
Rittler, Alois, 282
Romanes Lecture, 349, 398–400
Romantic School, 45, 46–47, 322
Romola (Eliot), 304

Roscher, Wilhelm, 135

Roscreans, Sylvester, Bishop, 194

Rose, George, 205

Rosebery, Archibald Philip Primrose, 5th Earl of, 336, 346, 369, 396; and Acton's Cambridge appointment, 365–68, 382; as foreign secretary, 337–38, 340, 352; successor to Gladstone, 354, 355, 356, 358

Roskell, Richard, Bishop, 139

Rosmini, Serbati, 76–77, 112, 145, 178, 430n.41

Rospigliosi, Françoise de Nompère de Champagny, 205

Rospigliosi, Prince, 205

Rossi, Giovanni de, 200, 237

Rossi, Pellegrino, 76, 77

Rothe, Richard, 286, 321

Rothschild, Nathan, 250, 395

Rottmanner, Otto, 401

Rousseau, Jean-Jacques, 285

Royer Collard, Pierre-Paul, 135

Ruskin, John, 346

Russell, Arthur, 295, 351

Russell, Charles William, 112, 119

Russell, Emily Theresa Villiers, Lady Ampthill, 206

Russell, John, 81, 91, 106, 164

Russell, Odo William Leopold, 1st Baron Ampthill, 178, 199, 201, 204, 206–7, 208, 213, 215, 216, 217, 222–23, 253, 351

Russia: coronation of Alexander II, 67–70; and Vatican Council, 215

St. Bartholomew Massacre, 184–85, 220

St. George's Cathedral, 24

St. Mary's College, Oscott, 18–19, 20–22, 24, 55

St. Nicholas du Chardonnet School, Gentilly, 19–20

Salisbury, Robert Arthur Talbert

Gascoyne-Cecil, 3d Marquess of, 294, 341

Salviati, Anton Maria, 185

Salviati, Duchess, 205

Salviati, Scipione, Duke, 204

Sandwith, Dr. Humphrey, 67

Sandys, Sir John, 375

San Marzano, Carlo de, 175

San Matino, Ponza di, 238

San Stefano, Treaty of, 360, 489n.127

Sarpi, Paolo, 161, 183–84, 189–90

Saturday Review, 111, 379–80, 439n.65

Savigny, Friedrich Karl von, 49–50

Savonarola, Girolamo, 299, 326

Sayn-Wittgenstein, Caroline von, 199

Schatz, Klaus, 233, 408, 409

Schelling, Friedrich Wilhelm von, 36, 155

Schema de Ecclesia, 212

Scherer, Edmond, 286, 313, 323–24

Scherr, Gregor von, Archbishop: excommunication of Döllinger, 228; and submission to Council dogma, 226–28; at Vatican Council, 222

Schiller, Friedrich von, 60, 63, 289

Schlegel, Friedrich von, 35, 46

Schleiermacher, Friedrich Daniel Ernst, 46

Schlözer, Kurd von, 175, 178

Schulte, Johann Friedrich von, 230

Schwarzenberg, Friedrich, Prince von, Cardinal, 191, 210, 219, 243–44

Scott, Christopher, 403–4

Scotus, Duns, 58

Seckendorff, Götz von, 356

"Secret History of Charles II, The" (Acton), 135

Seeley, John Robert, 366, 368, 371–73, 377, 381, 383

Sendschreiben (Acton), 243–48

Sepp, Johann Nepomuk, 148

Seripando, Girolamo, 179

Sermoneta, Michail Angelo Caetani,

Prince of Teano, Duke of, 177–78, 205, 241

Seymour, Horace, 351

Seymour, Lord Robert, 67

Shaftesbury, Anthony Ashley Cooper, 7th Earl of, 249

Short History of Napoleon the First (Seeley), 371

Shrewsbury, John Talbot, 16th Earl of, 113

Sickel, Theodor von, 237, 238

Sidgwick, Eleanor "Nora," 384

Sidgwick, Henry, 367, 372, 376, 384, 385, 389, 390

Simpson, Richard, 83, 91, 92, 163, 186, 265, 403; death of, 274; and *Home and Foreign Review,* 136, 137, 151; and *Rambler,* 115, 119, 120, 131, 133, 134, 137, 389

Singulari Nos, 145

Sixtus V, Pope, 123

Slavery, 88–89

Smith, Goldwin, 396

Smith, Robertson, 297, 389

Socialism, 410–11

Society of St. Vincent de Paul, 41

Spain: Acton's visit to, 353–54; and Vatican Council, 215

Spalding, Martin John, Archbishop, 194

Sparks, Jared, 65

Speaker, The, 325

Spectator, The, 379

Spencer, George (Father Ignatius), 22

Spencer, Herbert, 304

Spencer, John Poyntz, 5th Earl, 339, 340, 348, 355

Spencer Northcote, J., 139

Spink, Charles Anselm, 19, 40

Spinola, Marquise de, 205

Staël, Germaine Necker, Madame de, 46, 327

Stafford, Lord, 176

Stahl, Friedrich Julius, 321

Stahl, Georg Anton von, 135

Stamp tax, 111

Standard, The, 111

Stanley, Arthur Penrhyn, 166, 232

Stanley, Eugene Michaud, 232

Stanley, Henry Morton, 166

Stead, William Thames, 316

Stephens, Henry Morse, 397

Stevenson, Joseph, 135, 186

Stokes, Scott Nasmyth, 429n.26

Stolz, Alban, 49

Stonor, Edmund, 205

Stonor, Thomas, 374

Stonyhurst, 20–21

Stourton, Albert J., 205

Strachey, Lytton, 262

Strauss, David Friedrich, 148, 304

Strossmayer, Josef, Bishop, 195, 196, 198, 202, 203, 210, 217, 222, 225, 244, 271; career of, 460n.22; and intimidation at Vatican Council, 455n.39; on majority voting, 218–19; as Slavophile, 460–61n.25; and Theiner, 241; on universalization of Church, 219

Stubbs, William, Bishop, 388, 397, 495n.79

Sun, The, 111

Sutherland, George Granville William Sutherland Leveson-Gower, 3d Duke of, 94

Sutherland, Harriet Elizabeth Georgiana Leveson-Gower, Duchess of, 69, 105, 107

Swaythling family, 293

Swetchine, Anna Sophie Soymonoff, Mme, 33

Swinburne, Algernon Charles, 345–46

Switzerland, *Kulturkampf* in, 258

Sybel, Heinrich von, 414

Syllabus Errorum, 113, 143, 174, 189, 190, 409

Synopsis observationum, 243

Tablet, The, 71, 113–14, 126, 261, 403

Talbot, George, 79, 176, 178, 262–63

Talleyrand, Charles Maurice de, 8, 19

Tauffkirchen-Guttenburg, Karl, Count, 201, 202, 222, 452n.15

Tegernsee, Villa Arco at, 27, 28, 40, 235, 308–9, 328, 401–2

Temporal power of papacy, 127, 131, 132–33, 143, 432n.43

Tennyson, Alfred, Lord, 113, 166, 306, 344–45

Theiner, Augustin, 74, 180–82, 185, 186, 209–10, 240–41

Theologische Ethik (Rothe), 286

Thiers, Louis Adolphe, 181, 236, 239, 240, 361

Thornely, Thomas, 388–89

Throckmorton, Elizabeth Acton, 2, 13, 18, 79, 287–88

Throckmorton, Emily. *See* Dease, Emily Throckmorton

Throckmorton, Sir John, 198

Throckmorton, Minnie, 24, 31, 43, 102, 236–37, 250

Throckmorton, Sir Nicholas William George, 9th Baronet, 164

Throckmorton, Sir Robert George, 8th Baronet, 13, 52, 79, 142

Throckmorton family, 23–24

Thurston, Herbert, 403

Times, The, 83–84, 110–11, 112, 415; Acton's reply to Gladstone in, 259, 260, 261, 270; on Inaugural Address, 379; on *Sendschreiben,* 246–47

Tocqueville, Alexis de, 111

Todd, William Gowan, 119

To Rome and Back (Capes), 121

Tosa, Tommaso della, 181

Tractarians, 21, 39, 119

Trautmannsdorff, Ferdinand, Count, 202, 214, 241

Travellers Club, 293

Treitschke, Heinrich von, 414

Trevelyan, George Macaulay, 372, 382, 396, 413

Trevelyan, Sir George Otto, 294, 363, 367, 372, 374, 384

Trinity Historical Society, 388

Trollope, Anthony, 166

Turnbull, William, 93–94

Ullathorne, William Bernard, Bishop, 71, 118, 126, 265, 267, 347; attack on *Rambler,* 134–35, 137

Ultramontanism, 22, 34, 74, 114, 259; of *Civiltà Cattolica,* 77–78; and Döllinger, 36, 38–39, 127; of *Dublin Review,* 113; of Lamennais, 144–45; of Maistre, 144; of Manning, 133; and papal authority, 142–45, 188–89, 319; true Ultramontanism, 146–47

United States: Acton's visit to, 63–67; bishops at Vatican Council, 194, 224; Civil War, 87–88, 387; and federal system, 415; and slavery, 88–89

Universal History (Ranke), 105

Universal News, 441–42n.105

Universe, 114

Valente, Pietro, 2

Vallicelliana library, 174–75

Vallombrosa, Duchess of, 283

Van Dyck, Anthony, 42

Vatican Archives, 74, 175, 180, 185, 186, 209–10, 237–38, 240–41

Vatican Council of *1870,* 143, 170, 173; acoustic system at, 216; Acton's attitude towards Infallibility, 197–99, 209, 220; and Acton's departure, 221–22; Acton's history of (*Sendschreiben*), 243–48; Acton's influence on minority bishops, xxii–xxiii, 202–3, 207–8, 217, 223; announcement of, 188–89; cloak-and-dagger atmosphere at, 199–200, 208, 455n.39; division among minority bishops,

194–95; Döllinger-Acton reports on, xxii–xxiii, 200–202, 217, 221, 224, 246; and governmental policy, 207–8, 212–16; histories of, 233; Infallibility debate in, 217–22; in-opportunist group at, 208–9, 212; leadership of infallibilists, 195; leadership of minority bishops, 190–91, 195–97; modern view of, 408–9; Montalembert's death during, 203–4; regulation of debate in, 216–17; social life during, 204–7; and submission to decrees of, 225, 226–35, 259–61, 264–72; vote of, 223–24

Vatican Council, Second, xxiii, 127, 269

Vaticanism (Gladstone), 270

Vaughan, Herbert, Cardinal, 114, 373–74, 403, 404

Vaux, Lord. *See* Mostyn, George Charles of Kiddington

Ventura di Raulica, Gioacchino, 135

Vera, Augusto, 178–79

Veuillot, Louis, 33–34, 114, 135, 177, 180, 204, 222

Victor Emmanuel II, King, 178, 215, 237, 240

Victoria, Queen, 17, 66, 68, 85, 86, 103, 106, 277; and Acton-Arco engagement, 100; and Acton's Cambridge appointment, 367–68, 374–75; and Acton's court appointment, 342–44, 348, 356–57; attitude towards Catholicism, 53; attitude towards Gladstone, 249, 341–42, 343; and Catholic peers, 192; Diamond Jubilee, 390–91; Gladstone's resignation to, 354, 355–56; on Riviera, 284

Victor of Hohenlohe-Schillingfürst, Prince, 64

Vienna World's Fair, 249–51

Villa Acton (Naples), 1–2, 4–5, 7

Villiers, Lord, 67

Vinet, Alexandre, 321, 323–24, 410

Vinogradoff, Paul, 366–67

Visconti-Venosta, Emilio, 239, 240

Voltaire, François Marie Arouet de, 141

Vorzak, Nikolaus, 241

Waitz, Georg, 61

Wales, Prince of. *See* Edward VII

Wallis, John Edward, 114

Walsh, Michael, 114

Ward, Adolphus William, 297, 385, 394–95, 397

Ward, Bernard, 453n.31

Ward, Horatio James, 96

Ward, William George, 112–13, 119–20, 122, 139

Waterworth, William, 139

Watson, William, 346

Watts, George Frederick, 106

Weekly Register, The, 71, 114, 124

Weekly Register and Catholic Standard, The, 114

Weinzierl-Fischer, Erika, 215

Wessenberg, Heinrich Ignaz von, 140, 198

West, Sir Algernon, 336–37

Westcott, Brooke Foss, 385

Westmacott the Younger, Richard, 15

Westminster Review, 111

Wetherell, Thomas Frederick, 136, 137, 154, 155, 169, 232, 331

Whibley, Leonard, 393

White, Andrew D., 290

Whytford, Richard, 404

Wilberforce, Henry William, 70–71, 114

William I, King of Prussia, 103

William II, Emperor of Germany, 352, 357, 468n.2

Williams, Francis, 112

Williams and Norgate, 132

Wilson, Woodrow, 413

Windischmann, Friedrich, 31

Wiseman, Nicholas, Cardinal, 70, 72, 82, 113, 118, 123, 126, 142, 145; attack on *Home and Foreign Review,* 137–38; attack on *Rambler,* 120, 123, 124, 132, 133–34, 429n.28; on authority of Church, 153; and Döllinger, 26, 39; and *Dublin Review,* 112, 119, 120; at opening of St. George's Cathedral, 24; as Oscott rector, 18–19, 21–22; and Oxford converts, 21; successor to, 177

Wolff, Sir Henry Drummond, 353

Wolseley, Sir Garnet Joseph, 1st Viscount, 294, 391, 396

Women's education, 384

Women's suffrage, 384

Woodruff, Marie Immaculée Antoinette, "Mia," 59, 479n.22

Wright, Richard, 392, 394

Ximenes de Cisneros, Francisco, Cardinal, 354

Yussef, Gregorius, 210

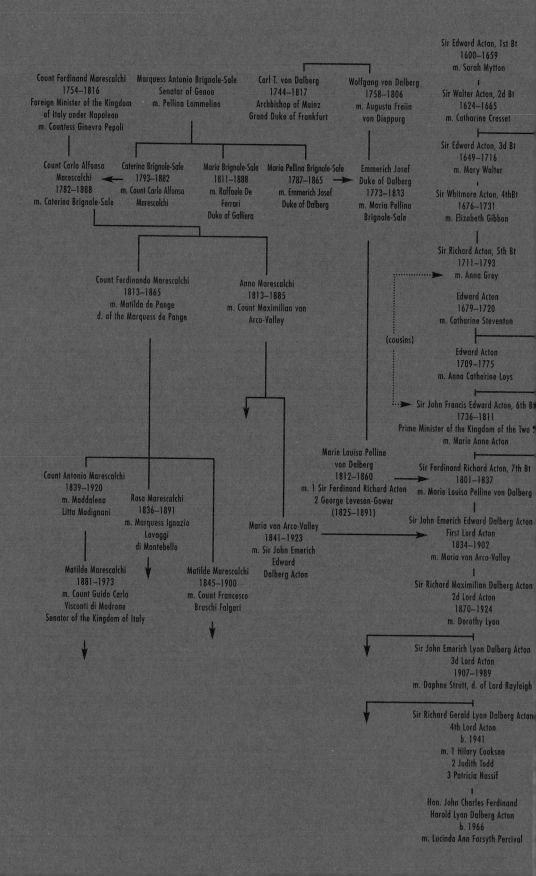

Sir Edward Acton, 1st Bt
1600–1659
m. Sarah Mytton

Sir Walter Acton, 2d Bt
1624–1665
m. Catharine Cresset

Sir Edward Acton, 3d Bt
1649–1716
m. Mary Walter

Sir Whitmore Acton, 4thBt
1676–1731
m. Elizabeth Gibbon

Sir Richard Acton, 5th Bt
1711–1793
m. Anna Grey

Edward Acton
1679–1720
m. Catharine Steventon

Edward Acton
1709–1775
m. Anna Cathe'rine Loys

Sir John Francis Edward Acton, 6th Bt
1736–1811
Prime Minister of the Kingdom of the Two S
m. Marie Anne Acton

Count Ferdinand Marescalchi
1754–1816
Foreign Minister of the Kingdom
of Italy under Napoleon
m. Countess Ginevra Pepoli

Marquess Antonio Brignole-Sale
Senator of Genoa
m. Pellina Lommelino

Carl T. von Dalberg
1744–1817
Archbishop of Mainz
Grand Duke of Frankfurt

Wolfgang von Dalberg
1758–1806
m. Augusta Freiin
von Dieppurg

Count Carlo Alfonso
Marescalchi
1782–1888
m. Caterina Brignole-Sale

Caterina Brignole-Sale
1793–1882
m. Count Carlo Alfonso
Marescalchi

Maria Brignole-Sale
1811–1888
m. Raffaele De
Ferrari
Duke of Galliera

Maria Pellina Brignole-Sale
1787–1865
m. Emmerich Josef
Duke of Dalberg

Emmerich Josef
Duke of Dalberg
1773–1833
m. Maria Pellina
Brignole-Sale

(cousins)

Count Ferdinando Marescalchi
1813–1865
m. Matilda de Pange
d. of the Marquess de Pange

Anna Marescalchi
1813–1885
m. Count Maximilian von
Arco-Valley

Marie Louisa Pelline
von Dalberg
1812–1860
m. 1 Sir Ferdinand Richard Acton
2 George Leveson-Gower
(1825–1891)

Sir Ferdinand Richard Acton, 7th Bt
1801–1837
m. Marie Louisa Pelline von Dalberg

Count Antonio Marescalchi
1839–1920
m. Maddalena
Litta Modignani

Rosa Marescalchi
1836–1891
m. Marquess Ignazio
Lavaggi
di Montebello

Maria von Arco-Valley
1841–1923
m. Sir John Emerich
Edward
Dalberg Acton

Sir John Emerich Edward Dalberg Acton
First Lord Acton
1834–1902
m. Maria von Arco-Valley

Matilde Marescalchi
1881–1973
m. Count Guido Carlo
Visconti di Modrone
Senator of the Kingdom of Italy

Matilde Marescalchi
1845–1900
m. Count Francesco
Bruschi Falgari

Sir Richard Maximilian Dalberg Acton
2d Lord Acton
1870–1924
m. Dorothy Lyon

Sir John Emerich Lyon Dalberg Acton
3d Lord Acton
1907–1989
m. Daphne Strutt, d. of Lord Rayleigh

Sir Richard Gerald Lyon Dalberg Acton
4th Lord Acton
b. 1941
m. 1 Hilary Cookson
2 Judith Todd
3 Patricia Nassif

Hon. John Charles Ferdinand
Harold Lyon Dalberg Acton
b. 1966
m. Lucinda Ann Forsyth Percival